P O O L[E]
A HIDDEN TREAS[URE]

GOLD ANCHOR

POOLE QUAY BOAT HAVEN

PORT OF POOLE MARINA

★★★★★★★
MARINA
OF THE YEAR
═ 2016 · 2017 · 2019 ═

POOLE HARBOUR
BOAT SHOW

HOME OF THE
POOLE HARBOUR
BOAT SHOW

PERMANENT BERTHS

It's in a private position that makes the most of the views and gorgeous sunsets, yet it's still close to Poole's historic quay, old town and vibrant shopping centre.

- 90 permanent berths
- Superyacht berths
- Floating docks for jet skis and RIB sparking up to 6.1m
- 24 hour security
- Deep water: 2.5 - 6m
- Water taxi service, parking

SWINGING MOORINGS

Relax with a glass of wine, on a sunny afternoon, on your own swinging mooring in Poole Harbour overlooking Brownsea Island. Away from the madding crowd, these offer you ultimate privacy, peace & tranquillity.

Poole Town Quay, Poole, Dorset BH15 1HJ
t: 01202 649488 | **poolequayboathaven.co.uk**

VISITOR MARINA

Use your boat as a holiday home; entertain family, friends, colleagues or customers on board; sail the stunning Jurassic Coast.

Enjoy all the attractions of Poole, Bournemouth and beautiful Dorset. A warm welcome always awaits!

- 125 visitor berths all year for vessels up to 75m in length and up to 4.8m draft
- On the Port estate we can accommodate vessels up to 210m in length with a maximum draft of 9m.

VHF Channel 80 call sign "Poole Quay Boat Haven"

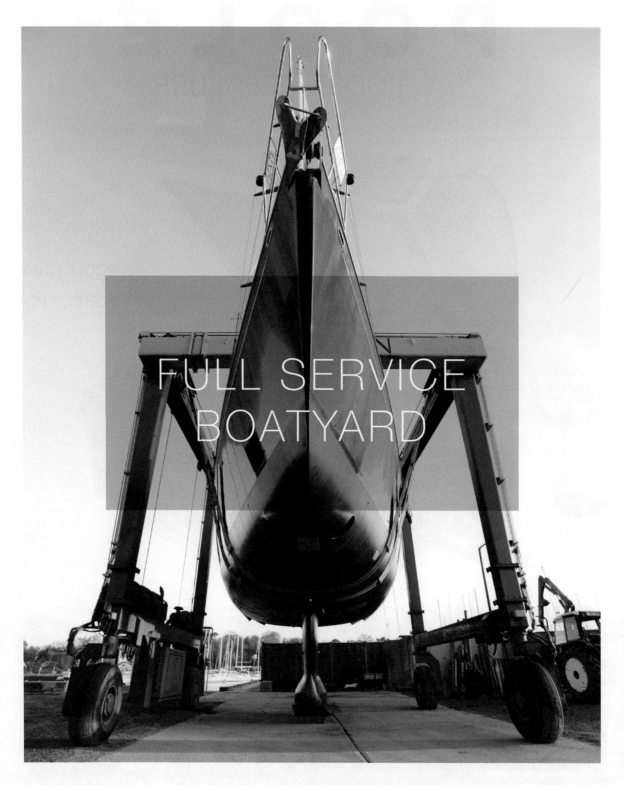

FULL SERVICE
BOATYARD

Our highly skilled staff take care of all boat needs, from
electronics to resprays, in our state of the art facilities.

Unrivalled experience   Small repairs to major refits   Quality, assured

refitsrepairs@berthon.co.uk | 01590 213141

BERTHON

MARINA | BOATYARD | COMMERCIAL | YACHT SALES

REEDS
EASTERN
ALMANAC
2022

ADLARD COLES NAUTICAL

EDITORS **Perrin Towler and Mark Fishwick**

Free updates are available at www.reedsalmanacs.co.uk

IMPORTANT SAFETY NOTE AND LEGAL DISCLAIMER

This Almanac provides basic navigational data for planning and executing passages. The tidal prediction data has been reproduced by permission of national hydrographic offices. Chartlets illustrate items in the text, orientate the user and highlight key features; they should not be relied on for navigational purposes and must always be used in conjunction with a current, corrected navigational chart. Any waypoint or position listed in this Almanac must first be plotted on the appropriate chart to assess its accuracy, safety in the prevailing circumstances and relevance to the Skipper's intentions.

Navigational guidance or suggestions are based on the accumulated experience of editors, agents, harbour masters and users. They are generic and in compiling a passage plan or pilotage notebook all other available publications and information should be consulted. They take no account of the characteristics of individual vessels nor the actual or forecast meteorological conditions, sea or tidal state. These need to be checked with appropriate local authorities for the intended area of operation prior to departure.

While every care has been taken in compiling the Almanac, it is a human endeavour with many contributors. Despite rigorous checking there may be inadvertent errors or inaccuracies, and omissions resulting from the time of notification in relation to the publication date. To the extent that the editors or publishers become aware of these, corrections will be published on the website www.reedsalmanacs.co.uk (requires registration). Readers should therefore regularly check the website between January and June for any such corrections. Data in this Almanac is corrected up to Weekly Edition 25/2021 of Admiralty Notices to Mariners.

The publishers, editors and their agents accept no responsibility for any errors or omissions, or for any accident, loss or damage (including without limitation any indirect, consequential, special or exemplary damages) arising from the use or misuse of, or reliance upon, the information contained in this Almanac.

The use of any data in this Almanac is entirely at the discretion of the Skipper or other individual with responsibility for the command, conduct or navigation of the vessel in which it is relied upon.

ADVERTISEMENT SALES
Enquiries about advertising space should be addressed to:
adlardcoles@bloomsbury.com

Managing editor Chris Stevens

Reeds Nautical Almanac
An imprint of Bloomsbury Publishing Plc
50 Bedford Square, London, WC1B 3DP

29 Earlsfort Terrace, Dublin 2, Ireland

Tel: +44 (0)1865 411010
info@reedsalmanacs.co.uk
editor.britishisles@reedsalmanacs.co.uk
editor.continental@reedsalmanacs.co.uk
www.reedsalmanacs.co.uk

REEDS, ADLARD COLES NAUTICAL and the Buoy logo are trademarks of Bloomsbury Publishing Plc

First published 2021

Bloomsbury Publishing Plc does not have any control over, or responsibility for, any third-party websites referred to or in this book. All internet addresses given in this book were correct at the time of going to press. The author and publisher regret any inconvenience caused if addresses have changed or sites have ceased to exist, but can accept no responsibility for any such changes.

Reeds Eastern Almanac 2022 – ISBN 978 1 4729 9054 9

British Library Cataloguing-in-Publication Data
A catalogue record for this book is available from the British Library.

Library of Congress Cataloguing-in-Publication data has been applied for.

Bloomsbury Publishing Plc makes every effort to ensure that the papers used in the manufacture of our books are natural, recyclable products made from wood grown in well-managed forests. Our manufacturing processes conform to the environmental regulations of the country of origin.

To find out more about our authors and books visit www.bloomsbury.com. Here you will find extracts, author interviews, details of forthcoming events and the option to sign up for our newsletters.

Typeset in Frutiger
Printed and bound in the UK by Bell & Bain Ltd

Reference Contents

Navigational Contents

WORLD CLASS SKIPPERS WANTED

NO PRESSURE

Sir Robin Knox-Johnston
Founder of the Clipper Round the World Yacht Race

Join the elite and take on the world's longest yacht race, crewed exclusively by novice crew embarking on the race of their lives.

Clipper Race Skippers are exceptional. These men and women have the fortitude to take on the toughest of mental challenges, and the physical endurance to successfully lead a team through Mother Nature's extreme environments on a 40,000 mile lap around the globe.

We are recruiting experienced professional Skippers for the next edition of the Clipper Race. To qualify you must hold a valid Yachtmaster Ocean certificate [commercial endorsed] or International Yacht Training Master of Yachts.

↘ APPLY NOW

clipperroundtheworld.com/careers
raceskipper@clipper-ventures.com
+44 (0) 2392 526000

transeurope
MARINAS

VISITORS BERTHING 50% DISCOUNT

Revised December, 2020. Please refer to the website
www.transeuropemarinas.com
for a current list of members.

The European marina network uniting over 80 marinas.

TransEurope Marinas cardholders benefit from a 50% visitor's berthing discount
in each associated marina for up to five days a year.

For a current list of members and further information, please visit
www.transeuropemarinas.com

UK
1. Bangor Marina
2. Rhu Marina
3. Troon Yacht Haven
4. Royal Quays Marina
5. Whitehaven Marina
6. Fleetwood Haven Marina
7. Liverpool Marina
8. Conwy Marina
9. Neyland Yacht Haven
10. Penarth Marina
11. Upton Marina
12. Portishead Marina
13. Mylor Yacht Harbour
14. Mayflower Marina
15. Dart Marina
16. Poole Quay Boat Haven
17. Buckler's Hard Yacht Harbour
18. Town Quay Marina
19. Universal Marina
20. Cowes Yacht Haven
21. Royal Clarence Marina
22. Emsworth Yacht Harbour
23. Birdham Pool Marina
24. Dover Marina
25. Gillingham Marina
26. Fambridge Yacht Haven
27. Tollesbury Marina
28. Fox's Marina
29. Brundall Bay Marina
30. Beaucette Marina

Germany
1. Sonwik Marina
2. Ancora Marina
3. Marina Boltenhagen
4. Marina Wiek auf Rügen
5. Baltic Sea Resort
6. Naturhafen Krummin
7. Lagunenstadt Ueckermünde

France
1. Dunkerque
2. Boulogne-sur-mer
3. Saint Valery sur Somme
4. Dieppe
5. Saint Valery en Caux
6. Fécamp
7. Le Havre Plaisance
8. Port-Deauville
9. Dives-Cabourg-Houlgate
10. Ouistreham/Caen
11. Granville
12. Saint-Quay Port d'Armor
13. Perros-Guirec
14. Roscoff
15. Marinas de Brest
16. Douarnenez-Tréboul
17. Loctudy
18. Port la Forêt
19. Concarneau
20. Ports de Nantes

Spain
1. Puerto Deportivo Gijón
2. Marina Combarro
3. Nauta Sanxenxo
4. Marina La Palma
5. Puerto Calero
6. Alcaidesa Marina
7. Pobla Marina

Belgium
1. VNZ Blankenberge
2. VY Nieuwpoort

Netherlands
1. Marina Den Oever
2. Jachthaven Waterland
3. Jachthaven Wetterwille
4. Marina Port Zélande
5. Jachthaven Biesbosch
6. Delta Marina Kortgene

Portugal
1. Douro Marina
2. Marina de Portimão
3. Quinta do Lorde Marina

Italy
1. Porto Romano
2. Venezia Certosa Marina
3. Marina del Cavallino

Ireland
1. Malahide Marina

Croatia
1. Marina Punat

Greece
1. Linariá Marina
2. Kos Marina

Madeira

Canarias

Oban, the gateway to the isles, the sea food capital of Scotland

Oban's new transit berth facility, puts you right in the centre of the town, ideal for shopping, a lovely meal out or picking up/dropping off crew.

Enjoy all Oban has to offer by spending from a few hours, up to 3 nights at the North Pier Pontoons.

We have 39 serviced finger pontoons plus a long breakwater with serviced berths, with secure access and a new harbour building with showers etc for your use.

We do not take bookings for berths, we operate a first come, first served policy, but by all means contact us to see what is available on the day.

For all vessels transiting through Oban Harbour there is a Code of Practice that the Harbour Authorities request you abide by for a safe and enjoyable visit, this can be found on the Oban Harbour website.

VHF Ch 12
Tel. 01631 562 892
M. 07388 808 061

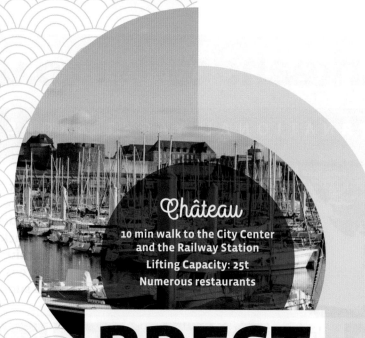

Château
10 min walk to the City Center
and the Railway Station
Lifting Capacity: 25t
Numerous restaurants

BREST
THE PERFECT GETAWAY
CITY CENTER OR BEACH-FRONT, JUST PICK WHERE YOU'LL STAY !

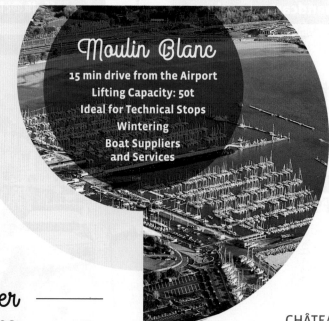

Moulin Blanc
15 min drive from the Airport
Lifting Capacity: 50t
Ideal for Technical Stops
Wintering
Boat Suppliers
and Services

We're here

Both marinas offer
the following facilities:

🛜 Free Wi-Fi ♻ Recycling Containers ⚡ Pump Station

⚠ Careening Area 💧 Toilets, Showers, Laundry ⚡ Fuel Station 24/7

🚲 Free bicycle hire

CHÂTEAU
☎ +33 (0) 298 33 12 50
@ chateau@marinasbrest.fr

MOULIN BLANC
☎ +33 (0) 298 02 20 02
@ moulinblanc@marinasbrest.fr

www.marinasbrest.fr/en f @marinasbrest

Yacht Havens

MARINAS · BOATYARDS · DRY STACK · BOAT CLUBS

WELCOME ABOARD

Welcome aboard the Yacht Havens family!

We'll help you **get the best** from your boating experience, whether you're passing through or looking for a longer stay.

Come boating with Yacht Havens at one of our **9 destinations**

1. Largs Yacht Haven
2. Troon Yacht Haven
3. Neyland Yacht Haven
4. Fambridge Yacht Haven
5. Lymington Yacht Haven
   Haven Quay – Dry Stack, Lymington
   Plymouth Yacht Haven
   Yacht Haven Quay – Dry Stack, Plymouth
   Jachthaven Biesbosch, The Netherlands

YACHTHAVENS.COM
01590 677071

PORT CHANTEREYNE
AN IRRESISTIBLE PORT OF CALL

A WARM WELCOME TO
CHERBOURG-EN-COTENTIN

Port Chantereyne
CHERBOURG

- Located in the biggest artificial harbour of Europe
- Accessible 24/7
- Deep water harbour with a total of 1,600 berths, 190 of which are designated for visitors
- Ideally positioned on the Channel coast, close to England, the Channel Islands and Brittany
- 5 Gold Anchors label
- Close to the dynamic city-center and its many shops and restaurants
- Many opportunities to enjoy yourself onland :
  - Oceanographic park of La Cité de la Mer
  - Remarkable gardens including the Emmanuel-Liais Park
  - Ravalet castle and its gardens
  - Museums, like the Thomas-Henry museum

Tel: +33 (0)2 33 87 65 70
portchantereyne@cherbourg.fr
VHF Channel 9

www.portchantereyne.fr

Reference data

0.1 THE ALMANAC

• Acknowledgements

The Editors thank the many official bodies and individuals for information and advice given in the compilation of this Almanac. These include: UKHO, Trinity House, Northern Lighthouse Board, HM Nautical Almanac Office, HMSO, HM Revenue & Customs, Meteorological Office, BBC, IBA, MCA, RNLI, PLA, ABP, Koninklijke Nederlandse Redding Maatschappij (KNRM), countless Harbourmasters and our many individual Harbour Agents.

• Permissions

Chartlets, tidal stream diagrams and curves are reproduced from Admiralty charts and publications (ALL, ATT and ALRS) by permission of the UKHO (Licence No GB DQ – 001 – Adlard Coles) and the Controller of HMSO.

UK and foreign tidal predictions are supplied by and with the permission of UKHO and by the German and Dutch HOs with permission to use the tidal predictions stated:

BSH (German HO): Helgoland. (Authorisation 11123/2012-10).

Rijkswaterstaat, Netherlands: Vlissingen, Hoek van Holland.

Vlaamse Hydrografie, Belgium: Zeebrugge.

Extracts from the *International Code of Signals 1969* and *Meteorological Office Weather Services for Shipping* are published by permission of the Controller of HMSO.

Ephemerides are derived from HM Nautical Almanac by permission of HM Nautical Almanac Office and the Council for the Central Laboratory of the Research Councils.

• Disclaimer

No National HO has verified the information in this product and none accepts liability for the accuracy of reproduction or any modifications made thereafter. No National HO warrants that this product satisfies national or international regulations regarding the use of the appropriate products for navigation.

Chartlets in this Almanac are not intended to be used for navigation. Always consult fully corrected official charts. See 0.32, Harbour Information, for more details.

• Improvements

Suggestions, however minor, for improving or correcting this Almanac are always welcome, especially if based on personal experience. All will be carefully considered. Please send your comments by email, if possible, direct to the relevant Editor (see below) or to info@reedsalmanacs.co.uk. Otherwise, a note to Adlard Coles Nautical (see page v) will be forwarded as necessary.

Perrin Towler (editor.britishisles@reedsalmanacs.co.uk) is responsible for Areas 1, 3, 4 and 5 (the east coasts of the UK); Mark Fishwick (editor.continental@reedsalmanacs.co.uk) is responsible for Area 2 (Netherlands and Belgium). We share the compilation of the Reference Data chapter.

• Notifying errors

Although every care has been taken in compiling this Almanac, errors may still occur. Please let us know if you spot any.

• Harbour Agents

Our harbour agents provide invaluable local information which may not appear in official sources. If this is of interest and you would like to earn a free copy of Reeds Nautical Almanac please apply to the relevant editor, giving brief details of your experience and the area(s) you would be able cover.

• Sources of corrections

This Almanac is corrected to Weekly edition No. 25/2021 of Admiralty Notices to Mariners.

Corrections to Admiralty charts and publications can be downloaded from the UKHO website or obtained from Admiralty Chart Agents (ACA) and certain Port Authorities.

• Updates

It is important that this Almanac is kept up to date to maintain its accuracy. For free monthly updates from January to June, please visit: www.reedsnauticalalmanac.co.uk/update

0.2 SYMBOLS AND ABBREVIATIONS

The following more common Symbols and Abbreviations feature in Reeds Almanacs and in some Admiralty charts and publications. Those symbols in the tinted box immediately below are frequently used within the text describing each port.

	Alongside berth
ⓒ	Automatic telling machine (ATM), cashpoint
Ⓑ	Bank
	Bottled gas available, Calor Gas, Camping Gaz,or Kosangas
	Boatyard
	Boat hoist (+tons)
	Crane (+ tons)
	Chandlery
	Customs
	Diesel (supply by hose)
	Diesel (in cans)
	Electrical repairs
Ⓔ	Electronic repairs
	Fresh water supply
	Food shop/supermarket
Ⓗ	Hospital
≠	In transit with, ie ldg marks/lts
@	Internet café/access
	Landing place/steps/ladder
	Laundry facilities available
LB, ♦	Lifeboat, inshore lifeboat
	Light float, minor
	Lt float, major; Light vessel or Lanby
	Licensed bar, Public house, Inn
©	National Coastwatch Institution (NCI)
	Marine engineering repairs
	Mooring buoy
	Petrol (supply by hose)
	Petrol (in cans)
⊠	Post Office
	Pump out facility
×	Restaurant/cafe
	Rigger
△	Sailmaker
	Shipwright (esp wooden hulls)
	Shower
	Shore power (electrical)
	Slipway
Ⓥ	Visitors' berths
	Visitors' mooring
	Wind turbine
	Weather forecast available
	Yacht Club/(YC), Sailing Club(SC)

abm	Abeam
ABP	Associated British Ports
ACA	Admiralty Chart, AC Agent
ACN	Adlard Coles Nautical (Publisher)
Aff Mar	Affaires Maritimes

AIS	Automatic Identification System
aka	Also known as
ALL	Admiralty List of Lights
ALRS	Admiralty List of Radio Signals
Al	Alternating light
ANWB	Association of road & waterway users (Dutch)
ATT	Admiralty Tide Tables
ATT	Atterisage (landfall/SWM) buoy
Auto	Météo Répondeur Automatique
B.	Bay, Black
BE	Belgian chart
Bk	Broken (nature of seabed)
Bkwtr	Breakwater
BMS	Bulletin Météorologique Spécial (Strong wind/Gale warning)
	Bn, bcn(s) Beacon, beacon(s)
BSH	German Hydrographic Office/chart(s)
BST	British Summer Time (= DST)
Bu	Blue
By(s)	Buoy, buoys
C.	Cape, Cabo, Cap
c	Coarse (sand; nature of seabed)
ca	Cable (approx 185m long)
Cas	Castle
CD	Chart datum (tidal)
CEVNI	Code Européen de Voies de la Navigation Intérieure (inland waterway signs etc)
cf	Compare, cross-refer to
CG	Coast Guard, HM Coastguard (in the UK)
CGOC	Coast Guard Operations Centre (UK)
chan	Channel (navigational)
Ch	Channel (VHF)
Ch, ⊕	Church
Chy	Chimney
Co	Coral (nature of seabed)
Col	Column, pillar, obelisk
CPA	Closest Point of Approach
CROSS	Centre Régional Opérationnel de Surveillance et Sauvetage (= MRCC)
CRS	Coast Radio Station
CRT	Canal and River Trust
C/S	COSPAS/SARSAT (satellite)
Cy	Clay (nature of seabed)
Dec	Declination (of the Sun) abbr: December
Defib	Automated External Defibrillator
dest	Destroyed
DF, D/F	Radio Direction Finding
DG	De-gaussing (range)
DGPS	Differential GPS
Dia	Diaphone (fog signal)
Dir Lt	Directional light
discont	Discontinued
DLR	Dockland Light Railway
Dn(s)	Dolphin(s)
DR	Dead Reckoning or Dries (secondary tides)
DSC	Digital Selective Calling
DST	Daylight Saving Time
DW	Deep Water (route)
DYC	Dutch Yacht Chart(s)
DZ	Danger Zone (buoy)
E	East
ECM	East cardinal mark (buoy/beacon)
ED	Existence doubtful. European Datum
EEA	European Economic Area
Elev	Elevation
Ent	Entrance, entry, enter
EP, △	Estimated position
ETA	Estimated Time of Arrival
ETD	Estimated Time of Departure
F	Fixed light
f	Fine (eg sand; nature of seabed)
F&A	Fore and aft (berth/mooring)
FFL	Fixed and Flashing light
Fl	Flashing light
FM	Frequency Modulation
Foc	Free of charge
Fog Det lt	Fog Detector light
Freq, Fx	Frequency
FS	Flagstaff, Flagpole
ft	Foot, feet
Ft,	Fort
FV	Fishing vessel
G	Gravel (nature of seabed), Green
GC	Great Circle
GDOP	Geometric Dilution of Precision (GPS)
GHA	Greenwich Hour Angle
GLA	General Lighthouse Authority
GMDSS	Global Maritime Distress & Safety System
grt	Gross Registered Tonnage
Gy	Grey
H, h, Hrs	Hour(s)
H−, H+	Minutes before, after the whole hour
H24	Continuous
Hd,hd	Headland, head (breakwater/mole)
HAT	Highest Astronomical Tide
HF	High Frequency
HFP	High Focal Plane (buoy)
HIE	Highlands & Islands Enterprise
HJ	Day service only, sunrise to sunset
HM	Harbour Master
HMRC	HM Revenue & Customs
HMSO	Her Majesty's Stationery Office
HN	Night service only, sunset to sunrise
HO	Office hours, Hydrographic Office
(hor)	Horizontally disposed (lights)
hPa	Hectopascal (= 1millibar)
HT	High Tension (overhead electricity line)
HW	High Water
HX	No fixed hours
IALA	International Association of Marine Aids to Navigation and Lighthouse Authorities
IDM	Isolated Danger Mark (buoy/beacon)
IHO	International Hydrographic Organisation
IMO	International Maritime Organisation
INMARSAT	International Maritime Satellite Organisation
intens	Intensified (light sector)
IPTS	International Port Traffic Signals
IQ	Interrupted quick flashing light
IRPCS	International Regulations for the Prevention of Collisions at Sea
Is, I	Island, Islet
ISAF	International Sailing Federation
Iso	Isophase light
ITU	International Telecommunications Union
ITZ	Inshore Traffic Zone (TSS)
IUQ	Interrupted ultra quick flashing light
IVQ	Interrupted very quick flashing light
kn	Knot(s)
kW	Kilowatts
L	Lake, Loch, Lough
Lat	Latitude
LAT	Lowest Astronomical Tide
Lanby, ⌐	Large automatic navigational buoy
Ldg	Leading (light)
LF	Low frequency
L Fl	Long flash

LH	Left hand
LNG	Liquefied Natural Gas
LNTM	Local Notice To Mariners
LOA	Length overall
Long, lng	Longitude
LPG	Liquefied Petroleum Gas
LT	Local time
Lt(s), ☆ ☆	Light(s)
M	Moorings. Nautical (sea) mile(s). Mud
m	Metre(s)
Mag	Magnetic. Magnitude (of star)
Mb, mb	Millibar (= 1 hectopascal, hPa)
MCA	Maritime and Coastguard Agency
Met/Météo	Meteorology/Météorologie (weather)
MHWN	Mean High Water Neaps
MHWS	Mean High Water Springs
MHz	Megahertz
ML	Mean Level (tidal)
MLWN	Mean Low Water Neaps
MLWS	Mean Low Water Springs
MMSI	Maritime Mobile Service Identity
Mo	Morse
Mon	Monument. Abbrev: Monday
MRCC	Maritime Rescue Co-ordination Centre
MRSC	Maritime Rescue Sub-Centre (not in the UK)
MSI	Maritime Safety Information
N	North
Navi	Navicarte (French charts)
NB	Nota Bene. Notice Board
NCM	North Cardinal Mark (buoy/beacon)
ND	No Data (secondary tides)
NGS	Naval Gunfire Support (buoy)
NM	Notice(s) to Mariners
NMOC	National Maritime Operations Centre (HMCG)
np	Neap tides
NP	Naval Publication (plus number)
NRT	Net registered tonnage
NT	National Trust (land/property)
Obscd	Obscured
Obstn	Obstruction
Oc	Occulting light
ODAS	Ocean Data Acquisition System (buoy)
Or	Orange (see also Y)
OT	Other times
P	Pebbles
(P)	Preliminary (NM)
PA	Position approximate
Pax	Passenger(s)
PC	Portuguese chart
PD	Position doubtful
PHM	Port-hand Mark (buoy/beacon)
PLA	Port of London Authority
Pos	Position
Prog	Prognosis (weather charts)
prom	Prominent
PSSA	Particularly Sensitive Sea Area
Pt(e).	Point(e)
Pta	Punta (point)
Q	Quick flashing light
QHM	Queen's Harbour Master
qv	Refer to (quod vide)
R	Red. River.
Racon	Radar transponder beacon
Ramark	Radar beacon
RCD	Recreational Craft Directive
RG	Emergency RDF station
RH	Right hand
Rk, Rky	Rock, Rocky (nature of seabed)

RNLI	Royal National Lifeboat Institution
ROI	Republic of Ireland
R/T	Radiotelephony
Ru	Ruins
RYA	Royal Yachting Association
S	South, Sand (nature of seabed)
S, St, Ste	Saint(s)
SAMU	Service d'Aide Médicale Urgente (ambulance)
SAR	Search and Rescue
SBM	Single buoy mooring
SC	Sailing Club. Spanish chart
SCM	South Cardinal Mark (buoy/beacon)
SD	Sailing Directions,Semi-diameter (of sun) Sounding of doubtful depth
Sh	Shells (nature of seabed). Shoal
SHM	Starboard-hand Mark (buoy/beacon); Simplified Harmonic Method (tides)
SHOM	Service Hydrographique et Océanographique de la Marine (FrenchHO/Chart)
Si	Silt (nature of seabed)
SIGNI	Signalisation de la Navigation Intérieure
SMS	Short Message Service (mobile texting)
so	Soft (eg mud; nature of seabed)
SOLAS	Safety of Life at Sea (IMO Convention)
Sp	Spire
sp	Spring tides
SPM	Special Mark (buoy/beacon)
SR	Sunrise
SRR	Search and Rescue Region
SS	Sunset. Signal Station
SSB	Single Sideband (radio)
St	Stones (nature of seabed)
Stbd	Starboard
subm	Submerged
SWM	Safe Water Mark (buoy/beacon)
sy	Sticky (eg mud; nature of seabed)
(T), (Temp)	Temporary
tbc	To be confirmed
tbn	To be notified
TD	Temporarily Discontinued (fog signal)
TE	Temporarily Extinguished (light)
tfn	Till further notice
Tr, twr	Tower
T/R	Traffic Report (route notification)
TSS	Traffic Separation Scheme
uncov	Uncovers
UQ	Ultra Quick flashing light
UT	Universal Time (= approx GMT)
Var	Variation (magnetic)
(vert)	Vertically disposed (lights)
Vi	Violet
vis	Visibility, visible
VLCC	Very large crude carrier (Oil tanker)
VNF	Voie Navigable de France (canals)
VQ	Very Quick flashing light
VTS	Vessel Traffic Service
W	West. White
WCM	West Cardinal Mark (buoy/beacon)
Wd	Weed (nature of seabed)
wef	With effect from
WGS	World Geodetic System (GPS datum)
wi-fi	Wireless Fidelity (internet access)
WIG	Wing in ground effect (craft)
WIP	Work in progress
Wk, ⌐ ⊕	Wreck (see also Fig 1(1))
WMO	World Meteorological Organisation
WPT, ⊕	Waypoint
WZ	Code for UK coastal navigation warning
Y	Yellow, Amber, Orange

0.3   PASSAGE PLANNING FORM

DATE:............................   FROM: ....   TO: ....   DIST: ....nm

ALTERNATIVE DESTINATION(S): ....

WEATHER FORECAST: ....

....

FORECASTS AVAILABLE DURING PASSAGE: ....

....

TIDES

DATE:..	DATE:..	DATE: ....
PLACE:...	PLACE:...	PLACE:...
HW	HW	HW ....
LW	LW	LW ....
HW	HW	HW ....
LW	LW	LW ....

COEFFICIENT: ....

HEIGHT OF TIDE AT: ....

.... hrs   .... m   .... hrs   .... m   .... hrs   .... m

DEPTH CONSTRAINTS: ....

TIDAL STREAMS AT: ....

TURNS .... AT .... TOTAL SET (FM .... TO ....): ....° .... M

TURNS .... AT .... TOTAL SET (FM .... TO ....): ....° .... M

NET TIDAL STREAM FOR PASSAGE: ....° .... M

ESTIMATED TIME: ....hrs   ETD: ....   ETA: ....

SUN/MOON	SUNRISE:	SUNSET:	
	MOONRISE:	MOONSET:	PHASE: ....

WAYPOINTS	NO	NAME	TRACK/DISTANCE (TO NEXT WAYPOINT)
	....	....	.... / ....
	....	....	.... / ....
	....	....	.... / ....
	....	....	.... / ....
	....	....	.... / ....

DANGERS   CLEARING BEARINGS/RANGES/DEPTHS

....

....

....

LIGHTS/MARKS EXPECTED ....

....

....

....

COMMUNICATIONS	PORT/MARINA	VHF	☎ ....
	PORT/MARINA	VHF	☎ ....

NOTES (CHARTS PREPARED & PAGE NUMBERS OF RELEVANT PILOTS / ALMANACS / ETC): ....

....

....

0.4   PASSAGE PLANNING

All passages by any vessel that goes to sea *must* be planned. This is defined as proceeding beyond sheltered waters. Full passage planning requirements may be found in Chapter V of the International Convention for Safety of Life at Sea (SOLAS), but more digestible guidance for small craft is in the MCA's Pleasure Craft Information Pack at: **https://www.gov. uk/government/uploads/system/uploads/attachment_data/ file/282631/pleasure_craft_information_packdec07-2.pdf.**

Although the passage plan does not have to be recorded on paper, in the event of legal action a written plan is clear proof that the required planning has been completed. A suggested passage planning form is on the previous page. When completed this would constitute a reasonable passage plan. The blank form may be photocopied and/or modified.

Although spot checks on small craft are unlikely, the MCA could, following an accident or incident, take action under the Merchant Shipping Act if it could be proved that the skipper did not have a reasonable passage plan.

All passage plans should at least consider the following:

- **Weather.** Check the weather forecast and know how to get regular updates during the passage.
- **Tides.** Check tidal predictions and determine if there are any limiting depths at your port of departure, during the passage and at the port of arrival (and at alternative ports, if applicable). Tidal streams will almost certainly affect the plan.
- **Vessel.** Confirm she is suitable for the intended trip, is properly equipped, and has sufficient fuel, water and food on board.
- **Crew.** Take into account your crew's experience, expertise and stamina. Cold, tiredness and seasickness can be debilitating – and skippers are not immune.
- **Navigation.** Make sure you are aware of all navigational dangers by consulting up to date charts, pilot books and this Almanac. Never *rely* on GPS for fixing your position.
- **Contingency plan.** Consider bolt holes which can be entered *safely* in an emergency.
- **Information ashore.** Make sure someone ashore knows your plans, when they should become concerned and what action to take if necessary. Be sure to join the Coastguard Voluntary Identification Scheme.

0.5   POSITIONS FROM GPS

GPS employs World Geodetic System 84 (WGS84). Galileo works to the ETRS 89. With the exception of some areas of Ireland and the west coast of Scotland, AC of UK waters use the ETRS 89 datum. Harbour chartlets reflect this.

If the chart in use is not referenced to ETRS 89/WGS84, positions read from the GPS receiver must be converted to the datum of the chart in use. This is printed on the chart and gives the Lat/Long corrections to be applied. They can be significant. There are two options:

- Set the receiver to WGS84. Before plotting positions, manually apply the corrections given on the chart. This option is advised by UKHO.
- Set the receiver to the datum of the chart in use; the datum corrections will be applied by the receiver's software. This method is not the most accurate due to the random nature of the differences.

0.6   VHF COMMUNICATIONS

Radio Telephony (R/T)

VHF radio (Marine band 156·00–174·00 MHz) is used by most vessels. Range is slightly better than the line of sight between aerials, typically about 20M between yachts and up to 65M to a shore station depending on aerial heights. It always pays to fit a good aerial, as high as possible.

VHF sets may be **Simplex**, ie transmit and receive on the same frequency, so only one person can talk at a time. **Semi-Duplex** (most modern sets), transmit and receive on different frequencies, or **full Duplex**, ie simultaneous Semi-Duplex, so conversation is normal, but two aerials are needed.

Marine VHF frequencies are known by their international channel number (Ch), as shown below.

Channels are grouped according to three main purposes, but some have more than one purpose.

Public correspondence: **(via Coast radio stations)**
Ch 26, 27, 25, 24, 23, 28, 04, 01, 03, 02, 07, 05, 84, 87, 86, 83, 85, 88, 61, 64, 65, 62, 66, 63, 60, 82, 78, 81.
All channels can be used for Duplex.

Inter-ship:
Ch 06*, 08*, 10, 13, 09, 72*, 73, 69, 77*, 15, 17.
These are all Simplex channels. * for use in UK.

Port Operations:
Simplex: Ch 12, 14, 11, 13, 09, 68, 71, 74, 69, 73, 17, 15.
Duplex: Ch 20, 22, 18, 19, 21, 05, 07, 02, 03, 01, 04, 78, 82, 79, 81, 80, 60, 63, 66, 62, 65, 64, 61, 84.

The following channels have one specific purpose:

Ch 0 (156·00 MHz): SAR ops, not available to yachts.

Ch 10 (156·50 MHz), **62** (160·725 MHz), **63** (160·775 MHz) and **64** (160·825 MHz): MSI broadcasts. The optimum channel number is stated on Ch 16 in an announcement prior to the broadcast itself.

Ch 13 (156·650 MHz): Inter-ship communications relating to safety of navigation; a possible channel for calling a merchant ship if no contact on Ch 16.

Ch 16 (156·80 MHz): Distress, Safety and calling. Ch 16, in parallel with DSC Ch 70, will be monitored by ships, CG rescue centres (and, in some areas, any remaining Coast Radio Stations) for Distress and Safety until further notice. Yachts should monitor Ch 16. After an initial call, stations concerned **must** switch to a working channel, except for Distress and Safety matters.

Ch 67 (156·375 MHz): Small craft safety channel used by all UK CG centres, accessed via Ch 16.

Ch 70 (156·525 MHz): Digital Selective Calling for Distress and Safety purposes under GMDSS.

Ch 80 (157·025 MHz): Primary working channel between yachts and UK marinas.

Ch M (157·85 MHz): Secondary working channel, formerly known as Ch 37. For use in UK territorial waters only.

Ch M2 (161·425 MHz): for race control, with Ch M as stand-by. YCs often use Ch M2. For use in UK waters only

Your position should be given as Lat/Long or the vessel's bearing and distance *from* a charted object, eg 'My position 225° Isle of May 4M' means you are 4M SW of the Isle of May (*not* 4M NE). Use the 360° True bearing notation and the 24-hour clock (0001–2359), specifying UT or LT.

0.7   DISTRESS CALLS

Distress signal - MAYDAY

Distress only applies to a situation where a *vessel or person is in grave and imminent danger and requires immediate assistance*. A MAYDAY call should usually be sent on VHF Ch 16 or MF 2182 kHz, but any frequency may be used if help would thus be obtained more quickly.

Distress, Urgency and Safety messages from vessels at sea are free of charge. A Distress call has priority over all other transmissions. If heard, cease all transmissions that may interfere with the Distress call or messages, and listen on the frequency concerned.

Brief your crew so they are all able to send a Distress message. The MAYDAY message format (below) should be displayed near the radio. Before making the call:

- Switch on radio (check main battery switch is ON)
- Select HIGH power (25 watts)
- Select VHF Ch 16 (or 2182 kHz for MF)
- Press and hold down the transmit button, and say slowly and distinctly:

- **MAYDAY MAYDAY MAYDAY**
- **THIS IS** ....
(name of boat, spoken three times)
- **MAYDAY** ....
(name of boat spoken once)
- **CALLSIGN / MMSI Number** ....
(Following a DSC alert)
- **MY POSITION IS** ....
(latitude and longitude, true bearing and
    distance *from* a known point, or general location)
- **Nature of distress** ....
(sinking, on fire etc)
- **Help required** ....
(immediate assistance)
- **Number of persons on board** ....
- **Any other important, helpful information** ....
(you are taking to the liferaft; distress rockets are
    being fired etc)
- **OVER**

On completion of the Distress message, release the transmit button and listen. The boat's position is of vital importance and should be repeated if time allows. If an acknowledgement is not received, check the set and repeat the Distress call.

Vessels with GMDSS equipment should make a MAYDAY call on Ch 16, including their MMSI and callsign, *after* sending a DSC Distress alert on VHF Ch 70 or MF 2187·5 kHz.

0.7.1   MAYDAY acknowledgement

In coastal waters an immediate acknowledgement should be expected, as follows:

MAYDAY ....
(name of station sending the Distress message, spoken three times)
THIS IS ....
(name of station acknowledging, spoken three times)
RECEIVED MAYDAY

If you hear a Distress message, write down the details and, if you can help, acknowledge accordingly - but only after giving an opportunity for the nearest Coastguard station or some larger vessel to do so.

0.7.2   MAYDAY relay

If you hear a Distress message from a vessel, and it is not acknowledged, you should pass on the message as follows:

MAYDAY RELAY ....
(spoken three times)
THIS IS ....
(name of vessel re-transmitting the Distress message, spoken three times), followed by the intercepted message.

0.7.3   Control of MAYDAY traffic

A MAYDAY call imposes general radio silence until the vessel concerned or some other authority (eg the nearest Coastguard) cancels the Distress. If necessary the station controlling Distress traffic may impose radio silence as follows:

SEELONCE MAYDAY, followed by its name or other identification, on the Distress frequency.

If some other station nearby believes it necessary to do likewise, it may transmit:

SEELONCE DISTRESS, followed by its name or other identification.

0.7.4   Relaxing radio silence

When complete radio silence is no longer necessary, the controlling station may relax radio silence as follows, indicating that restricted working may be resumed:

MAYDAY
ALL STATIONS, ALL STATIONS, ALL STATIONS
THIS IS ....
(name or callsign)
The time ....
The name of the vessel in distress ....
PRUDONCE

Normal working on the Distress frequency may then be resumed, having listened carefully before transmitting. Subsequent calls from the casualty should be prefixed by the Urgency signal (0.8).

If Distress working continues on other frequencies these will be identified. For example, PRUDONCE on 2182 kHz, but SEELONCE on VHF Ch 16.

0.7.5   Cancelling radio silence

When the problem is resolved, the Distress call must be cancelled by the co-ordinating station using the prowords SEELONCE FEENEE as follows:

MAYDAY
ALL STATIONS, ALL STATIONS, ALL STATIONS
THIS IS ....(name or callsign)
The time ....
The name of the vessel in distress ....
SEELONCE FEENEE

0.8 URGENCY AND SAFETY CALLS

Urgency signal - PAN PAN

The radio Urgency prefix, consisting of the words PAN PAN spoken three times, indicates that a vessel, or station, has *a very urgent message concerning the safety of a ship or person*. It may be used when urgent medical advice is needed. This is an example of an Urgency call:

> **PAN PAN, PAN PAN, PAN PAN**
>
> **ALL STATIONS, ALL STATIONS, ALL STATIONS**
>
> **THIS IS YACHT SEABIRD, SEABIRD, SEABIRD**
>
> Two nine zero degrees Needles lighthouse two miles
>
> Dismasted and propeller fouled
>
> Drifting east north east towards Shingles Bank
>
> Require urgent tow
>
> **OVER**

PAN PAN messages take priority over all traffic except Distress, and are sent on Ch 16 or 2182 kHz. They should be cancelled when the urgency is over.

If the message is long (eg a medical call) or communications traffic is heavy, it may be passed on a working frequency after an initial call on Ch 16 or 2182 kHz. At the end of the initial call you should indicate that you are switching to a working frequency.

An PAN PAN call warrants a similar reaction to a Distress call.

0.8.1 Safety signal - SÉCURITÉ

The word SÉCURITÉ (pronounced SAY-CURE-E-TAY) spoken three times, indicates that the station is about to transmit an important navigational or meteorological warning. Messages usually originate from the CG or Coast Radio Station, and are transmitted on a working channel after an announcement on the distress/calling channel (Ch 16 or 2182 kHz).

Safety messages are usually addressed to 'All stations', and are often transmitted at the end of the first available silence period. An example of a Sécurité message is:

> **SÉCURITÉ, SÉCURITÉ, SÉCURITÉ** ....
>
> **THIS IS** ....
> (CG Centre or Coast Radio Station callsign, spoken three times)
>
> **ALL STATIONS** ....
> (spoken three times) followed by instructions to change channel, then the message.

0.9 GMDSS

The Global Maritime Distress and Safety System (GMDSS) came into force in 1999. Seagoing vessels over 300 gross tons are required by SOLAS to comply with GMDSS. However, it is important that the principles of the system are understood, and you should at least consider fitting compliant equipment depending on your cruising area. Full details may be found in ALRS Vol 5 (NP 285).

0.9.1 Purpose

GMDSS enables a coordinated SAR operation to be mounted rapidly and reliably anywhere at sea. To this end, terrestrial and satellite communications and navigation equipment is used to alert SAR authorities ashore and ships in the vicinity to a Distress incident or Urgency situation. GMDSS also promulgates Maritime Safety Information (MSI).

0.9.2 Sea areas

The type of equipment carried by a vessel depends of her operating area. The four GMDSS Areas are:

A1	An area within R/T coverage of at least one VHF Coastguard or Coast radio station in which continuous VHF alerting is available via DSC. Range: 20–50M from the CG/CRS.
A2	An area, excluding sea area A1, within R/T coverage of at least one MF CG/CRS in which continuous DSC alerting is available. Range: approx 50–250M from the CG/CRS.
A3	An area between 76°N and 76°S, excluding sea areas A1 and A2, within coverage of HF or an Inmarsat satellite in which continuous alerting is available.
A4	An area outside sea areas A1, A2 and A3, ie the polar regions, within coverage of HF.

In each Area, in addition to a Navtex receiver, certain types of radio equipment must be carried by GMDSS vessels: In A1, VHF DSC; A2, VHF and MF DSC; A3, VHF, MF and HF or SatCom; A4, VHF, MF and HF.

0.9.3 Digital Selective Calling (DSC)

GMDSS comprises 'sub-systems' which are coordinated through Maritime Rescue Coordination Centres (MRCC) to ensure safety at sea. DSC is one of the 'sub-systems' of GMDSS. It uses terrestrial communications for making initial contact and, in a distress situation, provides the vessel's identity, nature of distress and position (entered manually or automatically if linked with the GPS). In all DSC messages every vessel and relevant shore station has a 9-digit Maritime Mobile Service Identity (MMSI) which is in effect an automatic electronic callsign. Dedicated frequencies are: VHF Ch 70, MF 2187·5 kHz. A thorough working knowledge of the following procedure is needed.

A typical VHF/DSC Distress alert might be sent as follows:

- Briefly press the (red, guarded) Distress button. The set automatically switches to Ch 70 (DSC Distress channel). Press again for 5 seconds to transmit a basic Distress alert with position and time. The radio then reverts to Ch 16.
- If time permits, select the nature of the distress from the menu, eg Collision, then press the Distress button for 5 seconds to send a full Distress alert.

A CG/CRS should automatically send an acknowledgement on Ch 70 before replying on Ch 16. Ships in range should reply directly on Ch 16. When a DSC Distress acknowledgement has been received, or after about 15 seconds, the vessel in distress should transmit a MAYDAY message by voice on Ch 16, including its MMSI.

0.10 NATIONAL COASTWATCH INSTITUTION

The National Coastwatch Institution (NCI) – www.nci.org.uk a national charity, is a voluntary organisation keeping visual watch along the coast of England and Wales, assisting the preservation and protection of life at sea and along the shore. The National Office is 17 Dean St, Liskeard, Cornwall, PL14 4AB ☎(01579) 347392. There are 56 operational stations (2021) manned by over 2600 volunteers. They are marked on the Area maps by the symbol © and maintain direct contact with HM CG, which also certify NCI stations and watchkeepers.

Stations monitor VHF Ch **65** 16, HM CG channels and local operational VHF channels. **65** is the NCI dedicated channel.

Seafarers can call directly for radio checks, AIS checks, actual weather, sea state, current hazards and local information. Call sign: name of selected station, (see full list at: www.nci. org.uk) plus abbreviation NCI, e.g: *Froward Point NCI*. Do **not** call on Ch 16 or use call sign *National Coastwatch*.

0.11   THE SEA SAFETY GROUP

The Sea Safety Group – www.seasafetygroup.org – a charity, is an association of independent coastal watch stations, each authorised by HM CG (MCA) to provide additional lookout and communications cover around the UK. They are similar in ethos but separate from the NCI.

0.12   HM COASTGUARD - CONTACT DETAILS OF CG CENTRES

EASTERN REGION
DOVER COASTGUARD
50°08'N 01°20'E. DSC MMSI 002320010
Langdon Battery, Swingate, Dover CT15 5NA.
☎ 01304 210008. ▨ 01304 202137. (Note: use call signs *Thames Coastguard* or *Dover Coastguard*, both on Ch 16)
Area: Camber Sands to Southwold.
Operates Channel Navigation Information Service (CNIS).

LONDON COASTGUARD
51°30'N 00°03'E. MMSI 002320063
Thames Barrier Navigation Centre, Unit 28,
34 Bowater Road, Woolwich, London SE18 5TF.
☎ 02083 127380. ▨ 02083 127679.
Area: River Thames from Shell Haven Pt (N bank) & Egypt Bay (S bank) up-river to Teddington Lock.

†HUMBER COASTGUARD
54°06'N 00°11'W. MMSI 002320007
Lime Kiln Lane, Bridlington, E Yorkshire YO15 2LX.
☎ 01262 672317. ▨ 01262 606915.
Area: Southwold to the Scottish border.

EASTERN AND NORTHERN SCOTLAND REGION
†ABERDEEN COASTGUARD
57°08'N 02°05'W. MMSI 002320004
Marine House, Blaikies Quay, Aberdeen AB11 5PB.
☎ 01224 592334. ▨ 01224 212862.
Area: English border to Cape Wrath, incl Pentland Firth.

†SHETLAND COASTGUARD
60°09'N 01°08'W. MMSI 002320001
Knab Road, Lerwick ZE1 0AX.
☎ 01595 692976. ▨ 01595 694810.
Area: Orkney, Fair Isle and Shetland.

NOTE: †Monitors DSC MF 2187.5 kHz.

0.13   NETHERLANDS COAST GUARD

The national SAR agency is: SAR Commission, Directorate Transport Safety (DGG), PO Box 20904, 2500 EX The Hague, Netherlands.

The Netherlands CG at Den Helder, co-located with the Navy HQ, coordinates SAR operations as the Dutch JRCC for A1 and A2 Sea Areas. (JRCC = Joint Rescue Coordination Centre – marine & aeronautical.) Call sign is *Netherlands Coast Guard*, but *Den Helder Rescue* is used during SAR operations.

The JRCC keeps a listening watch H24 on DSC Ch 70, and MF DSC 2187·5 kHz (but not on 2182 kHz); MMSI 002442000.

Coast Guard Operations can be contacted H24 via:

> **In emergency:**
> ☎ + 31 9000 111 or dial 112.
>
> **Operational telephone number:**
> ☎ + 31 223 542300. ▨ + 31 223 658358; ccc@kustwacht.nl If using a mobile phone, call 9000 111, especially if the International emergency number 112 is subject to delays.
>
> **Admin/info (HO):**
> ☎+31 223 658300. ▨+31 223 658303. info@kustwacht.nl PO Box 10.000/MPC 10A, 1780 CA Den Helder.

Remote Coast Guard stations are shown on Fig 0(6). Working channels are VHF 23 and 83.

0.13.1   Medical advice
Call initially on Ch 16, DSC Ch 70 or 2187·5 kHz (MMSI 002442000). Working chans are VHF Ch 23 & 83 or MF 2824 kHz (transmit), 2520 kHz (receive).

0.13.2   Resources
The Dutch Lifeboat Ass'n (KNRM) manages 26 lifeboat stations and 13 inshore lifeboat stations along the coast. The 60 lifeboats include 13m LOA water-jet, rigid inflatables capable of 36 kn. Helicopters, fixed wing aircraft and ships of the RNLN can be called upon; also Air Force helos at Leeuwarden. The area of activity extends across the Dutch Continental Shelf and into the Waddenzee, IJsselmeer and estuaries of Zuid Holland and Zeeland.

0.14   BELGIAN COAST GUARD

The Belgian Coast Guard coordinates SAR operations from Oostende MRCC, callsign *Coast Guard Oostende*. The MRCC and *Oostende Radio* (Coast Radio Station) both keep listening watch H24 on Ch 16, 67, 2182 kHz and DSC Ch 70 and 2187·5 kHz.

> **Coast Guard stations**
> **MRCC OOSTENDE**
> ☎ +32 59 701000; ▨ +32 59 703605
> MMSI 002059981
> mrcc@mrcc.be
>
> **RCC Brussels** (Point of contact for COSPAS/SARSAT)
> ☎ +32 2 751 4615; ▨ +32 2 7524201
> rcc@mil.be
>
> **Coast radio stations**
> **OOSTENDE Radio**
> ☎ +32 59 255493   ▨ +32 59 255467   rmd@mil.be
> MMSI 002050480 Ch 16, MF 2182 kHz, DSC Ch 70 and 2187·5 kHz (H24)
> MF: Tx 2484, Rx 3178 kHz. VHF Ch 07, 24, 27, 63, 78, 81 85

Zeebrugge	Ch 27
Oudenburg (Oostende)	Ch 85
De Panne (French border)	Ch 78
Antwerp	Chs 07,24,27
Ghent	Chs 24, 81
Rest of Belgium	Ch 24

0.14.1   Resources
Offshore and inshore lifeboats are based at Nieuwpoort, Oostende and Zeebrugge.
The Belgian Air Force provides helicopters from Koksijde near the French border. The Belgian Navy also participates in SAR operations as required.

Fig 0(1) Distress and life saving signals

(1) Signals to be used by Ships, Aircraft or Persons in Distress

Fire rocket vertically

If windy fire 15° downwind

NEVER fire a parachute flare if a helicopter is approaching

In low cloud fire at 45°

WIND

NEVER fire into the wind

Handheld pinpoint flare shows exactly where you are - use inshore or in sight of other vessels

Orange smoke for use by day - especially in bright conditions

For use at night or in dull conditions to pinpoint position

Red hand flare

Floating orange smoke

Buoyant smoke

Long range signal for use offshore

Red parachute rocket

White collision warning flare

White pinpoint

Handheld orange smoke

Orange hand smoke

(2) Replies from life-saving stations etc. to distress signals made by ships or persons

Orange smoke signal

White star rocket - three single signals fired at intervals of about one minute

Meaning
'You are seen - assistance will be given as soon as possible'

(3) Surface to Air Signals

Message	International Code of Signals		ICAO Visual Signals
'I require assistance'	'V' ⊠	(· · · —)	V
'I require medical assistance'	'W' ▣	(· — —)	X
'No' or 'negative'	'N'	(— ·)	N
'Yes' or 'affirmative'	'C'	(— · — ·)	Y
'Proceed in this direction'			↑

(4) Air to Surface replies

'Message understood'

or   or   or 'T' (—)
                         or 'R' (· — ·)

Drop a message   Rocking wings   Flash landing or navigation lights twice   Morse code signal by light

'Message not understood - repeat'

or 'RPT'
(· — · · — · —)

Straight and level flight   Circling   Morse code signal by light

(5) Air to Surface Direction Signals

Sequence of 3 manœuvres meaning proceed in this direction

(1) Circle Vessel at least once

(2) Cross low ahead of vessel, rocking wings

(3) Overfly vessel and head in required direction

Your assistance is no longer required

Cross low astern of vessel rocking wings

Note: as an alternative to rocking wings, the aircraft engine pitch or volume may be varied

(6) Surface to Air replies

'Message understood - I will comply'

Change course or direction

or

'T' (—)   Morse Code signal by light

or

Code and answering pennant 'Close up'

'I am unable to comply'

'N' (— ·)   Morse Code signal by light

or

International flag 'N'

0.15 NAVTEX

NAVTEX is the prime method of disseminating MSI to at least 200 miles offshore. A dedicated aerial and receiver with an LCD screen (or integrated printer) are required. The user selects which stations and message categories are recorded for automatic display or printing.

Two frequencies are used. On the international frequency, 518kHz, messages are always available in English with excellent coverage of Europe. Interference between stations is minimised by scheduling time slots and and by limiting transmission power; see Fig 6(3). NAVTEX information applies only to the geographical area for which each station is responsible.

On the national frequency 490kHz (for clarity, shown in red throughout this section) the UK issues inshore waters forecasts and coastal station actuals. Elsewhere it is used mainly for transmissions in the national language. 490khz stations have different identification letters from 518kHz stations. NAVTEX is particularly useful if preoccupied handling your vessel as you will not miss potentially important information.

0.15.1 Message categories

A*	Navigational warnings
B*	Meteorological warnings
C	Ice reports
D*	SAR info and Piracy attack warnings
E	Weather forecasts
F	Pilot service
G	AIS
H	LORAN
I	Spare
J	SATNAV
K	Other electronic Navaids
L	Navwarnings additional to **A**
M-U	Spare
V-Y	Special services – as allocated
Z	No messages on hand

* These categories cannot be rejected by the receiver.

Fig 0(2) NAVTEX stations/areas – North Sea

0.15.4 Message numbering

Each message is prefixed by a group of four characters:

The 1st character is the ident of the station (eg **E** for Niton). The 2nd is the message category, see 0.13.1. The 3rd and 4th are message serial numbers from 01 to 99, then re-starting at 01. The serial number 00 is used for urgent messages which are always printed.

Messages which are corrupt or have already been printed are rejected. Weather messages, and certain other message types, are dated and timed. All NAVTEX messages end with NNNN.

0.15.2 UK 518 kHz stations

The times (UT) of weather messages are in bold; the times of an extended outlook (a further 2 or 3 days beyond the shipping forecast period) are in italics.

E – Niton	*0040*	0440	**0840**	1240	1640	**2040**
Thames clockwise to Fastnet, excluding Trafalgar.						

G – Cullercoats	*0100*	0500	**0900**	1300	1700	**2100**
Fair Isle clockwise to Thames, excluding N and S Utsire, Fisher and German Bight.						

0.15.3 UK 490 kHz stations

These provide forecasts for UK inshore waters (to 12M offshore), a national 3 day outlook for inshore waters and, at times in bold, reports of actual weather at the places listed below. To receive these reports select message category 'V' (0.13.1) on your NAVTEX receiver. Times (UT) of transmissions are listed in chronological order.

Actual Met data includes: Sea level pressure (mb), wind direction and speed (kn), weather, visibility (M), air and sea temperatures (°C), dewpoint temperature (°C) and mean wave height (m).

I – Niton	Gibraltar Point to St David's Head	0120	0520	**0920**	1320	1720	**2120**
Sandettie Lt V and other places westwards along the English Channel.							

U – Cullercoats	C. Wrath & Shetland to N Foreland	0320	0720	**1120**	**1520**	1920	**2320**
Sandettie Lt V, Manston, Shoeburyness, Weybourne, Donna Nook or Bridlington, Boulmer, Leuchars, Aberdeen, Lossiemouth, Wick, Kirkwall, Lerwick, Foula, K7 Met buoy, Sule Skerry.							

0.15.5   NAVTEX coverage abroad

Selected NAVTEX stations in Metarea I, identity codes and times. Weather messages in **bold**. Gale warnings are usually 4 hourly.

METAREA I (Co-ordinator – UK)		Transmission times (UT)					
B – **Oostende**, Belgium (Mostly Dutch)	**0010**	0410	0810	**1210**	1610	2010
P – **Netherlands CG**, Den Helder	**0230**	0630	1030	**1430**	1830	2230
L – **Pinneberg**, Hamburg (In German)	**0150**	0550	0950	1350	**1750**	2150
S – **Pinneberg**, Hamburg	**0300**	**0700**	**1100**	**1500**	**1900**	**2300**
V – Oostende, Belgium (Note 2)	0330	0730	1130	1530	1930	2330
L – **Rogaland**, Norway	**0150**	0550	0950	**1350**	1750	2150

Note 1   Forecasts and strong wind warnings for Thames and Dover, plus nav info for the Belgian coast.
2   No weather information, only Nav warnings.

0.16   MSI BROADCASTS BY HM COASTGUARD

CGOC routinely broadcast Maritime Safety Information (MSI) every 3 hours from the start times in the Table below, but these can sometimes vary during busy operational times and emergencies. The VHF broadcast channel, either 10, 62, 63 or 64 is announced first on Ch 16. Each broadcast contains one of 3 different Groups of MSI:

Group A, Shipping forecast, new Inshore waters forecast and 24 hrs outlook, Gale warnings, Navigational (WZ) warnings and Subfacts & Gunfacts where appropriate ‡. Times of 'A' broadcasts are in bold.

Group B, New Inshore waters forecast, previous outlook, and Gale warnings. 'B' broadcast times are in plain type.

Group C Repeat of Inshore forecast and Gale warnings plus new Strong wind warnings. 'C' broadcast times are italicised.
‡ Subfacts and Gunfacts (occas) by Aberdeen Coastguard.

INSHORE WATERS FORECAST AREAS (In broadcast sequence) MSI TRANSMITTERS/START TIMES AND VHF WORKING CHANNELS

1) Cape Wrath to Rattray Head inc Orkney. 2) Rattray Head to Berwick-upon-Tweed.
ABERDEEN CG, every 3 hours commencing 0130

Durness (Loch Eriboll)	63	58°34'N 04°44'W
Noss Head (Wick)	62	58°29'N 03°03'W
Rosemarkie (Cromarty)	64	57°38'N 04°05'W
Windyheads Hill	63	57°39'N 02°14'W
Gregness *MF 2226kHz*, 64		57°08'N 02°03'W
Inverbervie	63	56°51'N 02°16'W
Fife Ness	62	56°17'N 02°35'W
Craigkelly (Burntisland)	63	56°04'N 03°14'W
St Abbs Head/Cross Law	64	55°54'N 02°12'W

3) Berwick-upon-Tweed to Whitby. 4) Whitby to Gibraltar Point.
HUMBER CG, every 3 hours commencing 0150

Newton	63	55°31'N 01°37'W
Cullercoats(Blyth) MF *1925kHz* 64		55°04'N 01°28'W
Boulby	63	54°34'N 00°51'W
Ravenscar	64	54°24'N 00°30'W
Flamborough	63	54°07'N 00°05'W
Easington (Spurn Hd)	64	53°39'N 00°06'E

Mablethorpe	62	53°21'N 00°16'E
Guy's Head (Wisbech)	63	52°48'N 00°13'E
Langham (Blakeney)	64	52°57'N 00°58'E
Trimingham (Cromer)	63	52°54'N 01°21'E
Caister (Great Yarmouth) 64		52°36N 01°43E
Lowestoft	63	52°29'N 01°46'E

5) Gibraltar Point to North Foreland.
6) North Foreland to Selsey Bill.
DOVER CG, every 3 hours commencing 0110

Bawdsey (R Deben)	62	52°00'N 01°25'E
Walton-on-the-Naze	63	51°51'N 01°17'E
Bradwell (R Blackwater)	64	51°44'N 00°53'E
Shoeburyness	63	51°31'N 00°47'E
Langdon (Dover)	64	51°08'N 01°21'E
Fairlight (Hastings)	62	50°52'N 00°39'E

18) Shetland Isles and 60 NM radius.
SHETLAND CG, 0110

Fitful Head (Sumburgh)	63	59°54'N 01°23'W
Saxavord (Unst)	63	60°42'N 00°51'W
Lerwick (Shetland)	62	60°10'N 01°08'W
Collafirth *MF 1770kHz*, 64		60°32'N 01°23'W
Wideford Hill (Kirkwall)	64	58°59'N 03°01'W

NOTE: Information on this page is subject to change. Check the MCGA Maritime Safety Information leaflet (MCA/064) at www.mcga.gov.uk, and the free monthly pdf updates from January to June for download at www.reedsnauticalalmanac.co.uk/update

0.17   OTHER UK WEATHER BROADCASTS

BBC Radio 4 Shipping forecast is broadcast at:

0048, 0520 LT[1]		LW FM
1203 LT	weekdays only	LW FM
1754 LT		LW only
0048, 0520,1754 LT (Sat/Sun)	LW, FM	

[1] Includes weather reports from coastal stations

Frequencies

LW		198 kHz
FM	England:	92·4–94·6 MHz
	Scotland:	91·3–96·1 MHz
		103·5–104·9 MHz

Broadcasts of shipping and inshore waters forecasts by HM Coastguard

Coastguard	Shipping forecast areas	Inshore areas	B	C	A	C	B	C	A	C
Dover	Humber,Thames, Dover, Wight.	5, 6	0110	*0410*	**0710**	*1010*	1310	*1610*	**1910**	*2210*
Humber	Tyne, Dogger, Fisher,Humber, German Bight.,	3,4,5	0150	*0450*	**0750**	*1050*	1350	*1650*	**1950**	*2250*
Aberdeen‡	Tyne, Forties, Forth, Cromarty, Fair Is.	1, 2	0130	*0430*	**0730**	*1030*	1330	*1630*	**1930**	*2230*
Shetland	Cromarty, Viking, Fair Isle, Faeroes.	1, 18	0110	*0410*	**0710**	*1010*	1310	*1610*	**1910**	*2210*

Broadcast times LT

The Shipping Forecast contains:

Time of issue; summary of gale warnings in force at that time; a general synopsis of weather systems and their expected development and movement over the next 24 hours; sea area forecasts for the same 24 hours, including wind direction/force, weather and visibility in each; and an outlook for the following 24 hours. **Gale warnings** for all affected areas are broadcast at the earliest break in Radio 4 programmes after receipt, as well as after the next news bulletin.

Weather reports from coastal stations follow the 0048 and 0520 shipping forecasts. They include wind direction and force, present weather, visibility, and sealevel pressure and tendency, if available. The stations are shown in Fig 0(4).

0.17.1   BBC Radio 4 Inshore waters forecast

The forecast for UK inshore waters up to 12M offshore (for relevant areas, see 0.15), valid for 24 hrs, is broadcast after the 0048 and 0520 coastal station reports. It includes forecasts of wind direction and force, weather, visibility and sea state.

Reports of actual weather are broadcast from all the stations below after the 0048 inshore waters forecast and also after the 0520 forecast, except those in italics: Lerwick. *Wick**; *Aberdeen*, Leuchars, *Boulmer*; Bridlington; Sandettie LV*, Greenwich LV*.

These stations are shown in Fig 0(4). An asterisk* denotes an automatic station.

0.17.2   Terms used in weather bulletins

Speed of movement of pressure systems	
Slowly	< 15 knots
Steadily	15–25 knots
Rather quickly	25–35 knots
Rapidly	35–45 knots
Very rapidly	> 45 knots

Visibility	
Good	> 5 miles
Moderate	2–5 miles
Poor	1000 metres–2 miles
Fog	Less than 1000 metres

Timing of gale warnings	
Imminent:	Within 6 hrs from time of issue
Soon:	6–12 hrs from time of issue
Later:	>12 hrs from time of issue

Barometric pressure changes (tendency)

Rising or falling slowly: Pressure change of 0·1 to 1·5 hPa/mb in the preceding 3 hours.

Rising or falling: Pressure change of 1·6 to 3·5 hPa/mb in the preceding 3 hours.

Rising or falling quickly: Pressure change of 3·6 to 6 hPa/mb in the preceding 3 hours.

Rising or falling very rapidly: Pressure change of more than 6 hPa/mb in the preceding 3 hours.

Now rising (or falling): Pressure has been falling (rising) or steady in the preceding 3 hours, but at the observation time was definitely rising (falling).

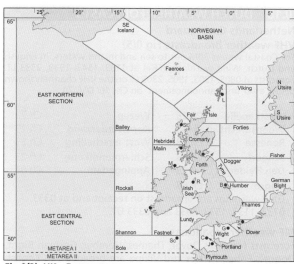

Fig 0(3) UK - Forecast areas

Fig 0(4) Stations reporting actual weather via BBC Radio 4, telephone recordings or NAVTEX

0.18   DUTCH WEATHER FORECASTS

Netherlands Coastguard
VHF weather broadcasts Fig 0(5)

For Coastal waters 30M out to sea and inland waters, in English and Dutch. Wind warnings, (F6+) at 1133, 1543, 1933, 2333 LT. Forecasts at 0805, 1305, 1905, 2305 LT on the VHF channels shown below after prior announcement on Chs 16/ DSC 70.

Westkapelle	Ch 23	Wezep	Ch 23
Woensdrecht	Ch 83	Kornwerderzand	Ch 23
Renesse	Ch 83	West Terschelling	Ch 83
Schoorl	Ch 83	Schiermonnikoog	Ch 23
Den Helder	Ch 23	Appingedam	Ch 83
Hoorn	Ch 83		

Gale warnings are broadcast on receipt and at 0333, 0733, 1133, 1533, 1933 and 2333 UT.

MF weather broadcasts

Forecasts for areas Dover, Thames, Humber, German Bight, Dogger, Fisher, Forties and Viking are broadcast in **English** by Scheveningen at 0940 and 2140 UT on 3673 kHz. Gale warnings for these areas are broadcast in **English** on receipt and at 0333, 0733, 1133, 1533, 1933 and 2333 UT.

Fig 0(5) Netherlands CRS broadcasts, showing the boundaries and names of coastal areas referred to above

0.17.1   Radio Noord-Holland (FM)

Coastal forecasts for northern areas, gale warnings and wind strength are broadcast in Dutch, Mon-Fri at 0730, 0838, 1005, 1230 and 1705LT; Sat/Sun 1005, by:

Wieringermeer 93.9 MHz and **Haarlem** 97.6 MHz.

0.17.2   Omroep Zeeland (FM)

Coastal forecasts for southern areas, synopsis, gale warnings and wind strength are broadcast in Dutch, Mon-Fri at 0715, 0915, 1215 and 1715LT; Sat/Sun 1015, by:

Philippine 97.8 MHz and **Goes** 101.9 MHz.

0.19   BELGIAN WEATHER FORECASTS

Coast Radio Stations

After prior notice on VHF16, DSC70 and 2182kHz, **Oostende Radio.** broadcasts in **English** and Dutch on VHF Ch 27 and 2761 kHz: Strong wind warnings on receipt and at 0820 and 1720 UT, together with a forecast for sea areas Thames and Dover.

Oostende Radio also broadcasts in **English** and Dutch on VHF Ch 24 for the Schelde estuary: Gale and strong wind warnings (F6+) on receipt and every H+48.

Zeebrugge Traffic Centre broadcasts weather bulletins for the Westerschelde.on VHF CH 69 every H+10 LT.

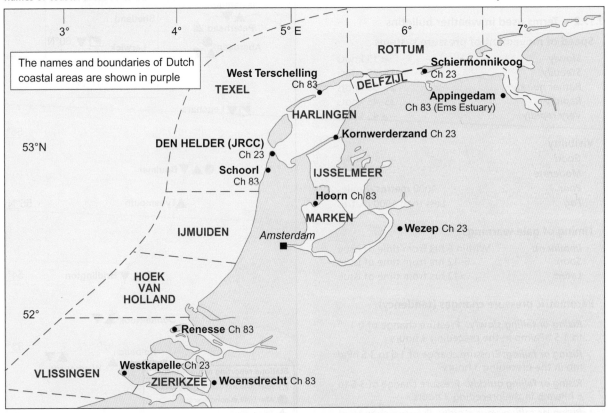

0.20 AUTOMATIC IDENTIFICATION SYSTEM (AIS)

Automatic Identification System (AIS) allows information to be provided to other ships and shore authorities; it is required by SOLAS to be fitted to most vessels over 300 GRT. AIS is widely used to automatically and continuously identify, track and display other vessels and their movements.

Each ship's course and speed vector is shown by a symbol on an AIS screen or overlaid on radar, chart plotter or PC. This data may also appear in a text box as heading, COG & SOG, range, CPA, position, ship's name, and her status – under power or sail, anchored, constrained by draught, restricted in her ability to manoeuvre, not under command, fishing etc.

Many lights, buoys and other aids to navigation (AtoN) are now fitted with AIS, and the number is growing rapidly. On Admiralty charts, these are shown by a magenta circle and the notation 'AIS'. Not all transmitted information is available to all users; it depends on the display system fitted.

AIS Class B transmitters/transceivers for non-SOLAS vessels are available, but are not mandatory. Later sets can receive aids to navigation (A2N) data, showing virtual marks and MMSI numbers from buoys and lighthouses.

Caveats: Many vessels are not fitted with AIS, and some may not have it switched on; some only display 3 lines of text, not a plot; in busy areas only the strongest signals may be shown; AIS may distract a bridge watchkeeper from his visual and radar watch; unlike eyes and radar, AIS does not yet feature in the Colregs; GPS/electronic failures invalidate AIS.

In areas of traffic concentration Class B transmitters may be excluded from the network if no time slots are available. *It is not a radar* despite what some advertisments may imply.

0.21 TIDE TABLES AND COMPUTER PREDICTIONS

The Almanac uses UKHO Standard Port tide prediction curves prepared for Admiralty Tide Tables. Standard Port predictions are replacing some established Secondary Ports in ATT to better support offshore activity. The Almanac continues to replicate the existing differences to provide the data in a compact format for planning. These are in italics where alternative information is available at reedstides.co.uk. The printed tidal curve is drawn to a mean Spring curve and, in dashed line, a mean Neap curve, with boxes for associated times of HW and LW. The curve does not take account of the differing arguments (geometrical positions) of the sun, moon and planets on a daily basis. Nor does it take account of differences which owe to the differing volume passing constrictions or obstructions.

The printed tables give condensed planning information. This is refinable from computer generated predictions, such as Easytide, which are accessible on-line and easy to use.

0.21.1 Clearances Below Overhead Objects

A diagram often helps when calculating vertical clearance below bridges, power cables etc. Fig 0(6) shows the relationship to CD. The height of such objects as shown on the chart is usually measured above HAT, so the actual clearance will almost always be more. The height of HAT above CD is given at the foot of each page of the tide tables. Most Admiralty charts now show clearances above HAT, but check the **Heights** block below the chart title.

To calculate clearances, insert the dimensions into the following formula, carefully observing the conventions for brackets:

> Masthead clearance = (Height of object above HAT + height of HAT above CD) minus (height of tide at the time + height of the masthead above waterline)

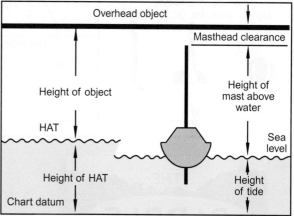

Fig 0(6) Calculating masthead clearance

0.22   IALA BUOYAGE

LATERAL MARKS – Port Hand
Topmark – can shape
(optional on can buoys)
Lights – red, any rhythm

R   R   R

LATERAL MARKS – Starboard Hand
Topmark –one shape
(optional on conical buoys)
Lights – green, any rhythm

G   G   G

SAFE WATER MARKS
Topmark – spherical (none
on spherical buoys)
Lights – white, Iso, Oc, or LFl.10s

RW   RW   RW

CARDINAL MARKS

NW   NE

North
Topmarks – 2 black cones, points up
Lights – white, VQ or Q

BY   BY

N

POINT OF INTEREST
(Shoal or Danger)

W   E

S

West
Topmarks –
2 black cones,
points inward
Lights – white,
VQ(9)10s
or Q(9)15s

East
Topmarks –
2 black cones,
points outward
Lights – white,
VQ(3)5s
or Q(3)10s

YBY YBY   BYB   BYB

South
Topmarks – 2 black cones,
points down
Lights – white, VQ(6) +
LFl.10s
Q(6) + LFl.15s

SW   YB   YB   SE

EMERGENCY WRECK MARKS
Topmark – Upright yellow cross
Lights – Al BuY 3s 4M

PREFERRED CHANNELS

Preferred chan to stbd
Light – red,
Rhythm: Fl(2+1)

Preferred chan to port
Light – green,
Rhythm: F(2+1)

ISOLATED DANGER MARKS
Topmark – 2 black spheres
Lights – white, Fl(2)

BRB   BRB

SPECIAL MARKS
Topmark – X (when fitted)
Lights – yellow, Fl.Y or Fl(4)Y

Y   Y   Y

Y   Y

0.23 FLAGS AND ENSIGNS

UK WHITE ENSIGN

UK BLUE ENSIGN

UK RED ENSIGN

AUSTRALIA

AUSTRIA

BASQUE FLAG

BELGIUM

CANADA

CYPRUS

DENMARK

FINLAND

FRANCE

GERMANY

GREECE

GUERNSEY

JERSEY

IRELAND

ISRAEL

ITALY

LIBERIA

MALTA

MONACO

MOROCCO

NETHERLANDS

NEW ZEALAND

NORWAY

PANAMA

POLAND

PORTUGAL

SOUTH AFRICA

SPAIN

SWEDEN

SWITZERLAND

TUNISIA

TURKEY

USA

Lights and shapes – Nav lights

0.24 LIGHTS AND SHAPES

Vessels being towed and towing

Vessel towed shows sidelights (forward) and sternlight

Tug shows two masthead lights, sidelights, sternlight, yellow towing light

Towing by day — Length of tow more than 200m

Towing vessel and tow display diamond shapes. By night, the towing vessel shows three masthead lights instead of two as for shorter tows

Motor sailing

Cone point down, forward. At night the lights of a power-driven vessel underway

Vessel fishing

All-round red light over all-round white, plus sidelights and sternlight when making way

Fishing/Trawling

A shape consisting of two cones point to point in a vertical line one above the other

Vessel trawling

All-round green light over all-round white, plus sidelights and sternlight when making way

Vessel restricted in her ability to manoeuvre

All-round red, white, red lights vertically, plus normal steaming lights when making way

Three shapes in a vertical line: ball, diamond, ball

Not under command

Two all-round red lights, plus sidelights and sternlight when making way

Two balls vertically

Dredger

All round red, white, red lights vertically, plus two all-round red lights (or two balls) on foul side, and two all-round green (or two diamonds) on clear side

Divers down

Letter 'A' International Code

Constrained by draught

Three all-round red lights in a vertical line, plus normal steaming lights. By day — a cylinder

Pilot boat

All-round white light over all-round red, plus sidelights and sternlight when underway, or anchor light

Vessel at anchor

All-round white light; if over 50m, a second light aft and lower

Ball forward

Vessel aground

Anchor light(s), plus two all-round red lights in a vertical line

Three balls in a vertical line

0.25 NAVIGATION LIGHTS

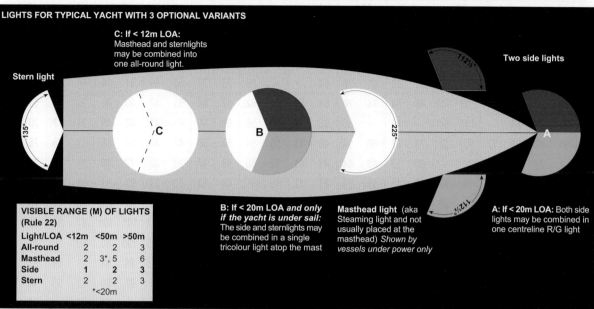

LIGHTS FOR TYPICAL YACHT WITH 3 OPTIONAL VARIANTS

C: If < 12m LOA: Masthead and sternlights may be combined into one all-round light.

Stern light

135°

225°

112½°

112½°

Two side lights

A

B

C

VISIBLE RANGE (M) OF LIGHTS (Rule 22)			
Light/LOA	<12m	<50m	>50m
All-round	2	2	3
Masthead	2	3*, 5	6
Side	1	2	3
Stern	2	2	3
		*<20m	

B: If < 20m LOA *and only if the yacht is under sail:* The side and sternlights may be combined in a single tricolour light atop the mast

Masthead light (aka Steaming light and not usually placed at the masthead) *Shown by vessels under power only*

A: If < 20m LOA: Both side lights may be combined in one centreline R/G light

---

PLAN VIEWS OF LIGHTS FOR SAILING VESSELS UNDERWAY AND UNDER SAIL ONLY
Note: If motor-sailing, the lights appropriate for a power-driven vessel must be shown, as below

Sailing vessel <7m shows, if practicable, side and sternlights; if not, a white light to prevent collision. Rule 25 d i

Sailing vessel <20m may show:
Either tricolour light atop the mast. Rule 25 b

Or combined centreline side lights plus stern light. Rule 25 a

Sailing vessel >20m Separate sidelights and sternlight. Rule 25 a

Sailing vessel under sail may show (in addition to other lights) two all-round lights, red over green, near the top of the mast, **but never** at the same time as a tricolour light atop the mast. Rule 25 c

---

PLAN VIEWS OF LIGHTS FOR POWER-DRIVEN VESSELS UNDERWAY AND SAILING CRAFT UNDER POWER

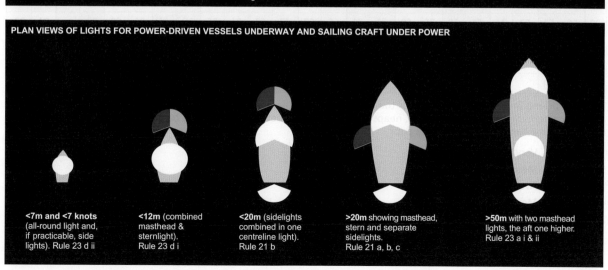

<7m and <7 knots (all-round light and, if practicable, side lights). Rule 23 d ii

<12m (combined masthead & sternlight). Rule 23 d i

<20m (sidelights combined in one centreline light). Rule 21 b

>20m showing masthead, stern and separate sidelights. Rule 21 a, b, c

>50m with two masthead lights, the aft one higher. Rule 23 a i & ii

Tidal Coefficients – Tidal stream rates

CHERBOURG TIDAL COEFFICIENTS 2022

Date	Jan am	Jan pm	Feb am	Feb pm	Mar am	Mar pm	Apr am	Apr pm	May am	May pm	June am	June pm	July am	July pm	Aug am	Aug pm	Sept am	Sept pm	Oct am	Oct pm	Nov am	Nov pm	Dec am	Dec pm
1	81	86	94	98	82	88	97	98	88	87	74	72	70	69	--	77	83	79	78	72	52	47	54	53
2	91	94	101	102	94	98	98	97	86	84	70	67	68	67	76	75	75	70	65	58	45	45	53	55
3	97	99	102	100	101	103	95	92	81	78	64	--	--	66	73	70	65	59	51	44	48	53	57	60
4	99	99	98	94	103	102	88	84	74	70	61	58	64	62	67	64	53	47	40	40	59	65	63	67
5	97	95	89	--	100	96	--	79	--	65	55	51	60	58	60	56	43	41	42	49	71	77	70	72
6	91	87	84	77	92	87	73	67	60	54	48	45	56	54	53	50	42	47	56	65	82	86	75	76
7	--	81	71	64	80	--	60	53	49	44	43	41	52	50	48	47	53	62	73	80	88	90	78	78
8	76	70	57	50	74	67	46	40	39	34	41	42	49	49	48	52	70	79	87	93	91	91	79	78
9	64	58	44	38	60	52	33	28	31	30	44	47	50	52	56	63	86	93	97	100	90	89	78	77
10	53	48	33	31	45	38	24	24	31	34	51	56	56	60	69	77	98	102	101	101	87	84	75	73
11	44	42	30	32	31	26	26	31	39	45	61	67	64	69	83	90	104	105	100	98	80	76	71	68
12	41	41	36	41	24	24	38	45	51	58	72	78	75	80	95	99	105	103	95	91	71	66	65	61
13	42	45	46	51	28	34	52	60	65	72	83	87	85	89	102	103	100	95	86	80	61	55	58	--
14	48	52	57	63	40	47	67	75	78	84	91	93	93	95	103	102	--	90	--	74	50	--	54	51
15	55	59	68	73	54	61	81	87	90	94	95	96	97	98	--	99	84	77	67	61	44	39	47	44
16	62	66	77	81	68	75	92	97	97	99	96	94	97	--	95	90	69	62	53	46	35	31	42	40
17	69	72	85	88	80	86	100	102	100	100	92	--	96	93	84	77	54	46	39	33	30	30	40	40
18	74	76	90	91	91	95	103	102	98	95	89	85	89	85	70	63	39	32	27	24	32	36	42	45
19	78	79	92	92	98	100	101	97	--	91	81	76	79	74	55	48	27	24	24	26	42	48	49	53
20	80	80	90	88	100	100	--	93	86	80	71	66	67	62	41	36	25	28	31	37	54	60	59	64
21	79	78	85	--	99	96	86	80	74	68	62	58	56	51	32	30	34	40	45	51	67	73	70	75
22	77	75	81	76	92	86	72	64	62	57	55	52	46	43	31	34	47	54	59	65	79	84	80	85
23	--	72	70	64	--	80	57	50	53	51	51	51	41	41	39	44	60	67	72	78	88	92	89	92
24	69	66	58	52	72	65	45	43	51	52	52	53	42	44	49	55	73	78	83	88	94	96	95	96
25	62	59	47	44	57	50	45	48	54	57	55	56	47	50	60	65	83	87	92	95	97	96	97	96
26	55	52	43	46	44	40	54	60	61	64	59	61	54	57	70	74	90	93	97	98	94	91	95	92
27	50	50	52	59	41	45	66	71	67	69	63	65	61	64	78	81	95	95	98	97	88	83	89	--
28	51	54	67	74	51	59	76	80	72	74	66	67	67	69	84	86	95	94	94	90	78	--	84	80
29	59	65			67	74	84	86	75	76	69	69	72	74	87	88	92	88	85	--	72	66	75	69
30	71	77			81	86	87	88	76	76	70	70	75	76	88	87	--	84	80	73	62	57	64	60
31	84	89			91	95			76	75			77	77	--	85			66	59			56	53

Tidal coefficients indicate the magnitude of the tide on any particular day without having to look up and calculate the range, and thus determine whether it is springs, neaps or somewhere in between. This table, based on Brest, is valid for all areas covered by this Almanac. Typical values are:

120	Very big spring tide
95	**Mean spring tide**
70	Average tide
45	**Mean neap tide**
20	Very small neap tide

0.27 CALCULATING TIDAL STREAM RATES

The tidal stream rate at any time may be calculated, assuming that it varies with the range of the tide at Dover. In tidal stream atlases, and on the tidal stream chartlets in this Almanac, the rates are shown in tenths of a knot. Thus '05,27' translates as 0·5k at Neaps and 2·7kn at Springs.

Example: Calculate the tidal stream rate off the north tip of Skye at 0420 UT on a day when the tide at Dover is:

UT	Ht (m)
0328	1·4
0819	6·3
1602	1·1
2054	6·4

The tidal stream chartlet for Skye [Dover HW–4] shows '08,18'. This is a mean Neap rate of 0·8kn and Spring rate of 1·8kn.

On the left hand figure identify the Spring (Red) and Neap (Blue) axes. On these mark the rate of 1.8kn and 0.8kn respectively, using the upper or lower scales.

Draw a diagonal line through these.

Calculate the tidal ranges for Dover:

(6·3 -1·4) = 4·9m   (6·4-1·1)=5·3m

The mean range = (4·9+5·3)/2 = 5·1m

On the vertical axis identify 5·1m and draw a horizontal line cutting the diagonal just drawn. From this intersection read off the required rate on either horizontal axis.

In the example this is 15 (1·5kn).

Times are in UT - add 1 hour in non-shaded areas to convert to BST

0.28 SUNRISE/SET TIMES 2022

The table shows times of Sunrise (SR) and Sunset (SS) for every 3rd day as the times of Sunrise and Sunset never change by more than 8 minutes (and often by only 1–3 minutes) between the given dates.

The table is based on Longitude 0°, so longitude corrections are required. To calculate this add 4 minutes of time for every degree West of Greenwich; subtract if East.

LATITUDE 56°N

	Rise JANUARY	Set	Rise FEBRUARY	Set	Rise MARCH	Set	Rise APRIL	Set	Rise MAY	Set	Rise JUNE	Set
1	08 31	15 36	07 55	16 33	06 52	17 34	05 31	18 38	04 16	19 39	03 22	20 34
4	08 30	15 40	07 49	16 39	06 44	17 40	05 23	18 44	04 10	19 45	03 19	20 38
7	08 28	15 44	07 43	16 46	06 36	17 47	05 15	18 50	04 03	19 51	03 17	20 42
10	08 26	15 49	07 37	16 53	06 29	17 53	05 07	18 56	03 57	19 57	03 15	20 45
13	08 23	15 54	07 30	16 59	06 21	17 59	05 00	19 03	03 51	20 03	03 14	20 47
16	08 20	16 00	07 23	17 06	06 13	18 05	04 52	19 09	03 46	20 08	03 13	20 49
19	08 16	16 06	07 16	17 12	06 05	18 12	04 45	19 15	03 40	20 14	03 13	20 50
22	08 12	16 12	07 09	17 19	05 57	18 18	04 37	19 21	03 35	20 19	03 13	20 51
25	08 07	16 18	07 02	17 25	05 49	18 24	04 30	19 27	03 31	20 24	03 14	20 51
28	08 02	16 24	06 54	17 32	05 41	18 30	04 23	19 33	03 27	20 29	03 16	20 50
31	07 57	16 31			05 34	18 36			03 23	20 33		

	JULY		AUGUST		SEPTEMBER		OCTOBER		NOVEMBER		DECEMBER	
1	03 18	20 49	04 04	20 08	05 04	18 55	06 03	17 35	07 07	16 20	08 07	15 31
4	03 21	20 47	04 09	20 02	05 10	18 47	06 09	17 28	07 13	16 13	08 11	15 29
7	03 24	20 45	04 15	19 55	05 16	18 39	06 15	17 20	07 20	16 07	08 16	15 27
10	03 28	20 42	04 21	19 48	05 22	18 31	06 21	17 12	07 26	16 01	08 20	15 26
13	03 32	20 39	04 27	19 42	05 27	18 23	06 27	17 05	07 32	15 56	08 23	15 25
16	03 36	20 35	04 33	19 35	05 33	18 15	06 33	16 57	07 38	15 50	08 26	15 25
19	03 41	20 31	04 39	19 27	05 39	18 07	06 39	16 50	07 44	15 46	08 28	15 26
22	03 46	20 26	04 44	19 20	05 45	17 59	06 46	16 42	07 50	15 41	08 30	15 27
25	03 51	20 21	04 50	19 13	05 51	17 51	06 52	16 35	07 56	15 37	08 31	15 29
28	03 56	20 15	04 56	19 05	05 57	17 43	06 58	16 28	08 02	15 34	08 32	15 32
31	04 02	20 10	05 02	18 57			07 05	16 22			08 31	15 35

LATITUDE 50°N

	Rise JANUARY	Set	Rise FEBRUARY	Set	Rise MARCH	Set	Rise APRIL	Set	Rise MAY	Set	Rise JUNE	Set
1	07 58	16 09	07 34	16 54	06 44	17 42	05 37	18 32	04 37	19 19	03 56	20 00
4	07 58	16 12	07 29	16 59	06 37	17 47	05 31	18 36	04 31	19 23	03 54	20 03
7	07 57	16 16	07 24	17 04	06 31	17 52	05 24	18 41	04 26	19 28	03 52	20 06
10	07 56	16 19	07 19	17 10	06 25	17 57	05 18	18 46	04 22	19 32	03 51	20 08
13	07 54	16 24	07 14	17 15	06 18	18 02	05 12	18 51	04 17	19 37	03 50	20 10
16	07 52	16 28	07 09	17 20	06 12	18 06	05 05	18 55	04 13	19 41	03 50	20 11
19	07 49	16 33	07 03	17 25	06 05	18 11	04 59	19 00	04 09	19 45	03 50	20 12
22	07 46	16 37	06 58	17 30	05 59	18 16	04 53	19 05	04 05	19 49	03 51	20 13
25	07 43	16 42	06 52	17 35	05 52	18 21	04 48	19 09	04 02	19 53	03 52	20 13
28	07 39	16 47	06 46	17 40	05 46	18 25	04 42	19 14	03 59	19 56	03 53	20 13
31	07 35	16 52			05 39	18 30			03 57	19 59		

	JULY		AUGUST		SEPTEMBER		OCTOBER		NOVEMBER		DECEMBER	
1	03 55	20 13	04 29	19 43	05 15	18 44	06 00	17 39	06 49	16 37	07 37	16 01
4	03 57	20 11	04 33	19 38	05 19	18 38	06 04	17 32	06 54	16 32	07 40	16 00
7	04 00	20 10	04 38	19 33	05 24	18 31	06 09	17 26	06 59	16 27	07 44	15 59
10	04 02	20 08	04 42	19 28	05 28	18 25	06 14	17 19	07 04	16 23	07 47	15 58
13	04 05	20 06	04 47	19 22	05 33	18 18	06 18	17 13	07 09	16 19	07 50	15 58
16	04 09	20 03	04 51	19 17	05 37	18 12	06 23	17 07	07 14	16 15	07 53	15 58
19	04 12	20 00	04 55	19 11	05 42	18 05	06 28	17 01	07 19	16 11	07 55	15 59
22	04 16	19 56	05 00	19 05	05 46	17 58	06 33	16 55	07 24	16 08	07 56	16 01
25	04 20	19 53	05 04	18 59	05 51	17 52	06 38	16 50	07 28	16 05	07 58	16 03
28	04 24	19 49	05 09	18 53	05 55	17 45	06 43	16 44	07 32	16 03	07 58	16 05
31	04 28	19 44	05 13	18 46			06 48	16 39			07 59	16 08

Times are in UT - add 1 hour in non-shaded areas to convert to BST

0.29 MOONRISE/SET TIMES 2022

The table gives the times of Moonrise (MR) and Moonset (MS) for every 3rd day; interpolation is necessary for other days. The aim is simply to indicate whether the night in question will be brightly moonlit, partially moonlit or pitch black – depending, of course, on the level of cloud cover. The table is based on Longitude 0°. To correct for longitude, add 4 minutes of time for every degree West; subtract if East. ** Indicates that the phenomenon does not occur.

LATITUDE 56°N

	Rise JANUARY	Set	Rise FEBRUARY	Set	Rise MARCH	Set	Rise APRIL	Set	Rise MAY	Set	Rise JUNE	Set
1	07 27	13 49	08 49	16 34	07 11	15 35	06 02	18 57	04 37	20 41	04 07	23 11
4	10 26	17 37	09 30	21 04	07 45	19 59	06 29	23 00	05 32	** **	07 08	00 23
7	11 15	22 07	09 56	** **	08 12	** **	07 34	01 31	08 08	01 54	11 06	01 07
10	11 40	00 46	10 40	03 37	09 05	02 36	10 27	03 52	12 05	02 49	15 18	01 31
13	12 17	04 36	12 44	06 43	11 34	05 20	14 32	04 41	16 20	03 15	20 09	02 10
16	13 57	07 59	16 34	08 02	15 35	06 22	18 53	05 07	21 09	03 49	23 30	04 37
19	17 29	09 39	20 44	08 34	19 51	06 51	23 42	05 46	00 05	05 44	00 12	09 21
22	21 34	10 17	** **	09 03	** **	07 24	02 16	08 00	01 51	10 10	00 39	13 35
25	00 21	10 44	04 09	10 16	03 18	09 03	03 43	12 26	02 22	14 27	01 05	17 33
28	04 57	11 41	06 50	14 00	05 18	13 11	04 12	16 39	02 46	18 26	02 08	21 06
31	08 20	14 58			05 54	17 35			03 34	22 13		

	Rise JULY	Set	Rise AUGUST	Set	Rise SEPTEMBER	Set	Rise OCTOBER	Set	Rise NOVEMBER	Set	Rise DECEMBER	Set
1	04 57	22 49	08 00	21 41	11 19	20 23	13 40	19 34	14 54	22 29	13 38	** **
4	08 52	23 24	12 04	22 04	15 50	21 36	16 25	23 11	15 28	01 34	13 59	03 36
7	12 54	23 48	16 39	23 01	18 21	** **	17 10	02 22	15 50	05 52	14 38	07 46
10	17 31	00 12	19 53	00 58	19 01	04 51	17 33	06 49	16 34	10 04	16 41	11 02
13	21 22	02 08	20 45	05 51	19 25	09 17	18 10	11 05	18 53	13 06	20 25	12 15
16	22 29	06 51	21 10	10 19	20 08	13 27	20 03	14 29	22 43	14 08	** **	12 40
19	22 55	11 19	21 46	14 26	22 18	16 33	23 45	15 49	01 22	14 32	03 05	13 02
22	23 25	15 21	23 30	17 51	00 47	17 41	02 27	16 16	05 39	14 56	07 51	13 59
25	00 09	19 01	01 48	19 19	04 51	18 07	06 40	16 38	10 27	16 09	11 00	17 42
28	02 47	20 55	05 48	19 50	09 04	18 30	11 23	17 33	13 00	20 12	11 46	22 33
31	06 41	21 33	09 52	20 12			14 31	20 54			12 08	01 24

LATITUDE 50°N

	Rise JANUARY	Set	Rise FEBRUARY	Set	Rise MARCH	Set	Rise APRIL	Set	Rise MAY	Set	Rise JUNE	Set
1	06 45	14 32	08 17	17 03	06 45	15 59	06 03	18 52	04 57	20 15	04 53	22 23
4	09 50	18 11	09 24	21 07	07 43	19 58	06 52	22 31	06 15	23 36	07 46	** **
7	11 04	22 14	10 10	** **	08 30	23 37	08 19	00 47	08 51	01 11	11 19	00 52
10	11 50	00 39	11 16	03 02	09 46	01 56	11 06	03 12	12 23	02 29	15 07	01 37
13	12 48	04 06	13 29	05 58	12 16	04 37	14 46	04 25	16 14	03 17	19 28	02 42
16	14 42	07 14	16 57	07 37	15 53	06 02	18 43	05 13	20 34	04 16	22 50	05 24
19	17 58	09 09	20 44	08 31	19 46	06 52	23 01	06 18	** **	06 33	** **	09 40
22	21 38	10 09	** **	09 22	23 54	07 49	01 27	08 48	01 24	10 35	00 41	13 30
25	00 11	10 57	03 25	11 01	02 30	09 51	03 19	12 48	02 19	14 27	01 28	17 04
28	04 19	12 21	06 14	14 35	04 48	13 39	04 10	16 37	03 03	18 03	02 52	20 18
31	07 39	15 37			05 48	17 37			04 15	21 28		

	Rise JULY	Set	Rise AUGUST	Set	Rise SEPTEMBER	Set	Rise OCTOBER	Set	Rise NOVEMBER	Set	Rise DECEMBER	Set
1	05 37	22 16	08 10	21 35	11 00	20 44	12 53	20 21	14 22	23 00	13 29	** **
4	09 08	23 14	11 51	22 20	15 02	22 25	15 46	23 49	15 21	01 46	14 12	03 25
7	12 47	23 58	15 58	23 43	17 45	00 43	16 58	02 40	16 06	05 38	15 16	07 09
10	16 56	00 39	19 12	01 46	18 53	05 04	17 44	06 41	17 15	09 25	17 29	10 14
13	20 38	02 57	20 33	06 09	19 40	09 05	18 46	10 31	19 39	12 18	20 51	11 47
16	22 13	07 14	21 21	10 12	20 48	12 49	20 52	13 40	23 06	13 43	** **	12 35
19	23 01	11 16	22 20	13 54	23 05	15 45	** **	15 19	01 29	14 29	02 52	13 18
22	23 54	14 55	** **	17 02	01 19	17 15	02 38	16 10	05 21	15 16	07 07	14 44
25	00 52	18 14	02 25	18 49	04 58	18 03	06 27	16 54	09 38	16 58	10 20	18 20
28	03 29	20 19	06 00	19 42	08 48	18 50	10 40	18 18	12 24	20 46	11 35	22 41
31	06 59	21 20	09 42	20 26			13 48	21 35			12 19	01 16

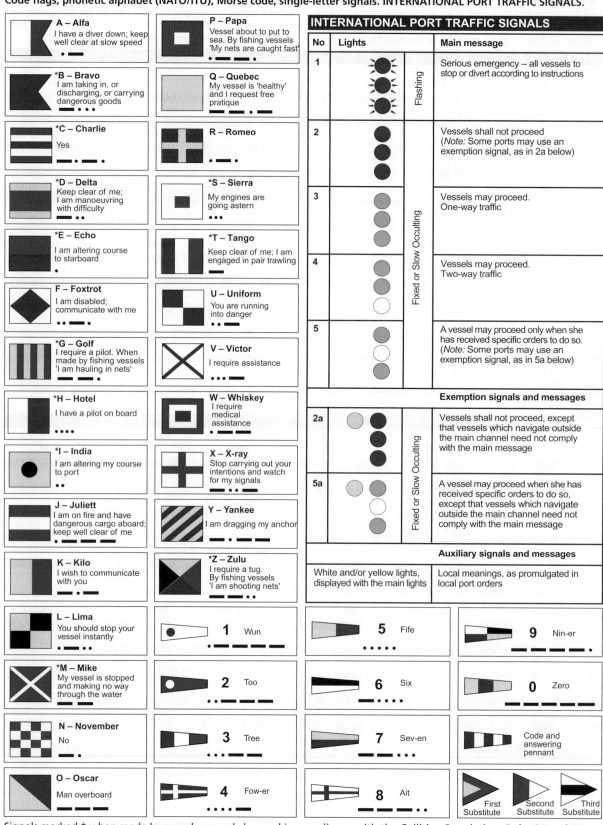

0.30 INTERNATIONAL CODE OF SIGNALS

Code flags, phonetic alphabet (NATO/ITU), Morse code, single-letter signals. INTERNATIONAL PORT TRAFFIC SIGNALS.

INTERNATIONAL PORT TRAFFIC SIGNALS

No	Lights		Main message
1		Flashing	Serious emergency – all vessels to stop or divert according to instructions
2		Fixed or Slow Occulting	Vessels shall not proceed (Note: Some ports may use an exemption signal, as in 2a below)
3			Vessels may proceed. One-way traffic
4			Vessels may proceed. Two-way traffic
5			A vessel may proceed only when she has received specific orders to do so. (Note: Some ports may use an exemption signal, as in 5a below)

Exemption signals and messages

| 2a | | Fixed or Slow Occulting | Vessels shall not proceed, except that vessels which navigate outside the main channel need not comply with the main message |
| 5a | | | A vessel may proceed when she has received specific orders to do so, except that vessels which navigate outside the main channel need not comply with the main message |

Auxiliary signals and messages

| White and/or yellow lights, displayed with the main lights | Local meanings, as promulgated in local port orders |

Flags:

A – Alfa: I have a diver down; keep well clear at slow speed
*B – Bravo: I am taking in, or discharging, or carrying dangerous goods
*C – Charlie: Yes
*D – Delta: Keep clear of me; I am manoeuvring with difficulty
*E – Echo: I am altering course to starboard
F – Foxtrot: I am disabled; communicate with me
*G – Golf: I require a pilot. When made by fishing vessels 'I am hauling in nets'
*H – Hotel: I have a pilot on board
*I – India: I am altering my course to port
J – Juliett: I am on fire and have dangerous cargo aboard; keep well clear of me
K – Kilo: I wish to communicate with you
L – Lima: You should stop your vessel instantly
*M – Mike: My vessel is stopped and making no way through the water
N – November: No
O – Oscar: Man overboard
P – Papa: Vessel about to put to sea. By fishing vessels 'My nets are caught fast'
Q – Quebec: My vessel is 'healthy' and I request free pratique
R – Romeo
*S – Sierra: My engines are going astern
*T – Tango: Keep clear of me; I am engaged in pair trawling
U – Uniform: You are running into danger
V – Victor: I require assistance
W – Whiskey: I require medical assistance
X – X-ray: Stop carrying out your intentions and watch for my signals
Y – Yankee: I am dragging my anchor
*Z – Zulu: I require a tug. By fishing vessels 'I am shooting nets'

1 Wun, 2 Too, 3 Tree, 4 Fow-er, 5 Fife, 6 Six, 7 Sev-en, 8 Ait, 9 Nin-er, 0 Zero

Code and answering pennant. First Substitute, Second Substitute, Third Substitute

Signals marked * when made by sound may only be used in compliance with the Collision Regulations Rules 34 and 35.

0.31   AREA INFORMATION

The 5 geographic Areas are arranged as follows:

An Area map which includes harbours, principal lights, TSS, MRCCs, NCI stations, airports, main ferry routes, magnetic variation and a distance table. Wind farms and other offshore energy installations are not routinely shown.

Tidal stream chartlets showing hourly rates and set.

Lights, buoys and waypoints (LBW) listing positions and characteristics of selected lights and other marks, their daytime appearance, fog signals and Racons. Arcs of visibility and alignment of sector/leading lights are true bearings as seen from seaward. Lights are white unless otherwise stated; any colours are shown between the bearings of the relevant arcs. AIS is widely fitted to navigational marks, but not normally shown in LBW. See the relevant official charts/publications for details.

Passage Information (PI) is at Section 4 in each Area. Further information is geographically arranged between the harbour entries.

Special notes giving data specific to a country or area.

Harbour information (see below).

0.32   HARBOUR INFORMATION

Each harbour entry is arranged as follows:

HARBOUR NAME followed by the County or Unitary Council (or foreign equivalent) and the lat/long of the harbour entrance, or equivalent, for use as the final waypoint.

Harbour ratings (⚙ 👌 ✿), inevitably subjective, which grade a port based on the following criteria:

Ease of access:

⚙⚙⚙   *Can be entered in almost any weather from most directions and at all states of tide, by day or night.*

⚙⚙   *Accessible in strong winds from most directions; possible tidal or pilotage constraints.*

⚙   *Only accessible in calm, settled conditions by day with little or no swell; possible bar and difficult pilotage.*

Facilities available:

👌👌👌   *Good facilities for vessel and crew.*

👌👌   *Most domestic needs catered for, but limited boatyard facilities.*

👌   *Possibly some domestic facilities, but little else.*

Ambience:

✿✿✿   *An attractive place; well worth visiting.*

✿✿   *Average for this part of the coast.*

✿   *Holds no particular attraction.*

CHARTS show Admiralty (AC), Imray, and foreign charts, all smallest scale first. Admiralty Leisure Folios (56XX), which cover most of the UK, Channel Islands and Ireland, and Imray 2000 series folios (2X00) are also shown.

TIDES include a time difference (usually on Dover in the UK), ML, Duration and the harbour's Standard Port. Time and height differences for Secondary Ports are also shown. Computer prediction is replacing some Secondary Port data in ATT. The Almanac continues to replicate these differences in italics when alternative information is available at www.reedstides.co.uk. Tidal coefficients are at 0.26.

SHELTER assesses how protected a harbour is from wind, sea, surge and swell. It warns of any access difficulties and advises on safe berths and anchorages.

NAVIGATION gives guidance on the approach and entry, and shows the position of the approach waypoint with its bearing and distance to the harbour entrance or next significant feature. Some waypoints may not be shown on the chartlet. Access times are only stated where a lock, gate, sill or other obstruction restricts entry. Otherwise the minimum charted depth of water in the approaches, where it is less than 2m, is usually shown, but always consult up to date official charts.

Chartlets are based on official charts augmented with local information. Due to their scale, they may not cover the whole area referred to in the text nor do they show every depth, mark, light or feature.

The chartlets are not intended to be used for navigation; positions taken from them should not be used as waypoints in chart plotters. The publisher and editors disclaim any responsibility for resultant accidents or damage if they are so used. The largest scale official chart, properly corrected, should always be used.

Drying areas and an indicative 5m depth contour are shown as: Dries ▦   <5m ▦   >5m

Wrecks around the UK which are of archaeological or historic interest are protected by law. Sites are listed under harbour entries or in Passage Information. Unauthorised interference, including anchoring and diving on these sites, may lead to a substantial fine.

LIGHTS AND MARKS describes, in more detail than is shown on the chartlets, any unusual characteristics of marks, their appearance by day and features not listed elsewhere.

COMMUNICATIONS shows the telephone area code followed by local telephone and VHF contact details for: CG, weather, police, doctor/medical, harbourmaster/office, other. Marina contact details are not usually duplicated if they are shown under the marina entry. International telephone calls from/to the UK are described in Special Notes, as are national numbers for emergency services: normally 112 in the EU; 999 in the UK. Radio callsigns, if not obvious, are in *italics*.

FACILITIES describes berthing options and facilities in harbours, marinas and yacht clubs (see the **Reeds Marina Guide** for detailed marina plans in the UK, Channel Islands and Ireland). Water, electricity, showers and toilets are available in marinas unless otherwise stated. Most yacht clubs welcome visiting crews who belong to a recognised club and arrive by sea. Any rail and air links are also shown.

The overnight cost of a visitor's alongside berth (AB) *is for comparison only and based on information supplied at the time of going to press (Summer 2021)* is the average charge per metre LOA (unless otherwise stated) during high season, usually June to Sept. It includes VAT, harbour dues and, where possible, any tourist taxes (per head). The cost of pile moorings, 🛥s or ⚓s, where these are the norm, may also be given. Shore electricity is usually free abroad but extra in the UK.

The number of 🅥 berths is a marina's estimate of how many visitors may be accommodated at any one time. It is always advisable to call the marina beforehand.

TransEurope Marinas (www.transeuropemarinas.com) is a group of independent marinas in the UK and abroad. Many hold Blue Flags and 4 or 5 Gold Anchor Awards; it is a condition of membership that they are well-equipped and maintain high standards. They operate a discounted reciprocal berthing scheme and are shown by the symbol ⓐ.

Rover Tickets, offering good discounts, are available for many berthing facilities in Scotland and the offlying islands.

0.33 ENVIRONMENTAL GUIDANCE

- Comply with regulations for navigation and conduct within Marine Nature Reserves, Particularly Sensitive Sea Areas (PSSA) and National Water Parks.
- In principle never ditch rubbish at sea, keep it on board and dispose of it in harbour refuse bins.
- Readily degradable foodstuffs may be ditched at sea when >3M offshore (>12M in the English Channel).
- Foodstuffs and other materials which are not readily degradable should never be ditched at sea.
- Sewage. If you do not have a holding tank, only use the onboard heads when well offshore. A holding tank should be fitted as soon as possible as many countries require them. Pump-out facilities (⚓) are shown in the text. Do not pump out holding tanks until more than 3M offshore.
- Do not discharge foul water into a marina, anchorage or moorings area and minimise on washing-up water.
- Deposit used engine oil and oily waste ashore at a recognised facility. Do not allow an automatic bilge pump to discharge oily bilge water overboard.
- Dispose of toxic waste, (eg some antifoulings, cleaning chemicals, old batteries) at an approved disposal facility.
- Row ashore whenever possible – to minimise noise, wash and disturbance. Land at recognised places.
- Respect wild birds, plants, fish and marine animals. Avoid protected nesting sites and breeding colonies.
- Do not anchor or dry out on vulnerable seabed species, eg soft corals, eel grass.

0.34 DISTANCES (M) ACROSS THE NORTH SEA

Approximate distances in nautical miles are by the most direct route, avoiding dangers and allowing for TSS.

UK \ Norway to France	Bergen	Stavanger	Lindesnes	Skagen	Esjberg	Sylt (List)	Brunsbüttel	Helgoland	Bremerhaven	Willhelmshaven	Delfzijl	Den Helder	IJmuiden	Scheveningen	Roompotsluis	Vlissingen	Zeebrugge	Oostende	Nieuwpoort	Dunkerque
Lerwick	210	226	288	403	428	442	517	470	510	500	493	486	497	505	551	550	552	555	562	588
Kirkwall	278	275	323	438	439	452	516	467	507	497	481	460	473	481	515	514	516	519	526	545
Wick	292	283	323	437	428	440	498	449	489	479	458	433	444	451	485	484	486	489	496	514
Inverness	356	339	381	485	461	462	529	479	519	509	487	460	471	478	513	512	514	517	524	542
Fraserburgh	288	266	296	410	383	384	451	404	444	434	412	385	396	403	430	429	431	434	441	456
Aberdeen	308	279	298	411	371	378	433	382	432	412	386	353	363	369	401	400	402	405	412	426
Dundee	362	329	339	451	394	401	448	396	436	426	395	352	359	364	390	389	385	388	395	412
Port Edgar	391	355	362	472	409	413	457	405	445	435	401	355	361	366	391	390	386	389	396	413
Berwick	374	325	320	431	356	361	408	355	395	385	355	310	315	320	342	341	337	340	347	364
Hartlepool	409	353	340	440	340	331	367	312	352	342	302	241	243	247	266	265	261	264	271	288
Grimsby	463	395	362	452	324	318	342	291	332	325	288	187	182	185	199	198	190	191	201	198
Kings Lynn	485	416	379	466	330	333	343	292	344	336	283	184	183	183	197	195	187	188	198	195
Lowestoft	508	431	380	453	308	300	295	262	284	271	218	118	104	98	95	99	87	87	89	106
Harwich	540	461	410	483	330	331	320	287	309	296	243	147	126	114	94	100	84	77	80	80
Brightlingsea	558	479	428	501	348	349	338	305	327	314	261	165	144	105	108	106	92	88	86	87
Burnham/Crouch	567	488	437	510	357	358	347	314	336	323	270	174	151	112	109	115	99	92	93	95
London Bridge	620	543	490	560	400	408	395	361	382	374	320	222	199	149	153	149	134	125	126	114
Sheerness	580	503	450	520	360	367	353	319	340	334	280	180	157	109	113	109	94	85	86	74
Ramsgate	575	498	446	516	368	346	339	305	323	315	262	161	144	121	89	85	77	65	58	42
Dover	588	511	459	529	378	359	352	328	336	328	275	174	155	132	101	92	79	65	58	44

Eastern England

Ramsgate to Berwick-upon-Tweed

E England

1.1

East England
North Foreland to Great Yarmouth

EMERGENCY 999
HMCG NATIONAL – 02392 552100
HMCG LONDON – 0208 312 7380
HM CUSTOMS – 0845 010 9000
POLICE – 101   MEDICAL – 111

Map labels:

- 2°E, 52°30'N, 30', 20', 10', 1°E, 30'
- See 3.1
- Winterton-on-Sea
- Caister-on-Sea
- Gt YARMOUTH 1.25
- Gorleston ©
- Middle Scroby Wind Farm
- LOWESTOFT 1.24
- Magnetic Variation 1·0°E
- SOUTHWOLD 1.23
- Minsmere
- Aldeburgh
- RIVER ORE/ALDE 1.22
- Orford Ness
- NORFOLK BROADS 1.25
- Woodbridge

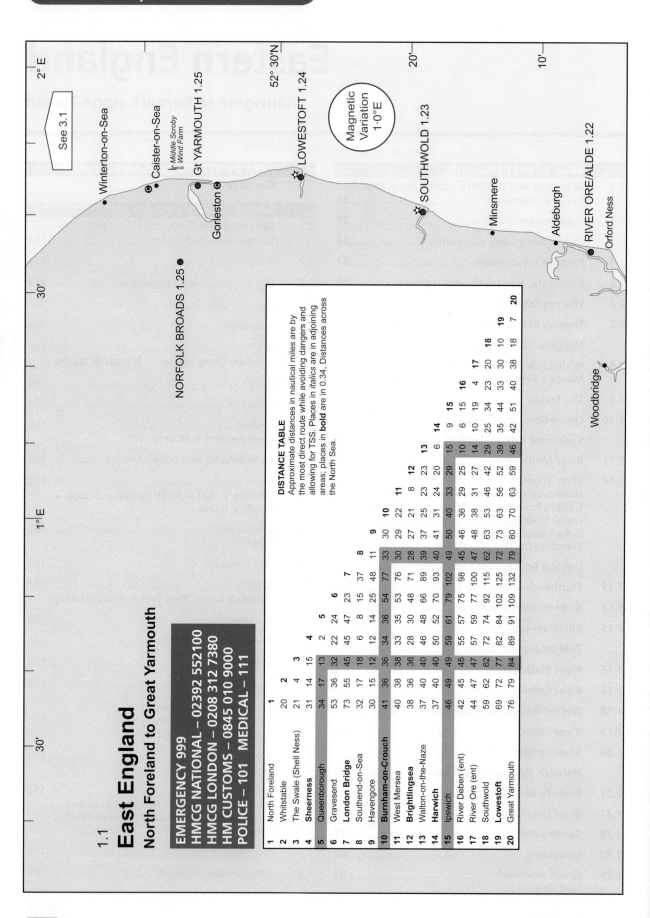

DISTANCE TABLE
Approximate distances in nautical miles are by the most direct route while avoiding dangers and allowing for TSS. Places in *italics* are in adjoining areas; places in **bold** are in 0.34, Distances across the North Sea.

	1	2	3	4	5	6	7	8	9	10	11	12	13	14	15	16	17	18	19	20
1 North Foreland	1																			
2 Whitstable	20	2																		
3 The Swale (Shell Ness)	21	4	3																	
4 **Sheerness**	31	14	15	4																
5 Queenborough	34	17	13	2	5															
6 Gravesend	53	36	32	22	24	6														
7 **London Bridge**	73	55	45	45	47	23	7													
8 Southend-on-Sea	32	17	18	6	8	15	37	8												
9 Havengore	30	15	12	12	14	25	48	11	9											
10 **Burnham-on-Crouch**	41	36	36	34	36	54	77	33	30	10										
11 West Mersea	40	38	38	33	35	53	76	30	29	22	11									
12 **Brightlingsea**	38	36	36	28	30	48	71	28	27	21	8	12								
13 Walton-on-the-Naze	37	40	40	46	48	66	89	39	37	25	23	23	13							
14 **Harwich**	37	40	40	50	52	70	93	40	41	31	24	20	6	14						
15 Ipswich	46	49	49	59	61	79	102	49	50	40	33	29	15	6	15					
16 River Deben (ent)	42	45	45	55	57	75	98	45	46	36	29	25	10	9	9	16				
17 River Ore (ent)	44	47	47	57	59	77	100	48	48	38	31	27	14	10	19	15	17			
18 Southwold	59	62	62	72	74	92	115	62	63	53	46	42	29	25	34	19	4	18		
19 **Lowestoft**	69	72	72	82	84	102	125	72	73	63	56	52	39	35	44	30	20	10	19	
20 Great Yarmouth	76	79	79	89	91	109	132	79	80	70	63	59	46	42	51	40	38	18	7	20

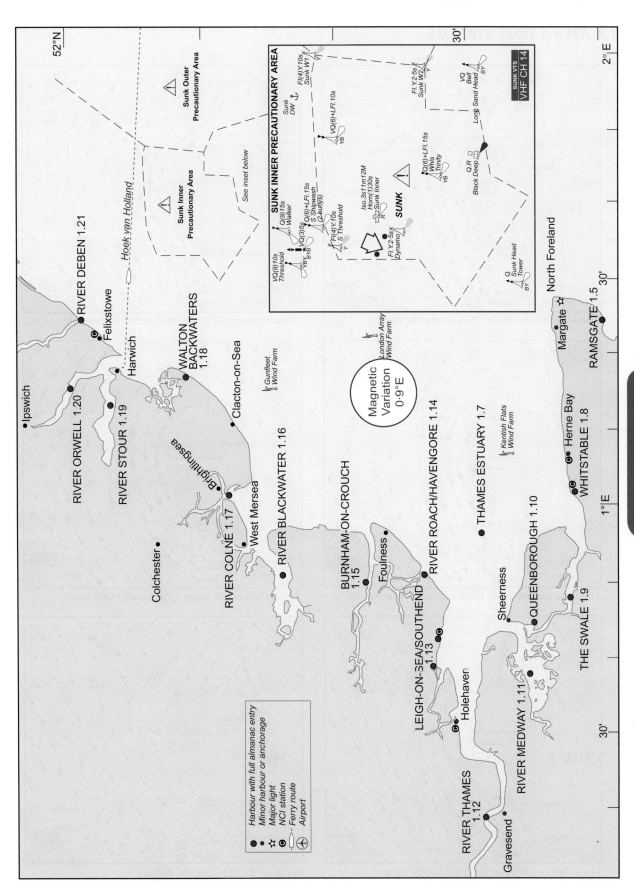

Sat Aug 6 = HW Dover @ 17:50 ≈ 6pm

1.2 AREA 1 TIDAL STREAMS

5 Hours before HW Dover (0530 before HW Walton) *1pm*

4 Hours before HW Dover (0430 before HW Walton) *2pm*

3 Hours before HW Dover (0330 before HW Walton) *3pm*

2 Hours before HW Dover (0230 before HW Walton) *4pm*

1 Hour before HW Dover (0130 before HW Walton) *5pm*

HW Dover (0030 before HW Walton) *6pm*

Thames Estuary 1.7   Northward 3.2   Eastward 2.2

1 Hour after HW Dover (0030 after HW Walton)

2 Hours after HW Dover (0130 after HW Walton)

3 Hours after HW Dover (0230 after HW Walton)

4 Hours after HW Dover (0330 after HW Walton)

5 Hours after HW Dover (0430 after HW Walton)

6 Hours after HW Dover (0530 after HW Walton)

E England

1.3 LIGHTS, BUOYS AND WAYPOINTS

Bold print = light with a nominal range of 15M or more. CAPITALS = place or feature. *CAPITAL ITALICS* = light-vessel, light float or Lanby. *Italics* = Fog signal. ***Bold italics*** = Racon. Some marks/buoys are fitted with AIS (<u>MMSI No</u>); see relevant charts.

IMPORTANT NOTE. Regular changes are made to Thames Estuary buoyage. Check Notices to Mariners for the latest information.

THAMES ESTUARY – SOUTHERN

(Direction of buoyage generally East to West)

APPROACHES to THAMES ESTUARY
Foxtrot 3 � 51°24'·15N 02°00'·38E; Fl 10s 12m **15M**; *Racon (T) 10M*; *Horn 10s*; <u>992351033</u>.
Falls Hd ⌕ Q; 51°28'·23N 01°49'·89E.
Drill Stone ⌕ Q (3) 10s; 51°25'·88N 01°42'·89E.
Thanet N ⌕ VQ 15s; 51°28'·28N 01°38'·06E.
NE Spit ⌕ VQ (3) *Racon (T) 10M*; 51°27'·93N 01°29'·89E; <u>992351037</u>
East Margate ⌕ Fl R 2·5s; 51°27'·03N 01°26'·40E.
Elbow ⌕ Q; 51°23'·23N 01°31'·59E.
Foreness Pt Outfall ⌕ Fl R 5s; 51°24'·58N 01°26'·12E.
Longnose ⌕ 51°24'·15N 01°26'·08E.
Longnose Spit ⌕ Fl R 2·5s 5m 2M; 51°23'·93N 01°25'·68E.

MARGATE and GORE CHANNEL
SE Margate ⌕ Q (3) 10s; 51°24'·05N 01°20'·40E.
S Margate ⌕ Fl G 2·5s; 51°23'·83N 01°16'·65E.
Copperas ⌕ QG; 51°23'·81N 01°11'·18E.
Reculver ⌕ QR; 51°23'·63N 01°12'·56E.

HERNE BAY
Beltinge Bay Bn ⌕ Fl Y 5s; 51°22'·73N 01°08'·63E.
Landing Stage ⌕ Q 18m 4M, (isolated); 51°22'·91N 01°06'·89E.
N Pier Hd ⌕ 2 FR (vert); 51°22'·43N 01°07'·27E.

WHITSTABLE
Whitstable Street ⌕ ; 51°24'·00N 01°01'·54E. (See The Swale.)
Oyster ⌕ Fl (2) R 10s; 51°22'·14N 01°01'·16E.
W Quay Dn ⌕ Fl G 5s 2m.

THE SWALE
Whitstable Street ⌕ Fl R 2s; 51°24'·00N 01°01'·54E.
Columbine ⌕ Fl G 2s; 51°24'·26N 01°01'·34E.
Columbine Spit ⌕ Fl (3) G 10s; 51°23'·86N 01°00'·03E.
Ham Gat ⌕ Q G; 51°23'·08N 00°58'·32E.
Pollard Spit ⌕ Q R; 51°22'·98N 00°58'·57E.
Sand End ⌕ Fl G 5s; 51°21'·43N 00°55'·90E.
Receptive Point ⌕ Fl G 10s; 51°20'·86N 00°54'·41E.
Queenborough Spit ⌕ Q (3) 10s; 51°25'·81N 00°43'·93E.
South Oaze ⌕ Fl R 2s; 51°21'·34N 00°56'·01E.

QUEENS CHANNEL and FOUR FATHOMS CHANNEL
E Margate ⌕ Fl R 2·5s; 51°27'·03N 01°26'·40E.
Spaniard ⌕ Q (3) 10s; 51°26'·23N 01°04'·00E.
Spile ⌕ Fl G 2·5s; 51°26'·43N 00°55'·70E.

PRINCES CHANNEL
Tongue Sand E ⌕ VQ (3) 5s; 51°29'·48N 01°22'·21E.
Tongue Sand N ⌕ Q; 51°29'·68N 01°22'·03E.
Princes Outer ⌕ VQ (6) + L Fl 10s; 51°28'·79N 01°19'·87E.
Princes North ⌕ Q G; 51°29'·25N 01°18'·35E.
Princes South ⌕ Q R; 51°28'·74N 01°18'·26E.
Princes No 1 ⌕ Fl (4) G 15s; 51°29'·23N 01°16'·02E.
Princes No 2 ⌕ Fl (2) R 5s; 51°28'·81N 01°13'·08E.
Princes No 3 ⌕ Fl (2) G 5s; 51°29'·33N 01°13'·10E.
Princes No 4 ⌕ Fl (3) R 10s; 51°28'·83N 01°09'·90E.
Princes No 5 ⌕ Fl (3) G 10s; 51°29'·39N 01°10'·00E.
Princes Mid ⌕ Fl Y 5s; 51°29'·19N 01°09'·00E.
Shivering Sand Twr N ⌕ Q; 51°30'·01N 01°04'·76E.
Shivering Sand Twr S ⌕ Q (6)+L Fl 15s; *Bell*; 51°29'·75N 01°04'·83E.
Princes No 8 ⌕ Fl (2) R 5s; 51°29'·14N 01°03'·00E.
Princes Inner ⌕ Fl Y 2·5s; 51°29'·59N 01°03'·47E.

FOULGER'S GAT and KNOB CHANNEL
N Edinburgh Channel is not buoyed. Foulger's Gat, lies within the boundary of the London Array Wind Farm.
Long Sand Outer ⌕ Iso 2s; 51°34'·61N 01°28'·34E.
Long Sand Middle ⌕ Iso 5s; 51°35'·60N 01°26'·45E.
Long Sand Inner ⌕ Iso 2s; 51°38'·78N 01°25'·44E.
SE Knob ⌕ Fl G 5s; 51°30'·89N 01°06'·41E.
Knob ⌕ Iso 5s; *Whis*; 51°30'·69N 01°04'·28E.

OAZE DEEP
Oaze Deep ⌕ Fl (2) G 5s; 51°29'·18N 00°56'·77E.
Red Sand Trs N ⌕ Fl (3) R 10s; *Bell*; 51°28'·73N 00°59'·32E.
N Oaze ⌕ QR; 51°30'·03N 00°57'·65E.
Oaze ⌕ Fl (4) Y 10s; 51°29'·06N 00°56'·93E.
W Oaze ⌕ Iso 5s; 51°29'·06N 00°55'·43E.
Oaze Bank ⌕ Q G 5s; 51°29'·18N 00°56'·77E.
Cant ⌕ (unlit); 51°27'·77N 00°53'·36E.
East Cant ⌕ QR; 51°28'·53N 00°55'·60E.

MEDWAY, SHEERNESS
Medway ⌕ Mo (A) 6s; 51°28'·83N 00°52'·81E.
No 1 ⌕ Fl G 2·5s; 51°28'·55N 00°50'·50E.
No 2 ⌕ Q; 51°28'·33N 00°50'·52E.
No 7 ⌕ Fl G 10s; 51°27'·91N 00°47'·52E.
No 9 ⌕ Fl G 5s; 51°27'·74N 00°46'·61E.
No 11 ⌕ Fl (3) G 10s; 51°27'·51N 00°45'·80E.
Grain Hard ⌕ Fl G 5s; 51°26'·98N 00°44'·17E.
Isle of Grain ⌕ Q 20m 13M; RW ◊ on R twr; 51°26'·70N 00°43'·38E.
Queenborough Spit ⌕ Q (3) 10s; 51°25'·81N 00°43'·93E.

RIVER THAMES

SEA REACH, NORE and YANTLET
Sea Reach 1 (N) ⌕ Fl Y 2·5s; *Racon (T) 10M*; 51°29'·59N 00°52'·71E.
Sea Reach 1 (S) ⌕ Fl R 2·5s; 51°29'·39N 00°52'·45E.
Sea Reach 2 (N) ⌕ Fl R 2·5s; 51°29'·49N 00°49'·73E.
Sea Reach 2 (S) ⌕ Fl R 2·5s; 51°29'·30N 00°49'·75E.
Sea Reach 3 (N) ⌕ Q G (sync); 51°29'·41N 00°46'·80E.
Sea Reach 3 (S) ⌕ Q R (sync); 51°29'·22N 00°46'·71E.
Sea Reach 4 (N) ⌕ Fl (2) G 5s; 51°29'·69N 00°44'·19E.
Sea Reach 4 (S) ⌕ Fl (2) R 5s; 51°29'·50N 00°44'·12E.
Sea Reach 5 (N) ⌕ VQ G; 51°30'·04N 00°41'·47E.
Sea Reach 5 (S) ⌕ VQ R; 51°29'·85N 00°41'·43E.
Sea Reach 6 (N) ⌕ Fl G 5s; 51°30'·13N 00°39'·87E.
Sea Reach 6 (S) ⌕ Fl R 5s; 51°29'·93N 00°39'·84E.
Sea Reach 7 (N) ⌕ Fl Y 2·5s; 51°30'·21N 00°36'·94E.
Sea Reach 7 (S) ⌕ Fl R 2·5s; *Racon (T) 10M*; 51°30'·01N 00°36'·91E.
Nore Swatch ⌕ Fl (4) R 15s; 51°28'·28N 00°45'·55E.
Mid Swatch ⌕ Fl G 5s; 51°28'·68N 00°44'·16E.
W Nore Sand ⌕ Fl (3) R 10s; 51°29'·48N 00°40'·87E.
East Blyth ⌕ Q; 51°29'·73N 00°37'·81E.
Mid Blyth ⌕ Q; 51°30'·08N 00°32'·38E.

LEIGH-ON-SEA and SOUTHEND-ON-SEA
Leigh ⌕; 51°31'·09N 00°42'·72E.
Southend Pier E End ⌕ 2 FG (vert) 7m; *Horn Mo (N) 30s, Bell (1)*.

LOWER HOPE REACH
West Blyth ⌕ Q R; 51°29'·57N 00°28'·39E.
Mucking 1 ⌕ Q G; 51°29'·70N 00°37'·28E.
Lower Hope ⌕ Fl R 5s; 51°29'·32N 00°28'·02E.
Mucking 3 ⌕ Fl G 2·5s; 51°29'·33N 00°27'·68E.
Mucking 5 ⌕ Fl (3) G 10s; 51°28'·76N 00°27'·19E.
Mucking 7 ⌕ Fl G 5s; 51°28'·03N 00°26'·77E.
Bell Ovens ⌕ Q G; 51°27'·50N 00°26'·35E.
Higham ⌕ Fl (2) R 5s; 51°27'·40N 00°26'·85E.
Tilbury ⌕ Q(6) + L Fl 15s; 51°27'·16N 00°25'·50E.

GRAVESEND
Shornmead ⌕ Fl (2) WR 10s 12m, W11/7M, R11M; vis 070°-W-084°-R(Intens)-089°-W(Intens)-094°-W-250°; 51°26'·92N 00°26'·24E.
Northfleet Upper ⌕ Oc WRG 10s 30m W10M, R7M, G7M; vis:126°-R-149°-W-159°-G-268°-W-279°; 51°26'·93N 00°20'·06E.

THAMES TIDAL BARRIER
Spans B, C, D, E, F, G are navigable. Spans C – F are for large ships. Eastbound small craft/yachts use Span B (51°29'·73N 00°02'·23E) Westbound small craft/yachts use Span G (51°29'·91N 00°02'·21E). **Red X** indicates span closed Green → indicates span open. W lights show either side of open spans in poor visibility.

KENTISH KNOCK
Kentish Knock ⚲ Q (3) 10s; 51°38'·08N 01°40·43E.
S Knock ⚲ Q (6) + L Fl 15s; *Bell*; 51°34'·13N 01°34'·29E.

KNOCK JOHN CHANNEL
No 7 ⚲ Fl (4) G 15s; 51°32'·03N 01°06'·40E.
No 5 ⚲ Fl (3) G 10s; 51°32'·49N 01°07'·75E.
No 4 ⚲ QR 10s; 51°32'·40 N 01°08'·08E.
No 2 ⚲ Fl (3) R 10s; 51°33'·03N 01°09'·63E.
No 3 ⚲ Q (6) + L Fl 15s; 51°33'·29N 01°09'·83E.
No 1 ⚲ Fl G 5s; 51°33'·75N 01°10'·72E.
Knock John ⚲ Fl (2) R 5s; 51°33'·61N 01°11'·37E.

BLACK DEEP
No 12 ⚲ Fl (4) R 15s; 51°33'·83N 01°13'·50E.
No 11 ⚲ Fl (3) G 10s; 51°34'·33N 01°13'·40E.
No 10 ⚲ Fl (3) R 10s; 51°34'·74N 01°15'·60E.
No 9 ⚲ Q (6) + L Fl 15s; 51°35'·13N 01°15'·09E.
No 8 ⚲ Q (9) 15s; 51°36'·36N 01°20'·43E.
No 7 ⚲ QG. 51°37'·08N 01°17'·69E.
No 6 ⚲ Fl R 2·5s; 51°38'·53N 01°24'·40E.
No 5 ⚲ VQ (3) 5s; 51°39'·53N 01°23'·00E.
No 4 ⚲ Fl (2) R 5s; 51°41'·42N 01°28'·49E.
Long Sand Bcn ⊥ ; 51°41'·48N 01°29'·49E.
No 3 ⚲ Fl (3) G 15s; 51°42'·39N 01°26'·65E.
No 1 ⚲ Fl G 5s; 51°44'·03N 01°28'·09E.
No 2 ⚲ Fl (4) R 15s; 51°45'·63N 01°32'·20E.
SHM ⚲ Fl Y 2·5s; *Racon (T) 10M*; 51°29'·59N 00°52'·71E.

SUNK
Sunk Head Tower ⚲ Q; *Bell*; 51°46'·63N 01°30'·51E.
Black Deep ⚲ QR; 51°48'·32N 01°36'·96E.
Long Sand Head ⚲ VQ; *Bell*; 51°48'·12N 01°39'·39E.
SUNK CENTRE ⚑ 51°50'·11N 01°46'·02E; Fl (2) 20s 12m **16M**; *Racon (C) 10M*; *Horn (2) 60s*; 992351094.
Dynamo ⚲ Fl Y 2·5s; 51°29'·59N 00°52'·71E.
Trinity ⚲ Q (6) + L Fl 15s; 51°49'·03N 01°36'·39E.
SUNK INNER ⚑ 51°51'·17N 01°34'·40E; Fl(5) 15s 11m 12M; *Racon (C) 10M*; *Horn 30s*; 992351027.

FISHERMANS GAT
Outer Fisherman ⚲ Q (3) 10s; 51°34'·02N 01°25'·10E.
Fisherman No 1 ⚲ Fl G 2·5s (sync); 51°34'·50N 01°23'·52E.
Fisherman No 2 ⚲ Fl R 2·5s (sync); 51°34'·30N 01°23'·50E.
Fisherman No 3 ⚲ Fl G 5s; 51°34'·78N 01°22'·65E.
Fisherman No 4 ⚲ Fl (2) R 5s; 51°34'·77N 01°22'·08E.
Fisherman No 5 ⚲ Fl (2) G 5s; 51°35'·25N 01°21'·84E.
Fisherman No 6 ⚲ Fl (3) R 10s; 51°35'·08N 01°21'·56E.
Inner Fisherman ⚲ Q R; 51°36'·15N 01°20'·08E.

BARROW DEEP
SW Barrow ⚲ Q(9) 15s; 51°32'·12N 01°00'·12E.
Alice Wk ⚲ Fl (2) 5s; 51°32'·33N 01°04'·22E.
Barrow No 14 ⚲ Fl R 2·5s; 51°31'·83N 01°00'·43E.
Barrow No 13 ⚲ Fl (2) G 5s; 51°32'·82N 01°03'·07E.
Barrow No 12 ⚲ Fl (2) R 5s; 51°33'·24N 01°05'·94E.
Barrow No 11 ⚲ Fl (3) G 10s; 51°34'·08N 01°06'·70E.
Barrow No 9 ⚲ VQ (3) 5s; 51°35'·34N 01°10'·30E.
Barrow No 8 ⚲ Fl (2) R 5s; 51°35'·05N 01°11'·36E.
Barrow No 7 ⚲ Fl G 2·5s; 51°37'·49N 01°13'·47E.
Barrow No 6 ⚲ Fl (4) R 15s; 51°37'·30N 01°14'·68E.
Barrow No 5 ⚲ Fl G 10s; 51°40'·03N 01°16'·20E.
Barrow No 4 ⚲ VQ (9) 10s; 51°39'·88N 01°17'·48E.
Barrow No 3 ⚲ Q (3) 10s; *Racon (M)10M*; 51°42'·02N 01°20'·24E.
Barrow No 2 ⚲ Fl (2) R 5s; 51°41'·98N 01°22'·89E.

WEST SWIN and MIDDLE DEEP
Blacktail Spit ⚲ Fl (3) G 10s; 51°31'·47N 00°56'·75E.
Maplin ⚲ Q G (sync with W Swin); 51°33'·66N 01°01'·40E.
W Swin ⚲ Q R (sync with Maplin); 51°33'·40N 01°01'·97E.
Maplin Edge ⚲ Fl G 2.5s; 51°35'·33N 01°03'·64E.
Maplin Bank ⚲ Fl (3) R 10s; 51°35'·50N 01°04'·70E.
Maplin Middle ⚲ Fl G 5s; *Bell*; 51°36'·78N 01°05'·50E.
E Maplin ⚲ 51°38'·29N 01°08'·86E.
Maplin Approach ⚲ Fl (2) G 10s; 51°39'·54N 01°09'·39E.

EAST SWIN and KING'S CHANNEL
N Middle ⚲ Q; 51°41'·35N 01°12'·61E.
W Sunk ⚲ Q (9) 15s; 51°44'·33N 01°25'·80E.
Gunfleet Spit ⚲ Q (6) + L Fl 15s; *Bell*; 51°45'·33N 01°21'·70E.

WHITAKER CHANNEL and RIVER CROUCH
Whitaker ⚲ Q (3) 10s; *Bell*; 51°41'·43N 01°10'·51E.
Inner Whitaker ⚲ VQ (6) + L Fl 10s; 51°40'·76N 01°08'·40E.
Swin Spitway ⚲ Iso 10s; *Bell*; 51°41'·95N 01°08'·35E.
Whitaker 1 ⚲ FlG 5s (sync Whit 2), 51° 40'·69N 01° 06'·67E.
Whitaker 2 ⚲ FlR 5s (sync Whit 1), 51° 40'·41N 01° 06'·78E.
Whitaker 3 ⚲ Fl(2) G 5s (sync Whit 4) 51° 40'·41N 01° 04'·74E.
Whitaker 4 ⚲ Fl(2) R 5s (sync Whit 4) 51° 40'·16N 01° 04'·91E.
Whitaker 5 ⚲ Fl(3) G 10s (sync Whit 6) 51° 40'·03N 01° 03'·22E.
Whitaker 6 ⚲ Fl(3) R 10s(sync Whit 5) 51° 39'·77N 01° 03'·43E.
Whitaker 7 ⚲ Fl(4) G 10s(sync Whit 8) 51° 39'·54N 01° 02'·00E.
Whitaker 8 ⚲ Fl(4) R 10s(sync Whit 7), 51° 39'·35N 01° 02'·00E.
Swallowtail 1 ⚲ Fl Y 5s, 51° 41'·38N 01° 08'·20E.
Swallowtail 2 ⚲ Fl Y 10s, 51° 41'·19N 01° 06'·28E.
Swallowtail 3 ⚲ Fl Y 15s, 51° 40.84N 01° 04.39E.
Swallowtail 4 ⚲ (2) Y 10s, 51° 40'·52N 01° 03'·47E.
Buxey Edge ⚲ Fl G 10s, 51° 40'·65N 01° 03'·48E.
Swallowtail 5 ⚲ VQ (9) 10s, 51° 40'·04N 01° 02'·65E.
Sunken Buxey ⚲ VQ; 51°39'·59N 01°00'·77E.
Buxey No 1 ⚲ VQ (6) + L Fl 10s; 51°39'·18N 01°01'·13E.
Buxey No 2 ⚲ Q; 51°39'·08N 01°00'·23E.
Outer Crouch 1 ⚲ Fl G 5s (sync Cro 2) 51° 38'·71N 00° 59'·00E.
Outer Crouch 2 ⚲ Fl R 5s (sync Cro 1) 51° 38'·62N 00° 59'·20E.
Outer Crouch 3 ⚲ Fl G 10s (sync Cro 4) 51° 38'·10N 00° 57'·83E.
Outer Crouch 4 ⚲ Fl R 10s (sync Cro 3) 51° 38'·00N 00° 58'·00E.
Crouch ⚲ Q.Fl, 51° 37.650N 00° 56.582E.
Inner Crouch ⚲ L Fl 10s, 51° 37'·19N 00° 55'·09E.
Branklet (RGR) **Pref Chan to Stbd,** Comp grp Fl (R) 2+1 10s, 51° 36'·99N 00° 52'·10E.

GOLDMER GAT and WALLET
NE Gunfleet ⚲ Q (3) 10s; 51°49'·93N 01°27'·79E.
Wallet No 2 ⚲ Fl R 5s; 51°48'·88N 01°22'·99E.
Wallet No 4 ⚲ Fl (4) R 10s; 51°46'·53N 01°17'·23E.
Wallet Spitway ⚲ L Fl 10s; *Bell*; 51°42'·86N 01°07'·30E.
Knoll ⚲ Q; 51°43'·88N 01°05'·07E.
Eagle ⚲ QG; 51°44'·10N 01°03'·63E.
N Eagle ⚲ Q; 51°44'·71N 01°04'·32E.
NW Knoll ⚲ Fl (2) R 5s; 51°44'·29N 01°02'·14E.
Colne Bar ⚲ Fl (2) G 5s; 51°44'·61N 01°02'·57E.
Bench Head ⚲ Fl (3) G 10s; 51°44'·56N 01°01'·18E.

RIVER BLACKWATER
The Nass ⚲ VQ (3) 5s 6m 2M; 51°45'·83N 00°54'·83E.
Thirslet ⚲ Fl (3) G 10s; 51°43'·73N 00°50'·39E.
No 1 ⚲ ; 51°43'·44N 00°48'·02E.

RIVER COLNE and BRIGHTLINGSEA
Inner Bench Head No 2 ⚲ Fl (2) R 5s; 51°45'·96N 01°01'·74E.
Colne Pt No 1 ⚲ Fl G 3s; 51°46'·01N 01°01'·92E.
No 8 ⚲ Fl R 3s; 51°46'·90N 01°01'·30E.
No 9 ⚲ Fl G 3s; 51°47'·36N 01°01'·07E.

Ldg lts 041°. Front, FR 7m 4M; W □, R stripe on post; vis: 020°-080°; 51°48'·39N 01°01'·20E. Rear, 50m from front, FR 10m 4M; W □, R stripe on post. FR lts are shown on 7 masts between 1·5M and 3M NW when firing occurs.

WALTON BACKWATERS
Pye End ⚓ L Fl 10s; 51°55'·03N 01°17'·90E.
No 2 ⚓ Fl (2) 5s; 51°54'·62N 01°16'·80E.
Crab Knoll No 3 ⚓ Fl G 5s; 51°54'·41N 01°16'·41E.
No 16 ⚓ 51°53'·17N 01°15'·52E.

HARWICH APPROACHES
(Direction of buoyage is North to South)
MEDUSA CHANNEL
Medusa ⚓ Fl G 5s; 51°51'·23N 01°20'·35E.
Stone Banks ⚓ FlR 5s; 51°53'·19N 01°19'·23E.
Pennyhole ⚓ ; 51°53'·55N 01°18'·00E (Mar–Sep).

CORK SAND and ROUGH SHOALS
S Cork ⚓ Q (6) + L Fl 15s; 51°51'·33N 01°24'·09E.
SE Roughs Tower ⚓ Q (3) 10s; 51°53'·64N 01°28'·94E.
NW Roughs Tower ⚓ VQ (9) 10s; 51°53'·81N 01°28'·77E.
Cork Sand ⚓ Fl (3) R 10s; 51°55'·51N 01°25'·42E.

HARWICH CHANNEL
S Threshold ⚓ Fl (4) Y 10s; 51°52'·20N 01°33'·14E.
S Shipwash ⚓⚓ 2 By(s) Q (6) + L Fl 15s; 51°52'·71N 01°33'·97E.
Outer Tidal Bn ⚓ Mo (U) 15s 2m 3M; 51°52'·85N 01°32'·34E.
E Fort Massac ⚓ VQ (3) 5s; 51°53'·36N 01°32'·79E.
W Fort Massac ⚓ VQ (9) 10s; 51°53'·36N 01°32'·49E.
Walker ⚓ Q (9)15s; 51°53'·79N 01°33'·90E.
N Threshold ⚓ Fl Y 5s; 51°54'·49N 01°33'·47E.
SW Shipwash ⚓ Fl Y 2·5s; 51°54'·75N 01°34'·21E.
Haven ⚓ Mo (A) 5s; 51°55'·76N 01°32'·56E.
W Shipwash ⚓ Fl (2) R 10s; 51°57'·13N 01°35'·89E.
NW Shipwash ⚓ Fl R 5s; 51°58'·98N 01°37'·01E.
Harwich App (HA) ⚓ Iso 5s; 51°56'·75N 01°30'·66E.
Cross ⚓ Fl (3) Y 10s; 51°56'·23N 01°30'·48E.
Harwich Chan No 1 ⚓ Fl Y 2·5s; *Racon (T) 10M*; 51°56'·13N 01°27'·06E.
Harwich Chan No 3 ⚓ Fl (3) Y 10s; 51°56'·04N 01°25'·54E.
Harwich Chan No 5 ⚓ Fl (5) Y 10s; 51°55'·96N 01°24'·01E.
Harwich Chan No 7 ⚓ Fl (3) Y 10s; 51°55'·87N 01°22'·49E.
S Bawdsey ⚓ Q (6) + L Fl 15s; *Whis*; 51°57'·23N 01°30'·19E.
Washington ⚓ QG; 51°56'·52N 01°26'·59E.
Felixstowe Ledge ⚓ Fl (3) G 10s; 51°56'·30N 01°23'·72E.
Wadgate Ledge ⚓ Fl (4) G 15s; 51°56'·16N 01°21'·99E.
Platters ⚓ Q (6) + L Fl 15s; 51°55'·64N 01°20'·97E.
Rolling Ground ⚓ QG; 51°55'·55N 01°19'·75E.
Beach End ⚓ Fl (2) G 5s; 51°55'·62N 01°19'·21E.
Cork Sand Yacht Bn ⚓ VQ 2M; 51°55'·21N 01°25'·20E.
Rough ⚓ VQ; 51°55'·19N 01°31'·00E.
Pitching Ground ⚓ Fl (4) R 15s; 51°55'·43N 01°21'·05E.
Inner Ridge ⚓ QR; 51°55'·38N 01°20'·20E.
Deane ⚓ L Fl R 6s; 51°55'·36N 01°19'·28E.
Landguard ⚓ Q; 51°55'·45N 01°18'·84E.

RIVERS STOUR AND ORWELL
RIVER STOUR and HARWICH
Shotley Spit ⚓ Q (6) + L Fl 15s; 51°57'·21N 01°17'·69E.
Shotley Marina Lock E side Dir lt 339·5° 3m 1M (uses Moiré pattern); Or structure; 51°57'·46N 01°16'·60E.
Guard ⚓ Fl R 5s; *Bell*; 51°57'·07N 01°17'·86E.

RIVER ORWELL and IPSWICH
Suffolk Yacht Harbour. Ldg lts Front Iso Y 1M; 51°59'·73N 01°16'·09E. Rear Oc Y 4s 1M.

HARWICH TO ORFORD NESS
FELIXSTOWE, R DEBEN and WOODBRIDGE HAVEN
Woodbridge Haven ⚓ Mo(A)15s; 51°57'·99N 01°23'·63E.
Deben ⚓ ; 51°59'·30N 01°23'·53E.

RIVERS ORE and ALDE
Orford Haven ⚓ L Fl 10s; *Bell*. 52°02'·00N 01°28'·20E.

OFFSHORE MARKS
S Galloper ⚓ Q (6) L Fl 15s; *Racon (T) 10M*; 51°43'·98N 01°56'·43E.
N Galloper ⚓ Q; 51°49'·84N 01°59'·99E.
S Inner Gabbard ⚓ Q (6) + L Fl 15s. 51°49'·92N 01°51'·89E.
N Inner Gabbard ⚓ Q; 51°59'·20N 01°56'·00E.
NHR-SE ⚓ Fl G 5s; 51°45'·39N 02°39'·89E.

SHIPWASH and BAWDSEY BANK
E Shipwash ⚓ VQ (3) 5s; 51°57'·08N 01°37'·89E.
NW Shipwash ⚓ Fl R 5s; 51°58'·98N 01°37'·01E.
N Shipwash ⚓ Q 7M; *Racon (M) 10M*; *Whis*; 52°01'·73N 01°38'·27E; 992351069.
S Bawdsey ⚓ Q (6) + L Fl 15s; *Bell*; 51°57'·23N 01°30'·19E.
Mid Bawdsey ⚓ Fl (3) G 10s; 51°58'·88N 01°33'·59E.
NE Bawdsey ⚓ Fl G 10s; 52°01'·73N 01°36'·09E.

CUTLER and WHITING BANKS
Cutler ⚓ QG; 51°58'·51N 01°27'·48E.
SW Whiting ⚓ Q (6) + L Fl 10s; 52°00'·96N 01°30'·69E.
Whiting Hook ⚓ Fl R 10s; 52°02'·98N 01°31'·82E.
NE Whiting ⚓ Q (3) 10s; 52°03'·61N 01°33'·32E.

ORFORD NESS TO WINTERTON
(Direction of buoyage is South to North)
Orford Ness Lt Ho (dis) 52°05'·04N 01°34'·45E; W ○ twr, R bands.
Aldeburgh Ridge ⚓ QR; 52°06'·49N 01°36'·95E.

SOUTHWOLD
Southwold ☆ 52°19'·63N 01°40'·89E; Fl 10s 37m **W24M**; vis 204°-W-032·5°, 992351019.

LOWESTOFT and APPR VIA STANFORD CHANNEL
E Barnard ⚓ Q (3) 10s; 52°25'·14N 01°46'·38E.
Newcome Sand ⚓ QR; 52°26'·33N 01°47'·16E.
S Holm ⚓ VQ (6) + L Fl 10s; 52°26'·63N 01°47'·11E.
Stanford ⚓ Fl R 2·5s; 52°27'·35N 01°46'·67E.
SW Holm ⚓ Fl (2) G 5s; 52°27'·87N 01°46'·99E.
Kirkley ⚓ Dir WRG 17m 10M, vis: 222°-OcG 10s -225°-FlG 2·5s-226°-FlW 2·5s-227°-OcW 10s-229°-FlW 2·5s-230°-FlR 2·5s-231°-OcR 10s-232°; 52°27'·71N 01°44'·54E.
Outer Hbr S Pier Hd ⚓ Oc R 5s 12m 6M; *Horn (4) 60s*; tfc sigs; 52°28'·29N 01°45'·36E.
N Newcome ⚓ Fl (4) R 15s; 52°28'·39N 01°46'·37E.
Lowestoft ☆ 52°29'·22N 01°45'·35; Fl 15s 37m **23M**; W twr; part obscd 347°- shore.

LOWESTOFT NORTH ROAD and CORTON ROAD
Lowestoft Ness SE ⚓ Q (6) + L Fl 15s; 52°28'·84N 01°46'·25E.
Lowestoft Ness N ⚓ VQ (3) 5s; *Bell*; 52°28'·89N 01°46'·23E.
W Holm ⚓ Fl (3) G 10s; 52°29'·50N 01°46'·99E.
NW Holm ⚓ Fl (4) G 15s; 52°30'·90N 01°46'·50E.

GREAT YARMOUTH APPROACH via HOLM CHANNEL
E Newcome ⚓ Fl (2) R 5s; 52°28'·51N 01°49'·21E.
Holm Approach ⚓ Q (3) 10s; 52°30'·88N 01°50'·22E.
Holm Sand ⚓ Q (9) 15s; 52°33'·28N 01°46'·62E.
S Corton ⚓ Q (6) + L Fl 15s; *Bell*; 52°33'·32N 01°48'·41E.
NE Holm ⚓ Fl R 2·5s; 52°33'·06N 01°48'·43E.
Mid Corton ⚓ Fl G 2·5s; 52°33'·61N 01°47'·98E.
N Holm ⚓ Q 52°33'·73N 01°47'·29E.
W Corton ⚓ Fl (3) G 10s; 52°34'·12N 01°47'·50E.

GREAT YARMOUTH and GORLESTON
Gorleston South Pier Hd ⚓ Fl R 3s 11m 11M; vis: 235°-340°; 52°34'·33N 01°44'·28E.
N Pier Hd ⚓ QG 8m 6M; vis: 176°-078°; *Horn(3) 60s*; 52°34'·38N 01°44'·38E.
Outer Hbr S Pier ⚓ Q R 17m 3M; 52°34'·61N 01°44'·73E.
Outer Hbr N Pier ⚓ Q G 17m 3M; 52°34'·70N 01°44'·74E.

1.4 PASSAGE INFORMATION

See 0.34 for distances across the North Sea. Admiralty Leisure Folios: 5606 Thames Estuary from Ramsgate to Tower Bridge, London; 5607 Northern Thames Estuary to Orford Ness; 5614 Orford Ness to Whitby. **Bibliography:** *East Coast Rivers* (Fernhurst/Harber); *East Coast Pilot* (Imray/Jarman,Holness,Cooper); *Dover Strait Pilot* (Admiralty NP28) and *North Sea (West) Pilot* (Admiralty NP54); *North Sea Passage Pilot* (Imray/Navin).

THE THAMES ESTUARY

(AC 1183, 1975, 1607, 1606, 1609) The sandbanks shift constantly in the Thames Estuary; charted depths cannot be relied upon, and an accurate echo sounder is vital. Up to date charts showing the latest buoyage changes and a detailed tidal stream atlas are essential. The commercial deep water route from the Sunk Inner precautionary area to the Yantlet runs through Black Deep and Knock John Channel. It is well marked, as are Barrow Deep, Princes Channel and Fisherman's Gat. The lesser channels and swatchways, which are convenient for yachtsmen, particularly when crossing the estuary, are mainly unmarked and unlit. They should be used with great caution. Good visibility is needed to pick out buoys and marks, and to avoid shipping. Care should be exercised when plotting electronic waypoints. Many former navigation marks and towers have been removed or allowed to disintegrate. Those that are still standing may be in very shallow water.

Newcomers to the estuary are advised to choose a period of neap tides when minimum depths are greater and tidal streams weaker. If a crossing at springs is unavoidable, keep in deep water even if that involves a longer passage.

Wind strength and direction needs careful consideration for each of the course changes during a typical crossing to avoid becoming trapped between shoals, downwind and downstream of safe water.

▶ *Study the tides so as to work the streams to best advantage and to ensure sufficient depth at the times and places where you expect to be, or might be later. In principle it is best to make most of the crossing on a rising tide. However, a typical passage from N Foreland to the Blackwater will take 7–9hrs, so some adverse stream is almost inevitable. The stream at springs runs at 3kn in places, mostly along the channels but sometimes across the intervening banks. A short, steep sea may be raised with the wind against tide.* ◀

CROSSING THE THAMES ESTUARY

(AC 1183, 1975, 1607, 1606, 1609) *Crossing the Thames Estuary* (Imray) gives 32 suggested routes. Making N from N Foreland to Orford Ness or beyond it may be better to keep to seaward of the main banks, via Kentish Knock and Long Sand Head buoys, thence to N Shipwash lt buoy, 14M further N.

Bound NW from North Foreland it is approximately 35M to the mouths of the Rivers Crouch, Blackwater or Colne. One route is through the Princes Channel, thence N of the Oaze Deep precautionary area and S of the Knob and West Barrow banks to the West Swin, before turning NE into Middle Deep and the East Swin. The Wallet Spitway then leads NW to the Colne and Blackwater. Many routes may be followed, depending on wind direction, tidal conditions and confidence in electronic aids in the absence of marks. Passage over Sunk Sand and Knock John bank is best avoided, particularly in winds >F5.

Southbound from the Colne or Blackwater, leave 1–2hrs before HW and make best speed to skirt or cross the shoals while there is sufficient depth of water. The latter part of the passage will be in generally deeper water of Edinburgh

Channel, Fisherman's or Foulger's Gat or (keeping clear of the turbines in the London Array), with a favourable S-going stream just starting off North Foreland.

From the NE follow Goldmer Gat and the Wallet (for Rivers Colne/Blackwater) or King's Channel and Whittaker Channel for the River Crouch.

London VTS has radar coverage from Greenwich to a line between the Naze and Margate. Keep a listening watch on VHF Ch 69 to monitor shipping activity. If really necessary, *London VTS* may be able to give navigational help to yachts.

NORTH FORELAND TO LONDON BRIDGE

North Foreland lt ho is conspic (AC 1828), with buoys offshore.

▶ *From HW Dover –0120 to +0045 the stream runs N from The Downs and W into Thames Estuary. From HWD +0045 to +0440 the N-going stream from The Downs meets the E-going stream from Thames Estuary, which in strong winds causes a bad sea. From HWD –0450 to –0120 the streams turn W into Thames Estuary and S towards The Downs. If bound for London, round N Foreland against the late ebb in order to carry a fair tide from Sheerness onward.* ◀

The most direct route from North Foreland to the Thames and Medway is via South, Gore and Copperas Channels, then Overland Passage, Four Fathoms Channel and The Cant. Minimum depth is about 2m but may be significantly less off Reculver and leaving Copperas Channel. It is not well marked. Beware of Kentish Flats wind farm (30 turbines) with submarine cables to Herne Bay. An alternative, deeper route is east of Margate Sand and the Tongue, via the Princes Channel to the Oaze Deep. The N and S Edinburgh Channels are unmarked but navigable with caution.

▶ *W-going streams begin at approx HW Sheerness –0600 and E-going at HW Sheerness +0030.* ◀

Margate or Whitstable afford little shelter for yachts. The Swale provides an interesting inside route S of the Isle of Sheppey with access to Sheerness and the R Medway. If sailing from N Foreland to the Thames, Queenborough offers the first easily accessible, all-tide, deep-water shelter. In the east part of The Swale, Harty Ferry provides a sheltered ⚓, but not in strong winds from N or E. The Medway Channel is the main approach to Sheerness from The Warp.

SHOEBURYNESS TO RIVER COLNE

(Charts 1185, 1975) Maplin and Foulness Sands extend nearly 6M NE from Foulness Pt, the extremity marked by Whitaker bn. On the N side of Whitaker channel leading to the R Crouch and R Roach lies Buxey Sand. Inshore of this Ray Sand channel (dries), may be a convenient short cut between the Rivers Crouch and Blackwater with sufficient rise of tide.

To seaward of Buxey Sand and the Spitway, Gunfleet Sand extends 10M NE. It is marked by buoys and dries in places. Gunfleet Sands Wind Farm, lies along the shoal between Swin Spitway and Gunfleet Old Lt Ho. 50 turbines are marked by Fl Y lts and R Aero obstn lts, the northernmost sounds a horn every 10s in fog.

▶ *A conspic disused lt tr stands on SE side of Gunfleet Sand, about 6M SSE of the Naze tr, and here the SW-going (flood) stream begins about HW Sheerness +0600, and the NE-going stream at about HW Sheerness –0030, Sp rates 2kn.* ◀

The Rivers Blackwater and Colne share a common estuary which is approached from the NE from NE Gunfleet lit buoy; thence along Goldmer Gat and the Wallet towards Knoll and Eagle lt buoys. For the Colne turn NNW via Colne Bar buoy towards Inner Bench Hd buoy keeping in mid-chan.

Continued overleaf

For R Blackwater, head WNW for NW Knoll and Bench Hd buoys. From the S or SE, make for the Whitaker ECM buoy, thence through the Spitway, via Swin Spitway and Wallet Spitway buoys to reach Knoll buoy and deeper water.

HARWICH

(Chart AC 1975, 1593) 4M SW of the Naze twr at Hollands Haven a conspic radar twr (67m, unlit) is an excellent daymark. From the S, approach Walton and Harwich via the Medusa chan about 1M E of the twr. Beware pot buoys and drift nets off the Naze. At the N end of this chan, 1M off Dovercourt, Pye End buoy marks chan SSW to Walton Backwaters. Harwich and Landguard Pt are close to the N. Making Harwich from the SE beware the drying Cork Sand, which lies N/S.

Sunk Inner SWM buoy, 11M E of The Naze, marks the outer apps to Harwich, an extensive and well sheltered hbr accessible at all times (chart AC 2693).

- Harwich, Felixstowe Docks and Ipswich are referred to collectively as the Haven Ports.
- Small craft should give plenty of sea room to shipping manoeuvring to board/disembark Pilots in the Sunk Inner Precautionary Area, see Thames Estuary chartlet.
- Harwich Deep Water chan runs N from 1·5M NNW of Sunk Inner between Rough and Shipwash shoals, then W past the Cork Sand PHM. Constantly used by commercial shipping, small craft should use the recommended track for yachts.

Approaching from NE and 2M off the ent to R Deben, beware Cutler shoal, with least depth of 1·2m, marked by SHM buoy on E side; Wadgate Ledge and the Platters are about 1·5M ENE of Landguard Point; beware pot buoys off Cobbolds Point.

▶ South of Landguard Point the W-going (flood) stream begins at HW Harwich +0600, and the E-going stream at HW Harwich, Sp rates about 1·5kn. Note: HW Harwich is never more than 7 mins after HW Walton; LW times are about 10 mins earlier. ◀

HARWICH TO ORFORD NESS

(Chart AC 2052) Shipwash shoal, buoyed and with a drying patch, runs NNE from 9M E of Felixstowe to 4M SSE of Orford Ness. Inshore of this is Shipway Chan, then Bawdsey Bank, buoyed with depths of 2m, on which the sea breaks in E'ly swell.

The Sledway Chan lies between Bawdsey Bank and Whiting Bank (buoyed) which is close SW of Orford Ness, and has depths less than 1m. Hollesley Chan, about 1M wide, runs inshore W and N of this bank. In the SW part of Hollesley B is the ent to Orford Haven and the R Ore/Alde.

▶ There are overfalls S of Orford Ness on both the ebb and flood streams. 2M E of Orford Ness the SW-going stream begins at HW Harwich +0605, Sp rate 2·5kn; the NE-going stream begins at HW Harwich –0010, Sp rate 3kn. ◀

Note: The direction of local buoyage becomes S to N off Orford Ness (52°05'N).

ORFORD NESS TO GREAT YARMOUTH

(Chart AC 1543) N of Orford Ness seas break on Aldeburgh Ridge (1·3m), but the coast is clear of offlying dangers past Aldeburgh and Southwold, as far as Benacre Ness, 5M S of Lowestoft. Sizewell power station (conspic) 3 bldg 1·5M N of Thorpe Ness. Keep 1·5M offshore to avoid fishing floats and outfalls marked by lit PHMs.

▶ Lowestoft is best approached from both S and E by the buoyed/lit Stanford chan, passing E of Newcome Sand and SW of Holm Sand; beware possible strong set across harbour entrance. ◀

From the N, approach through Cockle Gatway, Caister Road, Yarmouth Road, passing Great Yarmouth (beware of prohibited area N of harbour entrance); then proceed S through Gorleston, Corton and Lowestoft North Roads (buoyed).

▶ 1M E of hbr ent, the S-going stream begins at HW Dover –0600, and the N-going at HW Dover, Sp rates 2·6kn. ◀

Scroby Sands Wind Farm consists of 30 turbines centred on 52°39'·00N 01°47'·00E. Each turbine is 61m high, with 80m diameter blades and clearance height of 18m and six of the perimeter ones are lit. Vessels are to keep clear of turbines.

In the approaches to Great Yarmouth from seaward the banks are continually changing; use the buoyed chans which, from N and S, are those described in the preceding paragraph. But from the E the shortest approach is via Corton ECM lt buoy and the Holm Channel leading into Gorleston Road.

▶ The sea often breaks on North Scroby, Middle Scroby and Caister Shoal (all of which dry), and there are heavy tide rips over parts of Corton and South Scroby Sands, Middle and South Cross Sands, and Winterton Overfalls. ◀

▶ 1M NE of ent to Gt Yarmouth the S-going stream begins at HW Dover –0600, and the N-going at HW Dover –0015, Sp rates 2·3kn. Breydon Water (tidal) affects streams in the Haven; after heavy rain the out-going stream at Brush Quay may exceed 5kn. ◀

About 12M NE of Great Yarmouth lie Newarp Banks, on which the sea breaks in bad weather.

CROSSING FROM THAMES/ORWELL TO BELGIUM OR THE NETHERLANDS

(ACs 1408, 1406, 1610, 1630, 1872, 1183) Up to date charts are *essential*. Thanet Wind Farm is now established 6Nm ENE of N Foreland and bounded by cardinal buoys. The southern North Sea is an extremely busy area with several large and complex Traffic Separation Schemes and associated Precautionary Areas which should be avoided if at all possible. Where practicable, navigate outside the schemes using any available ITZs, and always cross a TSS on a heading at 90° to the traffic flow in accordance with the Collision Regulations. From the Thames to Zeebrugge, the most direct route crosses the Nord Hinder South TSS in the vicinity of F3 light float. This is a focal point for dense crossing traffic. The very busy area around West Hinder must then be negotiated. A longer but much safer route (or if bound for Dunkerque, Nieuwpoort or Oostende) via S Falls, Sandettié and Dyck minimises time spent in the TSS and provides the option of breaking the passage in Ramsgate.

From the Orwell (or adjacent rivers) to the Netherlands, it may be best to pass north of the Sunk Inner and Sunk Outer TSS/Precautionary Areas before setting course for Hoek van Holland. From S Shipwash make for N Inner Gabbard before setting course for NHR-S to cross the North Hinder TSS to NHR-SE, then pass S of the Maas-West TSS leaving MW1, MW3 and MW5 buoys to port before shaping up for MV-N buoy.

▶ Care must be taken throughout with the tidal streams, which may be setting across the yacht's track. ◀

The whole area is relatively shallow, and in bad weather seas are steep and short. (See also Area 2.)

1.5 RAMSGATE

Kent **51°19'·51N 01°25'·50E** ✵✵✵✵ⓘⓘ❀❀❀

CHARTS AC 323, 1828, 1827, 5605/6; Imray C30, C8, C1, 2100

TIDES +0030 Dover; ML 2·7; Duration 0530

SHELTER Options: (a) Inner Marina, min depth 2m. Access approx HW±2 via flap gate and lifting bridge; (b) W Marina, min 2m, access H24; (c) E Marina, min 2m, access H24. Larger vessels can berth on outer wavebreak pontoons of both W and E marinas.

NAVIGATION WPT 51°19'·43N 01°27'·70E, 270°/1·45M to S bkwtr. Commercial shipping uses the well-marked main E-W chan dredged 7·5m. *Due to silting, depths may be significantly less than shown; parts of Eastern Marina, particularly, almost dry at LWS*. Latest information may be obtained from Port Control.

For ent/dep yachts must use the Recommended Yacht Track on the S side of the main buoyed chan. Ent/dep under power, or advise Port Control if unable to motor. Ent/dep Royal Hbr directly; cross the turning basin without delay **keeping close to the W Pier to avoid shoal patch alongside E Pier**. Holding area to the S of the S bkwtr must be used by yachts to keep the hbr ent clear for freight vessels. Beware Dike Bank to the N and Quern Bank close S of the chan. Cross Ledge and Brake shoals are further S. Speed limit 5kn. See www.rma.eu.com.

LIGHTS AND MARKS Ldg lts 270°: front Dir Oc WRG 10s 10m 5M; rear, Oc 5s 17m 5M. N bkwtr hd = QG 10m 5M; S bkwtr hd = VQ R 10m 5M. At E Pier, **IPTS** (Sigs 2 and 3) visible from seaward and from within Royal Hbr, control appr into hbr limits (abeam Nos 1 & 2 buoys) and ent/exit to/from Royal Hbr. In addition a Fl Orange lt = ferry is under way; no other vessel may enter Hbr limits from seaward or leave Royal Hbr. Ent to inner marina controlled by separate IPTS to stbd of ent. Siren sounded approx 10 mins before gate closes; non-opening indicated by red ball or light.

COMMUNICATIONS (Code 01843) Dr 852853 Ⓗ 225544. Hbr Office ☎572100; Broadstairs HM ☎861879.

Listen and contact *Ramsgate Port Control* on Ch 14 when intending to enter or leave Royal Hbr. Only when in Royal Hbr call *Ramsgate Marina* Ch 80 for a berth. Ramsgate Dock Office must be called on Ch 14 for information on Inner Marina Lock.

FACILITIES Marina www.portoframsgate.co.uk ☎572100, ⏻ £32/craft<5t; 510 ⛵+300ⓥ £2.96; ⚓⚓🔌🛢🔧🗜🚿🛒Ⓔ⚠ 🅿(40t) ⛴ ACA.

Royal Hbr 🛥🏴(0600-2200).

Royal Temple YC ☎591766, 🍴.

Town 🛢✉Ⓑ🛒🍴✕🗑🚃.

HM Ch 14

RAMSGATE

ADJACENT HARBOUR
SANDWICH, Kent, 51°16'·83N 01°21'·20E. AC 1827 1828. Richborough differences above; ML 1·4m; Duration 0520. HW Sandwich Town quay is HW Richborough +1. Access via narrow drying channel to Sandwich; arrive off ent at HW Dover. SWM, LFL 10s, 51° 18'·532N 1° 23'·320E. Visitors should seek local knowledge before arriving by day; night ent definitely not advised. The chan is marked by small lateral buoys. Visitors' berths on S bank of the R Stour at Town Quay ☎(01304) 612162. Limited turning room before the swing bridge (opens 1hr notice ☎01304 620644 or Mobile 0860 378792), 1·7m clearance when closed. Facilities: ⏻ HW±2 ✉Ⓑ🛒✕🗑🚃✈ (Manston).

Marina ☎613783, ⏻ 50⛵+ⓥ £2.20 (<18m, 2·1m draught) ⚓🔧🗜🔧🚿⚠ 🅿(15t) 🛢⛴.

Sandwich Sailing and Motorboat Club ☎617650 and **Sandwich Bay Sailing and Water Ski Clubs** offer some facilities. The port is administered by Sandwich Port & Haven Commissioners.

STANDARD TIME (UT)
For Summer Time add ONE hour in **non-shaded areas**

RAMSGATE   LAT 51°20′N   LONG 1°25′E
TIMES AND HEIGHTS OF HIGH AND LOW WATERS

Dates in red are SPRINGS
Dates in blue are NEAPS

YEAR 2022

JANUARY

Day	Time	m	Time	m	Time	m	Time	m
1 SA	0420	0.8	0948	4.9	1652	0.5	2221	4.9
16 SU	0502	0.9	1048	4.5	1720	0.9	2309	4.7
2 SU	0524	0.7	1044	5.0	1753	0.5	●2312	5.0
17 M	0544	0.8	1124	4.6	1759	0.8	○2344	4.8
3 M	0623	0.5	1138	5.1	1850	0.5		
18 TU	0623	0.7	1159	4.7	1838	0.7		
4 TU	0002	4.9	0718	0.4	1231	5.1	1942	0.5
19 W	0015	4.8	0702	0.6	1231	4.8	1916	0.7
5 W	0050	5.0	0807	0.3	1323	5.0	2029	0.6
20 TH	0045	4.8	0739	0.5	1304	4.8	1954	0.7
6 TH	0137	5.0	0854	0.2	1413	4.9	2113	0.7
21 F	0116	4.9	0816	0.5	1337	4.8	2029	0.7
7 F	0223	4.9	0938	0.3	1502	4.7	2154	0.8
22 SA	0148	4.8	0852	0.5	1413	4.7	2102	0.8
8 SA	0311	4.8	1022	0.3	1553	4.5	2236	0.9
23 SU	0224	4.8	0928	0.5	1452	4.6	2136	0.9
9 SU	0402	4.6	1108	0.5	1648	4.3	☽2323	1.0
24 M	0305	4.7	1008	0.6	1538	4.4	2218	1.0
10 M	0459	4.4	1159	0.7	1750	4.1		
25 TU	0353	4.6	1057	0.7	1634	4.2	☽2313	1.2
11 TU	0016	1.1	0605	4.2	1255	0.9	1856	4.0
26 W	0453	4.4	1156	0.8	1742	4.1		
12 W	0115	1.2	0714	4.1	1356	1.0	2001	4.0
27 TH	0019	1.3	0607	4.3	1303	0.9	1900	4.1
13 TH	0219	1.2	0820	4.2	1457	1.1	2059	4.2
28 F	0134	1.3	0726	4.3	1418	0.9	2015	4.2
14 F	0321	1.1	0918	4.2	1552	1.1	2149	4.3
29 SA	0257	1.2	0841	0.8	1538	0.8	2121	4.5
15 SA	0416	1.0	1006	4.4	1638	1.0	2232	4.5
30 SU	0418	0.9	0947	4.6	1652	0.7	2219	4.8
31 M	0526	0.6	1046	4.8	1754	0.5	2310	4.8

FEBRUARY

Day	Time	m	Time	m	Time	m	Time	m
1 TU	0623	0.3	1138	5.0	1848	0.4	●2356	5.0
16 W	0605	0.5	1138	4.8	1824	0.6	○2352	4.9
2 W	0714	0.1	1227	5.0	1936	0.4		
17 TH	0646	0.4	1210	4.9	1905	0.5		
3 TH	0039	5.0	0759	0.0	1311	5.0	2017	0.4
18 F	0022	4.9	0726	0.3	1241	5.0	1944	0.5
4 F	0120	5.1	0840	0.0	1353	4.9	2053	0.4
19 SA	0052	5.0	0804	0.3	1312	4.9	2019	0.5
5 SA	0201	5.1	0916	0.0	1435	4.8	2126	0.5
20 SU	0123	5.0	0839	0.3	1346	4.9	2050	0.6
6 SU	0243	5.1	0951	0.2	1517	4.6	2159	0.6
21 M	0159	5.0	0912	0.4	1424	4.8	2119	0.8
7 M	0327	5.0	1028	0.4	1603	4.3	2237	0.8
22 TU	0239	4.9	0947	0.5	1508	4.6	2156	0.9
8 TU	0416	4.5	1108	0.7	1655	4.1	☽2322	1.1
23 W	0326	4.8	1030	0.7	1601	4.3	☽2246	1.1
9 W	0512	4.2	1155	1.1	1757	3.8		
24 TH	0424	4.5	1125	0.9	1709	4.1	2350	1.3
10 TH	0015	1.3	0621	3.9	1251	1.3	1911	3.7
25 F	0541	4.2	1234	1.1	1835	4.0		
11 F	0121	1.5	0738	3.8	1359	1.5	2023	3.9
26 SA	0114	1.4	0716	4.1	1406	1.2	2006	4.1
12 SA	0237	1.5	0848	3.9	1511	1.4	2121	4.1
27 SU	0258	1.3	0844	4.3	1543	1.1	2118	4.3
13 SU	0345	1.3	0943	4.1	1610	1.2	2206	4.4
28 M	0422	0.9	0951	4.5	1654	0.8	2214	4.6
14 M	0438	1.0	1026	4.4	1659	1.0	2245	4.6
15 TU	0523	0.7	1103	4.6	1742	0.8	2320	4.8

MARCH

Day	Time	m	Time	m	Time	m	Time	m
1 TU	0524	0.5	1045	4.8	1750	0.5	2301	4.8
16 W	0455	0.7	1033	4.7	1719	0.8	2248	4.8
2 W	0615	0.2	1131	5.0	1837	0.4	●2342	5.0
17 TH	0540	0.5	1108	4.9	1803	0.5	2320	4.9
3 TH	0700	0.0	1212	5.0	1918	0.3		
18 F	0622	0.3	1140	5.1	1844	0.4	○2351	5.1
4 F	0020	5.1	0740	-0.1	1249	5.0	1953	0.3
19 SA	0703	0.2	1211	5.1	1922	0.4		
5 SA	0057	5.2	0815	0.0	1326	5.0	2023	0.3
20 SU	0023	5.2	0743	0.2	1243	5.1	1958	0.5
6 SU	0135	5.2	0846	0.1	1402	4.9	2051	0.4
21 M	0057	5.2	0818	0.3	1319	5.1	2030	0.6
7 M	0212	5.1	0915	0.3	1440	4.7	2121	0.6
22 TU	0135	5.2	0851	0.4	1359	4.9	2102	0.7
8 TU	0251	4.9	0945	0.6	1519	4.5	2154	0.8
23 W	0218	5.1	0927	0.6	1445	4.8	2141	0.8
9 W	0332	4.6	1018	0.9	1602	4.2	2233	1.1
24 TH	0307	4.8	1010	0.8	1539	4.5	2230	1.1
10 TH	0418	4.2	1057	1.3	1654	3.9	☽2320	1.4
25 F	0409	4.5	1104	1.1	1647	4.1	☽2335	1.3
11 F	0519	3.8	1146	1.6	1806	3.7		
26 SA	0532	4.1	1218	1.4	1819	3.9		
12 SA	0020	1.7	0645	3.6	1253	1.8	1932	3.7
27 SU	0110	1.4	0718	4.0	1409	1.5	1957	4.0
13 SU	0142	1.7	0809	3.7	1422	1.7	2041	3.9
28 M	0259	1.2	0844	4.3	1540	1.2	2106	4.3
14 M	0306	1.4	0909	4.1	1538	1.4	2131	4.2
29 TU	0412	0.7	0945	4.6	1642	0.9	2158	4.6
15 TU	0406	1.1	0955	4.4	1633	1.1	2212	4.5
30 W	0507	0.3	1032	4.8	1731	0.6	2241	4.9
31 TH	0554	0.1	1112	5.0	1813	0.4	2319	5.1

APRIL

Day	Time	m	Time	m	Time	m	Time	m
1 F	0635	0.0	1148	5.1	1849	0.3	●2356	5.2
16 SA	0550	0.4	1105	5.1	1812	0.5	○2318	5.2
2 SA	0711	0.0	1223	5.1	1921	0.3		
17 SU	0633	0.3	1139	5.2	1853	0.5	2354	5.3
3 SU	0031	5.2	0743	0.2	1256	5.0	1949	0.4
18 M	0714	0.3	1216	5.2	1931	0.5		
4 M	0106	5.2	0811	0.3	1330	4.9	2017	0.6
19 TU	0033	5.3	0754	0.4	1256	5.2	2010	0.6
5 TU	0141	5.1	0837	0.6	1405	4.8	2045	0.7
20 W	0116	5.3	0832	0.5	1341	5.0	2049	0.7
6 W	0216	4.9	0903	0.8	1439	4.6	2116	1.0
21 TH	0205	5.1	0913	0.7	1430	4.8	2133	0.8
7 TH	0252	4.6	0932	1.1	1514	4.4	2151	1.2
22 F	0301	4.8	0959	1.0	1527	4.6	2224	1.0
8 F	0332	4.3	1005	1.4	1557	4.1	2233	1.4
23 SA	0408	4.5	1055	1.3	1636	4.2	☽2332	1.2
9 SA	0425	3.9	1050	1.6	1658	3.9	☽2328	1.6
24 SU	0533	4.2	1216	1.6	1803	4.0		
10 SU	0545	3.7	1153	1.8	1824	3.7		
25 M	0108	1.2	0711	4.1	1359	1.5	1933	4.1
11 M	0045	1.7	0717	3.8	1326	1.8	1946	3.9
26 TU	0238	1.0	0827	4.3	1516	1.2	2040	4.4
12 TU	0216	1.4	0825	4.1	1454	1.6	2044	4.2
27 W	0344	0.6	0922	4.6	1613	0.9	2131	4.6
13 W	0325	1.1	0915	4.4	1556	1.2	2129	4.5
28 TH	0437	0.3	1007	4.8	1659	0.6	2214	4.9
14 TH	0418	0.7	0956	4.7	1645	0.8	2208	4.8
29 F	0523	0.2	1046	4.9	1739	0.5	2254	5.1
15 F	0506	0.5	1031	5.0	1730	0.6	2243	5.0
30 SA	0603	0.2	1122	5.0	1815	0.4	●2331	5.1

Chart Datum: 2·58 metres below Ordnance Datum (Newlyn). HAT is 5·7 metres above Chart Datum.

》》 FREE monthly updates. Register at 《
www.reedsnauticalalmanac.co.uk

STANDARD TIME (UT)
For Summer Time add ONE hour in **non-shaded areas**

RAMSGATE LAT 51°20'N LONG 1°25'E
TIMES AND HEIGHTS OF HIGH AND LOW WATERS

Dates in red are **SPRINGS**
Dates in blue are **NEAPS**

YEAR **2022**

MAY

Time	m		Time	m
1 0638	0.3	**16**	0601	0.4
1156	5.0		1112	5.2
SU 1847	0.5	M 1824	0.6
		○ 2331	5.3
2 0006	5.1	**17**	0648	0.5
0708	0.5		1156	5.2
M 1230	5.0	TU 1911	0.6
1918	0.6		
3 0041	5.0	**18**	0017	5.3
0735	0.7		0735	0.5
TU 1303	4.9	W 1242	5.2
1947	0.8	1958	0.6
4 0115	4.9	**19**	0108	5.2
0801	0.8		1332	5.0
W 1336	4.8	TH 1332	5.0
2016	0.9	2044	0.6
5 0148	4.7	**20**	0203	5.0
0826	1.0		0908	0.8
TH 1408	4.7	F 1425	4.9
2046	1.0	2132	0.7
6 0223	4.6	**21**	0302	4.8
0855	1.1		0957	1.0
F 1441	4.5	SA 1521	4.6
2120	1.1	2225	0.8
7 0302	4.4	**22**	0407	4.5
0929	1.3		1055	1.3
SA 1521	4.4	SU 1624	4.5
2159	1.3	◑ 2330	0.9
8 0352	4.2	**23**	0523	4.3
1012	1.5		1207	1.4
SU 1612	4.2	M 1738	4.2
2250	1.3		
9 0458	4.0	**24**	0047	0.9
1111	1.7		0644	4.3
M 1721	4.0	TU 1324	1.4
◑ 2358	1.4	1857	4.3
10 0619	3.9	**25**	0200	0.8
1234	1.7		0753	4.4
TU 1841	4.0	W 1432	1.2
		2003	4.4
11 0122	1.3	**26**	0304	0.6
0733	4.1		0848	4.5
W 1401	1.6	TH 1529	1.0
1949	4.2	2058	4.6
12 0235	1.0	**27**	0358	0.5
0828	4.4		0936	4.7
TH 1507	1.3	F 1619	0.7
2041	4.5	2146	4.8
13 0334	0.8	**28**	0446	0.5
0913	4.6		1018	4.8
F 1601	1.0	SA 1703	0.7
2126	4.8	2230	4.9
14 0425	0.6	**29**	0528	0.5
0953	4.9		1058	4.8
SA 1649	0.8	SU 1743	0.7
2207	5.0	2310	4.9
15 0513	0.5	**30**	0604	0.6
1032	5.1		1135	4.9
SU 1736	0.6	M 1819	0.7
2248	5.2	● 2348	4.9
		31	0636	0.8
			1210	4.9
		TU 1852	0.8

JUNE

Time	m		Time	m
1 0023	4.8	**16**	0013	5.2
0706	0.9		0728	0.6
W 1243	4.8	TH 1236	5.1
1924	0.9	1954	0.5
2 0057	4.7	**17**	0108	5.1
0734	1.0		0818	0.7
TH 1316	4.8	F 1327	5.0
1956	0.9	2043	0.4
3 0130	4.7	**18**	0203	5.0
0803	1.0		0907	0.7
F 1347	4.8	SA 1418	4.9
2027	1.0	2131	0.4
4 0206	4.6	**19**	0259	4.9
0834	1.1		0955	0.9
SA 1420	4.7	SU 1510	4.8
2101	1.0	2221	0.4
5 0245	4.5	**20**	0356	4.7
0909	1.2		1045	1.0
SU 1458	4.6	M 1605	4.7
2139	1.0	2315	0.5
6 0329	4.4	**21**	0457	4.5
0951	1.3		1139	1.1
M 1542	4.4	TU 1706	4.5
2225	1.0	◑	
7 0422	4.2	**22**	0012	0.6
1042	1.4		0603	4.4
TU 1635	4.3	W 1237	1.1
◑ 2323	1.1	1814	4.4
8 0526	4.1	**23**	0113	0.7
1149	1.5		0709	4.3
W 1741	4.2	TH 1338	1.1
		1922	4.4
9 0033	1.1	**24**	0215	0.7
0636	4.1		0809	4.3
TH 1304	1.5	F 1438	1.1
1851	4.3	2024	4.5
10 0143	1.0	**25**	0315	0.8
0738	4.3		0904	4.4
F 1412	1.3	SA 1536	1.0
1953	4.5	2120	4.5
11 0245	0.8	**26**	0409	0.8
0832	4.5		0954	4.5
SA 1513	1.1	SU 1630	0.9
2047	4.7	2210	4.6
12 0342	0.7	**27**	0456	0.9
0921	4.7		1038	4.7
SU 1610	1.0	M 1716	0.9
2138	4.9	2255	4.6
13 0439	0.6	**28**	0536	1.0
1008	4.9		1118	4.7
M 1708	0.8	TU 1757	0.9
2228	5.1	2334	4.6
14 0536	0.6	**29**	0611	1.0
1056	5.1		1154	4.8
TU 1806	0.7	W 1834	0.9
○ 2319	5.2	●	
15 0633	0.6	**30**	0009	4.6
1145	5.1		0645	1.0
W 1901	0.6	TH 1227	4.8
		1909	0.9

JULY

Time	m		Time	m
1 0043	4.7	**16**	0105	5.1
0718	1.0		0815	0.5
F 1259	4.8	SA 1318	5.1
1942	0.8	2039	0.1
2 0116	4.7	**17**	0155	5.1
0752	1.0		0859	0.5
SA 1330	4.8	SU 1404	5.1
2016	0.8	2122	0.1
3 0150	4.7	**18**	0243	5.0
0826	0.9		0940	0.6
SU 1401	4.8	M 1450	5.0
2050	0.7	2204	0.1
4 0225	4.7	**19**	0331	4.8
0900	1.0		1020	0.7
M 1434	4.8	TU 1538	4.9
2125	0.7	2247	0.3
5 0303	4.6	**20**	0422	4.6
0935	1.1		1101	0.8
TU 1513	4.7	W 1631	4.8
2205	0.7	◑ 2332	0.5
6 0347	4.4	**21**	0517	4.4
1017	1.2		1148	1.0
W 1558	4.6	TH 1731	4.5
2253	0.8		
7 0439	4.3	**22**	0023	0.8
1109	1.3		0620	4.2
TH 1653	4.4	F 1242	1.2
◑ 2350	0.9	1838	4.3
8 0542	4.2	**23**	0121	1.0
1213	1.4		0727	4.1
F 1759	4.4	SA 1346	1.3
		1949	4.4
9 0054	1.0	**24**	0226	1.2
0651	4.2		0833	4.2
SA 1321	1.4	SU 1456	1.3
1911	4.4	2057	4.2
10 0200	1.0	**25**	0332	1.3
0757	4.3		0931	4.3
SU 1432	1.3	M 1602	1.2
2018	4.5	2153	4.3
11 0308	0.9	**26**	0428	1.3
0858	4.5		1019	4.5
M 1545	1.1	TU 1655	1.1
2121	4.7	2239	4.4
12 0419	0.8	**27**	0513	1.2
0955	4.7		1059	4.7
TU 1657	0.9	W 1738	1.0
2220	4.9	2318	4.6
13 0528	0.7	**28**	0552	1.1
1049	4.9		1135	4.8
W 1802	0.7	TH 1816	0.8
○ 2318	5.0	● 2353	4.7
14 0630	0.7	**29**	0630	0.9
1141	5.0		1208	4.9
TH 1859	0.5	F 1853	0.7
15 0012	5.1	**30**	0025	4.8
0726	0.6		0707	0.8
F 1231	5.1	SA 1238	4.9
1951	0.3	1929	0.6
		31	0057	4.9
			0744	0.8
		SU 1307	4.9
		2004	0.5

AUGUST

Time	m		Time	m
1 0128	4.9	**16**	0216	5.1
0818	0.8		0912	0.4
M 1336	4.9	TU 1423	5.3
2038	0.5	2136	0.1
2 0159	4.8	**17**	0258	4.9
0859	0.8		0945	0.5
TU 1407	4.9	W 1507	5.1
2111	0.5	2211	0.3
3 0233	4.8	**18**	0342	4.7
0919	1.0		1020	0.7
W 1442	4.9	TH 1554	4.9
2144	0.6	2249	0.6
4 0312	4.6	**19**	0430	4.4
0951	1.1		1101	0.9
TH 1524	4.8	F 1647	4.5
2224	0.7	◑ 2332	1.0
5 0359	4.4	**20**	0528	4.1
1035	1.2		1150	1.3
F 1614	4.6	SA 1751	4.2
◑ 2313	0.9		
6 0457	4.3	**21**	0023	1.4
1133	1.4		0639	3.9
SA 1719	4.4	SU 1252	1.6
		1911	3.9
7 0013	1.1	**22**	0129	1.7
0611	4.1		0757	3.9
SU 1243	1.5	M 1412	1.7
1839	4.3	2030	3.9
8 0126	1.2	**23**	0251	1.7
0733	4.2		0903	4.1
M 1409	1.5	TU 1533	1.5
2004	4.3	2130	4.1
9 0253	1.2	**24**	0400	1.6
0848	4.4		0952	4.3
TU 1542	1.3	W 1629	1.2
2119	4.5	2216	4.4
10 0419	1.1	**25**	0449	1.3
0951	4.6		1033	4.6
W 1659	0.9	TH 1713	1.0
2222	4.8	2253	4.6
11 0529	0.8	**26**	0531	1.0
1045	4.9		1108	4.8
TH 1801	0.5	F 1753	0.7
2317	5.0	2327	4.9
12 0627	0.6	**27**	0611	0.8
1133	5.0		1141	5.0
F 1853	0.3	SA 1831	0.6
○		● 2359	5.0
13 0006	5.1	**28**	0650	0.7
0717	0.5		1210	5.0
SA 1217	5.2	SU 1909	0.5
1941	0.0		
14 0051	5.2	**29**	0028	5.1
0801	0.4		0727	0.6
SU 1300	5.3	M 1238	5.1
2023	-0.1	1946	0.4
15 0134	5.2	**30**	0057	5.1
0838	0.4		0801	0.7
M 1341	5.3	TU 1306	5.1
2100	0.0	2020	0.5
		31	0127	5.0
			0831	0.8
		W 1337	5.2
		2050	0.5

E England

Chart Datum: 2·58 metres below Ordnance Datum (Newlyn). HAT is 5·7 metres above Chart Datum.

Ramsgate tides – Thames Estuary

RAMSGATE LAT 51°20'N LONG 1°25'E
TIMES AND HEIGHTS OF HIGH AND LOW WATERS

YEAR **2022**

SEPTEMBER

Day	Time	m	Day	Time	m
1 TH	0201 / 0857 / 1413 / 2120	4.9 / 0.9 / 5.1 / 0.6	**16** F	0301 / 0940 / 1515 / 2203	4.8 / 0.9 / 4.9 / 1.0
2 F	0240 / 0927 / 1455 / 2156	4.8 / 1.1 / 5.0 / 0.8	**17** SA	0344 / 1016 / 1602 / ◐2239	4.5 / 1.2 / 4.5 / 1.4
3 SA	0326 / 1009 / 1546 / ◑2243	4.6 / 1.2 / 4.7 / 1.0	**18** SU	0434 / 1101 / 1700 / 2323	4.2 / 1.5 / 4.1 / 1.7
4 SU	0424 / 1107 / 1653 / 2345	4.3 / 1.4 / 4.4 / 1.3	**19** M	0540 / 1158 / 1821	3.9 / 1.8 / 3.8
5 M	0543 / 1222 / 1826	4.1 / 1.6 / 4.1	**20** TU	0025 / 0706 / 1319 / 1951	2.0 / 3.8 / 1.9 / 3.8
6 TU	0108 / 0720 / 1408 / 2006	1.5 / 4.1 / 1.6 / 4.2	**21** W	0158 / 0821 / 1450 / 2055	2.0 / 4.0 / 1.7 / 4.1
7 W	0259 / 0843 / 1547 / 2121	1.5 / 4.2 / 1.2 / 4.5	**22** TH	0322 / 0915 / 1553 / 2142	1.7 / 4.3 / 1.3 / 4.4
8 TH	0422 / 0944 / 1655 / 2219	1.2 / 4.6 / 0.7 / 4.8	**23** F	0417 / 0957 / 1639 / 2220	1.4 / 4.6 / 0.9 / 4.7
9 F	0523 / 1033 / 1749 / 2306	0.8 / 4.9 / 0.4 / 5.1	**24** SA	0502 / 1033 / 1721 / 2254	1.0 / 4.8 / 0.7 / 5.0
10 SA	0613 / 1116 / 1836 / ○2349	0.6 / 5.1 / 0.1 / 5.2	**25** SU	0543 / 1105 / 1802 / ●2325	0.8 / 5.0 / 0.5 / 5.1
11 SU	0656 / 1156 / 1918	0.4 / 5.3 / 0.0	**26** M	0622 / 1135 / 1841 / 2354	0.6 / 5.2 / 0.4 / 5.2
12 M	0027 / 0734 / 1235 / 1956	5.3 / 0.3 / 5.4 / 0.0	**27** TU	0700 / 1204 / 1918	0.6 / 5.2 / 0.4
13 TU	0105 / 0807 / 1313 / 2030	5.3 / 0.4 / 5.5 / 0.1	**28** W	0023 / 0735 / 1235 / 1953	5.2 / 0.7 / 5.3 / 0.5
14 W	0143 / 0837 / 1353 / 2101	5.2 / 0.5 / 5.4 / 0.3	**29** TH	0056 / 0805 / 1310 / 2024	5.2 / 0.8 / 5.3 / 0.6
15 TH	0222 / 0907 / 1433 / 2131	5.0 / 0.6 / 5.2 / 0.6	**30** F	0132 / 0835 / 1349 / 2057	5.1 / 0.9 / 5.2 / 0.8

OCTOBER

Day	Time	m	Day	Time	m
1 SA	0215 / 0910 / 1435 / 2136	5.0 / 1.1 / 5.0 / 1.0	**16** SU	0302 / 0937 / 1521 / 2150	4.6 / 1.3 / 4.4 / 1.5
2 SU	0304 / 0956 / 1531 / 2225	4.7 / 1.2 / 4.7 / 1.3	**17** M	0344 / 1018 / 1613 / ◐2231	4.3 / 1.5 / 4.1 / 1.8
3 M	0405 / 1056 / 1646 / ◑2331	4.4 / 1.4 / 4.3 / 1.6	**18** TU	0441 / 1110 / 1727 / 2330	4.0 / 1.7 / 3.8 / 2.0
4 TU	0528 / 1220 / 1829	4.1 / 1.6 / 4.1	**19** W	0600 / 1225 / 1856	3.9 / 1.8 / 3.8
5 W	0113 / 0710 / 1415 / 2007	1.7 / 4.1 / 1.4 / 4.3	**20** TH	0100 / 0724 / 1356 / 2008	2.0 / 3.9 / 1.6 / 4.0
6 TH	0300 / 0830 / 1537 / 2114	1.5 / 4.3 / 1.0 / 4.6	**21** F	0232 / 0826 / 1505 / 2059	1.8 / 4.2 / 1.3 / 4.4
7 F	0409 / 0926 / 1636 / 2204	1.1 / 4.7 / 0.5 / 4.9	**22** SA	0334 / 0913 / 1558 / 2140	1.4 / 4.5 / 0.9 / 4.7
8 SA	0501 / 1012 / 1725 / 2246	0.8 / 5.0 / 0.2 / 5.1	**23** SU	0423 / 0952 / 1643 / 2216	1.0 / 4.8 / 0.7 / 5.0
9 SU	0546 / 1052 / 1809 / ○2324	0.5 / 5.2 / 0.1 / 5.2	**24** M	0506 / 1026 / 1726 / 2248	0.8 / 5.0 / 0.5 / 5.1
10 M	0625 / 1130 / 1848	0.4 / 5.4 / 0.0	**25** TU	0547 / 1059 / 1807 / ●2320	0.7 / 5.2 / 0.5 / 5.2
11 TU	0000 / 0700 / 1208 / 1923	5.3 / 0.4 / 5.5 / 0.2	**26** W	0626 / 1133 / 1846 / 2354	0.7 / 5.3 / 0.5 / 5.3
12 W	0036 / 0732 / 1245 / 1954	5.2 / 0.5 / 5.4 / 0.4	**27** TH	0704 / 1209 / 1924	0.7 / 5.4 / 0.6
13 TH	0112 / 0801 / 1323 / 2022	5.1 / 0.6 / 5.3 / 0.6	**28** F	0031 / 0742 / 1250 / 2003	5.2 / 0.8 / 5.3 / 0.7
14 F	0148 / 0831 / 1401 / 2049	5.0 / 0.8 / 5.1 / 0.9	**29** SA	0113 / 0821 / 1336 / 2043	5.2 / 0.9 / 5.2 / 0.9
15 SA	0224 / 0902 / 1439 / 2117	4.8 / 1.0 / 4.8 / 1.2	**30** SU	0200 / 0904 / 1429 / 2127	5.0 / 1.0 / 4.9 / 1.1
			31 M	0254 / 0955 / 1531 / 2221	4.7 / 1.1 / 4.6 / 1.4

NOVEMBER

Day	Time	m	Day	Time	m
1 TU	0357 / 1058 / 1649 / ◐2334	4.4 / 1.3 / 4.3 / 1.6	**16** W	0357 / 1034 / 1640 / ◐2250	4.2 / 1.4 / 4.0 / 1.7
2 W	0516 / 1226 / 1827	4.2 / 1.3 / 4.2	**17** TH	0500 / 1139 / 1757	4.0 / 1.5 / 3.9
3 TH	0114 / 0650 / 1359 / 1951	1.6 / 4.2 / 1.1 / 4.3	**18** F	0008 / 0618 / 1300 / 1912	1.8 / 4.0 / 1.4 / 4.0
4 F	0237 / 0804 / 1509 / 2051	1.4 / 4.4 / 0.7 / 4.6	**19** SA	0136 / 0728 / 1413 / 2011	1.7 / 4.1 / 1.2 / 4.2
5 SA	0338 / 0900 / 1605 / 2139	1.0 / 4.7 / 0.4 / 4.9	**20** SU	0243 / 0823 / 1511 / 2057	1.4 / 4.4 / 0.9 / 4.5
6 SU	0428 / 0946 / 1653 / 2220	0.7 / 4.9 / 0.2 / 5.0	**21** M	0336 / 0908 / 1601 / 2137	1.1 / 4.7 / 0.7 / 4.8
7 M	0511 / 1027 / 1736 / 2259	0.6 / 5.2 / 0.2 / 5.1	**22** TU	0424 / 0948 / 1647 / 2214	0.9 / 5.0 / 0.6 / 5.0
8 TU	0551 / 1107 / 1815 / ○2335	0.5 / 5.3 / 0.3 / 5.1	**23** W	0509 / 1028 / 1732 / ●2252	0.8 / 5.2 / 0.5 / 5.1
9 W	0627 / 1145 / 1849	0.5 / 5.3 / 0.4	**24** TH	0555 / 1109 / 1818 / 2333	0.7 / 5.3 / 0.5 / 5.2
10 TH	0011 / 0700 / 1222 / 1919	5.1 / 0.7 / 5.2 / 0.7	**25** F	0642 / 1153 / 1905	0.7 / 5.3 / 0.6
11 F	0046 / 0731 / 1259 / 1945	5.0 / 0.8 / 5.0 / 0.9	**26** SA	0017 / 0730 / 1241 / 1953	5.2 / 0.7 / 5.2 / 0.7
12 SA	0121 / 0801 / 1335 / 2012	4.9 / 1.0 / 4.8 / 1.1	**27** SU	0104 / 0818 / 1334 / 2040	5.1 / 0.7 / 5.0 / 0.9
13 SU	0156 / 0832 / 1412 / 2040	4.8 / 1.1 / 4.6 / 1.2	**28** M	0155 / 0906 / 1431 / 2130	4.9 / 0.7 / 4.8 / 1.0
14 M	0231 / 0906 / 1452 / 2113	4.6 / 1.2 / 4.4 / 1.4	**29** TU	0249 / 0959 / 1532 / 2226	4.7 / 0.8 / 4.6 / 1.2
15 TU	0310 / 0945 / 1540 / 2155	4.4 / 1.3 / 4.2 / 1.6	**30** W	0349 / 1102 / 1643 / ◑2334	4.5 / 0.9 / 4.4 / 1.3

DECEMBER

Day	Time	m	Day	Time	m
1 TH	0458 / 1214 / 1804	4.3 / 0.9 / 4.3	**16** F	0413 / 1103 / 1659 / ◐2324	4.3 / 1.1 / 4.0 / 1.5
2 F	0047 / 0617 / 1325 / 1919	1.3 / 4.3 / 0.7 / 4.3	**17** SA	0513 / 1210 / 1808	4.1 / 1.1 / 3.9
3 SA	0156 / 0729 / 1430 / 2019	1.2 / 4.4 / 0.6 / 4.5	**18** SU	0037 / 0624 / 1319 / 1915	1.5 / 4.1 / 1.0 / 4.0
4 SU	0255 / 0828 / 1528 / 2111	1.0 / 4.6 / 0.4 / 4.6	**19** M	0146 / 0729 / 1421 / 2012	1.4 / 4.3 / 0.9 / 4.3
5 M	0349 / 0920 / 1619 / 2157	0.8 / 4.8 / 0.4 / 4.8	**20** TU	0247 / 0826 / 1518 / 2102	1.2 / 4.5 / 0.8 / 4.5
6 TU	0437 / 1007 / 1705 / 2239	0.7 / 5.0 / 0.4 / 4.9	**21** W	0344 / 0918 / 1613 / 2149	1.0 / 4.8 / 0.7 / 4.8
7 W	0521 / 1050 / 1746 / 2318	0.6 / 5.0 / 0.6 / 4.9	**22** TH	0440 / 1007 / 1708 / 2236	0.9 / 4.9 / 0.6 / 4.9
8 TH	0601 / 1130 / 1821 / ○2355	0.6 / 4.9 / 0.7 / 4.9	**23** F	0537 / 1058 / 1804 / ●2323	0.7 / 5.1 / 0.6 / 5.0
9 F	0637 / 1208 / 1851	0.8 / 4.8 / 0.9	**24** SA	0633 / 1149 / 1859	0.6 / 5.1 / 0.6
10 SA	0029 / 0710 / 1243 / 1919	4.9 / 0.9 / 4.7 / 1.0	**25** SU	0011 / 0727 / 1241 / 1952	5.1 / 0.5 / 5.1 / 0.6
11 SU	0103 / 0742 / 1319 / 1948	4.8 / 0.9 / 4.6 / 1.1	**26** M	0101 / 0819 / 1334 / 2042	5.0 / 0.4 / 5.0 / 0.7
12 M	0135 / 0813 / 1354 / 2018	4.8 / 1.0 / 4.6 / 1.1	**27** TU	0150 / 0908 / 1428 / 2131	4.9 / 0.3 / 4.9 / 0.7
13 TU	0209 / 0847 / 1431 / 2053	4.7 / 1.0 / 4.5 / 1.2	**28** W	0240 / 0958 / 1523 / 2220	4.8 / 0.3 / 4.7 / 0.8
14 W	0244 / 0924 / 1512 / 2133	4.6 / 1.0 / 4.3 / 1.3	**29** TH	0333 / 1050 / 1622 / 2312	4.7 / 0.4 / 4.5 / 0.9
15 TH	0324 / 1008 / 1601 / 2221	4.4 / 1.0 / 4.2 / 1.4	**30** F	0432 / 1145 / 1727 / ◑	4.6 / 0.4 / 4.3
			31 SA	0007 / 0539 / 1244 / 1836	1.0 / 4.4 / 0.5 / 4.2

Chart Datum: 2·58 metres below Ordnance Datum (Newlyn). HAT is 5·7 metres above Chart Datum.

42

》》 **FREE** monthly updates. Register at 《
www.reedsnauticalalmanac.co.uk

1.6 THAMES ESTUARY

This chartlet is for general orientation. Due to scale many lights, buoys, marks and depths have been omitted.

⚠ Keep well clear of Precautionary Areas

Depth up to 10m

Depth over 10m

Depths in metres

1.7 THAMES ESTUARY TIDAL STREAMS

Due to very strong rates of tidal streams in some areas, eddies may occur. Where possible, some indication of these is shown, but in many areas there is insufficient information or eddies are unstable.

5 Hours before HW Sheerness (0335 before HW Dover)

4 Hours before HW Sheerness (0235 before HW Dover)

3 Hours before HW Sheerness (0135 before HW Dover)

2 Hours before HW Sheerness (0035 before HW Dover)

1 Hour before HW Sheerness (0025 after HW Dover)

HW Sheerness (0125 after HW Dover)

Due to very strong rates of tidal streams in some areas, eddies may occur. Where possible, some indication of these is shown, but in many areas there is insufficient information or eddies are unstable.

1 Hour after HW Sheerness (0225 after HW Dover)

2 Hours after HW Sheerness (0325 after HW Dover)

3 Hours after HW Sheerness (0425 after HW Dover)

4 Hours after HW Sheerness (0525 after HW Dover)

5 Hours after HW Sheerness (0600 before HW Dover)

6 Hours after HW Sheerness (0500 before HW Dover)

E England

45

MARGATE

MEAN SPRING
AND NEAP CURVES

MEAN RANGES	
Springs	4.3m
Neaps	2.5m

STANDARD TIME (UT)
For Summer Time add ONE hour in **non-shaded areas**

MARGATE   LAT 51°23′N   LONG 1°23′E
TIMES AND HEIGHTS OF HIGH AND LOW WATERS

Dates in red are **SPRINGS**
Dates in blue are **NEAPS**

YEAR **2022**

E England

JANUARY

#	Day	Time	m	Time	m	#	Day	Time	m	Time	m
1	SA	0415 1018 1640 2254	1.0 4.6 0.7 4.6			16	SU	0511 1111 1718 2331	1.0 4.3 1.1 4.4		
2	SU ●	0513 1117 1733 2344	0.8 4.7 0.7 4.6			17	M ○	0553 1151 1756	0.9 4.4 1.1		
3	M	0610 1213 1824	0.6 4.8 0.7			18	TU	0005 0631 1226 1829	4.5 0.8 4.4 1.0		
4	TU	0033 0705 1305 1914	4.7 0.5 4.9 0.8			19	W	0039 0704 1302 1901	4.5 0.7 4.5 1.0		
5	W	0121 0757 1357 2000	4.7 0.4 4.9 0.9			20	TH	0115 0738 1340 1935	4.6 0.6 4.5 0.9		
6	TH	0208 0846 1447 2043	4.7 0.4 4.7 1.0			21	F	0152 0813 1419 2012	4.6 0.6 4.5 0.9		
7	F	0253 0932 1536 2126	4.6 0.5 4.6 1.1			22	SA	0228 0850 1457 2050	4.6 0.6 4.4 1.0		
8	SA	0338 1017 1626 2210	4.5 0.6 4.4 1.3			23	SU	0302 0928 1534 2129	4.6 0.6 4.4 1.1		
9	SU ◑	0425 1105 1719 2259	4.4 0.8 4.2 1.4			24	M	0337 1008 1612 2212	4.4 0.7 4.3 1.2		
10	M	0519 1157 1817	4.3 0.9 4.0			25	TU ◑	0419 1052 1657 2301	4.4 0.8 4.2 1.2		
11	TU	0000 0623 1256 1917	1.5 4.1 1.1 4.0			26	W	0510 1146 1752	4.3 0.9 4.1		
12	W	0118 0727 1356 2016	1.6 4.0 1.2 4.0			27	TH	0003 0612 1255 1905	1.3 4.2 1.0 4.0		
13	TH	0226 0829 1453 2113	1.5 4.0 1.2 4.0			28	F	0126 0731 1413 2031	1.3 4.2 1.0 4.1		
14	F	0327 0930 1546 2206	1.4 4.1 1.2 4.2			29	SA	0249 0857 1525 2144	1.2 4.2 1.0 4.2		
15	SA	0422 1025 1635 2252	1.2 4.2 1.1 4.3			30	SU	0403 1013 1630 2246	1.0 4.4 0.9 4.4		
						31	M	0512 1117 1728 2340	0.8 4.6 0.9 4.5		

FEBRUARY

#	Day	Time	m	Time	m	#	Day	Time	m	Time	m
1	TU ●	0611 1212 1820	0.6 4.7 0.8			16	W ○	0612 1212 1814	0.7 4.4 1.0		
2	W	0028 0703 1302 1906	4.7 0.4 4.8 0.8			17	TH	0025 0646 1246 1846	4.5 0.6 4.5 0.8		
3	TH	0113 0749 1349 1947	4.7 0.3 4.8 0.8			18	F	0059 0719 1322 1920	4.6 0.5 4.6 0.8		
4	F	0156 0831 1433 2026	4.8 0.3 4.7 0.9			19	SA	0134 0753 1400 1955	4.7 0.4 4.6 0.8		
5	SA	0236 0909 1513 2101	4.7 0.4 4.6 1.0			20	SU	0209 0828 1436 2032	4.7 0.4 4.6 0.8		
6	SU	0313 0942 1550 2137	4.7 0.6 4.4 1.1			21	M	0241 0902 1509 2108	4.7 0.5 4.5 0.9		
7	M	0349 1015 1625 2215	4.5 0.7 4.2 1.2			22	TU	0314 0937 1543 2146	4.6 0.6 4.3 1.0		
8	TU ◑	0427 1052 1705 2259	4.4 1.0 4.0 1.4			23	W	0353 1016 1625 2232	4.5 0.7 4.2 1.1		
9	W	0514 1141 1801	4.1 1.2 3.8			24	TH	0442 1107 1719 2333	4.4 0.9 4.0 1.2		
10	TH	0000 0620 1250 1918	1.6 3.9 1.4 3.7			25	F	0546 1222 1836	4.2 1.2 3.9		
11	F	0131 0741 1407 2030	1.6 3.8 1.5 3.8			26	SA	0103 0717 1355 2015	1.3 4.0 1.3 3.9		
12	SA	0249 0857 1515 2135	1.5 3.8 1.4 3.9			27	SU	0239 0856 1518 2136	1.2 4.1 1.2 4.1		
13	SU	0356 1004 1614 2230	1.3 4.0 1.3 4.1			28	M	0406 1017 1628 2243	1.0 4.3 1.1 4.3		
14	M	0451 1056 1702 2314	1.0 4.2 1.2 4.3								
15	TU	0535 1137 1741 2351	0.9 4.3 1.1 4.4								

MARCH

#	Day	Time	m	Time	m	#	Day	Time	m	Time	m
1	TU	0514 1118 1723 2335	0.7 4.6 0.9 4.5			16	W	0505 1113 1717 2327	0.8 4.3 1.1 4.4		
2	W ●	0606 1208 1808	0.5 4.7 0.9			17	TH	0543 1148 1751	0.7 4.4 1.0		
3	TH	0019 0650 1252 1848	4.7 0.3 4.8 0.8			18	F ○	0001 0619 1222 1824	4.5 0.5 4.6 0.8		
4	F	0058 0729 1332 1926	4.8 0.3 4.7 0.8			19	SA	0035 0652 1258 1859	4.7 0.4 4.7 0.7		
5	SA	0135 0804 1409 2001	4.8 0.3 4.7 0.8			20	SU	0109 0726 1334 1935	4.8 0.3 4.7 0.7		
6	SU	0210 0834 1441 2034	4.8 0.4 4.5 0.8			21	M	0144 0800 1410 2011	4.8 0.4 4.6 0.7		
7	M	0243 0900 1509 2106	4.7 0.6 4.4 0.9			22	TU	0218 0833 1444 2048	4.8 0.4 4.5 0.8		
8	TU	0315 0928 1537 2138	4.6 0.8 4.2 1.1			23	W	0253 0909 1519 2128	4.7 0.6 4.4 0.9		
9	W	0349 0959 1611 2216	4.4 1.0 4.1 1.2			24	TH	0336 0950 1603 2216	4.6 0.8 4.2 1.0		
10	TH ◑	0429 1040 1654 2305	4.1 1.2 3.8 1.4			25	F ◑	0430 1045 1701 2323	4.3 1.1 4.0 1.2		
11	F	0521 1139 1756	3.8 1.5 3.6			26	SA	0542 1208 1827	4.1 1.4 3.8		
12	SA	0023 0639 1311 1920	1.6 3.6 1.7 3.6			27	SU	0100 0722 1349 2008	1.3 3.9 1.4 3.8		
13	SU	0205 0820 1442 2058	1.6 3.6 1.6 3.7			28	M	0242 0900 1514 2128	1.1 4.1 1.3 4.1		
14	M	0322 0936 1548 2159	1.3 3.9 1.4 4.0			29	TU	0403 1014 1619 2231	0.8 4.4 1.1 4.3		
15	TU	0421 1031 1638 2247	1.1 4.1 1.2 4.2			30	W	0502 1109 1708 2320	0.6 4.6 1.0 4.5		
						31	TH	0548 1154 1747	0.4 4.7 0.9		

APRIL

#	Day	Time	m	Time	m	#	Day	Time	m	Time	m
1	F ●	0000 0626 1232 1823	4.6 0.4 4.7 0.8			16	SA ○	0544 1150 1757	0.5 4.6 0.8		
2	SA	0034 0658 1305 1900	4.7 0.4 4.6 0.7			17	SU	0002 0620 1227 1835	4.7 0.4 4.7 0.7		
3	SU	0107 0727 1335 1935	4.8 0.4 4.6 0.7			18	M	0039 0656 1305 1914	4.8 0.3 4.7 0.6		
4	M	0140 0755 1403 2009	4.8 0.5 4.5 0.7			19	TU	0118 0732 1344 1953	4.9 0.4 4.7 0.6		
5	TU	0213 0822 1431 2040	4.7 0.6 4.4 0.8			20	W	0159 0809 1423 2034	4.8 0.5 4.6 0.7		
6	W	0246 0849 1501 2110	4.5 0.8 4.3 1.0			21	TH	0243 0849 1505 2119	4.7 0.7 4.4 0.8		
7	TH	0319 0919 1534 2143	4.3 1.0 4.1 1.1			22	F	0332 0936 1554 2214	4.5 0.9 4.2 0.9		
8	F	0357 0956 1614 2228	4.1 1.2 3.9 1.3			23	SA ◑	0432 1038 1656 2329	4.3 1.2 4.0 1.0		
9	SA ◑	0445 1049 1707 2334	3.8 1.5 3.7 1.5			24	SU	0549 1203 1821	4.1 1.4 3.9		
10	SU	0551 1207 1827	3.6 1.7 3.5			25	M	0102 0723 1339 1950	1.0 4.0 1.4 3.9		
11	M	0111 0727 1353 2010	1.5 3.6 1.7 3.6			26	TU	0232 0848 1456 2104	0.9 4.2 1.3 4.1		
12	TU	0237 0852 1508 2116	1.3 3.8 1.5 3.9			27	W	0343 0954 1555 2205	0.7 4.4 1.1 4.3		
13	W	0338 0950 1600 2207	1.2 4.1 1.2 4.2			28	TH	0437 1046 1641 2253	0.5 4.5 1.0 4.5		
14	TH	0426 1035 1642 2249	0.8 4.3 1.0 4.4			29	F	0519 1128 1720 2331	0.5 4.5 0.9 4.6		
15	F	0506 1113 1719 2326	0.6 4.5 0.9 4.6			30	SA ●	0552 1203 1756	0.5 4.5 0.8		

Chart Datum: 2·5 metres below Ordnance Datum (Newlyn). HAT is 5·2 metres above Chart Datum.

>> **FREE** monthly updates. Register at <<
www.reedsnauticalalmanac.co.uk

MARGATE LAT 51°23′N LONG 1°23′E
TIMES AND HEIGHTS OF HIGH AND LOW WATERS
YEAR 2022

STANDARD TIME (UT) — For Summer Time add ONE hour in **non-shaded areas**

Dates in red are SPRINGS
Dates in blue are NEAPS

MAY

Day	Time	m	Time	m	Time	m	Time	m	Phase
1 SU	0003	4.7	0621	0.5	1232	4.5	1834	0.7	
2 M	0036	4.7	0651	0.5	1259	4.5	1911	0.7	
3 TU	0111	4.7	0721	0.6	1329	4.5	1946	0.7	
4 W	0147	4.6	0750	0.7	1401	4.4	2018	0.8	
5 TH	0221	4.5	0819	0.9	1434	4.3	2048	0.9	
6 F	0256	4.3	0850	1.0	1508	4.2	2122	1.0	
7 SA	0335	4.1	0928	1.2	1547	4.0	2205	1.1	
8 SU	0421	3.9	1017	1.4	1636	3.9	2304	1.2	
9 M	0518	3.8	1123	1.6	1738	3.7			◐
10 TU	0021	1.3	0631	3.7	1244	1.6	1902	3.7	
11 W	0142	1.2	0755	3.8	1410	1.5	2020	3.9	
12 TH	0248	0.9	0859	4.1	1512	1.3	2116	4.2	
13 F	0341	0.7	0949	4.3	1601	1.1	2204	4.4	
14 SA	0426	0.6	1034	4.5	1645	0.9	2247	4.6	
15 SU	0508	0.5	1116	4.6	1728	0.8	2329	4.7	
16 M	0549	0.4	1158	4.6	1812	0.7			○
17 TU	0012	4.8	0630	0.4	1240	4.7	1857	0.6	
18 W	0059	4.9	0712	0.5	1325	4.7	1942	0.6	
19 TH	0149	4.9	0755	0.6	1410	4.6	2029	0.6	
20 F	0240	4.8	0840	0.8	1458	4.5	2121	0.6	
21 SA	0334	4.6	0932	1.0	1549	4.3	2220	0.7	
22 SU	0434	4.4	1034	1.2	1650	4.2	2332	0.8	◑
23 M	0547	4.2	1150	1.4	1806	4.1			
24 TU	0051	0.8	0707	4.2	1313	1.4	1921	4.1	
25 W	0205	0.7	0818	4.2	1423	1.3	2027	4.2	
26 TH	0308	0.6	0920	4.3	1521	1.2	2126	4.3	
27 F	0359	0.6	1012	4.4	1609	1.1	2216	4.4	
28 SA	0440	0.7	1055	4.4	1651	0.9	2258	4.5	
29 SU	0513	0.7	1130	4.4	1732	0.8	2335	4.5	
30 M	0546	0.7	1200	4.5	1812	0.7			●
31 TU	0011	4.6	0621	0.7	1230	4.5	1851	0.7	

JUNE

Day	Time	m	Time	m	Time	m	Time	m	Phase
1 W	0048	4.6	0654	0.8	1303	4.5	1927	0.7	
2 TH	0125	4.5	0726	0.8	1339	4.4	2000	0.7	
3 F	0202	4.4	0757	0.9	1414	4.4	2033	0.8	
4 SA	0240	4.3	0831	1.0	1451	4.3	2109	0.9	
5 SU	0319	4.2	0910	1.1	1530	4.3	2151	0.9	
6 M	0402	4.1	0956	1.3	1613	4.1	2242	1.0	
7 TU	0451	4.0	1050	1.4	1703	4.1	2342	1.0	◐
8 W	0547	3.9	1153	1.5	1803	4.0			
9 TH	0048	1.0	0654	4.0	1305	1.4	1913	4.0	
10 F	0155	0.9	0804	4.1	1418	1.3	2021	4.2	
11 SA	0255	0.7	0905	4.3	1520	1.1	2119	4.4	
12 SU	0348	0.6	0958	4.4	1614	0.9	2212	4.5	
13 M	0437	0.6	1048	4.5	1705	0.8	2304	4.7	
14 TU	0525	0.6	1136	4.6	1756	0.7	2356	4.8	○
15 W	0612	0.6	1224	4.6	1848	0.6			
16 TH	0050	4.9	0701	0.6	1313	4.7	1940	0.5	
17 F	0144	4.9	0749	0.7	1402	4.6	2032	0.5	
18 SA	0237	4.8	0837	0.8	1451	4.6	2125	0.5	
19 SU	0331	4.7	0927	1.0	1542	4.5	2221	0.5	
20 M	0428	4.5	1021	1.1	1637	4.4	2320	0.6	
21 TU	0530	4.3	1122	1.3	1739	4.3			
22 W	0022	0.7	0636	4.2	1231	1.3	1843	4.3	
23 TH	0124	0.8	0738	4.2	1339	1.4	1944	4.2	
24 F	0222	0.8	0836	4.2	1440	1.3	2042	4.2	
25 SA	0313	0.9	0931	4.2	1535	1.2	2138	4.3	
26 SU	0359	0.9	1019	4.3	1625	1.0	2229	4.3	
27 M	0442	0.9	1101	4.3	1712	0.9	2314	4.4	
28 TU	0522	0.9	1137	4.4	1756	0.8	2354	4.4	
29 W	0600	0.9	1211	4.4	1836	0.7			●
30 TH	0031	4.5	0636	0.9	1245	4.5	1912	0.7	

JULY

Day	Time	m	Time	m	Time	m	Time	m	Phase
1 F	0108	4.5	0709	0.9	1321	4.5	1946	0.7	
2 SA	0146	4.4	0741	0.9	1359	4.5	2020	0.7	
3 SU	0225	4.4	0817	1.0	1436	4.4	2056	0.7	
4 M	0304	4.3	0855	1.0	1513	4.4	2135	0.8	
5 TU	0343	4.2	0936	1.1	1551	4.3	2218	0.8	
6 W	0424	4.1	1020	1.2	1632	4.2	2305	0.9	
7 TH	0509	4.1	1111	1.3	1721	4.2			◐
8 F	0000	0.9	0603	4.1	1212	1.4	1818	4.2	
9 SA	0104	0.9	0709	4.1	1327	1.3	1927	4.2	
10 SU	0212	0.9	0823	4.1	1443	1.2	2041	4.3	
11 M	0316	0.8	0929	4.3	1549	1.0	2149	4.5	
12 TU	0415	0.8	1029	4.4	1650	0.9	2252	4.6	
13 W	0510	0.8	1123	4.5	1749	0.7	2350	4.8	○
14 TH	0604	0.7	1214	4.6	1846	0.5			
15 F	0045	4.8	0656	0.7	1304	4.7	1939	0.4	
16 SA	0139	4.9	0744	0.7	1353	4.7	2029	0.4	
17 SU	0230	4.8	0829	0.8	1440	4.7	2117	0.4	
18 M	0320	4.7	0913	0.9	1526	4.7	2203	0.5	
19 TU	0409	4.6	0956	1.0	1611	4.6	2248	0.6	
20 W	0458	4.4	1043	1.2	1659	4.5	2336	0.8	◑
21 TH	0551	4.2	1137	1.3	1754	4.3			
22 F	0030	1.0	0649	4.0	1245	1.4	1856	4.2	
23 SA	0129	1.1	0749	4.0	1356	1.5	2001	4.1	
24 SU	0229	1.2	0849	4.0	1502	1.4	2106	4.1	
25 M	0326	1.2	0947	4.1	1603	1.2	2208	4.2	
26 TU	0419	1.2	1038	4.2	1658	1.0	2259	4.3	
27 W	0505	1.1	1120	4.3	1743	0.9	2342	4.4	
28 TH	0546	1.1	1157	4.4	1821	0.8			●
29 F	0018	4.4	0621	1.0	1230	4.5	1856	0.7	
30 SA	0052	4.5	0653	1.0	1305	4.6	1929	0.6	
31 SU	0128	4.5	0726	0.9	1341	4.6	2002	0.6	

AUGUST

Day	Time	m	Time	m	Time	m	Time	m	Phase
1 M	0205	4.5	0800	0.9	1418	4.6	2037	0.6	
2 TU	0243	4.5	0836	1.0	1451	4.5	2112	0.7	
3 W	0319	4.4	0913	1.0	1525	4.5	2148	0.7	
4 TH	0353	4.3	0951	1.1	1600	4.4	2226	0.8	
5 F	0432	4.2	1034	1.2	1644	4.4	2312	0.9	◐
6 SA	0520	4.1	1128	1.3	1739	4.3			
7 SU	0015	1.1	0624	4.0	1244	1.4	1850	4.2	
8 M	0137	1.1	0749	4.0	1416	1.3	2018	4.2	
9 TU	0255	1.1	0911	4.1	1535	1.1	2140	4.4	
10 W	0404	1.0	1018	4.3	1645	0.9	2250	4.6	
11 TH	0504	0.9	1116	4.5	1747	0.6	2348	4.8	
12 F	0557	0.8	1207	4.7	1840	0.4			○
13 SA	0040	4.9	0645	0.8	1253	4.8	1928	0.3	
14 SU	0129	4.9	0729	0.8	1338	4.9	2012	0.3	
15 M	0215	4.8	0809	0.8	1420	4.9	2053	0.4	
16 TU	0258	4.7	0848	0.9	1459	4.8	2129	0.5	
17 W	0337	4.5	0925	1.0	1536	4.7	2202	0.7	
18 TH	0412	4.3	1002	1.1	1614	4.6	2237	0.9	
19 F	0450	4.1	1045	1.3	1659	4.3	2323	1.2	◑
20 SA	0541	3.9	1143	1.5	1759	4.1			
21 SU	0027	1.4	0654	3.8	1307	1.6	1917	3.9	
22 M	0145	1.6	0808	3.8	1428	1.5	2037	3.9	
23 TU	0258	1.5	0916	3.9	1541	1.3	2149	4.1	
24 W	0400	1.4	1014	4.2	1639	1.1	2244	4.2	
25 TH	0450	1.3	1101	4.3	1723	0.9	2326	4.4	
26 F	0530	1.1	1139	4.5	1800	0.8			
27 SA	0001	4.5	0603	1.1	1211	4.6	1833	0.7	●
28 SU	0032	4.5	0634	1.0	1244	4.7	1905	0.6	
29 M	0105	4.6	0706	0.9	1318	4.7	1937	0.6	
30 TU	0140	4.6	0740	0.9	1352	4.7	2009	0.6	
31 W	0215	4.6	0814	0.9	1425	4.7	2041	0.6	

Chart Datum: 2·5 metres below Ordnance Datum (Newlyn). HAT is 5·2 metres above Chart Datum.

STANDARD TIME (UT)
For Summer Time add ONE
hour in **non-shaded areas**

MARGATE   LAT 51°23'N   LONG 1°23'E

TIMES AND HEIGHTS OF HIGH AND LOW WATERS

Dates in **red** are SPRINGS
Dates in **blue** are NEAPS

YEAR 2022

SEPTEMBER

Time	m		Time	m
1 0248	4.5	**16** 0322	4.4
0848	1.0	0927	1.1
TH 1455	4.6	F 1535	4.5
2113	0.7	2145	1.1
2 0319	4.4	**17** 0354	4.2
0924	1.1	1004	1.3
F 1529	4.5	SA 1616	4.3
2148	0.9	☽ 2223	1.4
3 0356	4.2	**18** 0437	3.9
1004	1.2	1052	1.5
SA 1614	4.4	SU 1708	4.0
☽ 2232	1.1	2320	1.7
4 0445	4.1	**19** 0538	3.7
1059	1.3	1210	1.6
SU 1713	4.3	M 1824	3.7
2339	1.3		
5 0553	3.9	**20** 0053	1.9
1221	1.4	0719	3.6
M 1833	4.1	TU 1348	1.6
		2004	3.7
6 0117	1.4	**21** 0227	1.8
0732	3.8	0841	3.8
TU 1404	1.4	W 1507	1.4
2015	4.1	2121	4.0
7 0247	1.4	**22** 0336	1.6
0901	4.0	0942	4.0
W 1533	1.1	TH 1607	1.1
2144	4.4	2216	4.2
8 0359	1.2	**23** 0426	1.3
1012	4.3	1031	4.3
TH 1643	0.8	F 1651	0.9
2250	4.6	2258	4.4
9 0456	1.0	**24** 0504	1.2
1108	4.5	1110	4.5
F 1738	0.5	SA 1728	0.8
2343	4.8	2332	4.5
10 0543	0.9	**25** 0537	1.1
1154	4.7	1143	4.6
SA 1824	0.4	SU 1801	0.7
○		●	
11 0028	4.9	**26** 0002	4.6
0625	0.8	0609	1.0
SU 1235	4.8	M 1214	4.7
1906	0.3	1834	0.6
12 0110	4.9	**27** 0034	4.7
0705	0.8	0642	0.9
M 1313	4.9	TU 1247	4.8
1943	0.4	1905	0.5
13 0148	4.8	**28** 0108	4.7
0743	0.8	0716	0.8
TU 1351	4.9	W 1321	4.8
2017	0.5	1937	0.6
14 0223	4.7	**29** 0143	4.7
0819	0.9	0750	0.9
W 1426	4.9	TH 1354	4.8
2046	0.6	2009	0.6
15 0254	4.5	**30** 0215	4.6
0854	1.0	0826	0.9
TH 1500	4.7	F 1428	4.7
2114	0.8	2042	0.8

OCTOBER

Time	m		Time	m
1 0248	4.4	**16** 0314	4.2
0848	1.0	0903	1.2
SA 1507	4.6	SU 1543	4.2
2120	1.0	2140	1.4
2 0329	4.3	**17** 0354	4.0
0947	1.1	1014	1.4
SU 1558	4.4	M 1631	4.0
2210	1.2	☽ 2230	1.7
3 0424	4.1	**18** 0447	3.8
1048	1.3	1118	1.5
M 1705	4.2	TU 1735	3.7
☽ 2324	1.5	2346	1.9
4 0540	3.8	**19** 0604	3.6
1220	1.4	1254	1.6
TU 1838	4.0	W 1913	3.7
5 0109	1.6	**20** 0137	1.9
0724	3.8	0751	3.7
W 1403	1.2	TH 1420	1.4
2020	4.2	2037	3.9
6 0240	1.5	**21** 0255	1.7
0850	4.1	0857	3.9
TH 1526	0.9	F 1521	1.1
2140	4.5	2133	4.2
7 0347	1.2	**22** 0346	1.4
0958	4.4	0948	4.2
F 1629	0.6	SA 1608	0.9
2239	4.7	2216	4.4
8 0439	1.0	**23** 0427	1.2
1050	4.6	1029	4.4
SA 1719	0.5	SU 1648	0.8
2326	4.8	2253	4.5
9 0521	0.9	**24** 0503	1.1
1132	4.7	1105	4.6
SU 1759	0.4	M 1724	0.7
○		2327	4.7
10 0006	4.8	**25** 0539	0.9
0600	0.8	1140	4.7
M 1208	4.9	TU 1758	0.6
1835	0.4	●	
11 0041	4.8	**26** 0000	4.7
0638	0.8	0615	0.9
TU 1243	4.9	W 1214	4.8
1906	0.5	1832	0.6
12 0113	4.7	**27** 0036	4.8
0716	0.7	0652	0.8
W 1318	4.9	TH 1251	4.9
1937	0.6	1906	0.4
13 0142	4.7	**28** 0112	4.7
0753	0.8	0730	0.8
TH 1354	4.8	F 1330	4.8
2006	0.8	1942	0.7
14 0211	4.6	**29** 0149	4.6
0827	0.9	0809	0.8
F 1429	4.7	SA 1413	4.6
2034	1.0	2021	0.8
15 0241	4.4	**30** 0230	4.5
0858	1.0	0853	0.9
SA 1504	4.5	SU 1502	4.6
2103	1.2	2106	1.1
		31 0318	4.3
		0944	1.0
		M 1559	4.4
		2202	1.3

NOVEMBER

Time	m		Time	m
1 0417	4.1	**16** 0412	3.9
1052	1.1	1044	1.3
TU 1710	4.2	W 1659	3.8
☽ 2320	1.6	☽ 2258	1.8
2 0535	3.9	**17** 0511	3.8
1222	1.1	1155	1.4
W 1841	4.1	TH 1807	3.8
3 0057	1.6	**18** 0013	1.9
0708	3.9	0630	3.7
TH 1352	1.0	F 1316	1.3
2010	4.3	1932	3.9
4 0220	1.5	**19** 0144	1.7
0826	4.1	0756	3.9
F 1505	0.8	SA 1425	1.1
2120	4.5	2037	4.1
5 0323	1.3	**20** 0253	1.5
0930	4.4	0854	4.1
SA 1603	0.6	SU 1519	0.9
2215	4.6	2127	4.3
6 0413	1.1	**21** 0342	1.3
1022	4.6	0942	4.3
SU 1650	0.6	M 1604	0.8
2300	4.7	2211	4.5
7 0455	1.0	**22** 0426	1.1
1103	4.7	1025	4.5
M 1727	0.6	TU 1646	0.7
2338	4.7	2252	4.6
8 0534	1.0	**23** 0508	1.0
1139	4.8	1106	4.7
TU 1759	0.6	W 1725	0.7
○		● 2331	4.7
9 0008	4.7	**24** 0550	0.8
0613	0.7	1147	4.8
W 1214	4.8	TH 1804	0.7
1831	0.7		
10 0037	4.7	**25** 0010	4.7
0652	0.7	0633	0.8
TH 1251	4.8	F 1231	4.9
1903	0.7	1845	0.7
11 0107	4.6	**26** 0052	4.7
0730	0.7	0717	0.7
F 1328	4.7	SA 1319	4.9
1934	0.9	1927	0.8
12 0140	4.6	**27** 0137	4.7
0804	0.9	0803	0.7
SA 1405	4.6	SU 1410	4.8
2004	1.0	2012	0.9
13 0213	4.4	**28** 0224	4.6
0836	0.9	0853	0.7
SU 1441	4.4	M 1504	4.7
2034	1.2	2102	1.1
14 0247	4.3	**29** 0315	4.4
0909	1.1	0950	0.8
M 1520	4.2	TU 1602	4.5
2111	1.4	2159	1.3
15 0325	4.1	**30** 0412	4.3
0950	1.2	1057	0.8
TU 1605	4.0	W 1710	4.3
2157	1.6	☽ 2308	1.5

DECEMBER

Time	m		Time	m
1 0523	4.1	**16** 0435	4.0
1212	0.9	1112	1.1
TH 1827	4.3	F 1718	3.9
		☽ 2320	1.6
2 0030	1.5	**17** 0528	4.0
0642	4.1	1212	1.1
F 1326	0.8	SA 1817	3.9
1942	4.3		
3 0146	1.5	**18** 0025	1.6
0751	4.2	0632	3.9
SA 1432	0.8	SU 1318	1.1
2046	4.4	1928	4.0
4 0249	1.3	**19** 0141	1.5
0853	4.3	0745	4.0
SU 1528	0.8	M 1422	1.0
2142	4.4	2035	4.1
5 0342	1.2	**20** 0251	1.4
0947	4.5	0851	4.2
M 1614	0.8	TU 1520	0.9
2230	4.5	2132	4.3
6 0429	1.0	**21** 0349	1.2
1034	4.5	0948	4.4
TU 1653	0.8	W 1611	0.8
2309	4.5	2223	4.5
7 0512	1.0	**22** 0442	1.0
1116	4.6	1040	4.6
W 1727	0.8	TH 1700	0.8
2342	4.5	2311	4.6
8 0554	0.8	**23** 0533	0.8
1154	4.6	1132	4.7
TH 1803	0.9	F 1747	0.8
○		● 2357	4.6
9 0012	4.6	**24** 0624	0.7
0635	0.7	1224	4.8
F 1232	4.6	SA 1834	0.8
1838	0.9		
10 0045	4.6	**25** 0043	4.7
0713	0.7	0715	0.6
SA 1310	4.6	SU 1316	4.9
1911	1.0	1923	0.8
11 0119	4.5	**26** 0131	4.5
0748	0.8	0806	0.5
SU 1347	4.5	M 1410	4.8
1943	1.1	2010	0.9
12 0155	4.5	**27** 0220	4.7
0820	0.8	0858	0.5
M 1424	4.4	TU 1503	4.8
2015	1.2	2059	1.0
13 0231	4.4	**28** 0310	4.6
0854	0.9	0951	0.5
TU 1503	4.2	W 1558	4.6
2052	1.3	2150	1.1
14 0308	4.3	**29** 0402	4.5
0933	1.0	1046	0.6
W 1543	4.1	TH 1656	4.4
2134	1.4	2245	1.3
15 0348	4.1	**30** 0500	4.4
1018	1.1	1145	0.7
TH 1628	4.0	F 1758	4.3
2223	1.5	☽ 2347	1.4
		31 0604	4.3
		1246	0.8
		SA 1901	4.2

Chart Datum: 2·5 metres below Ordnance Datum (Newlyn). HAT is 5·2 metres above Chart Datum.

E England

》》 **FREE** monthly updates. Register at 《
www.reedsnauticalalmanac.co.uk

49

1.8 WHITSTABLE

Kent **51°21'·86N 01°01'·46E** ❁❁♨♨❀❀

CHARTS AC 5606, 1607, 2571; Imray C1, 2100

TIDES +0135 Dover; ML 3·0; Duration 0605

Standard Port MARGATE (←)

Times				Height (metres)			
High Water		Low Water		MHWS	MHWN	MLWN	MLWS
0100	0700	0100	0700	4·8	3·9	1·4	0·5
1300	1900	1300	1900				
Differences HERNE BAY							
+0022	+0020	+0019	+0017	+0·6	+0·3	+0·2	+0·1
WHITSTABLE APPROACHES							
+0042	+0029	+0025	+0050	+0·6	+0·6	+0·1	0·0

SHELTER Good, except in strong winds from NNW to NE. Harbour dries up to 0·4m. Yacht berths are limited since priority is given to commercial shipping. Fender board needed against piled quays or seek a mooring to NW of harbour (controlled by YC).

NAVIGATION WPT 51°22'·65N 01°01'·10E, 345°/0·83M to W Quay dolphin. From E keep well seaward of Whitstable Street, a hard drying sandspit, which extends 1M N from the coast; shoals a further 1M to seaward are marked by Whitstable Street NCM lt buoy. From W avoid Columbine and Pollard Spits.

Approach, not before half flood, via Oyster PHM lt buoy to harbour entrance. Entry best at HW±1.

LIGHTS AND MARKS Off head of W Quay on a dolphin, ⚡ Fl G 5s, covers the approaches.

COMMUNICATIONS (Code 01227) Dr 594400. HM 274086. *Whitstable Harbour Radio* VHF Ch **09** 12 16 (Mon–Fri: 0830–1700 LT. Other times: HW –3 to HW+1). Tidal info on request.

FACILITIES www.canterbury.gov.uk HM ☎274086, ⌒ £10 ⏚ 🛊.
Whitstable YC ☎272942, ⚓ ⚓ HW ±3 ⚓ ⏚✕ ▯.
Services ▯⚓Ⓔ⚓⚓⚓ ACA.
Town 🏧✉Ⓑ🛒▯✕▯⚋✈ Lydd/Manston.

MINOR HARBOURS WEST OF NORTH FORELAND
MARGATE, Kent, **51°23'·43N 01°22'·65E**. AC 5606, 1 827, 1828, 323; Imray Y7, C1; Stanfords 5, 8. HW+0045 on Dover; ML 2·6; Duration 0610; Standard Port (←). Small hbr drying 3m, inside bkwtr (Stone Pier) FR 17m 4M; exposed to NW'lies. Appr: from E, via Longnose NCM buoy, keeping about 5ca offshore; from N, via Margate PHM lt buoy; from W via Gore Chan and S Chan to SE Margate ECM. Facilities: Margate YC ☎(01843) 292602, ▯.
Town 10 ⚓ HW±2, book at Foreshore Office ☎(01843) 577529, 🏧🏧✉Ⓑ🛒✕▯⚋✈ Manston.

HERNE BAY, Kent, **51°22'·40N 01°07'·22E**. AC 5606, 1607. Close E of Pavilion (old pier), 400m long bkwtr 'Neptunes Arm' gives well sheltered drying ⚓ for craft <8m. Exposed to strong NE'lies at HW springs when Thames Barrier closed as seas may then top the bkwtr. 3 ⚓ (HW±2½ to HW±3). Foreshore Manager ☎(01227) 266719. Herne Bay SC ☎(01227) 375650. Lts: QW 8m 4M is 6ca offshore (former pier hd); bkwtr hd 2FR (vert); pier hd 2FG (vert); R bn on B dolphin, Fl Y 5s, is approx 1M ENE of bkwtr hd. Reculvers twrs are conspic 3M to the E.
Town 🏧🏧Ⓔ✉Ⓑ▯🛒✕▯⚋✈ Lydd/Manston.

1.9 THE SWALE
Kent ✿✿◊◊◊◊✿✿

CHARTS AC 5606, 2482, 2571, 2572, 1834, 3683; Imray Y18, C1, 2100

TIDES Queenborough +0130 Dover; Harty Ferry +0120 Dover; ML (Harty Ferry) 3·0; Duration 0610. Faversham HW differences are –0·2m on Sheerness; no other data.

Standard Port SHEERNESS (→)

Times				Height (metres)			
High Water		Low Water		MHWS	MHWN	MLWN	MLWS
0200	0800	0200	0700	5·8	4·7	1·5	0·6
1400	2000	1400	1900				

Differences R. SWALE (Grovehurst Jetty)

| –0007 | 0000 | 0000 | +0016 | 0·0 | 0·0 | 0·0 | –0·1 |

Grovehurst Jetty is close N of the ent to Milton Creek.

SHELTER Excellent in the Swale, the 14M chan between the Isle of Sheppey and the N Kent coast, from Shell Ness in the E to Queenborough in the W. Yachts can enter the drying creeks of Faversham, Oare, Conyer, and Milton. Beware wrecks at ent to Faversham Creek. Many moorings line the chan from Faversham to Conyer Creeks. See Queenborough for all-tide access.

NAVIGATION E ent WPT: Whitstable Street lit PHM, 51°24'·00N 01°01'·54E, at ent to well marked buoyed chan. Speed limit 8kn. The middle section from 1·5M E of Conyer Creek to 0·5M E of Milton Creek is narrowed by drying mudbanks and carries least depths of 0·4m. At Milton Creek direction of buoyage changes. There are numerous oyster beds in the area. Kingsferry Bridge opens for masted craft on request, but subject to railway trains; temp ⚓s off SW bank. The power lines crossing SE of the br have a clearance of 30m. **W ent** is marked by Queenborough Spit ECM buoy, Q (3) 10s, 1M S of Garrison Pt, at 51°25'·81N 00°43'·93E.

LIGHTS AND MARKS See chartlet and 1.3. In W Swale lights intended for large coasters using the narrow chan are:

No 5 Bn Oc WRG 6s; vis: 161°-G-166°-W-167°-R-172°. Round Loden Hope bend: two Q WG and one Q WRG on bns; keep in G sectors. See Queenborough chartlet. Horse Reach ldg lts 113°: front QG 7m 5M; rear Fl G 3s 10m 6M. Dir lt 098°, VQ (4) R 5s 6m 5M. Kingsferry Bridge: Dir WRG, 142°-G-147°-W-148°-R-153° 9m. Lts on bridge: two x 2 FG (vert) on SW buttresses; two x 2 FR (vert) on NE. Road bridge has a vertical clearance of 28m.

Kingsferry Bridge traffic sigs:

No lts	= Bridge down (3·35m MHWS).
Al Q ●/◐	= Centre span lifting.
F ●	= Bridge open (29m MHWS).
Q ●	= Centre span lowering. Keep clear.
Q ◌	= Bridge out of action.

Request bridge opening on VHF Ch 10 (or Ch 74 if no response).

COMMUNICATIONS (Code 01795) Dr or Ⓗ via Medway Navigation Service 663025. HM (Medway Ports Ltd) 596593.

Medway VTS VHF Ch **74** 16 22 (H24); Kingsferry Bridge Ch 10 (H24).

FACILITIES FAVERSHAM: Town ⚓✉Ⓑ🛒✕🖃⛽✈(Gatwick).
OARE CREEK ⚓◡⚒⚓Ⓒ🖃(8t)🅿.
Hollow Shore Cruising Club 🖃.

CONYER CREEK: Swale Marina ☎521562, 🖊 ◡(dredged 2m) £14/craft, ⚓🕁🅿🛢🛉⚒⚓🏴(30t)🅿(30t); **Conyer CC.**
Conyer Marina ☎521711, 🖊◡£10, 🅿⚒⚓Ⓒ🇪⚓🅿🅿🅿.

MILTON CREEK (Sittingbourne): **Crown Quay** ⚓🕁.
Town ✉Ⓑ🛒✕🖃⇌✈ (Gatwick); also the Dolphin Yard Sailing Barge Museum.

SHEERNESS

MEAN SPRING ———
AND NEAP CURVES – – –

MEAN RANGES
Springs 5.2m
Neaps 3.2m

1.10 QUEENBOROUGH

Kent (Isle of Sheppey) 51°25'·04N 00°44'·19E ❄❄❄◊◊◊✿✿

CHARTS AC 5606, 1834, 2572, 3683; Imray C1, Y18, 2100

TIDES Use 1.11 Sheerness, 2M to the N. +0130 Dover; ML 3·0; Duration 0610

SHELTER Good, except near HW in strong N'ly winds. The first deep-water refuge W of N Foreland, accessible at all tides from Garrison Pt (1.11); or from the Swale (1.9) on the tide.

An all-tide walk ashore pontoon (5m depth at end) on E bank is available for overnight/short stay; both sides of the jetty are foul. A pair Gy ⚓s (raft up to 6 craft <10m each) lie to the S; also single visitors Y ⚓s Nos 14-24 for craft <10m, with HM's permission craft >10m berth on W side of Concrete Lighter. When ⚓s are full the hbr controller will offer spare buoys. Smaller R buoys (numbered) are for locals. ⚓ owing to commercial traffic. Speed limit 8kn.

NAVIGATION See River Medway for appr via Garrison Pt. Enter the river at Queenborough Spit ECM, Q (3) 10s, 51°25'·75N 00°43'·93E. The channel narrows between drying banks and moorings.

See The Swale if approaching from the E.

LIGHTS AND MARKS Lights as chartlet. Note: No 5 Bn Dir Oc WRG 6s, vis 161°-G-166°-W-167°-R-172°, on river bend covers the appr chan. All-tide landing 2 FR (vert). Concrete lighter Fl G 3s.

COMMUNICATIONS (Code 01795) Dr 583828; Ⓗ (01634) 830000 (Gillingham). HM 662051 and mob 07456 459754 (trot boat).

Monitor *Medway VTS* VHF Ch **74** for traffic. HM Ch **08**. Call *Sheppey One* for trot boat.

FACILITIES **Queenborough Hbr Trust CIC** (www.queenborough-harbour.co.uk) manages the hbr, walk ashore pontoon, ⚓ and ⌖ on concrete lighter and town quay. ⚓ are serviced by a free 'Trot Boat'.

Queenborough Hbr ⌖ (all-tide) <10m £20 (+£2/m), short stay <3hrs £10 (+£2/m), ⚓. ⌖ Quay/concrete ltr/⚓ <10m £12, s/s £6.

Queenborough YC Wed, Fri, Sat evenings, Sat, Sun lunchtimes, ⚓🚿🛠🎣✕🛒.

The Creek ☎07974 349018, ⚓ (HW±1½) Scrubbing grid ⚓ 🛠 🛠.

Services ⛽✕🔧 ⬚🚿📷(10t).

Town 🏦🏧✉🛒✕🛒⇌✈ (Gatwick).

HM Ch 09

QUEENBOROUGH

SHEERNESS   LAT 51°27'N   LONG 0°45'E
TIMES AND HEIGHTS OF HIGH AND LOW WATERS

YEAR 2022

JANUARY

#	Day	Time	m		#	Day	Time	m
1	SA	0435	1.1		16	SU	0524	1.2
		1051	5.6				1144	5.2
		1715	0.8				1741	1.2
		2325	5.6					
2	SU	0540	0.9		17	M	0002	5.3
		1148	5.7				0609	1.0
		1812 ●	0.8				1224	5.3
							○1819	1.1
3	M	0017	5.7		18	TU	0039	5.4
		0641	0.7				0649	0.9
		1242	5.9				1301	5.4
		1904	0.7				1855	1.1
4	TU	0106	5.7		19	W	0114	5.4
		0736	0.6				0727	0.8
		1334	6.0				1336	5.5
		1951	0.8				1930	1.0
5	W	0154	5.7		20	TH	0148	5.5
		0828	0.5				0805	0.7
		1424	6.0				1411	5.6
		2036	0.9				2006	0.9
6	TH	0240	5.7		21	F	0222	5.5
		0916	0.5				0844	0.7
		1513	5.9				1447	5.6
		2117	1.0				2043	1.0
7	F	0326	5.6		22	SA	0256	5.5
		1001	0.6				0923	0.7
		1601	5.7				1524	5.5
		2157	1.2				2118	1.0
8	SA	0411	5.5		23	SU	0331	5.4
		1044	0.7				0958	0.8
		1650	5.4				1603	5.4
		2236	1.3				2152	1.1
9	SU	0458	5.3		24	M	0409	5.4
		1126	0.9				1031	0.9
		1740	5.2				1646	5.3
		◑2320	1.5				2228	1.2
10	M	0549	5.1		25	TU	0451	5.3
		1214	1.1				1106	0.9
		1833	5.0				1734	5.2
							◑2312	1.3
11	TU	0013	1.6		26	W	0542	5.2
		0646	4.9				1153	1.0
		1310	1.3				1832	5.0
		1933	4.8					
12	W	0119	1.7		27	TH	0010	1.4
		0750	4.8				0648	5.0
		1413	1.4				1258	1.2
		2036	4.7				1942	4.9
13	TH	0230	1.7		28	F	0127	1.5
		0858	4.7				0808	5.0
		1514	1.4				1430	1.3
		2139	4.8				2057	5.0
14	F	0335	1.5		29	SA	0300	1.4
		1002	4.9				0927	5.1
		1609	1.3				1552	1.2
		2234	5.0				2209	5.1
15	SA	0433	1.3		30	SU	0421	1.2
		1057	5.0				1040	5.3
		1658	1.3				1701	1.0
		2322	5.1				2313	5.3
					31	M	0536	0.9
							1144	5.6
							1803	0.9

FEBRUARY

#	Day	Time	m		#	Day	Time	m
1	TU	0009	5.5		16	W	0021	5.3
		0640	0.6				0635	0.8
		1238	5.8				1243	5.5
		●1856	0.8				○1840	1.0
2	W	0058	5.7		17	TH	0057	5.5
		0734	0.4				0714	0.7
		1328	6.0				1318	5.6
		1942	0.8				1916	0.9
3	TH	0143	5.8		18	F	0131	5.6
		0821	0.3				0752	0.6
		1413	6.0				1353	5.7
		2023	0.8				1953	0.8
4	F	0226	5.8		19	SA	0204	5.7
		0903	0.3				0831	0.5
		1457	5.9				1428	5.8
		2100	0.9				2030	0.8
5	SA	0306	5.7		20	SU	0237	5.7
		0941	0.5				0908	0.5
		1538	5.7				1504	5.7
		2134	1.0				2103	0.9
6	SU	0344	5.6		21	M	0311	5.7
		1013	0.6				0940	0.6
		1617	5.5				1541	5.6
		2205	1.1				2133	0.9
7	M	0422	5.5		22	TU	0347	5.6
		1042	0.7				1007	0.7
		1657	5.2				1620	5.5
		2237	1.3				2203	1.0
8	TU	0501	5.2		23	W	0427	5.4
		1111	1.1				1036	0.9
		1738	5.0				1703	5.2
		◑2316	1.4				◑2243	1.1
9	W	0547	4.9		24	TH	0515	5.3
		1152	1.3				1119	1.1
		1826	4.7				1757	5.0
							2339	1.3
10	TH	0007	1.6		25	F	0620	5.0
		0645	4.6				1226	1.3
		1252	1.6				1909	4.7
		1928	4.5					
11	F	0125	1.8		26	SA	0100	1.5
		0801	4.5				0747	4.8
		1418	1.7				1410	1.5
		2043	4.5				2035	4.7
12	SA	0255	1.7		27	SU	0251	1.4
		0924	4.5				0919	5.0
		1532	1.6				1541	1.4
		2157	4.6				2158	4.9
13	SU	0406	1.5		28	M	0423	1.1
		1033	4.8				1039	5.3
		1632	1.5				1656	1.2
		2256	4.9				2306	5.2
14	M	0505	1.2					
		1125	5.1					
		1722	1.3					
		2342	5.2					
15	TU	0553	1.0					
		1207	5.3					
		1803	1.1					

MARCH

#	Day	Time	m		#	Day	Time	m
1	TU	0539	0.8		16	W	0528	1.0
		1141	5.6				1140	5.3
		1756	1.0				1739	1.1
							2355	5.4
2	W	0000	5.5		17	TH	0611	0.8
		0636	0.5				1218	5.6
		1231	5.8				1818	1.0
		●1844	0.8					
3	TH	0045	5.7		18	F	0031	5.5
		0722	0.4				0651	0.6
		1315	6.0				1253	5.7
		1925	0.8				○1856	0.8
4	F	0126	5.8		19	SA	0105	5.7
		0803	0.3				0731	0.5
		1355	6.0				1329	5.8
		2002	0.7				1934	0.7
5	SA	0204	5.8		20	SU	0139	5.8
		0839	0.3				0809	0.4
		1433	5.9				1404	5.9
		2036	0.7				2011	0.7
6	SU	0239	5.8		21	M	0214	5.8
		0911	0.4				0846	0.4
		1508	5.7				1440	5.9
		2107	0.8				2045	0.7
7	M	0313	5.7		22	TU	0249	5.8
		0937	0.6				0918	0.5
		1541	5.5				1517	5.7
		2134	0.9				2116	0.8
8	TU	0346	5.5		23	W	0327	5.8
		1000	0.8				0946	0.7
		1613	5.3				1556	5.5
		2200	1.1				2147	0.9
9	W	0420	5.3		24	TH	0409	5.6
		1024	1.1				1017	0.9
		1646	5.0				1639	5.2
		2232	1.3				2230	1.0
10	TH	0459	5.0		25	F	0501	5.3
		1058	1.3				1104	1.2
		1726	4.7				1734	4.9
		◑2315	1.5				◑2329	1.3
11	F	0550	4.6		26	SA	0611	5.0
		1149	1.7				1218	1.5
		1821	4.4				1851	4.6
12	SA	0019	1.7		27	SU	0103	1.4
		0703	4.3				0744	4.8
		1313	1.9				1405	1.6
		1942	4.3				2024	4.6
13	SU	0208	1.8		28	M	0256	1.3
		0840	4.3				0918	5.0
		1455	1.9				1533	1.5
		2115	4.4				2149	4.9
14	M	0335	1.5		29	TU	0424	1.0
		1002	4.7				1033	5.4
		1603	1.6				1646	1.2
		2224	4.8				2253	5.2
15	TU	0438	1.2		30	W	0530	0.6
		1057	5.0				1129	5.7
		1656	1.3				1740	1.0
		2313	5.1				2344	5.5
					31	TH	0619	0.5
							1215	5.8
							1823	0.9

APRIL

#	Day	Time	m		#	Day	Time	m
1	F	0025	5.7		16	SA	0621	0.6
		0700	0.4				1223	5.8
		1254	5.9				1828	0.8
		●1901	0.8				○	
2	SA	0102	5.8		17	SU	0035	5.7
		0736	0.4				0703	0.5
		1330	5.9				1301	5.9
		1935	0.7				1910	0.7
3	SU	0137	5.8		18	M	0112	5.9
		0807	0.4				0743	0.4
		1404	5.8				1338	5.9
		2008	0.7				1950	0.7
4	M	0210	5.8		19	TU	0150	6.0
		0836	0.5				0821	0.4
		1435	5.7				1417	5.9
		2039	0.7				2029	0.7
5	TU	0242	5.7		20	W	0230	5.9
		0901	0.7				0857	0.6
		1505	5.5				1456	5.7
		2106	0.9				2106	0.7
6	W	0314	5.5		21	TH	0313	5.8
		0923	0.9				0931	0.8
		1533	5.4				1537	5.5
		2131	1.0				2145	0.8
7	TH	0348	5.3		22	F	0401	5.6
		0947	1.1				1010	1.1
		1604	5.1				1625	5.2
		2159	1.2				2233	1.0
8	F	0425	5.0		23	SA	0459	5.3
		1019	1.4				1103	1.4
		1641	4.8				1724	4.9
		2238	1.4				◑2339	1.2
9	SA	0511	4.7		24	SU	0613	5.0
		1106	1.7				1219	1.6
		1730	4.5				1843	4.7
		◑2336	1.6					
10	SU	0615	4.4		25	M	0119	1.2
		1217	2.0				0741	5.0
		1844	4.3				1354	1.6
							2011	4.7
11	M	0109	1.7		26	TU	0251	1.1
		0747	4.3				0905	5.2
		1404	2.0				1513	1.4
		2024	4.3				2129	5.0
12	TU	0253	1.5		27	W	0408	0.8
		0914	4.6				1013	5.5
		1522	1.7				1620	1.2
		2139	4.7				2230	5.3
13	W	0358	1.2		28	TH	0507	0.6
		1015	5.0				1106	5.7
		1618	1.4				1712	1.0
		2234	5.1				2318	5.5
14	TH	0451	0.9		29	F	0552	0.6
		1103	5.4				1150	5.7
		1704	1.1				1754	0.9
		2318	5.4				2359	5.6
15	F	0537	0.7		30	SA	0629	0.6
		1144	5.6				1228	5.7
		1747	1.0				1830 ●	0.8
		2358	5.6					

E England

Chart Datum: 2·90 metres below Ordnance Datum (Newlyn). HAT is 6·3 metres above Chart Datum.

FREE monthly updates. Register at www.reedsnauticalalmanac.co.uk

53

STANDARD TIME (UT)
For Summer Time add ONE hour in **non-shaded areas**

SHEERNESS LAT 51°27′N LONG 0°45′E
TIMES AND HEIGHTS OF HIGH AND LOW WATERS

Dates in red are SPRINGS
Dates in blue are NEAPS

YEAR **2022**

MAY

Day	Time m		Day	Time m	
1 SU	0035 5.7 / 0701 0.6 / 1302 5.7 / 1906 0.7		**16** M ○	0005 5.8 / 0633 0.5 / 1233 5.9 / 1846 0.7	
2 M	0109 5.7 / 0731 0.6 / 1334 5.7 / 1941 0.7		**17** TU	0048 5.9 / 0717 0.5 / 1315 5.9 / 1933 0.6	
3 TU	0143 5.7 / 0800 0.7 / 1404 5.6 / 2013 0.7		**18** W	0132 6.0 / 0800 0.6 / 1357 5.8 / 2018 0.6	
4 W	0216 5.6 / 0827 0.8 / 1433 5.5 / 2042 0.9		**19** TH	0217 6.0 / 0841 0.7 / 1440 5.7 / 2103 0.6	
5 TH	0249 5.5 / 0852 1.0 / 1502 5.4 / 2109 1.0		**20** F	0306 5.8 / 0922 0.9 / 1527 5.5 / 2151 0.7	
6 F	0323 5.3 / 0919 1.2 / 1533 5.2 / 2138 1.1		**21** SA	0359 5.6 / 1008 1.1 / 1619 5.3 / 2244 0.8	
7 SA	0401 5.0 / 0952 1.4 / 1610 4.9 / 2217 1.3		**22** SU ◑	0500 5.4 / 1102 1.4 / 1720 5.1 / 2352 0.9	
8 SU	0446 4.8 / 1037 1.6 / 1657 4.7 / 2311 1.4		**23** M	0609 5.2 / 1210 1.5 / 1831 4.9	
9 M ◑	0543 4.6 / 1139 1.8 / 1801 4.5		**24** TU	0112 1.0 / 0724 5.2 / 1327 1.6 / 1946 5.0	
10 TU	0025 1.5 / 0658 4.5 / 1302 1.9 / 1927 4.5		**25** W	0226 0.9 / 0837 5.2 / 1438 1.5 / 2056 5.1	
11 W	0156 1.4 / 0818 4.7 / 1425 1.7 / 2045 4.7		**26** TH	0333 0.9 / 0941 5.4 / 1540 1.3 / 2156 5.2	
12 TH	0307 1.2 / 0925 5.0 / 1527 1.4 / 2145 5.0		**27** F	0430 0.8 / 1035 5.5 / 1634 1.2 / 2247 5.4	
13 F	0404 0.9 / 1019 5.4 / 1620 1.2 / 2236 5.3		**28** SA	0515 0.8 / 1120 5.5 / 1719 1.1 / 2330 5.4	
14 SA	0457 0.7 / 1107 5.6 / 1710 1.0 / 2322 5.6		**29** SU	0552 0.8 / 1200 5.5 / 1800 0.9	
15 SU	0546 0.6 / 1151 5.8 / 1758 0.9		**30** M ●	0009 5.5 / 0625 0.8 / 1234 5.6 / 1839 0.8	
			31 TU	0046 5.5 / 0657 0.9 / 1307 5.6 / 1916 0.8	

JUNE

Day	Time m		Day	Time m	
1 W	0122 5.5 / 0729 0.9 / 1338 5.5 / 1952 0.8		**16** TH	0120 5.9 / 0745 0.7 / 1344 5.8 / 2014 0.5	
2 TH	0157 5.5 / 0759 1.0 / 1409 5.4 / 2024 0.9		**17** F	0211 6.0 / 0831 0.8 / 1432 5.7 / 2105 0.5	
3 F	0231 5.4 / 0829 1.1 / 1440 5.3 / 2055 1.0		**18** SA	0303 5.9 / 0916 0.9 / 1520 5.6 / 2155 0.5	
4 SA	0307 5.3 / 0900 1.2 / 1513 5.2 / 2129 1.0		**19** SU	0356 5.8 / 1002 1.1 / 1611 5.5 / 2248 0.6	
5 SU	0345 5.1 / 0936 1.4 / 1551 5.1 / 2208 1.1		**20** M	0452 5.6 / 1051 1.2 / 1706 5.3 / 2343 0.7	
6 M	0428 5.0 / 1018 1.5 / 1635 4.9 / 2256 1.2		**21** TU ◑	0550 5.4 / 1145 1.4 / 1805 5.2	
7 TU ◑	0518 4.9 / 1109 1.6 / 1729 4.8 / 2353 1.3		**22** W	0043 0.8 / 0653 5.3 / 1246 1.5 / 1908 5.1	
8 W	0617 4.8 / 1212 1.7 / 1834 4.7		**23** TH	0145 0.9 / 0756 5.2 / 1350 1.5 / 2013 5.1	
9 TH	0100 1.2 / 0725 4.9 / 1322 1.6 / 1947 4.8		**24** F	0245 1.0 / 0859 5.1 / 1453 1.5 / 2116 5.1	
10 F	0211 1.1 / 0833 5.1 / 1432 1.5 / 2054 5.0		**25** SA	0341 1.1 / 0957 5.2 / 1551 1.4 / 2213 5.1	
11 SA	0316 1.0 / 0935 5.3 / 1535 1.3 / 2154 5.3		**26** SU	0430 1.1 / 1048 5.3 / 1645 1.2 / 2304 5.2	
12 SU	0416 0.8 / 1031 5.5 / 1634 1.1 / 2248 5.5		**27** M	0513 1.1 / 1133 5.3 / 1804 1.1 / 2350 5.3	
13 M	0512 0.7 / 1122 5.7 / 1732 1.0 / 2340 5.7		**28** TU	0553 1.1 / 1212 5.4 / 1818 1.0	
14 TU ○	0606 0.7 / 1211 5.8 / 1828 0.8		**29** W ●	0030 5.4 / 0630 1.1 / 1248 5.4 / 1859 0.9	
15 W	0030 5.8 / 0657 0.7 / 1258 5.8 / 1922 0.6		**30** TH	0108 5.4 / 0704 1.1 / 1321 5.4 / 1936 0.9	

JULY

Day	Time m		Day	Time m	
1 F	0143 5.4 / 0738 1.1 / 1354 5.4 / 2012 0.9		**16** SA	0206 6.0 / 0822 0.8 / 1423 5.8 / 2102 0.3	
2 SA	0218 5.4 / 0812 1.1 / 1427 5.4 / 2047 0.9		**17** SU	0255 6.0 / 0906 0.9 / 1509 5.8 / 2148 0.3	
3 SU	0254 5.4 / 0847 1.1 / 1501 5.3 / 2124 0.9		**18** M	0343 5.9 / 0948 1.0 / 1554 5.7 / 2232 0.5	
4 M	0330 5.3 / 0923 1.2 / 1537 5.3 / 2202 0.9		**19** TU	0431 5.7 / 1028 1.1 / 1640 5.6 / 2315 0.7	
5 TU	0410 5.3 / 1001 1.3 / 1616 5.2 / 2240 1.0		**20** W ◑	0520 5.5 / 1109 1.3 / 1728 5.4 / 2358 0.9	
6 W	0453 5.2 / 1041 1.4 / 1659 5.1 / 2322 1.1		**21** TH	0611 5.2 / 1156 1.5 / 1821 5.2	
7 TH ●	0542 5.1 / 1128 1.5 / 1750 5.0		**22** F	0046 1.1 / 0707 5.0 / 1253 1.6 / 1922 5.0	
8 F	0010 1.1 / 0640 5.0 / 1225 1.5 / 1854 5.0		**23** SA	0145 1.3 / 0808 4.9 / 1403 1.6 / 2031 4.8	
9 SA	0112 1.1 / 0746 5.0 / 1335 1.5 / 2006 5.0		**24** SU	0248 1.4 / 0914 4.9 / 1512 1.6 / 2141 4.9	
10 SU	0228 1.1 / 0855 5.1 / 1454 1.4 / 2117 5.2		**25** M	0348 1.4 / 1016 5.0 / 1617 1.4 / 2243 5.0	
11 M	0341 1.1 / 0959 5.3 / 1607 1.2 / 2223 5.4		**26** TU	0442 1.4 / 1109 5.1 / 1715 1.2 / 2334 5.2	
12 TU	0447 1.0 / 1100 5.5 / 1714 1.0 / 2325 5.6		**27** W	0530 1.3 / 1153 5.3 / 1804 1.1	
13 W ○	0547 0.9 / 1155 5.6 / 1819 0.8		**28** TH ●	0017 5.3 / 0611 1.2 / 1232 5.4 / 1846 0.9	
14 TH	0021 5.8 / 0644 0.8 / 1247 5.7 / 1918 0.6		**29** F	0055 5.4 / 0647 1.2 / 1307 5.5 / 1923 0.9	
15 F	0115 6.0 / 0735 0.8 / 1336 5.8 / 2012 0.4		**30** SA	0129 5.5 / 0722 1.1 / 1340 5.5 / 1959 0.8	
			31 SU	0203 5.5 / 0757 1.0 / 1413 5.5 / 2036 0.7	

AUGUST

Day	Time m		Day	Time m	
1 M	0237 5.6 / 0833 1.0 / 1445 5.5 / 2112 0.7		**16** TU	0320 5.9 / 0924 0.9 / 1528 5.9 / 2203 0.5	
2 TU	0311 5.6 / 0908 1.1 / 1518 5.5 / 2147 0.8		**17** W	0401 5.7 / 0957 1.1 / 1606 5.7 / 2234 0.8	
3 W	0347 5.6 / 0941 1.2 / 1552 5.4 / 2218 0.9		**18** TH	0441 5.5 / 1030 1.2 / 1646 5.5 / 2304 1.0	
4 TH	0425 5.4 / 1012 1.3 / 1630 5.3 / 2249 1.0		**19** F ◑	0522 5.2 / 1106 1.4 / 1730 5.2 / 2339 1.3	
5 F ◑	0508 5.2 / 1049 1.4 / 1714 5.2 / 2326 1.1		**20** SA	0608 4.9 / 1153 1.6 / 1826 4.8	
6 SA	0559 5.1 / 1139 1.5 / 1811 5.1		**21** SU	0033 1.6 / 0707 4.8 / 1304 1.8 / 1940 4.6	
7 SU	0020 1.3 / 0704 5.0 / 1247 1.6 / 1927 5.0		**22** M	0154 1.8 / 0822 4.6 / 1437 1.8 / 2108 4.6	
8 M	0146 1.4 / 0820 4.9 / 1424 1.6 / 2052 5.0		**23** TU	0313 1.7 / 0942 4.7 / 1554 1.5 / 2222 4.9	
9 TU	0319 1.3 / 0936 5.1 / 1552 1.3 / 2210 5.3		**24** W	0418 1.6 / 1044 5.0 / 1657 1.3 / 2335 5.2	
10 W	0432 1.2 / 1046 5.3 / 1709 1.0 / 2319 5.6		**25** TH	0511 1.4 / 1131 5.2 / 1746 1.1 / 2358 5.4	
11 TH	0538 1.0 / 1146 5.5 / 1817 0.7		**26** F	0553 1.3 / 1211 5.4 / 1827 0.9	
12 F ○	0017 5.8 / 0635 0.9 / 1237 5.7 / 1914 0.5		**27** SA ●	0034 5.5 / 0629 1.2 / 1245 5.6 / 1903 0.7	
13 SA	0108 6.0 / 0724 0.8 / 1323 5.9 / 2003 0.3		**28** SU	0107 5.6 / 0703 1.1 / 1318 5.6 / 1939 0.7	
14 SU	0154 6.1 / 0808 0.8 / 1407 5.9 / 2047 0.2		**29** M	0140 5.7 / 0738 1.0 / 1350 5.7 / 2015 0.6	
15 M	0238 6.1 / 0847 0.8 / 1448 5.9 / 2127 0.3		**30** TU	0213 5.8 / 0814 0.9 / 1421 5.7 / 2051 0.6	
			31 W	0247 5.7 / 0848 1.0 / 1453 5.7 / 2124 0.7	

Chart Datum: 2·90 metres below Ordnance Datum (Newlyn). HAT is 6·3 metres above Chart Datum.

》 **FREE** monthly updates. Register at
www.reedsnauticalalmanac.co.uk 《

STANDARD TIME (UT)
For Summer Time add ONE hour in **non-shaded areas**

SHEERNESS LAT 51°27'N LONG 0°45'E
TIMES AND HEIGHTS OF HIGH AND LOW WATERS

Dates in red are **SPRINGS**
Dates in blue are **NEAPS**

YEAR 2022

SEPTEMBER

Time	m	Time	m
1 0321	5.7	**16** 0358	5.4
0918	1.1	0952	1.2
TH 1527	5.6	F 1606	5.5
2151	0.9	2214	1.2
2 0357	5.5	**17** 0432	5.2
0944	1.2	1022	1.4
F 1603	5.5	SA 1646	5.1
2215	1.0	2245	1.5
3 0437	5.3	**18** 0511	4.9
1018	1.3	1102	1.6
SA 1647	5.3	SU 1735	4.8
2250	1.2	2332	1.8
4 0525	5.1	**19** 0603	4.6
1108	1.4	1205	1.8
SU 1744	5.1	M 1847	4.4
2349	1.5		
5 0630	4.8	**20** 0051	2.1
1221	1.6	0724	4.4
M 1905	4.9	TU 1356	1.9
		2026	4.4
6 0127	1.7	**21** 0238	2.0
0755	4.7	0859	4.5
TU 1416	1.6	W 1525	1.6
2041	4.9	2150	4.7
7 0308	1.6	**22** 0349	1.8
0923	4.9	1010	4.8
W 1550	1.3	TH 1628	1.3
2208	5.3	2245	5.1
8 0424	1.3	**23** 0443	1.5
1037	5.2	1100	5.2
TH 1709	0.9	F 1717	1.0
2314	5.7	2328	5.4
9 0529	1.1	**24** 0525	1.3
1134	5.6	1140	5.5
F 1811	0.6	SA 1757	0.9
10 0007	5.9	**25** 0004	5.6
0621	0.9	0602	1.1
SA 1222	5.8	SU 1215	5.6
○ 1900	0.4	● 1834	0.8
11 0053	6.1	**26** 0038	5.7
0705	0.8	0637	1.0
SU 1304	5.9	M 1248	5.7
1943	0.3	1911	0.7
12 0135	6.1	**27** 0111	5.8
0745	0.8	0713	0.9
M 1343	6.0	TU 1321	5.8
2022	0.3	1947	0.6
13 0213	6.0	**28** 0145	5.9
0821	0.8	0750	0.9
TU 1420	6.0	W 1354	5.8
2056	0.4	2023	0.6
14 0250	5.9	**29** 0219	5.9
0854	0.9	0824	0.9
W 1456	5.9	TH 1428	5.8
2126	0.7	2056	0.7
15 0325	5.7	**30** 0254	5.8
0925	1.0	0855	1.0
TH 1531	5.7	F 1504	5.8
2150	0.9	2123	0.9

OCTOBER

Time	m	Time	m
1 0330	5.6	**16** 0350	5.2
0924	1.1	0947	1.3
SA 1544	5.6	SU 1612	5.1
2151	1.1	2202	1.5
2 0411	5.3	**17** 0425	4.9
1002	1.2	1023	1.5
SU 1632	5.4	M 1657	4.8
2233	1.4	◑ 2247	1.8
3 0501	5.0	**18** 0512	4.6
1057	1.4	1119	1.7
M 1735	5.1	TU 1801	4.5
◑ 2339	1.7	2354	2.1
4 0610	4.7	**19** 0624	4.4
1222	1.6	1251	1.9
TU 1901	4.9	W 1931	4.4
5 0124	1.8	**20** 0141	2.2
0742	4.7	0804	4.4
W 1421	1.5	TH 1441	1.7
2039	5.0	2058	4.6
6 0258	1.6	**21** 0305	1.9
0912	4.9	0921	4.7
TH 1549	1.1	F 1544	1.3
2200	5.4	2159	5.0
7 0412	1.4	**22** 0401	1.6
1022	5.3	1016	5.1
F 1700	0.8	SA 1635	1.1
2301	5.7	2246	5.4
8 0511	1.1	**23** 0446	1.3
1115	5.6	1059	5.4
SA 1753	0.5	SU 1718	0.9
2349	5.9	2326	5.6
9 0558	1.0	**24** 0526	1.1
1159	5.8	1138	5.6
SU 1837	0.5	M 1758	0.8
○			
10 0031	6.0	**25** 0003	5.8
0639	0.9	0606	1.0
M 1238	5.9	TU 1215	5.7
1915	0.5	● 1838	0.7
11 0108	6.0	**26** 0040	5.9
0715	0.8	0645	0.9
TU 1315	6.0	W 1251	5.9
1948	0.5	1917	0.6
12 0144	5.9	**27** 0116	5.9
0750	0.8	0725	0.9
W 1350	6.0	TH 1328	5.9
2019	0.6	1954	0.7
13 0217	5.8	**28** 0153	5.9
0824	0.9	0803	0.9
TH 1425	5.9	F 1406	5.9
2046	0.8	2029	0.8
14 0249	5.7	**29** 0231	5.8
0854	1.0	0840	0.9
F 1459	5.7	SA 1448	5.8
2109	1.1	2103	1.0
15 0319	5.4	**30** 0310	5.6
0920	1.2	0918	1.0
SA 1534	5.4	SU 1534	5.6
2132	1.3	2140	1.2
		31 0355	5.3
		1004	1.1
		M 1628	5.4
		2230	1.5

NOVEMBER

Time	m	Time	m
1 0450	5.0	**16** 0437	4.8
1106	1.3	1050	1.5
TU 1736	5.1	W 1725	4.6
● 2340	1.7	◑ 2312	1.9
2 0603	4.8	**17** 0537	4.5
1239	1.4	1159	1.6
W 1900	5.0	TH 1835	4.5
3 0113	1.8	**18** 0027	2.0
0730	4.8	0659	4.5
TH 1415	1.2	F 1329	1.6
2026	5.1	1952	4.6
4 0236	1.6	**19** 0155	1.9
0851	5.0	0818	4.7
F 1532	1.0	SA 1445	1.4
2139	5.4	2100	4.9
5 0344	1.6	**20** 0302	1.7
0956	5.3	0921	5.0
SA 1636	0.7	SU 1542	1.1
2237	5.7	2155	5.2
6 0441	1.2	**21** 0356	1.4
1048	5.5	1013	5.3
SU 1726	0.6	M 1632	0.9
2324	5.8	2244	5.5
7 0527	1.1	**22** 0445	1.2
1132	5.7	1059	5.5
M 1806	0.7	TU 1719	0.8
		2328	5.7
8 0004	5.8	**23** 0532	1.1
0607	0.9	1143	5.7
TU 1211	5.8	W 1804	0.8
○ 1840	0.7	●	
9 0040	5.8	**24** 0010	5.8
0645	0.9	0618	0.9
W 1248	5.8	TH 1225	5.8
1911	0.7	1848	0.7
10 0114	5.8	**25** 0051	5.8
0721	0.8	0704	0.8
TH 1324	5.8	F 1308	5.9
1941	0.8	1930	0.7
11 0147	5.7	**26** 0133	5.8
0756	0.8	0750	0.8
F 1400	5.7	SA 1353	5.9
2009	1.0	2012	0.8
12 0217	5.6	**27** 0215	5.7
0828	1.0	0836	0.8
SA 1435	5.6	SU 1440	5.8
2035	1.1	2053	1.0
13 0247	5.4	**28** 0300	5.6
0855	1.1	0923	0.8
SU 1510	5.3	M 1531	5.7
2101	1.3	2138	1.2
14 0318	5.2	**29** 0349	5.4
0923	1.2	1016	0.9
M 1548	5.1	TU 1628	5.5
2132	1.5	2229	1.4
15 0353	5.0	**30** 0446	5.2
0959	1.4	1118	1.0
TU 1631	4.9	W 1733	5.3
2215	1.7	◑ 2332	1.6

DECEMBER

Time	m	Time	m
1 0552	5.0	**16** 0502	4.8
1233	1.1	1122	1.3
TH 1844	5.2	F 1749	4.8
		◑ 2335	1.7
2 0045	1.6	**17** 0600	4.7
0705	5.0	1222	1.4
F 1348	1.0	SA 1851	4.8
1958	5.2		
3 0157	1.6	**18** 0039	1.8
0817	5.1	0710	4.7
SA 1457	1.0	SU 1331	1.3
2105	5.3	1959	4.9
4 0303	1.5	**19** 0152	1.7
0921	5.2	0821	4.9
SU 1558	0.9	M 1442	1.2
2204	5.4	2104	5.1
5 0401	1.3	**20** 0302	1.5
1017	5.3	0924	5.1
M 1649	0.9	TU 1546	1.1
2254	5.5	2203	5.3
6 0452	1.2	**21** 0405	1.3
1105	5.4	1022	5.3
TU 1729	0.9	W 1643	1.0
2337	5.5	2256	5.5
7 0537	1.1	**22** 0502	1.1
1148	5.5	1116	5.5
W 1804	0.9	TH 1736	0.9
		2346	5.6
8 0015	5.5	**23** 0558	0.9
0619	0.9	1207	5.7
TH 1228	5.6	F 1826	0.8
○ 1837	1.0	●	
9 0051	5.6	**24** 0033	5.7
0658	0.9	0653	0.8
F 1306	5.6	SA 1257	5.9
1910	1.0	1915	0.8
10 0124	5.5	**25** 0120	5.7
0736	0.9	0746	0.6
SA 1343	5.5	SU 1346	5.9
1941	1.1	2002	0.8
11 0155	5.5	**26** 0206	5.7
0809	0.9	0838	0.5
SU 1419	5.4	M 1437	5.9
2010	1.2	2049	0.8
12 0226	5.4	**27** 0254	5.7
0840	1.0	0929	0.5
M 1454	5.3	TU 1528	5.9
2041	1.3	2134	1.0
13 0258	5.2	**28** 0342	5.6
0911	1.1	1019	0.6
TU 1531	5.2	W 1621	5.7
2114	1.4	2220	1.2
14 0334	5.1	**29** 0434	5.4
0948	1.2	1110	0.7
W 1611	5.0	TH 1716	5.5
2153	1.5	2310	1.3
15 0414	5.0	**30** 0528	5.3
1031	1.3	1205	0.8
TH 1656	4.9	F 1815	5.3
2240	1.6	◑	
		31 0004	1.5
		0629	5.2
		SA 1304	1.0
		1918	5.1

Chart Datum: 2·90 metres below Ordnance Datum (Newlyn). HAT is 6·3 metres above Chart Datum.

E England

1.11 RIVER MEDWAY (SHEERNESS TO ROCHESTER)

Kent **51°27'·03N 00°44'·50E** (Off Garrison Pt) ❀❀❀✿✿✿✿✿✿

CHARTS AC 5606, 1835, 1834, 1185, 2482, 3683; IMRAY C1, Y18, 2100

TIDES +0130 Dover; ML 3·1; Duration 0610
Standard Port SHEERNESS (←—)

Times				Height (metres)			
High Water		Low Water		MHWS	MHWN	MLWN	MLWS
0200	0800	0200	0700	5·8	4·7	1·5	0·6
1400	2000	1400	1900				
Differences BEE NESS							
+0002	+0002	0000	+0005	+0·2	+0·1	0·0	0·0
BARTLETT CREEK							
+0016	+0008	ND	ND	+0·1	0·0	ND	ND
DARNETT NESS							
+0004	*+0004*	*0000*	*+0010*	*+0·2*	*+0·1*	*0·0*	*–0·1*
CHATHAM (Lock Approaches)							
+0010	+0012	+0012	+0018	+0·3	+0·1	–0·1	–0·2
UPNOR							
+0015	+0015	+0015	+0025	+0·2	+0·2	–0·1	–0·1
ROCHESTER (STROOD PIER)							
+0018	+0018	+0018	+0028	+0·2	+0·2	–0·2	–0·3
WOULDHAM							
+0030	+0025	+0035	+0120	–0·2	–0·3	–1·0	–0·3
NEW HYTHE							
+0035	+0035	+0220	+0240	–1·6	–1·7	–1·2	–0·3
ALLINGTON LOCK							
+0050	+0035	ND	ND	–2·1	–2·2	–1·3	–0·4

SHELTER There are 4 marinas downriver of Rochester Bridge and 5 above. Sheerness is solely a commercial hbr. See Queenborough for access to/from The Swale. Lower reaches of the Medway are exposed to strong NE winds, but Stangate and Half Acre Creeks are secure in all winds and give access to lesser creeks. There are good ⚓s in Sharfleet Creek; with sufficient rise of the tide it is possible to go via the 'back-door' into Half Acre Creek. Speed limit is 6kn W of Folly Pt (Hoo Island).

NAVIGATION WPT 51°28'·84N 00°52'·78E, SWM buoy, 253°/4·5M to No 11 SHM, then follow recommended route 240°/1M to Grain Hard SHM. The wreck of *Richard Montgomery* is visible 2M NE of estuary ent and E Bulwark SHM marks a wreck (2₂m) in Kethole Reach. Observe restrictions off Grain LNG Terminal keeping >150m from berths and >250m from ships offloading; speed limit 7½kn. There is a huge area to explore, although much of it dries to mud. Some minor creeks are buoyed. The river is tidal up to Allington Lock (21·6M) and well marked to Rochester. Above the bridge the river shoals markedly and the upper reaches have only about 1m at LW.

Bridge Clearances (HAT), going upriver:	
Rochester	5·4m
Medway (M2)	16·2m
Holborough Reach	5.0m
New Hythe (footbridge)	10·7m
Aylesford (pedestrian)	2·3m
Aylesford (road)	2·7m
Maidstone bypass (M20)	8·9m

LIGHTS AND MARKS See 1.3 and chartlet for details of most lts. NB: not all buoys are shown due to small scale. Isle of Grain lt Q 20m 13M. Power stn chy (242m) Oc and FR lts. Tfc Sigs: Powerful lt, Fl 7s, at Garrison Pt means large vessel >130m under way: if shown up river = Inbound; If to seaward = outbound.

COMMUNICATIONS (Codes 01634 Medway) Medway Navigation Service (01795) 663025; Sheerness HM (01795) 596593.
Medway VTS VHF Ch **74** 16 (H24). Monitor Ch 74 underway and Ch 16 at ⚓. Radar assistance is available on request Ch 22. Ch **80** M for marinas: Gillingham, Hoo (H24), Chatham Maritime (H24), Medway Bridge (0900-1700LT) and Port Medway (0800-2000LT).

YACHT CLUBS Sheppey YC ☎(01795) 663052.
Lower Halstow YC ☎(01227) 458554.
Medway Cruising Club (Gillingham) ☎856489, ⚓⛵🛥️🏠.
Hoo Ness YC ☎250052, ⚓⛵⚓✕🏠.
Hundred of Hoo SC ☎250102.
Medway Motor CCl ☎827194.
Medway Motor YC ☎(01622) 737647.
Medway YC (Upnor) ☎718399; **Upnor SC** ☎718043.
Royal Engineers YC ☎844555; **RNSA Medway** ☎200970.
Rochester CC ☎841350, ⚓⛵⚓🅿✕🏠.
Strood YC ☎718261, ⚓⛵⛵⚓🅿(1½t) 🏠.

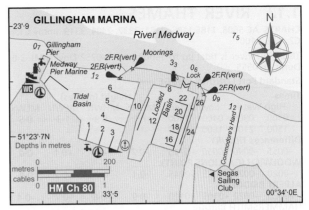

FACILITIES (☎ code 01634 unless otherwise stated). All moorings run by YCs or marinas. Slips at Commodores Hard, and Gillingham.

Marinas (From seaward to Rochester Bridge)
Gillingham Marina cross-tide, esp. the ebb, off the lock ent are reduced by a timber baffle at 90° to the stream (close W of lock). An angled pontoon deflects the stream and is also the fuel berth; the outboard end is lit by 2FR (vert).④ (252+12Ⓥs) ☎280022, pre-book. £3·20 locked basin (access via lock (width 6m) HW±4½), £2·10 tidal basin HW±2, ⚓⛵⚓✕🔧🅿Ⓔ🛒(65t) ⛴(1t) ⚓🚿🍴.

SEGAS SC ☎01304 362842 www.segassailingclub.co.uk on the 'Strand' the club has 90 members and a mix of buoys and drying berths available by prior arrangement.
Medway Pier Marine ☎851113, ⚓⚓⛴🏠ℝⒺ⛴(6t).

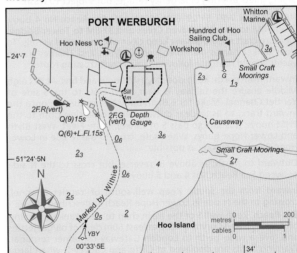

Port Werburgh (120+ residential ⛵ only), ☎252107 access to W basin HW±2½; HW±3 to E basin (via sill 1m above CD); an unlit WCM buoy marks chan ent; 4 waiting buoys in river; 🅿ℝ🅿.

Chatham Maritime Marina – see inset on previous page (←—) www.chathammaritimemarina.co.uk ☎899200 (300⛵), access via lock H24 and sill 1.3m above CD (1.5m at MLWS), £3.20. ⛴(15t), ⚓-⏚🅿⚓⛵✕⚓🅿⚓.
Victory Marina ☎07785 971797, Ⓥ⚓-⏚.

Marinas (Upriver from Rochester Bridge)
Medway Bridge Marina ☎843576, ⚓160⛵+4Ⓥ £1.20, ⚓⛵⚓✕✕Ⓔ⚓⛴(3t)🛒(10t)⚓🍴✕🏠.
Port Medway Marina ☎720033, 50⛵ inc Ⓥ✕🛒(16t) ⚓.
Cuxton Marina ☎721941, ⚓150⛵+Ⓥ✕✕Ⓔ Ⓔ🛒(12t)⚓.
Elmhaven Marina ☎240489, 60⛵✕✕Ⓔ⚓.
Allington Lock operates HW–3 to +2, ☎(01622) 752864.
Allington Marina ☎(01622) 752057, above the lock; ⚓120⛵⚓⚓⛵⚓✕✕Ⓔ🛒(10t)⚓.
Towns All facilities ✉🛒🅿✕⇌✈ (Gatwick).

E England

1.12 RIVER THAMES

CHARTS AC 5606, 1185,1186, 2151, 3337, 2484, 3319. Imray C1, C2, Y18, 2100

TIDES The river is tidal up to Teddington. +0252 Dover; ML 3·6; Duration 0555.

Standard Port LONDON BRIDGE (→)

Times				Height (metres)			
High Water		Low Water		MHWS	MHWN	MLWN	MLWS
0300	0900	0400	1100	7·1	5·9	1·3	0·5
1500	2100	1600	2300				
Differences TILBURY							
−0055	−0040	−0050	−0115	−0·7	−0·5	+0·1	0·0
WOOLWICH (GALLIONS POINT)							
−0020	−0020	−0035	−0045	−0·1	0·0	+0·2	0·0
ALBERT BRIDGE							
+0025	+0020	+0105	+0110	−0·9	−0·8	−0·7	−0·4
HAMMERSMITH BRIDGE							
+0040	+0035	+0205	+0155	−1·4	−1·3	−1·0	−0·5
KEW BRIDGE							
+0055	+0050	+0255	+0235	−1·8	−1·8	−1·2	−0·5
TEDDINGTON (RICHMOND) LOCK							
+0105	+0055	+0325	+0305	−2·2	−2·7	−0·9	−0·5

Tide Boards, showing height of tide above CD, are at Lower Pool (Met Police Boatyard), King's Reach (Temple Stairs), Nine Elms Reach (Cringle Wharf) and Battersea Reach (Plantation Wharf). Above Putney the height of LW may be below CD if the water flow over Teddington Weir is low; warnings are broadcast by London VTS. Thames Barrier closure will alter predicted water levels greatly.

SHELTER Very good in marinas. PLA Drawdocks, arrowed, are drying inlets offering emergency refuge, but subject to wash.

NAVIGATION WPT 51°29'·62N 00°44'·17E, Sea Reach No 4 buoy, 276°/6·8M to abm Holehaven Creek and 37·8M to Tower Bridge. Pleasure craft should always keep clear of commercial vessels. To clear tanker berths off Holehaven, Coryton and Thames Haven yachts should navigate following small craft crossing routes:

Inward from north: Keep close to SHM buoys and bns. At W Leigh Middle ensure the fairway is clear, then cross to the S side of Yantlet Channel. Make for E Blyth buoy before turning onto the inward track, so as to clear outward vessels passing close to the PHM buoys. It is safe to pass S of Tanker, Cliffe Fleet, West Blyth and Lower Hope buoys. When safe, cross to the N side in Lower Hope Reach as quickly as possible.

Outward to north: as above in reverse, but cross to the N side between Sea Reach Nos 4 and 5 buoys.

Inward from the south: Keep well south of Yantlet Channel, crossing to the N side in Lower Hope Reach as described above.

Sea Reach, keep well S of the main chan to clear tankers turning off Canvey Is and Coryton. Keep at least 60m clear of oil/gas jetties and give a wide berth to London Gateway container terminal. Warning lights are displayed at Cliffe and Canvey Is when large ships are manoeuvring.

Lower Hope Reach, hold the NW bank until Ovens SHM; long groynes extend from the N bank for the next 2M. Tilbury Landing Stage is used by the Gravesend ferry and cruise liners.

Gravesend Reach, beware 6 groynes off the N bank, WSW of Coalhouse Pt, which project almost into the fairway. Outer ends marked by SHM beacons, Fl G 2·5s. *No inside passage exists.*

Above **Gravesend** keep to stbd side of channel – do not cut corners.

Northfleet Hope, beware ships/tugs turning into Tilbury Docks; container berths and a grain terminal are close upriver. A light, Iso 6s, on Tilbury Cargo Jetty (51°27'·06N 00°20'·95E) is shown when vessels are manoeuvring off Tilbury Dock locks or for a berth in Northfleet Hope. *Proceed with caution.*

Above **Cherry Garden Pier** vessels > 40m LOA and tugs/tows always have priority. Very heavy traffic/frequent River Ferries from/to

Greenwich, Tower of London and Westminster. Police and PLA launches are always willing to assist.

Speed limits. Minimise wash. 8kn speed limit applies at Canvey Is, Coryton and Thurrock when gas tankers are berthed, in all creeks and above Wandsworth Bridge. Voluntary 12kn speed limit to Wandsworth Bridge.

Exclusion Zones. These are in place off the Houses of Parliament on the North Embankment and government offices below Vauxhall Br on the S side of the river.

> The Port of London Authority (PLA), London River House, Royal Pier Road, Gravesend, Kent DA12 2BG, ☎01474 562200, publish (download free from www.pla.co.uk) *Recreational Users' Guide; General Directions; Permanent Notices to Mariners; Port of London River Byelaws; Tide Tables* and a *Port Handbook.*

LIGHTS AND MARKS See 1.3 and chartlets. Glare from shore lts can make navigation by night difficult or even hazardous. Some ▲s show F.Bu lights; High Speed Craft show Fl.Y lights.

COMMUNICATIONS Port of London Authority: www.pla.co.uk HM: lower district ☎01474 562200, upper district ☎020 7743 7912; Port Controller Gravesend ☎01474 560311, Police Marine Support Unit ☎020 7275 4421; Thames Barrier Navigation Centre ☎020 3260 7711; Tower Bridge ☎020 7940 3984; Richmond lock ☎020 8940 0634; Teddington lock ☎020 8940 8723.

London VTS works from centres at Gravesend and the Thames Barrier, dividing the estuary/river into three sectors. Routine MSI broadcasts are made at the times shown (in brackets) below.

Sector 1: Outer limits – Sea Reach No 4 buoy. Ch **69** (H +15, H +45)
Sector 2: Sea Reach 4 – Crayfordness. Ch **68 (**H and H +30)
Sector 3: Crayfordness – Teddington. Ch **14** (H +15 and H +45)

PLA launches *Thames Patrol* Ch 69, 68, 14. Police launches *Thames Police* Ch 14. **Do not** use tug Channels 8, 10, 13, 36, 72, 77. **In emergency** call *London Coastguard* Ch 16, 67, co-located with London VTS at the Thames Barrier Navigation Control and covering from Canvey Island to Teddington. *Thames Coastguard* covers the area to seaward of Canvey Island. The RNLI operates four LB stations at Gravesend, Victoria Embankment (Waterloo Br), Chiswick and Teddington.

HARBOURS IN SEA REACH and GRAVESEND REACH
HOLEHAVEN CREEK, Essex, 51°30'·57N 00°33'·16E. AC 2484, 1186. HW +0140 on Dover; use differences for Coryton (at 1.13); ML 3·0m; Duration 0610. Shelter is good, but beware swell from passing traffic. Keep to Canvey Is side on ent. Temp ⚓ in lee of Chainrock jetty or call PLA ☎01474 562462 for possible mooring. 5ca N of ent an overhead oil pipe (2 FY horiz) crosses chan with 11m clearance, plus 2 FG (vert) on all jetty heads, plus Chainrock SHM buoy Fl G 5s. ⚓ from Lobster Smack pub, ⌂ ⌂ from Canvey Village (1M); all other facilities on Canvey Is.

GRAVESEND, Kent, 51°26'·61N 00°22'·92E. AC 1186, 2151.
HW +0150 on Dover; ML 3·3m; Duration 0610. Use Tilbury diffs. ⚓ E of Club's Jetty close to S shore, but remote from town.

Gravesend SC www.gravesendsailingclub.co.uk ☎07506 367699.

PLA ⚓s are upriver, £25/night. **London River Moorings** ☎01474 535700 All tide ⚓s £25/night, half tide ⚓. New all tide landing stage available.

Embankment Marina www.theembankmentmarina.co.uk ☎01474 535700; £25/night. Lock into Canal Basin HW −1 to HW Tilbury by arrangement: 1 Apr-31 Oct, 0800-2000; Winter 1000-1600. Lock closes at local HW. Out of hours openings up to HW by arrangement with lock keeper. Facilities: ▲ ⚓ 🔧🚿⌂ 🔨 🔧 ⛽ Ⓔ.

Town Tourist info ☎(01474) 337600, ⌂ ⌂ 🔨 🔧 ⛽ Ⓔ ⚓(70t) at Denton Wharf, 🚊 ✕.

Thurrock YC 51°28'·28N 00°19'·47E at Grays, ☎01375 373720. 1⚓ ⌂ ⌂ (2M), ⚓ ✕ (occas). M-F 1000-1500; Thu 2000-2300.

CANVEY ISLAND TO CRAYFORDNESS (AC 1185, 1186, 2484, 2151)

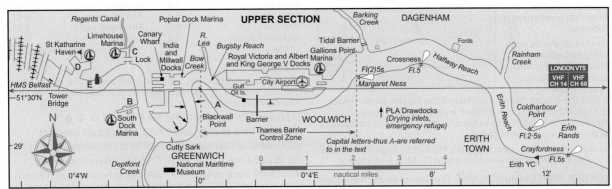

CRAYFORDNESS TO TOWER BRIDGE (AC 2484, 2151, 3337)

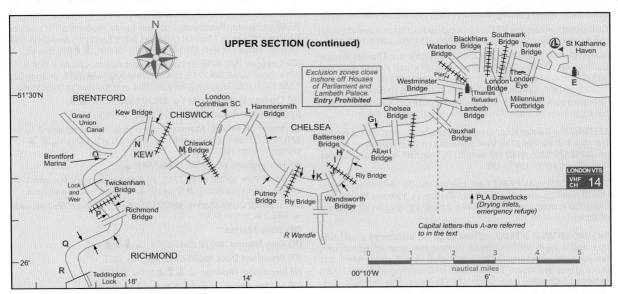

TOWER BRIDGE TO TEDDINGTON (AC 3319)

E England

OBSTRUCTIONS

THAMES TIDAL BARRIER 51°29'·91N 00°02'·21E (Span G), AC 5606, 2484, 3337. At Woolwich Reach are 9 piers between which gates can be rotated upwards from the river bed to form a barrier. Piers are numbered 1-9 from N to S; Spans are lettered A–K from S to N (see diagram). A, H, J & K are not navigable. C–F, with depth 5·8m and 61m wide, are for larger ships. Spans B and G, with 1·25m, are for small craft: W-bound via G and E-bound via B (51°29'·73N 00°02'·24E). On N side of river (Spans E and F) a cross-tide component is reported.

Small craft should not navigate between Thames Refinery Jetty and Gulf Oil Island, unless intending to transit the barrier. Yachts must transit the barrier under power, not sail. When all spans are closed, keep 200m clear to avoid turbulence. It is dangerous to transit a span closed to navigation as the gate may be semi-raised.

In reduced visibility, open spans are marked by high intensity lts. *London VTS* broadcasts information on Ch **14** at H+15/H+45.

CONTROL AND COMMUNICATIONS The Thames Barrier Navigation Centre controls all traffic in a Zone from Margaret Ness (51°30'·5N 00°05'·56E) to Blackwall Point (51°30'·3N 00°00'·2E), using the callsign *London VTS* on VHF Ch **14**, 22, 16.

Inbound call *London VTS* to obtain clearance to proceed through the Barrier when passing Margaret Ness (51°30'·54N 00°05'·50E).

Outbound call *London VTS* to obtain clearance to proceed through the Barrier when passing Blackwall Point (51°30'·30N 00°00'·18E).

Non-VHF craft should, if possible, pre-notify the Thames Barrier Control ☎020 8855 0315; then observe all visual signals, proceed with caution keeping clear of larger vessels and use spans B or G as appropriate. Call before and after transiting the barrier.

There are fixed warning noticeboards (CEVNI) at: Barking Creek (N bank), Blackwall Stairs (N bank), Blackwall Point (S bank).

TESTING The Barrier is completely closed for testing once a month for about 3hrs, LW ±1½. Visit www.pla.co.uk (navigation safety) or call ☎020 8305 4188 for details. In Sept/Oct an annual closure lasts about 10hrs, LW to LW.

THAMES GATEWAY CABLE CAR Joining the O2 Millennium Dome site at Greenwich with the Excel Centre at Victoria Docks, the Cable Car crosses the river between 2 pylons giving an air draught of 60m.

RICHMOND WEIR & TEDDINGTON LOCK At **Richmond** a half-tide lock and a weir with overhead sluice gates give access upriver; fee payable. 3 R discs (3 ● lts at night) in a ▽ show when the sluice gates are down (closed) and maintaining at least 1·72m between Richmond and Teddington bridges. The half-tide lock, on the Surrey bank, must then be used. At other times (approx HW ±2) two ● lights at each arch = weir open to navigation. Pass freely below the 3 central arches.

Teddington lock marks the end of the tidal Thames (semi-tidal above Richmond). Red/green lights indicate which of the launch or barge locks is in operation.

BRIDGES Craft approaching a bridge against the tide give way to those approaching with the tide. All bridges above Tower Bridge are fixed. A ▽ of R discs (● lts) below a bridge span = this arch closed; a bundle of straw = reduced headroom. Clearances (m) above HAT are as follows:

Tower Bridge: when bascules are open high intensity white signal lts on arches between Tower and Wandsworth bridges are electronically triggered by one or more large vessels approaching. Iso W 4s means a single large vessel, VQ a second large vessel, nearing the same bridge. Other vessels keep clear of that arch. NB air-draught boards are at Harrods Depository and Chiswick Eyot for Hammersmith Bridge.

Dartford (QEII)	53	Albert	4·5
Tower (closed)	8·0	Battersea road	5·0
Tower (open)	42	Battersea rail	5·5
London	8·2	Wandsworth	5·3
Cannon St	6·7	Fulham	6·3
Southwark	6·8	Putney	4·8
Millennium	8·4	Hammersmith	3·1
Blackfriars rail	6·8	Barnes	4·9
Blackfriars road	6·5	Chiswick	6·1
Waterloo	8·1	Kew rail	5·0
Charing Cross	6·5	Kew road	4·7
Westminster	4·8	Richmond foot	5·0
Lambeth	5·9	Twickenham	8·5*
Vauxhall	5·2	Richmond rail	8·0*
Victoria Railway	5·5	Richmond road	7·9*
Chelsea	6·1	* Above maintained water level	

FACILITIES

Marinas See overleaf for Gallions Point and Poplar Dock. Other marinas and YCs (Bold red letters in brackets appear on River Thames chartlets):

(A) Greenwich YC ☎0844 736 5846, VHF Ch M. ⚓ ⚙ ✎.

(B) South Dock Marina ☎020 7252 2244 (details overleaf).

(C) Limehouse Marina ☎020 7308 9930 (details overleaf).

(D) St Katharine Haven ☎020 7264 5312 (details overleaf).

West India Dock ☎020 7517 5500; group bookings (min 6) only.

Hermitage Moorings (3·5ca downstream of Tower bridge) ☎020 7481 2122; VHF Ch M/80. 2♥ on pontoons (max 40m LOA) £30/£40 per night, ⚓ 🔌 ⛽ ⚐/🚻.

(E) Fuel Barge ☎020 7481 1774; VHF Ch 14 *Heiko*. 🔵 ⚓ M–F 0630-1430. W/ends Apr-Oct, HW±2, between 0600 and 1800.

(F) Westminster Petroleum Ltd Fuel barge moored off Houses of Parliament. Open Mon-Fri (and Sat from Easter to mid-Oct). Call *Thames Refueller* VHF Ch 14, ☎07831 110681, 🔵 ⚓ dry stores.

(G) Cadogan 020 8748 2715, give 24hrs notice. Chiswick 020 8742 2713. Dove 020 8748 2715. St Katharine 020 7488 0555. Putney 020 7378 1211. 020 7930 2062 for Kew Pier and Richmond Lndg Stage.

(H) Chelsea Yacht & Boat Co ☎020 7352 1427, ⚓ ⚓.

(I) Chelsea Harbour ☎020 7225 9100 (p 302).

(J) Imperial Wharf Marina pier@imperialwharfmarina.co.uk. ☎ 07932 603284, 270m pontoon, 2m at MLWS, £4/m/night, ⚓ 🔌, visitors welcome.

(K) Hurlingham YC ☎020 8788 5547, ⚓.

Chiswick Pier ☎020 8742 2713, all tide access, max draught 1·4m £0.95m, long pontoon, 2FG (vert), ⚓ 🔌 ✕. Visitors welcome.

(L) Chiswick Quay Marina ☎020 8994 8743, Access HW±2 via lock, ⚓ 50☐ ⚓ ✕ ✎ 🛒 🚽.

(M) Dove Marina.

(N) Kew Marina ☎020 8940 8364, ⚓ ⚓ 🔵 ⚓ 🏴 🚽.

(O) Brentford Dock ☎020 8232 8941 (p 302).

(P) Richmond Slipway ⚓ ⚓ 🔵 ⚓ ✕ ✎ 🛒 🚦 🚽.

(Q) Eel Pie Island ⚓ ⚓ 🔌 🏴 ✕ ✎ 🛒 🚦(6t) 🚽.

(R) Swan Island Hbr ⚓ ⚓ ☐ ⚓ 🔵 ⚓ ✕ ✎ 🛒 🚦(30t) 🚽.

Piers where landing may be possible, by prior arrangement: Call London River Services ☎020 7941 2400 for: Greenwich, Tower Millennium, Embankment, Bankside, Festival, Westminster, Millbank, Blackfriars and Waterloo.

MARINAS ON THE TIDAL THAMES, from seaward to Brentford
AC 2484, 3337, 3319

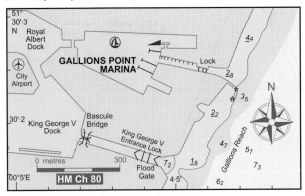

GALLIONS POINT MARINA, 51°30'·30N 00°04'·66E sited in the entry basin for Royal Albert Dock. www.gallionspoint marina.co.uk ☎ 020 7476 7054. Ch M/80, when vessel expected. 2 x ☆s 2FG (vert) on river pier. 8m depth in basin. Access via lock (width 7·6m) HW±5; Locking £5 each way; H24 security, ⌂ from £12/yacht, 🏴 ⚏ ⚓ 🚿 🛁 ⚓ ⚒ slip. DLR from N Woolwich to central London, until 0030. Woolwich ferry & foot tunnel 15 mins walk. ✈ (City) is adjacent.

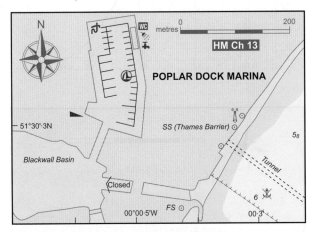

POPLAR DOCK MARINA, 51°30'·07N 00°00'·50W (lock entrance). ☎020 7308 9930, *but no visitors berths*. Tides: India and Millwall Docks ent. 4·5M below Tower Bridge. Canary Wharf twrs (244m) are conspic 4ca W of marina. Enter via West India Entrance Lock (spanned by Docklands 'Blue Bridge'). Lock (300m x 24m) opens 0700-1700LT at HW for outbound and HW-1 to HW+1 for arrivals, foc, but OT £20. Least width 12·1m into marina. VHF Ch 13 (H24).

Facilities ⚏ ⚓ ⚒ ⚓ 🚿 ✕ 🛁; Dr ☎020 7237 1078; 🅗 020 7955 5000. ⇄ Blackwall DLR, Canary Wharf Tube, ✈ City.

SOUTH DOCK MARINA (B), 51°29'·65N 00°01'·97W. ☎020 7252 2244 Mob 0795 662 10710 (OH 0700-1900 Mon-Fri / 0800-1700 w/e) Tides as for Surrey Dock Greenland Ent. 1·1M above Greenwich,

2·5M below Tower Bridge. Baltic Quay building at SW end of marina is conspic with five arched rooftops. Waiting pontoon at Greenland Pier. Approx access via lock (width 6·4m) HW-2 to HW+1½ for 2m draught. 250 + ⓥ, £22·62< 9·5m>£24·89<15m>£33·89<20m>£39·60. VHF Ch M 80; Dr ☎237 1078; 🅗 ⚓ ☎020 7955 5000; Police 101. **Facilities** ⚏ ⚓ ⚒ ✕ ⚏ 🛁 ⚓(20t) ⚓ ⚒ ✕ 🛁 ⇄ Surrey Quays and Canada Water tube, ✈ City Airport.

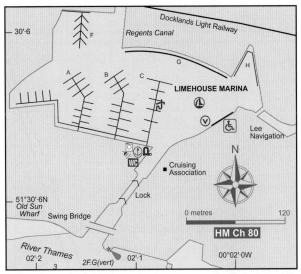

LIMEHOUSE MARINA (C), 51°30'·57N 00°02'·27W www.bwml.co.uk ☎020 7308 9930. Entry HW±3 via swing bridge/lock (width 8m) 0800-1800LT daily Apr-Sep; 0800-1600 Oct-Mar; other times by prior arrangement (24hrs notice) to BWML Lock control ☎020 7308 9930, beware cross-tide at lock cut, mid flood/ebb. Waiting pontoon in lock entrance is accessible outside LW±2. Call VHF Ch 80 *Limehouse Marina*.

Facilities 90⌂ from £28·00/craft ⓥ H24 security, ⚏ ⚓ ⚒ ⚓ ⚏ ⚓ ✕ ⚏ 🛁 ✕ 🛁 DLR; also entry to Regents Canal and Lee Navigation. Visitors welcome at CA clubhouse.

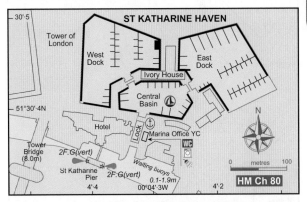

ST KATHARINE HAVEN (D), 51°30´·36N 00°04'·35W www.skdocks. co.uk ☎020 7264 5312 HW +0245 on Dover. Tides as London Bridge. Beware of cross-tide at mid-flood/ebb. Good shelter under all conditions. Tower Bridge and the Tower of London are uniquely conspic, close upriver. Six Y waiting buoys are close downstream of entrance. Berthing on St Katharine Pier, 30m upriver, is strictly by prior arrangement and only for shoal draught vessels with permission. Pleasure launches berth on S side of pier.

St Katharine Haven Ch **80** M. Lock (41m x 12·5m with 2 small lifting bridges), access HW –2 to HW +1½, season 0600-2030, winter 0800-1800LT; other times by prior arrangement. R/G traffic lights at entrance.

Facilities 160⌂ inc ⓥ in 3 basins £8·20+ 🔌 – usually Centre Basin or East Dock; ⚓ ⚏ 🛒 🚿 ✕ 🛁 wi-fi ⚓. ⚓ at fuel barge Heiko 500m downstream ☎020 3793 9925 / 07827 816400.

LONDON BRIDGE

MEAN SPRING ————
AND NEAP CURVES - - - -

MEAN RANGES	
Springs	6.6m
Neaps	4.6m

CHELSEA HARBOUR MARINA (I), London, **51°28´·48N 00°10´·82W**. Tides: see Albert Bridge. Good shelter in all conditions, 5M above Tower Bridge, reached via 14 fixed bridges. Battersea railway bridge is 120m upstream. Belvedere Tower (80m high with tide ball) is conspic, next to the lock and bascule bridge. Max sizes for lock: LOA 24m, beam 5·5m, draught 1·8m. Lock opens when there is 2·5m water above sill; tide gauge outside; R/G traffic lights. Limited waiting berths and shore access on Chelsea Hbr Pier (1·7m) close upriver. **Marina** Mobile ☎07770 542783. VHF Ch 80. 50⌑+10🅥 £25<12m>£30, ♿ ♂ 🐾 🅆🅒 🔲 🅑 🛒 ✕ 🖵.

BRENTFORD DOCK MARINA (O), **51°28´·92N 00°18´·05W**, 1100m beyond Kew bridge. AC 3319. Tides, see Kew Bridge. 60⌑ inc 🅥, £20 for all LOA. Mobile ☎07970 143 987. No VHF. Access approx HW±2½ via lock 4·8m x 9·8m (longer LOA during freeflow); 15m waiting pontoon.

Facilities ⫶🛢 ♂ 🔲 🛢 ✕ 🔧 🪝 🅒🅗 🛒 ✕ 🖵; Gunnersbury and Ealing Underground. Ent to Grand Union Canal via lock is nearby: ⚓ ⌑.

STANDARD TIME (UT)
For Summer Time add ONE
hour in **non-shaded areas**

LONDON BRIDGE   LAT 51°30'N   LONG 0°05'W
TIMES AND HEIGHTS OF HIGH AND LOW WATERS

Dates in red are **SPRINGS**
Dates in blue are NEAPS

YEAR **2022**

JANUARY

Time	m		Time	m
1 0623	1.1	**16** 0040	6.3	
1212	6.9	0700	1.0	
SA 1850	0.8	SU 1300	6.6	
		1915	1.1	
2 0045	6.8	**17** 0124	6.5	
0734	0.8	0749	0.8	
SU 1308	7.2	M 1342	6.7	
● 1956	0.7	○ 2000	1.1	
3 0140	6.9	**18** 0204	6.6	
0835	0.6	0833	0.7	
M 1403	7.3	TU 1421	6.7	
2052	0.7	2041	1.1	
4 0232	6.9	**19** 0240	6.7	
0930	0.4	0915	0.7	
TU 1455	7.4	W 1456	6.8	
2142	0.8	2119	1.1	
5 0321	7.0	**20** 0314	6.7	
1019	0.3	0955	0.6	
W 1545	7.3	TH 1530	6.8	
2227	0.8	2155	1.0	
6 0407	6.9	**21** 0347	6.7	
1104	0.3	1033	0.5	
TH 1633	7.2	F 1604	6.9	
2307	0.9	2231	1.0	
7 0452	6.8	**22** 0420	6.7	
1144	0.4	1107	0.5	
F 1720	7.0	SA 1640	6.8	
2344	1.1	2305	1.0	
8 0536	6.6	**23** 0454	6.6	
1220	0.5	1136	0.6	
SA 1807	6.7	SU 1718	6.7	
		2337	1.1	
9 0020	1.2	**24** 0531	6.6	
0621	6.4	1202	0.7	
SU 1254	0.7	M 1759	6.5	
◑ 1856	6.4			
10 0059	1.4	**25** 0011	1.2	
0709	6.2	0612	6.5	
M 1335	0.9	TU 1234	0.8	
1948	6.2	◑ 1846	6.3	
11 0146	1.6	**26** 0052	1.4	
0804	6.1	0700	6.4	
TU 1425	1.1	W 1317	0.9	
2042	6.0	1942	6.1	
12 0248	1.7	**27** 0144	1.5	
0905	6.0	0802	6.3	
W 1524	1.3	TH 1418	1.1	
2140	5.9	2056	6.0	
13 0359	1.7	**28** 0301	1.6	
1008	6.0	0925	6.2	
TH 1625	1.3	F 1552	1.3	
2244	5.9	2214	6.1	
14 0504	1.5	**29** 0439	1.5	
1113	6.1	1046	6.4	
F 1725	1.3	SA 1716	1.2	
2348	6.1	2328	6.3	
15 0604	1.2	**30** 0606	1.2	
1211	6.3	1158	6.6	
SA 1822	1.2	SU 1838	1.0	
		31 0036	6.5	
		0727	0.8	
		M 1302	6.9	
		1949	0.9	

FEBRUARY

Time	m		Time	m
1 0134	6.7	**16** 0146	6.6	
0830	0.4	0816	0.7	
TU 1358	7.2	W 1403	6.7	
● 2046	0.8	○ 2030	1.1	
2 0225	6.9	**17** 0223	6.7	
0924	0.2	0900	0.5	
W 1448	7.3	TH 1438	6.8	
2135	0.7	2112	1.0	
3 0310	7.0	**18** 0258	6.8	
1011	0.0	0942	0.4	
TH 1534	7.3	F 1512	6.9	
2219	0.7	2151	0.9	
4 0353	7.1	**19** 0330	6.9	
1052	0.0	1020	0.3	
F 1617	7.2	SA 1546	7.0	
2256	0.7	2227	0.8	
5 0432	7.1	**20** 0403	6.9	
1127	0.2	1054	0.3	
SA 1658	7.0	SU 1621	7.0	
2329	0.9	2300	0.9	
6 0510	6.9	**21** 0435	6.9	
1154	0.4	1121	0.4	
SU 1737	6.7	M 1657	6.8	
2356	1.0	2328	1.0	
7 0546	6.7	**22** 0510	6.8	
1215	0.6	1143	0.6	
M 1814	6.4	TU 1735	6.6	
		2357	1.1	
8 0021	1.2	**23** 0550	6.5	
0625	6.5	1211	0.8	
TU 1238	0.9	W 1818	6.3	
◑ 1854	6.1	◑		
9 0052	1.4	**24** 0032	1.3	
0708	6.2	0637	6.5	
W 1311	1.2	TH 1248	1.0	
1940	5.8	1911	6.0	
10 0135	1.7	**25** 0119	1.5	
0805	5.9	0737	6.2	
TH 1402	1.5	F 1343	1.4	
2038	5.6	2024	5.8	
11 0242	1.8	**26** 0234	1.7	
0915	5.7	0903	6.0	
F 1530	1.7	SA 1530	1.6	
2149	5.5	2153	5.7	
12 0418	1.8	**27** 0423	1.6	
1031	5.7	1034	6.1	
SA 1649	1.7	SU 1705	1.5	
2309	5.7	2321	6.0	
13 0529	1.4	**28** 0605	1.2	
1143	6.0	1156	6.4	
SU 1756	1.5	M 1835	1.2	
14 0014	6.1			
0633	1.1			
M 1239	6.3			
1856	1.3			
15 0104	6.4			
0728	0.8			
TU 1324	6.6			
1946	1.2			

MARCH

Time	m		Time	m
1 0033	6.4	**16** 0034	6.3	
0724	0.6	0659	0.8	
TU 1259	6.8	W 1255	6.5	
1940	0.9	1921	1.2	
2 0128	6.7	**17** 0117	6.6	
0821	0.2	0750	0.6	
W 1351	7.1	TH 1334	6.7	
● 2033	0.7	2008	1.1	
3 0213	6.9	**18** 0155	6.8	
0909	0.0	0836	0.5	
TH 1435	7.2	F 1411	6.9	
2119	0.6	○ 2052	1.0	
4 0253	7.1	**19** 0230	6.9	
0952	0.0	0918	0.3	
F 1516	7.2	SA 1447	7.0	
2159	0.6	2133	0.8	
5 0330	7.2	**20** 0305	7.1	
1028	0.1	0957	0.3	
SA 1553	7.2	SU 1523	7.1	
2234	0.7	2211	0.6	
6 0405	7.2	**21** 0339	7.2	
1056	0.3	1031	0.3	
SU 1628	7.0	M 1559	7.1	
2303	0.8	2245	0.8	
7 0439	7.1	**22** 0414	7.1	
1115	0.5	1058	0.4	
M 1700	6.7	TU 1635	6.8	
2325	0.9	2315	0.9	
8 0512	6.9	**23** 0451	7.0	
1130	0.7	1121	0.6	
TU 1731	6.4	W 1713	6.5	
2346	1.1	2343	1.0	
9 0545	6.6	**24** 0532	6.8	
1152	0.9	1150	0.9	
W 1803	6.1	TH 1756	6.2	
10 0013	1.3	**25** 0018	1.1	
0623	6.2	0622	6.5	
TH 1221	1.2	F 1230	1.2	
◑ 1841	5.8	◑ 1851	5.9	
11 0047	1.5	**26** 0106	1.4	
0708	5.8	0727	6.1	
F 1259	1.6	SA 1332	1.6	
1933	5.5	2008	5.6	
12 0137	1.8	**27** 0227	1.6	
0816	5.5	0858	5.9	
SA 1402	2.0	SU 1520	1.8	
2053	5.3	2143	5.6	
13 0322	1.9	**28** 0415	1.5	
0947	5.4	1029	6.1	
SU 1610	2.0	M 1658	1.6	
2226	5.4	2313	5.9	
14 0453	1.6	**29** 0603	1.0	
1108	5.7	1149	6.5	
M 1727	1.7	TU 1821	1.1	
2341	5.8			
15 0600	1.2	**30** 0020	6.4	
1209	6.2	0709	0.4	
TU 1828	1.4	W 1247	6.9	
		1921	0.8	
		31 0111	6.8	
		0800	0.2	
		TH 1334	7.1	
		2010	0.7	

APRIL

Time	m		Time	m
1 0152	7.0	**16** 0119	6.8	
0844	0.1	0801	0.5	
F 1414	7.1	SA 1338	6.9	
● 2053	0.6	○ 2023	1.0	
2 0228	7.1	**17** 0158	7.1	
0921	0.2	0847	0.4	
SA 1450	7.1	SU 1418	7.1	
2131	0.6	2108	0.8	
3 0301	7.2	**18** 0236	7.2	
0952	0.3	0928	0.4	
SU 1523	7.0	M 1457	7.1	
2204	0.6	2149	0.7	
4 0334	7.2	**19** 0315	7.3	
1015	0.5	1004	0.4	
M 1554	6.9	TU 1537	7.0	
2231	0.7	2227	0.7	
5 0407	7.1	**20** 0355	7.3	
1030	0.6	1034	0.5	
TU 1623	6.7	W 1617	6.8	
2252	0.8	2300	0.7	
6 0439	6.9	**21** 0436	7.1	
1050	0.8	1103	0.7	
W 1653	6.4	TH 1658	6.5	
2315	1.0	2332	0.8	
7 0512	6.6	**22** 0522	6.8	
1115	1.0	1138	1.0	
TH 1722	6.2	F 1745	6.1	
2341	1.1			
8 0546	6.2	**23** 0010	0.9	
1142	1.2	0618	6.5	
F 1755	5.9	SA 1224	1.3	
		◑ 1844	5.8	
9 0009	1.3	**24** 0103	1.2	
0626	5.9	0729	6.2	
SA 1214	1.6	SU 1334	1.7	
◑ 1840	5.5	2003	5.7	
10 0049	1.6	**25** 0227	1.3	
0720	5.5	0852	6.1	
SU 1302	2.0	M 1507	1.7	
1946	5.2	2129	5.8	
11 0201	1.8	**26** 0402	1.1	
0850	5.3	1012	6.3	
M 1452	2.2	TU 1634	1.5	
2134	5.2	2249	6.1	
12 0407	1.6	**27** 0535	0.8	
1019	5.6	1126	6.6	
TU 1638	1.9	W 1751	1.1	
2254	5.7	2354	6.5	
13 0515	1.2	**28** 0639	0.5	
1123	6.1	1224	6.8	
W 1743	1.5	TH 1849	0.9	
2352	6.1			
14 0614	0.9	**29** 0043	6.7	
1214	6.5	0728	0.4	
TH 1840	1.2	F 1309	6.9	
		1938	0.8	
15 0038	6.5	**30** 0123	6.9	
0711	0.6	0808	0.4	
F 1257	6.8	SA 1347	6.9	
1934	1.1	● 2021	0.7	

Chart Datum: 3·20 metres below Ordnance Datum (Newlyn). HAT is 7·7 metres above Chart Datum.

》》 **FREE** monthly updates. Register at
www.reedsnauticalalmanac.co.uk 《

E England

STANDARD TIME (UT)
For Summer Time add ONE hour in **non-shaded areas**

LONDON BRIDGE   LAT 51°30'N   LONG 0°05'W
TIMES AND HEIGHTS OF HIGH AND LOW WATERS

Dates in red are **SPRINGS**
Dates in blue are NEAPS

YEAR 2022

MAY

Day	Time	m	Time	m	Time	m	Time	m
1 SU	0158	7.0	0842	0.5	1420	6.9	2058	0.7
2 M	0231	7.1	0909	0.6	1451	6.9	2130	0.6
3 TU	0304	7.2	0929	0.7	1521	6.8	2157	0.7
4 W	0338	7.1	0951	0.8	1551	6.7	2222	0.8
5 TH	0411	6.8	1018	0.8	1621	6.5	2248	0.9
6 F	0444	6.5	1045	1.0	1652	6.2	2316	1.0
7 SA	0518	6.3	1113	1.2	1725	6.0	2344	1.4
8 SU	0558	6.0	1147	1.4	1808	5.7		
9 M ◐	0021	1.3	0648	5.7	1232	1.7	1906	5.5
10 TU	0119	1.5	0756	5.6	1346	1.9	2030	5.4
11 W	0305	1.5	0924	5.7	1527	1.8	2159	5.7
12 TH	0421	1.2	1030	6.1	1642	1.5	2301	6.1
13 F	0521	0.8	1127	6.5	1747	1.3	2354	6.6
14 SA	0619	0.7	1219	6.8	1850	1.1		
15 SU	0041	6.9	0718	0.6	1306	6.9	1950	1.0
16 M ○	0127	7.2	0812	0.5	1352	7.0	2042	0.8
17 TU	0211	7.3	0859	0.5	1436	7.0	2129	0.6
18 W	0256	7.4	0941	0.5	1521	6.9	2212	0.5
19 TH	0341	7.3	1019	0.7	1606	6.7	2251	0.5
20 F	0429	7.1	1055	0.8	1653	6.5	2330	0.6
21 SA	0520	6.9	1137	1.0	1743	6.2		
22 SU ◑	0012	0.7	0619	6.6	1226	1.3	1843	6.0
23 M	0108	0.9	0725	6.4	1330	1.5	1952	6.0
24 TU	0220	0.9	0832	6.3	1445	1.5	2103	6.0
25 W	0333	0.9	0943	6.4	1559	1.4	2212	6.2
26 TH	0444	0.7	1051	6.5	1708	1.2	2315	6.4
27 F	0550	0.7	1151	6.6	1809	1.0		
28 SA	0008	6.6	0643	0.7	1238	6.7	1902	0.9
29 SU	0051	6.8	0724	0.7	1318	6.7	1946	0.8
30 M ●	0129	6.9	0758	0.8	1352	6.7	2025	0.7
31 TU	0205	7.0	0827	0.8	1424	6.8	2100	0.7

JUNE

Day	Time	m	Time	m	Time	m	Time	m
1 W	0240	7.0	0855	0.8	1456	6.7	2131	0.7
2 TH	0316	6.9	0924	0.9	1528	6.6	2201	0.8
3 F	0350	6.8	0955	0.9	1601	6.5	2232	0.8
4 SA	0425	6.6	1027	1.0	1634	6.4	2304	0.9
5 SU	0501	6.4	1100	1.2	1710	6.1	2336	1.0
6 M	0540	6.2	1136	1.3	1752	6.0		
7 TU ◑	0012	1.1	0627	6.1	1220	1.5	1841	5.8
8 W	0101	1.1	0722	6.0	1318	1.6	1942	5.8
9 TH	0206	1.2	0832	6.0	1430	1.6	2101	5.9
10 F	0322	1.0	0944	6.1	1546	1.5	2213	6.2
11 SA	0431	0.8	1047	6.4	1700	1.3	2314	6.6
12 SU	0534	0.7	1145	6.7	1812	1.1		
13 M	0010	6.9	0638	0.6	1240	6.8	1921	0.9
14 TU ○	0102	7.2	0742	0.6	1332	6.9	2021	0.7
15 W	0153	7.3	0838	0.6	1422	6.9	2115	0.5
16 TH	0244	7.4	0928	0.7	1511	6.9	2205	0.4
17 F	0334	7.4	1014	0.7	1600	6.8	2251	0.3
18 SA	0425	7.3	1058	0.7	1648	6.7	2335	0.3
19 SU	0516	7.1	1140	0.9	1738	6.6		
20 M	0019	0.4	0611	6.8	1225	1.1	1831	6.4
21 TU ◑	0106	0.5	0707	6.6	1316	1.2	1928	6.3
22 W	0158	0.6	0806	6.4	1414	1.3	2028	6.3
23 TH	0254	0.7	0906	6.3	1517	1.4	2129	6.3
24 F	0351	0.8	1007	6.3	1621	1.3	2230	6.3
25 SA	0447	0.9	1109	6.3	1722	1.2	2328	6.4
26 SU	0543	1.0	1204	6.4	1821	1.0		
27 M	0020	6.6	0636	1.0	1250	6.5	1912	0.8
28 TU	0105	6.7	0722	1.0	1330	6.6	1958	0.7
29 W ●	0147	6.8	0803	1.0	1408	6.6	2038	0.7
30 TH	0226	6.8	0840	1.0	1443	6.6	2116	0.7

JULY

Day	Time	m	Time	m	Time	m	Time	m
1 F	0302	6.8	0914	1.0	1517	6.6	2153	0.6
2 SA	0337	6.7	0948	1.0	1551	6.6	2228	0.6
3 SU	0411	6.7	1024	1.0	1624	6.5	2303	0.6
4 M	0446	6.6	1100	1.1	1659	6.4	2335	0.7
5 TU	0524	6.5	1135	1.2	1736	6.3		
6 W	0006	0.8	0605	6.3	1211	1.3	1818	6.2
7 TH ◑	0041	0.9	0651	6.2	1254	1.4	1906	6.1
8 F	0125	0.9	0747	6.1	1348	1.5	2007	6.1
9 SA	0225	1.0	0859	6.1	1458	1.5	2126	6.2
10 SU	0344	1.0	1011	6.2	1624	1.4	2239	6.5
11 M	0500	0.9	1118	6.4	1745	1.1	2345	6.8
12 TU	0611	0.8	1221	6.6	1900	0.8		
13 W ○	0045	7.0	0724	0.8	1318	6.8	2009	0.6
14 TH	0142	7.2	0829	0.7	1412	6.9	2109	0.3
15 F	0235	7.4	0924	0.7	1503	7.0	2202	0.1
16 SA	0326	7.4	1013	0.7	1550	7.0	2250	0.0
17 SU	0415	7.4	1056	0.7	1636	7.0	2332	0.0
18 M	0503	7.2	1136	0.7	1720	6.9		
19 TU	0009	0.1	0551	7.0	1212	0.9	1806	6.8
20 W ◑	0044	0.3	0639	6.7	1251	1.1	1852	6.6
21 TH	0121	0.6	0728	6.4	1333	1.3	1944	6.4
22 F	0204	0.9	0820	6.2	1426	1.4	2041	6.2
23 SA	0257	1.2	0916	6.0	1530	1.5	2142	6.1
24 SU	0357	1.2	1019	5.9	1637	1.4	2248	6.2
25 M	0459	1.3	1128	6.0	1742	1.2	2352	6.3
26 TU	0602	1.2	1226	6.3	1843	0.9		
27 W	0046	6.6	0701	1.1	1313	6.5	1937	0.7
28 TH ●	0133	6.7	0750	1.1	1354	6.6	2023	0.6
29 F	0213	6.8	0832	1.1	1432	6.7	2104	0.6
30 SA	0250	6.8	0911	1.1	1506	6.7	2143	0.5
31 SU	0323	6.8	0948	1.0	1538	6.7	2221	0.4

AUGUST

Day	Time	m	Time	m	Time	m	Time	m
1 M	0355	6.8	1023	0.9	1609	6.7	2255	0.4
2 TU	0427	6.8	1057	1.0	1641	6.6	2325	0.5
3 W	0501	6.7	1127	1.1	1714	6.5	2350	0.7
4 TH	0538	6.5	1157	1.2	1751	6.4		
5 F ◐	0015	0.8	0619	6.3	1230	1.4	1834	6.4
6 SA	0049	0.9	0708	6.1	1314	1.5	1928	6.2
7 SU	0137	1.1	0814	5.9	1417	1.6	2043	6.1
8 M	0259	1.3	0938	5.9	1557	1.6	2212	6.2
9 TU	0438	1.3	1056	6.1	1727	1.3	2328	6.5
10 W	0559	1.1	1209	6.4	1854	0.8		
11 TH	0036	6.9	0720	0.9	1310	6.7	2006	0.4
12 F ○	0135	7.2	0823	0.7	1403	6.9	2103	0.1
13 SA	0226	7.4	0916	0.6	1450	7.1	2152	-0.1
14 SU	0313	7.4	1002	0.6	1533	7.2	2236	-0.2
15 M	0358	7.4	1043	0.6	1614	7.2	2313	-0.1
16 TU	0440	7.2	1118	0.7	1653	7.1	2344	0.2
17 W	0521	7.0	1149	0.8	1731	6.9		
18 TH	0008	0.5	0600	6.6	1217	1.1	1811	6.7
19 F ◑	0031	0.8	0639	6.3	1246	1.3	1854	6.4
20 SA	0100	1.1	0723	5.9	1325	1.5	1946	6.0
21 SU	0145	1.5	0817	5.7	1427	1.7	2053	5.8
22 M	0304	1.7	0927	5.5	1555	1.7	2210	5.8
23 TU	0427	1.7	1050	5.7	1710	1.4	2326	6.0
24 W	0539	1.5	1200	6.0	1817	1.0		
25 TH	0025	6.4	0642	1.3	1250	6.4	1914	0.8
26 F	0112	6.6	0733	1.1	1333	6.6	2002	0.6
27 SA ●	0152	6.8	0817	1.1	1410	6.7	2044	0.5
28 SU	0227	6.8	0857	1.1	1444	6.8	2124	0.4
29 M	0259	6.9	0935	1.0	1515	6.9	2201	0.4
30 TU	0330	6.9	1011	0.9	1545	6.9	2235	0.4
31 W	0402	6.9	1044	1.0	1616	6.9	2303	0.5

Chart Datum: 3·20 metres below Ordnance Datum (Newlyn). HAT is 7·7 metres above Chart Datum.

》》 FREE monthly updates. Register at 《
www.reedsnauticalalmanac.co.uk

STANDARD TIME (UT)
For Summer Time add ONE hour in **non-shaded areas**

LONDON BRIDGE   LAT 51°30′N   LONG 0°05′W
TIMES AND HEIGHTS OF HIGH AND LOW WATERS

Dates in red are SPRINGS
Dates in blue are NEAPS

YEAR 2022

SEPTEMBER

Day	Time / m		Day	Time / m
1	0435 6.7 / 1113 1.1 / TH 1649 6.8 / 2324 0.7		**16**	0516 6.5 / 1139 1.1 / F 1731 6.7 / 2341 1.0
2	0510 6.5 / 1138 1.2 / F 1725 6.6 / 2346 0.9		**17**	0548 6.2 / 1203 1.3 / SA 1808 6.3 ☽
3	0549 6.2 / 1208 1.4 / SA 1808 6.5 ☽		**18**	0006 1.3 / 0624 5.8 / SU 1235 1.5 / 1854 5.9
4	0017 1.1 / 0636 6.0 / SU 1247 1.5 / 1903 6.2		**19**	0042 1.7 / 0711 5.5 / M 1322 1.8 / 1958 5.5
5	0103 1.4 / 0739 5.7 / M 1349 1.7 / 2019 6.0		**20**	0144 2.1 / 0827 5.2 / TU 1506 2.0 / 2128 5.4
6	0231 1.8 / 0913 5.6 / TU 1542 1.7 / 2157 6.0		**21**	0351 2.2 / 1007 5.3 / W 1637 1.6 / 2251 5.7
7	0426 1.7 / 1043 5.8 / W 1724 1.3 / 2321 6.4		**22**	0512 1.8 / 1124 5.7 / TH 1743 1.2 / 2354 6.2
8	0558 1.3 / 1202 6.2 / TH 1854 0.7		**23**	0612 1.5 / 1218 6.2 / F 1840 0.8
9	0030 6.8 / 0713 0.9 / F 1300 6.7 / 1956 0.2		**24**	0041 6.5 / 0704 1.2 / SA 1301 6.5 / 1930 0.7
10	0125 7.2 / 0809 0.7 / SA 1348 7.0 / ○ 2047 -0.1		**25**	0120 6.7 / 0749 1.1 / SU 1338 6.7 / ● 2014 0.6
11	0211 7.3 / 0858 0.6 / SU 1430 7.1 / 2131 -0.1		**26**	0154 6.8 / 0831 1.1 / M 1412 6.9 / 2055 0.5
12	0254 7.3 / 0941 0.6 / M 1508 7.3 / 2210 0.0		**27**	0227 6.9 / 0911 1.0 / TU 1444 7.0 / 2133 0.5
13	0333 7.3 / 1019 0.6 / TU 1545 7.3 / 2242 0.2		**28**	0300 7.0 / 0949 0.9 / W 1517 7.1 / 2207 0.5
14	0410 7.1 / 1052 0.7 / W 1620 7.2 / 2307 0.5		**29**	0335 6.9 / 1024 0.9 / TH 1550 7.1 / 2234 0.6
15	0444 6.9 / 1118 0.9 / TH 1655 7.0 / 2322 0.7		**30**	0410 6.8 / 1054 1.0 / F 1626 7.0 / 2255 0.8

OCTOBER

Day	Time / m		Day	Time / m
1	0445 6.5 / 1120 1.1 / SA 1705 6.8 / 2322 1.0		**16**	0505 6.2 / 1128 1.2 / SU 1731 6.3 / 2326 1.4
2	0524 6.2 / 1151 1.2 / SU 1751 6.5 / 2358 1.3		**17**	0535 5.9 / 1155 1.4 / M 1810 5.9 / ☽ 2356 1.7
3	0613 5.9 / 1233 1.4 / M 1849 6.2 ☽		**18**	0615 5.5 / 1232 1.7 / TU 1902 5.5
4	0048 1.7 / 0720 5.6 / TU 1339 1.6 / 2014 5.9		**19**	0040 2.1 / 0716 5.2 / W 1342 2.0 / 2028 5.3
5	0232 2.0 / 0859 5.5 / W 1536 1.6 / 2149 6.1		**20**	0226 2.4 / 0907 5.1 / TH 1551 1.8 / 2200 5.5
6	0416 1.8 / 1032 5.8 / TH 1721 1.1 / 2311 6.5		**21**	0423 2.1 / 1033 5.5 / F 1657 1.4 / 2304 6.0
7	0545 1.3 / 1146 6.3 / F 1837 0.5		**22**	0526 1.7 / 1132 6.0 / SA 1753 1.0 / 2355 6.4
8	0016 6.9 / 0652 1.0 / SA 1241 6.7 / 1933 0.2		**23**	0620 1.4 / 1219 6.4 / SU 1845 0.8
9	0107 7.1 / 0744 0.7 / SU 1325 7.0 / ○ 2019 0.1		**24**	0037 6.7 / 0710 1.3 / M 1258 6.7 / 1934 0.7
10	0149 7.2 / 0831 0.7 / M 1404 7.1 / 2100 0.2		**25**	0116 6.8 / 0757 1.1 / TU 1335 6.9 / ● 2018 0.6
11	0227 7.2 / 0912 0.6 / TU 1439 7.3 / 2135 0.3		**26**	0154 7.0 / 0842 1.0 / W 1412 7.1 / 2059 0.6
12	0302 7.1 / 0949 0.7 / W 1513 7.3 / 2202 0.5		**27**	0232 7.0 / 0924 0.9 / TH 1450 7.2 / 2135 0.7
13	0335 7.0 / 1019 0.7 / TH 1548 7.3 / 2219 0.7		**28**	0311 6.9 / 1002 0.9 / F 1529 7.2 / 2206 0.8
14	0406 6.8 / 1042 0.9 / F 1622 7.0 / 2236 0.9		**29**	0349 6.8 / 1036 0.9 / SA 1609 7.0 / 2234 0.9
15	0436 6.5 / 1103 1.1 / SA 1656 6.7 / 2259 1.1		**30**	0428 6.5 / 1108 0.9 / SU 1653 6.9 / 2309 1.1
			31	0511 6.2 / 1144 1.1 / M 1744 6.5 / 2352 1.4

NOVEMBER

Day	Time / m		Day	Time / m
1	0604 5.9 / 1231 1.2 / TU 1848 6.2 / ☽		**16**	0544 5.8 / 1203 1.4 / W 1828 5.8 ☽
2	0052 1.8 / 0716 5.6 / W 1346 1.4 / 2012 6.1		**17**	0010 1.9 / 0636 5.5 / TH 1254 1.6 / 1928 5.6
3	0226 1.9 / 0847 5.7 / TH 1525 1.3 / 2133 6.2		**18**	0113 2.1 / 0746 5.3 / F 1431 1.7 / 2052 5.6
4	0355 1.7 / 1008 6.0 / F 1653 0.9 / 2247 6.5		**19**	0250 2.2 / 0927 5.5 / SA 1557 1.4 / 2204 5.9
5	0514 1.1 / 1117 6.3 / SA 1805 0.6 / 2351 6.8		**20**	0414 1.9 / 1035 5.9 / SU 1657 1.1 / 2301 6.3
6	0619 1.1 / 1213 6.7 / SU 1859 0.4		**21**	0522 1.6 / 1129 6.3 / M 1752 0.9 / 2353 6.6
7	0041 6.9 / 0713 0.9 / M 1257 6.9 / 1944 0.4		**22**	0622 1.4 / 1217 6.7 / TU 1846 0.8
8	0123 7.0 / 0759 0.8 / TU 1334 7.0 / ○ 2022 0.6		**23**	0041 6.6 / 0720 1.2 / W 1302 7.0 / ● 1939 0.7
9	0159 7.0 / 0840 0.7 / W 1409 7.2 / 2053 0.7		**24**	0126 6.9 / 0813 1.0 / TH 1346 7.2 / 2027 0.7
10	0231 6.9 / 0915 0.7 / TH 1444 7.2 / 2115 0.8		**25**	0211 6.9 / 0901 0.9 / F 1430 7.3 / 2111 0.8
11	0302 6.9 / 0945 0.8 / F 1519 7.1 / 2134 0.9		**26**	0255 6.9 / 0946 0.7 / SA 1515 7.3 / 2151 0.9
12	0333 6.7 / 1010 0.9 / SA 1554 6.9 / 2200 1.0		**27**	0339 6.7 / 1028 0.7 / SU 1602 7.2 / 2230 1.0
13	0404 6.5 / 1034 1.0 / SU 1629 6.6 / 2229 1.2		**28**	0424 6.5 / 1108 0.7 / M 1652 7.0 / 2312 1.1
14	0434 6.3 / 1101 1.1 / M 1703 6.3 / 2258 1.4		**29**	0512 6.3 / 1150 0.8 / TU 1746 6.7
15	0505 6.0 / 1130 1.3 / TU 1741 6.0 / 2329 1.6		**30**	0000 1.3 / 0606 6.1 / W 1242 0.9 / ☽ 1849 6.5

DECEMBER

Day	Time / m		Day	Time / m
1	0058 1.5 / 0711 6.0 / TH 1349 1.0 / 1958 6.4		**16**	0613 5.9 / 1235 1.2 / F 1852 6.0 ☽
2	0209 1.6 / 0824 6.0 / F 1500 0.9 / 2107 6.4		**17**	0046 1.7 / 0705 5.8 / SA 1326 1.3 / 1951 5.9
3	0323 1.6 / 0934 6.2 / SA 1608 0.9 / 2214 6.5		**18**	0146 1.8 / 0810 5.7 / SU 1432 1.3 / 2104 5.9
4	0433 1.4 / 1039 6.3 / SU 1715 0.8 / 2317 6.6		**19**	0257 1.8 / 0933 5.9 / M 1551 1.2 / 2213 6.1
5	0539 1.2 / 1138 6.5 / M 1814 0.8		**20**	0420 1.7 / 1042 6.2 / TU 1701 1.0 / 2315 6.4
6	0011 6.6 / 0637 1.0 / TU 1226 6.7 / 1902 0.8		**21**	0539 1.4 / 1141 6.6 / W 1804 0.9
7	0056 6.7 / 0726 0.9 / W 1308 6.8 / 1942 0.9		**22**	0012 6.7 / 0648 1.1 / TH 1236 6.9 / 1907 0.9
8	0134 6.7 / 0809 0.8 / TH 1346 6.9 / ○ 2014 1.0		**23**	0106 6.9 / 0750 0.9 / F 1328 7.2 / ● 2007 0.8
9	0208 6.7 / 0847 0.8 / F 1423 7.0 / 2042 1.0		**24**	0157 6.9 / 0848 0.7 / SA 1419 7.3 / 2101 0.8
10	0240 6.7 / 0920 0.8 / SA 1500 6.9 / 2109 1.1		**25**	0246 6.9 / 0941 0.5 / SU 1509 7.3 / 2151 0.8
11	0313 6.6 / 0950 0.9 / SU 1535 6.8 / 2140 1.1		**26**	0335 6.9 / 1030 0.4 / M 1559 7.3 / 2237 0.9
12	0346 6.5 / 1019 0.9 / M 1610 6.6 / 2212 1.2		**27**	0422 6.8 / 1116 0.3 / TU 1649 7.2 / 2320 0.9
13	0418 6.4 / 1050 1.0 / TU 1645 6.4 / 2246 1.3		**28**	0509 6.7 / 1159 0.3 / W 1741 7.0
14	0452 6.2 / 1122 1.1 / W 1722 6.3 / 2321 1.4		**29**	0003 1.0 / 0559 6.6 / TH 1243 0.4 / 1835 6.8
15	0529 6.1 / 1155 1.1 / TH 1804 6.1 / 2359 1.6		**30**	0050 1.2 / 0652 6.5 / F 1330 0.6 / ☽ 1933 6.5
			31	0142 1.3 / 0751 6.4 / SA 1422 0.8 / 2032 6.4

Chart Datum: 3·20 metres below Ordnance Datum (Newlyn). HAT is 7·7 metres above Chart Datum.

》》FREE monthly updates. Register at 《
www.reedsnauticalalmanac.co.uk

E England

1.13 SOUTHEND-ON-SEA/LEIGH-ON-SEA

Essex 51°31'·07N 00°42'·57E ✻✻⌂✿✿

CHARTS AC 5606, 1183, 1185; Imray C1, C2, Y18, 2100

TIDES +0125 Dover; ML 3·0; Duration 0610

Standard Port SHEERNESS (←—)

Times				Height (metres)			
High Water		Low Water		MHWS	MHWN	MLWN	MLWS
0200	0800	0200	0700	5·8	4·7	1·5	0·6
1400	2000	1400	1900				
Differences SOUTHEND-ON-SEA							
−0005	−0005	−0005	−0005	+0·1	0·0	−0·1	−0·1
CORYTON							
+0005	+0010	+0010	+0010	+0·4	+0·3	0·0	0·0

SHELTER The whole area dries soon after half ebb, except Ray Gut (0·4–4·8m) which leads to Leigh Creek and Hadleigh Ray, either side of Two Tree Island, thence to Benfleet Creek where the limit of W navigation is the Tidal Barrier just above Benfleet YC; all are buoyed, but echo-sounder is essential. Craft can take the ground alongside Bell Wharf or Victoria Wharf. It is also possible to secure at the end of Southend Pier to collect stores, ⚓. NOTE: Southend-on-Sea and Leigh-on-Sea are both part of the lower PLA Area and an 8kn speed limit is enforced in inshore areas.

NAVIGATION WPT 51°31'·07N 00°42'·57E, Leigh SHM buoy, at ent to Ray Gut; Lateral marks guard the channel to the Ray, the sands move frequently as do the buoys. The appr to Old Leigh is also buoyed but care needs to be taken as they too move often. Appr from Shoeburyness, keep outside the W Shoebury SHM buoy.

Beware some 300 small boat moorings 4M either side of Southend Pier. Speed limit in Canvey Island/Hadleigh Ray areas is 8kn.

LIGHTS AND MARKS See chartlet. Ray channel and approach to Old Leigh are marked; buoys move frequently.

COMMUNICATIONS (Code 01702) Essex Police Marine Section (01268) 775533; Dr 225500; Ⓗ 348911. HM 215620; HM Leigh-on-Sea 710561.

Port Control London: *London VTS* VHF Ch 68 inward from Sea Reach No 4, *London VTS* VHF Ch 69 seaward from Sea Reach No 4.

FACILITIES
SOUTHEND-ON-SEA: Southend Pier ☎215620, ⌓ (craft to be attended), £20<40'>£40<50'>£50/night (short stay free) ⚓⛟.
Alexandra YC ☎340363, ⚓🏠; **Thorpe Bay YC** ☎587563, ⛟⚓✕🏠; **Thames Estuary YC** ☎345967; **Halfway YC** ☎582025, book 1⌂⚓; **Town** Ⓔ 🏧 ACA ✉ Ⓑ 🛒 ✕ 🏠 ⚞ ✈.

LEIGH-ON-SEA: Essex YC ☎478404, ⚓🏠; **Leigh on Sea SC** ☎476788, ⚓🏠; **Bell Wharf** ⌓ 24hrs free then £11/night; **Victoria Wharf** ⌓ 24hrs free then £11/night, 🛢⛽⛟ (Two Tree Is HW±2½).
Town 🔧🔨 🏧 ⛺ 🚮 🏧.

CANVEY ISLAND: (Code 01268) Access via drying channels.
Island YC ☎510360, ⌓ (max 9m), dries; **Benfleet YC** (on S side of Benfleet Creek on Canvey Island) ☎792278, ⚓⛟🛢👤 (by day), **Services** 🛢🔧🔨 🏧 🚮 🏧 🛒 🗑 🏠.

WORLD CLASS SKIPPERS WANTED

NO PRESSURE

Sir Robin Knox-Johnston
Founder of the Clipper Round the World Yacht Race

Join the elite and take on the world's longest yacht race, crewed exclusively by novice crew embarking on the race of their lives.

Clipper Race Skippers are exceptional. These men and women have the fortitude to take on the toughest of mental challenges, and the physical endurance to successfully lead a team through Mother Nature's extreme environments on a 40,000 mile lap around the globe.

We are recruiting experienced professional Skippers for the next edition of the Clipper Race. To qualify you must hold a valid Yachtmaster Ocean certificate [commercial endorsed] or International Yacht Training Master of Yachts.

↘ APPLY NOW

clipperroundtheworld.com/careers
raceskipper@clipper-ventures.com
+44 (0) 2392 526000

CLIPPER | **ROUND THE WORLD**

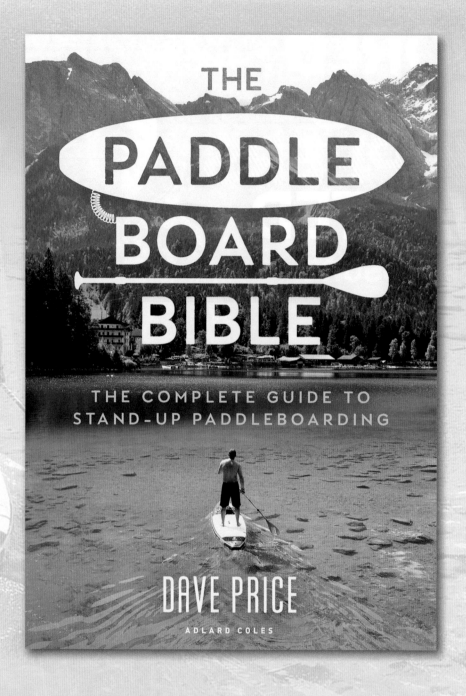

THE
PADDLE
BOARD
BIBLE

THE COMPLETE GUIDE TO
STAND-UP PADDLEBOARDING

DAVE PRICE

ADLARD COLES

The complete guide
to the world's fastest growing watersport:
stand-up paddleboarding

1.14 RIVER ROACH/HAVENGORE

Essex **51°36′·98N 00°52′·14E** (Branklet SPM buoy), R Roach ❀❀❀⚓❁❁❁. **51°33′·62N 00°50′·52E**, Havengore Bridge ❀⚓❁

CHARTS AC 5607, 1185, 3750; Imray C1, Y17, 2100, 2000

TIDES +0110 Dover; ML 2·7; Duration 0615

Standard Port WALTON-ON-THE-NAZE (→)

Times				Height (metres)			
High Water		Low Water		MHWS	MHWN	MLWN	MLWS
0000	0600	0500	1100	4·2	3·4	1·1	0·4
1200	1800	1700	2300				
Differences ROCHFORD							
+0050	+0040	DR	DR	–0·8	–1·1	DR	DR

SHELTER Good. The Roach gives sheltered sailing and access to a network of secluded creeks, including Havengore (the 'backdoor' from the Crouch to the Thames Estuary). No � available in the area. ⚓s behind sea-walls can be found for all winds at: Quay Reach (often more protected than the Crouch), Paglesham Reach, West Reach, Barling Reach and Yokes Fleet. An ⚓ light is essential due to freighters H24. Speed limit 8kn. Crouch Hbr Authority controls R Roach and Crouch, out to Foulness Pt.

NAVIGATION Normal access H24 to the Roach is from R Crouch; the ent between Branklet buoy and Nase Pt is narrowed by mudbanks. Unlit buoys upriver to Barling Ness, above which few boats go. To exit at Havengore Creek, appr via Middleway and Narrow Cuts to reach the bridge before HW.

Entry via **Havengore Creek** is possible in good weather, with great care and adequate rise of tide (max draught 1·5m at HW sp). Shoeburyness Range is usually active Mon-Fri 0600-1700LT; give 24hrs notice to Range Officer by ☎. Subsequent clearance on VHF by Havengore lifting bridge (☎HW±2, HJ); no passage unless bridge raised. Least water is over the shifting bar, just inside creek ent. From the S, cross Maplin Sands at HW –1 from S Shoebury SHM buoy, leaving Pisces wreck (conspic, 1M from ent) to port.

LIGHTS AND MARKS Unlit, but night entry to R Roach may be possible.

COMMUNICATIONS (Code 01702 Southend) Dr 218678. Crouch HM (01621) 783602; Range Officer 383211; Havengore Br 383436; Swing Br to Potton Island 219491.

VHF Ch 72 16 is worked by Range Officer (*Shoe Base*) (HO); Radar Control (*Shoe Radar*) (HO); and Bridge keeper (*Shoe Bridge*) (HW±2 by day). Radar guidance may be available.

FACILITIES Paglesham (East End) ⊼ ⚓ ♠ ⚒ ⚓ ⑤ (at ⨄) ⨄ ◻.
Gt Wakering ♠ ⊼ ⚓ ⚓ ⚒ ⚓ ⑤ ◻ ⚓ (from ⨄ at Rochford)
Wakering YC ☎530926, ⚓⚓ ◻. **Towns** Gt Wakering & Rochford; 🛒 ✕ ◻ ✉ (Great Wakering and Barling); most facilities, Ⓑ and ⚍ in Rochford and Shoeburyness, ✈ (Southend).

1.15 BURNHAM-ON-CROUCH

Essex **51°37'·50N 00°48'·23E** (Yacht Hbr) ✿✿✿⚓⚓⚓✿✿

CHARTS AC 5607, 1183, 1975, 3750; Imray C1, Y17, 2100, 2000

TIDES +0115 Dover; ML 2·5; Duration 0610

Standard Port WALTON-ON-THE-NAZE (——)

Times				Height (metres)			
High Water		Low Water		MHWS	MHWN	MLWN	MLWS
0000	0600	0500	1100	4·2	3·4	1·1	0·4
1200	1800	1700	2300				
Differences WHITAKER BEACON							
+0022	+0024	+0033	+0027	+0·6	+0·5	+0·2	+0·1
HOLLIWELL POINT							
+0034	+0037	+0100	+0037	+1·1	+0·9	+0·3	+0·1
NORTH FAMBRIDGE							
+0115	+0050	+0130	+0100	+1·1	+0·8	0·0	−0·1
HULLBRIDGE							
+0115	+0050	+0135	+0105	+1·1	+0·8	0·0	−0·1
BATTLESBRIDGE							
+0120	+0110	DR	DR	−1·8	−2·0	DR	DR

SHELTER River is exposed to most winds. Cliff Reach (off W edge of lower chartlet) is sheltered from SW'lies. ⚓ prohib in fairway but possible just E or W of the moorings.

NAVIGATION Appr from East Swin or the Wallet via Swin Spitway SWM / Whitaker ECM, into the well-marked Whitaker Channel.

Near Sunken Buxey seas can be hazardous with strong wind over tide. Ray Sand Chan (dries 1·7m), usable on the tide by shoal draught boats as a short cut from/to the Blackwater. Shoeburyness Artillery ranges lie E and S of Foulness Pt, clear of fairway. The buoyed chan leads either side of shoal patch 0·7 marked by Sunken Buxey NCM and Buxey No 1 SCM. R Crouch is navigable to Battlesbridge, 10M beyond Burnham. No landing on Foulness or Bridgemarsh Is. Wallasea Wetlands are being developed; keep well clear of ships using unloading pontoon at Ringwood Pt. ⚓ in swinging area between Horse Shoal and No 3 SHM buoy. Work is expected to be complete by 2019.

LIGHTS AND MARKS There are few landmarks to assist entry, but Whitaker Chan, Swallow Tail Bank and the river are well lit/buoyed to 0·5M W of Essex Marina. From Buxey No2 steer 240° in buoyed channel past Foulness Pt, N of Crouch NCM into the river. There is a 1·3M unlit gap between Inner Crouch SWM lit buoy, and the entrance to R Roach, which is marked by Pinto PHM and Branklet PCM en-route Horse Shoal NCM.

COMMUNICATIONS (Code 01621 Maldon) Dr 782054. HM 783602. VHF Ch 80 for: Crouch HM Launch (0900-1700LT, w/e); Essex Marina; Burnham Yacht Harbour; W Wick Marina (1000-1700), also Ch M.

FACILITIES There are five marinas or yacht hbrs. Speed limit 8kn.

BURNHAM, Burnham Yacht Hbr ☎782150, access H24, some ⚓s, ⚓ 350⚓ £2·50 ⚡+£2, ⚒🛒🚿🔧⚓ ⚓🗲🛢(30t) ✗ ⚓.

Royal Corinthian YC ☎782105, ⚓⚓⚓⚓✗⚓.

Royal Burnham YC ☎782044, ⚓✗⚓.

Crouch YC ☎782252,⚓⚓⚓🛢⚓🔧⚓🗲🛒⚓🛢(15t)⚓ ACA ✗⚓. **Town** ✉Ⓑ🛒✗⚓⚡✈ (Southend).

ALTHORNE, Bridgemarsh Marina ☎740414, ⚓ ⚓£20/craft/night 🛢⚓🔧⚓🛒.

WALLASEA ISLAND, Essex Marina ☎(01702) 258531, ⚓ 400⚓ £2·13, ⚓🛢LPG⚓🔧⚓🗲⚓⚓🛢(40t)⚓(13t)⚓✗⚓. Ferry to Burnham Hard at w/ends in season, ☎07704 060482. **Essex YC** ACA.

FAMBRIDGE, Fambridge Yacht Haven ⚓ www.yachthavens. com ☎740370; Min 1m depth in approach, Stow Cr marked by bn Q(4)Y 8s and ldg bns (F W lts) in line 356°; pontoon Fl(3) G 4s. ⚓s £1·50, ⚓ (£6-£15) 170⚓+⚓ £2·80, short stay <3hrs<15m £5, ⚓ 🛢⚓🔧⚓🗲 (£6-£15) 🛒🛢(40t)(25t)(20t) ⚓(30t) ⚓🛒 YC ⚓ wi-fi.

Fambridge Yacht Station ⚓ pontoon £2/m, ⚓⚡.

Brandy Hole Yacht Stn ☎(01702) 230248, Access via drying channel ⚓⚓⚓ 120⚓🛢⚓🔧⚓🛒⚓.

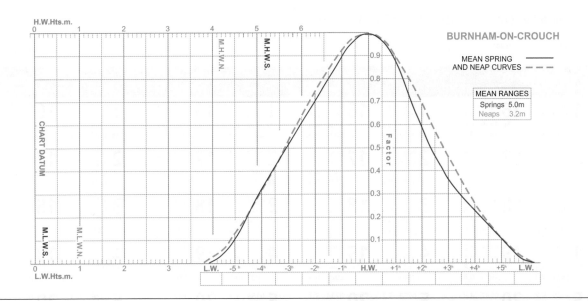

BURNHAM-ON-CROUCH

MEAN SPRING
AND NEAP CURVES

MEAN RANGES	
Springs	5.0m
Neaps	3.2m

BURNHAM-ON-CROUCH LAT 51°37'N LONG 0°48'E
TIMES AND HEIGHTS OF HIGH AND LOW WATERS

STANDARD TIME (UT)
For Summer Time add ONE hour in **non-shaded areas**

Dates in red are SPRINGS
Dates in blue are NEAPS

YEAR 2022

JANUARY

Time	m		Time	m
1 SA 0451 / 1053 / 1722 / 2323	0.8 / 4.9 / 0.5 / 5.0	**16** SU 0525 / 1135 / 1739 / 2354	0.8 / 4.5 / 0.9 / 4.7	
2 SU 0550 / 1149 / 1814 ●	0.6 / 5.1 / 0.4	**17** M 0610 / 1218 / 1817 ○	0.6 / 4.6 / 0.9	
3 M 0014 / 0645 / 1241 / 1904	5.2 / 0.3 / 5.3 / 0.3	**18** TU 0032 / 0650 / 1255 / 1851	4.8 / 0.5 / 4.7 / 0.8	
4 TU 0103 / 0736 / 1332 / 1951	5.2 / 0.1 / 5.4 / 0.4	**19** W 0106 / 0727 / 1330 / 1923	4.8 / 0.4 / 4.8 / 0.8	
5 W 0149 / 0826 / 1422 / 2038	5.2 / 0.0 / 5.4 / 0.4	**20** TH 0137 / 0802 / 1404 / 1956	4.8 / 0.4 / 4.8 / 0.7	
6 TH 0235 / 0915 / 1511 / 2123	5.1 / -0.1 / 5.3 / 0.5	**21** F 0210 / 0838 / 1440 / 2033	4.9 / 0.4 / 4.9 / 0.7	
7 F 0320 / 1003 / 1600 / 2209	5.0 / 0.0 / 5.1 / 0.7	**22** SA 0246 / 0916 / 1520 / 2112	4.9 / 0.4 / 4.9 / 0.7	
8 SA 0405 / 1052 / 1651 / 2256	4.8 / 0.1 / 4.8 / 0.8	**23** SU 0325 / 0957 / 1603 / 2153	4.9 / 0.4 / 4.9 / 0.8	
9 SU 0452 / 1141 / 1743 / ☽2345	4.6 / 0.4 / 4.6 / 1.0	**24** M 0409 / 1041 / 1650 / 2237	4.8 / 0.5 / 4.8 / 0.9	
10 M 0544 / 1231 / 1838	4.4 / 0.5 / 4.4	**25** TU 0455 / 1128 / 1741 / ☽2325	4.7 / 0.7 / 4.6 / 1.1	
11 TU 0037 / 0643 / 1324 / 1937	1.1 / 4.2 / 0.7 / 4.3	**26** W 0547 / 1222 / 1837	4.5 / 0.8 / 4.5	
12 W 0133 / 0748 / 1419 / 2036	1.1 / 4.1 / 0.8 / 4.3	**27** TH 0021 / 0648 / 1328 / 1942	1.2 / 4.3 / 0.9 / 4.3	
13 TH 0233 / 0854 / 1515 / 2132	1.1 / 4.2 / 0.9 / 4.3	**28** F 0136 / 0803 / 1450 / 2056	1.3 / 4.2 / 1.0 / 4.3	
14 F 0335 / 0954 / 1608 / 2224	1.0 / 4.3 / 0.9 / 4.5	**29** SA 0318 / 0927 / 1610 / 2206	1.2 / 4.3 / 0.8 / 4.5	
15 SA 0433 / 1047 / 1656 / 2311	0.9 / 4.4 / 0.9 / 4.6	**30** SU 0443 / 1038 / 1714 / 2308	0.9 / 4.6 / 0.6 / 4.7	
		31 M 0546 / 1139 / 1808	0.6 / 5.0 / 0.4	

FEBRUARY

Time	m		Time	m
1 TU 0001 / 0640 / 1232 / 1857 ●	5.0 / 0.1 / 5.2 / 0.3	**16** W 0015 / 0635 / 1239 / 1844 ○	4.8 / 0.4 / 4.8 / 0.6	
2 W 0051 / 0730 / 1322 / 1942	5.2 / -0.2 / 5.4 / 0.2	**17** TH 0053 / 0715 / 1316 / 1919	4.9 / 0.2 / 4.9 / 0.6	
3 TH 0136 / 0816 / 1409 / 2024	5.3 / -0.3 / 5.4 / 0.2	**18** F 0127 / 0752 / 1351 / 1953	5.0 / 0.1 / 5.0 / 0.5	
4 F 0218 / 0900 / 1453 / 2104	5.3 / -0.2 / 5.3 / 0.3	**19** SA 0200 / 0827 / 1426 / 2026	5.0 / 0.1 / 5.1 / 0.5	
5 SA 0258 / 0941 / 1536 / 2143	5.2 / -0.2 / 5.1 / 0.4	**20** SU 0234 / 0903 / 1504 / 2059	5.1 / 0.2 / 5.1 / 0.5	
6 SU 0336 / 1021 / 1617 / 2220	5.0 / 0.0 / 4.8 / 0.6	**21** M 0310 / 0938 / 1544 / 2134	5.0 / 0.2 / 5.0 / 0.6	
7 M 0415 / 1059 / 1659 / 2259	4.8 / 0.3 / 4.5 / 0.8	**22** TU 0349 / 1014 / 1626 / 2211	5.0 / 0.4 / 4.9 / 0.7	
8 TU 0456 / 1138 / 1743 / ☽2341	4.6 / 0.6 / 4.2 / 1.0	**23** W 0433 / 1053 / 1713 / 2253	4.8 / 0.6 / 4.6 / 0.8	
9 W 0542 / 1138 / 1832	4.3 / 0.8 / 4.0	**24** TH 0522 / 1138 / 1804 / 2344	4.6 / 0.8 / 4.3 / 1.0	
10 TH 0028 / 0637 / 1308 / 1932	1.1 / 4.0 / 1.0 / 3.9	**25** F 0619 / 1236 / 1906	4.3 / 1.1 / 4.1	
11 F 0123 / 0751 / 1406 / 2041	1.2 / 3.8 / 1.2 / 3.9	**26** SA 0048 / 0736 / 1419 / 2030	1.2 / 4.1 / 1.2 / 3.9	
12 SA 0232 / 0913 / 1501 / 2147	1.2 / 3.9 / 1.2 / 4.1	**27** SU 0306 / 0916 / 1540 / 2154	1.2 / 4.1 / 1.2 / 4.1	
13 SU 0352 / 1019 / 1624 / 2244	1.1 / 4.0 / 1.1 / 4.3	**28** M 0439 / 1032 / 1706 / 2258	0.8 / 4.5 / 0.7 / 4.5	
14 M 0459 / 1113 / 1719 / 2333	0.9 / 4.3 / 1.0 / 4.6			
15 TU 0550 / 1159 / 1804	0.6 / 4.5 / 0.8			

MARCH

Time	m		Time	m
1 TU 0538 / 1131 / 1757 / 2351	0.3 / 4.9 / 0.3 / 4.9	**16** W 0521 / 1134 / 1740 / 2352	0.5 / 4.6 / 0.7 / 4.7	
2 W 0628 / 1222 / 1843 ●	-0.1 / 5.2 / 0.1	**17** TH 0608 / 1216 / 1822	0.2 / 4.9 / 0.5	
3 TH 0037 / 0714 / 1308 / 1925	5.1 / -0.4 / 5.4 / 0.0	**18** F 0031 / 0649 / 1254 / ○1900	4.9 / 0.1 / 5.1 / 0.4	
4 F 0120 / 0756 / 1351 / 2003	5.3 / -0.4 / 5.4 / 0.0	**19** SA 0107 / 0728 / 1330 / 1936	5.0 / 0.0 / 5.2 / 0.3	
5 SA 0158 / 0835 / 1430 / 2038	5.3 / -0.3 / 5.2 / 0.1	**20** SU 0142 / 0804 / 1407 / 2009	5.1 / 0.0 / 5.2 / 0.3	
6 SU 0233 / 0909 / 1505 / 2111	5.2 / -0.1 / 5.0 / 0.3	**21** M 0217 / 0839 / 1444 / 2043	5.2 / 0.1 / 5.2 / 0.3	
7 M 0306 / 0940 / 1539 / 2142	5.1 / 0.1 / 4.7 / 0.4	**22** TU 0254 / 0914 / 1522 / 2117	5.2 / 0.2 / 5.1 / 0.4	
8 TU 0338 / 1010 / 1612 / 2214	4.9 / 0.4 / 4.5 / 0.6	**23** W 0333 / 0948 / 1603 / 2154	5.1 / 0.4 / 4.8 / 0.5	
9 W 0414 / 1041 / 1647 / 2250	4.7 / 0.6 / 4.3 / 0.8	**24** TH 0417 / 1026 / 1648 / 2237	4.9 / 0.6 / 4.5 / 0.6	
10 TH 0453 / 1117 / 1727 / ☽2331	4.4 / 0.9 / 4.1 / 0.9	**25** F 0506 / 1112 / 1737 / ☽2330	4.6 / 0.9 / 4.2 / 0.8	
11 F 0539 / 1200 / 1815	4.1 / 1.1 / 3.9	**26** SA 0606 / 1212 / 1839	4.3 / 1.1 / 3.9	
12 SA 0021 / 0637 / 1255 / 1923	1.1 / 3.8 / 1.3 / 3.7	**27** SU 0039 / 0732 / 1401 / 2014	1.0 / 4.0 / 1.3 / 3.8	
13 SU 0128 / 0812 / 1413 / 2102	1.2 / 3.6 / 1.4 / 3.8	**28** M 0306 / 0914 / 1549 / 2142	1.0 / 4.2 / 1.0 / 4.1	
14 M 0300 / 0946 / 1546 / 2214	1.1 / 3.8 / 1.2 / 4.0	**29** TU 0424 / 1023 / 1648 / 2243	0.5 / 4.6 / 0.6 / 4.5	
15 TU 0425 / 1046 / 1652 / 2307	0.9 / 4.2 / 1.0 / 4.4	**30** W 0519 / 1117 / 1737 / 2334	0.1 / 5.0 / 0.3 / 4.8	
		31 TH 0606 / 1205 / 1820	-0.2 / 5.2 / 0.1	

APRIL

Time	m		Time	m
1 F 0018 / 0649 / 1248 / 1900 ●	5.1 / -0.3 / 5.3 / 0.0	**16** SA 0000 / 0616 / 1224 / ○1832	4.8 / 0.0 / 5.2 / 0.4	
2 SA 0058 / 0728 / 1327 / 1937	5.2 / -0.3 / 5.3 / 0.0	**17** SU 0039 / 0658 / 1304 / 1912	5.1 / 0.0 / 5.3 / 0.3	
3 SU 0134 / 0802 / 1402 / 2009	5.2 / -0.1 / 5.1 / 0.1	**18** M 0118 / 0737 / 1343 / 1949	5.2 / 0.0 / 5.3 / 0.3	
4 M 0206 / 0831 / 1432 / 2037	5.1 / 0.1 / 4.9 / 0.3	**19** TU 0158 / 0814 / 1422 / 2026	5.2 / 0.1 / 5.2 / 0.3	
5 TU 0236 / 0856 / 1459 / 2105	5.0 / 0.4 / 4.7 / 0.4	**20** W 0238 / 0850 / 1502 / 2105	5.2 / 0.3 / 5.0 / 0.3	
6 W 0306 / 0921 / 1528 / 2135	4.9 / 0.5 / 4.5 / 0.5	**21** TH 0321 / 0929 / 1544 / 2147	5.1 / 0.5 / 4.8 / 0.4	
7 TH 0339 / 0951 / 1600 / 2210	4.7 / 0.7 / 4.4 / 0.6	**22** F 0408 / 1012 / 1630 / 2236	4.9 / 0.7 / 4.5 / 0.6	
8 F 0418 / 1027 / 1639 / 2251	4.5 / 0.9 / 4.2 / 0.8	**23** SA 0502 / 1103 / 1721 / ☽2337	4.6 / 1.0 / 4.2 / 0.7	
9 SA 0503 / 1111 / 1725 / ☽2342	4.2 / 1.1 / 4.0 / 0.9	**24** SU 0608 / 1210 / 1827	4.3 / 1.2 / 4.0	
10 SU 0555 / 1206 / 1820	3.9 / 1.2 / 3.8	**25** M 0103 / 0735 / 1349 / 2000	0.8 / 4.2 / 1.2 / 3.9	
11 M 0046 / 0706 / 1319 / 1945	1.0 / 3.7 / 1.4 / 3.7	**26** TU 0249 / 0859 / 1518 / 2119	0.6 / 4.4 / 1.0 / 4.2	
12 TU 0214 / 0855 / 1456 / 2128	1.0 / 3.8 / 1.3 / 3.9	**27** W 0357 / 1002 / 1618 / 2218	0.3 / 4.7 / 0.6 / 4.5	
13 W 0342 / 1006 / 1612 / 2229	0.8 / 4.2 / 1.1 / 4.2	**28** TH 0451 / 1054 / 1707 / 2308	0.0 / 5.0 / 0.4 / 4.8	
14 TH 0443 / 1058 / 1706 / 2317	0.5 / 4.6 / 0.8 / 4.6	**29** F 0537 / 1140 / 1751 / 2352	-0.1 / 5.2 / 0.2 / 5.0	
15 F 0533 / 1143 / 1751	0.2 / 4.9 / 0.6	**30** SA 0618 / 1222 / 1831 ●	-0.1 / 5.2 / 0.1	

Chart Datum: 2·35 metres below Ordnance Datum (Newlyn). HAT is 5·8 metres above Chart Datum.

>> FREE monthly updates. Register at <<
www.reedsnauticalalmanac.co.uk

STANDARD TIME (UT)
For Summer Time add ONE hour in **non-shaded areas**

BURNHAM-ON-CROUCH   LAT 51°37'N   LONG 0°48'E
TIMES AND HEIGHTS OF HIGH AND LOW WATERS

Dates in red are **SPRINGS**
Dates in blue are NEAPS

YEAR 2022

MAY

Day	Time	m	Day	Time	m
1 SU	0032 / 0655 / 1259 / 1908	5.1 / 0.0 / 5.1 / 0.2	**16** M ○	0009 / 0628 / 1236 / 1848	5.0 / 0.1 / 5.2 / 0.4
2 M	0108 / 0726 / 1332 / 1940	5.0 / 0.2 / 4.9 / 0.3	**17** TU	0054 / 0711 / 1319 / 1932	5.2 / 0.1 / 5.3 / 0.3
3 TU	0140 / 0751 / 1359 / 2007	4.9 / 0.4 / 4.7 / 0.4	**18** W	0139 / 0753 / 1402 / 2016	5.3 / 0.2 / 5.2 / 0.3
4 W	0209 / 0813 / 1423 / 2033	4.8 / 0.6 / 4.6 / 0.5	**19** TH	0225 / 0835 / 1445 / 2102	5.2 / 0.4 / 5.0 / 0.3
5 TH	0238 / 0838 / 1450 / 2103	4.7 / 0.7 / 4.6 / 0.5	**20** F	0312 / 0919 / 1530 / 2152	5.1 / 0.6 / 4.8 / 0.3
6 F	0312 / 0911 / 1525 / 2140	4.6 / 0.8 / 4.5 / 0.6	**21** SA	0403 / 1008 / 1618 / 2248	4.9 / 0.8 / 4.6 / 0.4
7 SA	0351 / 0950 / 1605 / 2225	4.5 / 0.9 / 4.4 / 0.7	**22** SU ◑	0500 / 1104 / 1712 / 2352	4.7 / 0.9 / 4.4 / 0.4
8 SU	0437 / 1037 / 1652 / 2317	4.3 / 1.0 / 4.3 / 0.8	**23** M	0605 / 1209 / 1817	4.5 / 1.1 / 4.2
9 M ◑	0530 / 1133 / 1746	4.1 / 1.2 / 4.1	**24** TU	0105 / 0709 / 1323 / 1933	0.4 / 4.4 / 1.1 / 4.2
10 TU	0021 / 0633 / 1240 / 1851	0.9 / 4.0 / 1.3 / 3.9	**25** W	0219 / 0830 / 1436 / 2045	0.3 / 4.5 / 0.9 / 4.3
11 W	0139 / 0754 / 1404 / 2019	0.9 / 4.0 / 1.3 / 3.9	**26** TH	0322 / 0930 / 1538 / 2144	0.2 / 4.7 / 0.7 / 4.6
12 TH	0257 / 0913 / 1522 / 2136	0.7 / 4.3 / 1.2 / 4.2	**27** F	0416 / 1022 / 1632 / 2236	0.1 / 4.9 / 0.5 / 4.8
13 F	0401 / 1014 / 1624 / 2234	0.5 / 4.6 / 0.9 / 4.5	**28** SA	0503 / 1109 / 1719 / 2323	0.1 / 4.9 / 0.4 / 4.9
14 SA	0455 / 1105 / 1715 / 2323	0.3 / 4.9 / 0.7 / 4.8	**29** SU	0545 / 1152 / 1803	0.2 / 4.9 / 0.4
15 SU	0543 / 1152 / 1802	0.2 / 5.1 / 0.5	**30** M ●	0005 / 0623 / 1230 / 1842	4.9 / 0.4 / 4.9 / 0.4
			31 TU	0044 / 0654 / 1304 / 1915	4.8 / 0.6 / 4.7 / 0.5

JUNE

Day	Time	m	Day	Time	m
1 W	0118 / 0717 / 1331 / 1943	4.7 / 0.7 / 4.6 / 0.6	**16** TH	0123 / 0741 / 1345 / 2012	5.3 / 0.3 / 5.1 / 0.2
2 TH	0147 / 0737 / 1355 / 2009	4.6 / 0.8 / 4.6 / 0.6	**17** F	0213 / 0827 / 1431 / 2103	5.3 / 0.4 / 5.0 / 0.1
3 F	0216 / 0806 / 1423 / 2041	4.5 / 0.8 / 4.6 / 0.6	**18** SA	0303 / 0915 / 1517 / 2154	5.2 / 0.5 / 4.9 / 0.1
4 SA	0251 / 0842 / 1459 / 2120	4.5 / 0.8 / 4.6 / 0.6	**19** SU	0354 / 1004 / 1605 / 2248	5.0 / 0.6 / 4.8 / 0.1
5 SU	0331 / 0924 / 1541 / 2206	4.5 / 0.8 / 4.6 / 0.7	**20** M	0449 / 1056 / 1656 / 2343	4.9 / 0.7 / 4.6 / 0.1
6 M	0417 / 1012 / 1628 / 2259	4.4 / 0.9 / 4.5 / 0.7	**21** TU ◑	0546 / 1151 / 1753	4.7 / 0.8 / 4.5
7 TU ◑	0509 / 1106 / 1720 / 2359	4.4 / 1.0 / 4.3 / 0.7	**22** W	0041 / 0648 / 1249 / 1857	0.2 / 4.5 / 0.9 / 4.4
8 W	0606 / 1206 / 1818	4.3 / 1.2 / 4.2	**23** TH	0141 / 0751 / 1351 / 2004	0.3 / 4.5 / 0.9 / 4.4
9 TH	0106 / 0711 / 1316 / 1926	0.8 / 4.3 / 1.2 / 4.1	**24** F	0241 / 0851 / 1454 / 2107	0.3 / 4.5 / 0.8 / 4.4
10 F	0215 / 0822 / 1431 / 2043	0.7 / 4.4 / 1.2 / 4.2	**25** SA	0338 / 0946 / 1553 / 2204	0.4 / 4.6 / 0.7 / 4.5
11 SA	0321 / 0929 / 1541 / 2151	0.6 / 4.5 / 1.1 / 4.4	**26** SU	0429 / 1036 / 1648 / 2255	0.5 / 4.6 / 0.6 / 4.6
12 SU	0420 / 1028 / 1642 / 2249	0.5 / 4.8 / 0.9 / 4.7	**27** M	0515 / 1123 / 1737 / 2342	0.6 / 4.7 / 0.6 / 4.6
13 M	0514 / 1121 / 1738 / 2343	0.4 / 4.9 / 0.7 / 5.0	**28** TU	0556 / 1205 / 1821	0.7 / 4.6 / 0.6
14 TU ○	0605 / 1211 / 1831	0.3 / 5.1 / 0.5	**29** W ●	0024 / 0631 / 1241 / 1859	4.6 / 0.8 / 4.6 / 0.6
15 W	0034 / 0654 / 1259 / 1922	5.2 / 0.3 / 5.1 / 0.3	**30** TH	0101 / 0657 / 1312 / 1931	4.6 / 0.8 / 4.6 / 0.6

JULY

Day	Time	m	Day	Time	m
1 F	0133 / 0720 / 1338 / 1959	4.5 / 0.8 / 4.6 / 0.6	**16** SA	0201 / 0820 / 1416 / 2055	5.4 / 0.3 / 5.1 / -0.2
2 SA	0202 / 0749 / 1406 / 2031	4.5 / 0.8 / 4.6 / 0.6	**17** SU	0250 / 0904 / 1501 / 2142	5.4 / 0.3 / 5.1 / -0.2
3 SU	0236 / 0826 / 1441 / 2109	4.6 / 0.7 / 4.7 / 0.5	**18** M	0338 / 0949 / 1545 / 2229	5.2 / 0.4 / 5.0 / -0.2
4 M	0315 / 0907 / 1522 / 2152	4.6 / 0.7 / 4.7 / 0.5	**19** TU	0426 / 1033 / 1630 / 2316	5.0 / 0.5 / 4.8 / 0.0
5 TU	0359 / 0951 / 1607 / 2239	4.7 / 0.8 / 4.6 / 0.6	**20** W ◑	0516 / 1120 / 1719	4.7 / 0.6 / 4.6
6 W	0447 / 1039 / 1655 / 2331	4.6 / 0.9 / 4.6 / 0.7	**21** TH	0004 / 0608 / 1208 / 1813	0.2 / 4.5 / 0.8 / 4.4
7 TH ◑	0539 / 1130 / 1747	4.5 / 1.0 / 4.4	**22** F	0055 / 0705 / 1302 / 1916	0.5 / 4.3 / 0.9 / 4.2
8 F	0028 / 0636 / 1228 / 1847	0.7 / 4.4 / 1.1 / 4.3	**23** SA	0150 / 0805 / 1401 / 2025	0.7 / 4.2 / 1.0 / 4.1
9 SA	0132 / 0740 / 1338 / 1957	0.8 / 4.3 / 1.2 / 4.2	**24** SU	0251 / 0906 / 1509 / 2131	0.8 / 4.1 / 1.0 / 4.2
10 SU	0242 / 0850 / 1459 / 2114	0.8 / 4.4 / 1.2 / 4.3	**25** M	0352 / 1004 / 1616 / 2230	0.9 / 4.2 / 0.9 / 4.3
11 M	0352 / 0956 / 1618 / 2224	0.7 / 4.5 / 1.0 / 4.5	**26** TU	0447 / 1056 / 1714 / 2322	0.9 / 4.4 / 0.7 / 4.4
12 TU	0456 / 1057 / 1725 / 2324	0.6 / 4.7 / 0.7 / 4.8	**27** W	0534 / 1142 / 1803	0.9 / 4.5 / 0.6
13 W ○	0553 / 1152 / 1823	0.5 / 4.9 / 0.4	**28** TH ●	0007 / 0615 / 1223 / 1845	4.5 / 0.8 / 4.6 / 0.5
14 TH	0019 / 0645 / 1242 / 1917	5.1 / 0.3 / 5.0 / 0.1	**29** F	0047 / 0649 / 1258 / 1921	4.6 / 0.8 / 4.6 / 0.4
15 F	0111 / 0734 / 1330 / 2007	5.3 / 0.3 / 5.1 / -0.1	**30** SA	0121 / 0718 / 1328 / 1953	4.6 / 0.7 / 4.7 / 0.4
			31 SU	0152 / 0746 / 1356 / 2024	4.7 / 0.7 / 4.7 / 0.3

AUGUST

Day	Time	m	Day	Time	m
1 M	0223 / 0818 / 1428 / 2058	4.8 / 0.6 / 4.8 / 0.3	**16** TU	0314 / 0923 / 1518 / 2158	5.3 / 0.2 / 5.2 / -0.2
2 TU	0259 / 0854 / 1505 / 2134	4.9 / 0.6 / 4.8 / 0.4	**17** W	0356 / 1002 / 1558 / 2237	5.0 / 0.3 / 5.0 / 0.1
3 W	0339 / 0931 / 1545 / 2213	4.9 / 0.6 / 4.8 / 0.5	**18** TH	0438 / 1041 / 1639 / 2316	4.7 / 0.5 / 4.7 / 0.4
4 TH	0423 / 1011 / 1629 / 2255	4.8 / 0.7 / 4.7 / 0.6	**19** F ◑	0521 / 1122 / 1724 / 2358	4.4 / 0.7 / 4.4 / 0.7
5 F	0510 / 1054 / 1718 / 2341	4.7 / 0.8 / 4.6 / 0.8	**20** SA	0609 / 1208 / 1818	4.1 / 0.9 / 4.1
6 SA ◑	0602 / 1141 / 1812	4.5 / 1.0 / 4.3	**21** SU	0045 / 0706 / 1301 / 1930	1.0 / 3.9 / 1.1 / 3.8
7 SU	0038 / 0702 / 1302 / 1919	0.9 / 4.2 / 1.2 / 4.1	**22** M	0143 / 0818 / 1409 / 2057	1.2 / 3.8 / 1.2 / 3.8
8 M	0157 / 0813 / 1414 / 2046	1.1 / 4.1 / 1.3 / 4.1	**23** TU	0259 / 0930 / 1538 / 2207	1.3 / 3.9 / 1.1 / 4.0
9 TU	0334 / 0932 / 1608 / 2209	1.0 / 4.1 / 1.1 / 4.3	**24** W	0415 / 1030 / 1647 / 2302	1.2 / 4.1 / 0.8 / 4.2
10 W	0449 / 1040 / 1720 / 2314	0.8 / 4.4 / 0.6 / 4.7	**25** TH	0509 / 1120 / 1738 / 2348	1.0 / 4.4 / 0.6 / 4.5
11 TH	0546 / 1138 / 1817	0.5 / 4.7 / 0.2	**26** F	0553 / 1203 / 1821	0.8 / 4.6 / 0.3
12 F ○	0009 / 0636 / 1229 / 1907	5.1 / 0.3 / 5.0 / -0.2	**27** SA ●	0028 / 0631 / 1240 / 1858	4.7 / 0.7 / 4.7 / 0.2
13 SA	0100 / 0721 / 1315 / 1953	5.4 / 0.1 / 5.2 / -0.4	**28** SU	0103 / 0704 / 1312 / 1933	4.8 / 0.6 / 4.8 / 0.1
14 SU	0147 / 0804 / 1358 / 2037	5.5 / 0.0 / 5.3 / -0.5	**29** M	0135 / 0735 / 1342 / 2005	4.9 / 0.5 / 4.9 / 0.1
15 M	0232 / 0844 / 1439 / 2118	5.5 / 0.1 / 5.3 / -0.4	**30** TU	0207 / 0806 / 1413 / 2038	5.0 / 0.5 / 5.0 / 0.2
			31 W	0241 / 0837 / 1447 / 2110	5.1 / 0.5 / 5.0 / 0.2

E England

Chart Datum: 2·35 metres below Ordnance Datum (Newlyn). HAT is 5·8 metres above Chart Datum.

» FREE monthly updates. Register at «
www.reedsnauticalalmanac.co.uk

71

STANDARD TIME (UT)
For Summer Time add ONE hour in **non-shaded areas**

BURNHAM-ON-CROUCH LAT 51°37'N LONG 0°48'E
TIMES AND HEIGHTS OF HIGH AND LOW WATERS

Dates in red are **SPRINGS**
Dates in blue are **NEAPS**

YEAR 2022

SEPTEMBER

Time	m		Time	m
1 0318	5.0	**16** 0356	4.7
0910	0.5	1000	0.5
TH 1525	4.9	F 1600	4.8
2144	0.4	2223	0.6
2 0359	4.9	**17** 0432	4.4
0946	0.6	1036	0.7
F 1606	4.8	SA 1640	4.4
2219	0.6	◑ 2259	0.9
3 0443	4.7	**18** 0511	4.1
1025	0.7	1118	0.9
SA 1653	4.6	SU 1726	4.1
◐ 2300	0.8	2341	1.1
4 0531	4.4	**19** 0558	3.9
1113	0.9	1209	1.1
SU 1746	4.3	M 1825	3.7
2352	1.1		
5 0627	4.1	**20** 0035	1.4
1211	1.1	0704	3.7
M 1853	4.0	TU 1314	1.2
		2007	3.6
6 0106	1.3	**21** 0152	1.5
0741	3.9	0848	3.7
TU 1345	1.3	W 1449	1.1
2033	4.0	2137	3.8
7 0327	1.2	**22** 0330	1.4
0916	3.9	0959	4.0
W 1608	0.9	TH 1610	0.9
2203	4.3	2234	4.1
8 0440	0.9	**23** 0434	1.1
1029	4.3	1051	4.3
TH 1711	0.4	F 1704	0.5
2306	4.8	2320	4.5
9 0532	0.5	**24** 0521	0.8
1125	4.7	1135	4.6
F 1802	-0.1	SA 1748	0.3
2358	5.2		
10 0618	0.2	**25** 0000	4.8
1213	5.1	0601	0.6
SA 1848	-0.4	SU 1213	4.9
○		● 1827	0.1
11 0044	5.4	**26** 0036	5.0
0701	0.0	0638	0.5
SU 1256	5.3	M 1248	5.0
1931	-0.6	1904	0.0
12 0127	5.5	**27** 0110	5.1
0740	-0.1	0712	0.4
M 1336	5.4	TU 1321	5.1
2010	-0.5	1938	0.0
13 0208	5.4	**28** 0144	5.2
0817	0.0	0745	0.4
TU 1413	5.4	W 1354	5.1
2047	-0.3	2012	0.1
14 0246	5.2	**29** 0220	5.2
0852	0.1	0817	0.4
W 1449	5.3	TH 1429	5.1
2120	0.0	2044	0.3
15 0321	5.0	**30** 0257	5.1
0926	0.3	0850	0.5
TH 1524	5.0	F 1507	5.0
2151	0.3	2117	0.4

OCTOBER

Time	m		Time	m
1 0336	4.9	**16** 0346	4.4
0927	0.6	0956	0.8
SA 1550	4.9	SU 1604	4.4
2154	0.7	2210	1.0
2 0419	4.6	**17** 0422	4.2
1010	0.7	1038	0.9
SU 1638	4.6	M 1648	4.1
2239	0.9	◑ 2254	1.2
3 0507	4.3	**18** 0506	4.0
1101	0.9	1130	1.1
M 1734	4.3	TU 1741	3.8
◐ 2335	1.2	2349	1.4
4 0603	4.0	**19** 0601	3.8
1207	1.1	1237	1.2
TU 1847	4.0	W 1854	3.7
5 0056	1.4	**20** 0102	1.5
0723	3.8	0727	3.7
W 1417	1.1	TH 1402	1.1
2034	4.1	2043	3.8
6 0312	1.2	**21** 0233	1.4
0905	4.0	0911	3.9
TH 1555	0.7	F 1523	0.9
2153	4.5	2150	4.1
7 0419	0.8	**22** 0347	1.2
1013	4.4	1010	4.3
F 1651	0.4	SA 1621	0.6
2250	4.9	2239	4.5
8 0508	0.4	**23** 0441	0.9
1105	4.9	1057	4.6
SA 1739	-0.2	SU 1709	0.3
2338	5.3	2322	4.9
9 0553	0.2	**24** 0525	0.7
1150	5.2	1138	4.9
SU 1822	-0.4	M 1751	0.2
○			
10 0022	5.4	**25** 0002	5.1
0634	0.0	0607	0.5
M 1232	5.4	TU 1217	5.1
1902	-0.4	● 1832	0.1
11 0102	5.4	**26** 0041	5.2
0712	0.0	0645	0.4
TU 1310	5.5	W 1255	5.2
1938	-0.2	1910	0.1
12 0140	5.3	**27** 0119	5.3
0748	0.1	0722	0.4
W 1346	5.4	TH 1334	5.3
2010	0.0	1946	0.2
13 0214	4.8	**28** 0158	5.2
0820	0.2	0759	0.4
TH 1420	5.2	F 1414	5.2
2039	0.3	2022	0.4
14 0245	4.8	**29** 0237	5.1
0850	0.4	0837	0.5
F 1452	5.0	SA 1456	5.1
2105	0.5	2059	0.6
15 0315	4.6	**30** 0318	4.8
0922	0.6	0919	0.6
SA 1527	4.7	SU 1542	4.9
2135	0.8	2141	0.8
		31 0402	4.6
		1007	0.7
		M 1634	4.6
		2232	1.1

NOVEMBER

Time	m		Time	m
1 0452	4.3	**16** 0431	4.2
1107	0.9	1101	1.0
TU 1735	4.4	W 1712	4.1
◑ 2336	1.3	◑ 2315	1.4
2 0552	4.0	**17** 0524	4.0
1229	1.0	1207	1.1
W 1853	4.2	TH 1813	4.0
3 0104	1.3	**18** 0022	1.4
0715	4.0	0629	3.9
TH 1413	0.8	F 1321	1.0
2021	4.4	1930	4.0
4 0240	1.1	**19** 0141	1.4
0842	4.2	0753	4.0
F 1527	0.4	SA 1434	0.9
2129	4.7	2048	4.2
5 0346	0.7	**20** 0255	1.3
0946	4.6	0912	4.2
SA 1622	0.1	SU 1536	0.7
2223	5.0	2149	4.6
6 0437	0.5	**21** 0356	1.0
1038	5.0	1010	4.5
SU 1709	-0.1	M 1629	0.5
2311	5.3	2240	4.9
7 0523	0.2	**22** 0448	0.8
1124	5.2	1100	4.8
M 1752	-0.1	TU 1717	0.3
2355	5.3	2327	5.1
8 0605	0.1	**23** 0536	0.7
1206	5.3	1147	5.1
TU 1831	0.0	W 1802	0.3
○		●	
9 0035	5.3	**24** 0011	5.2
0645	0.1	0622	0.5
W 1246	5.3	TH 1231	5.2
1906	0.2	1845	0.3
10 0111	5.1	**25** 0055	5.3
0721	0.3	0706	0.5
TH 1322	5.2	F 1316	5.3
1936	0.4	1927	0.4
11 0143	4.9	**26** 0138	5.2
0752	0.4	0750	0.4
F 1355	5.0	SA 1401	5.3
2000	0.7	2009	0.6
12 0211	4.7	**27** 0221	5.0
0820	0.6	0836	0.5
SA 1426	4.8	SU 1448	5.2
2023	0.8	2052	0.7
13 0237	4.6	**28** 0305	4.9
0849	0.7	0925	0.5
SU 1459	4.6	M 1538	5.0
2054	1.0	2140	0.9
14 0307	4.5	**29** 0351	4.6
0924	0.8	1020	0.6
M 1536	4.4	TU 1632	4.8
2132	1.1	2236	1.1
15 0346	4.3	**30** 0443	4.4
1008	0.9	1123	0.6
TU 1621	4.2	W 1733	4.6
2219	1.2	◑ 2339	1.2

DECEMBER

Time	m		Time	m
1 0542	4.3	**16** 0455	4.3
1233	0.6	1137	0.9
TH 1841	4.5	F 1742	4.5
		◑ 2344	1.3
2 0049	1.2	**17** 0552	4.2
0654	4.2	1241	0.9
F 1345	0.5	SA 1844	4.3
1952	4.6		
3 0201	1.0	**18** 0051	1.4
0808	4.4	0657	4.2
SA 1451	0.3	SU 1347	0.9
2056	4.8	1952	4.4
4 0307	0.8	**19** 0202	1.3
0912	4.6	0811	4.2
SU 1548	0.2	M 1451	0.8
2151	5.0	2100	4.5
5 0403	0.6	**20** 0311	1.2
1007	4.9	0923	4.4
M 1637	0.2	TU 1552	0.7
2241	5.1	2201	4.8
6 0454	0.4	**21** 0415	1.0
1057	5.0	1028	4.6
TU 1722	0.2	W 1648	0.6
2327	5.1	2256	4.9
7 0540	0.3	**22** 0513	0.8
1143	5.1	1120	4.9
W 1803	0.4	TH 1740	0.5
		2347	5.1
8 0008	5.0	**23** 0607	0.6
0624	0.3	1212	5.1
TH 1225	5.1	F 1830	0.5
○ 1840	0.6	●	
9 0046	4.9	**24** 0035	5.2
0702	0.4	0659	0.4
F 1304	4.9	SA 1302	5.3
1909	0.8	1918	0.5
10 0119	4.7	**25** 0122	5.2
0735	0.6	0749	0.3
SA 1337	4.8	SU 1351	5.3
1929	0.9	2004	0.6
11 0144	4.6	**26** 0207	5.1
0802	0.7	0839	0.2
SU 1407	4.6	M 1440	5.3
1952	1.0	2051	0.6
12 0208	4.6	**27** 0253	5.0
0829	0.7	0930	0.1
M 1438	4.5	TU 1530	5.2
2024	1.0	2139	0.7
13 0240	4.6	**28** 0339	4.9
0904	0.8	1021	0.1
TU 1515	4.5	W 1622	5.1
2105	1.1	2229	0.8
14 0319	4.5	**29** 0428	4.8
0947	0.8	1115	0.2
W 1559	4.4	TH 1716	4.9
2151	1.1	2322	0.9
15 0405	4.4	**30** 0521	4.6
1038	0.9	1211	0.3
TH 1648	4.4	F 1814	4.7
2244	1.2	◑	
		31 0019	0.9
		0621	4.5
		SA 1309	0.4
		1916	4.6

Chart Datum: 2·35 metres below Ordnance Datum (Newlyn). HAT is 5·8 metres above Chart Datum.

1.16 RIVER BLACKWATER

Essex **51°45´·33N 00°54´·90E** ✪✪✪✪✬✬✬✿✿✿

CHARTS AC 5607, 1183, 1975, 3741; Imray C1, Y17, 2000

TIDES Maldon +0130 Dover; ML 2·8; Duration 0620)

Standard Port WALTON-ON-THE-NAZE (→)

Times				Height (metres)			
High Water		Low Water		MHWS	MHWN	MLWN	MLWS
0000	0600	0500	1100	4·2	3·4	1·1	0·4
1200	1800	1700	2300				
Differences SUNK HEAD							
0000	+0002	−0002	+0002	−0·3	−0·3	−0·1	−0·1
WEST MERSEA							
+0035	+0015	+0055	+0010	+0·9	+0·4	+0·1	+0·1
BRADWELL							
+0035	+0023	+0047	+0004	+1·0	+0·8	+0·2	0·0
OSEA ISLAND							
+0057	+0045	+0050	+0007	+1·1	+0·9	+0·1	0·0
MALDON							
+0107	+0055	ND	ND	−1·3	−1·1	ND	ND

SHELTER Good, as appropriate to wind. ‡ in creeks restricted by oyster beds and many moorings.

NAVIGATION WPT Knoll NCM, Q, 51°43´·88N 01°05´·07E, 287°/6·7M to Nass bn, ECM VQ (3) 5s. Speed limit 8kn W of Osea Is.

WEST MERSEA Min depth 0·6m in approach to Nass Bn. Avoid oyster beds between Cobmarsh and Packing Marsh Is and in Salcott Chan. ‡ in Mersea Quarters in 5-6m (exposed). Landing pontoon (limited waiting) with pile and pontoon moorings in Ray Channel.

TOLLESBURY FLEET Proceed via S Chan up Woodrolfe Creek. A tide gauge shows depth over marina ent sill (approx 2·4m at MHWS and 1·4m at MHWN). Speed limits: Tollesbury Fleet S Chan 8kn; Woodrolfe Creek upper reaches 4kn.

BRADWELL PHM N of ent marks obstn. Creek only suitable for small craft and gets very crowded. Ent has NCM bn Q with tide gauge in creek; leave to **STBD** on entry. 4 PHM buoys, 3 SHM withies and 2 B/W △ ldg bns mark the channel which doglegs past a SHM buoy to marina entrance. Min depth 0·2m in appr channel.

MALDON From S of Osea Is, 'The Doctor', No 3 SHM buoy on with Blackwater SC lt, Iso G 5s, lead 300° approx up the chan; or No 3 and No 8 buoys in line at 305°.

LIGHTS AND MARKS See chartlets and 1.3. Chan to Maldon has some lit marks.

COMMUNICATIONS (01206 Colchester/W Mersea) Dr 352015 (WM). Bradwell and Tollesbury Marinas Ch **80** M (HO); Blackwater Marina Ch M 0900-2300; Heybridge Lock Ch 80 HW −2+1; WMYC launch VHF37/M, c/s *YC1* or Clarke and Carter launch VHF 37/M, c/s *CC1*.

FACILITIES

WEST MERSEA (01206) W Mersea YC382947, launch service call *YC1* on Ch 37/M or ☎07752 309435, ⚓ ✕ ⚓. **Town** ⚓ 🅿 🚗 ⚓ 🅱 🏧 ✉ 🅱 🛒 ✕ 🍴 ≋ (bus to Colchester, Ⓗ01206-747474), ✈ (Southend/Stansted).

TOLLESBURY Marina ⚓ marina@woodrolfe.com ☎(01621) 869202, Sill to marina dries 1·9m. ⚓ 220⚓+20🅥: 1 tide £5, <8m £19, <10m £21, <12m £22, >12m £23 🅳 🔧 LPG ⚓ 🗡 ⚓ 🅿(20t) 🅿(5t) 🅿.

Tollesbury Cruising Club ☎869561, ⚓ ✕ 🍴.

Village 🏦 🏧 ✕ 🍴 ✉ (Tues, Thurs 1000-1430), ≋ (bus to Witham), ✈ (Southend/Stansted).

BRADWELL (01621). **Bradwell Marina** ☎776235. Min depth 0·2m in appr chan. 350⚓ 50🅥 '<22' £17, <25' £18·50, <30' £20·50, <35' £22, <40' £23·50, <49' £26·50; ⚓ 🅿 🗡 ⚓ 🅱 🅿(45t) 🅿 ✕ 🍴.

Bradwell Quay YC ☎890173, ⚓ ⚓ ⚓ 🍴.

Village ✉ ≋ (bus to Southminster), ✈ (Southend/Stansted).

MAYLANDSEA (01621). **Blackwater Marina** ☎740264, 150⚓ 230⚓ all dry <10m £15, >10m £1·5, short stay £4, ⚓ 🗡 ⚓ ✕ 🍴.

MALDON (01621). **Maldon Quay** Beyond No 8 buoy, shifting marked chan carries 0·2m. Access near HW; pontoons dry to soft mud. HM/River bailiff ☎875837, Mob 07771935306 / 07818 013723 ⚓ ⚓ ⚓ <7m £18, <10m £22, <13m £25, ⚓ 🅿. **Maldon Little Ship Club** ☎854139, 🍴.

Services 🗡 ⚓ 🅱 Ⓔ 🅿 ACA.

Town ✉ 🅱 🛒 ✕ 🍴 ≋ (bus to Chelmsford, Ⓗ(01245) 440761), ✈ (Southend/Stansted).

HEYBRIDGE BASIN Lock ☎853506 mob 07712079764, opens approx HW−1 to HW (0600-2000 1 May-30 Sep); winter 0800-1700 www.essexwaterways.com). SHM opposite the lock and withies to port mark deep water entrance. Book 24 hrs in advance. Charges <7m £19·50, <10m £23·50, <13m £26·50, <15m £29·50, <20m £33·50 ⚓ ⚓ 🅿 ⚓ 🅿. Ent to Chelmer & Blackwater Canal (small craft).

Blackwater SC ☎853923 ⚓ ⚓. **Services** at CRS Marine ☎854684, Mobile 07850 543873 (pontoon outside lock), ⚓ ⚓ ⚓ 🗡 ⚓ 🅱 🅿. Bus to Heybridge/Maldon.

1.17 RIVER COLNE

Essex **51°47'·98N 01°00'·60E** (Brightlingsea) ❀❀♨♨♨❁❁

CHARTS AC 5607, 1183, 1975, 3741; Imray C1, Y17, 2000

TIDES +0050 Dover; ML 2·5; Duration 0615

Standard Port WALTON-ON-THE-NAZE (→)

Times				Height (metres)			
High Water		Low Water		MHWS	MHWN	MLWN	MLWS
0000	0600	0500	1100	4·2	3·4	1·1	0·4
1200	1800	1700	2300				
Differences BRIGHTLINGSEA							
+0025	+0021	+0046	+0004	+0·8	+0·4	+0·1	0·0
COLCHESTER							
+0035	+0025	DR	DR	0·0	–0·3	DR	DR
CLACTON-ON-SEA							
+0012	+0010	+0025	+0008	+0·3	+0·1	+0·1	+0·1

SHELTER Suitable shelter can be found from most winds. Brightlingsea outer hbr is exposed to W'lies. In the creek S of Cindery Island are moorings and long pontoons in about 1·5m, with possible ⚓ for Ⓥs. ⚓ prohib in Brightlingsea Hbr, but allowed to the NW of Mersea Stone Pt and in Pyefleet Chan, E of Pewit Is. R Colne is navigable for 4·5m draught to Wivenhoe and Rowhedge, where it dries; and to The Hythe, Colchester (3m draught).

NAVIGATION WPT Colne Bar By, SHM Fl (2) G 5s, 51°44'·61N 01°02'·57E, 340°/3·6M to Mersea Stone. Extensive mud and sand banks flank the entrance channel. Coasters may be encountered in the appr to Brightlingsea and manoeuvring off the quay beyond the hard. At HW sand barges regularly visit Ballast Quay below the tidal barrier at Wivenhoe. The entrance to Brightlingsea Creek is narrow at LW and carries about 1m.

Tidal barrier 2ca below Wivenhoe church is usually open (30m wide) allowing unrestricted passage; keep to stbd, max speed 5kn. 3 F R (vert), shown on N Pier, visible up/downstream indicate barrier gates are shut; see also LIGHTS AND MARKS.

Speed limits in approaches and upriver (by buoy no): No 13–15 = 8kn; No 15–18 = no spd limit; No 18–31 = 8kn; No 31 – Colchester = 5kn; Brightlingsea Harbour = 4kn.

LIGHTS AND MARKS Bateman's Tr (conspic) by Westmarsh Pt Fl(3) 20s. Brightlingsea ldg lts/marks 041°; FR 7/10m 4M, W ☐ on R striped posts; adjusted to suit channel. Pass Spit SCM, and follow lateral marks to NCM (Q) where chan is divided by Cindery Is. Pyefleet Chan and other creeks are unlit.

Lit lateral buoys up to Wivenhoe. Passage through flood barrier marked by 2FR/FG (vert) each side and there are bns, QR/QG, up/downstream on the banks.

COMMUNICATIONS (Brightlingsea 01206) Dr 302522; HM (B'sea) 302200.
Brightlingsea Harbour Radio VHF Ch 68. *Waterside Marina* Ch 68. *Water Taxi* Ch 68.

FACILITIES
BRIGHTLINGSEA Town Hard www.brightlingseaharbour.org ☎302200 ⚓ ⚓ 🛥 ⚓ 🅿. Marina has facilities with walk ashore

access. Floating pontoons are serviced by water taxi.

Waterside Marina ☎302200, sill 1m above CD; ⚓ 🛢 🛥 🚻 🅿 wi-fi.

Colne YC ☎302594, ⚓ 🛥 ✕ 🍺 wi-fi.

Brightlingsea SC ⚓ 🍺.

Services 🔧 🅿(HO) 🛢 ✕ 🔩 🛒 Ⓔ ⚓ 🅿 🛒(mobile) 🅿 ACA.

Town ✉ Ⓑ 🛒 ✕ 🍺 bus (Wivenhoe or Colchester for ⮌), ✈ (Southend or Stansted).

WIVENHOE: Wivenhoe SC ☎822132. ⚓ (drying Ⓥ berths may be available on the inside pontoons – first come first served, no charge). **Village** 🔧 ✉ 🛒 🍺 ⮌.

ROWHEDGE: Quay ⚓ for small craft on pontoon above pub (drying) some Ⓥ. Water Bailiff; David Slavinskas 07472 043784. EDPC office 01206 729200. Restrictions on Pontoon – 30ft for 3hr maximum stay, no overnight mooring on pontoon. O/n fees Lion or Pearsons Quay £10; 🛒 ✕ 🍺.

WALTON ON THE NAZE

MEAN SPRING —————
AND NEAP CURVES – – – –

MEAN RANGES	
Springs	3.8m
Neaps	2.3m

1.18 WALTON BACKWATERS

Essex **51°54′·57N 01°16′·79E** (No 2 PHM buoy) ❀❀♨♨♨♨❀❀

CHARTS AC 5607, 2052, 2695; Imray C1, Y16, 2000

TIDES +0030 Dover; ML 2·2; Duration 0615. Walton is a Standard Port. Predictions are for Walton Pier, ie to seaward. Time differences for Bramble Creek (N of Hamford Water) are +10, −7, −5, +10 mins; height differences are all +0·3m.

SHELTER Good in all weather, but ent not advised if a big sea is running from the NE. Good ⚓s in Hamford Water (clear of Oakley Creek) and in N end of Walton Chan, 2ca S of Stone Pt on E side.

NAVIGATION From S, appr via Medusa Chan; from N and E via the Harwich recomended yacht track (1.19). WPT Pye End SWM buoy, L Fl 10s, 51°55′·05N 01°17′·89E, 234°/1·1M to Crab Knoll SHM at chan ent. NB this stretch carries only 0·9m. Beware lobster pots off the Naze and Pye Sands and oyster beds in the Backwaters. Buoys may be moved to suit channel changes.

At narrow ent to Walton Chan leave NCM buoy to stbd, and 3 PHM buoys close to port. Fm No 9 SHM expect significant shoaling, ebb>4kn and strong back eddies around Stone Pt. Best water to E side, with narrowest/shallowest water at No 16 PHM; stay in channel. Beware tidal sheer and vessels with strong tide under them.

LIGHTS AND MARKS Naze Tr (49m) is conspic 3M S of Pye End buoy. 2M NNE at Felixstowe, cranes and Y flood lts are conspic D/N. No 9 SHM Fl G 5s, No 10 PHM Q R.

COMMUNICATIONS (Code 01255) Ⓗ 421145; HM 851899. Titchmarsh Marina Ch 80, 0800-2000 in season.

FACILITIES
Titchmarsh Marina ☎672185, pontoons on R Twizzle. Access over sill 1·3m (tide gauge at ent) berths dredged to approx 2m. ⚓ 420◯ inc ♥, £18 <8m, £20 <10m, £22 <12m, £24 <13m < £26m; short stay (<3hrs) £6+£5/hr. ⚓ LPG ⚓🔧 ⊞ 🛥(10t) 🛥(35t) ⚓ ✕ 🏠.
Yacht Basin ☎675873; appr dries. ⚓ ⚓ 60◯ occ ♥, £18 for 10m ⛽🅿🚿🔧✕ ⊞ 🍴 🛥(½t) ⚓ wi-fi.
Walton & Frinton YC, ☎678161, ✕ 🏠.

Town ⛽ ✉ 🛒 ✕ 🏠 🚆 ✈ (Southend/Cambridge/Stansted).

HM Ch 80

STANDARD TIME (UT)
For Summer Time add ONE hour in **non-shaded areas**

WALTON-ON-THE-NAZE LAT 51°51'N LONG 1°17'E
TIMES AND HEIGHTS OF HIGH AND LOW WATERS

Dates in red are SPRINGS
Dates in blue are NEAPS

YEAR **2022**

JANUARY

Day	Time / m
1 SA	0345 0.8, 0958 4.2, 1610 0.5, 2233 4.1
16 SU	0444 0.8, 1043 3.8, 1655 0.9, 2312 3.9
2 SU ●	0443 0.6, 1053 4.3, 1705 0.6, 2325 4.2
17 M ○	0524 0.7, 1124 3.9, 1733 0.9, 2349 4.0
3 M	0540 0.5, 1145 4.4, 1757 0.6
18 TU	0601 0.6, 1202 4.0, 1806 0.9
4 TU	0015 4.2, 0635 0.5, 1235 4.5, 1848 0.7
19 W	0024 4.0, 0636 0.5, 1238 4.0, 1837 0.8
5 W	0103 4.3, 0727 0.3, 1325 4.4, 1935 0.8
20 TH	0100 4.1, 0710 0.4, 1314 4.1, 1908 0.8
6 TH	0151 4.2, 0816 0.2, 1415 4.3, 2019 0.9
21 F	0135 4.0, 0746 0.4, 1351 4.1, 1941 0.8
7 F	0237 4.2, 0903 0.3, 1505 4.2, 2102 1.0
22 SA	0210 4.0, 0821 0.4, 1428 4.0, 2018 0.8
8 SA	0324 4.0, 0949 0.4, 1556 4.0, 2147 1.1
23 SU	0246 4.0, 0857 0.4, 1507 3.9, 2057 0.9
9 SU ☽	0411 3.9, 1036 0.5, 1649 3.8, 2237 1.2
24 M	0323 4.0, 0936 0.5, 1550 3.9, 2141 1.0
10 M	0501 3.8, 1127 0.7, 1745 3.6, 2336 1.3
25 TU ☽	0405 3.9, 1022 0.6, 1638 3.8, 2235 1.1
11 TU	0557 3.6, 1223 0.8, 1844 3.5
26 W	0455 3.8, 1120 0.6, 1737 3.7, 2342 1.1
12 W	0043 1.3, 0700 3.5, 1321 0.9, 1950 3.5
27 TH	0559 3.7, 1231 0.7, 1847 3.6
13 TH	0151 1.3, 0807 3.5, 1422 1.0, 2053 3.5
28 F	0102 1.1, 0717 3.7, 1346 0.8, 2006 3.6
14 F	0258 1.1, 0908 3.6, 1522 1.0, 2146 3.7
29 SA	0222 1.0, 0838 3.8, 1456 0.8, 2122 3.7
15 SA	0357 1.0, 0959 3.7, 1612 1.0, 2231 3.8
30 SU	0334 0.8, 0948 3.9, 1601 0.8, 2227 3.9
31 M	0440 0.6, 1047 4.1, 1700 0.7, 2321 4.0

FEBRUARY

Day	Time / m
1 TU ●	0539 0.4, 1140 4.3, 1752 0.7
16 W ○	0541 0.5, 1146 3.9, 1749 0.8
2 W	0009 4.2, 0632 0.2, 1228 4.4, 1839 0.7
17 TH	0007 4.0, 0615 0.4, 1222 4.1, 1820 0.8
3 TH	0054 4.3, 0719 0.1, 1314 4.4, 1921 0.7
18 F	0043 4.1, 0650 0.3, 1258 4.1, 1852 0.7
4 F	0136 4.3, 0802 0.1, 1359 4.3, 2001 0.8
19 SA	0118 4.2, 0724 0.2, 1333 4.2, 1925 0.7
5 SA	0217 4.3, 0841 0.2, 1442 4.1, 2038 0.8
20 SU	0152 4.2, 0758 0.2, 1409 4.1, 2000 0.7
6 SU	0256 4.2, 0915 0.3, 1525 4.0, 2113 0.9
21 M	0226 4.2, 0831 0.3, 1447 4.0, 2037 0.8
7 M	0334 4.0, 0949 0.5, 1607 3.7, 2151 1.0
22 TU	0301 4.1, 0905 0.4, 1526 3.9, 2118 0.8
8 TU ☽	0414 3.8, 1027 0.7, 1652 3.5, 2237 1.1
23 W	0340 4.1, 0947 0.5, 1611 3.8, 2207 0.9
9 W	0501 3.6, 1116 0.9, 1743 3.4, 2338 1.3
24 TH	0427 3.9, 1043 0.7, 1706 3.6, 2313 1.0
10 TH	0559 3.4, 1220 1.1, 1844 3.3
25 F	0530 3.7, 1201 0.9, 1817 3.4
11 F	0055 1.3, 0711 3.3, 1332 1.2, 2000 3.3
26 SA	0038 1.1, 0656 3.5, 1329 1.0, 1950 3.3
12 SA	0215 1.2, 0830 3.3, 1448 1.2, 2114 3.4
27 SU	0211 1.0, 0833 3.6, 1449 1.0, 2120 3.5
13 SU	0331 1.0, 0935 3.5, 1552 1.1, 2208 3.6
28 M	0334 0.8, 0948 3.8, 1559 0.9, 2223 3.8
14 M	0425 0.8, 1025 3.7, 1639 1.0, 2252 3.8
15 TU	0505 0.6, 1108 3.8, 1716 0.9, 2331 3.9

MARCH

Day	Time / m
1 TU	0441 0.5, 1046 4.1, 1654 0.8, 2314 4.0
16 W	0436 0.6, 1043 3.8, 1650 0.9, 2303 3.9
2 W ●	0534 0.3, 1134 4.2, 1740 0.7, 2357 4.2
17 TH	0512 0.4, 1121 4.0, 1722 0.8, 2340 4.0
3 TH	0619 0.1, 1217 4.3, 1821 0.7
18 F ○	0546 0.3, 1157 4.1, 1754 0.7
4 F	0037 4.3, 0700 0.1, 1257 4.3, 1900 0.6
19 SA	0015 4.2, 0622 0.2, 1233 4.2, 1829 0.6
5 SA	0114 4.3, 0736 0.1, 1336 4.2, 1937 0.7
20 SU	0051 4.3, 0656 0.2, 1310 4.2, 1904 0.6
6 SU	0150 4.3, 0807 0.2, 1414 4.1, 2010 0.7
21 M	0127 4.3, 0729 0.2, 1347 4.2, 1940 0.6
7 M	0223 4.2, 0835 0.4, 1449 3.9, 2041 0.8
22 TU	0203 4.3, 0802 0.3, 1425 4.1, 2018 0.6
8 TU	0257 4.1, 0901 0.5, 1524 3.7, 2113 0.9
23 W	0240 4.2, 0837 0.4, 1505 3.9, 2100 0.7
9 W	0332 3.9, 0932 0.7, 1600 3.6, 2151 1.0
24 TH	0320 4.1, 0920 0.6, 1549 3.7, 2150 0.8
10 TH ☽	0414 3.6, 1013 1.0, 1645 3.3, 2242 1.1
25 F ☽	0410 3.9, 1021 0.9, 1644 3.5, 2259 0.9
11 F	0508 3.4, 1117 1.2, 1745 3.2, 2359 1.3
26 SA	0517 3.6, 1147 1.1, 1802 3.3
12 SA	0622 3.2, 1248 1.4, 1903 3.1
27 SU	0032 1.0, 0656 3.5, 1320 1.2, 1946 3.2
13 SU	0130 1.2, 0752 3.2, 1414 1.4, 2030 3.2
28 M	0209 0.9, 0832 3.6, 1442 1.1, 2110 3.5
14 M	0254 1.1, 0906 3.4, 1525 1.2, 2136 3.4
29 TU	0331 0.6, 0942 3.9, 1549 1.0, 2209 3.8
15 TU	0354 0.8, 1000 3.6, 1613 1.0, 2223 3.7
30 W	0430 0.4, 1035 4.1, 1638 0.8, 2256 4.0
31 TH	0516 0.2, 1118 4.2, 1719 0.7, 2336 4.2

APRIL

Day	Time / m
1 F ●	0556 0.2, 1156 4.2, 1757 0.7
16 SA ○	0512 0.3, 1126 4.1, 1725 0.7, 2343 4.2
2 SA	0012 4.3, 0631 0.2, 1232 4.2, 1834 0.6
17 SU	0549 0.2, 1205 4.2, 1803 0.6
3 SU	0045 4.3, 0702 0.2, 1308 4.2, 1910 0.6
18 M	0022 4.4, 0626 0.2, 1244 4.3, 1843 0.5
4 M	0118 4.3, 0730 0.3, 1342 4.1, 1943 0.6
19 TU	0101 4.4, 0701 0.2, 1325 4.2, 1923 0.5
5 TU	0150 4.2, 0755 0.5, 1414 3.9, 2013 0.7
20 W	0141 4.4, 0738 0.4, 1406 4.1, 2004 0.5
6 W	0223 4.1, 0820 0.6, 1444 3.8, 2042 0.7
21 TH	0223 4.3, 0818 0.5, 1449 3.9, 2051 0.6
7 TH	0258 3.9, 0848 0.8, 1516 3.6, 2117 0.8
22 F	0309 4.1, 0908 0.8, 1536 3.7, 2147 0.7
8 F	0336 3.7, 0924 1.0, 1556 3.4, 2201 1.0
23 SA ☽	0405 3.9, 1015 1.0, 1637 3.5, 2300 0.8
9 SA ☽	0423 3.4, 1015 1.3, 1651 3.2, 2308 1.1
24 SU	0520 3.6, 1139 1.2, 1758 3.3
10 SU	0532 3.2, 1151 1.5, 1811 3.1
25 M	0032 0.8, 0654 3.6, 1304 1.2, 1930 3.4
11 M	0043 1.2, 0708 3.1, 1332 1.5, 1937 3.2
26 TU	0159 0.7, 0817 3.7, 1422 1.2, 2046 3.6
12 TU	0206 1.0, 0824 3.3, 1443 1.3, 2048 3.4
27 W	0313 0.5, 0922 3.9, 1525 1.0, 2143 3.8
13 W	0308 0.8, 0921 3.6, 1534 1.1, 2141 3.6
28 TH	0408 0.4, 1012 4.1, 1613 0.9, 2229 4.0
14 TH	0355 0.6, 1007 3.8, 1613 0.9, 2225 3.9
29 F	0450 0.3, 1054 4.1, 1653 0.8, 2308 4.1
15 F	0435 0.4, 1047 4.0, 1649 0.8, 2304 4.1
30 SA ●	0526 0.3, 1131 4.1, 1730 0.7, 2343 4.2

Chart Datum: 2·16 metres below Ordnance Datum (Newlyn). HAT is 4·7 metres above Chart Datum.

>> FREE monthly updates. Register at <<
www.reedsnauticalalmanac.co.uk

STANDARD TIME (UT)
For Summer Time add ONE hour in **non-shaded areas**

WALTON-ON-THE-NAZE   LAT 51°51′N   LONG 1°17′E
TIMES AND HEIGHTS OF HIGH AND LOW WATERS

Dates in red are **SPRINGS**
Dates in blue are NEAPS

YEAR **2022**

E England

MAY

Day	Time	m	Time	m	Time	m	Time	m
1 SU	0556	0.4	1205	4.1	1808	0.6		
2 M	0015	4.2	0626	0.4	1239	4.1	1845	0.5
3 TU	0048	4.2	0655	0.5	1311	4.0	1919	0.6
4 W	0121	4.2	0722	0.6	1342	4.0	1949	0.6
5 TH	0155	4.0	0748	0.7	1413	3.8	2019	0.7
6 F	0230	3.9	0817	0.9	1445	3.7	2053	0.7
7 SA	0308	3.7	0853	1.0	1524	3.5	2135	0.8
8 SU	0352	3.5	0940	1.2	1614	3.4	2234	1.0
9 M	0450	3.3	1050	1.4	1724	3.4	2357	1.0
10 TU	0613	3.3	1231	1.4	1843	3.3		
11 W	0116	0.9	0730	3.4	1349	1.3	1953	3.4
12 TH	0218	0.7	0831	3.6	1444	1.1	2051	3.7
13 F	0309	0.5	0922	3.8	1530	0.9	2141	3.9
14 SA	0354	0.4	1009	4.0	1613	0.8	2227	4.1
15 SU	0437	0.3	1054	4.1	1657	0.7	2311	4.3
16 M	0518	0.3	1138	4.2	1741	0.6	2355	4.4
17 TU	0559	0.3	1222	4.3	1826	0.5		
18 W	0039	4.5	0642	0.4	1307	4.2	1912	0.5
19 TH	0125	4.5	0726	0.5	1353	4.1	2000	0.4
20 F	0213	4.4	0814	0.7	1441	4.0	2053	0.5
21 SA	0305	4.2	0908	0.9	1533	3.8	2152	0.5
22 SU	0405	3.9	1011	1.1	1635	3.6	2303	0.6
23 M	0517	3.8	1122	1.2	1745	3.6		
24 TU	0020	0.6	0634	3.7	1237	1.2	1900	3.6
25 W	0133	0.5	0747	3.8	1348	1.2	2010	3.7
26 TH	0241	0.5	0850	3.9	1451	1.1	2108	3.8
27 F	0336	0.5	0942	4.0	1542	0.9	2156	4.0
28 SA	0419	0.5	1025	4.0	1626	0.8	2237	4.0
29 SU	0453	0.6	1104	4.0	1706	0.7	2314	4.1
30 M	0524	0.6	1140	4.0	1745	0.6	2349	4.1
31 TU	0557	0.6	1214	4.0	1823	0.6		

JUNE

Day	Time	m	Time	m	Time	m	Time	m
1 W	0023	4.1	0630	0.7	1247	4.0	1859	0.6
2 TH	0059	4.1	0659	0.8	1319	4.0	1932	0.6
3 F	0134	4.0	0728	0.8	1352	3.9	2004	0.6
4 SA	0211	3.9	0759	0.9	1427	3.8	2040	0.7
5 SU	0249	3.8	0836	1.0	1506	3.7	2121	0.7
6 M	0331	3.6	0921	1.1	1552	3.6	2211	0.8
7 TU	0421	3.5	1016	1.3	1647	3.5	2314	0.8
8 W	0522	3.5	1126	1.3	1752	3.5		
9 TH	0023	0.8	0632	3.5	1242	1.3	1859	3.6
10 F	0128	0.7	0738	3.7	1351	1.1	2002	3.7
11 SA	0224	0.6	0838	3.8	1449	1.0	2100	3.9
12 SU	0316	0.5	0934	4.0	1542	0.8	2154	4.1
13 M	0406	0.4	1027	4.1	1634	0.7	2245	4.3
14 TU	0455	0.4	1117	4.2	1725	0.6	2335	4.4
15 W	0543	0.5	1206	4.2	1817	0.5		
16 TH	0024	4.5	0633	0.6	1255	4.2	1910	0.4
17 F	0115	4.5	0722	0.7	1344	4.2	2003	0.3
18 SA	0206	4.4	0812	0.8	1434	4.1	2056	0.3
19 SU	0300	4.3	0903	0.9	1526	4.0	2152	0.4
20 M	0357	4.1	0956	1.0	1621	3.9	2250	0.4
21 TU	0458	3.9	1055	1.1	1718	3.8	2352	0.5
22 W	0600	3.8	1159	1.2	1820	3.8		
23 TH	0053	0.6	0706	3.7	1304	1.2	1925	3.8
24 F	0155	0.7	0810	3.7	1408	1.1	2027	3.8
25 SA	0253	0.7	0907	3.8	1508	1.0	2121	3.8
26 SU	0342	0.8	0956	3.8	1601	0.9	2208	3.9
27 M	0423	0.8	1039	3.9	1647	0.8	2250	4.0
28 TU	0501	0.8	1119	3.9	1729	0.7	2329	4.0
29 W	0538	0.8	1156	4.0	1808	0.6		
30 TH	0006	4.0	0614	0.8	1231	4.0	1845	0.6

JULY

Day	Time	m	Time	m	Time	m	Time	m
1 F	0044	4.0	0646	0.9	1306	4.0	1920	0.5
2 SA	0121	4.0	0716	0.9	1341	4.0	1954	0.5
3 SU	0157	4.0	0748	0.9	1416	3.9	2029	0.6
4 M	0234	3.9	0824	0.9	1453	3.9	2106	0.6
5 TU	0313	3.8	0903	1.0	1532	3.8	2147	0.6
6 W	0355	3.7	0948	1.1	1615	3.8	2234	0.7
7 TH	0445	3.7	1042	1.2	1707	3.7	2331	0.7
8 F	0543	3.7	1147	1.2	1808	3.7		
9 SA	0036	0.7	0650	3.7	1302	1.2	1916	3.8
10 SU	0144	0.7	0759	3.7	1415	1.1	2025	3.9
11 M	0246	0.7	0906	3.8	1519	0.9	2130	4.0
12 TU	0345	0.7	1008	3.9	1619	0.7	2229	4.2
13 W	0442	0.7	1104	4.1	1718	0.6	2323	4.4
14 TH	0536	0.7	1157	4.2	1815	0.4		
15 F	0015	4.5	0628	0.7	1246	4.3	1909	0.3
16 SA	0106	4.5	0717	0.7	1334	4.3	2000	0.2
17 SU	0156	4.5	0803	0.8	1421	4.3	2048	0.2
18 M	0246	4.3	0847	0.9	1508	4.2	2134	0.3
19 TU	0336	4.2	0932	1.0	1554	4.2	2220	0.4
20 W	0427	4.0	1019	1.1	1642	4.0	2307	0.6
21 TH	0520	3.8	1113	1.2	1734	3.9	2359	0.7
22 F	0617	3.6	1214	1.2	1832	3.7		
23 SA	0055	0.9	0720	3.5	1320	1.2	1939	3.6
24 SU	0157	1.0	0827	3.5	1431	1.2	2046	3.7
25 M	0304	1.1	0928	3.6	1540	1.0	2143	3.7
26 TU	0401	1.0	1018	3.8	1634	0.8	2231	3.9
27 W	0446	1.0	1101	3.9	1717	0.7	2314	3.9
28 TH	0524	0.9	1140	4.0	1754	0.6	2353	4.0
29 F	0559	0.9	1217	4.1	1829	0.5		
30 SA	0030	4.1	0632	0.9	1252	4.1	1902	0.5
31 SU	0106	4.1	0702	0.9	1326	4.1	1936	0.5

AUGUST

Day	Time	m	Time	m	Time	m	Time	m
1 M	0141	4.1	0733	0.9	1400	4.1	2009	0.5
2 TU	0215	4.0	0807	0.9	1433	4.1	2042	0.5
3 W	0250	4.0	0842	0.9	1507	4.0	2115	0.6
4 TH	0328	3.9	0921	1.0	1544	4.0	2153	0.7
5 F	0412	3.8	1006	1.1	1629	3.9	2242	0.8
6 SA	0504	3.7	1105	1.2	1725	3.8	2350	0.9
7 SU	0609	3.6	1224	1.2	1837	3.7		
8 M	0111	1.0	0727	3.5	1350	1.1	2001	3.8
9 TU	0227	0.9	0849	3.6	1505	0.9	2117	3.9
10 W	0335	0.9	1000	3.8	1615	0.7	2222	4.1
11 TH	0436	0.8	1058	4.0	1717	0.5	2318	4.3
12 F	0530	0.8	1148	4.2	1811	0.3		
13 SA	0007	4.5	0618	0.7	1234	4.3	1900	0.2
14 SU	0054	4.5	0703	0.7	1318	4.4	1944	0.1
15 M	0139	4.5	0744	0.8	1400	4.4	2025	0.2
16 TU	0224	4.3	0824	0.8	1440	4.4	2102	0.3
17 W	0307	4.1	0902	0.9	1519	4.2	2137	0.5
18 TH	0349	3.9	0941	1.0	1559	4.1	2213	0.7
19 F	0434	3.7	1025	1.1	1644	3.9	2258	1.0
20 SA	0523	3.5	1121	1.2	1740	3.6	2357	1.2
21 SU	0623	3.4	1231	1.3	1850	3.5		
22 M	0108	1.3	0740	3.3	1352	1.3	2012	3.5
23 TU	0230	1.3	0857	3.5	1518	1.1	2121	3.6
24 W	0342	1.2	0955	3.7	1616	0.9	2213	3.8
25 TH	0429	1.1	1040	3.8	1657	0.7	2256	3.9
26 F	0506	1.0	1119	4.0	1732	0.6	2334	4.0
27 SA	0539	0.9	1155	4.1	1804	0.5		
28 SU	0009	4.1	0610	0.9	1228	4.2	1837	0.4
29 M	0043	4.2	0640	0.8	1302	4.2	1909	0.4
30 TU	0117	4.2	0711	0.8	1335	4.2	1940	0.4
31 W	0151	4.1	0744	0.8	1407	4.2	2010	0.5

Chart Datum: 2·16 metres below Ordnance Datum (Newlyn). HAT is 4·7 metres above Chart Datum.

STANDARD TIME (UT)
For Summer Time add ONE hour in **non-shaded areas**

WALTON-ON-THE-NAZE LAT 51°51'N LONG 1°17'E
TIMES AND HEIGHTS OF HIGH AND LOW WATERS

Dates in red are **SPRINGS**
Dates in blue are NEAPS

YEAR 2022

SEPTEMBER

	Time	m		Time	m
1 TH	0225	4.1	**16** F	0308	3.9
	0818	0.9		0904	0.9
	1439	4.2		1517	4.1
	2040	0.6		2119	0.9
2 F	0301	4.0	**17** SA	0344	3.7
	0855	0.9		0942	1.0
	1515	4.1		1558	3.8
	2115	0.7	◑	2158	1.1
3 SA	0341	3.8	**18** SU	0427	3.5
	0938	1.0		1031	1.2
◑	1558	4.0		1651	3.5
	2202	0.9		2259	1.4
4 SU	0430	3.7	**19** M	0526	3.3
	1036	1.1		1142	1.3
	1654	3.8		1805	3.3
	2315	1.1			
5 M	0536	3.5	**20** TU	0024	1.6
	1159	1.2		0646	3.2
	1813	3.6		1309	1.3
				1937	3.3
6 TU	0053	1.2	**21** W	0155	1.6
	0705	3.3		0814	3.3
	1337	1.1		1439	1.2
	1952	3.6		2052	3.5
7 W	0217	1.2	**22** TH	0311	1.4
	0844	3.5		0920	3.5
	1501	0.9		1542	0.9
	2116	3.9		2146	3.7
8 TH	0329	1.1	**23** F	0400	1.2
	0955	3.8		1008	3.8
	1612	0.6		1625	0.7
	2218	4.2		2229	3.9
9 F	0428	0.9	**24** SA	0438	1.0
	1048	4.0		1047	3.9
	1708	0.4		1659	0.6
	2309	4.4		2305	4.1
10 SA	0516	0.8	**25** SU	0510	0.9
	1133	4.2		1122	4.1
	1755	0.2		1731	0.5
○	2353	4.5	●	2340	4.2
11 SU	0559	0.8	**26** M	0540	0.9
	1214	4.4		1156	4.2
	1838	0.2		1803	0.4
12 M	0034	4.5	**27** TU	0013	4.2
	0640	0.7		0612	0.8
	1253	4.4		1230	4.3
	1917	0.2		1836	0.4
13 TU	0115	4.4	**28** W	0048	4.3
	0719	0.7		0646	0.7
	1330	4.5		1304	4.3
	1952	0.3		1906	0.4
14 W	0154	4.3	**29** TH	0123	4.2
	0756	0.7		0720	0.7
	1406	4.4		1338	4.3
	2022	0.5		1936	0.5
15 TH	0232	4.1	**30** F	0159	4.1
	0830	0.8		0755	0.8
	1441	4.3		1414	4.3
	2050	0.7		2008	0.6

OCTOBER

	Time	m		Time	m
1 SA	0236	4.0	**16** SU	0258	3.7
	0834	0.8		0907	0.9
	1453	4.2		1520	3.8
	2047	0.8		2108	1.2
2 SU	0316	3.8	**17** M	0335	3.5
	0920	0.9		0950	1.1
	1539	4.0		1607	3.5
	2139	1.1	◑	2158	1.5
3 M	0406	3.6	**18** TU	0427	3.3
	1023	1.0		1054	1.2
	1639	3.8		1717	3.3
◑	2301	1.3		2326	1.7
4 TU	0516	3.4	**19** W	0549	3.2
	1154	1.1		1223	1.3
	1808	3.6		1851	3.3
5 W	0042	1.4	**20** TH	0110	1.7
	0659	3.3		0717	3.2
	1332	1.0		1347	1.1
	1952	3.7		2006	3.4
6 TH	0206	1.3	**21** F	0226	1.5
	0833	3.5		0828	3.4
	1453	0.7		1451	0.9
	2109	4.0		2104	3.7
7 F	0316	1.1	**22** SA	0319	1.3
	0938	3.8		0922	3.7
	1558	0.5		1539	0.7
	2205	4.2		2149	3.9
8 SA	0409	1.0	**23** SU	0359	1.1
	1028	4.1		1005	3.9
	1649	0.3		1617	0.6
	2251	4.3		2227	4.1
9 SU	0453	0.9	**24** M	0433	0.9
	1110	4.3		1043	4.1
	1731	0.3		1653	0.6
○	2332	4.4		2304	4.2
10 M	0533	0.8	**25** TU	0507	0.8
	1148	4.4		1120	4.2
	1808	0.3		1727	0.4
			●	2341	4.3
11 TU	0009	4.4	**26** W	0543	0.7
	0613	0.7		1158	4.4
	1223	4.4		1801	0.4
	1843	0.3			
12 W	0046	4.3	**27** TH	0019	4.3
	0651	0.6		0621	0.7
	1257	4.4		1235	4.4
	1913	0.5		1835	0.5
13 TH	0121	4.2	**28** F	0058	4.3
	0728	0.7		0700	0.7
	1331	4.4		1314	4.4
	1941	0.6		1909	0.6
14 F	0155	4.1	**29** SA	0138	4.2
	0802	0.7		0740	0.7
	1405	4.2		1355	4.4
	2007	0.8		1947	0.7
15 SA	0227	3.9	**30** SU	0218	4.0
	0833	0.8		0824	0.7
	1441	4.0		1440	4.2
	2034	1.0		2034	0.9
			31 M	0303	3.8
				0917	0.8
				1532	4.0
				2135	1.2

NOVEMBER

	Time	m		Time	m
1 TU	0357	3.6	**16** W	0348	3.5
	1026	0.9		1017	1.0
	1639	3.8		1630	3.4
◑	2258	1.4	◑	2223	1.6
2 W	0513	3.4	**17** TH	0453	3.3
	1155	0.9		1130	1.1
	1810	3.7		1750	3.3
				2355	1.9
3 TH	0026	1.4	**18** F	0616	3.3
	0647	3.4		1251	1.0
	1319	0.8		1906	3.4
	1938	3.8			
4 F	0143	1.3	**19** SA	0124	1.5
	0808	3.6		0727	3.4
	1433	0.6		1355	0.9
	2048	4.0		2007	3.6
5 SA	0250	1.2	**20** SU	0225	1.3
	0911	3.9		0826	3.6
	1534	0.5		1447	0.7
	2142	4.2		2059	3.8
6 SU	0343	1.0	**21** M	0312	1.1
	1000	4.1		0917	3.8
	1622	0.4		1532	0.6
	2227	4.2		2145	4.0
7 M	0427	0.9	**22** TU	0354	1.0
	1042	4.2		1003	4.0
	1702	0.4		1613	0.5
	2306	4.3		2229	4.1
8 TU	0508	0.8	**23** W	0436	0.8
	1119	4.3		1046	4.2
	1736	0.5		1653	0.5
○	2343	4.3	●	2312	4.2
9 W	0547	0.7	**24** TH	0519	0.7
	1154	4.3		1130	4.4
	1808	0.5		1733	0.5
				2356	4.3
10 TH	0017	4.2	**25** F	0603	0.6
	0627	0.6		1214	4.5
	1228	4.3		1813	0.5
	1839	0.6			
11 F	0051	4.2	**26** SA	0040	4.3
	0704	0.6		0648	0.5
	1302	4.3		1258	4.5
	1908	0.8		1856	0.7
12 SA	0123	4.1	**27** SU	0125	4.2
	0738	0.7		0735	0.5
	1337	4.1		1345	4.4
	1934	0.9		1943	0.8
13 SU	0154	3.9	**28** M	0211	4.1
	0809	0.7		0826	0.5
	1413	4.0		1435	4.3
	2002	1.1		2036	1.0
14 M	0226	3.8	**29** TU	0301	3.9
	0842	0.8		0923	0.5
	1452	3.8		1532	4.1
	2036	1.2		2136	1.2
15 TU	0302	3.6	**30** W	0358	3.7
	0923	0.9		1030	0.6
	1535	3.6		1639	3.9
	2121	1.4	◑	2245	1.3

DECEMBER

	Time	m		Time	m
1 TH	0506	3.6	**16** F	0415	3.5
	1144	0.6		1042	0.9
	1753	3.8		1651	3.5
	2358	1.3	◑	2247	1.4
2 F	0619	3.6	**17** SA	0514	3.5
	1255	0.6		1146	0.9
	1907	3.8		1756	3.5
				2359	1.4
3 SA	0109	1.3	**18** SU	0621	3.5
	0732	3.7		1253	0.9
	1401	0.6		1903	3.6
	2015	3.9			
4 SU	0215	1.2	**19** M	0117	1.4
	0836	3.8		0728	3.6
	1501	0.6		1354	0.8
	2113	4.0		2007	3.7
5 M	0312	1.1	**20** TU	0223	1.2
	0929	4.0		0830	3.8
	1551	0.6		1449	0.7
	2200	4.0		2105	3.9
6 TU	0401	0.9	**21** W	0319	1.0
	1014	4.1		0926	4.0
	1631	0.7		1540	0.6
	2242	4.1		2200	4.0
7 W	0446	0.8	**22** TH	0411	0.8
	1054	4.1		1019	4.1
	1707	0.7		1629	0.6
	2320	4.1		2251	4.1
8 TH	0528	0.7	**23** F	0502	0.6
	1131	4.1		1110	4.3
	1741	0.7		1717	0.6
○	2356	4.1	●	2341	4.2
9 F	0608	0.6	**24** SA	0553	0.5
	1207	4.2		1200	4.4
	1814	0.6		1805	0.6
10 SA	0030	4.1	**25** SU	0029	4.2
	0647	0.6		0645	0.4
	1242	4.1		1249	4.5
	1847	0.9		1855	0.7
11 SU	0103	4.0	**26** M	0118	4.2
	0721	0.6		0737	0.5
	1319	4.0		1340	4.5
	1916	1.0		1944	0.8
12 M	0135	4.0	**27** TU	0207	4.2
	0754	0.6		0829	0.3
	1355	3.9		1431	4.4
	1945	1.0		2034	0.9
13 TU	0209	3.9	**28** W	0256	4.1
	0827	0.7		0922	0.3
	1433	3.8		1526	4.2
	2020	1.1		2125	1.0
14 W	0245	3.8	**29** TH	0348	4.0
	0905	0.7		1018	0.3
	1513	3.7		1623	4.0
	2100	1.2		2220	1.1
15 TH	0326	3.6	**30** F	0443	3.9
	0949	0.8		1116	0.4
	1558	3.6		1724	3.8
	2148	1.3	◑	2321	1.2
			31 SA	0542	3.8
				1216	0.5
				1827	3.7

Chart Datum: 2·16 metres below Ordnance Datum (Newlyn). HAT is 4·7 metres above Chart Datum.

》》 **FREE** monthly updates. Register at 《
www.reedsnauticalalmanac.co.uk 《

1.19 & 20 RIVERS STOUR AND ORWELL ✿✿✿✿✿✿✿✿

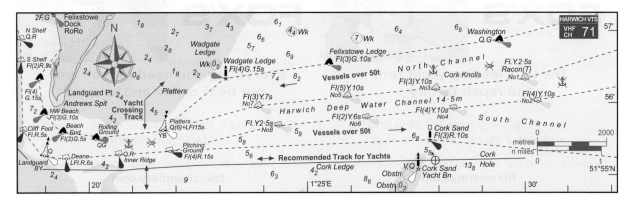

E England

1.19 RIVER STOUR

Essex/Suffolk 51°57'·06N 01°17'·77E (Guard PHM buoy)
❀❀❀♨♨♨❁❁❁

CHARTS AC 5607, 2052, 2693, 1491, 1594; Imray C29, C1, Y16, 2000

TIDES Harwich +0050 Dover; ML 2·1; Duration 0630
Standard Port HARWICH (⟶)

Times				Height (metres)			
High Water		Low Water		MHWS	MHWN	MLWN	MLWS
0000	0600	0000	0600	4·0	3·4	1·1	0·4
1200	1800	1200	1800				
Differences MISTLEY							
+0025	+0015	+0005	0000	+0·2	+0·1	−0·1	−0·1

SHELTER Good at Shotley Marina; access (H24) via chan dredged 2m, outer limits lit, to lock. Enter only on F.G tfc lt. ⚓ also at Halfpenny Pier (H24) and Manningtree (dries). No yachts at Parkeston Quay. ⚓s off Wrabness Pt (untenable in some wind against tide conditions), Holbrook Creek and Stutton Ness.

NAVIGATION WPT 51°55'·33N 01°25'·50E, on recommended yacht track, S of Cork Sand Bn (see also River Orwell page).

• Keep clear of commercial shipping and new container berth at Felixstowe. Outside the hbr, yachts should cross the DW chan at 90° between Rolling Ground and Platters buoys. Stay clear of the DW chan (Y lit SPMs) using Recommended Yacht Track, running S and W of DW chan to beyond Harwich.

• **Caution**: Bkwtr, ESE of Blackman's Hd, covers at HW; marked by PHM lit Bn, only 5ca W of main chan. Beware of passing W of Harwich Shelf ECM buoy without sufficient height of tide. The Guard Shoal (0·8m), about 2ca S of Guard PHM, lies close to the Recommended Yacht Track. R Stour is well marked; sp limit 8kn. Beware 'The Horse' 4ca NE and drying bank 1½ca NW of Wrabness Pt. Mistley Quay local knowledge advised for the narrow, tortuous chan to Manningtree.

Special local sound signals
Commercial vessels may use these additional signals:
Four short and rapid blasts followed by one short blast } = I am turning short around to stbd.
Four short and rapid blasts followed by two short blasts } = I am turning short around to port.
One prolonged blast = I am leaving dock, quay or ⚓.

LIGHTS AND MARKS The R Stour to Mistley is lit. Shotley Marina: a Dir lt at lock indicates the dredged chan (2·0m) by Inogen (or Moiré) visual marker lt which is a square, ambered display; a vert B line indicates on the appr centre line 339°. If off the centre line, arrows indicate the direction to steer to regain it.

COMMUNICATIONS (Code 01255) Dr 879400; 🏥 201200. Harwich HM 243030; Hbr Ops 243000.

Harwich VTS Ch **71** 11 20 (H24). Yachts should monitor Ch 71 for traffic info, but not transmit. ♨, tidal and (possibly) help in poor vis may be available on request. The Hbr Patrol launch listens on Ch 11 (summer weekends, 0800-1800). Hbr Radar Ch 20. Shotley Marina Ch **80** (lock master). Monitor Ch 14 for an information service by Dover CG for the Sunk TSS.

FACILITIES HARWICH Halfpenny Pier Available Apr–Oct, no reservations. Free 0900-1600; overnight: £10<5m>£15<10m>£20 <15m>£25<20m>£35, max 72hrs, ⚓ ⛽.

Town 🏧🏪🛒⚒🔧⛽🛢📮Ⓑ🛒✕🖃🚆. **Ferries** Hook of Holland: 2/day; 6¼hrs; Stena (www.stenaline.co.uk).

SHOTLEY (01473) Shotley Marina www.shotleymarina.com ☎ 788982 (H24), access H24 via lock (width 7m). 350⚓, ❶s welcome £3·00, 🅿🛢⚓(H24)⚒🔧⛽Ⓔ⚓🍴✕🖃 Ferries to Harwich.

Shotley SC ☎787500, ▬ ⚓ 🖃.

WRABNESS ⚓⚓🛒.

MANNINGTREE ⚓ (drying), ⚓. **Stour SC** ☎(01206) 393924, M (drying but free), ⚓⛽🖃. **Town** ⚓🛒.

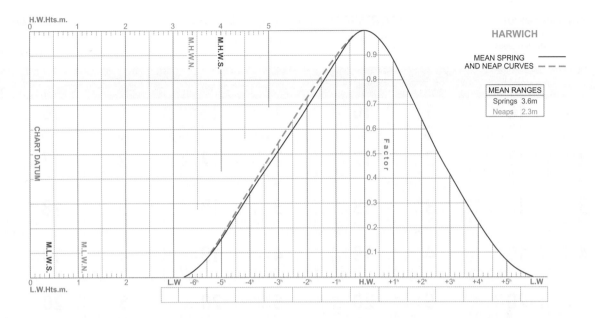

HARWICH

MEAN SPRING
AND NEAP CURVES - - - -

MEAN RANGES
Springs 3.6m
Neaps 2.3m

1.20 RIVER ORWELL

Suffolk **51°57′·06N 01°17′·77E** (Guard PHM by) ✹✹✹✹♨♨♨❀❀❀

CHARTS AC 5607, 2052, 2693, 1491; Imray C29, C1,Y16, 2000

TIDES Pin Mill +0100 Dover; Ipswich +0115 Dover; ML 2·4; Duration 0555

Standard Port HARWICH (→)

Times				Height (metres)			
High Water		Low Water		MHWS	MHWN	MLWN	MLWS
0000	0600	0000	0600	4·0	3·4	1·1	0·4
1200	1800	1200	1800				
Differences IPSWICH							
+0015	+0025	0000	+0010	+0·2	0·0	−0·1	−0·1

SHELTER Good. Ent and river well marked, but many unlit moorings line both banks. ⚓s above Shotley Pt on W side, or off Pinmill. No yacht facilities at Felixstowe. ❶'s (pre-book) at Suffolk Yacht Hbr, Woolverstone Marina, Fox's Marina (Ipswich), Neptune Marina, Ipswich Haven Marina, the latter two accessed via Prince Philip Lock; *call Ch 68 at Orwell Bridge.*

NAVIGATION Approach/entry from seaward as for R Stour. WPT Shotley Spit SCM buoy, Q (6)+L Fl 15s, 51°57′·21N 01°17′·68E, at river ent. A *Yachting Guide to Harwich Harbour and its Rivers* has much useful info; it can be obtained free from Harwich Haven Authority, The Quay, Harwich CO12 3HH; ☎(01255) 243030.

- Keep clear of the many large ships, ferries from/to Harwich, Felixstowe and Ipswich, especially container ships turning between Trinity container terminal, Shotley Spit and Guard buoys.
- Ch 71 should be monitored whilst in Harwich Harbour but only used in emergency. Call sign Harwich VTS. Harwich HM 01255 243030. Refer also to 1.19 River Stour.
- 6kn speed limit in R Orwell. Ipswich Dock ent closed when tide >4.6m above CD. Ipswich New Cut entrance: *Velocity Control Structure is raised from seabed when required with the top of it just below sea level*; 3 FR (vert) = no passage.

LIGHTS AND MARKS Suffolk Yacht Hbr appr marked by SWM then four bns and ldg lts: front Iso Y; rear Oc Y 4s.

A14 bridge lts: Centre FY (clearance 38m)
No 9 Pier 2 FR (vert) } shown up- and
No 10 Pier 2 FG (vert) } downstream.
● and ● tfc lts control ent to Ipswich Dock (H24).
Ipswich New Cut: 3 FR (vert) when closed to navigation.

COMMUNICATIONS (Code 01473) Ⓗ 712233; Orwell Navigation Service 211066, Ipswich HM 211771, Ipswich Lock Control 213526.
Ipswich Port Radio and *Ipswich Lock Control* VHF Ch 68 (H24). Once above Shotley Pt or anywhere in the area, monitor Ch 68 continuously in fog. Suffolk Yacht Hbr, Woolverstone Marina, Fox's Marina: Ch 80 M. Neptune Marina: Ch ⚓ 80 (0800-1730LT), Ipswich Haven Marina Ch M 80.

FACILITIES
LEVINGTON Suffolk Yacht Hbr (SYH) info@syharbour.co.uk ☎659240, Ch 80. Access H24. ⬛(launch £25) 550⬤+❶ £2·97, ⬛🔧 ⬛🚿 ♨(0815-1750) LPG ⬛⚒🔨 🔩 🅱️ Ⓔ ⚓ 🏗(10/60/75t) 🅰(15t) ⛽🛒.
Haven Ports YC ☎659658, ✕ 🍴.

Town ✉ Ⓑ (Felixstowe), ⇌ (bus to Ipswich), ✈ (Cambridge).

PIN MILL King's Boatyard ☎780258; ⚓ (<36′,£10 donation to RNLI, ☎ 07714 260568),⚓⬛🔧🔨 🅱️ 🏗(6t) 🛒(1M).
Pin Mill SC ☎780271.

WOOLVERSTONE Marina ☎780206 (H24), Mob 07803 968209. 235 ⬤, ❶ £3·40 inc ⛽, ⬛🚿 🅱️⬛(HO) ⬛🔩 🅱️⚓🅰 🏗(20t) ⛽ ✕.
Royal Harwich YC Marina www.royalharwichyachtclub.co.uk ☎ 780319 mob 07742 145994 (berths); ⬤ £2·60; ⚓⬛🔧⚓🅱️✕🍴.
Town Chelmondiston: ✉🍴.

IPSWICH, Fox's Marina ♨ www.foxsmarina.com ☎ 689111, Ch 80. 120⬤+❶ £2·94, ⬛⬛🚿(0800-1730) ⬛🔧 🔩 🅱️ Ⓔ ⚒ ♨ 🏗(44/70t) 🅰(7t) ⛽ ACA 🛒 wi-fi.
Marina YC ☎684111, 🍴 ✕.

Orwell YC ☎602288, ⚓⚓🛒🍴

Prince Philip Lock near city centre gives H24 access to:
Neptune Marina ☎215204, 150⬤+❶ £3·50, ⬛(0800-1700).

Ipswich Haven Marina ☎236644, ⚓ 320⬤+❶ £2·80, ⬛(0800-1900) ⬛🅱️ Ⓔ ♨ 🏗(75t) 🅰 ✕ 🍴 wi-fi.

Town 🎦🎦 ✉ Ⓑ ⇌ ✈ (Cambridge/Norwich).

STANDARD TIME (UT)
For Summer Time add ONE hour in **non-shaded areas**

HARWICH LAT 51°57'N LONG 1°17'E
TIMES AND HEIGHTS OF HIGH AND LOW WATERS

Dates in red are SPRINGS
Dates in blue are NEAPS

YEAR 2022

JANUARY

Day	Time m	Time m	Time m	Time m
1 SA	0329 0.8	0959 3.9	1601 0.6	2233 3.9
2 SU ●	0425 0.7	1055 4.0	1651 0.5	2325 4.0
3 M	0517 0.5	1148 4.1	1739 0.5	
4 TU	0014 4.0	0609 0.6	1239 4.2	1825 0.6
5 W	0102 4.0	0658 0.3	1329 4.2	1910 0.7
6 TH	0148 4.0	0748 0.3	1418 4.1	1955 0.8
7 F	0234 3.9	0837 0.3	1507 4.0	2039 0.9
8 SA	0319 3.8	0927 0.4	1555 3.8	2125 1.1
9 SU ☽	0405 3.7	1019 0.6	1646 3.6	2216 1.2
10 M	0455 3.5	1119 0.7	1740 3.4	2318 1.3
11 TU	0551 3.4	1221 0.9	1839 3.3	
12 W	0032 1.3	0654 3.3	1319 0.9	1942 3.3
13 TH	0140 1.3	0759 3.3	1414 1.0	2043 3.3
14 F	0240 1.1	0902 3.4	1504 1.0	2139 3.5
15 SA	0333 1.0	0958 3.5	1550 0.9	2227 3.6
16 SU	0419 0.9	1047 3.6	1631 0.9	2311 3.7
17 M ○	0459 0.7	1130 3.7	1709 0.7	2349 3.8
18 TU	0537 0.7	1208 3.7	1746 0.8	
19 W	0023 3.8	0615 0.6	1242 3.7	1822 0.8
20 TH	0055 3.7	0653 0.6	1316 3.7	1856 0.8
21 F	0127 3.7	0730 0.5	1351 3.8	1929 0.8
22 SA	0201 3.7	0806 0.5	1430 3.8	2005 0.8
23 SU	0237 3.7	0842 0.5	1512 3.7	2044 0.8
24 M	0317 3.7	0922 0.5	1558 3.7	2128 0.9
25 TU ☾	0401 3.6	1007 0.6	1649 3.5	2218 1.0
26 W	0454 3.5	1101 0.7	1749 3.4	2317 1.1
27 TH	0603 3.4	1212 0.8	1855 3.3	
28 F	0032 1.1	0720 3.4	1335 0.9	2006 3.3
29 SA	0159 1.1	0836 3.5	1447 0.8	2117 3.4
30 SU	0316 0.9	0947 3.6	1550 0.8	2221 3.6
31 M	0420 0.7	1048 3.9	1643 0.7	2316 3.8

FEBRUARY

Day	Time m	Time m	Time m	Time m
1 TU ●	0515 0.4	1142 4.1	1730 0.6	
2 W	0005 4.0	0605 0.3	1231 4.2	1814 0.6
3 TH	0051 4.0	0651 0.2	1317 4.2	1856 0.6
4 F	0133 4.0	0735 0.2	1401 4.1	1936 0.7
5 SA	0214 4.0	0816 0.3	1443 4.0	2015 0.8
6 SU	0252 3.9	0855 0.4	1523 3.8	2051 0.8
7 M	0330 3.8	0933 0.5	1602 3.6	2130 1.0
8 TU ☽	0410 3.7	1013 0.7	1643 3.4	2215 1.1
9 W	0456 3.5	1107 0.9	1728 3.2	2314 1.2
10 TH	0551 3.3	1217 1.1	1823 3.1	
11 F	0035 1.3	0658 3.1	1327 1.2	1935 3.1
12 SA	0158 1.2	0823 3.1	1430 1.1	2104 3.2
13 SU	0307 1.1	0937 3.3	1525 1.0	2204 3.4
14 M	0400 0.9	1030 3.5	1611 0.9	2251 3.6
15 TU	0441 0.7	1115 3.6	1652 0.8	2332 3.7
16 W ○	0519 0.6	1154 3.7	1729 0.8	
17 TH	0009 3.7	0557 0.5	1228 3.8	1805 0.7
18 F	0043 3.8	0634 0.4	1302 3.8	1839 0.7
19 SA	0114 3.8	0709 0.3	1335 3.8	1912 0.6
20 SU	0145 3.8	0743 0.3	1411 3.8	1946 0.6
21 M	0217 3.8	0817 0.3	1449 3.8	2024 0.6
22 TU	0253 3.8	0853 0.5	1530 3.7	2106 0.7
23 W ☾	0335 3.8	0936 0.5	1617 3.5	2153 0.8
24 TH	0424 3.6	1027 0.7	1711 3.3	2249 1.0
25 F	0528 3.4	1137 1.0	1820 3.1	
26 SA	0006 1.1	0657 3.2	1319 1.1	1944 3.1
27 SU	0152 1.1	0830 3.3	1441 1.0	2108 3.2
28 M	0318 0.8	0945 3.6	1543 0.9	2213 3.5

MARCH

Day	Time m	Time m	Time m	Time m
1 TU	0420 0.5	1043 3.9	1634 0.7	2305 3.8
2 W ●	0510 0.3	1133 4.1	1717 0.6	2351 3.9
3 TH	0554 0.1	1218 4.2	1758 0.6	
4 F	0033 4.0	0635 0.1	1300 4.1	1837 0.6
5 SA	0112 4.0	0713 0.2	1339 4.0	1914 0.6
6 SU	0148 4.0	0747 0.3	1415 3.9	1947 0.6
7 M	0222 3.9	0817 0.4	1447 3.8	2018 0.7
8 TU	0256 3.9	0846 0.6	1520 3.6	2052 0.8
9 W	0333 3.7	0919 0.7	1556 3.5	2132 0.9
10 TH ☽	0416 3.5	1002 1.0	1639 3.3	2223 1.1
11 F	0507 3.3	1107 1.2	1732 3.1	2340 1.2
12 SA	0610 3.0	1243 1.3	1837 3.0	
13 SU	0112 1.2	0733 3.0	1358 1.3	2008 3.0
14 M	0231 1.1	0913 3.2	1458 1.1	2134 3.3
15 TU	0329 0.9	1008 3.4	1547 1.0	2224 3.5
16 W	0413 0.7	1051 3.7	1628 0.8	2306 3.6
17 TH	0452 0.5	1130 3.8	1705 0.7	2343 3.7
18 F ○	0530 0.3	1205 3.9	1740 0.6	
19 SA	0018 3.8	0607 0.3	1239 3.9	1815 0.5
20 SU	0050 3.8	0642 0.2	1313 3.9	1850 0.5
21 M	0123 3.9	0716 0.2	1348 3.9	1926 0.4
22 TU	0157 4.0	0752 0.2	1425 3.9	2005 0.4
23 W	0235 3.9	0830 0.4	1505 3.7	2047 0.5
24 TH	0318 3.8	0913 0.6	1550 3.5	2135 0.7
25 F ☾	0409 3.6	1005 0.9	1642 3.2	2234 0.9
26 SA	0518 3.3	1121 1.2	1756 3.0	
27 SU	0007 1.1	0659 3.2	1316 1.2	1937 3.0
28 M	0158 0.9	0830 3.4	1431 1.1	2056 3.2
29 TU	0313 0.7	0936 3.7	1529 0.9	2156 3.5
30 W	0408 0.4	1028 3.9	1616 0.7	2245 3.8
31 TH	0453 0.2	1115 4.1	1658 0.6	2330 3.9

APRIL

Day	Time m	Time m	Time m	Time m
1 F ●	0533 0.1	1157 4.1	1737 0.5	
2 SA	0010 4.0	0610 0.2	1236 4.1	1815 0.5
3 SU	0047 4.0	0644 0.3	1312 3.9	1848 0.5
4 M	0120 3.9	0713 0.6	1343 3.8	1918 0.6
5 TU	0152 3.9	0738 0.5	1412 3.7	1948 0.6
6 W	0225 3.8	0805 0.6	1442 3.7	2021 0.7
7 TH	0301 3.7	0838 0.8	1518 3.5	2101 0.8
8 F	0343 3.5	0918 1.0	1601 3.4	2149 1.0
9 SA ☽	0433 3.3	1009 1.3	1655 3.2	2301 1.1
10 SU	0534 3.1	1155 1.4	1800 3.0	
11 M	0034 1.2	0648 3.0	1321 1.4	1917 3.0
12 TU	0148 1.0	0828 3.1	1423 1.2	2044 3.2
13 W	0246 0.8	0930 3.4	1513 1.0	2142 3.4
14 TH	0335 0.6	1015 3.7	1555 0.8	2228 3.6
15 F	0418 0.4	1055 3.8	1634 0.7	2308 3.7
16 SA ○	0459 0.3	1133 3.9	1712 0.6	2346 3.9
17 SU	0537 0.2	1210 4.0	1749 0.5	
18 M	0023 4.0	0614 0.2	1247 4.0	1828 0.4
19 TU	0100 4.0	0652 0.2	1326 4.0	1908 0.3
20 W	0140 4.1	0730 0.3	1405 3.9	1950 0.4
21 TH	0223 4.0	0812 0.5	1447 3.7	2036 0.5
22 F	0311 3.8	0858 0.7	1534 3.5	2128 0.6
23 SA ☾	0408 3.6	0953 1.0	1631 3.2	2236 0.8
24 SU	0526 3.3	1124 1.3	1755 3.1	
25 M	0021 0.9	0658 3.3	1301 1.3	1923 3.1
26 TU	0146 0.9	0812 3.5	1409 1.1	2031 3.4
27 W	0251 0.5	0912 3.8	1504 0.9	2128 3.6
28 TH	0343 0.3	1004 3.9	1551 0.8	2218 3.8
29 F	0426 0.3	1050 4.0	1634 0.6	2303 3.9
30 SA ●	0505 0.3	1132 4.0	1713 0.6	2343 3.9

Chart Datum: 2·02 metres below Ordnance Datum (Newlyn). HAT is 4·4 metres above Chart Datum.

FREE monthly updates. Register at
www.reedsnauticalalmanac.co.uk

STANDARD TIME (UT)
For Summer Time add ONE hour in **non-shaded areas**

HARWICH   LAT 51°57'N   LONG 1°17'E
TIMES AND HEIGHTS OF HIGH AND LOW WATERS

Dates in red are **SPRINGS**
Dates in blue are NEAPS

YEAR 2022

MAY

Day	Time m	Time m	Time m	Time m
1 SU	0541 0.4	1210 4.0	1750 0.6	
2 M	0020 3.9	0613 0.5	1244 3.9	1824 0.6
3 TU	0053 3.9	0640 0.6	1313 3.8	1853 0.6
4 W	0125 3.8	0705 0.7	1339 3.7	1924 0.6
5 TH	0158 3.8	0735 0.8	1410 3.7	1959 0.7
6 F	0235 3.7	0809 0.9	1447 3.6	2039 0.7
7 SA	0317 3.5	0848 1.0	1531 3.4	2127 0.9
8 SU	0405 3.3	0935 1.2	1624 3.2	2233 1.0
9 M	0503 3.2	1046 1.4	1727 3.1	◐ 2357 1.0
10 TU	0610 3.1	1233 1.4	1837 3.1	
11 W	0105 0.9	0723 3.2	1337 1.3	1947 3.2
12 TH	0202 0.7	0832 3.4	1430 1.1	2049 3.4
13 F	0255 0.5	0928 3.6	1517 0.9	2142 3.6
14 SA	0342 0.4	1015 3.8	1601 0.7	2230 3.8
15 SU	0426 0.3	1100 4.0	1643 0.6	2314 3.9
16 M	0508 0.2	1142 4.1	1725 0.4	○ 2358 4.1
17 TU	0550 0.2	1225 4.1	1808 0.3	
18 W	0042 4.1	0632 0.3	1307 4.0	1854 0.3
19 TH	0128 4.1	0715 0.4	1351 3.9	1941 0.3
20 F	0217 4.1	0800 0.6	1438 3.8	2031 0.4
21 SA	0310 3.9	0849 0.8	1529 3.6	2129 0.5
22 SU	0411 3.7	0949 1.1	1630 3.4	◑ 2243 0.6
23 M	0523 3.5	1109 1.3	1744 3.3	
24 TU	0008 0.7	0636 3.5	1230 1.3	1855 3.3
25 W	0118 0.6	0741 3.6	1335 1.2	1957 3.4
26 TH	0217 0.5	0840 3.7	1431 1.0	2054 3.6
27 F	0309 0.5	0933 3.8	1522 0.9	2146 3.7
28 SA	0354 0.5	1020 3.9	1607 0.7	2234 3.8
29 SU	0434 0.5	1104 3.9	1649 0.7	2317 3.8
30 M	0510 0.6	1143 3.8	1728 0.6	● 2356 3.8
31 TU	0543 0.7	1218 3.8	1803 0.6	

JUNE

Day	Time m	Time m	Time m	Time m
1 W	0031 3.8	0613 0.7	1247 3.7	1835 0.6
2 TH	0104 3.7	0642 0.8	1315 3.7	1909 0.6
3 F	0138 3.7	0714 0.9	1347 3.7	1946 0.6
4 SA	0215 3.6	0749 0.9	1424 3.6	2027 0.7
5 SU	0256 3.6	0828 1.0	1507 3.5	2113 0.8
6 M	0343 3.5	0913 1.1	1557 3.4	2208 0.8
7 TU	0436 3.4	1007 1.2	1654 3.3	◐ 2313 0.8
8 W	0535 3.3	1119 1.3	1758 3.3	
9 TH	0018 0.8	0638 3.4	1237 1.2	1902 3.3
10 F	0118 0.7	0741 3.5	1340 1.1	2003 3.4
11 SA	0214 0.6	0842 3.6	1435 1.0	2101 3.6
12 SU	0307 0.5	0938 3.8	1528 0.8	2156 3.8
13 M	0357 0.4	1030 3.9	1618 0.6	2248 4.0
14 TU	0445 0.4	1119 4.0	1707 0.5	○ 2339 4.1
15 W	0531 0.4	1207 4.0	1756 0.4	
16 TH	0029 4.2	0617 0.4	1254 4.0	1846 0.3
17 F	0120 4.2	0704 0.5	1342 4.0	1937 0.3
18 SA	0211 4.1	0751 0.7	1431 3.9	2030 0.3
19 SU	0305 4.0	0841 0.9	1522 3.8	2126 0.4
20 M	0401 3.9	0935 1.0	1617 3.6	2229 0.5
21 TU	0500 3.7	1037 1.2	1715 3.5	◑ 2336 0.5
22 W	0601 3.6	1148 1.2	1816 3.5	
23 TH	0040 0.6	0703 3.5	1255 1.2	1917 3.5
24 F	0137 0.6	0759 3.5	1355 1.1	2017 3.5
25 SA	0230 0.7	0858 3.6	1450 1.0	2113 3.6
26 SU	0319 0.7	0950 3.7	1542 0.9	2206 3.6
27 M	0403 0.8	1037 3.7	1628 0.8	2254 3.7
28 TU	0443 0.8	1120 3.8	1710 0.7	2337 3.7
29 W	0519 0.8	1158 3.8	1748 0.7	●
30 TH	0016 3.7	0554 0.9	1231 3.7	1824 0.6

JULY

Day	Time m	Time m	Time m	Time m
1 F	0051 3.7	0628 0.9	1301 3.7	1900 0.6
2 SA	0124 3.6	0702 0.9	1332 3.7	1937 0.6
3 SU	0159 3.6	0736 0.9	1408 3.7	2016 0.6
4 M	0238 3.6	0812 1.0	1447 3.6	2056 0.6
5 TU	0320 3.6	0852 1.0	1529 3.6	2138 0.6
6 W	0408 3.6	0937 1.1	1617 3.5	2226 0.7
7 TH	0501 3.5	1029 1.1	1714 3.4	◐ 2324 0.7
8 F	0559 3.5	1131 1.2	1817 3.4	
9 SA	0028 0.7	0701 3.5	1243 1.2	1922 3.4
10 SU	0134 0.7	0804 3.5	1355 1.1	2027 3.5
11 M	0236 0.7	0907 3.6	1501 0.9	2131 3.7
12 TU	0335 0.6	1007 3.8	1601 0.7	2231 3.9
13 W	0429 0.6	1102 3.9	1658 0.5	○ 2328 4.1
14 TH	0519 0.6	1155 4.0	1750 0.4	
15 F	0020 4.2	0607 0.6	1244 4.1	1842 0.2
16 SA	0112 4.2	0653 0.6	1332 4.1	1931 0.2
17 SU	0201 4.2	0739 0.7	1418 4.0	2020 0.2
18 M	0250 4.1	0824 0.8	1504 4.0	2108 0.2
19 TU	0338 4.0	0910 0.9	1549 3.8	2159 0.4
20 W	0427 3.8	0959 1.0	1637 3.7	◑ 2253 0.6
21 TH	0519 3.6	1055 1.2	1729 3.6	2353 0.7
22 F	0614 3.4	1204 1.2	1828 3.4	
23 SA	0053 0.9	0715 3.3	1314 1.2	1934 3.4
24 SU	0150 1.0	0819 3.3	1419 1.1	2041 3.4
25 M	0244 1.0	0919 3.4	1519 1.0	2143 3.5
26 TU	0335 1.0	1012 3.6	1612 0.9	2236 3.6
27 W	0420 1.0	1059 3.7	1656 0.7	2322 3.7
28 TH	0500 0.9	1141 3.8	1734 0.6	●
29 F	0003 3.7	0538 0.9	1218 3.8	1810 0.6
30 SA	0039 3.7	0613 0.9	1251 3.8	1845 0.5
31 SU	0112 3.7	0647 0.9	1321 3.7	1920 0.5

AUGUST

Day	Time m	Time m	Time m	Time m
1 M	0143 3.7	0720 0.9	1351 3.7	1956 0.5
2 TU	0217 3.7	0753 0.9	1423 3.7	2030 0.5
3 W	0255 3.7	0829 0.9	1459 3.7	2105 0.5
4 TH	0338 3.7	0909 0.9	1539 3.7	2145 0.6
5 F	0425 3.6	0955 1.0	1627 3.6	◐ 2233 0.7
6 SA	0520 3.5	1049 1.1	1729 3.5	2336 0.9
7 SU	0623 3.4	1158 1.2	1845 3.4	
8 M	0058 1.0	0732 3.3	1323 1.2	2002 3.4
9 TU	0216 1.0	0844 3.4	1447 1.0	2117 3.6
10 W	0324 0.9	0953 3.6	1558 0.8	2224 3.8
11 TH	0421 0.8	1052 3.8	1656 0.5	2321 4.1
12 F	0510 0.7	1144 4.0	1746 0.3	○
13 SA	0011 4.2	0555 0.6	1230 4.1	1833 0.1
14 SU	0058 4.3	0638 0.6	1315 4.2	1917 0.1
15 M	0143 4.2	0720 0.7	1356 4.1	1959 0.1
16 TU	0226 4.1	0800 0.7	1436 4.1	2039 0.3
17 W	0308 3.9	0839 0.8	1515 4.0	2119 0.5
18 TH	0348 3.7	0918 0.9	1554 3.8	2201 0.7
19 F	0429 3.5	1002 1.0	1639 3.6	◑ 2251 0.9
20 SA	0514 3.3	1059 1.2	1732 3.4	
21 SU	0000 1.1	0608 3.2	1223 1.3	1840 3.2
22 M	0109 1.2	0724 3.1	1347 1.3	2011 3.2
23 TU	0212 1.3	0849 3.3	1456 1.1	2124 3.4
24 W	0310 1.2	0949 3.5	1553 0.9	2218 3.6
25 TH	0359 1.1	1038 3.7	1636 0.7	2304 3.7
26 F	0439 1.0	1120 3.8	1712 0.6	2344 3.8
27 SA	0516 0.9	1158 3.8	1745 0.5	●
28 SU	0019 3.8	0551 0.8	1231 3.8	1820 0.5
29 M	0051 3.8	0624 0.8	1300 3.8	1854 0.4
30 TU	0121 3.8	0657 0.8	1327 3.8	1927 0.4
31 W	0152 3.8	0729 0.8	1356 3.9	1959 0.4

Chart Datum: 2·02 metres below Ordnance Datum (Newlyn). HAT is 4·4 metres above Chart Datum.

E England

»» FREE monthly updates. Register at www.reedsnauticalalmanac.co.uk ««

83

STANDARD TIME (UT)
For Summer Time add ONE hour in **non-shaded areas**

HARWICH LAT 51°57'N LONG 1°17'E
TIMES AND HEIGHTS OF HIGH AND LOW WATERS

Dates in red are SPRINGS
Dates in blue are NEAPS

YEAR **2022**

SEPTEMBER

Time	m		Time	m
1 0227	3.8	**16** 0306	3.7
0804	0.7	0839	0.9
TH 1429	3.9	F 1515	3.8
2033	0.5	2105	0.8
2 0306	3.8	**17** 0340	3.6
0843	0.8	0918	1.0
F 1508	3.8	SA 1556	3.6
2111	0.6	◑ 2144	1.1
3 0349	3.6	**18** 0420	3.4
0928	0.9	1007	1.2
SA 1553	3.7	SU 1647	3.4
◐ 2157	0.8	2245	1.3
4 0441	3.4	**19** 0512	3.2
1021	1.1	1127	1.3
SU 1652	3.5	M 1751	3.1
2257	1.1		
5 0547	3.2	**20** 0028	1.5
1131	1.2	0619	3.1
M 1818	3.3	TU 1310	1.3
		1936	3.1
6 0037	1.2	**21** 0141	1.4
0708	3.2	0810	3.1
TU 1315	1.2	W 1423	1.1
1953	3.3	2101	3.3
7 0210	1.2	**22** 0241	1.3
0834	3.3	0919	3.4
W 1449	1.0	TH 1519	0.9
2116	3.6	2154	3.6
8 0317	1.0	**23** 0331	1.1
0944	3.6	1008	3.6
TH 1557	0.7	F 1602	0.7
2218	3.9	2237	3.8
9 0410	0.8	**24** 0411	1.0
1039	3.8	1050	3.8
F 1648	0.4	SA 1638	0.6
2309	4.1	2316	3.9
10 0455	0.7	**25** 0448	0.9
1127	4.1	1127	3.9
SA 1733	0.2	SU 1713	0.5
○ 2356	4.3	● 2350	3.9
11 0537	0.6	**26** 0522	0.8
1210	4.2	1200	3.9
SU 1814	0.1	M 1748	0.4
12 0038	4.3	**27** 0021	3.9
0617	0.6	0557	0.7
M 1251	4.2	TU 1230	3.9
1853	0.1	1823	0.4
13 0119	4.2	**28** 0052	4.0
0656	0.6	0630	0.7
TU 1328	4.2	W 1259	3.9
1930	0.3	1856	0.4
14 0157	4.1	**29** 0125	4.0
0732	0.7	0705	0.7
W 1404	4.1	TH 1330	4.0
2003	0.4	1929	0.4
15 0232	3.9	**30** 0159	3.9
0806	0.8	0742	0.7
TH 1438	4.0	F 1406	4.0
2034	0.6	2005	0.5

OCTOBER

Time	m		Time	m
1 0237	3.8	**16** 0258	3.6
0823	0.7	0844	0.9
SA 1447	3.9	SU 1522	3.6
2046	0.7	2058	1.2
2 0319	3.6	**17** 0338	3.5
0909	0.8	0932	1.1
SU 1535	3.7	M 1611	3.4
2133	1.0	◑ 2146	1.4
3 0408	3.4	**18** 0430	3.3
1004	1.0	1043	1.3
M 1638	3.4	TU 1712	3.1
◐ 2235	1.3	2328	1.6
4 0518	3.1	**19** 0537	3.1
1124	1.2	1223	1.3
TU 1815	3.2	W 1831	3.0
5 0038	1.4	**20** 0102	1.6
0659	3.1	0701	3.1
W 1324	1.1	TH 1334	1.1
1956	3.4	2019	3.2
6 0201	1.3	**21** 0204	1.4
0823	3.3	0829	3.3
TH 1443	0.8	F 1430	0.9
2106	3.7	2115	3.5
7 0301	1.1	**22** 0253	1.2
0925	3.6	0924	3.5
F 1541	0.5	SA 1516	0.7
2201	4.0	2159	3.7
8 0351	0.9	**23** 0336	1.0
1017	3.9	1008	3.7
SA 1629	0.3	SU 1558	0.6
2249	4.2	2237	3.9
9 0434	0.7	**24** 0414	0.9
1103	4.1	1047	3.8
SU 1710	0.2	M 1638	0.5
○ 2333	4.3	2313	4.0
10 0514	0.7	**25** 0451	0.8
1145	4.1	1124	3.9
M 1748	0.2	TU 1715	0.4
		● 2348	4.0
11 0013	4.2	**26** 0528	0.7
0553	0.6	1159	4.0
TU 1223	4.2	W 1752	0.4
1824	0.3		
12 0051	4.1	**27** 0023	4.1
0630	0.6	0605	0.6
W 1259	4.1	TH 1234	4.1
1856	0.5	1828	0.4
13 0125	4.0	**28** 0100	4.0
0703	0.7	0644	0.6
TH 1332	4.0	F 1312	4.1
1924	0.6	1906	0.5
14 0155	3.9	**29** 0137	4.0
0734	0.7	0725	0.6
F 1406	4.0	SA 1353	4.1
1951	0.6	1945	0.6
15 0225	3.8	**30** 0217	3.8
0806	0.8	0809	0.6
SA 1442	3.8	SU 1439	3.9
2021	0.9	2029	0.9
		31 0301	3.6
		0859	0.8
		M 1533	3.7
		2119	1.1

NOVEMBER

Time	m		Time	m
1 0353	3.4	**16** 0356	3.4
1000	0.9	1011	1.1
TU 1644	3.5	W 1638	3.3
◑ 2228	1.4	◑ 2214	1.5
2 0511	3.2	**17** 0459	3.2
1138	1.0	1132	1.1
W 1818	3.4	TH 1744	3.2
3 0023	1.5	**18** 0001	1.6
0647	3.2	0612	3.1
TH 1312	0.9	F 1241	1.0
1938	3.5	1857	3.2
4 0137	1.3	**19** 0111	1.5
0758	3.4	0723	3.2
F 1419	0.7	SA 1339	0.9
2042	3.8	2007	3.4
5 0234	1.1	**20** 0206	1.3
0857	3.6	0825	3.4
SA 1514	0.5	SU 1430	0.7
2135	4.0	2104	3.6
6 0324	0.9	**21** 0253	1.1
0948	3.9	0918	3.6
SU 1600	0.4	M 1518	0.6
2223	4.1	2151	3.8
7 0408	0.8	**22** 0338	0.9
1035	4.0	1005	3.8
M 1641	0.4	TU 1603	0.5
2306	4.1	2235	4.0
8 0450	0.7	**23** 0420	0.8
1117	4.0	1049	3.9
TU 1718	0.4	W 1645	0.5
○ 2346	4.1	● 2318	4.1
9 0529	0.7	**24** 0502	0.7
1157	4.0	1132	4.1
W 1753	0.6	TH 1726	0.4
		2359	4.1
10 0022	4.0	**25** 0544	0.6
0606	0.7	1216	4.1
TH 1232	4.0	F 1807	0.5
1824	0.7		
11 0054	3.9	**26** 0041	4.1
0639	0.7	0629	0.5
F 1306	3.9	SA 1300	4.2
1851	0.8	1849	0.6
12 0123	3.8	**27** 0123	4.0
0710	0.7	0714	0.5
SA 1339	3.9	SU 1347	4.1
1919	0.9	1933	0.7
13 0151	3.8	**28** 0208	3.8
0743	0.8	0803	0.5
SU 1416	3.8	M 1439	4.0
1951	1.0	2020	0.9
14 0225	3.7	**29** 0256	3.7
0822	0.9	0858	0.6
M 1456	3.6	TU 1536	3.8
2029	1.2	2113	1.1
15 0306	3.6	**30** 0353	3.5
0909	1.0	1003	0.7
TU 1543	3.4	W 1643	3.6
2113	1.3	◑ 2219	1.3

DECEMBER

Time	m		Time	m
1 0504	3.4	**16** 0422	3.4
1125	0.8	1041	0.9
TH 1757	3.5	F 1704	3.4
2346	1.4	◑ 2238	1.4
2 0618	3.4	**17** 0524	3.3
1243	0.7	1146	0.9
F 1906	3.6	SA 1805	3.3
		2355	1.4
3 0059	1.3	**18** 0629	3.3
0724	3.5	1248	0.9
SA 1345	0.6	SU 1908	3.4
2008	3.7		
4 0200	1.2	**19** 0106	1.3
0823	3.6	0732	3.4
SU 1439	0.6	M 1345	0.8
2103	3.8	2010	3.5
5 0253	1.0	**20** 0205	1.2
0917	3.7	0832	3.5
M 1527	0.6	TU 1439	0.7
2153	3.9	2108	3.7
6 0342	0.9	**21** 0300	1.0
1007	3.8	0928	3.7
TU 1610	0.6	W 1531	0.6
2239	3.9	2202	3.8
7 0427	0.8	**22** 0352	0.8
1053	3.9	1022	3.9
W 1650	0.7	TH 1620	0.6
2321	3.9	2253	3.9
8 0509	0.7	**23** 0442	0.7
1135	3.9	1113	4.0
TH 1726	0.8	F 1707	0.6
○ 2359	3.9	● 2341	4.0
9 0548	0.7	**24** 0531	0.5
1213	3.8	1203	4.1
F 1758	0.8	SA 1753	0.6
10 0031	3.8	**25** 0028	4.0
0623	0.7	0620	0.4
SA 1248	3.8	SU 1253	4.2
1829	0.9	1838	0.6
11 0100	3.8	**26** 0115	4.0
0656	0.7	0710	0.3
SU 1322	3.7	M 1344	4.2
1859	1.0	1924	0.7
12 0129	3.8	**27** 0203	3.9
0730	0.7	0801	0.3
M 1357	3.7	TU 1435	4.1
1932	1.0	2012	0.8
13 0204	3.7	**28** 0252	3.8
0809	0.8	0853	0.4
TU 1436	3.6	W 1529	3.9
2009	1.1	2101	1.0
14 0244	3.6	**29** 0343	3.7
0853	0.8	0949	0.5
W 1519	3.5	TH 1624	3.8
2051	1.2	2155	1.1
15 0330	3.5	**30** 0438	3.6
0943	0.9	1053	0.6
TH 1608	3.4	F 1723	3.6
2139	1.3	◑ 2258	1.2
		31 0538	3.5
		1201	0.7
		SA 1825	3.5

Chart Datum: 2·02 metres below Ordnance Datum (Newlyn). HAT is 4·4 metres above Chart Datum.

1.21 RIVER DEBEN

Suffolk **51°59'·38N 01°23'·58E** (Felixstowe Ferry) ❀⚓♨♨❀❀❀

CHARTS AC 5607, 2052, 2693; Imray C29, C1, C28, Y16, 2000

TIDES Woodbridge Haven +0025 Dover; Woodbridge +0105 Dover; ML 1·9; Duration 0635

Standard Port WALTON-ON-THE-NAZE (←)

Times				Height (metres)			
High Water		Low Water		MHWS	MHWN	MLWN	MLWS
0100	0700	0100	0700	4·2	3·4	1·1	0·4
1300	1900	1300	1900				
Differences *FELIXSTOWE PIER* (51° 57'N 1° 21'E)							
–0005	–0007	–0018	–0020	–0·5	–0·4	0·0	0·0
BAWDSEY							
–0016	–0020	–0030	–0032	–0·8	–0·6	–0·1	–0·1
WOODBRIDGE HAVEN (Entrance)							
0000	–0005	–0020	–0025	–0·5	–0·5	–0·1	+0·1
WOODBRIDGE (Town)							
+0045	+0025	+0025	–0020	–0·2	–0·3	–0·2	0·0

SHELTER Good in Tide Mill Yacht Hbr (TMYH) Woodbridge. ⚓s upriver, clear of moorings: N of Horse Sand; off Ramsholt, The Rocks, Waldringfield, The Tips, Methersgate, Kyson Pt and Woodbridge.

NAVIGATION WPT 51°58'·20N 01°23'·85E Woodbridge Haven SWM buoy, thence NNW'ly past W Knoll PHM to Mid Knoll SHM and then head north upriver to the entrance hugging the sea wall/W bank until close to Deben PHM. Chartlet shows the ent at latest survey (2017), showing west'ly movement of the Knolls. Depths can change significantly and buoyage is often adjusted. Visitors may obtain updates at www.debenestuarypilot.co.uk.

Cross the shifting shingle bar HW–3 to HW+2 depending on draught. When Horse Sand is covered there is approx 2m at the bar. Best to enter after half-flood, and leave on the flood. The ent is only 1ca wide and in strong onshore winds gets dangerously choppy; channel is well buoyed/marked. Keep to the W shore until PHM opposite the SC, then move E of Horse Sand. No commercial traffic. 8kn max speed N of Green Reach.

LIGHTS AND MARKS See 1.3 and chartlets.

COMMUNICATIONS (Code 01473) HM mob 07803 476621, Asst HM mob 07860 191768.

Pilotage for river entrance, call *Odd Times* Ch 08 or HM on mobile.

FACILITIES

FELIXSTOWE FERRY (01394), ⚓🔧⚓⚒✎🛒🏪🚣✕🛁; Felixstowe Ferry SC ☎283785, 200⚓ ━(£10) 🚿🍴 ☎282173.

RAMSHOLT HM ☎07930 304061, ⚓⚓✕🛁.

WALDRINGFIELD AC 2693. Craft >11m should ⚓ at the Rocks (NW of Prettyman's Pt) or upriver at The Tips. Possibly ⚓ for <11m by arrangement with HM waldringfieldhm @ btinternet.com ☎736291 mob 07925 081062; 🍴 may have ⚓, ☎736260 VHF 80; ━🛁. Sailing Club www.waldringfieldsc.com 🛁 (Wed and Sat evenings only).

WOODBRIDGE (01394) Tide Mill Yacht Hbr, 200+♥ (max 24m) £2. info@tidemillyachtharbour.co.uk; ☎385745. Ent by No 26 PHM. Depth over sill, dries 1·5m, is 1·6m at MHWN and 2·5m MHWS, with very accurate tide gauge and 6 waiting buoys. ⚓🔧⚓🔟🗲 🚿🚻✎🛒🏪🅴⛺🍴🛁(18t)🚣🏪 ACA.

Woodbridge Cruising Club ☎386737.

Deben YC www.debenyachtclub.co.uk.

Town 🚿🏧✉Ⓑ🚣🏪✕🛁�➤✈ (Cambridge, Norwich).

WOODBRIDGE HAVEN

1.22 RIVER ORE/ALDE
Suffolk 52°02′·13N 01°27′·49E (Ent) ✲✿✿✿✿✿✿

CHARTS AC 5607, 1543, 2052, 2693, 2695; Imray C29, C28, 2000

TIDES Ent. +0015 Dover Slaughden Quay +0155 Dover; ML1·6; Duration 0620

Standard Port WALTON-ON-THE-NAZE (←—)

Times				Height (metres)			
High Water		Low Water		MHWS	MHWN	MLWN	MLWS
0100	0700	0100	0700	4·2	3·4	1·1	0·4
1300	1900	1300	1900				
Differences ORFORD HAVEN BAR							
−0026	−0030	−0036	−0038	−1·0	−0·8	−0·1	0·0
ORFORD QUAY							
+0040	+0040	+0055	+0055	−1·4	−1·1	0·0	+0·2
SLAUGHDEN QUAY							
+0105	+0105	+0125	+0125	−1·3	−0·8	−0·1	+0·2
IKEN CLIFF							
+0130	+0130	+0155	+0155	−1·3	−1·0	0·0	+0·2

SHELTER Good shelter within the river, but the entrance should not be attempted in strong E/ESE onshore winds and rough seas or at night. The only safe ⚓ is in Short Gull; ⚓ in mooring areas. Landing on Havergate Island bird sanctuary is prohibited. ⚓ at Orford have small pick-up buoys marked V. Possible use of private mooring via Upson's BY at Slaughden.

NAVIGATION WPT Orford Haven SWM buoy, 52°02′·00N 01°28′·21E, is moved as required. For latest position call London CG ☎020 8312 7380. Proceed NW'ly to Oxley PHM shaping a more NNW'ly course to leave Weir SHM and North Shoal carried to starboard.

Chartlet is based on surveys carried out in 2017, but depths can change significantly. North shoal is restablishing, the entrance moving further S towards its old position and South Shoal is consolidating. For regularly updated local information see *eastcoastsailing.co.uk*, call Small Craft Deliveries: ☎(01394) 387672, sales@scd-charts.co.uk; or local marinas or chandlers.

- The bar (approx 0·5m) shifts after onshore gales and is dangerous in rough or confused seas caused by tidal streams running against those within the shingle banks. Sp ebb runs up to 6kn.
- Without local info do not enter before half flood or at night. For a first visit, appr at about LW+2½ in settled conditions and at nps.
- Beware Horse Shoal close WNW of N Weir Pt and shoals S and SW of Dove Pt (SW tip of Havergate Island).

R Ore (re-named R Alde between Orford and Slaughden Quay) is navigable up to Snape. The upper reaches are shallow and winding, and marked by withies with red and green topmarks. Shellfish beds on the E bank centred on 52°08′·0N 01°35′·6E.

LIGHTS AND MARKS As chartlet. Ent and river are unlit. Oxley and Weir buoys are seasonal Apr-Oct and the Or bn on the shore of Oxley Marshes is not maintained. Shingle Street, about 2ca S of ent, is identified by Martello tr 'AA', CG Stn, terrace houses and DF aerial. Upriver, Orford Ch and Castle are conspic; also Martello Tr 'CC', 3ca S of Slaughden Quay.

COMMUNICATIONS (Codes 01394 Orford; 01728 Aldeburgh) Orford Dr 450315(HO); Aldeburgh Dr 452027(HO). HM 07528 092635; Small Craft Deliveries (pilotage info) 382655.

Chantry on Ch 08.

FACILITIES
ORFORD: Orford Quay for ⛴ phone HM for availability (max 1 hour with competent crew); M (marked 'V'; call HM. No rafting) £8/night collected by launch 'Chantry'; ⚓⚓ ☎ Orford SC (OSC) visitors may use ⚓ (£6 deposit, key held in Quay Office), ✕ ⌂ Internet (White Lion Hotel Aldeburgh).

Village (¼M) ✉ 🛒 ✕ ⌂ ⇌ (twice daily bus to Woodbridge).

ALDEBURGH: Slaughden Quay ⚓ ⚓ ⚓ ⚓(20t).
Aldeburgh YC (AYC) ☎452562 ⚓.

Slaughden SC (SSC). **Services** ⚓ (via Upson's BY if any vacant) £5. ✕ ⚓ ⚓ ⚓ ⚓ ⚓

Town (¾M) ☎ 🛒 ✕ ⌂ ✉ Ⓑ ⇌ (bus to Wickham Market), ✈ (Norwich).

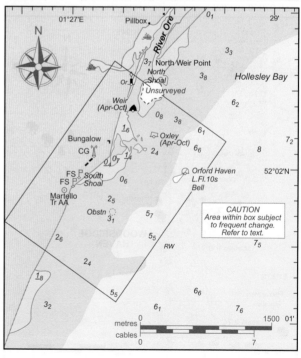

1.23 SOUTHWOLD

Suffolk 52°18'·78N 01°40'·54E ❀❀▲▲▲▲✿✿✿

CHARTS AC 5614, 1543, 2695; Imray C29, C28

TIDES –0105 Dover; ML 1·5; Duration 0620

Standard Port LOWESTOFT (→)

Times				Height (metres)			
High Water		Low Water		MHWS	MHWN	MLWN	MLWS
0300	0900	0200	0800	2·4	2·1	1·0	0·5
1500	2100	1400	2000				
Differences SOUTHWOLD							
+0105	+0105	+0055	+0055	0·0	0·0	–0·1	0·0
MINSMERE SLUICE							
+0110	+0110	+0110	+0110	0·0	–0·1	–0·2	–0·2
ALDEBURGH (seaward)							
+0130	+0130	+0115	+0120	+0·3	+0·2	–0·1	–0·2
ORFORD NESS							
+0135	+0135	+0135	+0125	+0·4	+0·6	–0·1	0·0

NOTE: HW time differences (above) for Southwold apply up the hbr. At the ent mean HW is HW Lowestoft +0035.

SHELTER Good, but the ent is dangerous in strong winds from N through E to S. Visitors berth (must book ahead) on pontoon by HM office or a staging 6ca from the ent, on N bank near to the Harbour Inn. If rafted, shore lines are essential due to current. Some larger vessels moor on N wall of Dock and may encroach channel.

NAVIGATION WPT 52°18'·09N 01°41'·69E, 315°/1M to N Pier lt.

- Enter on the flood as the ebb runs up to 6kn. Shoals are unpredictable up to ¼M offshore; a sand and shingle bar, extent/depth variable, lies off the ent and a shoal builds inside N Pier. Obtain details of appr chans from HM before entering.
- Enter between piers in midstream. When chan widens keep close to The Knuckle (2 FG vert), turn stbd towards [LB] House; keep within 3m of quay wall until it ends, then resume midstream.
- **Caution** Rowing ferry (which has right of way at all times) 3ca and unlit low footbridge 7.5ca upstream of ent.

LIGHTS AND MARKS See 1.3 and chartlet. Walberswick ✠ in line with N Pier lt ≠ 268°. Hbr ent opens on 300°. 3 FR (vert) at N pier ≠ port closed. Lt ho, W ○ tr, Fl 10s 24M, in Southwold town, 0·86M NNE of hbr ent.

COMMUNICATIONS(Code 01502) Dr 722326; Ⓗ 723333; HM 724712. *Southwold Port Radio* Ch **12** 16 (as reqd). HM for fuel 12.

FACILITIES Hbr southwoldharbour@waveney.gov.uk ⚓ HW±3 (Hbr due £8·00) ⚓ £17·50<20ft, £20·50<30ft, £25<40ft, £31<50ft (+£4·30 🕭) ⛽ ☎ also by bowser 100 l/min, ⚒ ⚓ ⛟ ▣(20t) ⬡. **Southwold SC; Town** (¾M) ⛽ ✉ Ⓑ 🛒 ✕ ⇌ (bus to Brampton/ Darsham), ✈ (Norwich).

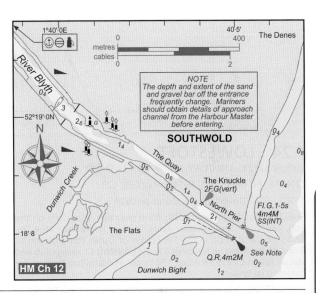

SOUTHWOLD

NOTE
The depth and extent of the sand and gravel bar off the entrance frequently change. Mariners should obtain details of approach channel from the Harbour Master before entering.

HM Ch 12

E England

LOWESTOFT

MEAN SPRING ——————
AND NEAP CURVES ― ― ―

MEAN RANGES	
Spring	1.9m
Neaps	1.1m

1.24 LOWESTOFT

Suffolk **52°28'·31N 01°45'·39E** ✤✤✤▲▲▲✿✿✿

CHARTS AC 1543, 1535, 5614; Imray C29, C28

TIDES –0133 Dover; ML 1·6; Duration 0620

SHELTER Good; accessible H24. Wind over tide, especially on the ebb, can make the entrance lively. Fairway is dredged to 4·7m. RN&S YC yacht basin in the SW corner of Outer Hbr with 2m to 2·5m; no berthing on N side of S Pier. Lowestoft Cruising Club and Haven Marina have facilities 1.5M upriver. Hamilton Dock is for commercial vessels.

NAVIGATION The main commercial approach runs in a SW direct on Kirkley bn; shoal exists at W edge of sector 700m NE of ent. Monitor Ch 14; req permission from *Harbour Control* to enter/leave harbour. Sands continually shift and buoys move to suit. Beware shoals and drying areas esp S of hbr ent; do not cross banks in bad weather, nor at mid flood/ebb. Speed limit in hbr is 4kn.

From S, WPT is E Barnard ECM buoy, Q (3) 10s, 52°25'·15N 01°46'·36E; thence via Stanford Chan E of Newcome Sand QR, Stanford Fl R 2.5s and N Newcome Fl (4) R 15s, all PHM buoys. S Holm SCM, VQ (6)+L Fl 10s, and SW Holm SHM, Fl (2) G 5s, buoys mark the seaward side of this channel.

From E, WPT is Holm Approach ECM buoy, Q (3) 10s, 52°30'·88N 01°50'·22E, then via Holm Chan (buoyed) into Corton Road. Or approach direct to S Holm SCM buoy for Stanford Channel.

From N, appr via Yarmouth, Gorleston and Corton Roads.

Bridge to Inner Hbr (Lake Lothing and Lowestoft CC) lifts at the following times (20 mins notice required): daily 0300, 0500, 0700, 0945, 1115, 1430, 1600, (1800 W/Es + BHs only) 1900, 2100 and 2400 and for commercial traffic. Small craft may pass under the bridge (clearance 2·2m) at any time but call on Ch 14. Craft are to await bridge opening on pontoon at E end of Trawl Dock. **Vessels may only transit bridge chan when G lights shown on N side of appr.**

Gull Wing Bridge is being built across Lake Lothing until 2023. A 32m wide chan will be maintained with details at ABP Lowestoft.

LIGHTS AND MARKS Lowestoft lt ho, W twr, is 1M N of entrance, Kirkley dir bn WRG Oc 10s (see 1.3) is 7ca to the S.

Traffic Signals E arm of RN & SYC yacht basin; S Pier (entry/exit):
3 FR (vert) = do not proceed
GWG (vert) = proceed only as/when instructed

Lift Bridge Iso Y 5s to either side of chan; **Signals** (on N bank):
● = bridge operating, keep 100m clear.
● = vessels may pass through bridge channel.
Oulton Rwy Br centre span lit Iso 10s, S side Fl R 2.5s, N side Fl G 2.5s.

COMMUNICATIONS (Code 01502) Ⓗ 01493 452452. HM & Bridge Control 572286; Mutford Bridge / Lock 531778 (Ansafone, checked daily at 0830, 1300 & 1730); Oulton Broad Yacht Stn 574946.
Lowestoft Hbr Control (ABP) VHF Ch **14** 16 11 (H24). *Lowestoft Haven Marina* Ch **80**, 37. *Oulton Broad YS and Mutford Lock Control* Ch 73. Pilot Ch 14. RN & SYC Ch 14, 80.

FACILITIES **Royal Norfolk & Suffolk YC** www.rnsyc.net ☎566726, ► ⬡ £3·05 inc YC facilities ⛽ ▲ ⟲ ✕ ◻.
Lowestoft Cruising Club www.lowestoftcruisingclub.co.uk, ☎07810 522515, ⬡(max 12m) £2·00, ⬔, ⟲ ► (emergency).
Lowestoft Haven Marina ⬥ www. lowestofthavenmarina.co.uk ☎580300, 140⬡ £2·57 ⬔ ⬚ @ ▲ ▲ ⬚ Ⓔ ▣(70t).
Town ✉ Ⓑ ⬚ ✕ ◻ ⇌ ✈ (Norwich).

Entry to the Broads: See Gt Yarmouth and www.norfolkbroads. com. Passage to Oulton Broad from Lake Lothing is via two bridges and Mutford Lock (width 5·9m). The lock is available 0800-1200 and 1300-1730 daily; 0800-1200 and 1300-1930 at weekends/Bank Holidays; 0900-1200 only 1 Nov to 31 Mar. Charge is £13/day. Booking 24hrs in advance is recommended, ☎(01502) 531778, Ch 73. Oulton Broad Yacht Station ☎(01502) 574946. From Oulton Broad, access into the R Waveney is via Oulton Dyke.

LOWESTOFT LAT 52°28′N LONG 1°45′E
TIMES AND HEIGHTS OF HIGH AND LOW WATERS

Dates in red are **SPRINGS**
Dates in blue are **NEAPS**

YEAR 2022

E England

JANUARY

Time	m	Time	m
1 0129	0.9	**16** 0226	1.0
0732	2.5	0848	2.2
SA 1400	0.7	SU 1431	1.0
2015	2.5	2054	2.4
2 0228	0.8	**17** 0306	0.9
0830	2.6	0927	2.3
SU 1453	0.7	M 1504	1.0
● 2101	2.5	○ 2125	2.4
3 0325	0.6	**18** 0344	0.8
0930	2.6	1001	2.3
M 1543	0.7	TU 1537	1.0
2148	2.6	2157	2.5
4 0419	0.5	**19** 0421	0.7
1026	2.6	1034	2.3
TU 1631	0.8	W 1613	0.9
2234	2.6	2233	2.5
5 0510	0.4	**20** 0500	0.7
1119	2.5	1108	2.3
W 1717	0.8	TH 1649	0.9
2320	2.6	2309	2.5
6 0559	0.4	**21** 0538	0.6
1211	2.5	1143	2.3
TH 1759	0.9	F 1727	0.9
		2347	2.5
7 0005	2.6	**22** 0616	0.6
0647	0.4	1220	2.3
F 1303	2.3	SA 1804	1.0
1841	1.0		
8 0051	2.6	**23** 0024	2.5
0736	0.5	0656	0.7
SA 1401	2.2	SU 1259	2.2
1923	1.1	1844	1.0
9 0137	2.5	**24** 0103	2.5
0829	0.6	0737	0.7
SU 1512	2.1	M 1342	2.2
☽ 2008	1.3	1928	1.1
10 0226	2.4	**25** 0146	2.5
0927	0.8	0823	0.7
M 1619	2.1	TU 1433	2.1
2103	1.3	☽ 2018	1.1
11 0326	2.3	**26** 0236	2.4
1030	0.9	0920	0.8
TU 1717	2.1	W 1547	2.1
2227	1.4	2117	1.2
12 0439	2.2	**27** 0340	2.4
1130	1.0	1034	0.8
W 1813	2.2	TH 1711	2.1
2348	1.3	2240	1.2
13 0546	2.2	**28** 0506	2.3
1224	1.0	1147	0.9
TH 1904	2.2	F 1810	2.2
14 0049	1.2	**29** 0008	1.1
0653	2.2	0620	2.4
F 1311	1.0	SA 1249	0.9
1947	2.3	1905	2.4
15 0141	1.1	**30** 0118	0.9
0758	2.2	0728	2.4
SA 1354	1.0	SU 1348	0.9
2023	2.3	1957	2.4
		31 0222	0.7
		0835	2.5
		M 1444	0.8
		2047	2.5

FEBRUARY

Time	m	Time	m
1 0321	0.5	**16** 0326	0.7
0932	2.5	0944	2.3
TU 1535	0.8	W 1524	0.9
● 2134	2.6	○ 2137	2.5
2 0412	0.4	**17** 0404	0.6
1021	2.5	1014	2.3
W 1621	0.8	TH 1600	0.8
2219	2.6	2212	2.5
3 0459	0.3	**18** 0441	0.6
1106	2.5	1046	2.4
TH 1701	0.8	F 1636	0.8
2302	2.7	2248	2.6
4 0542	0.3	**19** 0518	0.5
1150	2.4	1120	2.4
F 1739	0.8	SA 1712	0.8
2344	2.7	2324	2.6
5 0624	0.3	**20** 0555	0.5
1233	2.3	1155	2.3
SA 1815	0.9	SU 1747	0.8
6 0024	2.6	**21** 0000	2.6
0705	0.5	0631	0.5
SU 1315	2.2	M 1231	2.3
1850	1.0	1823	0.9
7 0105	2.5	**22** 0038	2.6
0745	0.6	0708	0.6
M 1401	2.1	TU 1312	2.2
1928	1.1	1903	0.9
8 0149	2.4	**23** 0121	2.5
0829	0.8	0750	0.7
TU 1459	2.0	W 1358	2.2
☽ 2012	1.2	☽ 1950	1.0
9 0240	2.3	**24** 0212	2.4
0925	1.0	0842	0.8
W 1612	2.0	TH 1457	2.1
2111	1.3	2050	1.1
10 0355	2.2	**25** 0322	2.3
1043	1.1	0957	1.0
TH 1713	2.0	F 1625	2.1
2302	1.3	2221	1.1
11 0519	2.1	**26** 0502	2.3
1152	1.2	1132	1.1
F 1812	2.1	SA 1740	2.1
12 0021	1.2	**27** 0001	1.0
0641	2.1	0625	2.3
SA 1248	1.2	SU 1242	1.0
1910	2.2	1843	2.2
13 0120	1.1	**28** 0114	0.8
0757	2.1	0742	2.4
SU 1336	1.2	M 1345	1.0
1955	2.2	1941	2.3
14 0208	0.9		
0841	2.2		
M 1416	1.1		
2031	2.3		
15 0249	0.8		
0915	2.2		
TU 1450	1.0		
2103	2.4		

MARCH

Time	m	Time	m
1 0219	0.6	**16** 0220	0.7
0841	2.4	0849	2.3
TU 1440	0.9	W 1429	1.0
2031	2.4	2033	2.3
2 0313	0.4	**17** 0258	0.6
0926	2.5	0918	2.3
W 1525	0.8	TH 1504	0.9
● 2117	2.5	2109	2.4
3 0358	0.3	**18** 0337	0.5
1006	2.6	0947	2.4
TH 1605	0.8	F 1540	0.8
2159	2.6	○ 2145	2.5
4 0440	0.2	**19** 0414	0.4
1045	2.4	1020	2.4
F 1641	0.7	SA 1616	0.7
2240	2.7	2222	2.6
5 0518	0.3	**20** 0452	0.3
1122	2.4	1054	2.4
SA 1715	0.7	SU 1653	0.7
2320	2.7	2259	2.6
6 0554	0.4	**21** 0528	0.4
1159	2.3	1129	2.4
SU 1748	0.8	M 1728	0.7
2358	2.6	2337	2.6
7 0628	0.5	**22** 0604	0.5
1233	2.2	1206	2.3
M 1820	0.8	TU 1805	0.7
8 0036	2.6	**23** 0018	2.6
0701	0.7	0642	0.6
TU 1307	2.1	W 1246	2.3
1856	0.9	1847	0.8
9 0117	2.3	**24** 0104	2.5
0735	0.9	0724	0.8
W 1345	2.1	TH 1332	2.2
1937	1.0	1936	0.8
10 0206	2.2	**25** 0202	2.3
0815	1.1	0816	1.0
TH 1433	2.0	F 1429	2.1
☽ 2029	1.1	☽ 2042	0.9
11 0317	2.1	**26** 0331	2.2
0910	1.3	0937	1.2
F 1547	2.0	SA 1549	2.1
2155	1.2	2231	0.9
12 0457	2.0	**27** 0515	2.2
1122	1.4	1125	1.2
SA 1708	2.0	SU 1712	2.1
2350	1.1	2358	0.8
13 0623	2.0	**28** 0639	2.3
1229	1.3	1237	1.2
SU 1814	2.1	M 1820	2.2
14 0051	1.0	**29** 0106	0.6
0736	2.1	0746	2.4
M 1318	1.2	TU 1338	1.1
1912	2.1	1921	2.3
15 0139	0.9	**30** 0206	0.5
0818	2.2	0832	2.4
TU 1356	1.1	W 1427	1.0
1956	2.2	2011	2.4
		31 0255	0.4
		0910	2.4
		TH 1507	0.8
		2055	2.5

APRIL

Time	m	Time	m
1 0336	0.3	**16** 0303	0.4
0945	2.4	0917	2.4
F 1543	0.7	SA 1513	0.7
● 2136	2.6	○ 2114	2.5
2 0414	0.3	**17** 0343	0.3
1019	2.4	0951	2.4
SA 1618	0.7	SU 1553	0.7
2216	2.6	2154	2.6
3 0449	0.4	**18** 0423	0.3
1053	2.4	1027	2.5
SU 1651	0.7	M 1633	0.6
2255	2.6	2235	2.6
4 0521	0.5	**19** 0502	0.4
1125	2.3	1105	2.4
M 1723	0.7	TU 1713	0.6
2333	2.5	2318	2.6
5 0551	0.6	**20** 0541	0.5
1156	2.3	1144	2.4
TU 1755	0.8	W 1754	0.6
6 0010	2.4	**21** 0004	2.5
0620	0.8	0622	0.7
W 1228	2.2	TH 1226	2.3
1830	0.8	1841	0.7
7 0051	2.3	**22** 0059	2.4
0649	1.0	0707	0.9
TH 1304	2.2	F 1314	2.3
1909	0.9	1937	0.7
8 0139	2.1	**23** 0209	2.3
0725	1.1	0802	1.1
F 1348	2.1	SA 1413	2.2
1958	1.0	☽ 2053	0.8
9 0247	2.0	**24** 0352	2.2
0812	1.3	0927	1.3
SA 1444	2.1	SU 1526	2.1
☽ 2108	1.1	2230	0.7
10 0433	2.0	**25** 0518	2.3
0921	1.4	1107	1.3
SU 1600	2.0	M 1645	2.1
2313	1.1	2342	0.6
11 0549	2.0	**26** 0632	2.3
1153	1.4	1216	1.2
M 1721	2.0	TU 1754	2.2
12 0011	0.9	**27** 0045	0.5
0654	2.1	0730	2.3
TU 1241	1.3	W 1314	1.1
1822	2.1	1855	2.3
13 0058	0.8	**28** 0141	0.5
0739	2.2	0813	2.4
W 1319	1.2	TH 1402	1.0
1912	2.2	1946	2.4
14 0141	0.7	**29** 0228	0.5
0813	2.3	0847	2.4
TH 1356	1.0	F 1442	0.9
1955	2.3	2030	2.4
15 0222	0.5	**30** 0307	0.4
0845	2.3	0920	2.4
F 1434	0.9	SA 1518	0.8
2035	2.4	● 2112	2.5

Chart Datum: 1·50 metres below Ordnance Datum (Newlyn). HAT is 2·9 metres above Chart Datum.

≫ **FREE** monthly updates. Register at
www.reedsnauticalalmanac.co.uk ≪

89

STANDARD TIME (UT)
For Summer Time add ONE hour in **non-shaded areas**

LOWESTOFT   LAT 52°28'N   LONG 1°45'E
TIMES AND HEIGHTS OF HIGH AND LOW WATERS

Dates in **red** are SPRINGS
Dates in blue are NEAPS

YEAR **2022**

MAY

Time	m		Time	m
1 0343	0.5	**16**	0312	0.4
0952	2.4		0924	2.5
SU 1553	0.7	M 1530	0.7
2153	2.5	○ 2130	2.6
2 0417	0.6	**17**	0356	0.4
1024	2.4		1003	2.5
M 1628	0.7	TU 1616	0.6
2233	2.4	2217	2.6
3 0447	0.7	**18**	0439	0.5
1055	2.4		1044	2.5
TU 1701	0.7	W 1702	0.5
2312	2.3	2307	2.6
4 0515	0.8	**19**	0523	0.6
1125	2.3		1127	2.5
W 1734	0.7	TH 1750	0.5
2350	2.3		
5 0542	0.9	**20**	0001	2.5
1157	2.3		0608	0.8
TH 1809	0.8	F 1213	2.4
		1843	0.5
6 0030	2.2	**21**	0102	2.4
0613	1.0		0656	1.0
F 1233	2.3	SA 1303	2.4
1849	0.8	1943	0.5
7 0117	2.1	**22**	0218	2.3
0650	1.2		0751	1.2
SA 1316	2.2	SU 1400	2.3
1936	0.9	◑ 2055	0.6
8 0218	2.0	**23**	0348	2.2
0737	1.3		0904	1.3
SU 1408	2.2	M 1504	2.3
2038	1.0	2210	0.6
9 0358	2.0	**24**	0502	2.3
0834	1.4		1030	1.3
M 1509	2.1	TU 1615	2.3
◐ 2213	1.0	2316	0.6
10 0508	2.0	**25**	0607	2.3
1002	1.4		1139	1.3
TU 1623	2.1	W 1724	2.3
2322	0.9		
11 0605	2.1	**26**	0014	0.6
1138	1.3		0702	2.3
W 1732	2.1	TH 1238	1.2
		1824	2.3
12 0012	0.8	**27**	0109	0.6
0653	2.2		0746	2.3
TH 1229	1.2	F 1330	1.1
1827	2.2	1918	2.3
13 0058	0.6	**28**	0155	0.6
0733	2.3		0823	2.3
F 1315	1.1	SA 1414	1.0
1915	2.3	2007	2.3
14 0143	0.5	**29**	0236	0.6
0810	2.3		0856	2.4
SA 1400	0.9	SU 1454	0.8
2000	2.4	2053	2.4
15 0228	0.4	**30**	0312	0.7
0846	2.4		0928	2.4
SU 1445	0.8	M 1532	0.8
2044	2.5	● 2136	2.3
		31	0345	0.8
			0959	2.4
		TU 1609	0.7
		2218	2.3

JUNE

Time	m		Time	m
1 0416	0.8	**16**	0423	0.6
1029	2.4		1028	2.5
W 1644	0.7	TH 1656	0.4
2258	2.3	2304	2.5
2 0444	0.9	**17**	0510	0.7
1100	2.4		1114	2.5
TH 1719	0.7	F 1748	0.4
2336	2.2		
3 0513	1.0	**18**	0000	2.5
1134	2.4		0557	0.9
F 1755	0.8	SA 1201	2.5
		1841	0.4
4 0015	2.2	**19**	0058	2.4
0547	1.0		0644	1.0
SA 1211	2.4	SU 1250	2.5
1835	0.8	1936	0.4
5 0058	2.1	**20**	0204	2.3
0626	1.1		0733	1.1
SU 1253	2.3	M 1341	2.5
1920	0.8	2035	0.5
6 0146	2.1	**21**	0323	2.2
0711	1.2		0827	1.2
M 1340	2.3	TU 1436	2.4
2013	0.9	◑ 2138	0.5
7 0248	2.0	**22**	0431	2.2
0803	1.3		0934	1.3
TU 1431	2.2	W 1540	2.4
◐ 2116	0.9	2241	0.6
8 0417	2.1	**23**	0531	2.2
0904	1.3		1050	1.3
W 1528	2.2	TH 1649	2.3
2226	0.8	2340	0.7
9 0517	2.1	**24**	0626	2.2
1020	1.3		1158	1.3
TH 1636	2.2	F 1753	2.3
2325	0.7		
10 0608	2.2	**25**	0034	0.8
1135	1.2		0715	2.3
F 1741	2.3	SA 1257	1.1
		1854	2.2
11 0018	0.6	**26**	0123	0.8
0654	2.3		0757	2.3
SA 1234	1.1	SU 1349	1.0
1837	2.3	1952	2.2
12 0108	0.6	**27**	0206	0.9
0736	2.3		0834	2.3
SU 1328	1.0	M 1435	0.9
1929	2.4	2045	2.3
13 0157	0.5	**28**	0245	0.9
0818	2.4		0907	2.4
M 1420	0.8	TU 1516	0.8
2020	2.5	2131	2.3
14 0246	0.5	**29**	0319	0.9
0900	2.5		0938	2.4
TU 1512	0.7	W 1555	0.8
○ 2113	2.5	● 2212	2.3
15 0335	0.6	**30**	0351	1.0
0943	2.5		1009	2.5
W 1604	0.5	TH 1632	0.7
2208	2.6	2248	2.2

JULY

Time	m		Time	m
1 0421	1.0	**16**	0458	0.8
1041	2.5		1100	2.7
F 1708	0.7	SA 1740	0.3
2323	2.2	2350	2.5
2 0453	1.0	**17**	0542	0.9
1117	2.5		1145	2.7
SA 1744	0.7	SU 1827	0.3
2358	2.2		
3 0529	1.0	**18**	0039	2.4
1154	2.5		0625	0.9
SU 1822	0.7	M 1230	2.7
		1915	0.3
4 0035	2.2	**19**	0132	2.3
0608	1.1		0706	1.0
M 1233	2.4	TU 1316	2.6
1903	0.7	2004	0.5
5 0114	2.1	**20**	0236	2.2
0649	1.1		0749	1.1
TU 1313	2.4	W 1404	2.5
1946	0.8	◑ 2057	0.6
6 0158	2.1	**21**	0347	2.2
0734	1.2		0839	1.2
W 1357	2.4	TH 1500	2.4
2034	0.8	2157	0.8
7 0252	2.1	**22**	0447	2.1
0826	1.2		0948	1.3
TH 1445	2.3	F 1613	2.3
◐ 2131	0.8	2301	0.9
8 0415	2.1	**23**	0543	2.2
0925	1.3		1118	1.3
F 1543	2.3	SA 1726	2.2
2237	0.8		
9 0522	2.2	**24**	0000	1.0
1041	1.2		0638	2.2
SA 1658	2.3	SU 1229	1.2
2341	0.8	1838	2.2
10 0615	2.2	**25**	0055	1.1
1159	1.2		0729	2.3
SU 1806	2.4	M 1330	1.1
		1953	2.2
11 0039	0.7	**26**	0143	1.1
0705	2.3		0811	2.3
M 1303	1.0	TU 1421	1.0
1907	2.4	2046	2.2
12 0134	0.7	**27**	0226	1.1
0752	2.4		0847	2.4
TU 1403	0.8	W 1503	0.9
2008	2.5	2126	2.3
13 0228	0.7	**28**	0302	1.1
0839	2.5		0918	2.4
W 1502	0.7	TH 1541	0.8
○ 2109	2.5	● 2201	2.3
14 0321	0.7	**29**	0333	1.0
0927	2.5		0949	2.5
TH 1558	0.5	F 1617	0.7
2207	2.6	2232	2.3
15 0411	0.8	**30**	0405	1.0
1013	2.6		1022	2.5
F 1650	0.3	SA 1652	0.6
2259	2.6	2302	2.3
		31	0438	0.9
			1057	2.6
		SU 1727	0.6
		2334	2.3

AUGUST

Time	m		Time	m
1 0513	0.9	**16**	0011	2.4
1133	2.6		0559	0.9
M 1802	0.6	TU 1205	2.8
		1845	0.4
2 0007	2.3	**17**	0053	2.3
0550	1.0		0636	1.0
TU 1208	2.6	W 1247	2.7
1838	0.6	1925	0.6
3 0042	2.3	**18**	0138	2.2
0626	1.0		0715	1.0
W 1245	2.5	TH 1331	2.5
1915	0.7	2008	0.8
4 0121	2.2	**19**	0231	2.2
0707	1.1		0758	1.2
TH 1325	2.5	F 1423	2.4
1956	0.7	◑ 2058	1.0
5 0206	2.2	**20**	0342	2.1
0752	1.1		0855	1.3
F 1410	2.5	SA 1538	2.2
◐ 2044	0.8	2211	1.2
6 0304	2.2	**21**	0447	2.1
0847	1.2		1037	1.3
SA 1506	2.4	SU 1705	2.2
2148	0.9	2331	1.3
7 0429	2.2	**22**	0547	2.2
0958	1.2		1207	1.2
SU 1628	2.3	M 1830	2.2
2310	0.9		
8 0538	2.2	**23**	0034	1.3
1136	1.1		0649	2.2
M 1750	2.3	TU 1310	1.1
		1948	2.2
9 0019	1.0	**24**	0128	1.3
0636	2.3		0741	2.3
TU 1249	1.0	W 1401	1.0
1902	2.4	2034	2.3
10 0119	1.0	**25**	0211	1.2
0730	2.4		0819	2.4
W 1354	0.8	TH 1442	0.9
2012	2.5	2109	2.3
11 0217	0.9	**26**	0245	1.1
0821	2.5		0851	2.5
TH 1456	0.6	F 1518	0.7
2110	2.5	2138	2.3
12 0312	0.9	**27**	0315	1.0
0910	2.6		0923	2.5
F 1550	0.4	SA 1553	0.7
○ 2200	2.6	● 2205	2.4
13 0400	0.8	**28**	0347	1.0
0956	2.7		0957	2.6
SA 1638	0.3	SU 1627	0.6
2245	2.6	2234	2.4
14 0442	0.8	**29**	0420	0.9
1040	2.8		1031	2.7
SU 1722	0.2	M 1701	0.5
2328	2.5	2305	2.4
15 0522	0.8	**30**	0454	0.9
1123	2.8		1106	2.7
M 1804	0.3	TU 1735	0.5
		2338	2.4
		31	0528	0.9
			1142	2.6
		W 1809	0.6

Chart Datum: 1·50 metres below Ordnance Datum (Newlyn). HAT is 2·9 metres above Chart Datum.

≫ **FREE** monthly updates. Register at ≪
www.reedsnauticalalmanac.co.uk

STANDARD TIME (UT)
For Summer Time add ONE
hour in **non-shaded areas**

LOWESTOFT LAT 52°28'N LONG 1°45'E
TIMES AND HEIGHTS OF HIGH AND LOW WATERS

Dates in red are **SPRINGS**
Dates in blue are **NEAPS**

YEAR **2022**

E England

SEPTEMBER
Time	m	Time	m
1 0012	2.4	**16** 0051	2.3
0604	0.9	0645	1.0
TH 1217	2.6	F 1301	2.5
1844	0.7	1919	0.9
2 0050	2.3	**17** 0130	2.3
0641	1.0	0726	1.1
F 1257	2.6	SA 1352	2.3
1921	0.8	◑ 1958	1.2
3 0132	2.3	**18** 0217	2.2
0726	1.1	0818	1.2
SA 1344	2.5	SU 1508	2.2
◐ 2007	0.9	2050	1.4
4 0224	2.2	**19** 0325	2.2
0821	1.1	0949	1.3
SU 1447	2.4	M 1646	2.1
2109	1.1	2301	1.5
5 0337	2.2	**20** 0445	2.2
0937	1.2	1140	1.2
M 1622	2.3	TU 1811	2.2
2248	1.2		
6 0502	2.2	**21** 0014	1.4
1128	1.1	0551	2.2
TU 1753	2.3	W 1239	1.1
		1923	2.2
7 0008	1.2	**22** 0106	1.4
0609	2.3	0650	2.3
W 1242	0.9	TH 1327	0.9
1912	2.4	2007	2.3
8 0112	1.1	**23** 0146	1.3
0708	2.4	0736	2.4
TH 1348	0.7	F 1408	0.8
2015	2.5	2039	2.4
9 0210	1.1	**24** 0218	1.2
0801	2.5	0814	2.5
F 1446	0.5	SA 1444	0.7
2102	2.6	2106	2.4
10 0259	1.0	**25** 0248	1.0
0849	2.7	0849	2.6
SA 1534	0.3	SU 1519	0.6
○ 2143	2.6	● 2133	2.4
11 0342	0.9	**26** 0320	0.9
0933	2.8	0925	2.6
SU 1617	0.3	M 1554	0.5
2222	2.6	2202	2.5
12 0420	0.8	**27** 0355	0.9
1016	2.8	1001	2.7
M 1657	0.3	TU 1630	0.5
2301	2.5	2235	2.5
13 0457	0.8	**28** 0431	0.8
1058	2.8	1038	2.7
TU 1734	0.4	W 1705	0.5
2339	2.4	2309	2.5
14 0532	0.8	**29** 0507	0.8
1138	2.7	1115	2.7
W 1810	0.5	TH 1739	0.6
		2344	2.5
15 0015	2.4	**30** 0543	0.8
0608	0.9	1154	2.6
TH 1218	2.6	F 1814	0.7
1845	0.7		

OCTOBER
Time	m	Time	m
1 0022	2.4	**16** 0048	2.4
0623	0.9	0700	1.0
SA 1238	2.6	SU 1327	2.2
1854	0.9	1910	1.3
2 0106	2.4	**17** 0131	2.3
0710	1.0	0749	1.1
SU 1331	2.4	M 1441	2.1
1942	1.1	◑ 1954	1.4
3 0158	2.3	**18** 0226	2.2
0811	1.0	0902	1.2
M 1446	2.3	TU 1621	2.1
◐ 2046	1.3	2055	1.6
4 0307	2.2	**19** 0337	2.2
0945	1.0	1101	1.1
TU 1638	2.3	W 1734	2.2
2237	1.4	2336	1.6
5 0430	2.3	**20** 0455	2.2
1123	0.9	1158	1.0
W 1802	2.4	TH 1839	2.2
2358	1.3		
6 0542	2.3	**21** 0025	1.4
1231	0.7	0558	2.3
TH 1913	2.5	F 1243	0.9
		1925	2.3
7 0100	1.2	**22** 0103	1.3
0644	2.4	0648	2.4
F 1333	0.6	SA 1324	0.8
2005	2.5	1959	2.4
8 0154	1.1	**23** 0137	1.2
0737	2.6	0732	2.5
SA 1426	0.5	SU 1403	0.7
2045	2.5	2028	2.4
9 0239	1.0	**24** 0212	1.1
0824	2.7	0812	2.5
SU 1510	0.4	M 1441	0.6
○ 2121	2.6	2058	2.5
10 0318	0.9	**25** 0250	0.9
0908	2.7	0851	2.6
M 1550	0.4	TU 1519	0.5
2156	2.5	● 2131	2.5
11 0355	0.8	**26** 0329	0.8
0951	2.8	0931	2.7
TU 1627	0.4	W 1557	0.5
2231	2.5	2205	2.6
12 0432	0.8	**27** 0408	0.8
1033	2.7	1011	2.7
W 1702	0.6	TH 1635	0.5
2306	2.5	2242	2.5
13 0507	0.8	**28** 0448	0.8
1114	2.6	1103	2.7
TH 1734	0.7	F 1713	0.6
2340	2.4	2320	2.5
14 0542	0.9	**29** 0530	0.8
1154	2.5	1138	2.6
F 1804	0.9	SA 1753	0.8
15 0013	2.4	**30** 0000	2.5
0619	0.9	0616	0.8
SA 1236	2.4	SU 1229	2.5
1835	1.1	1837	1.0
		31 0047	2.4
		0710	0.8
		M 1332	2.4
		1928	1.2

NOVEMBER
Time	m	Time	m
1 0142	2.4	**16** 0149	2.3
0818	0.9	0826	1.1
TU 1502	2.3	W 1538	2.1
◑ 2034	1.4	◐ 2009	1.5
2 0247	2.3	**17** 0247	2.3
0950	0.9	0955	1.1
W 1642	2.3	TH 1649	2.1
2217	1.4	2118	1.5
3 0402	2.3	**18** 0355	2.2
1107	0.7	1105	1.0
TH 1755	2.4	F 1746	2.2
2334	1.4	2306	1.5
4 0514	2.4	**19** 0505	2.3
1210	0.7	1154	0.9
F 1856	2.4	SA 1833	2.3
5 0034	1.3	**20** 0004	1.4
0616	2.4	0602	2.3
SA 1307	0.6	SU 1238	0.8
1944	2.5	1914	2.3
6 0126	1.2	**21** 0050	1.2
0710	2.5	0651	2.4
SU 1358	0.6	M 1321	0.7
2021	2.5	1950	2.4
7 0212	1.0	**22** 0135	1.1
0758	2.6	0736	2.5
M 1441	0.5	TU 1403	0.6
2056	2.5	2025	2.5
8 0253	0.9	**23** 0219	1.0
0844	2.6	0820	2.6
TU 1520	0.6	W 1446	0.6
○ 2129	2.5	● 2101	2.5
9 0332	0.8	**24** 0304	0.8
0929	2.6	0904	2.6
W 1556	0.6	TH 1528	0.6
2204	2.5	2139	2.6
10 0409	0.8	**25** 0350	0.7
1012	2.6	0951	2.6
TH 1629	0.8	F 1611	0.6
2237	2.5	2219	2.6
11 0446	0.8	**26** 0436	0.6
1054	2.5	1040	2.6
F 1659	0.9	SA 1655	0.7
2309	2.5	2301	2.6
12 0522	0.8	**27** 0525	0.6
1135	2.4	1133	2.6
SA 1728	1.0	SU 1739	0.9
2341	2.5	2346	2.6
13 0559	0.9	**28** 0616	0.6
1218	2.3	1231	2.5
SU 1757	1.1	M 1826	1.0
14 0016	2.4	**29** 0035	2.5
0639	1.0	0714	0.6
M 1305	2.2	TU 1336	2.4
1832	1.3	1918	1.2
15 0058	2.4	**30** 0128	2.5
0726	1.0	0820	0.7
TU 1406	2.1	W 1501	2.3
1916	1.4	◑ 2018	1.3

DECEMBER
Time	m	Time	m
1 0227	2.4	**16** 0208	2.3
0933	0.7	0849	1.0
TH 1626	2.3	F 1539	2.1
2135	1.4	◐ 2031	1.4
2 0332	2.4	**17** 0301	2.3
1041	0.7	0954	0.9
F 1731	2.3	SA 1650	2.1
2253	1.4	2136	1.4
3 0444	2.4	**18** 0403	2.3
1141	0.7	1058	0.9
SA 1828	2.3	SU 1743	2.2
2357	1.3	2256	1.4
4 0548	2.4	**19** 0513	2.3
1237	0.7	1153	0.8
SU 1916	2.4	M 1830	2.3
5 0054	1.2	**20** 0005	1.3
0645	2.4	0612	2.4
M 1327	0.7	TU 1243	0.7
1956	2.4	1913	2.3
6 0145	1.1	**21** 0101	1.1
0737	2.5	0704	2.4
TU 1412	0.7	W 1331	0.7
2032	2.4	1955	2.4
7 0230	1.0	**22** 0153	1.0
0827	2.5	0755	2.5
W 1451	0.8	TH 1419	0.7
2106	2.5	2036	2.5
8 0313	0.9	**23** 0245	0.8
0916	2.4	0847	2.5
TH 1527	0.8	F 1507	0.7
○ 2140	2.5	● 2118	2.5
9 0353	0.8	**24** 0338	0.7
1001	2.4	0942	2.6
F 1600	0.9	SA 1555	0.7
2213	2.5	2202	2.6
10 0431	0.8	**25** 0430	0.6
1044	2.4	1037	2.6
SA 1630	1.0	SU 1643	0.8
2245	2.5	2248	2.6
11 0508	0.8	**26** 0522	0.5
1124	2.3	1132	2.5
SU 1659	1.1	M 1730	0.9
2317	2.5	2335	2.6
12 0545	0.8	**27** 0614	0.4
1203	2.2	1226	2.5
M 1730	1.1	TU 1816	1.0
2353	2.5		
13 0623	0.9	**28** 0022	2.6
1243	2.2	0708	0.4
TU 1806	1.2	W 1323	2.4
		1903	1.1
14 0034	2.4	**29** 0111	2.6
0706	0.9	0803	0.5
W 1327	2.1	TH 1432	2.3
1849	1.2	1952	1.2
15 0119	2.4	**30** 0202	2.5
0754	0.9	0902	0.6
TH 1419	2.1	F 1553	2.2
1937	1.3	◑ 2047	1.3
		31 0259	2.5
		1005	0.7
		SA 1656	2.2
		2158	1.3

Chart Datum: 1·50 metres below Ordnance Datum (Newlyn). HAT is 2·9 metres above Chart Datum.

〉〉 **FREE** monthly updates. Register at 〈
www.reedsnauticalalmanac.co.uk 〈

1.25 GREAT YARMOUTH

Norfolk 52°34'·36N 01°44'·39E ✶✶❀✿✿

CHARTS AC 5614, 1543, 1535, 1534; Imray C29, C28

TIDES −0210 Dover; ML 1·5; Duration 0620

Standard Port LOWESTOFT (⟵)

Times				Height (metres)			
High Water		Low Water		MHWS	MHWN	MLWN	MLWS
0300	0900	0200	0800	2·4	2·1	1·0	0·5
1500	2100	1400	2000				
Differences *GORLESTON* (To be used for Great Yarmouth)							
−0035	−0035	−0030	−0030	0·0	0·0	0·0	0·0
CAISTER-ON-SEA							
−0120	−0120	−0100	−0100	0·0	−0·1	0·0	0·0
WINTERTON-ON-SEA							
−0225	−0215	−0135	−0135	+0·8	+0·5	+0·2	+0·1

• Rise of tide occurs mainly during 3½hrs after LW. From Lowestoft HW−3 until HW the level is usually within 0·3m of predicted HW. Flood tide runs until about HW+0015 and ebb until about LW+0025.

SHELTER Excellent on Town Hall Quay, close S of Haven Bridge; yachts and small craft are not allowed in the outer harbour and ⚓ prohibited in the commercial hbrs, R Yar and its approaches.

NAVIGATION WPT 52°34'·43N 01°45'·56E, 264°/1M to front ldg lt.

• Access is H24, subject to clearance, but small craft must not attempt ent in strong SE winds which cause dangerous seas, especially on the ebb. Except at local slack water, which occurs at HW+1½ and LW+1¾, tidal streams at the ent are strong.
• On the flood, the stream eddies NW past S pier, thence upriver; a QY tidal lt on S pier warns of this D/N. Beware being set onto the N pier.
• Temporary shoaling may occur in the ent during strong E'lies, with depths 1m less than those charted.
• Beware strong tidal streams that sweep through the Haven Bridge. Proceed slowly past Bure Marine.
• Harbour is for commercial vessels only.

LIGHTS AND MARKS See 1.3 and Chartlet. Gorleston Pier lt, Fl R 3s, is on R brick building (W lower half floodlit). Entrance and bend marked by five 2FG(vert) and seven 2FR(vert).

TRAFFIC SIGNALS Port operations advise on Ch 12, this should always be heeded. **Inbound:** now IALA sigs on S pier: 3 Fl ● = hbr closed; 3F ● = do not proceed; 3 F ● = vessels may proceed, oneway; ● ○ ● = proceed only when told to; **Outbound:** 3 ● (vert) = no vessel to go downriver south of LB shed. Haven and Breydon bridges: 3 ● (vert) = passage prohib.

COMMUNICATIONS (Code 01493) HM 335511; Breydon Bridge 651275.

Yarmouth Radio Ch **12** (H24). *Breydon Bridge* Ch **12** (HO).

FACILITIES **Town Hall Quay** (50m stretch) ⚓ £126.76 (all vessels). **Burgh Castle Marina** (top of Breydon Water 5M) ☎780331, access HW ±4 for 1m draught ⚓ 90+10♥ £16, ▢ ⛽ ⚓ ☒ ⚒ ⚓ ▣ diving ⚓ ACA ⚓ ✕ ⚓.
Goodchild Marine Services (top of Breydon Water 5M) ☎782301, access 6ft at LW. ⚓ ⚓ (27⚓+6♥ £12.50), ⚓ ⛽ ⚒ ⚓ ⚓ ▣ ⚓ ▷(32t, including mast stepping).
Town ⚓ ⚓ ⚓ ACA ✉ Ⓑ ⚓ ✕ ⚓ ⇌ ✈ (Norwich).

NORFOLK BROADS: The Broads comprise about 120 miles of navigable rivers and lakes in Norfolk and Suffolk. The main rivers (Bure, Yare and Waveney) are tidal, flowing into the sea at Great Yarmouth. The N Broads have a 2·3m headroom limit. Br clearances restrict cruising to R Yare (Great Yarmouth to Norwich, but note that 3M E of Norwich, Postwick viaduct on S bypass has 10.7m HW clearance) and River Waveney (Lowestoft to Beccles). The Broads may be entered also at Lowestoft (1.24). Broads Navigation Authority ☎(01603) 610734.

Entry to the Broads: Pass up R Yare at slack LW, under Haven Bridge (1·8m HAT) thence to Breydon Water via Breydon Bridge (4·0m) or to R Bure. Both bridges lift in co-ordination to pass small craft in groups. All br lifts on request to Hbr Office (01493) 335503 during office hrs. Weekend and bank holiday lifts to be requested working afternoon before. Call the Bridge Officer on VHF Ch 12. R Bure has two fixed bridges (2·3m MHWS).

Tidal data on the rivers and Broads is based on the time of LW at Yarmouth Yacht Stn (mouth of R Bure), which is LW Gorleston +0100 (see TIDES). Add the differences below to time of LW Yarmouth Yacht Stn to get local LW times:

R Bure		R Waveney		R Yare	
Acle Bridge	+0230	Berney Arms	+0100	Reedham	+0130
Horning	+0300	St Olaves	+0130	Cantley	+0200
Potter Heigham	+0300	Oulton Broad	+0300	Norwich	+0300

LW at Breydon (mouth of R Yare) is LW Yarmouth Yacht Stn +0100. Tide starts to flood on Breydon Water whilst still ebbing from R Bure. Max draught is 1·8m; 2m with care. Tidal range 0·6m to 1·8m.

Licences (compulsory) are obtainable from: The Broads Authority, 18 Colegate, Norwich NR3 1BQ, ☎01603 610734; the Info Centre, Yarmouth Yacht Stn or the River Inspectors. *Hamilton's Guide to the Broads* is recommended. www.hamilton publications.com.

Netherlands & Belgium

Delfzijl to Nieuwpoort

Netherlands

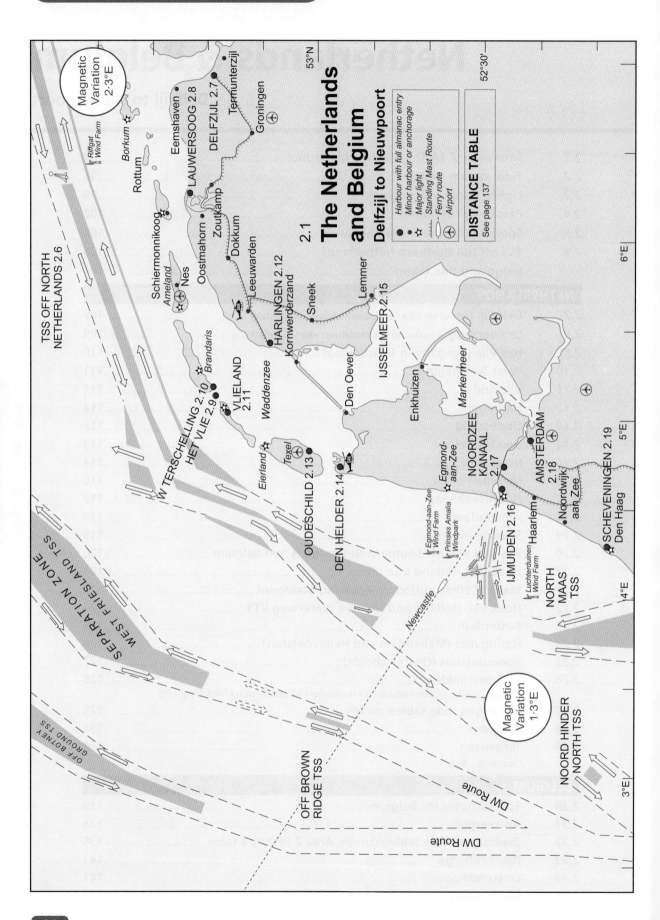

2.1

The Netherlands and Belgium
Delfzijl to Nieuwoort

- ● Harbour with full almanac entry
- • Minor harbour or anchorage
- ☆ Major light
- Standing Mast Route
- Ferry route
- ✈ Airport

DISTANCE TABLE
See page 137

Magnetic Variation 2·3°E

Magnetic Variation 1·3°E

53°N

52°30'

6°E

5°E

4°E

3°E

Riffgat Wind Farm

Borkum

Rottum

Eemshaven

LAUWERSOOG 2.8

DELFZIJL 2.7

Termunterzijl

Groningen

Schiermonnikoog

Ameland

Nes

Oostmahorn

Zoutkamp

Dokkum

Leeuwarden

Sneek

Lemmer

IJSSELMEER 2.15

HARLINGEN 2.12

Kornwerderzand

Brandaris

VLIELAND 2.11

W TERSCHELLING 2.10
HET VLIE 2.9

Waddenzee

Den Oever

Enkhuizen

Markermeer

Eierland

Texel

OUDESCHILD 2.13

DEN HELDER 2.14

Egmond-aan-Zee Wind Farm

Prinses Amalia Windpark

Egmond-aan-Zee

NOORDZEE KANAAL 2.17

AMSTERDAM

Noordwijk aan Zee

NOORDWIJK 2.18

Luchterduinen Wind Farm

IJMUIDEN 2.16

Haarlem

SCHEVENINGEN 2.19
Den Haag

Newcastle

NORTH MAAS TSS

TSS OFF NORTH NETHERLANDS 2.6

SEPARATION ZONE

WEST FRIESLAND TSS

OFF BOTNEY GROUND TSS

OFF BROWN RIDGE TSS

NOORD HINDER NORTH TSS

DW Route

DW Route

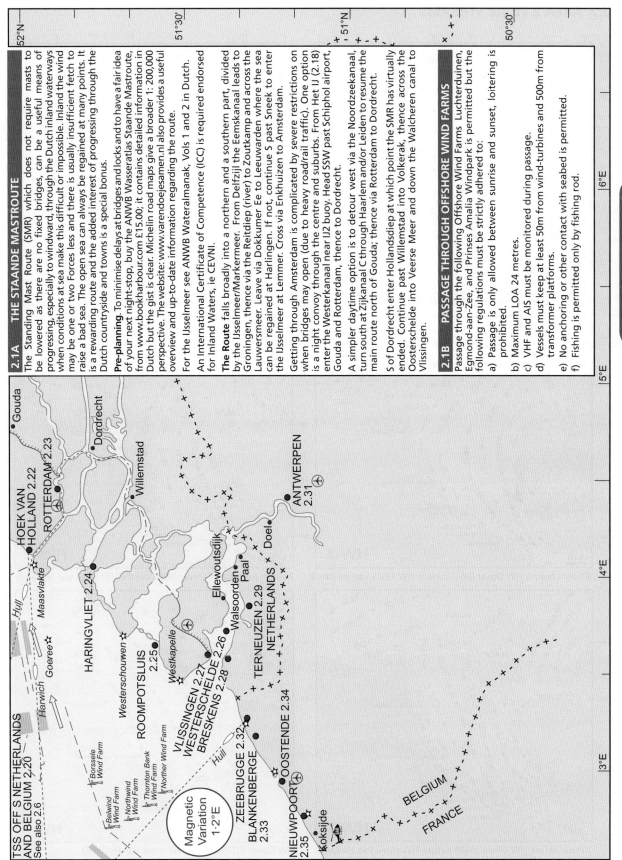

2.1A   THE STAANDE MASTROUTE

The Standing Mast Route (SMR) which does not require masts to be lowered as there are no fixed bridges, can be a useful means of progressing, especially to windward, through the Dutch inland waterways when conditions at sea make this difficult or impossible. Inland the wind may be one or two Forces less and there is usually insufficient fetch to raise a bad sea. The open sea can always be regained at many points. It is a rewarding route and the added interest of progressing through the Dutch countryside and towns is a special bonus.

Pre-planning. To minimise delays at bridges and locks and to have a fair idea of your next night-stop, buy the ANWB Wasseratlas Staande Mastroute, from www.bookharbour.com £15.00; it contains detailed information in Dutch but the gist is clear. Michelin road maps give a broader 1: 200,000 perspective. The website: www.varendoejesamen.nl also provides a useful overview and up-to-date information regarding the route.

For the IJsselmeer see ANWB Wateralmanak, Vols 1 and 2 in Dutch.

An International Certificate of Competence (ICC) is required endorsed for Inland Waters, ie CEVNI.

The Route falls broadly into a northern and a southern part, divided by the IJsselmeer/Markermeer. From Delfzijl the Eemskanaal leads to Groningen, thence via the Reitdiep (river) to Zoutkamp and across the Lauwersmeer. Leave via Dokkumer Ee to Leeuwarden where the sea can be regained at Harlingen. If not, continue S past Sneek to enter the IJsselmeer at Lemmer. Cross via Enkhuizen to Amsterdam.

Getting through Amsterdam is complicated by severe restrictions on when bridges may open (due to heavy road/rail traffic). One option is a night convoy through the centre and suburbs. From Het IJ (2.18) enter the Westerkanaal near IJ2 buoy. Head SSW past Schiphol airport, Gouda and Rotterdam, thence to Dordrecht.

A simpler daytime option is to detour west via the Noordzeekanaal, turn south at Zijkanaal C through Haarlem and/or Leiden to resume the main route north of Gouda; thence via Rotterdam to Dordrecht.

S of Dordrecht enter Hollandsdiep at which point the SMR has virtually ended. Continue past Willemstad into Volkerak, thence across the Oosterschelde into Veerse Meer and down the Walcheren canal to Vlissingen.

2.1B   PASSAGE THROUGH OFFSHORE WIND FARMS

Passage through the following Offshore Wind Farms Luchterduinen, Egmond-aan-Zee, and Prinses Amalia Windpark is permitted but the following regulations must be strictly adhered to:

a) Passage is only allowed between sunrise and sunset, loitering is prohibited.

b) Maximum LOA 24 metres.

c) VHF and AIS must be monitored during passage.

d) Vessels must keep at least 50m from wind-turbines and 500m from transformer platforms.

e) No anchoring or other contact with seabed is permitted.

f) Fishing is permitted only by fishing rod.

TSS OFF S NETHERLANDS AND BELGIUM 2.20
See also 2.6

Hull
Harwich
Goeree ☆

Borssele Wind Farm
Belwind Wind Farm
Northwind Wind Farm
Thornton Bank Wind Farm
Norther Wind Farm

Magnetic Variation 1·2°E

Gouda
Dordrecht
HOEK VAN HOLLAND 2.22
ROTTERDAM 2.23
Willemstad
Maasvlakte
Hull

HARINGVLIET 2.24
Westerschouwen
ROOMPOTSLUIS 2.25
Westkapelle
VLISSINGEN 2.27
WESTERSCHELDE 2.28
BRESKENS 2.26
Ellewoutsdijk
Walsoorden 2.29
Paal
TERNEUZEN
NETHERLANDS
Doel
ANTWERPEN 2.31

ZEEBRUGGE 2.32
BLANKENBERGE 2.33
OOSTENDE 2.34
NIEUWPOORT 2.35
Koksijde

Hull

BELGIUM
FRANCE

52°N
51°30'
51°N
50°30'

3°E   4°E   5°E   6°E

95

2.2 AREA 2 TIDAL STREAMS

5 Hours before HW Dover (0420 after HW Hoek van Holland)

4 Hours before HW Dover (0520 after HW Hoek van Holland)

3 Hours before HW Dover (0605 before HW Hoek van Holland)

2 Hours before HW Dover (0505 before HW Hoek van Holland)

1 Hour before HW Dover (0405 before HW Hoek van Holland)

HW Dover (0305 before HW Hoek van Holland)

Westward 1.2   North-westward 3.2

1 Hour after HW Dover (0205 before HW Hoek van Holland)

2 Hours after HW Dover (0105 before HW Hoek van Holland)

3 Hours after HW Dover (0005 after HW Hoek van Holland)

4 Hours after HW Dover (0055 after HW Hoek van Holland)

5 Hours after HW Dover (0155 after HW Hoek van Holland)

6 Hours after HW Dover (0255 after HW Hoek van Holland)

Netherlands

2.3 LIGHTS, BUOYS AND WAYPOINTS

Bold print = light with a nominal range of 15M or more. CAPITALS = place or feature. *CAPITAL ITALICS* = light-vessel, light float or Lanby. *Italics* = Fog signal. ***Bold italics*** = Racon. Many marks/buoys are fitted with AIS (MMSI No); see relevant charts.

TSS OFF NORTHERN NETHERLANDS

TERSCHELLING-GERMAN BIGHT TSS
TG1/Ems ℓ IQ G 13s; 53°43'·33N 06°22'·24E.
TE5 ⚓ Fl (3) G 10s; 53°37'·79N 05°53'·69E.
TE1 ⚓ Fl (3) G 10s; 53°29'·58N 05°11'·31E.

OFF VLIELAND TSS
VL-CENTER ⬚ Fl 5s 12M; ***Racon C, 12–15M***; 53°26'·93N 04°39'·88E. VL7 ⚓ L Fl G 10s; 53°26'·40N 04°57'·60E.
VL1 ⚓ Fl (2) G 10s; 53°10'·96N 04°35'·31E.

DELFZIJL TO HARLINGEN

DELFZIJL
PS3/BW26 ⚓ Fl (2+1) G 12s; 53°19'·25N 07°00'·32E.
W mole ⚓ FG; 53°19'·01N 07°00'·27E.
Ldg lts 203° both Iso 4s. Front, 53°18'·63N 07°00'·17E.

SCHIERMONNIKOOG AND LAUWERSOOG
WG (Westgat) ⚓ Iso 8s; ***Racon N***; 53°31'·96N 06°01'·84E .
WRG ℓ Q; 53°32'·87N 06°03'·24E.AM ℓ VQ; 53°30'·95N 05°44'·72E.
Schiermonnikoog ☆ Fl (4) 20s 43m **28M**; dark R ○ twr. Same twr: F WR 29m **W15M**, R12M; 210°-W-221°-R-230°. 53°29'·20N 06°08'·79E.
Lauwersoog W mole ⚓ FG; *Horn (2) 30s;* 53°24'·68N 06°12'·00E.

ZEEGAT VAN AMELAND
BR ℓ Q; 53°30'·66N 05°33'·52E.
TS ℓ VQ; 53°28'·15N 05°21'·53E.
WA ⚓ 53°28'·35N 05°28'·64E. (Westgat buoys are all unlit)
Ameland, W end ☆ Fl (3) 15s 57m **30M**; 53°26'·89N 05°37'·42E.

NES
VA2-R1 ℓ VQ(6) + L Fl 10s; 53°25'·71N 05°45'·88E.
Reegeul R3 ⚓ Iso G 4s; 53°25'·80N 05°45'·93E.
R7 ⚓ QG; 53°25'·91N 05°46'·21E.

HET VLIE (ZEEGAT VAN TERSCHELLING)
ZS (Zuider Stortemelk) ⚓ Iso 4s; ***Racon T***; 53°18'·28N 04°56'·23E.
ZS1 ⚓ VQ G; 53°18'·58N 04°57'·54E.
ZS3 ⚓ QG; 53° 19'·29N 04° 59'·49E
ZS5 ⚓ L Fl G 8s; 53°18'·55N 05°00'·83E.
ZS11-VS2 ℓ Q (9) 15s; 53°18'·63N 05°05'·94E.

NOORD MEEP/SLENK TO WEST TERSCHELLING
WM3 ⚓ Iso G 2s; 53°17'·45N 05°12'·28E.
NM 4-S 21 ℓ VQ (3) 5s; 53°19'·02N 05°15'·47E.
SG1 ℓ Q (9) 15s; 53°20'·44N 05°11'·70E.
Brandaris Twr ☆ Fl 5s 54m **29M**; Y ☐ twr partly obscured by dunes; 53°21'·62N 05°12'·86E.
W Terschelling W hbr mole ⚓ FR 5m 5M; R post, W bands; *Horn 15s;* 53°21'·26N 05°13'·09E. E pier hd ⚓ FG 4m 4M.

VLIELAND
VS3 (Vliesloot) ⚓ VQ G; 53°18'·27N 05°06'·25E.
VS14 ⚓ Iso R 4s; 53°17'·58N 05°05'62E.
VS16-VB1 ⚓ Fl (2+1) R 10s; 53°17'·62N 05°05'·19E.
E/W mole hds ⚓ FG and ⚓ FR; 53°17'·68N 05°05'·51E.
Ldg lts 282° ⚓ Iso 4s 10/16m 1M, synch; 53°17'·75N 05°04'·47W (100m apart); mainly for the ferry terminal at E Vlieland.
E Vlieland (Vuurduin) ☆ Iso 4s 54m **20M**; 53°17'·75N 05°03'·49E.

APPROACHES TO HARLINGEN (selected marks):

VLIESTROOM buoys are frequently moved.
VL1 ⚓ QG; 53°18'·99N 05°08'·82E. VL 2 ⚓ QR; 53°19'·40N 05°09'·19E.
VL 11 ⚓ Iso G 8s; 53°16'·42N 05°09'·70E.

BLAUWE SLENK
BS1-IN2 ℓ VQ (3) 5s; 53°15'·41N 05°09'·41E.
BS13 ⚓ QG; 53°13'·31N 05°17'·13E. BS19 ⚓ VQ G; 53°11'·90N 05°18'·28E.
BS23 ⚓ L Fl G 8s; 53°11'·42N 05°19'·60E.

POLLENDAM
Ldg lts 112°, both Iso 6s 8/19m 13M (H24); B masts, W bands. Front, 53°10'·52N 05°24'·19E. Use only between P2 and P6.
P2 ℓ; 53°11'·47N 05°20'·38E on the training wall.
P4, Iso R 8s; P6, Iso R 4s; P8, Iso R 8s; and P10, Iso R 2s.
Yachts should keep outboard of P1 thru 7 SHM buoys. P1 ⚓ Iso G 2s; 53°11'·39N 05°20'·32E. P7 ⚓ VQ G; 53°10'·68N 05°23'·45E.

HARLINGEN
S mole hd ⚓ FG 9m; 53°10'·56N 05°24'·18E.
N mole hd ⚓ FR 9m 4M; R/W pedestal; 53°10'·59N 05°24'·32E.

TEXEL AND THE WADDENZEE

TEXEL (from NW and W)
Eierland ☆ Fl (2) 10s 52m **29M**; R ○ twr; 53°10'·93N 04°51'·31E.
TX ℓ Q(9) 15s; 53°06'·81N 04°41'·19E

MOLENGAT (from the N)
Note: Positions/depths unreliable, see: Pl Terschelling to Texel and Den Helder.
Zinker-MG ℓ VQ(9) 10s; 53°02'·27N 04°40'·95E
MG-A,Y ⚓; 53°02'·61N 04°40'·28E.
MG-B, Y ℓ; 53°01'·99N 04°42'·00E
MG-D, Y ℓ; 53°00'·90N 04°42'·04E;
MG-G, Y ℓ; 52°59'·30N 04°42'·56E;
MG-H, Y ⚓; 52°58'·91N 04°43'·10E.

OUDESCHILD
T12 ⚓ Iso R 8s; 53°02'·23N 04°51'·52E.
Oudeschild Dir ⚓ Oc 6s; intens 291°; 53°02'·40N 04°50'·94E; leads 291° into hbr between N mole head FG 6m; and S mole head ⚓ FR 6m; 53°02'·33N 04°51'·17E.

APPROACHES TO KORNWERDERZAND SEALOCK

DOOVE BALG (From Texelstroom eastward)
T23 ⚓ VQ G; 53°03'·60N 04°55'·85E, 066°/3M from Oudeschild.
T29 ⚓ 53°03'·25N 05°00'·05E.
D1 ⚓ Iso G 4s; 53°02'·18N 05°03'·42E.
D21 ⚓ Iso G 8s; 53°03'·55N 05°15'·71E.
BO2-WG1 ℓ Q (6) + L Fl 10s; 53°05'·00N 05°17'·91E.

KORNWERDERZAND SEALOCK
W mole ⚓ FG 9m 7M; *Horn Mo(N) 30s;* 53°04'·78N 05°20'·03E.
E mole ⚓ FR 9m 7M; 53°04'·70N 05°20'·08E.
W mole elbow ⚓ Iso G 6s 6m 7M; 53°04'·61N 05°19'·90E.

APPROACHES TO DEN OEVER SEALOCK

MALZWIN and VISJAGERSGAATJE CHANS TO DEN OEVER
MH4-M1 ℓ VQ (9) 10s; 52°58'·14N 04°47'·49E, close N Den Helder.
M15 ⚓ QG; 52°59'·39N 04°55'·48E (thence use DYC 1811.3).
VG1-W2 ⚓ Fl (2+1) G 10s; 52°59'·00N 04°56'·85E.
O9 ⚓ Iso G 8s; 52°56'·63N 05°02'·38E.

DEN OEVER SEALOCK
Ldg lts 131°, both Oc 10s 6m 7M; 127°-137°. Front, 52°56'·32N 05°02'·98E. Rear, 280m from front.

E end of swing bridge, ⚡ Iso WRG 5s 14m 10/7M; 226°-G-231°-W-235°-R-290°-G-327°-W-335°-R-345°; 52°56'·12N 05°02'·52E.

ZEEGAT VAN TEXEL AND DEN HELDER

OFFSHORE MARKS W and SW OF DEN HELDER
NH (Noorderhaaks) ⚓ VQ; 53°00'·24N 04°35'·37E.
MR ⚓ Q (9) 15s; 52°56'·77N 04°33'·82E.
ZH (Zuiderhaaks) ⚓ VQ (6) + L Fl 10s; 52°54'·65N 04°34'·72E.
Vinca G wreck ⚓ Q (9) 15s; 52°45'·93N 04°12'·31E.

SCHULPENGAT (from the SSW)
Schulpengat Dir ☆ 026·5°, Dir WRG, Al WR, Al WG, **W22M R/G18M**, church spire; 025.1°-FG-025.6°-AlWG-026.3°-FW-026.7°-Al WR- 027.4° -F R- 027.9°; shown H24.
Licht van Troost ☆, delete entry in toto, substitute: Licht van Troost ⚡ FWRG 27m W3M (Green post on Texel), W8M 21m, R8M, G5M; 333°-W-026°-G-033°-W-038°-R-070°; 53°00'·50N 04°45'·70E.
SG ⚓ Mo (A) 8s; **Racon Z**; 52°52'·90N 04°37'·90E.
S1 ▲ Iso G 4s; 52°53'·53N 04°38'·82E.
S7 ▲ QG; 52°56'·25N 04°40'·92E. S6A ⚓ QR; 52°56'·52N 04°40'·51E.
S10 ⚓ Iso R 8s; 52°57'·59N 04°41'·57E. S14-MG17 ⚓, see Molengat.
S11 ▲ Iso G 8s; 52°57'·55N 04°43'·25E.
Kijkduin ☆ Fl (4) 20s 56m **30M**; vis 360°, except where obsc'd by dunes on Texel; brown twr; 52°57'·33N 04°43'·58E (mainland).

MARSDIEP and DEN HELDER
T1 ▲ Fl (3) G 10s; 52°57'·99N 04°44'·62E.
T3 ▲ Iso G 8s; 52°58'·07N 04°46'·42E.
Den Helder ldg lts 191°, both Oc G 5s 16/25m 3M, synch. Front, vis 183·5°-198·5°; B ▽ on bldg; 52°57'·37N 04°47'·08E.
Marinehaven, W bkwtr head ⚡ QG 11m 8M; *Horn 20s*; 52°57'·95N 04°47'·07E (Harssens Island).
W side, ⚡ Fl G 5s 9m 4M (H24); 180°-067°; 52°57'·78N 04°47'·08E.
Yacht hbr (KMYC) ent ⚡ FR & FG; 165m SW of ⚡ Fl G 5s, above.
E side, MH6 ⚓ Iso R 4s; 52°57'·99N 04°47'·41E.
Ent E side, ⚡ QR 9m 4M (H24); 52°57'·77N 04°47'·37E.

DEN HELDER TO AMSTERDAM

Zanddijk Grote Kaap ⚡ Oc WRG 10s 30m 8M; 041°-G-088°-W-094°-R-120°; brown twr; 52°52'·86N 04°42'·88E.
Petten ⚓ VQ (9) 10s; 52°47'·33N 04°36'·78E (Power stn outfall).
Egmond-aan-Zee ☆ Iso WR 10s 36m **W18M**, R14M; 010°-W-175°-R-188°; W ◯ twr; 52°36'·99N 04°37'·16E.

IJMUIDEN
Baloeran ⚓ Q (9) 15s; 52°29'·21N 04°32'·00E.
IJmuiden ⚓ Mo (A) 8s; **Racon Y, 10M**; 52°28'·45N 04°23'·92E.
Ldg lts 100·5° (FW 5M by day; 090·5°-110·5°). **Front** ☆ F WR 30m **W16M**, R13M; 050°-W-122°-R-145°-W-160°; (Tidal and traffic sigs); dark R ◯ twrs; 52°27'·70N 04°34'·47E. **Rear** ☆ Fl 5s 52m **29M**; 019°-199° (FW 5M by day; 090·5°-110·5°); 560m from front.
S bkwtr hd ⚡ FG 14m 10M (in fog Fl 3s); W twr, G bands; 52°27'·82N 04°31'·93E.
N bkwtr hd ⚡ FR 15m 10M; 52°28'·05N 04°32'·55E.
IJM1 ▲ Iso G 4s; 52°27'·75N 04°33'·59E.
S outer chan ⚡ Iso G 6s, 52°27'·75N 04°33'·81E. ⚡ Iso R 6s, 52°27'·84N 04°34'·39E (Forteiland). Kleine Sluis 52°27'·84N 04°35'·43E.

AMSTERDAM
IJ8 ⚓ Iso R 8s (for Sixhaven marina); 52°22'·86N 04°54'·37E.
Oranjesluizen, N lock 52°22'·93N 04°57'·60E (for IJsselmeer).

AMSTERDAM TO ROTTERDAM

Noordwijk-aan-Zee ☆ Oc (3) 20s 32m **18M**; W◻twr; 52°14'·88N 04°26'·02E.

SCHEVENINGEN
Lighthouse ☆ Fl (2) 10s 48m **29M**; 014°-244°; brown twr; 52°06'·23N 04°16'·13E, 5ca E of hbr ent.

Ldg lts 156°, both Iso 4s 14M, H24; synch; Gy masts. Front 52°05'·99N 04°15'·44E; rear 250m from front. Intens at night.
SCH ⚓ Iso 4s; 52°07'·76N 04°14'·12E.
KNS ⚓ Q (9)15s; 52°06'·48N 04°15'·27E.
W mole ⚡ FG 12m 9M; G twr, W bands; 52°06'·23N 04°15'·16E.
E mole ⚡, FR 12m 9M; R twr, W bands; 52°06'·24N 04°15'·37E.
Inner ldg lts 131°: both Iso G 4s synch; Gy posts. Front 52°05'·81N 04°15'·89E. Rear, 34m from front.

NOORD HINDER N & S TSS and JUNCTION
NHR-N ⚓ L Fl 8s; **Racon K, 10M**; 52°10'·91N 03°04'·76E.
Noord Hinder ⚓ Fl (2) 10s; *Horn (2) 30s*; **Racon T, 12-15M**; 52°00'·10N 02° 51'·11E.
NHR-S ⚓ Fl Y 10s; 51°49'·53N 02°25'·95E.
NHR-SE ▲ Fl G 5s; 51°43'·43N 02°37'·18E.
Birkenfels ⚓ Q (9) 15s; 51°38'·96N 02°32'·03E.
Twin ⚓ Fl (3) 9s; 51°32'·05N 02°22'·62E.
Garden City ⚓ Q (9) 15s; 51°29'·12N 02°17'·92E.

APPROACHES TO HOEK VAN HOLLAND
Europlatform ⛴ Mo (U) 15s; W structure, R bands; helicopter platform; *Horn Mo(U) 30s*; 51°55'·50N 03°40'·10E.
Goeree ☆ Mo(U)15s 32m **28M**; R/W chequered twr on platform; helicopter platform; *Horn Mo(U) 30s*; **Racon T, 12-15M**; 51°55'·42N 03°40'·03E.
Maasvlakte ☆ Fl (5) 20s 67m **28M**, H24; 340°-267°; W twr, B bands; 51°58'·20N 04°00'·84E, 1.5M SSW of Maas ent.
Maas Center ⚓ Iso 4s; **Racon M, 10M**; 52°00'·92N 03°48'·79E.
MO ⚓ Mo (A) 8s; 52°01'·10N 03°58'·19E.
MN3 ▲ Fl (3) G 10s; 52°07'·04N 04°00'·00E.
MN1 ▲ Fl G 5s; 52°02'·23N 04°01'·91E.

HOEK VAN HOLLAND
Maasmond ldg lts 112° (for deep draught vessels): both Iso 4s 30/46m **21M**; 101°-123°, synch; W twr, B bands. **Front**, 51°58'·88N 04°04'·88E (NW end of Splitsingsdam). Rear, 0·6M from front.
Indusbank N ⚓ Q; 52°01'·82N 04°03'·60E.
MVN ⚓ VQ; 51°59'·61N 04°00'·23E.
NETW ⚓ Q (9) 15s; 51°59'·32N 04°01'·24E.
Maas 1 ▲ L Fl G 5s; 51°59'·35N 04°01'·68E.
Nieuwe Waterweg ldg lts 107°: both Iso R 6s 29/43m **18M**; 099.5°-114.5°; R twr, W bands. Front, 51°58'·55N 04°07'·52E. Rear, 450m from front.
Noorderdam Head ⚡ FR 25m 10M (In fog Al Fl WR 6s; 278°-255°); R twr, W bands; 51°59'·67N 04°02'·80E.
Nieuwe Zuiderdam ⚡ FG 25m 10M, 330°-307°; (In fog Al Fl WG 6s); G twr, W bands; 51°59'·14N 04°02'·49E.

ROTTERDAM
Maassluis ⚡ FG 6m; 51°54'·94N 04°14'·81E; and FR.
Vlaardingen ⚡ FG; 51°53'·99N 04°20'·95E; and FR.
Spuihaven, W ent ⚡ FR; 51°53'·98N 04°23'·97E.
Veerhaven, E ent ⚡ FG; 51°54'·42N 04°28'·75E; and FR.
City marina ent, 51°54'·64N 04°29'·76E.

APPROACHES TO HARINGVLIET
Buitenbank , Iso 4s; 51°51'·16N 03°25'·71E.
Hinder ⚓ Q (9) 15s; 51°54'·55N 03°55'·42E.
SH ⚓ VQ (9) 10s; 51°49'·49N 03°45'·79E.
Westhoofd ☆ Fl (3) 15s 55m **30M**; R ◻ tr; 51°48'·79N 03°51'·85E.
Ooster ⚓ Q (9) 15s; 51°47'·90N 03°41'·27E.

SLIJKGAT
SG ⚓ Iso 4s; 51°51'·95N 03°51'·42E.
SG 2 ⚓ Iso R 4s; 51°51'·71N 03°53'·45E.
SG 5 ▲ Iso G 4s; 51°50'·00N 03°55'·56E.
SG 11 ▲ Iso G 4s; 51°50'·81N 03°58'·52E.
P1 ▲ Iso G 4s; 51°51'·30N 04°01'·12E.
P3 ▲ Iso G 8s; 51°51'·12N 04°01'·45E.
P9 ▲ Iso G 8s; 51°49'·98N 04°02'·15E.

STELLENDAM
N mole ⚲ FG; *Horn (2) 15s;* 51°49'·88N 04°02'·03E.
Buitenhaven ⚲ Oc 6s; 51°49'·73N 04°01'·75E.

APPROACHES TO OOSTERSCHELDE
OUTER APPROACHES
Schouwenbank ⬡ Mo (A) 8s; *Racon O, 10M;* 51°44'·94N 03°14'·32E.
Middelbank ⬡ Iso 8s; 51°40'·86N 03°18'·20E.
MW ⚲ Q (9) 15s; 51°44'·55N 03°24'·04E (Schouwendiep).
MD 3 ▲ Fl G 5s; 51°42'·70N 03°26'·98E.
Rabsbank ⬡ Iso 4s; 51°38'·25N 03°09'·93E.
Westpit ⬡ Iso 8s; 51°33'·65N 03°09'·92E.
ZSB ⚲ VQ (9) 10s; 51°36'·57N 03°15'·62E.
OG1 ▲ QG; 51°36'·14N 03°20'·08E.

WESTGAT, OUDE ROOMPOT and ROOMPOTSLUIS
West Schouwen ☆ Fl (2+1)15s 57m **30M**; Gy twr, R diagonals on upper part; 51°42'·52N 03°41'·50E, 5·8M N of Roompotsluis.
OG-WG ⚲ VQ (9) 10s; 51°37'·18N 03°23'·82E.
WG1 ▲ Iso G 8s; 51°38'·00N 03°26'·24E.
WG4 ⚲ L Fl R 8s; 51°38'·62N 03°28'·78E.
WG7 ▲ Iso G 4s 51°39'·40N 03°32'·67E.
WG-GB (Geul van de Banjaard) ◢ 51°39'·72N 03°32'·69E.
OR1 ▲ 51°39'·15N 03°33'·59E.
OR5 ▲ Iso G 8s; 51°38'·71N 03°35'·53E.
OR11 ▲ Iso G 4s; 51°36'·98N 03°38'·40E.
R11A ⚲ QG 51°36'·74N 03°39'·29E.
R11B ⚲ Iso G 4s 51°37'·00N 03°39'·82E.
OR12 ⬡ Iso R 4s; 51°37'·27N 03°39'·25E.
OR13 R14; ⚲ VQ (3) 5s 51°36'·61N 03°38'·67E.
Roompotsluis ldg lts 073·5°, both Oc G 5s; synch. Front, 51°37'·33N 03°40'·75E. Rear, 280m from front.
N bkwtr ⚲ FR 7m; 51°37'·31N 03°40'·09E.

WESTKAPELLE TO VLISSINGEN
OOSTGAT
Ldg lts 149·5°: Front, Noorderhoofd Oc WRG 10s 20m; W13M, R/G10M; 353°-R-008°-G-029°-W-169°; R ○ twr, W band; 51°32'·40N 03°26'·21E, 0·73M from rear (Westkapelle).
Westkapelle ☆, rear, Fl 3s 50m **28M**; obsc'd by land on certain brgs; □ twr, R top; 51°31'·75N 03°26'·83E.
Kaloo ⬡ Iso 8s; 51°35'·55N 03°23'·24E. Chan is well buoyed/lit.
OG5 ▲ Iso G 8s; 51°34'·10N 03°23'·88E.
OG 7 ▲ VQ G , 51°32'·76N 03° 24'·87E.
Molenhoofd ⚲ Oc WRG 6s 10m; 311·5°-R-330·5°-W-348·5°-R-008°-G-034·5°-W-036·5°-G-147.5°-W-168.5°-R-198°; W mast R bands; 51°31'·58N 03°26'·05E.
Zoutelande F 22m 12M; 321°-352°; R □ twr; 51°30'·28N 03°28'·41E.
Kaapduinen, ldg lts 130°: both Oc 5s 25/34m 13M; synch; Y □ twrs, R bands. Front, 122·5° - 137·5°; 51°28'·47N 03°30'·99E. Rear, 122·5° - 137·5°; 220m from front.
Fort de Nolle ⚲ Oc WRG 9s 11m W6M, R/G4M; 293°-R-309°-W-324·5°-G-336·5°-R-014°-G-064°-R-099·5°-W-110·5°-G-117°-R-130°; W col, R bands; 51°26'·94N 03°33'·12E.
Ldg lts 117°: Front, Leugenaar, Oc R 5s 6m 5M; intens 108°-126°; W&R pile; 51°26'·43N 03°34'·14E.
Rear, Sardijngeul ⚲ Oc WR 5s 10m 5M, synch; 245°-R-273°-W-123.5°-R-147°; R △, W bands on R & W mast; Koopmanshaven W Head, 550m from front; 51°26'·30N 03°34'·55E.

OFFSHORE: W HINDER TSS TO SCHEUR CHANNEL
West Hinder ☆ Fl (4) 30s 23m 13M; *Horn Mo (U) 30s; Racon W;* 51°23'·30N 02°26'·27E.
WH Zuid ⚲ Q (6) + L Fl 15s; 51°22'·78N 02°26'·25E.
OostdyckBk ⚲ Q; 51°21'·38N 02°31'·12E.
BerguesBk-N ⚲ Q; 51°19'·95N 02°24'·50E.

Oost-Dyck West ⚲ Q (9) 15s; 51°17'·15N 02°26'·32E.
Oostdyck radar twr; ⚲ Mo (U) 15s 15m 12M on 4 corners; *Horn Mo (U) 30s; Racon O*. R twr, 3 W bands, with adjacent red twr/helipad; 51°16'·49N 02°26'·85E.
A-N ⚲ Fl (4) R 20s; 51°23'·45N 02°36'·90E.
AS ▲ Fl (3) G 10s; 51°21'·15N 02°36'·92E.
KB2 ⚲ VQ; 51°21'·04N 02°42'·22E.
KB ⚲ Q; *Racon K;* 51°21'·03N 02°42'·83E.
MBN ⚲ Q; 51°20'·82N 02°46'·29E.
Akkaert-SW ⚲ Q (9) 15s; 51°22'·28N 02°46'·34E.
VG ⚲ Q ; 51°23'·38N 02°46'·21E, Vaargeul 1.
VG1 ▲ VQ G; 51°25'·03N 02°49'·04E.
VG2 ⬡ Q (6) + L Fl R 15s; *Racon V;* 51°25'·96N 02°48'·16E.
VG3 ⚲ QG; 51°25'·05N 02°52'·92E.
VG5 ▲ Fl G 5s; 51°24'·63N 02°57'·92E.
SVG ⚲ Q ; 51°24'·53N 02°59'·92E.
Goote Bank ⚲ Q (3) 10s; 51°26'·95N 02°52'·72E.
A1 ⚲ Iso 8s; 51°22'·36N 02°53'·33E.
A1bis ⚲ L Fl 10s; 51°21'·68N 02°58'·02E.

WESTERSCHELDE APPROACHES
SCHEUR CHANNEL
S1 ▲ Fl G 5s; 51°23'·14N 03°00'·12E.
S3 ⚲ Q; 51°24'·30N 03°02'·92E.
MOW 0 ⊙ Fl (5) Y 20s; *Racon S, 10M;* 51°23'·67N 03°02'·75E.
S5 ▲ Fl G 5s; 51°23'·70N 03°06'·30E.
S7 ▲ Fl G 5s; 51°23'·98N 03°10'·42E.
S9 ▲ QG; 51°24'·42N 03°14'·99E.
S12 ⬡ Fl (4) R 10s; 51°24'·67N 03°18'·22E.
S-W ⚲ Q; 51°24'·13N 03°18'·22E, here Wielingen chan merges.
S14 ⬡ Fl R 5s; 51°24'·58N 03°19'·67E.

WIELINGEN CHANNEL
BVH ⬡ Q (6) + L Fl R 15s; 51°23'·15N 03°12'·04E.
MOW3 tide gauge ⚲ Fl (5) Y 20s; *Racon H, 10M;* 51°23'·38N 03°11'·92E.
W ▲ Fl (3) G 15s; 51°23'·26N 03°14'·90E.
W1 ▲ Fl G 5s; 51°23'·46N 03°18'·21E.
Fort Maisonneuve ⚲ VQ (9) 10s; wreck; 51°24'·20N 03°21'·50E.
W3 ▲ Iso G 4s; 51°23'·95N 03°21'·48E.
W5 ▲ Iso G 8s; 51°24'·30N 03°24'·50E.
W7 ▲ Iso G 8s; 51°24'·59N 03°27'·27E.
W9 ▲ Q G; 51°24'·94N 03°30'·43E.
Nieuwe Sluis ⚲ Oc WRG 10s 26m W14M, R11M, G10M; 055°-R-089°-W-093°-G-105°-R-134°-W-136.5°-G-156.5°-R-236.5°-G-243°-W-254°-R-292°-W-055°; B 8-sided twr, W bands; 51°24'·41N 03°31'·29E.
Songa ▲ QG; 51°25'·26N 03°33'·66E.
W10 ⬡ QR; 51°25'·85N 03°33'·28E.

VLISSINGEN
Koopmanshaven, W mole root, ⚲ Iso WRG 3s 16m 8M; 253°-R-277°-W-284°-R-297°-W-306.5°-G-013°-W-024°-G-033°-W-035°-G-039°-W-055°-G-084.5°-R-092°-G-111°-W-114°; R pylon; 51°26'·37N 03°34'·52E.
Sardijngeul ⚲ Oc WR 5s; 51°26'·30N 03°34'·55E: see OOSTGAT last 3 lines. E mole head, ⚲ FG 7m; W mast; 51°26'·32N 03°34'·67E.
Buitenhaven ent, W side ⚲ FR 10m 5M; also Iso WRG 4s 6M; W073°-324°, G324°-352°, W352°-017°, G017°-042°, W042°-056°, R056°-073°; W post, R bands; tfc sigs; 51°26'·38N 03°36'·06E.
Buitenhaven ent, E side ⚲ FG 7m 4M; 51°26'·41N 03°36'·38E.
Schone Waardin ⚲ Oc WRG 9s 10m W13M, R10M, G9M; 235°-271°-W-283°-G-335°-R-341°-G-026°-W-079°-R-091°; R mast, W bands; 51°26'·54N 03°37'·91E (1M E of Buitenhaven ent).

BRESKENS TO CADZAND-BAD
Nieuwe Sluis ⚲ Oc 10s 28m 14M (priv); B/W banded 8 sided tr; 51°24'·43N 03°31'·26E.

Netherlands *(vertical tab)*

ARV-VH ↙ Q; 51°24′·71N 03°33′·89E.
VH2 (Vaarwaterlangs Hoofdplaat) ↙ Iso R 2s; 51°24′·34N 03°33′·90E.
Yacht hbr, W mole ⚓ FG 7m; in fog FY; Gy post; 51°24′·03N 03°34′·06E. E mole ⚓ FR 6m; Gy mast; 51°23′·95N 03°34′·09E.
Cadzand-Bad, marina approach, CZ ⚓ Mo (A) 8s; 51°23′·08N 03°23′·07E.

WESTERSCHELDE: TERNEUZEN TO PAAL

TERNEUZEN
Nieuw Neuzenpolder ldg lts 125°, both Oc 5s 6/16m 9/13M; intens 117°-133°; synch. Front, W col, B bands; 51°20′·97N 03°47′·24E. Rear, B & W twr; 365m from front.
Oost Buitenhaven E mole ⚓ FR 5M; 51°20′·56N 03°49′·19E.
Veerhaven (former ferry hbr, W part) & marinas (E part) W mole head ⚓ FG, Gy mast; 51°20′·57N 03°49′·64E. E mole, FR. W mole ⚓ Oc WRG 5s 15m W9M, R7M, G6M; 090°-R-115°-W-120°-G-130°-W-245°-G-249°-W-279°-R-004°; B & W post; 51°20′·54N 03°49′·58E, close SW of ⚓ FG.

HANSWEERT
W mole ⚓ Oc WRG 10s 9m W6M, R6M, G6M; (in fog FY); 288°-R-311°-G-320°-W-332·5°-G-348·5°-W-042·5°-R-061·5°-W-078°-G-099°-W-114·5°-R-127·5°-W-288°; R twr, W bands; 51°26′·42N 04°00′·53E.

BELGIUM
ZANDVLIET TO ANTWERPEN

ZANDVLIET
Dir ⚓ 118·3°,WRG 20m W4M, R/ G3M; 116·63°-Oc G-117·17°- FG-117·58°-Alt GW-118·63°-F-118·63°-Alt RW-119·18°-FR-119·58°-Oc R-120·13°; 51°20′·61N 04°16′·47E, near Zandvliet locks.

ANTWERPEN
No 107 ↙ Iso G 8s, 51°14′·12N 04°23′·80E (Kattendijksluis for Willemdok ⓐ).
Royerssluis, ldg lts 091°, both FR. Ent FR/FG.
No 109 ↙ Iso G 8s; 51°13′·88N 04°23′·87E, (off Linkeroever ⓐ).
Linkeroever marina ↙ F WR 9m W3M; R2M; shore-W-283°- R-shore; B ⊙, R lantern; 51°13′·91N 04°23′·70E. Marina ent, FR/FG.

COASTAL MARKS

AW2 ↙ Fl (4) R 20s; 51°21′·95N 03°00′·94E; Wandelaar.
AW1 ↙ QG; 51°21′·50N 03°02′·59E; Wandelaar.
Oostende Bank N ↙ Q; 51°21′·20N 02°52′·93E.
Wenduine Bank E ↙ QR; 51°18′·83N 03°01′·64E.
Wenduine Bank W ↙ Q (9) 15s; 51°17′·23N 02°52′·76E.
Nautica Ena wreck ↙ Q; 51°18′·08N 02°52′·79E.
Oostendebank E ↙ Fl G 5s; 51°17′·35N 02°51′·92E.
Oostendebank W ↙ Q (9)15s; 51°16′·20N 02°44′·74E.
LST 420 ↙ Q (9)15s; 51°15′·45N 02°40′·67E.
MBN ↙ Q; 51°20′·82N 02°46′·29E.
Middelkerke Bank ↙ Fl G 5s; 51°18′·19N 02°42′·75E.
Middelkerke Bank S ↙ Q (9) R 15s; 51°14′·73N 02°41′·89E.
D1 ↙ Q (3) 10s; 51°13′·95N 02°38′·59E.
BT Ratel ↙ Fl (4) R 15s; 51°11′·63N 02°27′·92E; Buiten Ratel.

ZEEBRUGGE TO THE FRENCH BORDER

ZEEBRUGGE
AW ↙ Iso 8s; 51°22′·41N 03°07′·05E.
Ldg lts 136°, both Oc 5s 22/45m 8M; 131°-141°; H24, synch; W cols, R bands. Front, 51°20′·71N 03°13′·11E. Rear, 890m SE.
SZ ↙ Q (3) 10s; 51°23′·30N 03°08′·65E (Scheur Channel).
Z ↙ QG; 51°22′·48N 03°09′·95E.

WZ ↙ Q (9) 15s; 51°22′·57N 03°10′·72E.
W outer mole ⚓ Oc G 7s 31m 7M; G vert strip lts visible from seaward; 057°-267°; *Horn (3) 30s;* IPTS; 51°21′·74N 03°11′·17E.
E outer mole ⚓ Oc R 7s 31m 7M; R vert strip lts visible from seaward; 087°-281°; *Bell 25s;* 51°21′·78N 03°11′·86E.
Ldg lts 154°: Front, Oc WR 6s 20m 3M, 135°-W-160°-R-169°; W pylon, R bands; 51°20′·33N 03°12′·89E. Rear, Oc 6s 38m 3M, H24, synch; 520m from front.
Leopold II mole ☆ Oc WR 15s 22m, **W20M, R18M**; 068°-W-145°-R-212°-W-296°; IPTS; 51°20′·85N 03°12′·17E.
Entrance to Marina and FV hbr 51°19′·88N 03°11′·85E.

BLANKENBERGE
Promenade pier Fl (3) Y 20s, 8m 4M; 51°19′·28N 03°08′·18E.
Lt ho ☆ Fl (2) 8s 30m **20M**; 065°-245°; W twr, B top; 51°18′·76N 03°06′·87E.
Ldg lts 134°, both FR 5/9m 3/10M, R cross (X) topmarks on masts; front 51°18′·70N 03°08′·82E; rear 81m from front.
E pier ⚓ FR 12m 11M; R290°-245°(315°); W ○ twr; 51°18′·91N 03°06′·56E.
W pier ⚓ FG 14m 11M; intens 065°-290°, unintens 290°-335°; W ○ twr; 51°18′·89N 03°06′·42E.
OBST 4 – OBST 14 are eleven ↙s Q approx 3ca offshore, marking Spoil Ground between Blankenberge and Oostende.

OOSTENDE
Wenduinebank West ↙ Q (9) 15s; 51°17′·23N 02°52′·76E.
Buitenstroombank ↙ Q; 51°15′·17N 02°51′·71E.
Binnenstroombank ↙ Q (3) 10s; 51°14′·47N 02°53′·65E.
Ldg lts 143°: both Iso 4s (triple vert) 36/46m 4M, 068°-218°; X on metal mast, R/W bands. Front, 51°13′·80N 02°55′·89E.
Oostende lt ho ☆ Fl (3) 10s 65m **27M**; obsc 069·5°-071°; Gy twr, 2 sinusoidal Bu bands; 51°14′·18N 02°55′·84E.
W bkwtr hd ⚓ FG 9m 3M G mast; 51°14′·44N 02° 54′·97E.
E bkwtr hd ⚓ FR 9m 3M + QY; R mast; 51°14′·51N 02° 55′·18E and Radar tr, 50m, vert R/W stripes, R top, 51°14′·51N 02°55′·19E.

NIEUWPOORT
Zuidstroombank ↙ Fl R 5s; 51°12′·28N 02°47′·37E.
Weststroombank ↙ Fl (4) R 20s; 51°11′·34N 02°43′·03E.
Wreck 4 ↙ Q (6) + L Fl 15s; 51°10′·98N 02°40′·10E.
Nieuwpoort Bank ↙ Q (9) 15s; 51°10′·16N 02°36′·09E.
Whitley ↙ Q; 51°09′·15N 02°39′·44E.
Lt ho ☆ Fl (2) R 14s 28m **16M**; R/W twr; 51°09′·28N 02°43′·80E.
E pier ⚓ FR 10m 10M; R025°-250°(225°) R307°-347°(40°); W ○ twr; 51°09′·41N 02°43′·08E.
W pier ⚓ FG 10m 9M; G025°-250°(225°) G284°-324°(40°); W ○ twr; 51°09′·35N 02°43′·00E.
⚓ QG 51°08′·65N 02°44′·31E marks the Y-junction where the channel forks stbd for KYCN and port for WSKLM and VVW-N.

WESTDIEP and PASSE DE ZUYDCOOTE
Den Oever wreck 2 ↙ Q; 51°08′·11N 02°37′·43E.
Wreck 1 ↙ Q; 51°08′·32N 02°35′·03E (adjacent to ⚓ next line).
Wave recorder ⚓ Fl (5) Y 20s; 51°08′·25N 02°34′·98E.
Trapegeer ↙ Fl G 10s; 51°08′·41N 02°34′·36E.
E12 ↙ VQ (6) + L Fl 10s; 51°07′·92N 02°30′·61E.

French waters, for continuity:
CME ↙ Q (3) 10s; 51°07′·30N 02°30′·00E.
E11 ↙ Fl G 4s; 51°06′·85N 02°30′·83E.
E10 ↙ Fl (2) R 6s; 51°06′·26N 02°30′·40E.
E9 ↙ Fl (2) G 6s; 51°05′·61N 02°29′·60E.
E8 ↙ Fl (3) R 12s; 51°05′·12N 02°28′·60E.

2.4 PASSAGE INFORMATION

Bibliography: *N Sea Passage Pilot* (Imray/Navin). *Cruising Guide to the Netherlands* (Imray/Navin). NP 55 *N Sea (East) Pilot*. NP 28 *Dover Strait Pilot*. *Hafenhandbuch Nordsee* (DSV-Verlag).

CHARTS, PSSA AND TSS

While AC 2182A, 1405/06/08, 1630/31/32/33, 1872 or the equivalent Royal Netherlands Navy Zeekaarten suffice for coastal passages and entry to the main ports, larger scale **Dutch yacht charts** (DYC 1800 series) are essential for exploring the cruising grounds and smaller hbrs along this coast. Inland, the ANWB booklet/chart (€19.95) of the *Staande-Mast Route* (Fixed Mast Route; see 2.1A) is very detailed with intelligible notes in Dutch.

From the Ems estuary west to Den Helder a **Particularly Sensitive Sea Area** (PSSA) extends 3M seaward from the West Frisian Islands. Yachts should carefully avoid damaging the maritime environment and marine organisms living in it.

The Terschelling-German Bight TSS, Off Vlieland TSS and Off Texel TSS lie between 5 and 10M to seaward of the West Frisian Islands. Cruising yachts are advised to navigate within this relatively narrow ITZ. Further offshore, and particularly in and near the Off Vlieland TSS, West Friesland TSS and Botney Ground TSS, navigation is further complicated by the many oil and gas fields. For general notes on North Sea oil and gas installations, see Area 3. Up to date charts are essential, particularly AC 1406, 1408 and 1423.

CROSSING THE NORTH SEA TO THE UK

From ports S of Hoek van Holland make for NHR-SE, to cross the TSS for destinations between Harwich and Great Yarmouth (AC 1406, 1408, 1872, 2449, 3371). From ports N of Hoek van Holland passages can be more problematic. For example, a route from IJmuiden to the Humber crosses two DW routes, N and NW of Brown Ridge, and then runs into extensive offshore Gas Fields. These might cause you to opt for two shorter legs, stopping a night at Great Yarmouth. Similar thinking might apply if coming out of Den Helder, even if a stop at Great Yarmouth might incur some southing. From east of Den Helder, make ground west via the ITZ before taking departure.

THE WEST FRISIAN ISLANDS

These islands stretch from the R Ems estuary W and SSW for some 85M along the Dutch coast to Den Helder (AC 1632, 1633). They have similar characteristics – being long, low and narrow, with the major axis parallel to the coast. Texel is the largest and, with Vlieland and Terschelling, lies furthest offshore.

Between the islands, narrow channels (*zeegat* in Dutch, *Seegat* in German) give access to/from the North Sea. Most of these channels are shallow for part of their length, and in these shoal areas a dangerous sea builds up in a strong onshore wind against the outgoing (ebb) tide. The Westerems and the Zeegaten van Terschelling and van Texel are safe for yachts in W–NE winds up to force 6. The rest are unsafe in strong onshore winds.

▶*The flood stream along this coast is E-going, so it starts to run in through the zeegaten progressively from W to E. Where the tide meets behind each island, as it flows in first at the W end and a little later at the E end, a bank is formed, called a wantij (Dutch) or Wattenhoch (German).*◀

These banks between the islands and the coast are major obstacles to E/W progress inside the islands. The chans are narrow and winding, marked by buoys and/or withies (⚲ ⚲) in the shallower parts, and they mostly dry; so that it is essential to time the tide correctly.

This is an area most suited to shallow-draft yachts that can take the ground easily. Whilst the zeegaten are described briefly below, the many channels inside the islands and across the Waddenzee are mentioned only for general orientation.

DELFZIJL TO AMELAND

The Ems estuary (AC 1633, 3631) flows seaward past the SW side of the German island of Borkum giving access to **Delfzijl**, **Termunterzijl** and **Emden**. Hubertgat, which runs parallel to and S of the main Westerems chan, though sparsely buoyed and unlit, is fine for yachts in fair weather and slightly more direct when bound to/from the W. In strong NW winds against the ebb both chans produce a dangerous sea.

Further offshore, the growing string of wind farms continues W with the Gemini 'twins' BuitenGaats and ZeeEnergie, 150 turbines, 54°02′·39N 05°57′·64E, 34M due north of Ameland. Bard 1, 80 turbines and Vega Mate 67 turbines, 50°20′·46N 05°56′·54E, are 18M further N, and EnBW Hohe See, 71 turbines, 54°28′·87N 06°21′·25E lies 15M to the NE.

▶*The E-going (flood) stream begins at HW Helgoland +0530, and the W-going (ebb) stream begins at HW Helgoland –0030, sp rates 1·5kn.*◀

Friesche Zeegat (DYC 1812.3 & .9) between Schiermonnikoog and Ameland, contains two channels: Westgat is marked by 'WG' buoys, but shoaling and shifting channels have made it increasingly hazardous without local knowledge and Plaatgat, an unmarked channel, which is dangerous. In strong winds the sea breaks across the whole estuary. Westgat trends SE past Wierumergronden and N7-FA-1 platform, the S past Het Rif and Engelsmanplaat (a prominent sandbank) into Zoutkamperlaag, the main channel (buoys prefixed 'Z') to **Lauwersoog**. Here locks give access to the Lauwersmeer and inland waterways.

Zeegat van Ameland (DYC 1811.6) between Ameland and Terschelling is fronted by the sandbank of Bornrif about 3M offshore. The main entrance is also called Westgat, with buoys prefixed by letters 'WA', all unlit except WA12 QR. The channel runs ESE close N of Terschelling, and divides into Boschgat (BG) at the E end of West Terschelling and Borndiep (BB) the wider, deeper channel. This skirts the W end of Ameland and at WA22-WG1 buoy gives access via the Molengat to the small ferry port and yacht hbr at Nes.

▶*In Westgat the flood stream begins at HW Helgoland +0425, and the ebb stream at HW Helgoland –0150, sp rates 2kn.*◀ A dangerous sea develops in strong onshore winds.

TERSCHELLING TO TEXEL AND DEN HELDER

Zeegat Het Vlie, aka Zeegat van Terschelling (AC 112 and DYC 1811.4, .5 and .9) between Terschelling and Vlieland, gives access to the hbrs of **Vlieland, West Terschelling and Harlingen**; it is also a northern approach to the sealock at Kornwerderzand. Shallow banks extend more than 5M seaward narrowing the ITZ to only 4M wide.

▶*The E-going (flood) stream begins at HW Helgoland +0325, while the W-going (ebb) stream begins at HW Helgoland –0230, sp rates 2·5kn.*◀

The main chan (buoyed/lit) through the banks is Zuider Stortemelk (buoys prefixed 'ZS') running ESE close N of Vlieland into Vliesloot (VS) which leads to **Oost Vlieland** hbr. The Stortmelk (SM) forks eastward at SM1-ZS10 buoy towards the deeper wider channel of Vliestroom.

In fair weather, and daylight, approach **West Terschelling** via the Schuitengat-Zuid, R and G lateral buoys (unlit), beginning at the RGR (preferred chan to stbd) VL2-SG1 buoy. At night, or in strong W or NW'lies and swell, it is advisable to go via Meep and Slenk. From Zuider Stortemelk the Vliestroom, a deep well-buoyed chan (buoys prefixed 'VL') runs S for about 4M to its junction with Blauwe Slenk (BS) and Inschot (IN). Blauwe Slenk runs ESE to **Harlingen**; from Harlingen a S-going channel 'Boontjes' leads via the locks at Kornwerderzand into the IJsselmeer.

Eierlandsche Gat (DYC 1811.7) between Vlieland and Texel, consists of dangerous shoals, shallow and unmarked chans used only by fishermen, *and should not be attempted by strangers*.

Zeegat van Texel (AC 1546/DYC 1811.2), lies between Texel and

Den Helder, and gives access to the **Waddenzee** and IJsselmeer via locks at Den Oever or Kornwerderzand. Haaksgronden shoals extend 5M seaward. The 2 appr channels are: Molengat from the N along the Texel shore (see next para) and from the SSW the well-marked/lit main chan Schulpengat, buoys prefixed 'S'. Small craft bound for Den Helder will find clear water and adequate depths E of the buoyed chan and, closing Kijkduin lt ho, should then keep an offing of 200m to avoid inshore hazards. Beware rough seas with strong SW wind against. ▶*the SW-going (ebb) stream which begins at HW Helgoland −0330, while the NE-going (flood) stream begins at HW Helgoland +0325, sp rates 1·5kn.*◀

Serious shoaling in the Molengat has reduced it to a fair weather channel for small craft in daylight only. It is no longer surveyed by the Dutch Hydrographic Service, and depths vary from those charted. Y SPM's mark the N and S entrances; keep close W of the line of Y spar bys marking the chan, submerged WWII bunkers lie E of these bys. Do not attempt in fresh NW'lies or swell.

▶*In Molengat the N-going (ebb) stream begins at HW Helgoland −0145, and the S-going (flood) stream at HW Helgoland +0425, sp rates 1·25kn.*◀

From the N the Schulpengat involves a southerly deviation of approx 15M and leads W of the very dangerous Zuider Haaks which should be avoided in bad weather.

E of **Den Helder** and the Marsdiep, the flood makes in three main directions through the SW Waddenzee:

- to E and SE through Malzwin and Visjagersgaatje (keeping to the ctr of the channel) to **Den Oever** (where the lock into IJsselmeer is only available during daylight hours); thence NE along the Afsluitdijk, and then N towards Harlingen;
- to NE and E through Texelstroom and Doove Balg towards Kornwerderzand; and
- from Texelstroom, NE and N through Scheurrak, Omdraai and Inschot, where it meets the flood stream from Zeegat van Terschelling. The ebb runs in reverse. The **Kornwerderzand** locks (available H24), near NE end of Afsluitdijk, also give access to the IJsselmeer.

DEN HELDER TO SCHEVENINGEN

South of Den Helder the coast is low, and, like most of the Dutch coast, not readily visible from seaward. Conspic landmarks include: chimneys of nuclear power station 1·5M NNE of Petten; Egmond aan Zee lighthouse; chimneys of steelworks N of IJmuiden; two light houses at IJmuiden; big hotels at Zandvoort; Noordwijk aan Zee light house; and Scheveningen lighthouse and big hotels.

Egmond aan Zee wind farm, 36 turbines, 52°36'·03N 04°26'·47E (about 6·7M W of the town it is named after) and 8M further W Prinses Amalia Windpark, 60 turbines, is centred on 52°35'·27N 04°13'·55E. Luchterduinen wind farm, 43 turbines, centred on 52°24'·16N 04°09'·31E is 14M WSW of IJmuiden. All show FR lts and Fl Y on perimeters: see AC 1631 and AC 1408.

▶*3M W of IJmuiden the N-going stream begins at HW Hoek van Holland −0120, and the S-going at HW Hoek van Holland +0430, sp rates about 1·5kn. Off ent to IJmuiden the stream turns about 1h earlier and is stronger, and in heavy weather there may be a dangerous sea.*◀ From **IJmuiden** the **Noordzeekanaal** leads east to **Amsterdam** and the **IJsselmeer.**

HOEK VAN HOLLAND TO THE WESTERSCHELDE

Off Hoek van Holland at the ent to Europoort and **Rotterdam** shipping is dense and fast-moving. Yachts must go upriver via the Nieuwe Waterweg which near Vlaardingen becomes the Nieuwe Maas.

The Slijkgat (lit) is the approach chan to **Stellendam** and entry to the Haringvliet. The Schaar, Schouwenbank, Middelbank and Steenbanken parallel the coast off the approaches to Oosterschelde. From the N, Geul van de Banjaard (partly lit) joins

Westgat and leads to Oude Roompot, and Roompot (unlit) the main, well-marked channels to the **Roompotsluis**, in S half of the barrage. Here the Oosterschelde (AC 192) is entered.

Rounding Walcheren via the Oostgat, close inshore, Westkapelle lt ho is conspic with two smaller lts nearby: Molenhoofd 5ca WSW and Noorderhoofd 7ca NNW. The Oostgat is the inshore link between Oosterschelde and Westerschelde and also the N approach to the latter.

Deurloo and Spleet are unlit secondary channels parallel to Oostgat and a mile or so to seaward. By day they keep yachts clear of commercial traffic in the Oostgat.

All channels converge between **Vlissingen** and **Breskens**. This bottleneck is declared a Precautionary Area where yachts have no rights of way over other vessels. An above-average lookout, and traffic avoidance is essential. Vessels <20m must give way to larger craft; yachts <12m must stay outside the buoyed chans.

The main approach chan to the Westerschelde from the W is the Scheur, which yachts may follow just outside the fairway. From **Zeebrugge** and the SW use the Wielingen chan, keeping close to S side of estuary until past **Breskens**.

If crossing the Precautionary Area there are two recommended routes. The W route runs to the W of Songa with a dogleg at W10 towards SG-W. The E route from Breskens, head up channel from ARV-VH, staying S of the G bys, turning N to cross the mini-TSS which runs E/W close off Vlissingen. Ensure you cross at right angles. The tide runs hard in the estuary, causing a bad sea in chans and overfalls on some banks in strong winds. There is shoaling.

The passage upriver to **Antwerpen** is best made in one leg, starting from Breskens, Vlissingen or **Terneuzen** in order to get the tidal timing right. Special inshore lanes for vessels <15m, known locally as 'fietspaden' (cycle paths!) are clearly marked by unlit Y bys. More exist between Harlingen and Terschelling.

HOEK VAN HOLLAND TO THE SOUTH EAST UK

Yachts out of Rotterdam/Hoek van Holland bound for the southern Thames Estuary should route 254°/52M from MV-N buoy to NHR-SE buoy, passing MW5, Goeree tower, MW3 and MW1 buoys. Cross the Noord Hinder South TSS between NHR-SE and NHR-S buoys. Thence depending on destination, set course 242°/44M to Outer Tongue for the R Thames; or 228°/46M to NE Goodwin for Ramsgate or points S.

If bound for the R Orwell or adjacent rivers, it may be best to pass N (rather than S) of the large and busy Sunk Outer and Inner Precautionary Areas and their associated TSS. From NHR-S buoy route via West Gabbard, North Inner Gabbard, S Shipwash and Rough buoys to pick up the recommended yacht track at Cork Sand Yacht beacon; it is a less direct route than going S via Galloper, but it avoids the worst of the commercial traffic.

THE BELGIAN COAST

Long shoals parallel this 36M coastline (AC 1872). The buoyed channels mostly run within 3M of the shore, the outer shoals giving some protection from strong W or SW winds, but dangerous in strong W to NE'lys with wind against tide.

▶*Off the Belgian coast the E-going stream begins at HW Vlissingen −0320 (HW Dover −0120), and the W-going at HW Vlissingen +0240 (HW Dover +0440), sp rates 2kn. Mostly the streams run parallel with the coast.*◀

From **Zeebrugge** stay 1M offshore inside Wenduine Bank past **Oostende**, then Kleine Rede or Grote Reede into West Diep off **Nieuwpoort**. At the French border West Diep narrows into Passe de Zuydcoote; stay close inshore for 25M to Dyck PHM.

Conversely, E-bound from the Thames, for **Oostende** or the **Westerschelde**, use W Hinder lt. From N, use NHR-S and NHR-SE buoys or N Hinder lt buoy. Enter the buoyed channels at Dyck. Wind farms lie 15M to 24M NW of Zeebrugge: Norther, 44 turbines, Thornton Bank/C Power 48 , Rentel 42, Northwind 72, Seamade 58, Belwind 55, Nobelwind 50, Northwester 23, Seastar 28. The adjacent Dutch wind farms Borssele 1,2,3 and 4, total 171 turbines. All show FR lts and Fl Y at perimeters. The TSS *Off North Hinder* then routes traffic W, S and E of these hazards via precautionary areas *At West Hinder, At Gootebank, Schouwenbank* and *Maas junctions*, see 2.20, 2.21A and AC 1872, 1630.

E bound, leave Oostende ►*HW Vlissingen – 0300 on a fair tide*◄. Keep 2M off **Blankenberge** and 1M off **Zeebrugge**, staying S of the Scheur channel to avoid much commercial traffic.

CROSSING THE NORTH SEA FROM BELGIUM

(AC 1406, 323) These four elements are useful for planning :

- Avoid N Hinder-Maas and W Hinder-Sandettie complexes.
- Cross TSS at their narrowest parts, ie between NHR-SE and Fairy W; and SW of Sandettie.
- Plan to cross the many offshore ridges at their extremities, zigzagging as necessary to achieve this.
- If bound for Dover or down-Channel use the coastal passage W to Dyck, then via MPC to SW Goodwin buoy. Or route via Sandettie to NE Goodwin buoy and into the southern Thames Estuary.

From the Scheur chan off Zeebrugge a fairly direct course via Fairy W, S Galloper leads into the N Thames Estuary or towards the Suffolk ports. Avoid shoals, particularly in rough weather when the sea-state and under-keel clearance may be crucial problems. For N Sea distances see 0.34.

2.5 SPECIAL NOTES: NETHERLANDS

PROVINCES are given in lieu of UK 'counties'.

CHARTS The following types of chart are available from agents. The Chart catalogue (HP7) is downloadable from www.hydro.nl:

- Zeekaarten (equivalent to AC) are issued by the Royal Netherlands Navy Hydrographer and corrected by Notices to Mariners (*Berichten aan Zeevarenden or BaZ*).
- 1800 series voor *Kust-en Binnenwateren* (coastal and inland waters) are yacht charts (DYC) issued annually in March by the Hydrographer in 8 folios (1801-1812, excluding 1802/4/6 & 8); about 9 loose double-sided sheets (54 x 38cm) per folio.

TIME ZONE is –0100, but add 1hr for DST in the summer months.

TIDES HP 33 *Waterstanden & Stromen* (Tide tables and tidal streams in **English** and Dutch, £16·90 www.bookharbour.com) is useful if cruising Dutch waters for any length of time. It contains tide tables for 15 Dutch and 2 Belgian coastal ports; and 8 tidal stream atlases, including Westerschelde, Oosterschelde and the Maas.

REGULATIONS Discharge of toilet waste from recreational boats is forbidden in all Dutch waters, including inland waterways, lakes and the Waddenzee. Carry evidence (receipts) that any red diesel in your tanks is duty paid.

MARINAS Most marinas are private YCs or Watersport Associations (WSV or WV): *Gemeentelijke (Gem)* = municipal. Marinas with >50 berths must have a pump-out unit ♻. Many Dutch Marinas use VHF Ch 30 or 31, not all UK VHF sets include these and will need to be modified. Sometimes (in Belgium also) berth-holders show a green tally if a berth is free, or red if returning same day, but check with HM. Red diesel is only allowed in main fuel tanks and NOT in cans. A tourist tax (Toeristenbelasting) is often levied at €0·30–1·90 pp/night. VAT (BTW) is 21%. Two very useful websites providing berthing availability at many ports are www. waddenhavens.nl and www.allejachthavens.nl. Blue water App for IOS and Android is increasingly popular to pre-book and pay for busy marina berths.

CUSTOMS Ports of entry are: Delfzijl, Lauwersoog, W Terschelling, Vlieland*, Harlingen, Kornwerderzand, Den Helder, IJmuiden, Scheveningen, Hoek van Holland, Maassluis, Schiedam, Vlaardingen, Rotterdam, Roompot*, Vlissingen, Terneuzen and Breskens. *Summer only. Den Oever and Stellendam are *not* Ports of entry.

FERRIES TO THE UK IJmuiden-Newcastle; Hoek van Holland-Harwich; Rotterdam (Europoort)-Hull.

BUOYAGE Buoys are often named by the abbreviations of the banks or chans which they mark (eg VL = Vliestroom). A division buoy has the abbreviations of both chans meeting there, eg VL2-SG2 = as above, plus Schuitengat.

Some minor, tidal channels are marked by withies: SHM bound ⚓; PHM unbound ⚓. On tidal flats (eg Friesland) where the direction of main flood stream is uncertain, bound withies are on the S side of a chan and unbound on the N side; the banks thus marked are steep-to. In minor chans marks can be moved without notice.

The SIGNI buoyage system is used in the IJsselmeer, but not in the Eems, Waddenzee and Westerschelde.

SIGNALS When **motor-sailing** yachts must by law hoist a ▼ and when **at anchor** a black ball ●; these laws are rigidly enforced.

IPTS are widely used at coastal ports. Local signals, if any, are given where possible.

Sluicing signals may be shown by day: A blue board, with the word 'SPUIEN' on it; by night 3 ● in a △; sometimes both at once.

Storm warning signals, lts only, are shown by day and night at West Terschelling, Den Helder and IJmuiden.

R/T In emergency call *Den Helder Rescue* Ch 16 for Netherlands CG; or the working channel of a VTS sector or nearest lock or bridge. Monitor TSS info broadcasts and VTS sector channels. Ch 30/31 is for Dutch marinas (UK VHF sets need to be modified). Note: Do not use Ch M in Dutch waters, where it is a salvage frequency. Ch 13 is for commercial ship-ship calling. English is the second language and widely spoken.

TELEPHONE To call UK from the Netherlands, dial 00-44; then the UK area code minus the prefix 0, followed by the number required. To call the Netherlands from UK dial 00-31 then the area code minus the prefix 0 followed by two or three digits, followed by a 7 or 6 digits subscriber. No Mobile phone Nos start 06.

Emergency: Fire, Police, Ambulance, dial 112 (free); Non-emergency 0900 8844 (local tariff).

PUBLIC HOLIDAYS New Year's Day, Easter Sun and Mon, King's Birthday (27 April) Liberation Day (5 May) Ascension Day, Whit Mon, Christmas and Boxing Days.

BRITISH CONSULS Contact British Consulate-General, Koningslaan 44, 1075 AE Amsterdam; ☎020 676 4343. Or British Embassy, Lange Voorhout 10, 2514 ED The Hague; ☎070 4270 427.

INLAND WATERWAYS The sealocks at Kornwerderzand, Den Oever (IJsselmeer) IJmuiden, Stellendam and Roompotsluis are fully covered. The Staandemast (mast-up) route (Area map) and the IJsselmeer are outlined. Lack of space precludes detailed coverage of other harbours in the very extensive and enjoyable inland seas, waterways and canals.

Regulations. All craft must carry a copy of waterway regulations, *Binnenvaartpolitiereglement (BPR)*, as given in Dutch in the annual ANWB *Wateralmanak Vol 1* or available separately. Vol 2, also in Dutch, is essential reading; it gives pictograph details of marinas and the opening hours of bridges and locks.

Qualifications. Craft >15m LOA or capable of more than 20kph (11kn) must be skippered by the holder of an RYA Coastal Skipper's Certificate or higher qualification; *plus* an International Certificate of Competence (ICC) endorsed for Inland waterways, ie CEVNI.

Bridges and locks mostly work VHF Ch 18, 20 or 22, but CEVNI light signals (shown up-/downstream) largely negate the need for R/T. The most commonly seen signals include:

● = Bridge closed (opens on request).

To request bridges to open, call on VHF low power (1 watt) or sound 'K' (−·−).

● over ● = Bridge about to open.   ● = Bridge open.

● over ● = No service.

2.6 TSS OFF THE NORTHERN NETHERLANDS

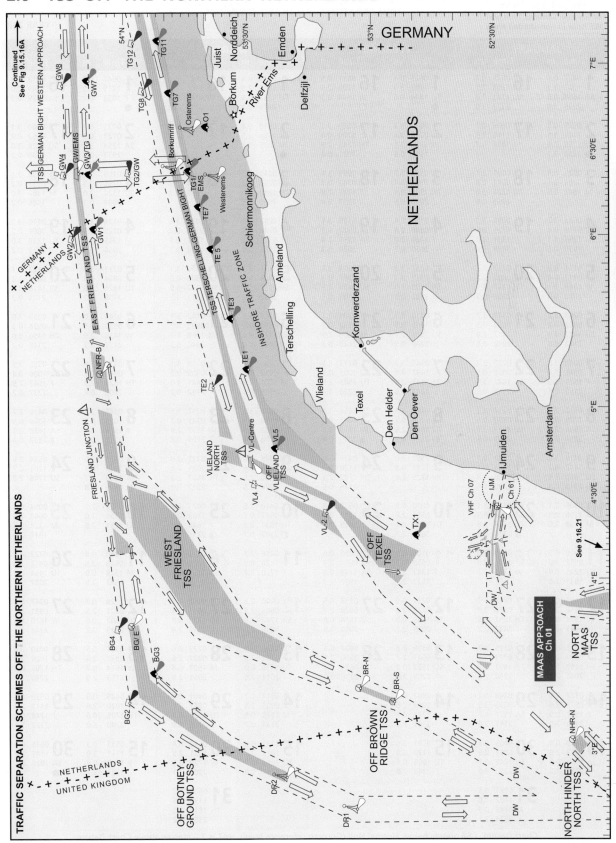

STANDARD TIME UT –01
Subtract 1 hour for UT
For German Summer Time add
ONE hour in **non-shaded areas**

HELGOLAND   LAT 54°11'N LONG 7°53'E
TIMES AND HEIGHTS OF HIGH AND LOW WATERS

Dates in red are **SPRINGS**
Dates in blue are **NEAPS**

YEAR 2022

JANUARY

Day	Time m	Day	Time m
1 SA	0427 0.6 / 1007 3.1 / 1658 0.6 / 2235 3.0	16 SU	0525 0.7 / 1103 2.9 / 1741 0.8 / 2322 3.0
2 SU	0529 0.5 / 1108 3.1 / 1755 0.6 / 2330 3.1 ●	17 M	0609 0.7 / 1146 2.9 / 1822 0.7 ○
3 M	0625 0.4 / 1203 3.1 / 1848 0.6	18 TU	0001 3.1 / 0647 0.6 / 1224 3.0 / 1859 0.6
4 TU	0022 3.2 / 0719 0.4 / 1256 3.1 / 1939 0.6	19 W	0037 3.1 / 0725 0.6 / 1301 3.0 / 1935 0.6
5 W	0114 3.3 / 0812 0.4 / 1348 3.1 / 2028 0.6	20 TH	0112 3.2 / 0802 0.5 / 1337 2.9 / 2009 0.5
6 TH	0203 3.3 / 0902 0.4 / 1437 3.0 / 2112 0.6	21 F	0147 3.2 / 0837 0.5 / 1412 2.9 / 2042 0.5
7 F	0249 3.3 / 0946 0.4 / 1521 2.9 / 2152 0.6	22 SA	0220 3.2 / 0912 0.5 / 1447 2.9 / 2118 0.5
8 SA	0332 3.3 / 1029 0.5 / 1604 2.9 / 2234 0.7	23 SU	0257 3.2 / 0950 0.5 / 1527 2.9 / 2159 0.6
9 SU	0418 3.2 / 1112 0.7 / 1650 2.8 / 2319 0.8 ☾	24 M	0337 3.1 / 1031 0.5 / 1608 2.8 / 2239 0.6
10 M	0506 3.1 / 1156 0.8 / 1738 2.8	25 TU	0417 3.1 / 1109 0.5 / 1648 2.8 / 2320 0.6 ☾
11 TU	0008 0.8 / 0557 3.0 / 1245 0.9 / 1831 2.8	26 W	0501 3.0 / 1151 0.6 / 1734 2.7
12 W	0105 0.9 / 0656 3.0 / 1344 0.9 / 1933 2.8	27 TH	0013 0.7 / 0558 2.9 / 1251 0.6 / 1837 2.7
13 TH	0215 0.9 / 0804 2.9 / 1451 0.9 / 2041 2.8	28 F	0125 0.7 / 0713 2.9 / 1407 0.7 / 1954 2.8
14 F	0327 0.9 / 0913 2.9 / 1557 0.9 / 2144 2.9	29 SA	0248 0.7 / 0835 2.9 / 1527 0.7 / 2111 2.9
15 SA	0432 0.8 / 1013 2.9 / 1654 0.9 / 2238 3.0	30 SU	0409 0.6 / 0953 2.9 / 1642 0.7 / 2222 3.0
		31 M	0521 0.5 / 1102 3.0 / 1748 0.6 / 2324 3.1

FEBRUARY

Day	Time m	Day	Time m
1 TU	0623 0.4 / 1202 3.0 / 1844 0.6 ●	16 W	0631 0.5 / 1209 2.9 / 1844 0.5 ○
2 W	0019 3.2 / 0716 0.4 / 1253 3.1 / 1932 0.6	17 TH	0020 3.1 / 0709 0.4 / 1245 2.9 / 1921 0.4
3 TH	0107 3.3 / 0805 0.4 / 1338 3.1 / 2016 0.5	18 F	0055 3.1 / 0747 0.3 / 1321 2.9 / 1957 0.4
4 F	0151 3.4 / 0848 0.4 / 1420 3.0 / 2056 0.5	19 SA	0129 3.1 / 0822 0.3 / 1355 2.9 / 2030 0.3
5 SA	0231 3.3 / 0927 0.4 / 1458 3.0 / 2132 0.5	20 SU	0204 3.1 / 0857 0.3 / 1429 2.9 / 2105 0.3
6 SU	0310 3.3 / 1003 0.5 / 1535 2.9 / 2208 0.5	21 M	0239 3.1 / 0932 0.3 / 1506 2.9 / 2142 0.3
7 M	0348 3.2 / 1037 0.6 / 1611 2.9 / 2243 0.6	22 TU	0317 3.1 / 1009 0.3 / 1543 2.9 / 2220 0.4
8 TU	0426 3.1 / 1108 0.7 / 1646 2.9 / 2317 0.7 ☾	23 W	0356 3.0 / 1043 0.4 / 1619 2.8 / 2256 0.4 ☽
9 W	0504 3.0 / 1141 0.8 / 1725 2.8	24 TH	0436 2.9 / 1120 0.5 / 1702 2.8 / 2345 0.5
10 TH	0000 0.8 / 0551 2.8 / 1230 0.9 / 1821 2.7	25 F	0531 2.8 / 1218 0.7 / 1805 2.7
11 F	0105 0.9 / 0659 2.7 / 1343 1.0 / 1937 2.7	26 SA	0059 0.6 / 0651 2.7 / 1342 0.8 / 1930 2.7
12 SA	0231 0.9 / 0823 2.6 / 1508 0.9 / 2059 2.7	27 SU	0233 0.6 / 0824 2.7 / 1514 0.6 / 2059 2.9
13 SU	0355 0.8 / 0941 2.7 / 1623 0.9 / 2209 2.8	28 M	0404 0.6 / 0950 2.8 / 1636 0.7 / 2216 3.0
14 M	0502 0.7 / 1043 2.8 / 1721 0.7 / 2301 2.9		
15 TU	0551 0.6 / 1130 2.9 / 1805 0.6 / 2343 3.0		

MARCH

Day	Time m	Day	Time m
1 TU	0519 0.4 / 1100 2.9 / 1742 0.6 / 2319 3.1	16 W	0527 0.4 / 1106 2.8 / 1741 0.6 / 2317 3.0
2 W	0619 0.4 / 1156 2.9 / 1836 0.5 ●	17 TH	0608 0.3 / 1145 2.9 / 1821 0.4 / 2355 3.0
3 TH	0010 3.2 / 0708 0.4 / 1242 3.0 / 1920 0.5	18 F	0646 0.3 / 1221 2.9 / 1859 0.3 ○
4 F	0053 3.3 / 0748 0.3 / 1320 3.0 / 1958 0.4	19 SA	0030 3.1 / 0723 0.2 / 1257 2.9 / 1936 0.3
5 SA	0131 3.3 / 0824 0.3 / 1354 3.0 / 2032 0.4	20 SU	0106 3.1 / 0800 0.2 / 1332 3.0 / 2011 0.2
6 SU	0206 3.3 / 0858 0.4 / 1428 3.0 / 2105 0.4	21 M	0142 3.1 / 0835 0.2 / 1406 3.0 / 2046 0.2
7 M	0241 3.2 / 0930 0.4 / 1501 2.9 / 2138 0.4	22 TU	0218 3.1 / 0909 0.2 / 1441 3.0 / 2122 0.2
8 TU	0316 3.1 / 0959 0.5 / 1532 2.9 / 2208 0.4	23 W	0257 3.1 / 0945 0.3 / 1517 2.9 / 2201 0.3
9 W	0348 3.0 / 1023 0.6 / 1600 2.9 / 2234 0.5	24 TH	0337 3.0 / 1021 0.4 / 1557 2.9 / 2242 0.3
10 TH	0418 2.8 / 1047 0.7 / 1631 2.8 / 2307 0.7 ☾	25 F	0423 2.8 / 1103 0.5 / 1644 2.8 / 2335 0.4 ☽
11 F	0458 2.7 / 1128 0.9 / 1720 2.7	26 SA	0523 2.7 / 1204 0.7 / 1751 2.8
12 SA	0006 0.8 / 0603 2.5 / 1242 1.0 / 1838 2.6	27 SU	0052 0.5 / 0645 2.6 / 1331 0.8 / 1919 2.8
13 SU	0136 0.8 / 0733 2.5 / 1418 0.9 / 2011 2.6	28 M	0229 0.6 / 0821 2.6 / 1507 0.8 / 2051 2.9
14 M	0314 0.7 / 0905 2.5 / 1548 0.8 / 2134 2.7	29 TU	0401 0.5 / 0947 2.7 / 1628 0.7 / 2208 3.0
15 TU	0433 0.6 / 1017 2.7 / 1654 0.7 / 2234 2.9	30 W	0512 0.4 / 1051 2.8 / 1729 0.6 / 2305 3.1
		31 TH	0604 0.3 / 1139 2.9 / 1817 0.5 / 2351 3.2

APRIL

Day	Time m	Day	Time m
1 F	0647 0.3 / 1219 2.9 / 1858 0.4 ●	16 SA	0613 0.2 / 1149 3.0 / 1829 0.3 ○
2 SA	0031 3.2 / 0723 0.3 / 1254 3.0 / 1933 0.3	17 SU	0000 3.1 / 0652 0.2 / 1226 3.0 / 1908 0.3
3 SU	0105 3.2 / 0755 0.3 / 1324 3.0 / 2004 0.3	18 M	0038 3.1 / 0731 0.2 / 1302 3.0 / 1946 0.2
4 M	0138 3.2 / 0825 0.4 / 1355 3.0 / 2036 0.3	19 TU	0116 3.1 / 0808 0.2 / 1339 3.0 / 2025 0.2
5 TU	0211 3.1 / 0854 0.4 / 1426 3.0 / 2108 0.3	20 W	0157 3.1 / 0846 0.2 / 1416 3.0 / 2105 0.2
6 W	0244 3.0 / 0922 0.5 / 1456 2.9 / 2137 0.3	21 TH	0239 3.0 / 0924 0.3 / 1456 3.0 / 2148 0.2
7 TH	0314 2.9 / 0946 0.5 / 1524 2.9 / 2203 0.4	22 F	0326 2.9 / 1006 0.4 / 1543 2.9 / 2237 0.2
8 F	0345 2.7 / 1010 0.7 / 1554 2.8 / 2233 0.6	23 SA	0419 2.7 / 1056 0.5 / 1638 2.9 / 2337 0.4 ☽
9 SA	0423 2.6 / 1047 0.9 / 1639 2.7 / 2326 0.8 ☾	24 SU	0524 2.6 / 1201 0.7 / 1748 2.8
10 SU	0522 2.5 / 1155 1.0 / 1751 2.6	25 M	0054 0.5 / 0643 2.6 / 1324 0.8 / 1911 2.9
11 M	0050 0.8 / 0648 2.5 / 1328 0.9 / 1922 2.6	26 TU	0223 0.5 / 0812 2.6 / 1454 0.7 / 2037 3.0
12 TU	0228 0.7 / 0821 2.5 / 1502 0.8 / 2049 2.7	27 W	0347 0.4 / 0931 2.7 / 1610 0.6 / 2148 3.1
13 W	0351 0.5 / 0937 2.6 / 1614 0.7 / 2153 2.9	28 TH	0450 0.4 / 1029 2.8 / 1705 0.5 / 2240 3.1
14 TH	0449 0.3 / 1030 2.8 / 1705 0.6 / 2240 3.0	29 F	0536 0.3 / 1111 2.9 / 1748 0.4 / 2323 3.1
15 F	0533 0.3 / 1111 2.9 / 1748 0.4 / 2321 3.1	30 SA	0615 0.3 / 1149 2.9 / 1829 0.4 ●

Chart Datum: 1·68 metres below Normal Null (German reference level). HAT is 3·0 metres above Chart Datum.

STANDARD TIME UT –01
Subtract 1 hour for UT
For German Summer Time add
ONE hour in **non-shaded areas**

HELGOLAND LAT 54°11'N LONG 7°53'E
TIMES AND HEIGHTS OF HIGH AND LOW WATERS

Dates in red are **SPRINGS**
Dates in blue are **NEAPS**

YEAR **2022**

Netherlands

MAY

Day	Time	m	Day	Time	m
1 SU	0003 / 0652 / 1224 / 1906	3.1 / 0.3 / 3.0 / 0.3	**16** M	0618 / 1152 / 1838 ○	0.2 / 3.0 / 0.3
2 M	0039 / 0723 / 1255 / 1938	3.1 / 0.4 / 3.0 / 0.3	**17** TU	0009 / 0700 / 1232 / 1922	3.1 / 0.2 / 3.1 / 0.3
3 TU	0111 / 0752 / 1325 / 2009	3.1 / 0.4 / 3.0 / 0.3	**18** W	0052 / 0743 / 1314 / 2007	3.1 / 0.2 / 3.1 / 0.2
4 W	0143 / 0821 / 1356 / 2041	3.0 / 0.5 / 3.0 / 0.4	**19** TH	0140 / 0828 / 1359 / 2055	3.1 / 0.3 / 3.1 / 0.1
5 TH	0216 / 0850 / 1428 / 2112	2.9 / 0.5 / 3.0 / 0.4	**20** F	0229 / 0912 / 1445 / 2143	3.0 / 0.3 / 3.1 / 0.1
6 F	0249 / 0917 / 1459 / 2142	2.8 / 0.6 / 3.0 / 0.5	**21** SA	0321 / 0959 / 1536 / 2237	3.0 / 0.4 / 3.0 / 0.2
7 SA	0323 / 0947 / 1532 / 2216	2.8 / 0.7 / 3.0 / 0.6	**22** SU	0417 / 1052 / 1634 / 2338 ☽	2.7 / 0.5 / 3.0 / 0.3
8 SU	0403 / 1025 / 1615 / 2304 ☽	2.7 / 0.9 / 2.9 / 0.8	**23** M	0520 / 1154 / 1741	2.6 / 0.6 / 3.0
9 M	0456 / 1123 / 1716	2.6 / 0.9 / 2.8	**24** TU	0046 / 0631 / 1307 / 1854	0.4 / 2.6 / 0.7 / 3.0
10 TU	0013 / 0608 / 1242 / 1833	0.8 / 2.6 / 0.9 / 2.8	**25** W	0202 / 0746 / 1425 / 2009	0.5 / 2.6 / 0.7 / 3.0
11 W	0137 / 0729 / 1408 / 1953	0.7 / 2.6 / 0.8 / 2.8	**26** TH	0314 / 0857 / 1536 / 2115	0.5 / 2.7 / 0.6 / 3.1
12 TH	0257 / 0844 / 1521 / 2101	0.5 / 2.7 / 0.7 / 2.9	**27** F	0414 / 0954 / 1631 / 2208	0.5 / 2.8 / 0.6 / 3.1
13 F	0358 / 0941 / 1618 / 2154	0.3 / 2.8 / 0.6 / 3.0	**28** SA	0459 / 1037 / 1717 / 2252	0.5 / 2.9 / 0.5 / 3.1
14 SA	0448 / 1027 / 1707 / 2241	0.3 / 2.9 / 0.5 / 3.1	**29** SU	0540 / 1117 / 1800 / 2334	0.5 / 3.0 / 0.5 / 3.1
15 SU	0534 / 1110 / 1754 / 2326	0.2 / 3.0 / 0.4 / 3.1	**30** M	0619 / 1155 / 1840 ●	0.5 / 3.0 / 0.4
			31 TU	0013 / 0654 / 1229 / 1915	3.0 / 0.5 / 3.1 / 0.4

JUNE

Day	Time	m	Day	Time	m
1 W	0048 / 0725 / 1301 / 1948	3.0 / 0.5 / 3.1 / 0.4	**16** TH	0038 / 0726 / 1258 / 1958	3.1 / 0.3 / 3.2 / 0.2
2 TH	0122 / 0756 / 1334 / 2022	3.0 / 0.5 / 3.1 / 0.5	**17** F	0131 / 0817 / 1349 / 2051	3.0 / 0.4 / 3.2 / 0.2
3 F	0156 / 0827 / 1408 / 2054	2.9 / 0.6 / 3.1 / 0.5	**18** SA	0224 / 0905 / 1439 / 2141	3.0 / 0.4 / 3.2 / 0.3
4 SA	0231 / 0859 / 1441 / 2128	2.9 / 0.6 / 3.1 / 0.6	**19** SU	0316 / 0952 / 1529 / 2232	2.9 / 0.4 / 3.2 / 0.3
5 SU	0308 / 0933 / 1517 / 2206	2.8 / 0.7 / 3.1 / 0.7	**20** M	0408 / 1042 / 1623 / 2326	2.8 / 0.5 / 3.2 / 0.4
6 M	0349 / 1013 / 1559 / 2250	2.8 / 0.8 / 3.1 / 0.7	**21** TU	0504 / 1137 / 1721 ☽	2.7 / 0.6 / 3.1
7 TU	0437 / 1102 / 1649 / 2343 ☽	2.7 / 0.9 / 3.0 / 0.7	**22** W	0022 / 0603 / 1244 / 1822	0.5 / 2.7 / 0.7 / 3.1
8 W	0531 / 1202 / 1748	2.7 / 0.8 / 2.9	**23** TH	0121 / 0704 / 1340 / 1926	0.6 / 2.7 / 0.7 / 3.0
9 TH	0047 / 0635 / 1312 / 1855	0.6 / 2.7 / 0.8 / 2.9	**24** F	0223 / 0807 / 1448 / 2031	0.6 / 2.7 / 0.7 / 3.0
10 F	0155 / 0743 / 1422 / 2002	0.5 / 2.7 / 0.7 / 2.9	**25** SA	0324 / 0908 / 1551 / 2131	0.6 / 2.8 / 0.7 / 3.0
11 SA	0259 / 0844 / 1526 / 2104	0.4 / 2.8 / 0.6 / 3.0	**26** SU	0418 / 1001 / 1645 / 2222	0.7 / 2.9 / 0.7 / 3.0
12 SU	0357 / 0939 / 1625 / 2201	0.4 / 2.9 / 0.5 / 3.1	**27** M	0507 / 1047 / 1734 / 2309	0.6 / 3.0 / 0.6 / 3.0
13 M	0453 / 1032 / 1721 / 2256	0.3 / 3.0 / 0.4 / 3.1	**28** TU	0551 / 1130 / 1818 / 2352	0.6 / 3.1 / 0.5 / 3.0
14 TU	0547 / 1121 / 1814 / 2347 ○	0.3 / 3.1 / 0.3 / 3.1	**29** W	0630 / 1209 / 1857 ●	0.6 / 3.1 / 0.5
15 W	0637 / 1209 / 1905	0.3 / 3.1 / 0.2	**30** TH	0031 / 0706 / 1244 / 1933	3.0 / 0.6 / 3.2 / 0.5

JULY

Day	Time	m	Day	Time	m
1 F	0107 / 0740 / 1319 / 2008	3.0 / 0.6 / 3.2 / 0.5	**16** SA	0126 / 0809 / 1341 / 2044	3.1 / 0.4 / 3.4 / 0.3
2 SA	0142 / 0813 / 1352 / 2041	2.9 / 0.6 / 3.2 / 0.6	**17** SU	0216 / 0856 / 1429 / 2132	3.0 / 0.4 / 3.4 / 0.3
3 SU	0216 / 0845 / 1425 / 2114	2.9 / 0.6 / 3.2 / 0.6	**18** M	0303 / 0939 / 1514 / 2215	2.9 / 0.4 / 3.3 / 0.3
4 M	0252 / 0920 / 1501 / 2152	2.9 / 0.7 / 3.2 / 0.6	**19** TU	0347 / 1021 / 1601 / 2300	2.9 / 0.5 / 3.3 / 0.4
5 TU	0332 / 1000 / 1542 / 2234	2.9 / 0.7 / 3.2 / 0.6	**20** W	0433 / 1107 / 1650 / 2343 ☽	2.8 / 0.5 / 3.2 / 0.6
6 W	0416 / 1043 / 1624 / 2315	2.8 / 0.7 / 3.1 / 0.6	**21** TH	0521 / 1153 / 1739	2.8 / 0.6 / 3.1
7 TH	0459 / 1128 / 1709 ●	2.8 / 0.7 / 3.0	**22** F	0027 / 0609 / 1244 / 1833	0.7 / 2.8 / 0.7 / 3.0
8 F	0000 / 0546 / 1220 / 1803	0.6 / 2.8 / 0.7 / 3.0	**23** SA	0120 / 0707 / 1349 / 1937	0.8 / 2.8 / 0.8 / 2.9
9 SA	0056 / 0644 / 1325 / 1908	0.6 / 2.8 / 0.7 / 2.9	**24** SU	0225 / 0814 / 1504 / 2049	0.8 / 2.8 / 0.8 / 2.9
10 SU	0202 / 0750 / 1437 / 2020	0.6 / 2.8 / 0.7 / 3.0	**25** M	0335 / 0923 / 1615 / 2155	0.8 / 2.9 / 0.8 / 2.9
11 M	0312 / 0857 / 1549 / 2130	0.6 / 2.9 / 0.6 / 3.0	**26** TU	0438 / 1022 / 1713 / 2250	0.8 / 3.0 / 0.7 / 2.9
12 TU	0421 / 1002 / 1658 / 2237	0.5 / 3.0 / 0.5 / 3.0	**27** W	0529 / 1111 / 1801 / 2336	0.7 / 3.0 / 0.6 / 2.9
13 W	0526 / 1102 / 1800 / 2337 ○	0.4 / 3.1 / 0.4 / 3.1	**28** TH	0613 / 1152 / 1841 ●	0.6 / 3.1 / 0.6
14 TH	0625 / 1158 / 1858	0.5 / 3.2 / 0.3	**29** F	0017 / 0651 / 1230 / 1918	2.9 / 0.6 / 3.2 / 0.5
15 F	0033 / 0718 / 1251 / 1952	3.1 / 0.5 / 3.3 / 0.3	**30** SA	0053 / 0727 / 1304 / 1953	3.0 / 0.6 / 3.2 / 0.5
			31 SU	0127 / 0800 / 1336 / 2026	3.0 / 0.6 / 3.2 / 0.5

AUGUST

Day	Time	m	Day	Time	m
1 M	0200 / 0831 / 1408 / 2057	3.0 / 0.6 / 3.2 / 0.5	**16** TU	0239 / 0916 / 1451 / 2148	3.0 / 0.4 / 3.3 / 0.4
2 TU	0233 / 0903 / 1442 / 2132	3.0 / 0.6 / 3.2 / 0.6	**17** W	0317 / 0953 / 1531 / 2223	2.9 / 0.4 / 3.2 / 0.5
3 W	0310 / 0941 / 1520 / 2211	3.0 / 0.6 / 3.2 / 0.6	**18** TH	0355 / 1030 / 1612 / 2257	2.9 / 0.5 / 3.1 / 0.6
4 TH	0350 / 1021 / 1559 / 2246	2.9 / 0.7 / 3.2 / 0.6	**19** F	0432 / 1106 / 1652 / 2330 ☽	2.8 / 0.6 / 3.0 / 0.7
5 F	0427 / 1057 / 1637 / 2320	2.9 / 0.7 / 3.1 / 0.6	**20** SA	0512 / 1147 / 1738	2.8 / 0.7 / 2.8
6 SA	0505 / 1139 / 1723	2.9 / 0.8 / 3.0	**21** SU	0014 / 0604 / 1248 / 1842	0.9 / 2.7 / 0.9 / 2.7
7 SU	0008 / 0557 / 1241 / 1829	0.7 / 2.8 / 0.8 / 2.9	**22** M	0123 / 0718 / 1412 / 2005	1.0 / 2.7 / 0.9 / 2.7
8 M	0119 / 0709 / 1403 / 1952	0.8 / 2.8 / 0.8 / 2.9	**23** TU	0250 / 0842 / 1541 / 2128	1.0 / 2.8 / 0.9 / 2.7
9 TU	0243 / 0830 / 1530 / 2116	0.8 / 2.9 / 0.7 / 3.0	**24** W	0410 / 0957 / 1653 / 2233	0.9 / 2.9 / 0.8 / 2.8
10 W	0404 / 0947 / 1648 / 2230	0.7 / 3.0 / 0.6 / 3.0	**25** TH	0510 / 1052 / 1743 / 2321	0.8 / 3.0 / 0.7 / 2.9
11 TH	0517 / 1054 / 1756 / 2335	0.7 / 3.2 / 0.5 / 3.0	**26** F	0554 / 1134 / 1822 / 2359	0.7 / 3.1 / 0.6 / 3.0
12 F	0618 / 1152 / 1853 ○	0.6 / 3.3 / 0.5	**27** SA	0632 / 1210 / 1858 ●	0.6 / 3.1 / 0.5
13 SA	0029 / 0711 / 1243 / 1944	3.1 / 0.5 / 3.4 / 0.3	**28** SU	0034 / 0707 / 1243 / 1932	3.0 / 0.6 / 3.2 / 0.5
14 SU	0116 / 0756 / 1328 / 2029	3.1 / 0.5 / 3.4 / 0.3	**29** M	0107 / 0741 / 1316 / 2005	3.0 / 0.6 / 3.2 / 0.5
15 M	0159 / 0838 / 1411 / 2110	3.1 / 0.4 / 3.4 / 0.3	**30** TU	0139 / 0812 / 1347 / 2035	3.0 / 0.6 / 3.3 / 0.5
			31 W	0210 / 0843 / 1419 / 2107	3.0 / 0.6 / 3.3 / 0.6

Chart Datum: 1·68 metres below Normal Null (German reference level). HAT is 3·0 metres above Chart Datum.

》 FREE monthly updates. Register at 《
www.reedsnauticalalmanac.co.uk

107

STANDARD TIME UT –01
Subtract 1 hour for UT
For German Summer Time add
ONE hour in **non-shaded areas**

HELGOLAND LAT 54°11′N LONG 7°53′E
TIMES AND HEIGHTS OF HIGH AND LOW WATERS

Dates in red are SPRINGS
Dates in blue are NEAPS

YEAR 2022

SEPTEMBER

Time	m		Time	m
1 0243	3.1		**16** 0315	2.9
0917	0.6		0953	0.5
TH 1455	3.3		F 1533	3.0
2141	0.6		2210	0.7
2 0319	3.0		**17** 0346	2.9
0954	0.7		1024	0.6
F 1533	3.2		SA 1608	2.9
2215	0.7		◑ 2238	0.8
3 0355	3.0		**18** 0421	2.8
1030	0.7		1059	0.8
SA 1611	3.1		SU 1650	2.7
◔ 2249	0.8		2318	1.0
4 0433	2.9		**19** 0510	2.7
1113	0.8		1155	1.0
SU 1659	3.0		M 1753	2.6
2338	0.9			
5 0528	2.9		**20** 0027	1.1
1218	0.9		0625	2.7
M 1810	2.9		TU 1322	1.1
			1920	2.6
6 0055	1.0		**21** 0201	1.2
0647	2.9		0758	2.7
TU 1349	0.9		W 1502	1.0
1942	2.8		2054	2.6
7 0229	1.0		**22** 0334	1.1
0818	3.0		0924	2.8
W 1525	0.8		TH 1624	0.8
2114	2.9		2208	2.8
8 0358	0.9		**23** 0443	0.9
0941	3.1		1025	3.0
TH 1647	0.7		F 1718	0.7
2229	3.0		2257	2.9
9 0510	0.8		**24** 0528	0.8
1048	3.2		1107	3.1
F 1751	0.5		SA 1755	0.6
2329	3.0		2332	3.0
10 0608	0.6		**25** 0604	0.7
1142	3.3		1142	3.2
SA 1843	0.4		SU 1829	0.6
○			●	
11 0017	3.1		**26** 0006	3.0
0655	0.5		0640	0.6
SU 1228	3.4		M 1216	3.2
1926	0.4		1904	0.5
12 0057	3.1		**27** 0039	3.1
0736	0.5		0715	0.6
M 1308	3.4		TU 1249	3.3
2004	0.4		1937	0.5
13 0133	3.1		**28** 0112	3.1
0812	0.4		0747	0.6
TU 1345	3.4		W 1321	3.3
2039	0.4		2009	0.5
14 0207	3.0		**29** 0143	3.1
0847	0.4		0819	0.6
W 1422	3.3		TH 1354	3.3
2112	0.5		2039	0.6
15 0242	3.0		**30** 0215	3.1
0920	0.4		0852	0.6
TH 1458	3.2		F 1430	3.2
2143	0.6		2112	0.6

OCTOBER

Time	m		Time	m
1 0249	3.1		**16** 0310	3.0
0930	0.6		0951	0.7
SA 1509	3.2		SU 1535	2.8
2147	0.7		2159	0.9
2 0328	3.0		**17** 0344	2.9
1011	0.7		1026	0.9
SU 1554	3.0		M 1616	2.7
◑ 2228	0.9		◑ 2237	1.1
3 0414	3.0		**18** 0431	2.9
1102	0.8		1117	1.1
M 1650	2.9		TU 1714	2.6
2325	1.0		2341	1.2
4 0516	2.9		**19** 0539	2.8
1213	0.9		1236	1.1
TU 1807	2.8		W 1835	2.6
5 0046	1.1		**20** 0110	1.2
0639	2.9		0708	2.8
W 1346	0.9		TH 1412	1.1
1940	2.8		2007	2.6
6 0223	1.1		**21** 0244	1.1
0813	3.0		0835	2.9
TH 1523	0.8		F 1538	0.9
2111	2.8		2125	2.7
7 0352	1.0		**22** 0358	1.0
0935	3.2		0942	3.0
F 1641	0.7		SA 1636	0.7
2222	2.9		2217	2.9
8 0458	0.7		**23** 0448	0.9
1036	3.3		1027	3.1
SA 1737	0.6		SU 1716	0.6
2313	3.0		2255	3.0
9 0548	0.7		**24** 0527	0.8
1124	3.3		1105	3.2
SU 1821	0.5		M 1751	0.6
○ 2354	3.0		2329	3.1
10 0631	0.6		**25** 0605	0.7
1205	3.3		1142	3.2
M 1859	0.5		TU 1828	0.5
			●	
11 0031	3.1		**26** 0005	3.1
0709	0.5		0643	0.6
TU 1243	3.3		W 1218	3.3
1933	0.5		1904	0.5
12 0103	3.1		**27** 0039	3.2
0744	0.5		0719	0.6
W 1318	3.3		TH 1253	3.3
2004	0.5		1939	0.5
13 0135	3.1		**28** 0114	3.2
0817	0.5		0756	0.6
TH 1353	3.2		F 1331	3.2
2035	0.6		2014	0.6
14 0208	3.0		**29** 0149	3.2
0850	0.5		0833	0.5
F 1427	3.1		SA 1411	3.2
2105	0.7		2050	0.6
15 0239	3.0		**30** 0227	3.1
0921	0.6		0915	0.6
SA 1500	3.0		SU 1455	3.1
2131	0.7		2131	0.7
			31 0312	3.1
			1003	0.6
			M 1547	2.9
			2219	0.9

NOVEMBER

Time	m		Time	m
1 0406	3.1		**16** 0404	3.0
1101	0.7		1052	1.0
TU 1649	2.8		W 1644	2.7
◑ 2321	1.0		◑ 2307	1.1
2 0512	3.0		**17** 0501	2.9
1213	0.8		1156	1.1
W 1805	2.7		TH 1750	2.6
3 0039	1.1		**18** 0020	1.1
0632	3.0		0614	2.9
TH 1340	0.9		F 1315	1.0
1931	2.7		1908	2.6
4 0209	1.1		**19** 0143	1.1
0759	3.1		0732	2.9
F 1508	0.8		SA 1434	0.8
2055	2.8		2022	2.7
5 0333	1.0		**20** 0257	1.0
0916	3.2		0842	3.0
SA 1619	0.8		SU 1537	0.7
2200	2.9		2121	2.8
6 0435	0.8		**21** 0355	0.9
1014	3.3		0936	3.1
SU 1710	0.7		M 1625	0.6
2247	3.0		2207	2.9
7 0522	0.8		**22** 0443	0.8
1059	3.3		1022	3.1
M 1750	0.7		TU 1709	0.6
2326	3.1		2248	3.0
8 0604	0.7		**23** 0528	0.7
1140	3.3		1105	3.2
TU 1828	0.6		W 1751	0.6
○			● 2329	3.1
9 0002	3.1		**24** 0612	0.6
0643	0.6		1147	3.2
W 1218	3.2		TH 1833	0.6
1902	0.6			
10 0036	3.1		**25** 0008	3.2
0718	0.5		0654	0.5
TH 1253	3.2		F 1229	3.2
1933	0.7		1914	0.6
11 0107	3.1		**26** 0049	3.2
0752	0.5		0738	0.5
F 1328	3.1		SA 1314	3.2
2004	0.7		1957	0.6
12 0140	3.1		**27** 0132	3.2
0826	0.6		0824	0.5
SA 1402	3.0		SU 1402	3.1
2035	0.7		2041	0.6
13 0214	3.1		**28** 0217	3.2
0859	0.6		0912	0.5
SU 1436	2.9		M 1452	3.0
2104	0.8		2126	0.6
14 0246	3.1		**29** 0306	3.2
0930	0.7		1003	0.5
M 1512	2.8		TU 1545	2.9
2134	0.9		2216	0.8
15 0320	3.0		**30** 0401	3.2
1006	0.9		1101	0.6
TU 1553	2.8		W 1645	2.8
2213	1.0		◑ 2315	0.9

DECEMBER

Time	m		Time	m
1 0504	3.1		**16** 0428	3.0
1206	0.8		1121	0.9
TH 1753	2.8		F 1708	2.7
			◑ 2334	0.9
2 0024	1.0		**17** 0522	2.9
0614	3.1		1217	0.8
F 1318	0.8		SA 1806	2.7
1906	2.8			
3 0140	0.9		**18** 0038	0.9
0729	3.1		0625	2.9
SA 1432	0.8		SU 1322	0.8
2019	2.8		1911	2.7
4 0256	0.9		**19** 0147	0.9
0842	3.2		0732	2.9
SU 1540	0.8		M 1427	0.7
2124	2.9		2015	2.8
5 0401	0.9		**20** 0254	0.9
0942	3.2		0837	3.0
M 1634	0.8		TU 1529	0.7
2214	3.0		2114	2.9
6 0452	0.8		**21** 0356	0.8
1031	3.2		0937	3.0
TU 1718	0.8		W 1626	0.6
2256	3.1		2208	3.0
7 0538	0.7		**22** 0454	0.7
1115	3.2		1033	3.1
W 1759	0.7		TH 1720	0.6
2336	3.1		2258	3.1
8 0621	0.6		**23** 0547	0.6
1156	3.1		1125	3.1
TH 1836	0.7		F 1811	0.6
○			● 2346	3.2
9 0013	3.1		**24** 0638	0.5
0659	0.6		1215	3.1
F 1233	3.1		SA 1900	0.6
1910	0.7			
10 0047	3.1		**25** 0034	3.2
0734	0.6		0729	0.4
SA 1309	3.0		SU 1306	3.1
1943	0.7		1950	0.6
11 0122	3.2		**26** 0124	3.3
0810	0.6		0822	0.4
SU 1345	2.9		M 1359	3.1
2016	0.7		2039	0.6
12 0156	3.2		**27** 0214	3.3
0844	0.6		0913	0.4
M 1420	2.9		TU 1450	3.0
2047	0.7		2125	0.6
13 0229	3.1		**28** 0302	3.3
0916	0.7		1002	0.5
TU 1455	2.8		W 1540	2.9
2119	0.8		2211	0.7
14 0303	3.1		**29** 0352	3.3
0952	0.8		1052	0.5
W 1533	2.8		TH 1631	2.9
2156	0.9		2302	0.7
15 0342	3.1		**30** 0447	3.2
1033	0.8		1145	0.7
TH 1618	2.7		F 1726	2.8
2241	0.9		◑ 2356	0.8
			31 0544	3.2
			1240	0.8
			SA 1824	2.8

Chart Datum: 1·68 metres below Normal Null (German reference level). HAT is 3·0 metres above Chart Datum.

>> FREE monthly updates. Register at <<
www.reedsnauticalalmanac.co.uk

2.7 DELFZIJL

Groningen 53°18'·99N 07°00'·45E ✿✿✿❅❅❁❁✿

CHARTS AC 3631, 3632; DYC 1812.6; Zeekaart 1555; Imray C26; ANWB A

TIDES –0025 Dover; ML 2·1; Duration 0605
Standard Port HELGOLAND (←—)

Times				Height (metres)			
High Water		Low Water		MHWS	MHWN	MLWN	MLWS
0200	0700	0200	0800	3·1	2·8	0·8	0·4
1400	1900	1400	2000				
Differences DELFZIJL							
+0020	–0005	–0040	0000	+0·6	+0·6	0·0	0·0
EEMSHAVEN							
–0025	–0045	–0115	–0045	*0·0*	*+0·1*	*–0·1*	*–0·1*
HUIBERTGAT							
–0150	–0150	–0210	–0210	–0·5	–0·4	–0·2	–0·2
SCHIERMONNIKOOG							
–0120	–0130	–0240	–0220	–0·3	–0·3	–0·2	–0·1

SHELTER Good in Handelshaven, where at Neptunus Marina, a floating jetty, acts as a wavebreak.

NAVIGATION From the E or N, WPT 53°38'·96N 06°27'·06E (Riffgat SWM buoy) 121°/4·2M to Nos 11/12 buoys. See also TSS off the Northern Netherlands.

From the W, WPT 53°36'·95N 06°17'·74E (Westerems SWM buoy) 091°/8·2M to join Riffgat at Nos 11/12 buoys.

Huibertgat lies parallel to and S of Westereems. It is marked by unlit R/W buoys H1-H5, least depths about 9m but prone to silt.

From Nos 11/12 buoys follow the well marked/lit river channel for approx 25M via Randzelgat or Alte Eems, Dukegat and Ostfriesisches Gatje to enter Zeehavenkanaal abeam Knock lt ho. Beware strong cross tides at the ent (Lat/Long under title).

INLAND ROUTE TO IJSSELMEER See Area Map and IJsselmeer.

LIGHTS AND MARKS See chartlet and Lights, buoys and waypoints. From the river, appr ldg lts 203°, both Iso 4s. Hbr ent, FG on W arm and FR on E arm (in fog, FY). Zeehavenkanaal, 2·5M long, has Fl G lts to N and Fl R to S. Entry sigs on both piers: 2 ● = No entry, unless cleared by Hbr office on VHF ch 14.

COMMUNICATIONS (Code 0596) All vessels, except leisure craft, must call *Delfzijl Radar* VHF Ch 03 (H24) for VTS, co-ordinated with *Ems Traffic*; Traffic, weather and tidal info is broadcast every even H+10 on VHF Ch 14 in Dutch and English on request; *Ems Traffic* VHF Ch 15, 18, 20 and 21 (H24) broadcasts every H + 50 weather and tidal info in German, and gale warnings for coastal waters between Die Ems and Die Weser, see also Emden; CG (Police) 613831; Police 112; ⊖ 0598 696560; Brit Consul (020) 6764343; Ⓗ 644444; Port HM 640400, VHF Ch 66; HM 't Dok 616560; Eemskanaal Sea locks 613293, VHF Ch 26.

FACILITIES Neptunus Yacht Hbr (4·4m, 53°19'·80N 06°55'·86E) ☎ 0612 386 446, ⬡€1·50, ▮ (0900-1700) ✕ ▯ ▮ ▧ 🚻 free wi-fi. **Yacht Hbr 't Dok** at N end of the Old Eemskanaal in 4m, ⬡ €0·80, ▮. Note: Eems (Dutch) = Ems (German). **Ems Canal** ⬡ ⚓ ⬡. **Motor Boat Club Abel Tasman** ☎616560, ⬡ ▮ ⬡. **Services** ▮ ⬡ ACA, DYC Agent, ⚒ ▯. **Town** ▮ ▮ ✕ ▯ 🛒 ✉ Ⓑ ⇌ ✈ (Groningen/Eelde). **Ferry** Hoek van Holland.

MINOR HARBOUR 1·3M ESE OF DELFZIJL ENTRANCE
TERMUNTERZIJL Groningen, **53°18'·20N 07°02'·21E**. AC 3632; Zeekaart 1555; DYC 1812.6. HW –0025 on Dover (UT); use Differences Delfzijl. Ent (1·3M ESE of Delfzijl ent) is close to BW13 SHM buoy Fl G 5s (53°18'·63N 07°02'·32E); then chan marked by 7 R and 7 G unlit bns. Yachts berth in Vissershaven (0·9m) stbd of ent, or on pontoons (1m) to port of ent, €1·10. HM ☎ 601 356 (Apr-Sept) VHF Ch 09, ⚓ ▯ ✕ ▯.

COMMERCIAL HARBOUR AT MOUTH OF THE EEMS (EMS)
EEMSHAVEN, Groningen, **53°27'·66N 06°50'·27E**. AC 3631, 3632, Zeekaart 1555, DYC 1812.5/.6. HW –0100 (approx) on Dover. Tides as for Borkum. Eemshaven is a modern commercial port, but may

be used by yachts as a port of refuge. Outer appr via Hubertgat (see TSS N Netherlands) or Westereems; inner appr via Randzelgat or Alte Eems, passing the outer anchorage for merchant ships. From the nearest buoy, A16 PHM Fl R 4s, the hbr ent bears 137°/1·6M. Call *Eemshaven Radar* Ch 01 (H24) for VTS info; and *Eemshaven Port Control* Ch 66 for info and clearance to enter.

There are many wind turbines S, W and NW of the port. A power stn chy (128m high) is conspic 2M ESE of the port; as are white-roofed bldgs at the port. Enter on 175°, ldg lts Iso 4s, between mole hds, FG and FR. Inner ldg lts, both Iso R 4s, leads 195° to S end of port. Here yachts turn 90° stbd into Emmahaven, marked by FG and FR, and berth on floating jetty in SW corner. HM ☎(Delfzijl Port Authority) (0596) 640400; ⊖ 0598 696560; other ☎numbers see Delfzijl. No special facilities for yachts, but dues are €0·24 per gross ton.

2.8 LAUWERSOOG

Friesland, **53°24'·68N 06°12'·04E**

CHARTS AC 1632/3; Imray C26; Zeekaart 1458; DYC 1812.3

TIDES HW –0150 on Dover; ML 1·7m. See Harlingen.

SHELTER Outer hbr suffers swell in bad weather; complete shelter in Noordergat Marina.

NAVIGATION See Schiermonnikoog (facing page); continue to Z15 SHM buoy for hbr ent. Await lock on pontoons on stbd side outer lock ent. Lock hrs (LT) **April-Oct**: Mon-Sat 0700-1830; Sun 0800-1930. **Nov-Mar**: Mon-Sat 0700-1200, 1300-1800; Sun shut. A firing range 1·5m ENE of hbr ent is marked by Fl Y 10s bcns, alternating W/R when the range is active; info broadcasts on Ch 71.

LIGHTS AND MARKS See chartlet and Lights, buoys and waypoints.

COMMUNICATIONS (Code 0519) HM 349023, VHF Ch 05, 11; Lock 349043, VHF Ch 84; Range broadcast Ch 71.

FACILITIES Noordergat Marina, ☎349040; www.noordergat.nl (2·4–2·8m). **Ⓥ**s berth on first pontoon, €1·50 + €1·15 pp/day tax. 🚿 (E end of hbr); 🚿 (ferry terminal, W end of hbr) ✗ 🍴🛒◎⚓ 🚽 🍴 🏪(30t) ⚓ YC. **Passantenhaven Lauwersoog**, ☎349023, 60 berths (visitors only) €2·00,🚽🚿🚿. The Staande Mastroute (Area map, Delfzijl-Harlingen) can be entered from the Lauwersmeer at Dokkum.

OTHER HARBOURS IN THE LAUWERSMEER
ZOUTKAMP, Groningen, **53°20'·38N 06°17'·55E**. AC 2593, Zeekaarten 1458, DYC 1812·4; non-tidal. Appr down the Zoutkamperril (2·6-4·5m); approx 2ca before lock/bridge, Hunzegat marina (1·5-2·1m) is to port. ☎(0595) 402875, SC ⚓. Beyond the lock (FR lts) and close to port is Oude Binnenhaven marina (2m) €1·50 + €1·15 pp/day tax. ⚓ 🍴 ✗ 🏪(20t) 🚽.

Town ⚓🚿✗🍴🛒⚓🚽⚓✉ Dr.

OOSTMAHORN, Friesland, **53°22'·94N 06°09'·63E**. AC 2593, Zeekaarten 1458, DYC 1812·4. Non-tidal hbr on W side of Lauwersmeer; lock in as for Lauwersoog. Floating bns with Y flags mark fishing areas. Main hbr with FR and FG lts at ent has marina (2·2-3·0m). HM ☎(0511) 408100, €1·50, 🚿🚿✗🍴🛒⚓⚓ 🍴🚽(15t) ⚓. Approx 450m to the SSE, next to the Voorm Veerhaven (ferry hbr) is a tiny marina with 1·5–2m.

MINOR HARBOURS IN THE WEST FRISIAN ISLANDS
SCHIERMONNIKOOG, Friesland, **53°28'·07N 06°10'·05E**. AC 3761; Zeekaart 1458; DYC 1812.3. HW –0150 on Dover. See Delfzijl. WPT 53°31'·96N 06°01'·84E (WG SWM buoy, Iso 8s, Racon N) 150°/1·0M to WG1 SHM buoy, VQ G, at ent to Westgat; though buoyed/lit, this approach should only be attempted by strangers in gentle, settled conditions and avoided completely in winds W-N-NE >F4, when the fast shifting shoals and chan make it very dangerous. **It is essential to call Schiermonnikoog ✦ on VHF Ch 05 for latest update**. Follow Westgat chan into Zoutkamperlaag either to Lauwersoog or Schiermonnikoog; leave at Z6 and Z6A bys, then use GVS chan bys for Gat van Schiermonnikoog. Follow GVS bys to ent of Groote Siege (GS bys), turn port at GS6 into Reegeul chan (aka Harms Geultje), R&G lateral bys (unlit), and east to the small drying yacht hbr of Schiermonnikoog, (1·3-1·5m) 1·5m max at HW in apprs, silting rptd 2016. Picturesque, busy in season, €0·70/m². HM VHF Ch 31; ☎(0519) 531544 (May-Sept). Facilities: ⚓ 🍴 ✗. Note: Lt ho Fl (4) 20s, R twr, conspic 1.35M NNW of yacht hbr. CG at lt ho, 48M radius radar surveillance of the Terschelling/German Bight TSS and coordinates local SAR operations. VHF Ch 05, 10, 16, 67 and 37 (all H24); ☎0519 531247.

NES, Ameland, Friesland, **53°26'·22N 05°46'·53E**. AC 2593, Zeekaart 1458, DYC 1811.10 & .2. HW –0155 on Dover; ML 1·6m; Duration 0625. See Harlingen. Shelter in all but E/S winds. Appr from WA SWM buoy via Westgat, Borndiep and Molengat to VA2-R1 SCM lt perch, VQ(6) + L Fl 10s, beware sandbanks; dangerous in >F6 from SW–N–NE. Lts: see Lights, buoys and waypoints. **Yacht hbr** ('t Leije Gat) HM ☎(0519) 542159. 140 berths. €0·75/m² + €1·60 pp/ day tax. L Fl R 8s and L Fl G 8s piles at ent. Pontoons N end hbr (0·8m) beyond ferry; W side dries. Facilities: ⚓ YC.

2.9 HET VLIE (ZEEGAT VAN TERSCHELLING)

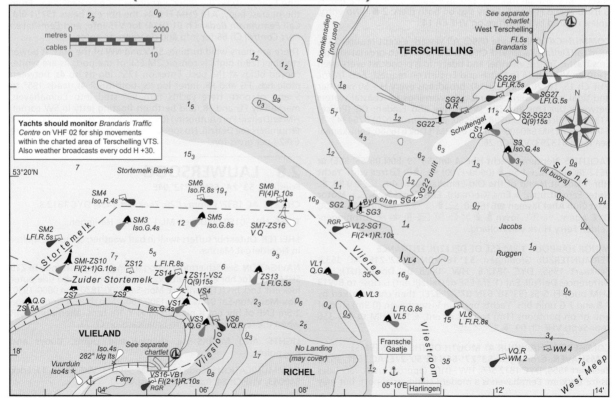

2.10 WEST TERSCHELLING

WEST FRISIAN ISLANDS 53°21'·26N 05°13'·13E ✿✿✿✿❍❍❍✿✿✿

CHARTS AC 1633, 112; Zeekaart 1456; DYC 1811.4/.5; Imray C25

TIDES –0300 Dover; ML 1·4; Duration No data

Standard Port HELGOLAND (←—)

Times				Height (metres)			
High Water		Low Water		MHWS	MHWN	MLWN	MLWS
0200	0700	0200	0800	3·1	2·8	0·8	0·4
1400	1900	1400	2000				
Differences WEST TERSCHELLING							
–0220	–0250	–0335	–0310	–0·7	–0·7	–0·2	–0·1
VLIELAND-HAVEN							
–0250	–0320	–0355	–0330	–0·7	–0·7	–0·2	–0·1

SHELTER Good in the marina; very crowded in season.

NAVIGATION WPT 53°19'·58N 04°55'·77E (ZS buoy) 099°/6·2M to ZS11-VS2 buoy via Zuider Stortemelk which is well marked/lit. In strong W/NW'lies beware dangerous seas from ZS to ZS5/6 buoys. Stortemelk, the deeper N'ly route, is no shorter and is more exposed.

In daylight use fair weather approach to West Terschelling via Schuitengat-Zuid from RGR (preferred chan to stbd) VL2-SG1 buoy and subsequent numbered R and G SG lateral bys SG3 to SG 31 (unlit until SG 23). In darkness, or strong W or NW'lies and swell, it is essential to go via West Meep and Slenk, longer, but wide, safe (3·2m) and much easier for visitors. Route: WM2, 4 and 6 buoys, NM4–S21 buoy to enter Slenk buoyed/lit chan (note: SHMs to port for this approach) leading NW into the Schuitengat (11m) at SG 23 buoy. (SHMs then to stbd to West Terschelling.) Expect much commercial traffic and ferries in Slenk.

Ameland can be reached if draft <1.5m by the inshore channels across the Waddenzee (Meep, Noorder Balgen and Oosterom; DYC 1811.4 and .6). Leave at HW –3 to arrive at HW.

LIGHTS AND MARKS Hbr lts as chartlet and Lights, buoys and waypoints. The square, yellow Brandaris light tower dominates the town and hbr.

COMMUNICATIONS (Code 0562) Coast Guard 442341; *Brandaris* (VTS) Ch 02, 04 broadcasts weather, visibility, traffic, tidal data at H+30 in Dutch and English. Yachts must monitor Ch 02; ⊜ 442884; Dr 442181; Port HM 443337 (H24) VHF Ch 12; Marina Ch 31 HO.

FACILITIES **Marina Stichting Passantenhaven** ☎443337 (H24 Apr-Oct) info@jachthaventerschelling.nl. www.waddenhavens.nl. Notices on pontoons A-G indicate berths by LOA and type of boat (yacht, motor cruiser or traditional craft). 500 ⌒ €0·70/m² + €1·30 pp/day tax, inc ⚡🔌📻🚰; 🛢 at marina ent, @ ⚓⚓⚓⚓ chart agent ⚒.

Village is an easy walk: ✗🏠🍴🏪⊠Ⓑ🔧 (5km). ✈ Amsterdam. Ferry to Harlingen, thence ⇌ for Hook-Harwich.

2.11 VLIELAND

WEST FRISIAN ISLANDS

Friesland 53°17'·68N 05°05'·49E ✿✿✿✿❍❍✿✿

CHARTS AC 1633, 112; Zeekaart 1456; DYC 1811.4/.5; Imray C26

TIDES –0300 Dover; ML 1·4; Duration 0610. See West Terschelling. The Dutch use Harlingen as a Standard Port.

SHELTER Good in yacht hbr. Two ⚓s, both affected by swell in strong SE–SW'lies near HW: (a) in up to 3m ½M S of the hbr or (b) in 4-9m 1M W of the hbr (beyond the ferry pier). Do not ⚓ in buoyed chan from hbr ent to ferry pier (no ⌒).

NAVIGATION From ZS buoy (WPT) follow W Terschelling Navigation, lines 1-3. At ZS11-VS2 and VS1 buoys turn S into Vliesloot (narrow and in places only 2·5m MLWS). Keep in mid-chan past VS3-VS7 buoys, then steer direct from VS14 buoy 200m to narrow13m wide hbr ent. Beware strong cross current, ideally arrive near HW slack. Tight berths are difficult in SW wind. It is a local tradition to give way to old Dutch boats, 'bruine vloot'!

LIGHTS AND MARKS A dk R lt ho (W lantern, R top) stands on Vuurduin, 1·2M W of hbr. Hbr lts as chartlet. Tfc sigs: R Flag or ●● at ent = hbr closed (full). The 282° ldg lts (Lights, bys and waypoints & W Terschelling) lead toward the ferry terminal in E Vlieland.

COMMUNICATIONS (Code 0562) CG 442341; All vessels in Zeegat van Terschelling and N Waddenzee must monitor Ch 02 for *Brandaris Traffic Centre VTS;* Police 451312; ⊜ 058 2949488 (Leeuwarden);

Brit Consul (020) 6764343; Dr 451307; HM 451729, mob 06 201 33086, VHF Ch 12.

FACILITIES **Yacht Hbr** ☎451729. www.waddenhavens.nl 300 inc ♥; on finger berths in 2m. €0·70 per m² + €1·35 pp/day tax; ⚓ 🛢 ⚒ 🔧🔧 (10 mins); 🛢 at Harlingen and Terschelling.
Village ✗🏠🍴🛢🔧 @ ⊠ Ⓑ ✈(Amsterdam). **Ferry** see West Terschelling.

2.12 HARLINGEN

Friesland 53°10'·58N 05°24'·23E ✿✿◊◊✿✿

CHARTS AC 1633, 112; Zeekaart 1454, 1456; DYC 1811·5; ANWB B; Imray C26

TIDES −0210 Dover; ML 1·2; Duration 0520

Standard Port HELGOLAND (←)

Times				Height (metres)			
High Water		Low Water		MHWS	MHWN	MLWN	MLWS
0200	0700	0200	0800	3·1	2·8	0·8	0·4
1400	1900	1400	2000				
Differences LAUWERSOOG							
−0130	−0145	−0235	−0220	−0·3	−0·2	−0·2	0·0
HARLINGEN							
−0155	−0245	−0210	−0130	−0·8	−0·7	−0·4	−0·1
NES (AMELAND)							
−0135	−0150	−0245	−0225	−0·3	−0·2	−0·2	0·0

SHELTER Very good in Noorderhaven. Beware strong flood stream across outer hbr ent, rough at HW in W/NW'lies.

NAVIGATION WPT 53°11'·48N 05°19'·63E (abeam BS23 buoy) 110°/2·8M to hbr ent. See West Terschelling for appr, thence to the WPT via buoyed Vliestroom and Blauwe Slenk chans; the latter is narrow for the last 2½M. A small craft chan, at least 1·8m, lies parallel to Pollendam trng wall and outboard of the main chan SHM buoys; it is marked by SPM buoys A–N in season. Beware ferries passing very close. Caution: When Pollendam is covered, tidal streams sweep across it.

LIGHTS AND MARKS See chartlet and Lights, buoys and waypoints. Ldg lts 111°, both Iso 6s, H24; B masts, W bands. 2 ch spires are conspic almost on ldg line.

COMMUNICATIONS (Code 0517) Coast Guard 0223 542300; Brandaris Traffic Ctre (088)7974640, VHF Ch 02; Police 0900 8844/112; ⊖ 088 151444; British Consul (020) 6764343; ⊞ 058 2866666; Doctor 412544; Harlingen Port Control 412512, VHF Ch 11; HM 723300, Tsjerk Hiddes Locks, VHF Ch 22 (ent to Van Harinxma Canal).

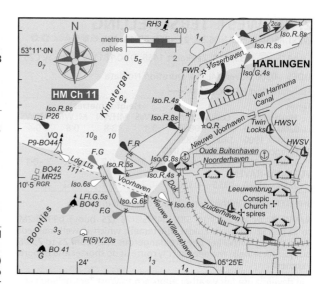

FACILITIES Lifting bridges across the Oude Buitenhaven and Noorderhaven open in unison 2 x per hr 0600-2200 in season (on request in winter) but not at times of boat trains/ferries and when tidal height exceeds LAT + 2·54m. 🔌🛢 H24 self service cr/debit cards at Multiship Holland Boatyard on S bank of Van Harinxma Canal, (accessed via locks NE end Nieuwe Voorhaven), then1·5M inland just beyond opening road bridge.

Noorderhaven Yacht Hbr ☎ 06-53846734 www.interharbours.com/harlingen, ✗⬜🛒📅🛢🔌🛢🔧⚓ Ⓔ Diving/salvage (call).

Harlinger Watersportvereningen (HWSV) ☎416898 info@harlingerwatersportvereningen.nl, useful small marina just inside the locks, 100+ 🛟 inc Ⓥ €1·10 + €0·75 pp/day tax, inc 🔌⚓🚩 🚽; 🛢 📞 @. **Town** ✗⬜🛒✉Ⓑ ≈ ✈ (Amsterdam). **Ferry** see Hoek van Holland.

2.13 OUDESCHILD

Texel, 53°02'·35N 04°51'·18E ✿✿✿◊◊◊✿✿

CHARTS AC 1631, 1546; Zeekaart 1546, 1454; DYC 1811·3

TIDES −0355 Dover; ML 1·1m; Duration 0625

Standard Port HELGOLAND (←)

Times				Height (metres)			
High Water		Low Water		MHWS	MHWN	MLWN	MLWS
0200	0700	0200	0800	3·1	2·8	0·8	0·4
1400	1900	1400	2000				
Differences OUDESCHILD							
−0310	−0420	−0445	−0400	−1·3	−1·2	−0·4	−0·1

SHELTER Very good in marina (2·4m) in far NE basin. ⚓ prohib. Visitors are always welcome.

NAVIGATION From Waddenzee appr via Doove Balg and Texelstroom. From seaward, app via Schulpengat or Molengat (fair weather and daylight only) into Marsdiep (Den Helder). Thence NE via Texelstroom for 3·5M to WPT 53°02'·26N 04°51'·55E (abeam T12 PHM buoy) 291°/400m to hbr ent, keeping the dir lt, Oc 6s, midway between FR and FG mole hd lts. Speed limit 5kn.

LIGHTS AND MARKS See chartlet and Lights, buoys and waypoints. Dir lt Oc 6s, on G mast, is vis only on brg 291°. FR/FG lts are on R/G masts with W bands.

COMMUNICATIONS (Code 0222) Coast Guard 316270; Police/ambulance 0900 8844 or 112; ⊖ via HM; Port HM 312710, mobile 06 1502 8380, VHF Ch 12 0800-2000LT; Marina VHF Ch 31; see Den Helder for VTS and radar assistance/info on request.

FACILITIES
Waddenhaven Texel Marina 250 berths ☎321227 info@waddenhaventexel.nl €0·70/m² + €1·60pp/day tax 🛢🛢✗⬜ mini 🛒 in season 🛢🛢@🚿 bike hire ◣.

YC WSV Texel, members only. Dry dock (FVs only).

Village (walking distance) ✗⬜🛒✉🔌⚓🛢Ⓑ. Ferry from 't Horntje to Den Helder. UK ferries from Hook/Rotterdam. ✈ Amsterdam.

2.14 DEN HELDER

Noord Holland 52°57'·94N 04°47'·24E

CHARTS AC 1408, 1631, 1546, 126; Zeekaart 1454, 1546; DYC 1811.2, 1801.10; ANWB F; Imray C25

TIDES –0430 Dover; ML 1·1; Duration 0540

Standard Port HELGOLAND (←)

Times				Height (metres)			
High Water		Low Water		MHWS	MHWN	MLWN	MLWS
0200	0700	0200	0800	3·1	2·8	0·8	0·4
1400	1900	1400	2000				
Differences DEN HELDER							
–0410	–0520	–0520	–0430	–1·3	–1·1	–0·4	–0·2
K13A PLATFORM (53°13'·0N 03°13'·1E; 58M WNW of Den Helder)							
–0420	–0430	–0520	–0530	–1·3	–1·4	–0·1	–0·1

SHELTER Good in all yacht hbrs (see Facilities). Hbr speed limit 5kn. Den Helder is the main base of the Royal Netherlands Navy which manages the Marinehaven Willemsoord and KMYC.

NAVIGATION Caution: fast ferries to/from Texel, many FVs and offshore service vessels, strong tidal streams across the hbr ent.

Schulpengat leads into Marsdiep for the hbr ent. It is well marked/ lit. WPT 52°52'·90N 04°37'·90E (SG (SWM) buoy, Mo (A) 8s, Racon Z) 026·5°/6M towards S14/MG17 SCM lt buoy.

Although closed as a shipping chan due to silting, the Molengat remains a viable fair weather chan for smaller craft, but depths are now unreliable as regular hydrographic surveys have been discontinued. Keep close W of Y bys marking E side. Do not attempt at night or in fresh NW–N wind or swell.

LIGHTS AND MARKS See chartlet and Lights, buoys and waypoints. Schulpengat: Dir lt Al WRG and F WRG. Kijkduin lt ho, R twr, is conspic 2·3M WSW of hbr. Hbr 191° ldg lts; front B ▲ on bldg; rear B ▼ on B lattice twr. A 60m radar twr is conspic on E side of hbr.

Entry sigs, from Hbr Control twr (W side of ent): ring of R lts = No entry/exit, except for the vessel indicated by Hbr Control Ch 62.

Bridges: Moorman bridge operates H24 7/7, except 0700-0845, 1200-1230, 1600-1700, giving access to Nieuwe Diep, Koopvaarder Lock and N Holland Canal.

Van Kinsbergen bridge is operated by HM, on request, Mon-Fri. All bridges are closed 0705-0810, 1200-1215, 1245-1300, 1600-1700, Mon-Fri. All LT.

COMMUNICATIONS (Code 0223) VTS 657522, monitor VHF Ch 62 *Den Helder Traffic* (VTS) in the Schulpengat and Marsdiep; info on request; Police 112/09008844; Water Police 616767; ⊖ 0255 566707; Immigration 08000543; British Consul (020) 676 4343; ⊞ 696969; HM 613955, VHF Ch 14 (H24) also remote control of van Kinsbergen bridge; *Koopvaarders Lock* VHF Ch 22 (H24) also remote control of Burgemeester Vissersbrug; Moorman bridge VHF Ch 18 (H24).

FACILITIES KMJC is hard to stbd on entering Naval Hbr. ☎652645, mob 0651007528, VHF Ch 31, www.kmjc.eu €2·10 + €1·24 pp/day tax draught <4m, 🔧 ✕ 🛒 📷 ⛽.

Willemsoord Marina through Zeedoksluis by arrangement with HM (Ch 14) 0800-1700, expect wait of 1-1·5 hours. ☎616100, www. willemsoord.nl €1·65 + €1·24pp/day tax, 🔧 ✕.

In or near **Binnenhaven**, YCs/marinas (MWV, HWN and Breewijd) can only be reached via the Rijkshaven, Moorman bridge, Nieuwe Diep and lock: **MWV YC** ☎652173, www.marinewatersport.nl €1·40 + €1·24pp/day tax. 🔧 📷 🛒. **HWN YC** ☎624422, www. wsvhwn.nl €1·00 + €1·24pp/day tax. **YC WSOV Breewijd** ☎615500 €0·75 + €1·20pp/day tax. **Council harbour** ☎613955 €1·30 + €1·24pp/day tax.

Services 🔧 ⚓ Floating dock ⚓. **Boatyard** Jachtwerf Den Helder ☎636964, 🏗(40t) ✕.

Town 🔧 ✕ 🛒 🏦 ✉ Ⓑ 🏧. ⇒ ✈ (Amsterdam). **Ferry** Hook–Harwich; Rotterdam–Hull, IJmuiden–Newcastle.

2.15 IJSSELMEER

CHARTS Zeekaart 1351, 1454; In-date DYC 1810, sheets 3-5, are essential to avoid live firing ranges, fishing areas and other hazards; 1810 also has many hbr chartlets.

TIDES The IJsselmeer is non-tidal. Tides seaward of Den Oever and Kornwerderzand locks: –0230 Dover; ML 1·2

Standard Port HELGOLAND (←)

Times				Height (metres)			
High Water		Low Water		MHWS	MHWN	MLWN	MLWS
0200	0700	0200	0800	3·1	2·8	0·8	0·4
1400	1900	1400	2000				
Differences DEN OEVER							
–0245	–0410	–0400	–0305	–1·2	–1·0	–0·5	–0·2
KORNWERDERZAND							
–0210	–0315	–0300	–0215	–1·0	–0·8	–0·4	–0·2

SHELTER Excellent in the marinas, but in the IJsselmeer strong winds can get up very quickly and often raise short, steep seas.

NAVIGATION Enter from sea by Den Oever or Kornwerderzand locks; also from IJmuiden via the Noordzeekanaal and Amsterdam.

Speed limits: 10·5kn in buoyed chans and <250m from shore. Hbr limits vary; see Special notes for the ANWB *Wateralmanak*.

A firing range, operational Tues to Thurs 1000–1900LT, extends S from Breezanddijk (53°01'·0N 05°12'·5E) to 3M NE of Medemblik then NNW to Den Oever (DYC 1811.3 & 1810.3). Call *Schietterrein Breezanddijk* (range control) Ch 71. Firing times are broadcast on VHF Ch 01 by Centrale Meldpost at H +15 on the day of firing, after weather forecasts.

R/T Nav info VHF Ch 01. Sealocks: Kornwerderzand 18; Den Oever 20. Enkhuizen naviduct 22; Lelystad 20; Oranjesluizen 18.

SEALOCKS Standard signals, see Special notes.

DEN OEVER SEALOCK AND MARINA Approach from seaward via the buoyed/lit Malzwin and Wierbalg channels. Enter on 131° ldg line, then 220° towards Buitenhaven. 2 swing bridges (52°56'·05N 05°02'·50E) and lock open in unison HO. If NW-bound, await lock opening in Binnenhaven. **Marina Den Oever BV** ⚓ HM ☎(0227) 511789, 310 ⌣inc ✓ (in 2-3m) €1·75 + €1·10 pp/day tax, ⚡ €0·45/kWh, 🚿 🛒 ⛽✕🛟 wi-fi 🅿 🛠(30t), bike hire. **Village** 20 mins easy walk, ✕ 🍴🛒 Ⓑ ✉.

KORNWERDERZAND SEALOCK From seaward approach from the W via Doove Balg; from NW via shallow Inschot chan; or from N via Boontjes. Entrance to Buitenhaven has FR/G and Iso G 6s lts. When two road bridges (53°04'·44N 05°20'·09E) have opened, yachts enter the smaller Lorentz E lock, operates H24. N-bound, follow 348° ldg lts, Iso 4s, to FR/G at ent. Await lock in Binnenhaven (3·6m). HM ☎(0517) 578170. ⊜ 058 2949444.

FACILITIES clockwise from Kornwerderzand. Overnight fees range from approx €0·80–1·80/metre LOA. Most berths are bows on to a pontoon, stern lines to piles; there are few ⚓s.

IJSSELMEER EASTERN SHORE

MAKKUM: 1M SE of Kornwerderzand, MA5 SHM by, Iso G4s, marks the byd chan. FR/FG lts lead 090·5° into Makkum. To stbd, **Marina Makkum** (2·5-2·8m) ☎(0515) 232828, ⚓🚿✕🛒🔧⚓⚓. 5 more marinas/YCs are to E; ⚓🔧🔌(40t)🛟(30t). **Town** ✕🛒🗲 Dr.

WORKUM: 5M S of Makkum; FW ldg lts 081° along buoyed chan to **It Soal Marina** ☎(0515) 542937, ⚓📞⚓🔧🗲.

HINDELOOPEN: WV Hylper Haven HM ☎ 06 4294 5342. ⚓⚓🔧📞🔨. **Old Hbr** ⚓⚓🔧📞🔨. **Jachthaven Hindeloopen** (500) HM ☎ 088 0504140. ⚓⚓✕🛒⚓🔌(65t).

STAVOREN: Ent Buitenhaven 048° on Dir lt Iso 4s between FR/G. Marina, €1·00, E of ent in Oudehaven; ☎(0514) 681216, VHF Ch 74. Or, 1km S, ent Nieuwe Voorhaven (FR/G & Fl 5s Dir lt) then via lock to **Marina Stavoren** (3m) ☎088 0504122. ⚓⚓⚓🔧🗲🔌(65t); **Outer Marina** (3·5m) close S of Nieuwe Voorhaven. Also 3 other marinas. **Town** ✕🛒🗲 (B) Dr ⚓.

LEMMER: Appr on ldg lts 038°, Iso 8s, to KL5/VL2 By; then ldg lts 083°, Iso 8s, through Lemstergeul. Lastly FG and Iso G 4s lead 065° into town and some 14 marinas. **Jachthaven Friese Hoek** (275) HM ☎ 088 0504130. 🔌⚓⚓🔧⚓(30t).

URK: Hbr ent ½M SE of lt ho. Dir lt Iso G 4s to hbr ent, FR/G. Hbr has 4 basins; keep NNW to berth in Nieuwe Haven, Westhaven or Oosthaven (3·3m). HM ☎(0527) 689970. **Westhaven** 📞📞; 🔌 at Hbr reception, ⚓; **Oosthaven** 🔌🔧📞🔨(E). **Town** EC Tues; 🗲 (B) Dr.

KETELHAVEN, E of Ketel bridge, (opens H+20/+50), for buoyed access chan to **Yachthaven Ketelmeer** ☎, 0321 312271, 300 inc🅥 in 3m most pile/pontoon, some ⚓€1·27.✕🔌⚓🔌🏴🔌⚓ wi-fi.

LELYSTAD: Flevo is 2M NNE of lock. (550) ☎ 088 0504180,⚓⚓✕🛒🔧🔌⚓🔌(50t)🗲. **Deko Marina** is close N of the lock; ☎(0320) 269000, ✕🔌⚓🗲. **WV Lelystad, Houtribhaven** (560) HM ☎(0320) 260198, ⚓✕🛒🔧🔌🔌(20t). S of lock **Bataviahaven** (150) Ch 14, HM ☎06 511 77049. **Marina Lelystadhaven** ☎(0320) 260326, ✕.

IJSSELMEER WESTERN SHORE

ENKHUIZEN: 036° ldg lts Iso 4s; 230° ldg lts Iso 8s. Here, the 13M Houtribdijk causeway between the Ijsselmeer and Markermeer is crossed by a double chamber lock above a road tunnel, minimising delays for boat and road traffic; call Ch 22. Boats <6m air clearance use Krabbersgat lock and bridge. **Compagnieshaven** (500) HM ☎(0228) 313353, ⚓⚓⚓🔌(12t); **Buyshaven** (195) ☎315660, 🔨🔌 🏴; **Buitenhaven** ☎312444. **Town** EC Mon; Market Wed; ✕🛒 🔌🔌🔌🗲 (B) Dr ⚓🔨⚓.

ANDIJK: Visitors use **Stichting Jachthaven Andijk**, the first of 2 marinas; (600) ☎(0228) 593075, narrow ent with tight turn between FR/G lts. ⚓🔌⚓⚓🔧⚓🗲(20t).

MEDEMBLIK: Ent on 232°, Dir lt Oc 5s between FR/G. Thence via Oosterhaven ⚓⚓ into Middenhaven (short stay) and via bridge to Westerhaven. **Pekelharinghaven** (120) HM ☎06 12335841; ent is to port by Castle, ✕🔌🔨. **Middenhaven** HM ☎541686, ⚓ **Stichting Jachthaven** HM ☎541681 in Westerhaven, 🔌🗲. **Town** ✕🛒🔌 🔌🔌⚓🔧🔨🗲 (B) Dr. **Regatta Centre** 0·5M S of hbr entr. HM ☎(0227) 547781, ⚓450, ✕🔌🗲(20t)🔨.

MARKERMEER This is accessed from the sea via IJmuiden, Noordzeekanaal, or Amsterdam/Oranjesluizen. **Caution,** dense propeller-disabling weed is a problem here; if offered a tow agree a price before accepting. S side of Houtribdijk, Marker Wadden islands nature reserve has a small harbour, 26 🅥⚓, max draft 2.9m, €1·30p/n + €6·00p/p. No facilities, pay by Blue water App.

DE BLOCQ VAN KUFFELER: (8·5M SW Lelystad) ☎06 2751 2497, ✕.

MUIDERZAND: S Markermeer, buoys IJM5 & IJM7/JH2, 1M N of bridge (12·7m cl'nce). **Marina** ☎(036) 5369151, ⚓⚓✕🔌🔧🗲.

MUIDEN: Ldg lts Q 181° into **KNZ & RV Marina** (2·6m) W of ent; home of Royal Netherlands YC (150 berths). HM ☎06 20146897, www.knzrv.nl €1·95, ✕🔌🔌📞🔨. On E bank **Stichting Jachthaven** (70) ☎(0294) 261223, €1·60, ⚓⚓.

DURGERDAM: ½M E of overhead power lines (70m); convenient for Oranjesluizen. Keep strictly in buoyed chan. **WV Durgerdam** Berth to stbd of ent (1·8m). ⚓ 06 51628873.

UITDAM Appr from MIJ5 buoy Fl Y 5s, via buoyed chan to FR/FG at ent. ⚓⚓🔨⚓(9t). HM (020) 4031433.

MARKEN (picturesque show piece): Ent Gouwzee from N, abeam Volendam, thence via buoyed chan; Dir FW lt 116° between FR/FG at hbr (2·2m). Lt ho, conspic, Oc 8s 16m 9M, on E end of island. HM ☎(0299) 601253, free 🅥⚓ on quay, ✕🛒📞📞(B).

MONNICKENDAM: Appr as for Marken, then W to MO10 Iso R 8s and 236° ldg lts FR. **Hemmeland Marina** ☎(0299) 655555, (2·0m) C. **Waterland Marina** ④ ☎652000, (2·5m) 🔌(15t) www. jachthavenwaterland.nl. **Marina Monnickendam** ☎652595, (2·0m) C. **Zeilhoek Marina** ☎651463, (2·5m) ⚓

VOLENDAM: Old hbr to stbd (2·4m). Dir lt Fl 5s 313°. FR/FG at ent. ☎06 51337494, ⚓⚓⚓⚓🔧🗲. To port via unlit buoyed chan, **Marina Volendam** (2·7m) HM (0299) 320262, ✕🛒 (B)⚓🗲(16t).

EDAM: Appr via unlit chan keeping Iso W 8s between FG /R at narrow ent; beware commercial traffic. **Jachthaven WSV De Zeevang** (2·2m) S side of outer hbr. ☎(0299) 350174, ⚓📞🔨. Or lock into the Oorgat and via S canal to Nieuwe Haven. **Town** ✕🔌🔌🗲 (B).

HOORN: Radio twr (80m) 1·5M ENE of hbr. Iso 4s 15m 10M and FR/G at W Hbr ent. Five options: To port **Grashaven** (700) HM ☎(0229) 215208, 🛒🔌🔧🔨⚓. To stbd ⚓ in **Buitenhaven** (1.6m). Ahead & to stbd **WSV Hoorn**, (100) ☎213540 ✕🏴🔌. **Kaap Hoorn marina,** 0.9M east of hbr ent, ☎0615906024, 50 inc 🅥 ✕ 🏴⚓🏴🔨. Ahead to **Binnenhaven** (2·5m) via narrow lock (open H24) ⚓⚓. **Town** ✕🔌🛒🔌📞📞⚓🗲 (B) Dr ⚓.

BROEKERHAVEN: Small yacht hbr 1·5M SW of Enkhuizen. Appr from KG15-BR2 buoy. WSV de Broekerhaven ☎(0228) 518798.

2.16 IJMUIDEN

N Holland 52°27'·94N 04°32'·39E (Hbr ent) SPM ❀❀⚓🌊🌊🌸🌸

CHARTS AC 1631, 124; Zeekaart 1450, 1543, 1035, 1350; DYC 1801.8; Imray C25

TIDES +0400 Dover; ML 1·0. Noordzeekanaal level may be above or below sea level

Standard Port VLISSINGEN (→)

Times				Height (metres)			
High Water		Low Water		MHWS	MHWN	MLWN	MLWS
0300	0900	0400	1000	5·0	4·1	1·1	0·5
1500	2100	1600	2200				
Differences IJMUIDEN							
+0145	+0140	+0305	+0325	–2·8	–2·4	–0·7	–0·3
PETTEN (SOUTH) 18M N of IJmuiden							
+0210	+0215	+0345	+0500	–2·9	–2·3	–0·6	–0·2

SHELTER Very good at Seaport (SPM) marina (2·9-4·8m).

NAVIGATION WPT 52°28'·10N 04°30'·94E, 100°/0·9M to ent. Beware strong tidal streams across hbr ent, scend inside Buitenhaven and commercial tfc – do not impede. Keep a good lookout, especially astern. 3 knots max speed in marina.

Marina access chan is buoyed/lit as per the chartlet.

LOCKS In IJmuiden the 4 locks are North, Middle, South and Small. Yachts normally use the S'most Small lock (Kleine Sluis) which opens H24 on request Ch 22; wait W or E of it.
Lock signals shown W and E from each lock are standard, ie:

● ● = Lock not in use; no entry.   ● = No entry/exit.

● ● ● = Prepare to enter/exit.   ● = Enter or exit.

Tidal and sluicing sigs may be shown from or near the conspic Hbr Ops Centre (HOC) bldg, near the front 100·5° ldg lt:

Tidal signals: ● over Ⓦ = rising tide; Ⓦ over ● = falling tide.

Sluicing sigs are a △ of 3 horiz lts and 1 lt at the apex. The sluices are N of the N lock, so unlikely to affect yachts.

LIGHTS AND MARKS Both ldg lt ho's 100·5° for Zuider Buitenkanaal are dark R twrs. The HOC bldg is conspic next to front lt; so are 6 chimneys (138-166m high) 7ca N and ENE of Small lock.

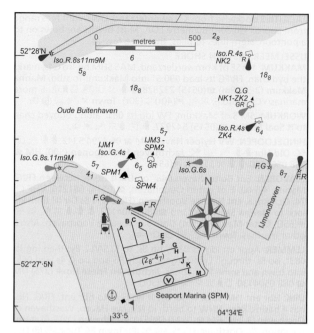

COMMUNICATIONS (Code 0255) Coast Guard 537644; Tfc Centre IJmuiden 564500, VHF Ch 07, see also VTS overleaf; Police 0900 8844; ⊖ 020 5813614; British Consul (020) 6764343; Ⓗ (023) 5453200; Hbr Ops 523934; Seaport Marina call *SPM* VHF Ch 74; Pilot 564503.

FACILITIES Seaport Marina (SPM) ☎560300. www.marinaseaport. nl info@ marinaseaport.nl ⚓ 600 incⓋ €2·20 inc ⚓ ⛽ 🚾 ⌂. Berth as directed, or on M pontoon in a slot with green tally. 🛥 🛥 ✕ 🗐 🛒 🅿 🛢 ⚓ ⛏ ✕ 🔧 🎦 Ⓔ ⚑(70t) ⚓. Buses to Amsterdam and Haarlem in summer.

Town ✕ 🗐 🚂 🛢 @ ✉ Ⓑ ⚓ (bus to Beverwijk) ✈ Amsterdam. **Ferry** IJmuiden-Newcastle.

2.17 NOORDZEEKANAAL

VTS Monitor the following VTS stns (H24) in sequence to approach, enter and transit the canal (see diagram below):

• *IJmuiden Traffic Centre*	Ch 07	W of IJM C buoy
• *IJmuiden Port Control*	Ch 61	IJM buoy to locks
• *IJmuiden Locks*	Ch 22	at the locks
• *Noordzeekanaal Traffic Centre*	Ch 03	Locks to km 14·8
• *Amsterdam Port Control*	Ch 04	Km 14·8 – Amsterdam
• *Sector Schellingwoude*	Ch 60	City centre (04°55'E) to Buiten IJ

Radar surveillance is available on request Ch 07. Visibility reports are broadcast on all VHF chans every H+00 when vis <1000m.

NAVIGATION Canal speed limit is 9kn. The 13·5M transit is simple, but there is much commercial traffic. Keep as far to stbd as possible. Keep a good lookout for vessels emerging from dock basins and side canals. The banks and ents to basins and side canals are well lit, so night navigation need be no problem apart from the risk of not being seen by other vessels against shore lights.

FACILITIES There are small marinas at IJmond beyond lifting bridge (Ch 18) in Zijkanaal ⊠ Km 10 (S bank); and at Nauerna (Zijkanaal ⬇ Km 12) (N bank).

WV IJmond ❀❀❀⬇⬇❀. Ch 31, HM ☎(023) 5375003, ⌣ €1.10. ⬇
⬇ ♺ ⬇(20t) ▢ ⬇ ✗.

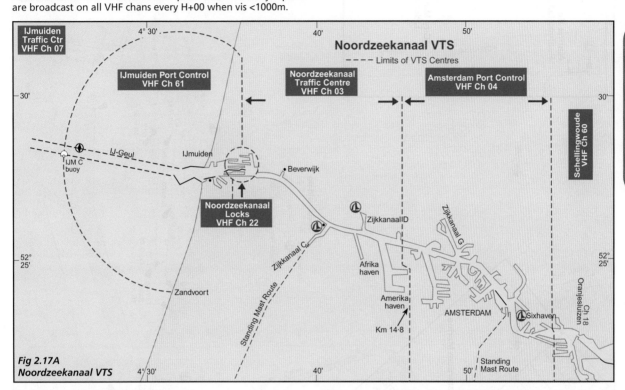

Noordzeekanaal VTS
- - - - Limits of VTS Centres

IJmuiden Traffic Ctr VHF Ch 07

IJmuiden Port Control VHF Ch 61

Noordzeekanaal Traffic Centre VHF Ch 03

Amsterdam Port Control VHF Ch 04

Schellingwoude VHF Ch 60

IJ-Geul · IJM C buoy · IJmuiden · Beverwijk

Noordzeekanaal Locks VHF Ch 22

Zijkanaal C · ZijkanaalID · Zijkanaal G · Ch 18 Oranjesluizen

Afrika haven

Amerika haven

Zandvoort

AMSTERDAM · Sixhaven

Km 14·8

Standing Mast Route · Standing Mast Route

Fig 2.17A
Noordzeekanaal VTS

2.18 AMSTERDAM

Noord Holland **52°22'·97N 04°53'·92E** Marinas ❀❀❀⬇⬇❀❀❀

CHARTS AC 124; DYC 1801.8, 1810.2; ANWB G, I

NAVIGATION Het IJ (pronounced eye) is the well-lit/buoyed chan through the city centre. From IJ 10/11 to IJ 14/15 buoys yachts must keep out of Het IJ, using a yacht chan between the lateral buoys and RW (N side) or GW (S side) buoys further outboard. A second recreational fairway, 100m wide and 5.5m deep (NAP), runs between IJ2 and IJ6.

Two yacht crossing points by YM 14-15 lead to Oranjesluizen, use the N lock, marked 'SPORT'; Ch 18, H24. Waiting piers/jetties either side. The Schellingwoude bridge (9m) opens on the hour and ±20 mins, except Mon-Fri 0600-0900 and 1600-1800; VHF Ch 18.

COMMUNICATIONS (Code 020) Emergency 112; Police 0900 8844; ⊖ 5867511; Brit Consul 6764343; Dr 0880 030600; Traffic Info VHF Ch 04; Port Control (East) 6221515; Port Control (West) 0255 514457; Port Info VHF Ch 14; Westerdoks-brug 6241457, VHF Ch 22; Oranjesluizen VHF Ch 18; Amsterdam Marina VHF Ch 31.

FACILITIES Complete shelter available in all yacht hbrs/marinas: **Amsterdam Marina** (52°24'·12N 04°53'·10E) VHF Ch 31, ☎6310767. info@marinaamsterdam.com www.marinaamsterdam.com 250+100❶, max LOA 30m, €2·50 inc ⬇ ✗ ⬇ ⬇ ▢.

City Marina IJdock 52°23'·04N 04°53'·63E, is centrally located in approach to Westerdok, due W of IJ6 buoy, within the IJdock high rise complex. Access through bridge opening on request, VHF Ch 22. Essential to book, HM ☎ 0687478290, www.citymarina.nl citymarina@outlook.com. 60⌣ inc ❶, €3·00 inc ⬇; ⬇ ❿ ⬇ ⬇ ✗ ⬇ ⬇ 5 mins walk to Haarlemmerstraat shopping centre and ⬇. Reports welcome.

Marina Het Realeneiland 52°23'·28N 04°53'·43E, in the Westerdok, ent lies W of Noordzee Canal IJ8 buoy, the two bridges open simultaneously on request: VHF Ch 22 or ☎0206241457. Must prebook berth. No VHF, ☎6238855 or hetrealeneiland@upcmail.nl

50 inc❶ max LOA 30m, €2·50, ⬇ ⬇ hose/cable from HM, ❿ no ❿ on site but possible at local squash club. All facilities nearby, easy walk, ⬇ 5 mins. Access by locked gate, key provided.

WVDS Sixhaven 52°22'·90N 04°54'·40E, close NE of IJ8 buoy and NE of conspic Central ⬇ Stn, is small, popular, and often full in season 1800-1100. ☎6329429, www.sixhaven.nl 100 +❶ max LOA 15m. €1·50 inc ⬇ ⬇(w/e) ⬇ ▢. Free ferries to N bank.

WV Aeolus 52°22'·91N 04°55'·17E. Few ❶ berths, rafting is strictly controlled. ☎6360791. Often full in season, no pre-booking, berth as directed. 45 + 8❶ €1·10, ⬇ ⬇ ⬇, YC. Free ferries to N bank.

Aquadam Twellegea 52°23'·04N 04°56'·63E, ent to Zijkanaal K. ☎6320616. €2·50, ⬇ ✗ ⬇(30t). www.aquadam.nl Full ♺ facilities.

WV Zuiderzee 52°22'·95N 04°57'·77E, 140m NE of Oranjesluizen. ☎6946884, www.wsv-dezuiderzee.nl €1·10, YC.

City All needs; ⬇ Ⓔ ACA, DYC Agent, Ⓑ @ ⊠ ⬇ ✈. Amsterdam gives access to the N Holland and Rijn canals.

Netherlands

2.19 SCHEVENINGEN

Zuid Holland 52°06'·24N 04°15'·26E 🌊🌊❄❄❄❄🌸🌸❄

CHARTS AC 1630, 125, 122; Zeekaart 1035, 1349, 1350, 1449; DYC 1801.7; ANWB H/J; Imray C25

TIDES +0320 Dover; ML 0·9; Duration 0445

Standard Port VLISSINGEN (→)

Times				Height (metres)			
High Water		Low Water		MHWS	MHWN	MLWN	MLWS
0300	0900	0400	1000	5·0	4·1	1·1	0·5
1500	2100	1600	2200				
Differences SCHEVENINGEN							
+0105	+0100	+0220	+0245	–2·7	–2·3	–0·7	–0·2

SHELTER Very good in marina. Ent difficult in SW–N F6 winds, and dangerous in NW F6-8 which cause scend in outer hbr.

NAVIGATION WPT 52°07'·75N 04°14'·12E (SCH buoy) 156°/1·6M to ent; access H24. Close west of the 156° leading line and 1M from the hbr ent, outfalls are marked by E and W cardinal light buoys and by 2 SPM buoys (off chartlet). The promenade pier, Iso 5s, is 1·2M NE of the hbr ent. Caution: Strong tidal streams set across the ent. Slack water is about HW Scheveningen –2 and +3. Beware large ships and FVs entering/leaving.

LIGHTS AND MARKS Daymarks include: the reddish-brown lt ho (5ca E of hbr ent); twr bldgs in Scheveningen and Den Haag.

Traffic signals (from signal mast, N side of ent to Voorhaven):

● over ○ = No entry. ○ over ● = No exit.
Fl ● = One or more large vessels are leaving the port.

Tide sigs (same mast): ● over ○ = tide rising. ○ over ● = tide falling.

Shown from SE end of narrow chan between 1st and 2nd Hbrs:
● = vessels must not leave the 2nd Hbr. The chan is generally blind, so go slowly and sound horn.

COMMUNICATIONS (Code 070) Call Traffic Centre Scheveningen Ch 21 (H24) prior to entry/departure to avoid FVs; Police 0900 8844; ⊜ 020 5813614; Brit Consul (020) 6764343; Dr 3450650; Port HM 3527711; Radar (info only) on request VHF Ch 21; When in 2nd Hbr call Yacht Club Scheveningen VHF Ch 31 for a berth.

FACILITIES YC Scheveningen ☎3520017, mob 0653 293137. www.jachtclubscheveningen.com info@jachtclubscheveningen.com 223 + 100Ⓥ €2·00 + €2·05 pp/day tax. Visitors *must* turn to berth/raft bows NE, for fire safety reasons. ✗ 🗔 ☎3520308, 🔲.

2nd Harbour Fuel barge GEO (0630-1600) 🛢 only. ⚓ DYC agent; 🔧🏪🍴🛒🔨⚓.

Town 🛥✗🏠🛒⊠ⒷⲺ✈ Rotterdam and Amsterdam. The town is effectively merged with Den Haag (The Hague), seat of Dutch government and well worth a visit by bus.

Port Control Ch 21

Netherlands

2.20 TSS AND VTS OFF SOUTH NETHERLANDS AND BELGIUM

2.21 MAAS TSS

Large ships bound up-Channel for Europoort route via the Dover Strait and the Noord Hinder South TSS to Noord Hinder Junction (a large pentagon roughly centred on 52°N 02°51'·1E). Here ships enter the MAAS TRAFFIC SEPARATION SCHEME.

Maas West Outer TSS starts some 33M offshore and funnels large ships 083°/27M via the TSS lanes or Eurogeul (DW route dredged 24·5m) towards a second pentagon 'Maas Precautionary Area' clear

of Maas West Inner TSS and 10M offshore. When abeam Maas Centre SWM buoy, ships enter the Maasgeul (Maas narrows) and track inbound 5·5M on the 112° leading lights to the Maasmond (Maas mouth, ie the harbour entrance).

Yachts should avoid the whole complex by using the ITZ and/or crossing the Maasgeul via the recommended track (see Hoek van Holland and www.maasvlakte2.com/uploads/crossing_route.pdf). Knowing the above is to be aware of what you are avoiding.

STANDARD TIME UT –01
Subtract 1 hour for UT
For Dutch Summer Time add
ONE hour in **non-shaded areas**

HOEK VAN HOLLAND   LAT 51°59'N   LONG 4°07'E
TIMES AND HEIGHTS OF HIGH AND LOW WATERS

Dates in red are **SPRINGS**
Dates in blue are **NEAPS**

YEAR **2022**

Netherlands

JANUARY

Time	m		Time	m
1 0059	2.2	**16**	0204	1.9
0624	0.5		0736	0.4
SA 1322	2.2	SU 1412	2.0
1842	0.4		2029	0.5
2 0150	2.2	**17**	0241	2.0
0708	0.4		0810	0.4
SU 1411	2.3	M 1448	2.1
● 1930	0.4	○ 2129	0.5
3 0239	2.2	**18**	0313	2.0
0751	0.3		0831	0.3
M 1458	2.4	TU 1523	2.2
2305	0.5		2228	0.6
4 0327	2.2	**19**	0345	2.0
0834	0.3		0855	0.3
TU 1545	2.4	W 1558	2.2
			2321	0.5
5 0002	0.5	**20**	0418	2.1
0415	2.1		0926	0.2
W 0918	0.2	TH 1632	2.3
1632	2.4		
6 0057	0.5	**21**	0008	0.5
0502	2.1		0453	2.1
TH 1005	0.2	F 1000	0.1
1720	2.4		1708	2.3
7 0149	0.5	**22**	0051	0.5
0551	2.1		0529	2.0
F 1056	0.1	SA 1037	0.1
1811	2.3		1745	2.2
8 0242	0.6	**23**	0133	0.5
0641	2.0		0606	2.0
SA 1153	0.1	SU 1117	0.1
1907	2.2		1825	2.2
9 0333	0.6	**24**	0210	0.5
0734	1.9		0648	2.0
SU 1257	0.1	M 1202	0.1
☽ 2006	2.1		1912	2.2
10 0423	0.6	**25**	0231	0.6
0829	1.9		0736	2.0
M 1403	0.2	TU 1255	0.1
2107	2.0		☽ 2008	2.1
11 0308	0.6	**26**	0233	0.5
0930	1.8		0836	1.9
TU 1523	0.3	W 1408	0.1
2217	1.9		2116	2.0
12 0416	0.6	**27**	0314	0.5
1042	1.8		0947	1.9
W 1642	0.3	TH 1523	0.2
2330	1.9		2226	2.0
13 0517	0.6	**28**	0415	0.5
1148	1.8		1100	1.9
TH 1746	0.4	F 1637	0.3
			2338	1.9
14 0028	1.9	**29**	0520	0.5
0608	0.5		1209	2.0
F 1244	1.9	SA 1744	0.4
1843	0.4		
15 0119	1.9	**30**	0045	2.0
0654	0.5		0613	0.4
SA 1332	1.9	SU 1308	2.1
1936	0.5		1839	0.4
		31	0142	2.0
			0658	0.3
		M 1400	2.2
			2200	0.4

FEBRUARY

Time	m		Time	m
1 0232	2.0	**16**	0256	2.0
0739	0.3		0803	0.3
TU 1448	2.3	W 1505	2.2
● 2254	0.5	○ 2313	0.5
2 0318	2.1	**17**	0326	2.0
0819	0.2		0826	0.3
W 1533	2.4	TH 1538	2.2
2346	0.5		2307	0.5
3 0402	2.1	**18**	0359	2.1
0900	0.1		0857	0.2
TH 1618	2.4	F 1612	2.3
			2347	0.5
4 0038	0.5	**19**	0433	2.1
0446	2.1		0930	0.1
F 0943	0.1	SA 1647	2.3
1702	2.4		
5 0130	0.5	**20**	0028	0.5
0528	2.1		0508	2.1
SA 1029	0.1	SU 1007	0.1
1747	2.3		1724	2.3
6 0220	0.5	**21**	0107	0.5
0611	2.1		0545	2.1
SU 1119	0.1	M 1047	0.1
1834	2.2		1803	2.3
7 0305	0.5	**22**	0140	0.5
0655	2.1		0624	2.1
M 1217	0.1	TU 1132	0.0
1923	2.1		1847	2.2
8 0110	0.5	**23**	0000	0.4
0742	2.0		0709	2.1
TU 1322	0.2	W 1226	0.1
☽ 2014	1.9	☽ 1939	2.1
9 0204	0.5	**24**	0050	0.4
0834	1.9		0803	2.0
W 1428	0.2	TH 1359	0.1
2109	1.8		2043	1.9
10 0326	0.5	**25**	0244	0.4
0934	1.8		0913	1.9
TH 1615	0.3	F 1521	0.2
2214	1.7		2159	1.7
11 0450	0.5	**26**	0354	0.4
1050	1.7		1008	1.9
F 1723	0.4	SA 1634	0.3
2357	1.6		2326	1.7
12 0545	0.4	**27**	0505	0.4
1213	1.7		1158	1.9
SA 1820	0.4	SU 1738	0.4
13 0059	1.6	**28**	0040	1.8
0634	0.4		0558	0.3
SU 1312	1.8	M 1301	2.0
1912	0.5		2110	0.4
14 0147	1.8		
0716	0.4		
M 1356	1.9		
2154	0.5		
15 0225	1.9		
0746	0.3		
TU 1432	2.1		
2245	0.5		

MARCH

Time	m		Time	m
1 0136	1.9	**16**	0158	1.8
0641	0.3		0718	0.3
TU 1352	2.2	W 1407	2.1
2203	0.4		2229	0.4
2 0222	2.0	**17**	0228	1.9
0720	0.2		0730	0.3
W 1436	2.3	TH 1438	2.2
● 2240	0.5		2314	0.5
3 0304	2.0	**18**	0259	2.0
0759	0.1		0755	0.2
TH 1518	2.3	F 1511	2.3
2324	0.5	○ 2019	0.5
4 0344	2.1	**19**	0332	2.1
0837	0.1		0827	0.1
F 1559	2.3	SA 1546	2.3
			2049	0.5
5 0013	0.5	**20**	0407	2.2
0423	2.1		0901	0.1
SA 0917	0.1	SU 1622	2.3
1640	2.3		2122	0.4
6 0104	0.5	**21**	0443	2.2
0502	2.2		0939	0.1
SU 1332	0.1	M 1701	2.3
1721	2.2		2159	0.4
7 0151	0.4	**22**	0521	2.2
0540	2.2		1021	0.1
M 1045	0.1	TU 1741	2.2
1801	2.1		2242	0.3
8 0229	0.5	**23**	0601	2.2
0618	2.1		1110	0.1
TU 1136	0.2	W 1825	2.1
1841	2.0		2331	0.3
9 0001	0.4	**24**	0645	2.2
0659	2.1		1213	0.2
W 1243	0.2	TH 1915	2.0
1924	1.9		
10 0105	0.4	**25**	0037	0.3
0745	1.9		0738	2.1
TH 1350	0.3	F 1421	0.2
☽ 2013	1.7	☽ 2019	1.8
11 0204	0.4	**26**	0227	0.3
0845	1.8		0853	1.9
F 1550	0.3	SA 1519	0.3
2113	1.6		2146	1.6
12 0427	0.4	**27**	0336	0.3
0957	1.7		1031	1.8
SA 1658	0.4	SU 1625	0.4
2230	1.5		2323	1.6
13 0522	0.3	**28**	0446	0.3
1135	1.6		1154	1.9
SU 1755	0.4	M 1952	0.4
14 0030	1.5	**29**	0033	1.7
0611	0.3		0537	0.3
M 1246	1.8	TU 1254	2.0
1848	0.4		2124	0.4
15 0120	1.7	**30**	0124	1.8
0654	0.3		0913	0.2
TU 1331	1.9	W 1339	2.2
2131	0.4		2244	0.4
		31	0206	1.9
			0659	0.2
		TH 1420	2.2
			2221	0.4

APRIL

Time	m		Time	m
1 0245	2.0	**16**	0226	2.0
0737	0.1		0724	0.2
F 1459	2.3	SA 1441	2.3
● 2257	0.5	○ 1951	0.4
2 0322	2.1	**17**	0302	2.1
0814	0.1		0758	0.1
SA 1538	2.3	SU 1518	2.4
2343	0.4		2023	0.3
3 0359	2.2	**18**	0339	2.2
0852	0.1		0835	0.1
SU 1616	2.2	M 1557	2.3
2359	0.4		2058	0.3
4 0435	2.2	**19**	0418	2.3
1255	0.2		0915	0.1
M 1653	2.1	TU 1638	2.3
2205	0.4		2138	0.3
5 0510	2.2	**20**	0458	2.3
1331	0.2		1001	0.2
TU 1729	2.0	W 1720	2.2
2232	0.3		2225	0.3
6 0545	2.1	**21**	0540	2.3
1327	0.3		1056	0.2
W 1803	1.9	TH 1805	2.0
2319	0.3		2320	0.2
7 0621	2.1	**22**	0626	2.2
1341	0.3		1334	0.2
TH 1837	1.9	F 1857	1.8
8 0018	0.3	**23**	0045	0.2
0659	2.0		0722	2.1
F 1406	0.3	SA 1414	0.3
1914	1.7	☽ 2008	1.6
9 0125	0.3	**24**	0206	0.2
0751	1.8		0851	1.9
SA 1528	0.4	SU 1510	0.4
☽ 2014	1.6		2144	1.5
10 0403	0.3	**25**	0314	0.2
0920	1.7		1026	1.9
SU 1632	0.4	M 1807	0.4
2140	1.4		2311	1.5
11 0457	0.3	**26**	0423	0.2
1045	1.6		1143	2.0
M 1729	0.4	TU 1947	0.4
2334	1.4		
12 0547	0.3	**27**	0014	1.7
1207	1.8		0742	0.2
TU 1823	0.4	W 1237	2.1
			2100	0.3
13 0040	1.6	**28**	0102	1.8
0629	0.3		0846	0.2
W 1256	2.0	TH 1320	2.2
2056	0.4		2158	0.4
14 0119	1.8	**29**	0144	1.9
0635	0.3		0929	0.2
TH 1332	2.1	F 1400	2.2
2159	0.4		2159	0.4
15 0152	1.9	**30**	0222	2.0
0654	0.2		0719	0.2
F 1406	2.2	SA 1439	2.2
2247	0.4	● 2229	0.4

Chart Datum is 0·92 metres below NAP Datum. HAT is 2·5 metres above Chart Datum.

FREE monthly updates. Register at
www.reedsnauticalalmanac.co.uk

STANDARD TIME UT −01
Subtract 1 hour for UT
For Dutch Summer Time add
ONE hour in **non-shaded areas**

HOEK VAN HOLLAND LAT 51°59'N LONG 4°07'E
TIMES AND HEIGHTS OF HIGH AND LOW WATERS

Dates in red are SPRINGS
Dates in blue are NEAPS

YEAR 2022

MAY

Time	m	Time	m
1 0259	2.1	**16** 0233	2.2
0757	0.2	0734	0.2
SU 1516	2.2	M 1452	2.3
2312	0.4	○ 2000	0.3
2 0334	2.1	**17** 0313	2.3
1111	0.2	0814	0.2
M 1553	2.1	TU 1534	2.3
2359	0.3	2039	0.3
3 0409	2.2	**18** 0355	2.3
1156	0.3	0859	0.2
TU 1628	2.0	W 1618	2.2
		2123	0.2
4 0443	2.2	**19** 0438	2.3
1234	0.3	0949	0.3
W 1701	2.0	TH 1703	2.1
2359	0.3	2212	0.2
5 0518	2.1	**20** 0523	2.3
1304	0.3	1307	0.3
TH 1733	1.9	F 1752	1.9
2255	0.2	2311	0.1
6 0552	2.1	**21** 0613	2.2
1335	0.4	1340	0.3
F 1804	1.8	SA 1848	1.8
2350	0.2		
7 0627	2.0	**22** 0025	0.1
1412	0.4	0715	2.1
SA 1841	1.8	SU 1415	0.4
		◗ 2005	1.7
8 0058	0.2	**23** 0138	0.1
0710	1.9	0846	2.0
SU 1507	0.4	M 1637	0.4
◗ 1930	1.6	2127	1.6
9 0159	0.2	**24** 0246	0.1
0840	1.7	1005	2.0
M 1606	0.4	TU 1752	0.4
2101	1.5	2242	1.6
10 0431	0.2	**25** 0604	0.1
1000	1.7	1116	2.0
TU 1701	0.4	W 1907	0.4
2220	1.5	2343	1.7
11 0520	0.2	**26** 0710	0.1
1111	1.8	1210	2.1
W 1755	0.4	TH 2019	0.4
2338	1.6		
12 0550	0.2	**27** 0033	1.8
1208	2.0	0804	0.2
TH 2011	0.4	F 1256	2.1
		2110	0.4
13 0031	1.7	**28** 0118	1.9
0542	0.2	0841	0.2
F 1252	2.1	SA 1339	2.1
2119	0.4	2143	0.4
14 0113	1.9	**29** 0158	2.0
0618	0.2	0714	0.3
SA 1331	2.2	SU 1419	2.1
2208	0.4	2214	0.4
15 0153	2.0	**30** 0236	2.0
0655	0.2	0933	0.3
SU 1411	2.3	M 1457	2.0
1925	0.4	● 2014	0.4
		31 0312	2.1
		1018	0.3
		TU 1533	2.0
		2332	0.3

JUNE

Time	m	Time	m
1 0347	2.1	**16** 0337	2.3
1108	0.4	1151	0.4
W 1607	2.0	TH 1604	2.1
		2110	0.2
2 0007	0.3	**17** 0423	2.3
0422	2.1	1245	0.4
TH 1157	0.4	F 1651	2.1
1640	1.9	2159	0.1
3 0035	0.2	**18** 0511	2.3
0457	2.1	1337	0.4
F 1240	0.4	SA 1742	1.9
1712	1.9	2253	0.1
4 0107	0.2	**19** 0603	2.2
0531	2.1	1430	0.4
SA 1320	0.4	SU 1838	1.8
1745	1.8	2355	0.1
5 0000	0.2	**20** 0705	2.1
0607	2.0	1525	0.4
SU 1402	0.4	M 1944	1.8
1823	1.8		
6 0022	0.2	**21** 0103	0.1
0648	1.9	0818	2.1
M 1448	0.4	TU 1625	0.4
1910	1.7	◗ 2050	1.7
7 0121	0.2	**22** 0212	0.1
0745	1.9	0926	2.0
TU 1539	0.5	W 1726	0.5
◗ 2019	1.6	2158	1.7
8 0216	0.2	**23** 0324	0.1
0912	1.9	1036	2.0
W 1630	0.5	TH 1824	0.4
2135	1.6	2303	1.8
9 0310	0.2	**24** 0633	0.2
1017	1.9	1138	2.0
TH 1718	0.5	F 1922	0.4
2242	1.7		
10 0405	0.2	**25** 0000	1.8
1116	2.0	0532	0.2
F 1712	0.4	SA 1230	2.0
2343	1.8	2025	0.4
11 0457	0.2	**26** 0050	1.9
1210	2.1	0627	0.3
SA 1747	0.4	SU 1319	2.0
		2125	0.4
12 0035	1.9	**27** 0136	1.9
0547	0.2	0721	0.5
SU 1259	2.2	M 1404	2.0
1825	0.4	1932	0.4
13 0123	2.1	**28** 0217	2.0
0633	0.2	0828	0.4
M 1345	2.2	TU 1444	2.0
1904	0.3	2012	0.3
14 0208	2.2	**29** 0254	2.0
0718	0.2	0933	0.4
TU 1431	2.2	W 1520	1.9
○ 1944	0.3	● 2045	0.3
15 0252	2.3	**30** 0330	2.1
0802	0.3	1031	0.5
W 1517	2.2	TH 1552	1.9
2025	0.2	2110	0.3

JULY

Time	m	Time	m
1 0405	2.1	**16** 0410	2.4
1129	0.5	1236	0.5
F 1625	1.9	SA 1640	2.0
2139	0.2	2140	0.1
2 0440	2.1	**17** 0458	2.3
1220	0.5	1328	0.5
SA 1658	1.9	SU 1727	2.0
2359	0.2	2229	0.1
3 0515	2.1	**18** 0547	2.3
1304	0.5	1421	0.5
SU 1732	1.9	M 1817	2.0
2254	0.2	2322	0.1
4 0550	2.1	**19** 0640	2.2
1346	0.5	1513	0.5
M 1809	1.8	TU 1909	1.9
2335	0.2		
5 0628	2.0	**20** 0024	0.1
1427	0.5	0738	2.1
TU 1850	1.8	W 1603	0.5
		◗ 2004	1.9
6 0021	0.1	**21** 0134	0.1
0714	2.0	0839	2.0
W 1506	0.5	TH 1650	0.5
1940	1.8	2102	1.8
7 0117	0.1	**22** 0246	0.2
0813	2.0	0943	1.9
TH 1505	0.5	F 1547	0.5
◗ 2045	1.8	2209	1.8
8 0222	0.1	**23** 0407	0.2
0925	2.0	1059	1.9
F 1536	0.5	SA 1652	0.5
2154	1.8	2321	1.8
9 0322	0.1	**24** 0516	0.3
1029	2.0	1205	1.9
SA 1623	0.5	SU 1745	0.4
2300	1.9		
10 0423	0.2	**25** 0024	1.8
1132	2.1	0614	0.4
SU 1716	0.4	M 1302	1.9
		1832	0.4
11 0002	2.0	**26** 0118	1.9
0525	0.2	0706	0.4
M 1232	2.1	TU 1353	1.9
1805	0.4	1915	0.4
12 0058	2.1	**27** 0205	2.0
0621	0.3	0754	0.5
TU 1326	2.1	W 1435	1.9
1850	0.3	1953	0.3
13 0149	2.2	**28** 0242	2.0
0710	0.4	0842	0.5
W 1417	2.1	TH 1509	1.9
○ 1932	0.3	● 2022	0.3
14 0237	2.3	**29** 0315	2.1
1049	0.4	1003	0.6
TH 1505	2.1	F 1538	2.0
2013	0.2	2044	0.3
15 0324	2.3	**30** 0348	2.1
1143	0.5	1113	0.6
F 1553	2.1	SA 1609	2.0
2055	0.2	2111	0.2
		31 0422	2.2
		1159	0.6
		SU 1641	2.0
		2144	0.2

AUGUST

Time	m	Time	m
1 0456	2.2	**16** 0524	2.3
1241	0.6	1403	0.6
M 1714	2.0	TU 1748	2.1
2219	0.2	2250	0.2
2 0529	2.2	**17** 0610	2.2
1321	0.5	1451	0.6
TU 1749	2.0	W 1832	2.1
2255	0.2	2345	0.2
3 0606	2.2	**18** 0659	2.1
1358	0.6	1531	0.6
W 1826	2.0	TH 1919	2.0
2336	0.1		
4 0647	2.2	**19** 0054	0.2
1428	0.6	0751	2.0
TH 1908	2.0	F 1341	0.6
		◗ 2011	2.0
5 0023	0.1	**20** 0209	0.3
0735	2.1	0847	1.9
F 1245	0.5	SA 1454	0.5
◗ 2000	2.0	2111	1.8
6 0125	0.1	**21** 0343	0.4
0837	2.1	0953	1.7
SA 1450	0.5	SU 1627	0.5
2107	1.9	2228	1.7
7 0251	0.2	**22** 0457	0.4
0949	2.0	1141	1.7
SU 1546	0.5	M 1724	0.5
2223	1.8		
8 0406	0.3	**23** 0000	1.8
1102	1.9	0555	0.5
M 1653	0.5	TU 1245	1.7
2338	1.9	1813	0.4
9 0518	0.4	**24** 0103	1.9
1215	1.9	0647	0.5
TU 1751	0.4	W 1337	1.8
		1856	0.4
10 0042	2.0	**25** 0150	2.0
0615	0.4	0955	0.6
W 1316	2.0	TH 1418	1.9
1836	0.3	1932	0.4
11 0137	2.2	**26** 0225	2.1
0944	0.5	1045	0.6
TH 1408	2.0	F 1449	2.0
1916	0.3	1954	0.4
12 0225	2.3	**27** 0256	2.2
1038	0.5	1125	0.6
F 1455	2.1	SA 1516	2.0
○ 1956	0.2	● 2013	0.3
13 0311	2.4	**28** 0326	2.2
1126	0.6	0832	0.6
SA 1539	2.1	SU 1545	2.1
2036	0.2	2040	0.3
14 0355	2.4	**29** 0358	2.3
1217	0.6	1131	0.6
SU 1622	2.1	M 1617	2.1
2117	0.1	2112	0.2
15 0439	2.4	**30** 0431	2.3
1310	0.6	1211	0.6
M 1705	2.1	TU 1650	2.1
2201	0.1	2146	0.2
		31 0505	2.3
		1251	0.6
		W 1724	2.1
		2222	0.2

Chart Datum is 0·92 metres below NAP Datum. HAT is 2·5 metres above Chart Datum.

〉〉 **FREE** monthly updates. Register at 〈
www.reedsnauticalalmanac.co.uk 〈

STANDARD TIME UT –01
Subtract 1 hour for UT
For Dutch Summer Time add
ONE hour in **non-shaded areas**

HOEK VAN HOLLAND   LAT 51°59'N   LONG 4°07'E
TIMES AND HEIGHTS OF HIGH AND LOW WATERS

Dates in red are SPRINGS
Dates in blue are NEAPS

YEAR **2022**

Netherlands

SEPTEMBER

Day	Time	m	Time	m	Time	m	Time	m
1 TH	0541	2.3	1040	0.6	1800	2.2	2303	0.2
2 F	0621	2.3	1122	0.5	1841	2.2	2351	0.2
3 SA ◑	0707	2.2	1211	0.5	1928	2.1		
4 SU	0052	0.3	0802	2.0	1521	0.5	2029	2.0
5 M	0251	0.3	0916	1.9	1521	0.5	2157	1.9
6 TU	0403	0.4	1043	1.7	1635	0.5	2324	1.9
7 W	0511	0.5	1208	1.8	1734	0.4		
8 TH	0034	2.1	0842	0.5	1309	1.9	1817	0.4
9 F	0127	2.2	0947	0.5	1357	2.0	1856	0.3
10 SA ○	0212	2.3	1024	0.6	1439	2.1	1934	0.2
11 SU	0254	2.4	1251	0.6	1520	2.2	2013	0.2
12 M	0336	2.4	1150	0.6	1600	2.2	2052	0.2
13 TU	0417	2.4	1242	0.6	1639	2.2	2134	0.2
14 W	0459	2.3	1333	0.6	1719	2.2	2218	0.3
15 TH	0540	2.2	1418	0.6	1758	2.2	2307	0.3
16 F	0622	2.1	1129	0.6	1839	2.2		
17 SA ◑	0010	0.4	0705	2.0	1234	0.5	1925	2.0
18 SU	0143	0.4	0754	1.8	1344	0.5	2024	1.9
19 M	0323	0.5	0853	1.7	1606	0.5	2138	1.7
20 TU	0436	0.5	1016	1.5	1702	0.4	2331	1.7
21 W	0534	0.6	1220	1.6	1752	0.4		
22 TH	0038	1.9	0627	0.6	1310	1.8	1837	0.4
23 F	0123	2.0	0925	0.6	1348	1.9	1911	0.4
24 SA	0158	2.1	1020	0.6	1418	2.0	1922	0.4
25 SU ●	0227	2.2	1107	0.6	1446	2.1	1941	0.4
26 M	0257	2.3	0804	0.6	1516	2.2	2009	0.3
27 TU	0329	2.4	0832	0.6	1549	2.2	2042	0.3
28 W	0403	2.4	0903	0.6	1623	2.3	2116	0.2
29 TH	0440	2.4	0937	0.5	1659	2.3	2155	0.2
30 F	0517	2.4	1016	0.5	1736	2.3	2239	0.2

OCTOBER

Day	Time	m	Time	m	Time	m	Time	m
1 SA	0558	2.3	1100	0.4	1817	2.3	2331	0.3
2 SU ●	0643	2.1	1154	0.4	1905	2.2		
3 M	0159	0.4	0738	1.9	1332	0.4	2006	2.0
4 TU	0251	0.5	0858	1.7	1459	0.5	2147	1.9
5 W	0356	0.6	1038	1.6	1612	0.5	2319	2.0
6 TH	0715	0.6	1201	1.7	1711	0.4		
7 F	0026	2.1	0852	0.5	1257	1.9	2043	0.4
8 SA	0114	2.2	0954	0.5	1340	2.0	2134	0.3
9 SU ○	0156	2.3	1005	0.6	1420	2.1	1913	0.3
10 M	0235	2.4	1033	0.7	1458	2.2	1951	0.3
11 TU	0315	2.4	1117	0.6	1536	2.3	2029	0.3
12 W	0355	2.4	1209	0.6	1614	2.3	2109	0.3
13 TH	0434	2.3	1259	0.6	1651	2.3	2135	0.3
14 F	0122	0.4	1010	0.5	1728	2.3		
15 SA	0155	0.5	0548	2.1	1055	0.5	1805	2.2
16 SU	0124	0.5	1149	0.4	1845	2.1		
17 M	0154	0.6	0701	1.8	1259	0.4	1935	1.9
18 TU	0304	0.6	0755	1.7	1543	0.5	2058	1.8
19 W	0412	0.6	0916	1.5	1638	0.4	2226	1.7
20 TH	0509	0.6	1133	1.5	1728	0.4	2359	1.9
21 F	0603	0.6	1229	1.7	1816	0.4		
22 SA	0045	2.0	0839	0.6	1307	1.8	1847	0.4
23 SU	0121	2.2	0942	0.6	1339	2.0	1844	0.4
24 M	0152	2.3	1031	0.6	1410	2.1	1909	0.4
25 TU ●	0225	2.4	0737	0.6	1444	2.2	1941	0.3
26 W	0300	2.5	0807	0.6	1519	2.3	2016	0.3
27 TH	0337	2.5	0840	0.5	1557	2.4	2053	0.3
28 F	0416	2.4	0916	0.4	1635	2.4	2135	0.3
29 SA	0457	2.3	0959	0.4	1716	2.4	2224	0.4
30 SU	0539	2.2	1048	0.4	1759	2.4		
31 M	0118	0.5	0627	2.0	1150	0.3	1849	2.2

NOVEMBER

Day	Time	m	Time	m	Time	m	Time	m
1 TU ◐	0154	0.5	0726	1.8	1320	0.4	1958	2.0
2 W	0243	0.6	0854	1.7	1433	0.4	2143	2.0
3 TH	0534	0.6	1028	1.6	1543	0.4	2307	2.0
4 F	0712	0.6	1142	1.7	1913	0.4		
5 SA	0009	2.2	0838	0.5	1234	1.9	2017	0.3
6 SU	0055	2.3	0932	0.6	1318	2.0	2103	0.3
7 M	0136	2.3	0941	0.6	1358	2.1	1856	0.4
8 TU ○	0216	2.3	1004	0.6	1436	2.2	1936	0.4
9 W	0256	2.3	1046	0.6	1514	2.3	2015	0.4
10 TH	0335	2.3	1137	0.5	1551	2.3	2332	0.5
11 F	0412	2.2	1226	0.5	1627	2.3		
12 SA	0021	0.5	0448	2.1	0952	0.5	1703	2.3
13 SU	0049	0.5	0521	2.0	1036	0.4	1739	2.2
14 M	0114	0.6	0554	2.0	1126	0.4	1816	2.1
15 TU	0149	0.6	0629	1.9	1228	0.4	1859	2.0
16 W ◑	0241	0.6	0714	1.8	1331	0.4	2014	1.8
17 TH	0343	0.7	0833	1.6	1611	0.4	2134	1.8
18 F	0440	0.6	0950	1.6	1702	0.4	2246	1.9
19 SA	0533	0.6	1110	1.7	1753	0.4	2349	2.0
20 SU	0744	0.6	1211	1.8	1734	0.4		
21 M	0034	2.2	0856	0.6	1255	2.0	1803	0.4
22 TU	0114	2.3	0949	0.6	1334	2.1	1840	0.4
23 W ●	0153	2.4	0711	0.5	1413	2.3	1918	0.3
24 TH	0233	2.4	0745	0.5	1453	2.4	1957	0.4
25 F	0314	2.4	0822	0.4	1534	2.4	2038	0.4
26 SA	0356	2.3	0902	0.4	1616	2.5	2124	0.4
27 SU	0440	2.3	0948	0.3	1700	2.4		
28 M	0043	0.5	0527	2.1	1040	0.3	1747	2.4
29 TU	0124	0.5	0618	2.0	1141	0.3	1841	2.2
30 W ◑	0203	0.6	0721	1.8	1252	0.2	1955	2.1

DECEMBER

Day	Time	m	Time	m	Time	m	Time	m
1 TH	0400	0.6	0841	1.7	1402	0.3	2122	2.1
2 F	0520	0.6	0958	1.7	1510	0.3	2236	2.1
3 SA	0640	0.6	1107	1.8	1846	0.3	2339	2.1
4 SU	0753	0.6	1203	1.9	1941	0.3		
5 M	0030	2.2	0848	0.6	1251	2.0	2024	0.3
6 TU	0116	2.2	0923	0.6	1335	2.1	2050	0.4
7 W	0159	2.2	0952	0.6	1416	2.2	2115	0.4
8 TH ○	0241	2.2	0758	0.5	1455	2.2	2154	0.5
9 F	0320	2.1	0835	0.5	1532	2.2	2242	0.5
10 SA	0356	2.1	1158	0.4	1608	2.2	2333	0.5
11 SU	0431	2.1	0944	0.4	1645	2.2		
12 M	0019	0.6	0503	2.0	1023	0.3	1721	2.2
13 TU	0059	0.6	0536	2.0	1107	0.3	1757	2.1
14 W	0137	0.6	0612	1.9	1155	0.3	1836	2.0
15 TH	0219	0.6	0654	1.8	1249	0.3	1924	2.0
16 F ◑	0307	0.6	0749	1.8	1346	0.3	2039	1.9
17 SA	0359	0.6	0902	1.7	1441	0.3	2147	2.0
18 SU	0448	0.6	1010	1.8	1537	0.3	2247	2.0
19 M	0452	0.6	1114	1.8	1633	0.3	2345	2.1
20 TU	0530	0.6	1211	2.0	1727	0.3		
21 W	0037	2.2	0610	0.5	1301	2.1	1816	0.3
22 TH	0125	2.3	0650	0.5	1347	2.2	1902	0.4
23 F ●	0211	2.3	0729	0.4	1432	2.3	1946	0.4
24 SA	0257	2.3	0809	0.4	1516	2.4	2029	0.5
25 SU	0343	2.2	0850	0.3	1601	2.4		
26 M	0009	0.5	0429	2.2	0936	0.2	1648	2.4
27 TU	0100	0.5	0517	2.1	1025	0.2	1737	2.4
28 W	0152	0.6	0609	2.0	1119	0.1	1831	2.3
29 TH	0246	0.6	0706	1.9	1221	0.1	1935	2.2
30 F ◑	0347	0.6	0809	1.9	1329	0.2	2045	2.1
31 SA	0453	0.6	0914	1.8	1437	0.2	2153	2.1

Chart Datum is 0·92 metres below NAP Datum. HAT is 2·5 metres above Chart Datum.

>> FREE monthly updates. Register at <<
www.reedsnauticalalmanac.co.uk

2.21A MAAS TSS, PRECAUTIONARY AREA AND MAASGEUL

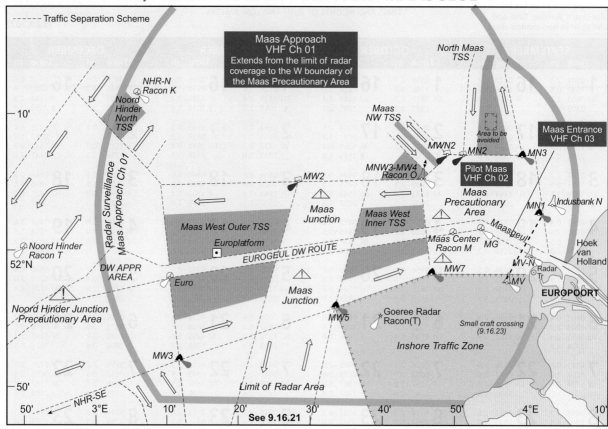

2.22 HOEK VAN HOLLAND AND NIEUWE WATERWEG VTS

Nieuwe Waterweg VTS and Nieuwe Maas *continued*

CROSSING THE MAASGEUL To cross the entrance (ie seaward of the bkwtrs) coasting yachts should advise *Maas Ent* Ch 03 of position/course/speed, then monitor Ch 03. Cross on the recommended track, 046° (226°) under power; see chartlet. Beware strong cross-tides. Keep a keen lookout for fast-moving merchantmen; Rules 18 d (ii) and 28.

HOEK VAN HOLLAND

CHARTS AC 122, 132; Zeekaart 1540, 1349, 1350, 1449; DYC 1801.6, 1801.7; Imray C30, Y5

TIDES +0251 Dover; ML 0·9; Duration 0505. HOEK VAN HOLLAND is a Standard Port (←), but has no Secondary ports; see also Rotterdam. Double LWs occur, more obviously at sp; in effect a LW stand. The 1st LW is about 5½hrs after HW and the 2nd LW about 4¼hrs before the next HW. Predictions are for the *lower* LW. Prolonged NW gales can raise levels by up to 3m.

SHELTER Entry safe, but in strong onshore winds heavy seas/swell develop. The first adequate shelter is 6M upriver at Maassluis (3m). Complete shelter 10-19M further E at Rotterdam.

NAVIGATION From N, WPT 52°02′·89N 04°03′·57E (Indusbank NCM lt buoy, Q) 190°/3·2M to Noorderdam lt, FR.

From S, WPT 51°59′·61N 04°00′·20E (MV-N buoy) 101°/3·0M to ent to Nieuwe Waterweg. *Yachts must on no account enter the Calandkanaal or Europoort. Stay in the Nieuwe Waterweg.*

LIGHTS AND MARKS See chartlet and Lights, buoys and waypoints for details. Outer ldg lts 112° to ent; then 107° R (ie keep to port) ldg lts into Nieuwe Waterweg, both R trs, W bands.

Hbr patrol vessels show a Fl Bu lt; additionally a Fl R lt = 'Stop'.

COMMUNICATIONS (Code 0174) TC/Port Authority (010) 2522801; Police (0900) 8844; Brit Consul (020) 6764343; Ⓗ 4112800.

FACILITIES Berghaven, use only in emergencies, HM 638850.

Hoek van Holland 🛥 🅟 ✕ ⌂ 🛒 ✉ Ⓑ ⇌ ✈ (Rotterdam). **Ferries** Hook–Harwich; Rotterdam (Vlaardingen)–Hull.

Maasluis Binnenhaven, bridge, (HM 5912852 Ch 68) ⌓ quay, picturesque town centre, only charge €6 for bridge transit.

NIEUWE WATERWEG VTS

Arrival procedure for yachts First report to *Maas Approach* or *Pilot Maas*, depending on distance offshore (or *Maas Ent* if within 4M of hbr ent) stating name/type of vessel, position and destination. Obey any instructions, monitoring the relevant Radar Ch's (limits as shown by W ☐ signboards on the riverbanks; Km signs are similar).

Rules for yachts in Nieuwe Waterweg/Nieuwe Maas:
Crossing the Nieuwe Waterweg S to N or vice versa is not permitted without VTS permission. Monitor VTS channels (see below); transmit only in emergency or if obliged to deviate from the usual traffic flow. Keep to extreme stbd limit of buoyed line, avoiding debris between buoys and bank. No tacking/beating; no ⚓. Engine ready for instant start. Able to motor at 3·24kn (6km/h). Hoist a radar reflector, esp in poor vis or at night. Cross chan quickly at 90°. All docks are prohib to yachts, except to access a marina. *Keep a good lookout, especially astern.*

The 3 **Traffic Centres (TC)** oversee their Radar surveillance stations and sub-sectors *(italics)*, on dedicated VHF chans below:

- **TC Hoek van Holland (VCH)** Ch 11. (See chart previous page)

Maas Approach	Ch 01	38 – 11M W of Hoek;
Pilot Maas	Ch 02	11 – 4M W of Hoek;
Maas Entrance	Ch 03	4M – km 1031.

  English is the primary language on Ch 01, 02 and 03.

Rozenburg	Ch 65	km 1031 – 1028;
Maassluis	Ch 80	km 1028 – 1017.

- **Botlek Information & Tracking system** Ch 14.

Botlek	Ch 61	km 1017 – 1011;
Eemhaven	Ch 63	km 1011 – 1007.

- **TC Rotterdam (VCR)** *Ch 11.*

Waalhaven	Ch 60	km 1007 – 1003·5;
Maasbruggen	Ch 81	km 1003·5 – 998;
Brienenoord	Ch 81	km 998 – 993.

Harbour Coordination Centre (HCC) administers and controls Rotterdam port, Ch 19 (H24).

MSI broadcasts by TCs Ch 11 and on request by Radar stns.

TRAFFIC CENTRE ROTTERDAM Ch 11 AND VTS RADAR SECTORS

2.23 ROTTERDAM

Zuid Holland **51°54'·00N 04°28'·00E** (610m S of Euromast)
❋❋❋⟡⟡⟡❀❀❀

CHARTS AC 122, 132, 133; Zeekaart 1540/1/2; DYC 1809.4, 1809.5

TIDES +0414 Dover; ML 0·9; Duration 0440
Standard Port VLISSINGEN (→)

Times				Height (metres)			
High Water		Low Water		MHWS	MHWN	MLWN	MLWS
0300	0900	0400	1000	5·0	4·1	1·1	0·5
1500	2100	1600	2200				

Differences EUROPLATFORM (30M W of Hoek van Holland)
+0005	−0005	−0030	−0055	−2·8	−2·3	−0·6	−0·2

MAASSLUIS (Km 1019)
| +0155 | +0115 | +0100 | +0310 | −2·9 | −2·4 | −0·8 | −0·3 |

VLAARDINGEN (Km 1011)
| +0150 | +0120 | +0130 | +0330 | −2·9 | −2·4 | −0·8 | −0·3 |

NOTE: Double LWs occur. Maasluis and Vlaardingen are referenced to Vlissingen, in UK ATT as above. The Dutch HP33 *Tidal heights and streams in Dutch coastal waters* shows the time differences below, relative to HW and the first LW at Hoek van Holland:

HOEK VAN HOLLAND	HW	1st LW
Maasluis	+0102	+0308
Vlaardingen	+0103	+0333
Rotterdam	+0111	+0341

SHELTER Good in the yacht hbrs where visitors are welcome (see Facilities). There is always a considerable chop/swell in the river due to constant heavy traffic to/from Europoort and Rotterdam.

NAVIGATION See 2.22 for WPTs (to enter Nieuwe Waterweg) and Yacht Rules. From the hbr ent to the conspic Euromast (51°54'·33N 04°28'·00E) is about 18M (33km). 6M W of the Euromast, the very busy Oude Maas joins at km 1013, giving access to Dordrecht and the Delta network of canals/lakes.

COMMUNICATIONS (Code 010) See chartlet above for VTS in central Rotterdam. In emergency call Rotterdam Tfc Centre Ch 11; Police (0900) 8844; ⊜ 2442266; Brit Consul (020) 676 4343; Ⓗ 4112800; Hbr Coordination Centre (HCC) 2522601, also Emergency; see Facilities for VHF Chans at locks/bridges, English is the second language.

FACILITIES Marinas/yacht harbours from seaward:
Vlaardingen YC, 51°53'·98N 04°20'·93E, 400m E of Delta Hotel in Buitenhaven.⟆(3·6-4·4m) or lock (Ch 20) into Oude Haven (2·7m). HM ☎2484333, ⬤⬤⬤⬤.

Spuihaven, 51°54'·00N 04°24'·00E, immediately E of the ent to Wilhelmina Haven. €1.25/m. No lock/bridge to transit. Schiedam YC mob 0644326722, ⟆(1·6-2·8m)⬤.

Coolhaven Yacht Hbr, 51°54'·12N 04°28'·00E; next to Euromast 185m. Access through Parkhaven via lock (Ch 22). ☎4764146, ⟆(2·7m)⬤.

Veerhaven. 51°54'·39N 04°28'·76E, 5ca E of Euromast. ☎4365446, mob 0653536107, www.veerhavenrotterdam.nl info@veerhavenrotterdam.nl Centre for traditional sea-going vessels. Ⓥ welcome, €2·20, ⎅€3·00 p/d. ⟆(3·9m), 350m N,⬤⬤, water taxi to S bank. **Royal Maas YC** ☎4137681 (clubhouse, members only).

City Marina, 51°54'·64N 04°29'·76E. Go under Erasmus bridge (Ch 18) via lifting section at SE end which only opens 1000, 1100, 1330, 1530 & 1900LT or on request Ch 18 2030-0700 1hr before req'd (11m clearance under fixed span). Ldg lts 056·7°, both Iso 2s; then 2nd ent to stbd, via lifting bridge. ☎4854096, mob 0622 215761, www.citymarinarotterdam.nl info@citymarinarotterdam.nl 130 ⟆ +40 Ⓥ in 4m. €2·00 night for 2 nights; €1·50 3rd-7th nights; €1·25 7 nights, ⎅€3·30 p/d. YC, water taxi to N bank, @.

WSV IJsselmonde, 51°54'·24N 04°33'·34E, on S bank at km 994, 800m E of Brienenoordbrug, Ch 20 (off chartlet). ☎4828333, ⟆(1·3-2·1m).

City All facilities, ACA, DYC Agent. **Ferry** Rotterdam (Vlaardingen)–Hull; Hook–Harwich.

2.24 HARINGVLIET (Stellendam and Hellevoetsluis)

Zuid Holland **51°49'·46N 04°02'·29E** (Goereesesluis). Stellendam ❋❀⟡⟡❀

Continued overleaf

HARINGVLIET *continued*

CHARTS AC 1630, 110; Zeekaart 1447, 1448; DYC 1801.6, 1807.6; Imray C30

TIDES +0300 Dover; ML 1·2; Duration 0510

Standard Port VLISSINGEN (→)

Times				Height (metres)			
High Water		Low Water		MHWS	MHWN	MLWN	MLWS
0300	0900	0400	1000	5·0	4·1	1·1	0·5
1500	2100	1600	2200				
Differences HARINGVLIETSLUIZEN							
+0015	+0015	+0015	−0020	−2·1	−1·9	−0·7	−0·3

NOTE: Double LWs occur. The rise after the 1st LW is called the Agger. Water levels on this coast are much affected by weather. Prolonged NW gales can raise levels by up to 3m. Water levels in the Haringvliet can drop by 0·5m an hour when the sluices are open.

SHELTER Good in all the marinas. The entrance to the Slijkgat can be rough in W/NW winds stronger than Force 6, and also with wind against tide. When there is heavy swell, entry into the Slijkgat is not advisable. Call Post Ouddorp, VHF Ch 25 if in doubt.

NAVIGATION WPT 51°51′·95N 03°51′·42E (SG SWM buoy, Iso 4s) 110°/2·7M to SG5/6 chan buoys. Note 1·4m shoal close N bys SG5/6, 7/8 and 9/10. Call Post Ouddorp VHF (see Comms) for latest silting info. Thence 2·4M via the well-buoyed/lit Slijkgat chan to SG15/16 bns. Follow Pampus chan P1,3,5,7,9 SHM buoys SSE for 2·2M to the Buitenhaven. In both these channels intermediate pairs of unlit pillar buoys are also used with suffix A, eg: SG7A, P3A.

Avoid the no-entry sluicing area marked by 4 SPM buoys in the approach to the 24/7 access lock. This has recessed bollards and the 2 bridges lift in sequence to minimise road tfc delays. Note: seaward, W bridge does not operate in winds >F7 and has 14m vertical clearance when lowered (indicated by digital gauge on seaward side of lock). The E bridge has only 5·4m vert clearance.

Hellevoetsluis is 2·6M E of Stellendam marina on the N bank. Three hbrs from W: Heliushaven, Het Groote Dok and Koopvaardijhaven,

a lt ho (see below) marks ent to Groote Dok.

LIGHTS AND MARKS Haringvlietsluizen: 3 ● in △ are shown from pier heads on dam when sluicing in progress. Groote Dok LtHo: Iso WRG 10s 16m W11M, R8M, G7M; W tower, R top; 266°-G-275°-W-294°-R-316°-W036°-G-058°-W-095°-R-140°.

COMMUNICATIONS Post Ouddorp (lighthouse) VHF Ch 25 for weather, advice and assistance, daily, 0800-1600, Thur/Fri H24 ⊖ Rotterdam (010) 4298088 or Vlissingen (0118) 484600; Emergencies 112; Brit Consul (020) 676 4343; Stellendam Port HM 0187 491000; Lock (Walcheren Canal) (0118) 412840; Lock 0187 497350, *Goereese Sluis* VHF Ch 20 for bridges and lock; Hellevoetsluis HM (and locks) VHF Ch 74.

FACILITIES Stellendam Marina ☎0187 493769, VHF Ch 31. www.marinastellendam.nl info@marinastellendam.nl 200 � inc⒱ €2·00 inc tourist tax ⚓ 🚻. Berth as directed in 3m; all pontoons have fingers. 🛢🏪✕🔧🛠⚓🔨(20t) ☎0187 492344, bike hire.

Town (4½km) ✕ 🏪 🚮 ✉. ✈ (Rotterdam). Bus to Vlissingen & Spijkenisse. **Ferry** Hoek of Holland-Harwich; Rotterdam-Hull.

Heliushaven On the E side is **Marina Cape Helius** ☎0181 310056, mob 0613181974. www.marina-capehelius.nl havenkantoor@marina-capehelius.nl €1·50 + €0·70 pp/day tax; 🛢. There are also 3 YCs situated on the W side of Heliushaven which may be able to help with berthing.

YC Helius ☎0181 316563, mob 0616 756515; €1·40 + €0·70 pp/day tax; 🛢.

YC Hellevoetsluis ☎0181 315868, €1·40 + €0·70 pp/day tax.

YC Haringvliet ☎0181 314748, €1·35 + €0·70 pp/day tax.

Groote Dok. ⒱ ⌣ before the bridge, ⌁🔨⚓. In summer the bridge opens every hour. After the bridge is **Marina Hellevoetsluis** ☎0181 312166. www.marina-capehelius.nl info@marina-capehelius.nl €1·50 + €0·70 pp/day tax; 🛢. Reports welcome.

Koopvaardijhaven. ⒱ berths with ⌁ on the W side, though there can also be a lot of commercial traffic here. Reports welcome.

Yagra BY (E bank) ☎0181 314748, mob 06 29403177. www.jachtservice-reparatie.nl Reports welcome.

Town ✕ 🏪 🚮 ✉.

2.25 ROOMPOTSLUIS (for Oosterschelde)

Zeeland **51°37′·11N 03°41′·08E** Roompot Lock

CHARTS AC 1630, 110; Zeekaart 1448; DYCs 1805.8, 1801.5; Imray C30

TIDES +0230 Dover

Standard Port VLISSINGEN (→)

Times				Height (metres)			
High Water		Low Water		MHWS	MHWN	MLWN	MLWS
0300	0900	0400	1000	5·0	4·1	1·1	0·5
1500	2100	1600	2200				
Differences ROOMPOT BUITEN							
−0015	+0005	+0005	−0020	−1·3	−1·1	−0·4	−0·1

SHELTER An approach in strong SW through NW winds is not advised. The Buitenhaven's inner part is sheltered.

NAVIGATION WPT 51°39′·35N 03°33′·65E (abeam OR1 SHM buoy) 122°/4·2M via Oude Roompot chan to the 073·5° ldg line, both Oc G 5s, into the Buitenhaven. The flood sets E from HW Vlissingen −3 to +1. See Passage information for the several offshore banks.

Alternatively Roompot chan, buoyed but unlit, is further south and closer inshore.

Keep clear of the buoyed areas, W and E of the storm-surge barrier, which are very dangerous due to strong tidal streams and many obstructions.

Netherlands

Roompotsluis lock, ☎0111659265 (H24), beware tide in approach, waiting pontoons (no overnight stays) W and E of lock with intercom to control centre. Custom clearance at lock in season.

The fixed bridge has 18·2m least clearance. At LW clearance is approx 21m. Check with tide gauges or lock-keeper if in doubt. Small bollards, fixed at vertical intervals, are recessed into the lock walls. Ent to/exit from the lock is controlled by R/G traffic lights.

LIGHTS AND MARKS See Lights, buoys and waypoints and chartlet.

COMMUNICATIONS (Code 0113) Lock *Roompotsluis* Ch 18. Roompot Marina Ch 31. Monitor Ch 68 which broadcasts local forecasts at H+15. Dr 372565; ⊖ (0118) 484600.

FACILITIES Roompot Marina Good shelter, 1·5M SE of lock. Beware cross tide and LW depth 1·5m-1·2m at ent. ☎405110, marina@roompot.nl. 250 + 80 Ⓥ, €2·00 + €1·60pp/day tax, 🅿🛠✕◻🛒▢🅱▬ Alternatively, follow G3-G17 buoys into **Betonhaven** about 1M NE of the lock. ⚓ in 3-6m, good holding in sticky black mud. Easy walk to the Delta Expo.

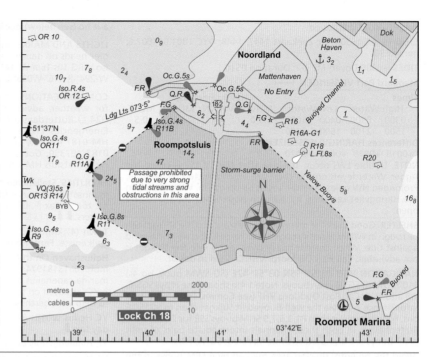

Lock Ch 18

Roompot Marina

2.26 WESTERSCHELDE

Zeeland mostly, but Belgium for the last 12M to Antwerpen

CHARTS AC 1874, 120, 128; Zeekaart 1443; BE 103, 104; DYC 1803; Imray C30

TIDES +0200 Dover; ML Hansweert 2·7, Westkapelle 2·0, Bath 2·8; Duration 0555

Standard Port VLISSINGEN (⟶)

Times				Height (metres)			
High Water		Low Water		MHWS	MHWN	MLWN	MLWS
0300	0900	0400	1000	5·0	4·1	1·1	0·5
1500	2100	1600	2200				
Differences WESTKAPELLE (8M NW of Vlissingen)							
−0025	−0015	−0010	−0025	−0·7	−0·6	−0·2	−0·1
HANSWEERT							
+0100	+0050	+0040	+0100	+0·6	+0·6	0·0	0·0
BATH							
+0125	+0115	+0115	+0140	+1·1	+1·0	0·0	0·0

SHELTER In strong winds a bad sea can be met in the estuary mouth. Conditions become easier further upriver. See Facilities.

NAVIGATION Westerschelde is the waterway to Antwerpen (and via canal to Gent) very full of ships and barges, especially in the last 15M. The main channel winds through a mass of well-marked sandbanks. It is essential to work the tides, which average 2½kn, more at springs. Best timing is most easily achieved by starting from Vlissingen, Breskens or Terneuzen. Yachts should keep to the edge of main chan. Use alternative chans with caution; Vaarwater langs Hoofdplat and de Paulinapolder/Thomasgeul are buoyed shortcuts popular with yachtsmen, but note that channels shift regularly.

Commercial shipping: Yachts should keep just outside the busy shipping chans, ie Wielingen from the SW, Scheur from the W, and Oostgat from the NW. A listening watch on Ch 10 (ship-to-ship) is compulsory above buoy 100 (near Antwerpen).

Be aware of large ship anchorages, Wielingen Noord and Zuid, either side of the fairway, as defined by buoys W6-Trawl-WN6 and W9-Songa. Further E, Flushing Roads anchorage is defined by Songa, SS1, SS5 and ARV-VH buoys. Ocean-going ships often manoeuvre off Vlissingen to transfer pilots.

S of Vlissingen (see Breskens) an E–W TSS (part of a Precautionary area) is best avoided by yachts which should cross the fairway via the recommended N–S track between Buitenhaven and ARV3 SPM lt buoy. Fast ferries, which have right of way, ply half-hourly from Vlissingen Buitenhaven to Breskens. *Keep a sharp lookout*.

Recommended small craft routes: From the SW there are few

dangers. After Zeebrugge, keep S of the Wielingen chan buoys (W1-9). Off Breskens avoid fast ferries to/from Vlissingen; continue E to SS1 buoy, then cross to Vlissingen on a N'ly track.

From the W, keep clear of the Scheur chan by crossing to the S of Wielingen as soon as practicable.

From the N, the narrow, busy Oostgat can be used with caution, keeping just outside the SW edge of the buoyed/lit chan.

Three lesser, unlit day-only N'ly routes which avoid Oostgat are:
• From Kaloo or DR1 buoys, follow the Geul van de Rassen, Deurloo & Spleet chans to SP4 buoy. Thence E via WN6 buoy.
• Or continue down Deurloo from DL5 by to join Oostgat at OG19 by; thence cross to the N shore when Oostgat tfc permits.
• Another route, slightly further offshore, is to skirt the NW side of Kaloo bank to Botkil-W buoy, thence SE via Geul van de Walvischstaart (PHM buoys only) to Trawl SCM buoy.

LIGHTS AND MARKS The apprs are well lit by lighthouses: on the S shore at Nieuwe Sluis, and on the N shore at Westkapelle; see Lights, buoys and waypoints. The main fairways are, for the most part, defined by ldg lts and by the W sectors of the many Dir lts.

SCHELDEMOND VTS (www.vts-scheldt.net) covers from the North Sea outer approaches upriver to Antwerpen; see the diagram below and TSS off S Netherlands. Yachts should monitor at all times the VHF Ch for the area in which they are, so as to be aware of other shipping and to be contactable if required. Do not transmit, unless called. 7 **Traffic Centres** control the Areas below, within which radar stations provide radar, weather and hbr info, as shown below:

Outer approaches: (*Traffic Centre* is the callsign prefix)		
Wandelaar	Ch 65	*Zeebrugge Radar* Ch 04.
Zeebrugge	Ch 69	*Radar* as in line above.
Steenbank	Ch 64	*Radar* also on Ch 64.
In the Westerschelde: (*Centrale* is the callsign prefix)		
Vlissingen	Ch 14	*Radar* Ch 21. Vlissingen to E2A/PvN SPR buoys (51°24'N 03°44'E).
Terneuzen	Ch 03	*Radar* Ch 03. Thence to Nos 32/ 35 buoys (51°23'N 03°57'E). Ch 11 Terneuzen-Gent Canal.
Hansweert	Ch 65	*Radar* Ch 65. Thence to Nos 46/ 55 buoys (51°24'N 04°02'E).
Zandvliet	Ch 12	Thence to Antwerpen. *Radar Waarde* 19; *Saeftinge* 21; *Zandvliet* 04; *Kruisschans* 66.

WESTERSCHELDE *continued*

In **emergency**, call initially on the working channel in use; state yacht's name, position and the nature of the problem. You may then be switched to Ch **67 (Emergency)** or another VHF channel.

Broadcasts of visibility, Met, tidal data and ship movements are made in Dutch at: H +00 by *Terneuzen* Ch 11; H +10 by *Zeebrugge* Ch 69; H +30 by *Zandvliet* Ch 12; H +50 by *Centrale Vlissingen* Ch 14; **H +55 by Radar Vlissingen Ch 21 in English.**

FACILITIES Some minor hbrs from Terneuzen to Antwerpen (38M) are listed below. They may be useful in emergency or offer shelter, but most dry. Yachts usually go non-stop to Antwerpen.

ELLEWOUTSDIJK, 51°23′·10N 03°49′·05E. BE 103; DYC 1803.2. HW +2 and +0.3m on Vlissingen; ML 2·6m. Small, unlit hbr, 27 ⌓ voluntary donation. 1·5m at MLWS. Strong cross-eddy on ebb. HM ☎(0113) 548431/06 251154766, ▮ @ ▷(10t) YC.

HOEDEKENSKERKE, 51°25′·11N 03°54′·90E. BE 103; DYC 1803.3. Disused ferry hbr (dries) abeam MG13 SHM buoy (Iso G 4s). €1·00/m (min €8·00/night) inc ⊅ ⚓. **YC WV Hoedekenskerke** ☎(0113) 639278, mob 0653794069. 33 + 6♥ ⚓ ▮ ⚠ ▷ at campsite 400m. **Town** ✉ ⑧ ⇌ (Goes).

HANSWEERT, 51°26′·37N 04°00′·66E. BE 103; DYC 1803.3. Tidal differences above. Temporary stop, but it is the busy ent to Zuid Beveland canal, lock Ch 22. Lt Oc WRG 10s, R lattice tr, W band, at ent. Waiting berths outside lock on E side. **No smoking or naked**

flames in, or near lock. Services: ▮ ▮ ✗ ⚓ ⚒ ♺ ▷(17t). **Town** ✉ ⑧ ⇌ (Kruiningen-Yerseke).

WALSOORDEN, 51°22′·93N 04°02′·10E. BE 103; DYC 1803.3. HW is +0110 and +0·7m on Vlissingen; ML 2·6m. Prone to swell. SHM buoy 57, Iso G 8s, is 500m N of ent where 16 silos are conspic. Ldg lts 220° both Oc 3s. Hbr ent FG & FR. Unmarked stone pier just outside E hbr pier, partly dries at LW. Yacht basin dead ahead on ent to hbr, depths 2 to 2·8m. 4/5 ⌓ €0·30/m, max stay 24hrs. *Zandvliet Radio* VHF Ch 12. WSV d'Ouwe Haven ☎(0114) 681235, ⚓ ▮ ▮ ⚠ ▷ ⑧ ♺ ▷(16t) ▃. **Town** ✗ ✉ ✉.

PAAL, 51°21′·25N 04°06′·65E. BE 103; DYC 1803.3. HW +0120 and +0·8m on Vlissingen; ML 2·7m. Appr via No 63 SHM buoy and tide gauge, across drying Speelmansgat. Unlit, drying yacht hbr on S bank at river mouth, ent marked by withy. HM ☎(0114) 314974, 0611 028174. *Zandvliet Radio* Ch 12. **Jachthaven** 150 ⌓ ⓟ €0·50, ▮ ⚒ ✗ ⛽ ⚓ in YC. ⑦ (10 mins walk). **Yachtclub** ☎(0114) 315548; www.wv-saeftinghe.nl

DOEL, 51°18′·67N 04°16′·11E. BE 103; DYC 1803.5. HW +0100 and +0·7m on Vlissingen. Small drying hbr next to 'ghost town' on W bank. Ldg lts 188·5°: front Fl WR 3s on N pier hd; rear Fl 3s, synch. HM ☎(03) 5758103; **YC de Noord** ☎7733669, open to visitors, ⚓ ✗ ▷.

LILLO, 51°18′·16N 04°17′·30E. BE 103; DYC 1803.5. 1M SE of Doel on opp bank; small drying hbr for shoal-draft only; Customs base. T-jetty has Oc WRG 10s. HM (035) 686456; small YC, Scaldis, is named after local restaurant original members used for meetings.

2.27 VLISSINGEN (FLUSHING)

Zeeland 51°26′·31N 03°34′·61E Koopmanshaven ❁❁⚓⚓⚓❀❀❀

CHARTS AC 1872, 1874, 120; Zeekaart 1442, 1443, 1533; BE 103; DYC 1803.2, 1801.4; Imray C30

TIDES +0210 Dover; ML 2·3; Duration 0555. Note: Vlissingen is a Standard Port (➡)

SHELTER Very good in both yacht hbrs.

NAVIGATION WPT 51°25′·16N 03°33′·66E (Songa SHM buoy, QG) 027°/1·29M to Koopmanshaven ent. Keep to W pier side, strong crossflow until piers. Study Westerschelde (previous page).

LIGHTS AND MARKS From North West, Oostgat 117° ldg lts: Front RW pile; rear Sardijngeul, Oc WR 5s, R/W banded mast, R △. Note: Conspic radar twr (close NW of Koopmanshaven) shows a Fl Y lt to warn when ships are approaching in the blind NW arc through the well buoyed Oostgat–Sardijngeul chan.

A conspic, floodlit R/W metal framework tr (50m) near de Ruyter Marina indicates the appr. Buitenhaven traffic signals from mole W side of ent: R flag or extra ● near FR on W mole lt = No entry.

COMMUNICATIONS (Code 0118) Emergency 112; Schelde Traffic Coordination Centre 424760; Police 0900-8844; ⊖ 484600; Brit Consul (020) 676 4343; Dr 412233; Port HM 414498, VHF Ch 14;

Walcheren Canal, 0118 412372; sealock VHF Ch 18; Canal bridges VHF Ch 22, see also Westerschelde; Michiel de Ruyter and Schelde Marinas, no VHF; use mobile.

FACILITIES
Michiel de Ruyter Marina (2·9m) ☎+31118414498; info@ brasserieevertsen.nl www.michielderuyterhaven.nl *Pre-booking in season is strongly advised.* 100 + 40♥ €2·20/m + €1·60pp/day tax. ✗ ▷ ◎ @ free wi-fi; ⊕ (22t) ⚒ ✗ ⑧.
Ent is 6m narrow, over a sill with 1·2m water at MLWS. Access HW±4. Check depth gauge on outer wall or with HM. 2 small footbridges (R/G tfc lts) are swiftly swung open by HM 0800-2200LT. They stay open 2200–0800LT, but only for yachts to leave; ●● (vert) tfc lts prohibit arrival from sea. Storm barrier is open 1/4-1/11. Beware high speed Pilot boats using the adjacent inlet.

VVW Schelde (2·8-4·1m) ☎,+31 118465912, HM mob 0615538515. www.vvwschelde.nl 80 + 80♥ €2·00 inc ⓟ wi-fi, + €1·60 pp/day tax. ⊅ €1·00/4kWh. 500m walk to ferry. ▮ ✗ ▷ ◎ ▃ (12t max) At ent to the Buitenhaven beware ferries; keep to port, pass S of the ferry terminal for the most N'ly and smallest sealock, which operates H24. Waiting possible on piles to SE.

Town ✗ ▷ ⥮ ⑦⚓ ✉ ⑧ ⇌ ✈ Antwerpen). Foot ferry to Breskens; road tunnel to Terneuzen. At Middelburg: ♺ ⚒ ✗ ⚠.

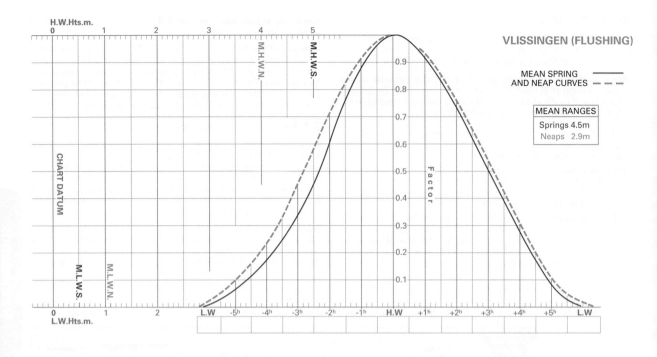

H.W.Hts.m.

CHART DATUM

M.H.W.N.

M.H.W.S.

M.L.W.S.

M.L.W.N.

Factor

VLISSINGEN (FLUSHING)

MEAN SPRING ——————
AND NEAP CURVES – – – – –

MEAN RANGES
Springs 4.5m
Neaps 2.9m

L.W.Hts.m.

L.W -5ʰ -4ʰ -3ʰ -2ʰ -1ʰ H.W +1ʰ +2ʰ +3ʰ +4ʰ +5ʰ L.W

VLISSINGEN *continued*

HM Ch 14

DE RUYTER MARINA
Small pedestrian
swing bridges

Building(80m)
conspic

VLISSINGEN

Disused Lock

Walcheren Canal

Middelburg 3·5M

RoRoTerminal

VVW Schelde

Oil tanks

Oil tanks

Schelde Shipyard

Binnenhaven No.2   No.1

Buitenhaven

Spire ⌖(conspic)
Michiel de Ruyter Marina

Schelde Tfc Centre Rdr Twr (conspic)

Radar Tr

Tr R/W (conspic)

Locks
Disused

Ferry Terminal

High buildings

Ldg Lts 117°

VQ(3)5s SG-W

BYB

OcR5s

Iso.WRG.3s

Oc.WR.5s
F.R

F.G

RV2
R

RV4
R

RV6
R
Iso.R.4s

W

IsoWRG4s10m
F.R

Q(9)15s

F.G

Oc.WR.5s

Recommended crossing track for yachts

Iso.WRG.3s

Recommended crossing track for yachts

metres cables

N edge of Precautionary TSS

STANDARD TIME UT –01
Subtract 1 hour for UT
For Dutch Summer Time add
ONE hour in **non-shaded areas**

VLISSINGEN   LAT 51°27′N   LONG 3°36′E
TIMES AND HEIGHTS OF HIGH AND LOW WATERS

Dates in red are **SPRINGS**
Dates in blue are **NEAPS**

YEAR **2022**

Netherlands

JANUARY

Time	m	Time	m
1 0012	4.8	**16** 0114	4.3
0635	0.8	0724	1.0
SA 1233	4.8	SU 1329	4.4
1905	0.6	1936	1.0
2 0104	4.9	**17** 0151	4.4
0731	0.7	0803	0.9
SU 1324	5.0	M 1405	4.6
● 1955	0.6	○ 2013	1.0
3 0154	4.9	**18** 0224	4.6
0822	0.5	0840	0.8
M 1414	5.1	TU 1439	4.7
2043	0.6	2048	0.9
4 0242	5.0	**19** 0257	4.7
0912	0.4	0917	0.7
TU 1503	5.2	W 1513	4.8
2129	0.7	2124	0.9
5 0330	4.9	**20** 0330	4.7
1001	0.4	0955	0.6
W 1552	5.1	TH 1547	4.8
2214	0.8	2200	0.9
6 0417	4.9	**21** 0404	4.7
1048	0.4	1033	0.5
TH 1641	5.0	F 1621	4.8
2258	0.9	2236	0.9
7 0505	4.8	**22** 0439	4.7
1135	0.4	1110	0.5
F 1732	4.9	SA 1657	4.8
2343	1.0	2312	0.9
8 0554	4.7	**23** 0516	4.7
1222	0.5	1148	0.6
SA 1824	4.7	SU 1737	4.7
		2351	0.9
9 0030	1.1	**24** 0557	4.6
0645	4.5	1228	0.6
SU 1310	0.7	M 1823	4.7
◑ 1919	4.5		
10 0122	1.3	**25** 0034	1.0
0739	4.3	0645	4.5
M 1403	0.8	TU 1314	0.6
2019	4.3	◑ 1919	4.5
11 0224	1.4	**26** 0126	1.0
0841	4.1	0744	4.4
TU 1504	1.0	W 1409	0.7
2129	4.1	2026	4.4
12 0334	1.4	**27** 0230	1.1
0951	4.0	0855	4.3
W 1618	1.1	TH 1515	0.9
2238	4.1	2137	4.3
13 0449	1.4	**28** 0346	1.1
1059	4.1	1009	4.3
TH 1724	1.1	F 1633	0.9
2338	4.1	2250	4.3
14 0551	1.3	**29** 0509	1.1
1157	4.2	1119	4.4
F 1815	1.1	SA 1750	0.9
		2357	4.4
15 0030	4.2	**30** 0623	0.9
0641	1.2	1222	4.7
SA 1247	4.3	SU 1852	0.8
1858	1.1		
		31 0055	4.6
		0722	0.6
		M 1318	4.9
		1944	0.7

FEBRUARY

Time	m	Time	m
1 0146	4.8	**16** 0206	4.6
0815	0.4	0823	0.7
TU 1408	5.0	W 1423	4.8
● 2032	0.7	○ 2029	0.9
2 0232	4.9	**17** 0238	4.7
0903	0.3	0859	0.5
W 1454	5.1	TH 1455	4.9
2116	0.7	2105	0.8
3 0317	5.0	**18** 0310	4.8
0948	0.2	0935	0.4
TH 1539	5.2	F 1527	5.0
2158	0.7	2141	0.7
4 0359	5.0	**19** 0343	4.9
1031	0.2	1013	0.4
F 1622	5.1	SA 1600	5.0
2238	0.8	2218	0.7
5 0441	4.9	**20** 0417	4.9
1112	0.3	1050	0.3
SA 1706	5.0	SU 1636	5.0
2316	0.9	2254	0.7
6 0523	4.9	**21** 0453	4.9
1150	0.4	1127	0.4
SU 1749	4.8	M 1714	4.9
2355	1.0	2331	0.7
7 0606	4.7	**22** 0532	4.9
1229	0.6	1206	0.4
M 1834	4.5	TU 1757	4.8
8 0036	1.1	**23** 0012	0.7
0650	4.5	0617	4.8
TU 1311	0.8	W 1249	0.5
◐ 1920	4.3	◑ 1849	4.6
9 0125	1.2	**24** 0101	0.8
0740	4.2	0713	4.6
W 1403	1.0	TH 1341	0.7
2013	4.0	1954	4.3
10 0234	1.3	**25** 0205	1.0
0841	4.0	0826	4.3
TH 1513	1.2	F 1449	0.9
2126	3.8	2110	4.1
11 0353	1.4	**26** 0326	1.1
1006	3.8	0949	4.2
F 1631	1.3	SA 1615	1.1
2259	3.8	2234	4.0
12 0508	1.4	**27** 0458	1.1
1126	3.9	1111	4.3
SA 1739	1.3	SU 1741	1.0
		2349	4.2
13 0003	3.9	**28** 0617	0.8
0613	1.2	1220	4.5
SU 1226	4.1	M 1845	0.9
1833	1.2		
14 0053	4.1		
0704	1.0		
M 1312	4.3		
1916	1.1		
15 0132	4.4		
0746	0.9		
TU 1350	4.6		
1954	1.0		

MARCH

Time	m	Time	m
1 0048	4.5	**16** 0105	4.3
0716	0.6	0721	0.8
TU 1314	4.8	W 1324	4.6
1935	0.8	1930	0.9
2 0136	4.7	**17** 0139	4.6
0805	0.3	0758	0.6
W 1359	5.0	TH 1357	4.8
● 2019	0.7	2005	0.8
3 0218	4.9	**18** 0210	4.8
0849	0.2	0833	0.4
TH 1440	5.1	F 1428	5.0
2059	0.7	○ 2041	0.7
4 0257	5.0	**19** 0242	4.9
0929	0.2	0909	0.3
F 1519	5.1	SA 1500	5.1
2137	0.7	2118	0.6
5 0336	5.0	**20** 0316	5.0
1008	0.2	0947	0.2
SA 1558	5.1	SU 1535	5.1
2214	0.7	2156	0.5
6 0414	5.0	**21** 0351	5.1
1044	0.3	1026	0.2
SU 1637	5.0	M 1612	5.1
2249	0.7	2234	0.5
7 0451	4.9	**22** 0429	5.1
1118	0.4	1104	0.3
M 1714	4.8	TU 1651	5.0
2322	0.8	2313	0.5
8 0529	4.8	**23** 0509	5.0
1150	0.6	1144	0.4
TU 1752	4.6	W 1735	4.8
2355	0.9	2356	0.6
9 0607	4.6	**24** 0555	4.9
1223	0.8	1228	0.5
W 1830	4.3	TH 1826	4.5
10 0030	1.1	**25** 0047	0.7
0650	4.3	0652	4.6
TH 1303	1.0	F 1322	0.8
◑ 1915	4.0	◑ 1933	4.2
11 0118	1.2	**26** 0153	0.9
0745	4.0	0811	4.2
F 1413	1.3	SA 1435	1.1
2013	3.7	2056	3.9
12 0310	1.4	**27** 0319	1.0
0902	3.7	0941	4.1
SA 1550	1.4	SU 1610	1.2
2149	3.5	2226	3.9
13 0429	1.4	**28** 0455	1.0
1051	3.7	1108	4.3
SU 1704	1.4	M 1737	1.1
2331	3.7	2342	4.1
14 0540	1.2	**29** 0610	0.7
1159	4.0	1216	4.6
M 1805	1.2	TU 1837	0.9
15 0024	4.0	**30** 0037	4.4
0638	1.0	0704	0.5
TU 1246	4.3	W 1305	4.8
1852	1.0	1922	0.8
		31 0120	4.6
		0749	0.3
		TH 1344	5.0
		2002	0.7

APRIL

Time	m	Time	m
1 0158	4.8	**16** 0137	4.8
0828	0.2	0802	0.4
F 1421	5.0	SA 1357	5.1
● 2039	0.7	○ 2013	0.6
2 0235	4.9	**17** 0212	5.0
0906	0.2	0840	0.3
SA 1457	5.0	SU 1432	5.2
2114	0.6	2052	0.5
3 0311	5.0	**18** 0248	5.1
0941	0.3	0920	0.2
SU 1533	5.0	M 1510	5.2
2150	0.6	2133	0.4
4 0346	5.0	**19** 0326	5.2
1015	0.4	1001	0.3
M 1608	4.9	TU 1549	5.1
2223	0.7	2215	0.4
5 0421	4.9	**20** 0407	5.2
1047	0.5	1042	0.3
TU 1642	4.7	W 1632	5.0
2255	0.7	2258	0.4
6 0455	4.8	**21** 0450	5.0
1116	0.7	1124	0.5
W 1715	4.5	TH 1718	4.7
2324	0.8	2345	0.5
7 0530	4.6	**22** 0540	4.8
1144	0.9	1212	0.7
TH 1749	4.3	F 1813	4.4
2354	0.9		
8 0609	4.3	**23** 0040	0.6
1219	1.0	0644	4.5
F 1829	4.1	SA 1310	0.9
		◑ 1925	4.1
9 0034	1.1	**24** 0150	0.8
0659	4.0	0808	4.3
SA 1309	1.3	SU 1428	1.1
◑ 1926	3.8	2047	3.9
10 0214	1.3	**25** 0315	0.9
0818	3.7	0934	4.2
SU 1514	1.5	M 1606	1.2
2046	3.5	2213	3.9
11 0351	1.3	**26** 0445	0.8
1001	3.7	1057	4.3
M 1627	1.4	TU 1725	1.1
2244	3.6	2324	4.1
12 0459	1.1	**27** 0554	0.6
1121	4.0	1159	4.6
TU 1729	1.2	W 1820	0.9
2345	3.9		
13 0600	0.9	**28** 0016	4.4
1211	4.3	0644	0.4
W 1819	1.0	TH 1245	4.8
		1903	0.8
14 0028	4.3	**29** 0058	4.6
0646	0.7	0726	0.4
TH 1250	4.7	F 1324	4.9
1858	0.9	1940	0.7
15 0103	4.6	**30** 0136	4.7
0725	0.5	0804	0.3
F 1323	4.9	SA 1400	4.9
1935	0.7	● 2016	0.7

Chart Datum is 2·56 metres below NAP Datum. HAT is 5·4 metres above Chart Datum.

STANDARD TIME UT –01
Subtract 1 hour for UT
For Dutch Summer Time add ONE hour in **non-shaded areas**

VLISSINGEN LAT 51°27'N LONG 3°36'E
TIMES AND HEIGHTS OF HIGH AND LOW WATERS

Dates in red are SPRINGS
Dates in blue are NEAPS

YEAR **2022**

MAY

#	Time	m		#	Time	m
1 SU	0211 / 0839 / 1435 / 2051	4.8 / 0.4 / 4.9 / 0.6		**16** M	0142 / 0812 / 1406 / ○2029	5.0 / 0.3 / 5.1 / 0.5
2 M	0246 / 0914 / 1509 / 2127	4.9 / 0.4 / 4.8 / 0.6		**17** TU	0223 / 0855 / 1447 / 2114	5.1 / 0.3 / 5.1 / 0.4
3 TU	0321 / 0947 / 1542 / 2202	4.9 / 0.5 / 4.7 / 0.6		**18** W	0305 / 0939 / 1531 / 2200	5.2 / 0.4 / 5.0 / 0.4
4 W	0355 / 1019 / 1614 / 2235	4.8 / 0.7 / 4.6 / 0.7		**19** TH	0350 / 1023 / 1617 / 2247	5.1 / 0.5 / 4.9 / 0.4
5 TH	0429 / 1049 / 1646 / 2304	4.7 / 0.8 / 4.6 / 0.8		**20** F	0438 / 1109 / 1708 / 2338	5.0 / 0.6 / 4.6 / 0.4
6 F	0503 / 1118 / 1720 / 2335	4.5 / 1.0 / 4.3 / 0.9		**21** SA	0533 / 1159 / 1807	4.8 / 0.8 / 4.4
7 SA	0540 / 1152 / 1759	4.3 / 1.1 / 4.1		**22** SU	0036 / 0643 / 1259 / ◐1916	0.5 / 4.6 / 1.0 / 4.2
8 SU	0016 / 0627 / 1239 / ◐1853	1.0 / 4.1 / 1.3 / 3.9		**23** M	0145 / 0758 / 1416 / 2028	0.6 / 4.4 / 1.1 / 4.1
9 M	0119 / 0743 / 1417 / 2010	1.1 / 3.9 / 1.4 / 3.7		**24** TU	0300 / 0914 / 1542 / 2144	0.7 / 4.3 / 1.2 / 4.0
10 TU	0308 / 0905 / 1544 / 2135	1.1 / 3.8 / 1.4 / 3.7		**25** W	0420 / 1029 / 1658 / 2252	0.7 / 4.4 / 1.1 / 4.2
11 W	0412 / 1027 / 1643 / 2251	1.0 / 4.0 / 1.2 / 3.9		**26** TH	0526 / 1129 / 1753 / 2346	0.6 / 4.6 / 1.0 / 4.4
12 TH	0511 / 1125 / 1734 / 2342	0.9 / 4.2 / 1.0 / 4.3		**27** F	0617 / 1218 / 1837	0.5 / 4.7 / 0.9
13 F	0602 / 1209 / 1819	0.7 / 4.7 / 0.9		**28** SA	0032 / 0659 / 1300 / 1915	4.5 / 0.5 / 4.7 / 0.8
14 SA	0024 / 0647 / 1247 / 1902	4.6 / 0.5 / 4.9 / 0.7		**29** SU	0113 / 0736 / 1339 / 1952	4.6 / 0.5 / 4.7 / 0.7
15 SU	0103 / 0729 / 1326 / 1945	4.8 / 0.4 / 5.1 / 0.6		**30** M	0150 / 0812 / 1415 / ●2029	4.7 / 0.6 / 4.7 / 0.7
				31 TU	0226 / 0847 / 1449 / 2106	4.7 / 0.6 / 4.7 / 0.6

JUNE

#	Time	m		#	Time	m
1 W	0301 / 0921 / 1522 / 2143	4.7 / 0.7 / 4.6 / 0.6		**16** TH	0251 / 0922 / 1518 / 2150	5.1 / 0.5 / 4.9 / 0.3
2 TH	0335 / 0955 / 1554 / 2220	4.7 / 0.8 / 4.5 / 0.7		**17** F	0339 / 1009 / 1607 / 2240	5.1 / 0.6 / 4.8 / 0.3
3 F	0410 / 1028 / 1627 / 2254	4.6 / 0.9 / 4.4 / 0.8		**18** SA	0430 / 1056 / 1700 / 2332	5.0 / 0.7 / 4.7 / 0.3
4 SA	0446 / 1100 / 1703 / 2328	4.5 / 1.0 / 4.3 / 0.8		**19** SU	0527 / 1146 / 1756	4.9 / 0.9 / 4.6
5 SU	0523 / 1136 / 1742	4.4 / 1.1 / 4.2		**20** M	0027 / 0629 / 1242 / 1855	0.4 / 4.7 / 1.0 / 4.4
6 M	0007 / 0607 / 1219 / 1830	0.8 / 4.2 / 1.2 / 4.1		**21** TU	0125 / 0733 / 1345 / ◐1957	0.5 / 4.6 / 1.1 / 4.3
7 TU	0059 / 0707 / 1316 / ◐1933	0.9 / 4.1 / 1.3 / 4.0		**22** W	0226 / 0839 / 1454 / 2103	0.6 / 4.4 / 1.2 / 4.2
8 W	0208 / 0818 / 1434 / 2044	0.9 / 4.1 / 1.3 / 3.9		**23** TH	0336 / 0949 / 1610 / 2210	0.7 / 4.4 / 1.2 / 4.2
9 TH	0315 / 0926 / 1544 / 2152	0.9 / 4.2 / 1.2 / 4.1		**24** F	0447 / 1052 / 1715 / 2311	0.7 / 4.5 / 1.1 / 4.3
10 F	0415 / 1030 / 1642 / 2253	0.8 / 4.4 / 1.1 / 4.3		**25** SA	0543 / 1147 / 1806	0.7 / 4.5 / 1.0
11 SA	0514 / 1125 / 1737 / 2345	0.7 / 4.6 / 0.9 / 4.6		**26** SU	0004 / 0629 / 1236 / 1850	4.4 / 0.7 / 4.5 / 0.9
12 SU	0609 / 1214 / 1830	0.6 / 4.8 / 0.7		**27** M	0052 / 0709 / 1320 / 1931	4.5 / 0.8 / 4.5 / 0.8
13 M	0032 / 0700 / 1300 / 1921	4.8 / 0.5 / 5.0 / 0.6		**28** TU	0135 / 0747 / 1359 / 2010	4.5 / 0.8 / 4.5 / 0.8
14 TU	0118 / 0748 / 1345 / ○2011	5.0 / 0.4 / 5.0 / 0.5		**29** W	0213 / 0823 / 1434 / ●2049	4.6 / 0.8 / 4.6 / 0.7
15 W	0204 / 0835 / 1431 / 2100	5.1 / 0.3 / 5.0 / 0.4		**30** TH	0248 / 0859 / 1507 / 2127	4.6 / 0.9 / 4.6 / 0.7

JULY

#	Time	m		#	Time	m
1 F	0322 / 0935 / 1539 / 2205	4.7 / 0.9 / 4.6 / 0.6		**16** SA	0330 / 0955 / 1556 / 2230	5.1 / 0.7 / 4.9 / 0.3
2 SA	0357 / 1010 / 1613 / 2242	4.6 / 1.0 / 4.5 / 0.7		**17** SU	0419 / 1041 / 1643 / 2318	5.1 / 0.8 / 4.9 / 0.3
3 SU	0432 / 1044 / 1648 / 2318	4.6 / 1.0 / 4.5 / 0.7		**18** M	0510 / 1127 / 1732	5.0 / 0.9 / 4.8
4 M	0507 / 1119 / 1724 / 2354	4.5 / 1.1 / 4.4 / 0.7		**19** TU	0004 / 0602 / 1213 / 1823	0.3 / 4.9 / 1.0 / 4.7
5 TU	0546 / 1157 / 1805	4.5 / 1.1 / 4.3		**20** W	0052 / 0656 / 1303 / ◐1916	0.4 / 4.7 / 1.1 / 4.5
6 W	0035 / 0632 / 1242 / 1854	0.7 / 4.4 / 1.1 / 4.3		**21** TH	0142 / 0754 / 1401 / 2014	0.6 / 4.5 / 1.2 / 4.3
7 TH	0123 / 0730 / 1335 / ◐1955	0.7 / 4.4 / 1.2 / 4.2		**22** F	0239 / 0859 / 1508 / 2122	0.8 / 4.3 / 1.2 / 4.2
8 F	0219 / 0836 / 1439 / 2103	0.8 / 4.4 / 1.1 / 4.3		**23** SA	0349 / 1010 / 1623 / 2233	0.9 / 4.2 / 1.3 / 4.1
9 SA	0322 / 0941 / 1549 / 2209	0.8 / 4.4 / 1.1 / 4.4		**24** SU	0501 / 1116 / 1732 / 2338	1.0 / 4.2 / 1.2 / 4.2
10 SU	0429 / 1046 / 1659 / 2312	0.8 / 4.5 / 1.0 / 4.5		**25** M	0558 / 1213 / 1827	1.0 / 4.3 / 1.1
11 M	0537 / 1146 / 1806	0.7 / 4.7 / 0.8		**26** TU	0035 / 0645 / 1303 / 1914	4.3 / 1.0 / 4.4 / 1.0
12 TU	0009 / 0638 / 1240 / 1905	4.7 / 0.6 / 4.8 / 0.6		**27** W	0123 / 0726 / 1345 / 1955	4.4 / 1.0 / 4.4 / 0.9
13 W	0102 / 0731 / 1331 / ○2000	4.9 / 0.6 / 4.9 / 0.5		**28** TH	0202 / 0803 / 1419 / ●2033	4.5 / 1.0 / 4.5 / 0.8
14 TH	0152 / 0821 / 1420 / 2051	5.0 / 0.6 / 4.9 / 0.4		**29** F	0235 / 0839 / 1451 / 2109	4.6 / 1.0 / 4.6 / 0.7
15 F	0241 / 0909 / 1508 / 2141	5.1 / 0.6 / 4.9 / 0.3		**30** SA	0308 / 0915 / 1522 / 2146	4.7 / 0.9 / 4.7 / 0.6
				31 SU	0340 / 0950 / 1555 / 2223	4.8 / 0.9 / 4.7 / 0.6

AUGUST

#	Time	m		#	Time	m
1 M	0412 / 1025 / 1627 / 2258	4.8 / 1.0 / 4.7 / 0.6		**16** TU	0444 / 1100 / 1702 / 2334	5.1 / 0.9 / 5.0 / 0.4
2 TU	0445 / 1058 / 1700 / 2333	4.8 / 1.0 / 4.7 / 0.6		**17** W	0529 / 1140 / 1746	4.9 / 1.0 / 4.8
3 W	0520 / 1133 / 1737	4.7 / 1.0 / 4.6		**18** TH	0013 / 0615 / 1222 / 1832	0.5 / 4.7 / 1.0 / 4.7
4 TH	0008 / 0600 / 1212 / 1819	0.6 / 4.7 / 1.0 / 4.6		**19** F	0055 / 0704 / 1310 / ◑1923	0.7 / 4.4 / 1.2 / 4.4
5 F	0049 / 0648 / 1258 / ◐1911	0.6 / 4.6 / 1.0 / 4.5		**20** SA	0146 / 0758 / 1416 / 2024	0.9 / 4.2 / 1.3 / 4.1
6 SA	0139 / 0751 / 1357 / 2019	0.7 / 4.5 / 1.1 / 4.4		**21** SU	0254 / 0912 / 1535 / 2150	1.2 / 3.9 / 1.4 / 3.9
7 SU	0241 / 0901 / 1510 / 2134	0.8 / 4.4 / 1.1 / 4.3		**22** M	0414 / 1043 / 1655 / 2314	1.3 / 3.8 / 1.4 / 4.0
8 M	0356 / 1015 / 1633 / 2248	0.9 / 4.3 / 1.1 / 4.4		**23** TU	0526 / 1151 / 1802	1.3 / 4.0 / 1.2
9 TU	0516 / 1127 / 1752 / 2356	0.9 / 4.4 / 0.9 / 4.6		**24** W	0017 / 0622 / 1243 / 1856	4.2 / 1.2 / 4.2 / 1.0
10 W	0624 / 1229 / 1857	0.8 / 4.6 / 0.7		**25** TH	0105 / 0707 / 1325 / 1938	4.4 / 1.1 / 4.4 / 0.9
11 TH	0054 / 0720 / 1322 / 1951	4.8 / 0.8 / 4.8 / 0.5		**26** F	0143 / 0744 / 1358 / 2013	4.6 / 1.1 / 4.6 / 0.8
12 F	0145 / 0809 / 1409 / ○2041	5.0 / 0.7 / 4.9 / 0.3		**27** SA	0215 / 0818 / 1428 / ●2047	4.8 / 1.0 / 4.7 / 0.7
13 SA	0231 / 0855 / 1453 / 2127	5.2 / 0.7 / 5.0 / 0.2		**28** SU	0245 / 0852 / 1458 / 2121	4.9 / 0.9 / 4.8 / 0.7
14 SU	0316 / 0938 / 1537 / 2212	5.2 / 0.8 / 5.0 / 0.2		**29** M	0315 / 0926 / 1528 / 2156	5.0 / 0.9 / 4.9 / 0.5
15 M	0400 / 1020 / 1619 / 2254	5.2 / 0.8 / 5.0 / 0.3		**30** TU	0346 / 1000 / 1600 / 2232	5.0 / 0.9 / 4.9 / 0.5
				31 W	0418 / 1035 / 1633 / 2306	5.0 / 0.9 / 4.9 / 0.5

Chart Datum is 2·56 metres below NAP Datum. HAT is 5·4 metres above Chart Datum.

》》 **FREE** monthly updates. Register at 《
www.reedsnauticalalmanac.co.uk 《

STANDARD TIME UT –01
Subtract 1 hour for UT
For Dutch Summer Time add
ONE hour in **non-shaded areas**

VLISSINGEN   LAT 51°27'N   LONG 3°36'E
TIMES AND HEIGHTS OF HIGH AND LOW WATERS

Dates in red are **SPRINGS**
Dates in blue are NEAPS

YEAR 2022

Netherlands

SEPTEMBER

#	Time	m	#	Time	m
1 TH	0453 / 1109 / 1709 / 2342	4.9 / 0.9 / 0.9 / 0.6	16 F	0536 / 1144 / 1751	4.7 / 1.0 / 4.7
2 F	0532 / 1147 / 1749	4.9 / 0.9 / 4.8	17 SA	0011 / 0616 / 1223 / 1835	0.9 / 4.4 / 1.2 / 4.4
3 SA	0021 / 0617 / 1232 / 1838	0.6 / 4.7 / 0.9 / 4.7	18 SU	0053 / 0701 / 1317 / 1930	1.2 / 4.1 / 1.4 / 4.1
4 SU	0110 / 0715 / 1330 / 1945	0.8 / 4.4 / 1.1 / 4.4	19 M	0202 / 0758 / 1457 / 2050	1.4 / 3.8 / 1.5 / 3.8
5 M	0213 / 0831 / 1449 / 2111	1.0 / 4.2 / 1.2 / 4.2	20 TU	0335 / 0957 / 1616 / 2244	1.6 / 3.6 / 1.5 / 3.8
6 TU	0336 / 0956 / 1621 / 2237	1.2 / 4.1 / 1.2 / 4.3	21 W	0451 / 1121 / 1729 / 2350	1.5 / 3.8 / 1.3 / 4.1
7 W	0507 / 1118 / 1746 / 2351	1.2 / 4.2 / 1.0 / 4.5	22 TH	0554 / 1215 / 1828	1.4 / 4.1 / 1.1
8 TH	0617 / 1221 / 1850	1.0 / 4.5 / 0.7	23 F	0037 / 0642 / 1255 / 1911	4.4 / 1.2 / 4.4 / 0.9
9 F	0049 / 0711 / 1311 / 1941	4.8 / 0.9 / 4.7 / 0.5	24 SA	0114 / 0719 / 1328 / 1945	4.7 / 1.1 / 4.6 / 0.8
10 SA	0135 / 0756 / 1353 / 2026	5.1 / 0.8 / 4.9 / 0.3	25 SU	0146 / 0751 / 1357 / 2017	4.9 / 1.0 / 4.8 / 0.6
11 SU	0216 / 0838 / 1433 / 2108	5.2 / 0.8 / 5.0 / 0.3	26 M	0215 / 0824 / 1427 / 2051	5.0 / 0.9 / 5.0 / 0.5
12 M	0256 / 0917 / 1513 / 2148	5.2 / 0.8 / 5.1 / 0.3	27 TU	0245 / 0858 / 1458 / 2126	5.1 / 0.8 / 5.1 / 0.5
13 TU	0336 / 0956 / 1552 / 2226	5.2 / 0.8 / 5.1 / 0.4	28 W	0317 / 0934 / 1531 / 2203	5.2 / 0.8 / 5.1 / 0.5
14 W	0416 / 1033 / 1632 / 2302	5.1 / 0.9 / 5.1 / 0.5	29 TH	0351 / 1011 / 1607 / 2240	5.1 / 0.8 / 5.1 / 0.5
15 TH	0456 / 1108 / 1711 / 2336	4.9 / 0.9 / 4.9 / 0.7	30 F	0428 / 1048 / 1644 / 2318	5.1 / 0.8 / 5.1 / 0.6

OCTOBER

#	Time	m	#	Time	m
1 SA	0508 / 1129 / 1726 / 2359	4.9 / 0.8 / 5.0 / 0.7	16 SU	0536 / 1147 / 1756	4.4 / 1.1 / 4.4
2 SU	0554 / 1216 / 1816	4.7 / 0.9 / 4.7	17 M	0007 / 0616 / 1227 / 1845	1.3 / 4.1 / 1.3 / 4.1
3 M	0049 / 0653 / 1317 / 1927	1.0 / 4.3 / 1.1 / 4.4	18 TU	0056 / 0709 / 1415 / 2000	1.6 / 3.8 / 1.5 / 3.8
4 TU	0156 / 0814 / 1441 / 2101	1.2 / 4.0 / 1.2 / 4.2	19 W	0256 / 0825 / 1535 / 2150	1.7 / 3.6 / 1.5 / 3.7
5 W	0328 / 0945 / 1617 / 2232	1.4 / 3.9 / 1.2 / 4.2	20 TH	0410 / 1034 / 1644 / 2310	1.6 / 3.6 / 1.4 / 4.0
6 TH	0504 / 1109 / 1740 / 2347	1.3 / 4.1 / 0.9 / 4.6	21 F	0514 / 1133 / 1747 / 2359	1.5 / 4.0 / 1.1 / 4.3
7 F	0610 / 1209 / 1839	1.1 / 4.4 / 0.7	22 SA	0605 / 1215 / 1833	1.3 / 4.3 / 0.9
8 SA	0039 / 0658 / 1254 / 1925	4.8 / 1.0 / 4.7 / 0.5	23 SU	0037 / 0644 / 1249 / 1909	4.6 / 1.1 / 4.6 / 0.8
9 SU	0120 / 0739 / 1333 / 2006	5.0 / 0.9 / 4.9 / 0.4	24 M	0110 / 0718 / 1321 / 1943	4.9 / 1.0 / 4.8 / 0.6
10 M	0158 / 0818 / 1411 / 2044	5.1 / 0.8 / 5.0 / 0.4	25 TU	0141 / 0753 / 1354 / 2019	5.1 / 0.9 / 5.0 / 0.5
11 TU	0235 / 0855 / 1449 / 2122	5.1 / 0.8 / 5.1 / 0.4	26 W	0214 / 0830 / 1428 / 2057	5.2 / 0.8 / 5.2 / 0.5
12 W	0313 / 0932 / 1526 / 2157	5.1 / 0.8 / 5.1 / 0.5	27 TH	0249 / 0909 / 1505 / 2136	5.2 / 0.7 / 5.2 / 0.5
13 TH	0350 / 1007 / 1603 / 2231	5.0 / 0.8 / 5.0 / 0.7	28 F	0327 / 0950 / 1544 / 2216	5.2 / 0.7 / 5.1 / 0.6
14 F	0426 / 1042 / 1639 / 2302	4.8 / 0.9 / 4.9 / 0.9	29 SA	0407 / 1032 / 1625 / 2257	5.1 / 0.7 / 5.1 / 0.7
15 SA	0501 / 1114 / 1716 / 2333	4.6 / 1.0 / 4.7 / 1.1	30 SU	0451 / 1117 / 1711 / 2342	4.9 / 0.7 / 5.0 / 0.9
			31 M	0540 / 1209 / 1806	4.6 / 0.8 / 4.7

NOVEMBER

#	Time	m	#	Time	m
1 TU	0035 / 0643 / 1313 / 1924	1.1 / 4.2 / 1.0 / 4.3	16 W	0020 / 0635 / 1302 / 1919	1.5 / 4.0 / 1.3 / 3.9
2 W	0145 / 0805 / 1436 / 2052	1.4 / 4.0 / 1.1 / 4.2	17 TH	0132 / 0743 / 1446 / 2037	1.7 / 3.8 / 1.4 / 3.8
3 TH	0320 / 0930 / 1606 / 2219	1.5 / 3.9 / 1.0 / 4.3	18 F	0320 / 0904 / 1550 / 2202	1.7 / 3.7 / 1.3 / 3.9
4 F	0451 / 1049 / 1724 / 2329	1.4 / 4.1 / 0.9 / 4.6	19 SA	0421 / 1028 / 1650 / 2306	1.5 / 3.9 / 1.1 / 4.2
5 SA	0553 / 1147 / 1819	1.2 / 4.4 / 0.7	20 SU	0514 / 1123 / 1743 / 2351	1.4 / 4.2 / 1.0 / 4.6
6 SU	0019 / 0639 / 1232 / 1903	4.8 / 1.1 / 4.6 / 0.6	21 M	0600 / 1205 / 1827	1.2 / 4.5 / 0.8
7 M	0100 / 0718 / 1312 / 1942	4.9 / 0.9 / 4.8 / 0.5	22 TU	0030 / 0641 / 1244 / 1907	4.8 / 1.0 / 4.8 / 0.7
8 TU	0138 / 0756 / 1350 / 2019	5.0 / 0.9 / 4.9 / 0.5	23 W	0107 / 0722 / 1323 / 1949	5.0 / 0.8 / 5.0 / 0.6
9 W	0215 / 0833 / 1427 / 2055	5.0 / 0.8 / 5.0 / 0.6	24 TH	0146 / 0805 / 1402 / 2031	5.1 / 0.7 / 5.2 / 0.5
10 TH	0252 / 0910 / 1503 / 2130	4.9 / 0.8 / 5.0 / 0.7	25 F	0226 / 0849 / 1443 / 2114	5.2 / 0.6 / 5.2 / 0.6
11 F	0327 / 0947 / 1539 / 2204	4.8 / 0.8 / 4.9 / 0.9	26 SA	0308 / 0935 / 1526 / 2157	5.1 / 0.6 / 5.2 / 0.6
12 SA	0401 / 1022 / 1615 / 2235	4.7 / 0.9 / 4.8 / 1.0	27 SU	0352 / 1021 / 1612 / 2242	5.0 / 0.6 / 5.1 / 0.8
13 SU	0434 / 1055 / 1651 / 2306	4.5 / 1.0 / 4.6 / 1.2	28 M	0440 / 1111 / 1702 / 2330	4.8 / 0.6 / 4.9 / 0.9
14 M	0509 / 1127 / 1729 / 2338	4.4 / 1.1 / 4.4 / 1.3	29 TU	0533 / 1205 / 1802	4.6 / 0.7 / 4.7
15 TU	0547 / 1204 / 1814	4.2 / 1.2 / 4.2	30 W	0024 / 0637 / 1308 / 1916	1.1 / 4.3 / 0.8 / 4.5

DECEMBER

#	Time	m	#	Time	m
1 TH	0130 / 0747 / 1419 / 2031	1.3 / 4.2 / 0.9 / 4.4	16 F	0043 / 0703 / 1329 / 1943	1.4 / 4.1 / 1.1 / 4.1
2 F	0251 / 0900 / 1536 / 2148	1.4 / 4.1 / 0.9 / 4.4	17 SA	0144 / 0808 / 1438 / 2051	1.5 / 4.0 / 1.1 / 4.1
3 SA	0416 / 1013 / 1654 / 2256	1.4 / 4.2 / 0.8 / 4.5	18 SU	0304 / 0918 / 1542 / 2158	1.5 / 4.0 / 1.1 / 4.2
4 SU	0523 / 1114 / 1751 / 2350	1.3 / 4.3 / 0.7 / 4.6	19 M	0410 / 1024 / 1644 / 2259	1.4 / 4.2 / 1.0 / 4.5
5 M	0613 / 1205 / 1837	1.1 / 4.5 / 0.7	20 TU	0509 / 1120 / 1742 / 2351	1.2 / 4.5 / 0.8 / 4.7
6 TU	0037 / 0655 / 1250 / 1917	4.7 / 1.0 / 4.7 / 0.7	21 W	0604 / 1210 / 1835	1.0 / 4.7 / 0.7
7 W	0119 / 0735 / 1332 / 1955	4.8 / 0.9 / 4.8 / 0.7	22 TH	0038 / 0656 / 1257 / 1924	4.9 / 0.8 / 4.9 / 0.6
8 TH	0159 / 0813 / 1411 / 2031	4.8 / 0.8 / 4.8 / 0.8	23 F	0124 / 0747 / 1343 / 2011	5.0 / 0.7 / 5.1 / 0.6
9 F	0236 / 0851 / 1448 / 2106	4.7 / 0.8 / 4.8 / 0.9	24 SA	0209 / 0836 / 1428 / 2057	5.0 / 0.5 / 5.2 / 0.6
10 SA	0311 / 0929 / 1524 / 2141	4.6 / 0.8 / 4.8 / 0.9	25 SU	0255 / 0925 / 1515 / 2144	5.0 / 0.5 / 5.2 / 0.7
11 SU	0344 / 1007 / 1559 / 2214	4.6 / 0.8 / 4.7 / 1.1	26 M	0342 / 1014 / 1604 / 2230	4.9 / 0.4 / 5.1 / 0.8
12 M	0417 / 1042 / 1635 / 2247	4.5 / 0.9 / 4.6 / 1.2	27 TU	0431 / 1104 / 1656 / 2318	4.8 / 0.4 / 5.0 / 0.9
13 TU	0451 / 1116 / 1712 / 2319	4.4 / 1.0 / 4.5 / 1.3	28 W	0523 / 1156 / 1752	4.7 / 0.5 / 4.9
14 W	0528 / 1151 / 1752 / 2356	4.3 / 1.0 / 4.3 / 1.4	29 TH	0008 / 0619 / 1250 / 1853	1.0 / 4.6 / 0.5 / 4.7
15 TH	0610 / 1233 / 1841	4.2 / 1.1 / 4.2	30 F	0103 / 0718 / 1346 / 1957	1.2 / 4.4 / 0.7 / 4.5
			31 SA	0206 / 0821 / 1449 / 2105	1.3 / 4.3 / 0.8 / 4.4

Chart Datum is 2·56 metres below NAP Datum. HAT is 5·4 metres above Chart Datum.

》 **FREE** monthly updates. Register at 《
www.reedsnauticalalmanac.co.uk

133

2.28 BRESKENS

Zeeland **51°24'·00N 03°34'·08E** ❄❄❄💧💧💧🌸🌸🌸

CHARTS AC 1874, 1872, 116; Zeekaart 120, 101; BE 103; DYC 1801.4, 1803.2; Imray C30

TIDES +0210 Dover; ML no data; Duration 0600

Standard Port VLISSINGEN (←) Use Vlissingen data.

SHELTER Good in all winds except N/NW. In fine weather ⚓ off Plaat van Breskens or in peaceful Vaarwater langs Hoofdplaat; no ⚓ in commercial/fishing hbr.

NAVIGATION WPT 51°24'·71N 03°33'·90E (ARV-VH NCM buoy, Q), 170°/7ca to hbr ent. Beware fast ferries and strong tides across the ent. Do not confuse the ent with the ferry port ent, 0·7M WNW, where yachts are prohib.

LIGHTS AND MARKS Large bldg/silo on centre pier in hbr and three apartment blocks (30m) SE of marina are conspic. See chartlet and Lights, buoys and waypoints. Nieuwe Sluis lt ho, a 28m B/W banded 8-sided twr, is 1·8M W of marina.

COMMUNICATIONS (Code 0117); Police 0900 8844; ⊖ (0118) 484614/484624; British Consul (020) 676 4343; Ⓗ (0117) 459000; Dr 384010, at night/weekends (0115) 643000; Marina VHF Ch 31.

FACILITIES Marina info@ jachthavenbreskenst.nl ☎381902. www. jachthavenbreskens.nl 580 ⌷ inc Ⓥ €1·95 + €1·20 pp/day tax. Enter marina between two wavebreak barges; access H24, 5m at ent. Berth on 1st pontoon where HM assigns a berth via an intercom ☎. 🍴🐟 (fuel berth in FV hbr) ⬚♿⚓⛽ ACA 🔧🗑Ⓔ🔨⚓🛟 🏳(70t) ⚓(30t) ⚓. **YC Breskens** ☎383278, ✕🗑 (book early) @.

Town ✕🗑🛒✉Ⓑ🛎🍴✈ (Oostende, Antwerp or Brussels). Pedestrian & bike ferry or car tunnel to Vlissingen for ⇌.

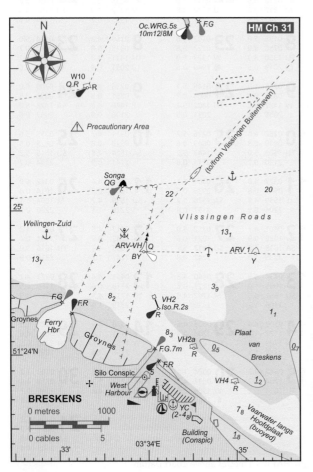

2.29 TERNEUZEN

Zeeland **51°20'·58N 03°49'·69E** ❄❄❄💧💧💧🌸🌸

CHARTS AC 120; Zeekaart 1443; BE 103, 105; DYC 1803.2; Imray C30

TIDES +0230 Dover; ML 2·5; Duration 0555

Standard Port VLISSINGEN (←)

Times				Height (metres)			
High Water		Low Water		MHWS	MHWN	MLWN	MLWS
0300	0900	0400	1000	5·0	4·1	1·1	0·5
1500	2100	1600	2200				
Differences *TERNEUZEN*							
+0020	+0020	+0020	+0030	+0·4	+0·3	+0·1	0·0

SHELTER Very good except in strong N'lies. Exposed ⚓ on N side of fairway between buoys WPT4, WPT6, PvT-ZE & ZE5. Strong currents.

NAVIGATION WPT 51°20'·82N 03°47'·96E (25B SHM buoy), 101°/1M, keep well to stbd and call *Traffic Centre Terneuzen* Ch 03 when 1·5M from hbr ent (and also when departing). Fairway only 500m wide and large ships pass very close; maintain a constant lookout E and W. Very busy traffic to/from the locks; call *Port Control Terneuzen*, Ch 11. If S-bound via Gent Canal transit the E lock to berth in Zijkanaal A. Strong eddy during ebb at Veerhaven ent.

LIGHTS AND MARKS Dow Chemical works and storage tanks are conspic 2M W of hbr. Lt Oc WRG 5s, B/W post, on W mole is a conspic mark for the Veerhaven.

When entry to E Buitenhaven is prohib, a second ● is shown below FR on E mole. For E lock: ● = no entry; ●● (vert) = get ready; ● = go. No yachts in W Buitenhaven, Middle and W locks.

COMMUNICATIONS (Code 0115) Police 0900 8844; ⊖ (0118) 484600; British Consul (020) 676 4343; Ⓗ 688000; Dr 616262; Port HM 612161, call *Port Control* Ch 11 (H24) for locks and Gent canal; also info broadcasts every H+00; East lock VHF Ch 18; No marina VHF.

FACILITIES Two marinas in SE corner of Veerhaven (former ferry hbr, 0·5M E of main hbr ent): **WV Honte Marina** where berths are more likely. ☎697089, mob 0651 168987. www.jachthaventerneuzen.nl 130 inc Ⓥ ⌷ €1·50. ⚡ (230v) €1·25, 🗑(6t). **WV Neusen Marina** is close ESE (and in Zijkanaal A) ☎696331; mob 0652182564 www.wvneusen.nl 100 ⌷ €1·00, 🗑♿ wi-fi. **Boatyards: Aricom** www.aricom.nl ☎614577, €1·00, ♿🛎🔧🗑🔨 ⚓(50t).

Town 🏪🏪 ✕🗑🛒🍴✉Ⓑ✈ (Antwerpen). Foot ferry Breskens to Vlissingen. Cars by road tunnel Terneuzen–Ellewoutsdijk. Road tunnel to Terneuzen. At Middelburg: 🚆🔧🔨⚓.

MARINA 8M WSW OF VLISSINGEN, Jachthaven Cadzand, WPT 51°23'·08N 03°23'·07E, CZ SWM buoy Mo(A), 198°/0·2M to hbr ent. and arrival pontoon A. ☎+31 611410975; www.rycb.be/jachthavens/cadzand/marina/ cadzand@rycb.be. VHF Ch 31, 125 inc 🅥◻ €2·30 inc 🏴 wi-fi; + €1·20 pp/day tax; ⛽ €3·00/day. Near to ✕ ◻ 🍴. Run by the Royal YC of Belgium and close to a tourist resort/luxury bathing facilities and large sandy beach.

JACHTHAVEN CADZAND HM Ch 31

2.30 SPECIAL NOTES FOR BELGIUM

PROVINCES are given in lieu of UK 'counties'.

LANGUAGES 1st, Flemish,(Flanders Dutch) used on the coast/N of Brussels. 2nd, French, in and S of Brussels. English is widely used.

CURRENCY is the Euro €. VAT (BTW/TVA) is 21%.

CHARTS 'Vlaamse Banken' (BE) issued by the Hydrografische Dienst der Kust are widely used. Dutch yacht charts (DYC 1800 series) cover all Belgian ports. Imray C30 is also popular.

TIME ZONE is –0100, which is allowed for in tidal predictions but no provision is made for daylight saving schemes.

HARBOURS Ports of entry are Nieuwpoort, Oostende and Zeebrugge; Blankenberge, early April–late Sep. Berths and moorings are administered by local YCs and municipal authorities.

SIGNALS IPTS, Oostende and Zeebrugge, and wind warnings (also Nieuwpoort and Blankenberge) for craft <6m LOA, Day, 2▼s, points together = onshore wind >F3; offshore wind >F4. Night, Fl Bu lt.

TELEPHONE To call UK from Belgium, dial 00 44 then the UK area code minus the prefix 0, followed by the number called. To call Belgium from UK, dial 00 32 then the code and 6/7 digit number.

Emergency: ☎101 Police; ☎100 Fire, Ambulance and Marine. ☎112 (EU emergency number) is also operational.

CONSUL British Embassy, Brussels, (consular) 02 287 6248.

MRCC Oostende co-ordinates SAR operations (5.14). If no contact, call *Oostende Radio* VHF Ch 16 or e100. For medical advice call *Radiomédical Oostende* on Ch 16.

PUBLIC HOLIDAYS New Year's Day, Easter Mon, Labour Day (1 May) Ascension Day, Whit Mon, National Day (21 July) Feast of the Assumption (15 Aug) All Saints' Day (1 Nov) Armistice Day (11 Nov) King's Birthday (15 Nov) Christmas Day.

RULES A ▼ when motor-sailing and a black ball ● at ⚓ are strictly enforced. Navigation within 200m of shore (MLWS) and through wind farm restricted areas prohibited. Red diesel in pleasure craft is illegal in Belgium, see 2.3.2. Radio Licences must be up-to-date and cover all relevant equipment including radar.

INLAND WATERWAYS See: www.mobilit.fgov.be for CEVNI based regulations in French or Dutch. ICC as for the Netherlands.

2.31 ANTWERPEN

Belgium, Antwerpen 51°13'·66N 04°23'·79E ✹✹◈◊◊✿✿✿✿

CHARTS AC 128; Zeekaart 1443; BE 103, 104; DYC 1803.5

TIDES +0342 Dover; ML 2·9; Duration 0605
Standard Port VLISSINGEN (←)

Times				Height (metres)			
High Water		Low Water		MHWS	MHWN	MLWN	MLWS
0300	0900	0400	1000	5·0	4·1	1·1	0·5
1500	2100	1600	2200				
Differences *ANTWERPEN*							
+0128	+0116	+0121	+0144	+1·2	+1·0	+0·1	+0·1

SHELTER Excellent in both marinas. ⚓ in the river is not advised.

NAVIGATION See Westerschelde. Best to check off the buoys coming upriver. There is a gap of 1·4M between No 116 PHM buoy and No 107 SHM buoy. The only access to Willemdok marina is via Kattendijksluis (abeam buoy 107), VHF 69, operating if tide between TAW 2.2–5.0m, or approximately 3±HW. Royerssluis was closed indefinitely 2020 for major lock and bridge enlargement.

COMMUNICATIONS (Code 03) VTS, Zandvliet Centre VHF Ch 12, lock Ch 79; Radar VHF Ch 04, 66 ⊜ 2292004; Police 5460730; Ⓗ 2852000 (W Bank) 234111 (E Bank); Antwerp Port Ops Ch 74 (H24); Royerssluis VHF Ch 22; Access bridges VHF Ch 62; Willemdok VHF Ch 23; Linkeroever VHF Ch 09 (HW±1).

ANTWERPEN

FACILITIES from seaward: **Willemdok Marina** 51°13'·78N 04°24'·43E. ☎2315066, mob 0495 535455. www.jachthaven-antwerpen.be jaw@pandora.be. Wait on inshore side of ferry pontoon S of No 107 buoy opposite the Kattendijksluis lock, accessible HW-/+ 3hrs Mon-Sat 0600-2200; Sun and hols between Easter and last w/end Sept 0900-1900. Call VHF Ch 69 'kattendijksluis'. London bridge VHF Ch 62, opens 0630, 0830, 1000, 1130, 1245, 1415, 1515, 1615*, 1730, 1845, 2015, 2145, 2245LT.*Sat/Sun/Public hols. To enter Dock areas and marina, pre-arrange an FD number via VHF Ch 20, ☎, or email. 200 + 🅥, €1·50, €8·00 week, 🔧🛒 ▣ 🗐.

Linkeroever Marina (W bank); lat/long under title. Access by gate HW ±1, 0800–2200 (1800 in winter). Y waiting buoy is off the ent. ☎2190895, mob 0475 643957. www.jachthaven-antwerpen.be jachthaven_linkeroever@skynet.be 200+🅥, €1·50, €8·00 week. 🔧 ✕ 🛒 🔋 🛢 🗐 ✕ ⚓(38t) ⛴(1·5t) ◻.

Royal YC van België ☎2195231. www.rycb.be rycb@rycb.be. 🔧🛢 ✕ ◻ 🛢 🍴 ◻.

Kon. Liberty YC ☎2191147. **Services** 🔧 🏴 ACA, DYC Agent.

City centre is ¾M from Linkeroever via St Annatunnel (pedestrian) 51°13'·22N. All facilities, @ ⇌ ✈.

Belgium

2.32 ZEEBRUGGE

Belgium, West Flanders **51°21'·83N 03°11'·39E** ✱✱✱♨♨♨✿✿

CHARTS AC 2449, 3371, 1872, 1874; Zeekaart 1441; BE 104; DYC 1801.3, 1803; Imray C30

TIDES +0135 Dover; ML 2·4; Duration 0535. Note: Zeebrugge is a Standard Port (⟶)

SHELTER Very good in the marina, access H24.

NAVIGATION WPT 51°22'·48N 03°09'·95E (Z SHM buoy, QG), 129°/1·1M to ent (lat/long under title). Lts on outer bkwtr heads show high-vis strip lts to seaward. Beware strong currents in hbr apprs (up to 4kn at HW −1). Caution on ent/dep due to limited vis; give all jetties a wide berth. A busy commercial, naval and fishing port and a ferry terminal. An inner WPT 51°20'·85N 03°12'·29E off Leopold II Dam head is useful to avoid getting 'lost' inside the vast outer hbr, especially in poor vis; see chartlet.

LIGHTS AND MARKS Big ship ldg marks (hard to see by day) and lts (as chartlet) lead in sequence to Vissershaven and the marina:

- 136°: Both W cols, R bands.
- 154°: Front, W pylon, R bands; rear, W bldg, R bands.
- 220°: Both W cols, B bands. • 193°: Both W cols, R bands.

IPTS are shown prominently from E and W outer bkwtrs and Leopold II Dam. Extra sigs: 3 Fl Y lts (vert) + IPTS No 2 or 5 = LNG

tanker entering/leaving. No exit/entry without specific permission from Port Control.

COMMUNICATIONS (Code 050) Coast Guard 545072; Sea Saving Service 544007; Police 544148; ⊖ 545455; British Consul 02 287 6248; Dr 544590; Port HM 543241; Port Control 546867/550801, VHF Ch 71 (H24); Lock 543231, VHF Ch 68; Marina VHF Ch 23.

FACILITIES Royal Belgian SC (VZW) ☎544903, mob 0496 789053. havenmeester@rbsc.be www.rbsc.be 100 + 100♥ €2·64 inc free ⚓♒ wi-fi, ⅅ (on coin meter) ♨ (0830-1200, 1300-1800) ⚓ ⚒ ⚓ ⚒ ☐ ☐ (Clubhouse Alberta) ☎544197.

BZYC Tijdokhaven Marina, HM VHF Ch 12, mob+32 472676394; havenmeester@bzyc.be www.bzyc.be 94 inc ♥ (max 20m) €2·67 inc ⚓ ⅅ ♒ wi-fi. Clubhouse 'ONA', ☎ +32 492397017.

Town ⓐ ⓑ ✗ ☐ ⌣ ▮ ⊠ Ⓑ ✗. ⇌ 15 mins to Brugge. Tram to Oostende for ✈. Ferries to Hull and Rosyth (Edinburgh).

BRUGGE Masted yachts transit Zeebrugge's eastern sealock to Brugge docks, 6M S, via the Boudewijnkanaal (Ch 68) and 2 lifting bridges to **Konninklijke Brugse Zeil en Yacht Club (BZYC)** on the E bank: www.bzyc.be info@bzyc.be €1·00/m; ⚓ ⅅ €2·00/day. 15 mins' walk to city centre. Unmasted boats can go clockwise on the Oostende-Gent Canal (Ch 18) to **Flandria Marina** (S of city): ☎380866, mob 0477 384456. www.yachtclubflandria.be 10 mins' walk to city centre; close to ⇌ (quick and easy by train).

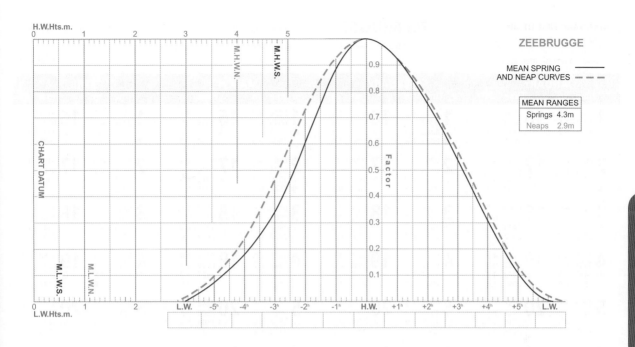

ZEEBRUGGE

MEAN SPRING ——————
AND NEAP CURVES – – – – –

MEAN RANGES	
Springs	4.3m
Neaps	2.9m

Belgium

1	*Borkum*	**1**																									
2	**Delfzijl**	22	**2**																								
3	Lauwersoog	30	46	**3**																							
4	Terschelling	65	85	43	**4**																						
5	Vlieland	72	92	52	7	**5**																					
6	Harlingen	80	102	67	19	18	**6**																				
7	Kornwerderzand	86	106	70	24	19	7	**7**																			
8	Den Oever	90	110	88	34	33	21	13	**8**																		
9	Oudeschild	94	114	79	38	34	25	18	10	**9**																	
10	**Den Helder**	95	115	81	39	33	30	24	11	5	**10**																
11	Medemblik	104	124	99	39	40	27	20	12	22	24	**11**															
12	Enkhuizen	112	132	106	47	41	28	23	18	28	29	10	**12**														
13	Amsterdam	139	159	123	83	84	81	47	62	52	51	38	26	**13**													
14	IJmuiden	126	146	109	70	71	68	57	49	38	38	58	37	13	**14**												
15	**Scheveningen**	151	171	132	95	96	93	79	74	60	63	80	62	38	25	**15**											
16	Rotterdam	185	205	159	129	130	127	113	108	94	97	114	96	72	59	34	**16**										
17	Hook of Holland	165	185	146	109	110	107	93	88	74	77	94	76	52	39	14	20	**17**									
18	Stellendam	181	201	157	125	126	123	109	104	90	93	110	92	68	55	30	36	16	**18**								
19	**Roompotsluis**	193	204	177	128	124	129	118	109	110	97	130	112	90	63	50	49	29	27	**19**							
20	**Vlissingen**	211	222	190	146	143	147	137	128	121	115	141	123	108	82	61	67	47	45	21	**20**						
21	Terneuzen	220	240	202	164	165	162	152	143	133	132	153	135	111	98	73	79	59	57	36	12	**21**					
22	Antwerpen	249	269	221	193	194	191	181	172	162	161	182	164	140	127	102	108	88	86	65	41	31	**22**				
23	Breskens	202	230	192	161	165	152	142	133	123	122	143	125	101	88	63	69	49	47	21	3	12	45	**23**			
24	**Zeebrugge**	219	239	194	163	164	161	147	142	128	131	148	130	106	93	68	74	54	50	25	16	28	57	13	**24**		
25	Blankenberge	224	244	196	168	169	166	152	147	133	136	153	135	111	98	73	79	59	55	33	21	33	62	18	5	**25**	
26	**Oostende**	233	239	205	163	164	161	160	142	141	131	161	143	110	106	81	87	67	72	36	27	41	70	26	13	9	**26**
27	**Nieuwpoort**	242	262	215	186	187	184	170	165	151	154	171	153	129	116	91	97	77	83	46	39	51	80	36	23	18	9	**27**
28	*Dunkerque*	257	277	228	201	202	199	185	180	166	169	186	168	144	131	106	112	92	90	57	50	67	96	52	40	35	26	15 **28**

DISTANCE TABLE
Approximate distances in nautical miles are by the most direct route while avoiding dangers and allowing for TSS. Places in *italics* are in adjoining areas; places in **bold** are in 0.34, Distances across the North Sea.

STANDARD TIME UT –01
Subtract 1 hour for UT
For Belgian Summer Time add
ONE hour in **non-shaded areas**

ZEEBRUGGE LAT 51°21'N LONG 3°12'E
TIMES AND HEIGHTS OF HIGH AND LOW WATERS

Dates in red are SPRINGS
Dates in blue are NEAPS

YEAR **2022**

JANUARY

Time	m	Time	m
1 0613	0.9	**16** 0054	4.2
1211	4.6	0713	1.0
SA 1837	0.7	SU 1310	4.3
		1921	1.1
2 0043	4.6	**17** 0131	4.3
0704	0.8	0744	0.9
SU 1303	4.7	M 1345	4.3
● 1926	0.7	○ 1947	1.1
3 0131	4.6	**18** 0202	4.3
0752	0.6	0810	0.9
M 1350	4.8	TU 1415	4.4
2012	0.7	2012	1.1
4 0215	4.6	**19** 0230	4.3
0838	0.5	0838	0.8
TU 1437	4.9	W 1443	4.5
2057	0.8	2043	1.0
5 0259	4.6	**20** 0257	4.4
0923	0.5	0911	0.7
W 1523	4.9	TH 1514	4.6
2142	0.8	2118	0.9
6 0344	4.6	**21** 0328	4.5
1010	0.4	0947	0.6
TH 1610	4.8	F 1549	4.7
2227	0.9	2156	0.9
7 0430	4.6	**22** 0404	4.6
1058	0.4	1027	0.5
F 1700	4.7	SA 1629	4.7
2315	1.0	2238	0.9
8 0520	4.5	**23** 0444	4.6
1149	0.5	1110	0.5
SA 1753	4.6	SU 1713	4.7
		2322	0.9
9 0006	1.1	**24** 0529	4.5
0613	4.4	1156	0.6
SU 1244	0.6	M 1802	4.6
◑ 1851	4.4		
10 0102	1.2	**25** 0011	1.0
0712	4.2	0621	4.4
M 1343	0.8	TU 1249	0.7
1953	4.2	◑ 1859	4.4
11 0206	1.4	**26** 0108	1.2
0816	4.1	0721	4.3
TU 1447	1.0	W 1352	0.8
2058	4.0	2004	4.3
12 0317	1.4	**27** 0219	1.3
0925	4.0	0830	4.2
W 1553	1.1	TH 1509	1.0
2207	4.0	2116	4.1
13 0430	1.4	**28** 0341	1.3
1035	4.0	0945	4.1
TH 1659	1.1	F 1620	1.0
2314	4.0	2231	4.1
14 0537	1.3	**29** 0457	1.2
1138	4.1	1059	4.2
F 1758	1.1	SA 1728	1.0
		2340	4.1
15 0009	4.1	**30** 0602	1.0
0631	1.1	1204	4.4
SA 1229	4.2	SU 1827	0.9
1846	1.1		
		31 0036	4.3
		0656	0.8
		M 1257	4.6
		1916	0.9

FEBRUARY

Time	m	Time	m
1 0121	4.4	**16** 0137	4.3
0742	0.6	0750	0.8
TU 1342	4.7	W 1351	4.5
● 2000	0.8	○ 1952	1.0
2 0202	4.6	**17** 0205	4.4
0826	0.4	0818	0.6
W 1424	4.9	TH 1421	4.7
2042	0.8	2024	0.8
3 0243	4.7	**18** 0234	4.6
0908	0.3	0852	0.4
TH 1507	4.9	F 1453	4.8
2123	0.7	2101	0.7
4 0325	4.7	**19** 0307	4.7
0952	0.2	0930	0.3
F 1550	4.9	SA 1530	4.9
2205	0.7	2141	0.6
5 0408	4.8	**20** 0344	4.8
1036	0.2	1010	0.3
SA 1635	4.6	SU 1608	4.9
2248	0.8	2221	0.7
6 0452	4.7	**21** 0423	4.8
1121	0.3	1051	0.5
SU 1722	4.7	M 1650	4.8
2330	0.9	2302	0.7
7 0537	4.6	**22** 0505	4.7
1206	0.5	1133	0.5
M 1809	4.4	TU 1734	4.7
		2345	0.9
8 0014	1.1	**23** 0552	4.6
0625	4.3	1219	0.6
TU 1256	0.8	W 1824	4.4
◑ 1900	4.1	◑	
9 0104	1.3	**24** 0034	1.0
0719	4.0	0646	4.4
W 1358	1.1	TH 1316	0.9
2000	3.8	1925	4.1
10 0224	1.5	**25** 0140	1.3
0827	3.8	0755	4.1
TH 1511	1.3	F 1437	1.1
2116	3.6	2046	3.8
11 0350	1.5	**26** 0318	1.4
0952	3.6	0925	3.9
F 1622	1.4	SA 1602	1.2
2238	3.6	2217	3.7
12 0504	1.4	**27** 0443	1.2
1109	3.7	1053	4.0
SA 1728	1.4	SU 1717	1.2
2343	3.8	2333	3.9
13 0606	1.3	**28** 0552	1.0
1206	3.9	1159	4.3
SU 1823	1.3	M 1818	1.0
14 0031	4.0		
0652	1.1		
M 1248	4.1		
1900	1.2		
15 0108	4.1		
0724	0.9		
TU 1322	4.3		
1925	1.1		

MARCH

Time	m	Time	m
1 0026	4.2	**16** 0033	4.1
0645	0.7	0649	0.9
TU 1248	4.5	W 1250	4.4
1904	0.9	1854	1.0
2 0107	4.4	**17** 0104	4.3
0728	0.5	0719	0.6
W 1328	4.7	TH 1321	4.6
● 1944	0.8	1926	0.8
3 0144	4.6	**18** 0134	4.6
0808	0.4	0752	0.4
TH 1407	4.9	F 1353	4.9
2023	0.7	○ 2002	0.6
4 0223	4.8	**19** 0207	4.8
0848	0.2	0829	0.2
F 1446	5.0	SA 1428	5.0
2101	0.6	2041	0.5
5 0302	4.9	**20** 0242	4.9
0929	0.1	0908	0.2
SA 1527	5.0	SU 1506	5.0
2140	0.6	2122	0.5
6 0342	4.9	**21** 0321	5.0
1009	0.1	0949	0.2
SU 1608	4.9	M 1545	5.0
2219	0.6	2202	0.5
7 0423	4.8	**22** 0400	4.9
1049	0.3	1029	0.3
M 1649	4.7	TU 1626	4.8
2255	0.7	2242	0.6
8 0502	4.6	**23** 0442	4.8
1126	0.6	1110	0.5
TU 1727	4.4	W 1709	4.6
2330	0.9	2323	0.6
9 0540	4.4	**24** 0528	4.6
1201	0.9	1155	0.7
W 1805	4.1	TH 1757	4.3
10 0004	1.2	**25** 0011	1.0
0620	4.0	0621	4.3
TH 1240	1.3	F 1251	1.1
◑ 1847	3.7	◑ 1857	3.9
11 0047	1.5	**26** 0119	1.2
0711	3.7	0735	4.0
F 1417	1.6	SA 1419	1.3
2002	3.4	2028	3.6
12 0308	1.6	**27** 0304	1.3
0856	3.4	0916	3.8
SA 1542	1.7	SU 1547	1.4
2150	3.3	2204	3.6
13 0422	1.6	**28** 0425	1.1
1029	3.5	1044	4.0
SU 1647	1.6	M 1701	1.2
2305	3.5	2316	3.9
14 0524	1.3	**29** 0533	0.9
1131	3.8	1146	4.3
M 1744	1.4	TU 1802	1.1
2356	3.8		
15 0614	1.1	**30** 0007	4.2
1215	4.1	0625	0.6
TU 1824	1.2	W 1232	4.6
		1846	0.9
		31 0047	4.4
		0708	0.4
		TH 1310	4.8
		1924	0.8

APRIL

Time	m	Time	m
1 0123	4.7	**16** 0101	4.7
0747	0.2	0722	0.3
F 1347	4.9	SA 1324	5.0
● 2001	0.6	○ 1937	0.5
2 0200	4.8	**17** 0138	4.9
0825	0.2	0803	0.2
SA 1424	4.9	SU 1402	5.1
2038	0.5	2019	0.4
3 0238	4.9	**18** 0217	5.0
0903	0.2	0844	0.2
SU 1503	4.9	M 1442	5.0
2114	0.5	2101	0.4
4 0317	4.9	**19** 0258	5.0
0941	0.3	0926	0.2
M 1541	4.8	TU 1523	4.9
2150	0.6	2142	0.5
5 0354	4.8	**20** 0340	4.9
1016	0.5	1008	0.4
TU 1617	4.6	W 1605	4.7
2223	0.7	2224	0.6
6 0429	4.7	**21** 0423	4.7
1047	0.7	1050	0.6
W 1649	4.3	TH 1649	4.4
2253	0.9	2307	0.8
7 0501	4.3	**22** 0511	4.5
1114	1.0	1137	0.9
TH 1719	4.0	F 1739	4.1
2322	1.1	2359	0.9
8 0534	4.0	**23** 0608	4.2
1144	1.3	1238	1.2
F 1751	3.8	SA 1844	3.8
2358	1.3	◑	
9 0616	3.7	**24** 0116	1.1
1225	1.6	0729	4.0
SA 1836	3.5	SU 1405	1.4
◑		2015	3.6
10 0059	1.6	**25** 0245	1.1
0734	3.4	0904	3.9
SU 1455	1.7	M 1524	1.4
2049	3.3	2141	3.7
11 0335	1.5	**26** 0358	0.9
0937	3.5	1023	4.1
M 1600	1.6	TU 1635	1.2
2212	3.4	2249	4.0
12 0434	1.3	**27** 0504	0.7
1044	3.8	1123	4.4
TU 1655	1.4	W 1737	1.1
2308	3.7	2341	4.3
13 0524	1.0	**28** 0600	0.5
1132	4.1	1209	4.6
W 1740	1.2	TH 1823	0.9
2350	4.1		
14 0606	0.8	**29** 0023	4.5
1212	4.5	0645	0.4
TH 1819	0.9	F 1249	4.7
		1902	0.8
15 0026	4.4	**30** 0102	4.6
0644	0.5	0724	0.3
F 1248	4.8	SA 1326	4.8
1858	0.7	● 1939	0.7

Chart Datum is 0·23 metres below TAW Datum. HAT is 5·6 metres above Chart Datum.

》》 FREE monthly updates. Register at 《
www.reedsnauticalalmanac.co.uk

STANDARD TIME UT –01
Subtract 1 hour for UT
For Belgian Summer Time add
ONE hour in **non-shaded areas**

ZEEBRUGGE LAT 51°21'N LONG 3°12'E
TIMES AND HEIGHTS OF HIGH AND LOW WATERS

Dates in red are **SPRINGS**
Dates in blue are **NEAPS**

YEAR **2022**

Belgium

MAY

Time m	Time m
1 0139 4.7 / 0802 0.3 / SU 1403 4.8 / 2015 0.6	**16** 0112 4.9 / 0737 0.3 / M 1338 4.9 / ○ 1957 0.5
2 0217 4.8 / 0838 0.4 / M 1440 4.7 / 2050 0.6	**17** 0155 4.9 / 0821 0.3 / TU 1421 4.8 / 2041 0.5
3 0254 4.7 / 0913 0.5 / TU 1516 4.5 / 2124 0.6	**18** 0238 4.9 / 0905 0.4 / W 1504 4.7 / 2125 0.5
4 0329 4.6 / 0944 0.7 / W 1549 4.4 / 2155 0.7	**19** 0323 4.8 / 0949 0.6 / TH 1548 4.5 / 2210 0.6
5 0401 4.4 / 1011 0.9 / TH 1617 4.2 / 2224 0.9	**20** 0410 4.7 / 1035 0.8 / F 1636 4.3 / 2258 0.7
6 0431 4.2 / 1038 1.1 / F 1645 4.0 / 2255 1.0	**21** 0502 4.5 / 1125 1.0 / SA 1729 4.1 / 2356 0.8
7 0504 4.1 / 1110 1.3 / SA 1718 3.9 / 2332 1.1	**22** 0603 4.3 / 1228 1.2 / SU 1834 3.9 / ☽
8 0547 3.9 / 1152 1.4 / SU 1804 3.7 / ☽	**23** 0107 0.8 / 0719 4.1 / M 1342 1.3 / 1952 3.8
9 0028 1.3 / 0654 3.7 / M 1311 1.6 / 1935 3.5	**24** 0219 0.8 / 0838 4.1 / TU 1452 1.3 / 2107 3.9
10 0244 1.3 / 0840 3.7 / TU 1509 1.5 / 2113 3.6	**25** 0325 0.8 / 0949 4.2 / W 1559 1.2 / 2213 4.1
11 0343 1.1 / 0950 3.9 / W 1606 1.3 / 2215 3.8	**26** 0430 0.7 / 1051 4.4 / TH 1704 1.1 / 2310 4.3
12 0435 0.9 / 1045 4.2 / TH 1657 1.1 / 2304 4.1	**27** 0530 0.6 / 1142 4.5 / F 1758 0.9 / 2358 4.4
13 0523 0.7 / 1132 4.5 / F 1744 0.9 / 2348 4.4	**28** 0620 0.5 / 1227 4.6 / SA 1841 0.8
14 0609 0.5 / 1215 4.8 / SA 1829 0.7	**29** 0042 0.5 / 0702 0.5 / SU 1308 4.6 / 1920 0.8
15 0030 4.7 / 0653 0.3 / SU 1256 4.9 / 1913 0.5	**30** 0122 4.6 / 0740 0.6 / M 1346 4.5 / ● 1956 0.7
	31 0200 4.5 / 0815 0.7 / TU 1423 4.5 / 2030 0.7

JUNE

Time m	Time m
1 0236 4.5 / 0846 0.8 / W 1457 4.3 / 2102 0.7	**16** 0224 4.8 / 0847 0.6 / TH 1449 4.6 / 2112 0.5
2 0310 4.4 / 0915 1.0 / TH 1527 4.2 / 2133 0.8	**17** 0311 4.8 / 0933 0.7 / F 1535 4.5 / 2200 0.5
3 0340 4.3 / 0943 1.1 / F 1554 4.1 / 2204 0.8	**18** 0400 4.7 / 1021 0.9 / SA 1624 4.4 / 2250 0.5
4 0411 4.2 / 1013 1.1 / SA 1624 4.1 / 2237 0.9	**19** 0453 4.6 / 1112 1.0 / SU 1716 4.3 / 2345 0.5
5 0447 4.2 / 1049 1.2 / SU 1700 4.0 / 2318 1.0	**20** 0550 4.5 / 1208 1.1 / M 1814 4.2
6 0531 4.1 / 1133 1.3 / M 1748 3.9	**21** 0045 0.6 / 0655 4.4 / TU 1309 1.2 / ☽ 1919 4.1
7 0013 1.0 / 0630 4.1 / TU 1236 1.4 / ☽ 1855 3.9	**22** 0147 0.6 / 0802 4.3 / W 1413 1.2 / 2026 4.1
8 0140 1.0 / 0746 4.0 / W 1406 1.4 / 2015 3.9	**23** 0249 0.7 / 0908 4.2 / TH 1519 1.2 / 2132 4.1
9 0251 0.9 / 0858 4.1 / TH 1516 1.2 / 2122 4.0	**24** 0354 0.7 / 1013 4.2 / F 1628 1.2 / 2236 4.2
10 0349 0.8 / 0958 4.3 / F 1614 1.1 / 2220 4.2	**25** 0458 0.8 / 1114 4.3 / SA 1731 1.1 / 2334 4.3
11 0444 0.7 / 1053 4.5 / SA 1710 0.9 / 2313 4.4	**26** 0555 0.8 / 1206 4.3 / SU 1824 1.0
12 0536 0.6 / 1144 4.6 / SU 1802 0.8 / 2359 4.6	**27** 0025 4.3 / 0643 0.8 / M 1252 4.4 / 1907 0.9
13 0627 0.5 / 1232 4.7 / M 1852 0.7	**28** 0108 4.4 / 0723 0.9 / TU 1332 4.3 / 1944 0.9
14 0051 4.7 / 0715 0.5 / TU 1319 4.7 / ○ 1939 0.6	**29** 0147 4.4 / 0755 1.0 / W 1408 4.3 / ● 2016 0.8
15 0138 4.8 / 0802 0.5 / W 1404 4.6 / 2026 0.5	**30** 0222 4.3 / 0823 1.1 / TH 1439 4.3 / 2045 0.8

JULY

Time m	Time m
1 0253 4.3 / 0850 1.1 / F 1508 4.2 / 2115 0.8	**16** 0259 4.9 / 0918 0.8 / SA 1520 4.6 / 2146 0.3
2 0323 4.3 / 0921 1.0 / SA 1536 4.3 / 2148 0.7	**17** 0346 4.9 / 1004 0.8 / SU 1606 4.7 / 2234 0.3
3 0355 4.4 / 0955 1.0 / SU 1608 4.3 / 2225 0.7	**18** 0435 4.8 / 1051 0.8 / M 1654 4.6 / 2324 0.3
4 0431 4.4 / 1034 1.0 / M 1645 4.3 / 2306 0.7	**19** 0526 4.7 / 1140 0.9 / TU 1745 4.6
5 0514 4.5 / 1117 1.0 / TU 1729 4.3 / 2354 0.7	**20** 0015 0.4 / 0621 4.6 / W 1231 1.0 / ☽ 1841 4.4
6 0603 4.4 / 1209 1.1 / W 1822 4.3	**21** 0110 0.6 / 0720 4.4 / TH 1328 1.2 / 1941 4.2
7 0051 0.8 / 0702 4.4 / TH 1310 1.2 / ☽ 1925 4.2	**22** 0211 0.8 / 0822 4.2 / F 1436 1.3 / 2047 4.1
8 0156 0.8 / 0808 4.3 / F 1421 1.2 / 2032 4.2	**23** 0317 1.0 / 0931 4.0 / SA 1552 1.3 / 2200 4.0
9 0303 0.8 / 0914 4.3 / SA 1533 1.2 / 2138 4.2	**24** 0426 1.1 / 1043 4.0 / SU 1704 1.3 / 2311 4.0
10 0408 0.8 / 1018 4.3 / SU 1640 1.1 / 2242 4.3	**25** 0531 1.1 / 1145 4.1 / M 1805 1.1
11 0509 0.8 / 1119 4.4 / M 1741 0.9 / 2342 4.4	**26** 0008 4.1 / 0625 1.1 / TU 1234 4.2 / 1854 1.0
12 0607 0.7 / 1215 4.4 / TU 1836 0.8	**27** 0053 4.3 / 0706 1.1 / W 1315 4.2 / 1931 0.9
13 0037 4.6 / 0658 0.7 / W 1305 4.5 / ○ 1926 0.7	**28** 0130 4.3 / 0736 1.1 / TH 1348 4.3 / ● 2000 0.9
14 0126 4.7 / 0746 0.7 / TH 1351 4.5 / 2013 0.5	**29** 0203 4.4 / 0801 1.1 / F 1418 4.3 / 2027 0.8
15 0213 4.8 / 0832 0.8 / F 1435 4.6 / 2059 0.4	**30** 0232 4.5 / 0829 1.0 / SA 1445 4.4 / 2057 0.7
	31 0302 4.6 / 0902 0.9 / SU 1515 4.5 / 2131 0.6

AUGUST

Time m	Time m
1 0335 4.7 / 0938 0.8 / M 1548 4.6 / 2209 0.5	**16** 0411 5.0 / 1025 0.7 / TU 1628 4.9 / 2256 0.2
2 0411 4.8 / 1018 0.8 / TU 1625 4.7 / 2248 0.5	**17** 0457 4.9 / 1108 0.8 / W 1713 4.8 / 2342 0.4
3 0451 4.8 / 1059 0.8 / W 1705 4.7 / 2330 0.5	**18** 0544 4.7 / 1151 0.9 / TH 1800 4.6
4 0535 4.7 / 1142 0.9 / TH 1751 4.6	**19** 0029 0.7 / 0634 4.4 / F 1238 1.1 / ☾ 1852 4.3
5 0016 0.6 / 0625 4.6 / F 1232 1.0 / 1845 4.5	**20** 0125 1.0 / 0730 4.0 / SA 1345 1.4 / 1956 4.0
6 0111 0.8 / 0723 4.4 / SA 1332 1.2 / 1948 4.3	**21** 0240 1.3 / 0843 3.8 / SU 1518 1.5 / 2120 3.8
7 0221 0.9 / 0832 4.2 / SU 1455 1.3 / 2102 4.2	**22** 0354 1.4 / 1008 3.7 / M 1633 1.4 / 2244 3.8
8 0339 1.0 / 0949 4.1 / M 1617 1.2 / 2221 4.2	**23** 0502 1.4 / 1119 3.8 / TU 1739 1.3 / 2346 4.0
9 0450 1.0 / 1103 4.1 / TU 1726 1.1 / 2331 4.3	**24** 0600 1.4 / 1210 4.0 / W 1830 1.1
10 0553 1.0 / 1205 4.2 / W 1825 0.9	**25** 0031 4.2 / 0643 1.3 / TH 1250 4.2 / 1907 0.9
11 0028 4.6 / 0646 0.9 / TH 1253 4.4 / 1914 0.6	**26** 0106 4.4 / 0711 1.2 / F 1322 4.4 / 1935 0.8
12 0115 4.8 / 0732 0.8 / F 1336 4.6 / ○ 1959 0.4	**27** 0137 4.6 / 0736 1.0 / SA 1350 4.5 / ● 2002 0.6
13 0159 4.9 / 0816 0.8 / SA 1418 4.8 / 2043 0.3	**28** 0206 4.7 / 0806 0.9 / SU 1418 4.7 / 2034 0.5
14 0242 5.0 / 0858 0.7 / SU 1500 4.9 / 2127 0.2	**29** 0237 4.9 / 0841 0.7 / M 1449 4.8 / 2109 0.4
15 0326 5.1 / 0941 0.7 / M 1543 5.0 / 2211 0.1	**30** 0311 5.0 / 0919 0.6 / TU 1524 4.9 / 2147 0.3
	31 0347 5.0 / 0958 0.6 / W 1601 4.9 / 2226 0.4

Chart Datum is 0·23 metres below TAW Datum. HAT is 5·6 metres above Chart Datum.

》》 FREE monthly updates. Register at 《
www.reedsnauticalalmanac.co.uk

139

STANDARD TIME UT −01
Subtract 1 hour for UT
For Belgian Summer Time add
ONE hour in **non-shaded areas**

ZEEBRUGGE LAT 51°21'N LONG 3°12'E
TIMES AND HEIGHTS OF HIGH AND LOW WATERS

Dates in red are **SPRINGS**
Dates in blue are NEAPS

YEAR 2022

SEPTEMBER

Day	Time	m	Time	m	Time	m	Time	m
1 TH	0425	5.0	1037	0.7	1640	4.9	2305	0.5
16 F	0508	4.6	1113	0.9	1722	4.6	2344	0.9
2 F	0506	4.8	1117	0.8	1723	4.8	2347	0.6
17 SA	0548	4.3	1150	1.1	1805	4.3		
3 SA ◑	0552	4.6	1201	1.0	1812	4.6		
18 SU	0025	1.3	0632	3.9	1234	1.4	1857	3.9
4 SU	0037	0.9	0646	4.3	1257	1.2	1913	4.3
19 M	0149	1.6	0737	3.6	1443	1.6	2033	3.6
5 M	0148	1.2	0757	4.0	1428	1.4	2037	4.1
20 TU	0320	1.7	0925	3.5	1557	1.6	2207	3.6
6 TU	0321	1.3	0930	3.8	1602	1.3	2211	4.1
21 W	0425	1.7	1042	3.6	1700	1.4	2312	3.9
7 W	0436	1.3	1053	4.0	1713	1.1	2324	4.3
22 TH	0523	1.5	1136	3.9	1753	1.1	2358	4.2
8 TH	0541	1.1	1152	4.2	1811	0.8		
23 F	0607	1.3	1216	4.2	1831	0.9		
9 F	0017	4.6	0633	1.0	1238	4.5	1859	0.5
24 SA	0034	4.5	0639	1.1	1248	4.5	1902	0.7
10 SA ○	0101	4.9	0716	0.8	1318	4.7	1941	0.3
25 SU ●	0105	4.8	0708	0.9	1318	4.7	1933	0.5
11 SU	0141	5.1	0756	0.7	1357	4.9	2022	0.2
26 M	0136	5.0	0742	0.7	1349	4.9	2007	0.3
12 M	0221	5.2	0837	0.6	1437	5.1	2104	0.1
27 TU	0209	5.1	0819	0.6	1422	5.0	2045	0.3
13 TU	0302	5.2	0917	0.5	1518	5.1	2146	0.1
28 W	0245	5.2	0858	0.5	1459	5.1	2124	0.3
14 W	0344	5.1	0957	0.6	1600	5.1	2227	0.3
29 TH	0322	5.1	0937	0.6	1537	5.1	2203	0.4
15 TH	0426	4.9	1036	0.7	1642	4.9	2306	0.6
30 F	0401	5.0	1016	0.7	1616	5.0	2242	0.6

OCTOBER

Day	Time	m	Time	m	Time	m	Time	m
1 SA	0441	4.8	1055	0.8	1659	4.8	2323	0.8
16 SU	0508	4.2	1112	1.1	1725	4.2	2333	1.4
2 SU ◑	0526	4.5	1139	1.0	1749	4.5		
17 M ◑	0542	3.9	1149	1.4	1808	3.9		
3 M	0013	1.1	0619	4.1	1237	1.2	1853	4.2
18 TU	0014	1.7	0628	3.6	1356	1.6	1932	3.6
4 TU	0130	1.4	0737	3.8	1418	1.4	2029	4.0
19 W	0237	1.9	0830	3.4	1516	1.6	2118	3.6
5 W	0306	1.5	0918	3.7	1545	1.2	2202	4.1
20 TH	0342	1.8	0952	3.6	1614	1.4	2225	3.9
6 TH	0420	1.4	1036	4.0	1654	1.0	2310	4.5
21 F	0437	1.5	1050	3.9	1706	1.1	2315	4.2
7 F	0524	1.2	1133	4.3	1752	0.7	2359	4.7
22 SA	0524	1.3	1133	4.2	1748	0.9	2356	4.6
8 SA	0615	1.0	1218	4.6	1839	0.5		
23 SU	0602	1.0	1210	4.5	1826	0.6		
9 SU ○	0043	5.0	0657	0.8	1257	4.8	1921	0.3
24 M	0031	4.9	0639	0.8	1244	4.8	1902	0.4
10 M	0122	5.1	0736	0.7	1336	5.0	2001	0.2
25 TU ●	0106	5.1	0717	0.6	1319	5.0	1940	0.3
11 TU	0200	5.1	0815	0.6	1415	5.1	2040	0.2
26 W	0142	5.2	0756	0.5	1356	5.1	2020	0.3
12 W	0240	5.1	0853	0.5	1455	5.1	2120	0.3
27 TH	0220	5.2	0837	0.5	1435	5.1	2101	0.4
13 TH	0320	5.0	0931	0.6	1535	5.0	2157	0.5
28 F	0259	5.0	0918	0.6	1516	5.1	2141	0.5
14 F	0358	4.8	1007	0.7	1613	4.8	2231	0.8
29 SA	0340	4.8	0958	0.7	1558	4.9	2222	0.7
15 SA	0435	4.5	1040	0.9	1649	4.5	2302	1.1
30 SU	0422	4.6	1040	0.8	1643	4.7	2306	1.0
31 M	0508	4.3	1128	1.0	1736	4.5	2359	1.3

NOVEMBER

Day	Time	m	Time	m	Time	m	Time	m
1 TU ◐	0606	4.0	1235	1.1	1847	4.2		
16 W ◐	0554	3.8	1218	1.4	1843	3.8		
2 W	0121	1.5	0729	3.8	1406	1.2	2020	4.1
17 TH	0046	1.8	0717	3.6	1425	1.4	2018	3.8
3 TH	0245	1.5	0858	3.8	1521	1.0	2142	4.3
18 F	0249	1.7	0851	3.7	1524	1.3	2129	4.0
4 F	0356	1.4	1011	4.1	1628	1.0	2248	4.5
19 SA	0347	1.5	0954	3.9	1616	1.1	2226	4.3
5 SA	0501	1.2	1108	4.4	1728	0.6	2340	4.7
20 SU	0439	1.3	1045	4.2	1705	0.9	2313	4.5
6 SU	0554	1.0	1156	4.6	1818	0.5		
21 M	0526	1.1	1130	4.5	1750	0.7	2356	4.8
7 M	0024	4.9	0638	0.8	1238	4.8	1901	0.4
22 TU	0610	0.8	1212	4.7	1833	0.5		
8 TU ○	0104	5.0	0718	0.7	1318	4.9	1941	0.4
23 W ●	0038	4.9	0653	0.7	1253	4.9	1916	0.4
9 W	0143	5.0	0756	0.7	1357	5.0	2019	0.5
24 TH	0119	5.0	0736	0.6	1334	5.0	1958	0.5
10 TH	0222	4.9	0833	0.6	1437	4.9	2056	0.6
25 F	0200	4.9	0819	0.6	1417	5.0	2041	0.6
11 F	0300	4.7	0910	0.7	1515	4.8	2130	0.8
26 SA	0242	4.7	0902	0.6	1500	4.9	2124	0.7
12 SA	0336	4.5	0943	0.8	1550	4.6	2200	1.0
27 SU	0324	4.7	0946	0.7	1546	4.8	2208	0.9
13 SU	0408	4.3	1015	0.9	1624	4.4	2228	1.2
28 M	0410	4.5	1032	0.7	1635	4.7	2256	1.1
14 M	0439	4.2	1046	1.1	1658	4.2	2259	1.4
29 TU	0500	4.3	1126	0.8	1732	4.5	2353	1.3
15 TU	0511	4.0	1123	1.2	1739	4.0	2338	1.6
30 W ●	0559	4.1	1231	0.9	1841	4.3		

DECEMBER

Day	Time	m	Time	m	Time	m	Time	m
1 TH ◐	0103	1.4	0711	4.0	1343	0.9	1959	4.3
16 F ◑	0010	1.5	0629	4.0	1308	1.2	1917	4.1
2 F	0214	1.4	0827	4.0	1450	0.8	2112	4.3
17 SA	0127	1.5	0742	3.9	1424	1.1	2028	4.1
3 SA	0323	1.3	0937	4.0	1556	0.8	2218	4.4
18 SU	0248	1.5	0853	4.0	1525	1.0	2132	4.3
4 SU	0431	1.2	1039	4.3	1701	0.7	2316	4.6
19 M	0352	1.3	0954	4.1	1622	0.9	2230	4.4
5 M	0533	1.1	1134	4.5	1757	0.6		
20 TU	0450	1.2	1050	4.3	1716	0.8	2324	4.5
6 TU	0006	4.7	0622	0.9	1222	4.6	1844	0.6
21 W	0544	1.0	1143	4.5	1807	0.7		
7 W	0051	4.7	0705	0.8	1306	4.7	1925	0.5
22 TH	0014	4.6	0634	0.8	1232	4.7	1855	0.7
8 TH ○	0131	4.7	0744	0.8	1346	4.7	2002	0.8
23 F ●	0100	4.7	0720	0.7	1319	4.8	1941	0.7
9 F	0210	4.6	0820	0.8	1425	4.6	2036	0.9
24 SA	0145	4.7	0806	0.6	1404	4.8	2026	0.7
10 SA	0246	4.5	0854	0.8	1501	4.5	2107	1.0
25 SU	0229	4.6	0851	0.6	1450	4.9	2111	0.8
11 SU	0319	4.4	0926	0.8	1534	4.4	2135	1.1
26 M	0313	4.6	0937	0.5	1537	4.9	2157	0.7
12 M	0349	4.3	0957	0.9	1606	4.2	2204	1.2
27 TU	0359	4.6	1026	0.5	1627	4.8	2245	1.0
13 TU	0419	4.2	1030	0.9	1640	4.3	2237	1.3
28 W	0448	4.5	1118	0.5	1721	4.7	2338	1.1
14 W	0452	4.1	1108	1.0	1720	4.2	2317	1.4
29 TH	0542	4.4	1214	0.6	1821	4.6		
15 TH	0534	4.1	1156	1.1	1810	4.1		
30 F ◐	0035	1.2	0643	4.3	1313	0.6	1926	4.4
31 SA	0136	1.3	0749	4.2	1416	0.7	2033	4.3

Chart Datum is 0·23 metres below TAW Datum. HAT is 5·6 metres above Chart Datum.

FREE monthly updates. Register at
www.reedsnauticalalmanac.co.uk

2.33 BLANKENBERGE

Belgium, West Flanders 51°18'·90N 03°06'·48E ✦✦◊◊◊✿✿

CHARTS AC 2449, 1872, 1874; DYC 1801.3; Imray C30

TIDES +0130 Dover; ML 2·5; Duration 0535
Standard Port ZEEBRUGGE (◄—)

Times				Height (metres)			
High Water		Low Water		MHWS	MHWN	MLWN	MLWS
0300	0900	0300	0900	4·8	4·0	1·2	0·5
1500	2100	1500	2100				
Differences BLANKENBERGE							
ND		ND		+0·1	0·0	-0·1	0·0
CADZAND							
+0005	−0010	+0000	+0010	0·0	0·0	-0·1	0·0

SHELTER Good, but entry is dangerous in NW'lies F6 and above.

NAVIGATION WPT 51°19'·60N 03°05'·31E, 134°/1M to pierheads. Caution: 4 unlit Y SPM buoys and one Fl (3) Y 20s lie E and W of hbr ent about 400m offshore. Beware strong tides (and fishing lines) across ent. Said to be dredged 2·5m during the season; but out of season it silts badly between piers and dries at LW. Do not try to ent/exit around low water, especially at springs and from Oct-end May, unless depths have been pre-checked. Call dredger Ch 10 for clearance to pass.

LIGHTS AND MARKS Conspic high-rise blocks E of lt ho, W twr B top. Ldg lts 134°, both FR, (Red X on front mast) show the best water. FG on W pier is more visible than FR (E pier). A water twr is conspic on E side of new Hbr. See also Lights, buoys and waypoints and chartlet.

COMMUNICATIONS (Code (0)50) *Blankenberge Rescue* Ch 08 or relay via Zeebrugge Traffic Centre VHF Ch 69, ⊖ 544223, Police 429842; Dr 333668; Ⓗ 413701; Brit Consul (02) 287 6248; VNZ, SYCB and VVW marinas VHF Ch 23; Dredger VHF Ch 10.

FACILITIES A port of entry, with Customs early Apr–late Sept. Keep to port, past the FV hbr, for the old Yacht Hbr (1·8m); VNZ pontoons are on N side and SYCB to the E. Or turn 90° stbd into new Hbr/marina (2·5m); 12 pontoons, run by VNZ, SYCB & VVW.

VNZ (YC Vrije Noordzeezeilers) ☎425292, mob 0497 565565. www. vnzblankenberge.be vnz@skynet.be 120 inc ⓥ▱, €2·50 inc ⚓ ⅅ◐ wi-fi, multihulls €3·80. ✕ ▱.

SYCB (Scarphout Royal YC) ☎411420, mob 0476971692 www. scarphout.be scarphout@skynet.be 250 inc ⓥ▱, €2·40 inc ⚓ wi-fi ⅅ◐ coin meters, multihulls +50%. ✕ ▱ ⓑ ▬ ⛴(10·5t).

VVW Marina ☎417536. www.vvwblankenberge.be info@ vvweblankenberge.be 350 inc ⓥ▱, €1·90 inc ⚓ ◐ wi-fi, ⅅ €2·00 p/d, multihulls +50%, ▮▲♂ ⅅ ⊡▣ ⚒ 🅿 ⚔ ⛴(20t).

Town ✕ ▱ 🛒 🛢 ✉ Ⓑ Ⓒ ≈ ✈ Oostende.

2.34 OOSTENDE

Belgium, West Flanders 51°14'·35N 02°55'·09E ✦✦◊◊◊✿✿✿

CHARTS AC 2449, 1872, 1874, 1873; SHOM 7214; Navi 1010; DYC 1801.2; Imray C30; BE D11

TIDES +0115 Dover; ML 2·79; Duration 0530
Standard Port ZEEBRUGGE (◄—)

Times				Height (metres)			
High Water		Low Water		MHWS	MHWN	MLWN	MLWS
0300	0900	0300	0900	4·8	4·0	1·2	0·5
1500	2100	1500	2100				
Differences OOSTENDE							
−0019	−0019	−0008	−0008	+0·4	+0·2	+0·2	+0·1

SHELTER Very good in Mercator Marina (5·0m) and Royal North Sea YC (2.2m). RYCO (2·7m) may be exposed in strong W/NW'lies.

NAVIGATION WPT 51° 15'·2N 02° 54'·23E, 143°/1M to ent. Avoid the offshore banks esp in bad weather: From the NE stay to seaward of Wenduinebank, except in calm weather. From the NW keep S of W Hinder TSS and approach from MBN buoy. From the SW appr via West Diep and Kleine Rede, inside Stroombank.

LIGHTS AND MARKS Europa Centrum bldg (105m; twice as high as other bldgs) is conspic 4ca SSW of ent. W lt ho, 5ca ESE of the ent, is conspic with 2 sinusoidal blue bands. E bkwtr hd, distinctive 50m high R/W Radar twr. 143° ldg marks are lattice masts with R/W bands and X topmarks. See chartlet and Lights, buoys and waypoints for lt details.

IPTS At blind exit from Montgomerydok, green and red arrows regulate exit.

COMMUNICATIONS (Code 059) HM 340711, Ch 09 (H24); 🌬 VHF Ch 27 at 0820 and 1720 UT (English and Dutch); Police 701111; ⊖ 242070; Brit Consul (02) 287 6248; Ⓗ 552000; Ch 09 (H24); Mercator lock 705762, VHF Ch 14; Marina VHF Ch 14 (lock hrs); Demey lock 340729, VHF Ch 22, gives access to Oostende-Brugge canal.

FACILITIES from seaward: **Royal North Sea YC (RNSYC)** ☎430694 HM 474688278. www.rnsyc.be simon@rnsyc.be No VHF. 150+50ⓥ €2·70/m inc ⅅ◐ (M/Cruisers €3.25/m). ✕ ▱ ▣ ⚒ 🅿 ⚔ ⊡ ⚠ wi-fi, grid.

Mercator lock Call Ch 14 for lock-in time and berth. Waiting pontoon N of lock. No freeflow. R/G tfc lts. Hrs (times in brackets are Fri-Sun & public hols): May/Jun 0800-2000 (2100); Jul/Aug 0700-2200, 7/7; Sep 0800-1800 (2000). Oct–Apr, see web.

Mercator Marina ☎+3259705762.www.mercatormarina.be info@ mercatormarina.be 300+50ⓥ (vessels < 8.99m €2·58m/day, >9m, surcharge of €2·58 m/day inc ⚓. Multihulls +50%). ◐ amend: €1·00, add: ▣ €5·00,dryer €4·00, ⅅ €1·00/1kw; pay cash/card before entering lock outbound.

Royal YC Oostende (RYCO) ☎32477 secretariaat@ryco.be www. ryco.be No VHF, Dockmaster 676391 or enquire in Clubhouse on arrival. 195, some ⓥ if available, €2·60 inc ◐ ⅅ ✕ ▱ ▬ (10t) grid ⛴(½t).

Town All needs, 🏧 🏪 only, ≈ ✈.

O5
Q.G
Q.R
O6
F.R.3M+Q.Y
F.G.3M
OH
Fl.G.5s
Radar tower
8₂
OH2
Q.R
14'·5
Lgd Lts 143°
OH1
Fl.G.5s
Fl(5)Y.20s
aKust6
OH6
Q.R
7g
Fort Napoleon
N
OH8
Q.R
Lt Ho
Fl(3)10s
65m27M
OH10
Q.R
MRCC
OH12
Q.R
Royal North Sea YC
2₇
Visserijdok
2₅
C
B A
F
E
D
Conspic
Centrum Bldg
(105m)
Montgomerydok
14'
5
8
F.R
Tijdok
G
RYCO
F.G
Naval Basin
Zeewezendok
V
V
V
V
K
J
I
H
Mercator
Lock
3₇
F
OOSTENDE
Cathedral
(twin spires)
Mercator
Marina
5
ISO4s
38m4M
8
Voorhaven
ISO4s
48m4M
8
5₂
2₇
RYCO
8
0 metres   600
0 cables   4
Demey Lock
4₂ Canal to Brugge
See inset
VVW
51°13'·5N
55'
02°56'E
HM Ch 09

Royal
North
Sea YC
Waiting
pontoon
N
MERCATOR MARINA
Dredged to 2·7m
I
H G
F
E
A
A
A
5
Montgomerydok
Mercator STS
D
5
B
1–27
Swing
bridge
B
B
C 35–1
B
Waiting
pontoon

2.35 NIEUWPOORT

Belgium, W Flanders **51°09'·38N 02°43'·04E** ❀❀❀❀♨♨♨❁❁❁

CHARTS AC 2449, 1872, 1873; Belgian 101, D11; SHOM 7214; Navicarte 1010; Imray C30

Belgium

TIDES +0105 Dover; ML 2·96; Duration 0515

Standard Port ZEEBRUGGE (←)

Times				Height (metres)			
High Water		Low Water		MHWS	MHWN	MLWN	MLWS
0300	0900	0300	0900	4·8	4·0	1·2	0·5
1500	2100	1500	2100				
Differences NIEUWPOORT							
−0031	−0031	−0010	−0010	+0·7	+0·5	+0·2	+0·1

SHELTER Good except in strong NW'lies. Access H24.

NAVIGATION WPT 51°10'·08N 02°41'·90E, 134°/1M to ent. The bar (1·5m) is liable to silting but usually ample water will be found. At sp beware 2kn stream across ent, and 3kn where inner approach chan reduces to 35m navigable width through Storm surge barrage (WIP 2021/22) (see chartlet inset). From here, the 1M chan to the 3 marinas, dredged 3·1m, is marked by white-topped piles and coloured arrows to each (WSKLuM–blue; VY-N–yellow; KYCN–grey). Speed limit between jetties, 5kn, within docks 3kn.

LIGHTS AND MARKS The high-rise blocks W of the entrance are in stark contrast to the sand dunes and flatlands to the E. The lt ho is a conspic 28m R twr, W bands; see chartlet and Lights, buoys and waypoints. The central, pyramidal white HM bldg at VY-N is conspic.

COMMUNICATIONS (Code 058) MRCC Oostende VHF Ch 16,27; (059) 701000, emergency direct line, SAR support ship (rescue/towing) 0475 630082;VTS Wandelaar appr VHF Ch 60; Coast Guard/Marine Police 224030; Police 101, emergency 112; Brit Consul (02) 287 6211; Med Emergency 1733; Port VHF Ch 09,16 (H24); Canal locks VHF Ch 10, 233050; Air Force Yacht Club (WSKLuM): VHF Ch 23. KYCN: VHF Ch 23. VY-N: VHF Ch 08.

FACILITIES 3 marinas: **WSKLuM**, N & E of Novus Portus. ☎233641, www.wsklum.be info@wsklm.be 453 inc 𝗩 on pontoon A, €2·20. ⏚ €2·60p/d, ⚓ 🛒 ♨ free wi-fi, 🔋 ⛽🔧⚓ (at fuel berth, see para 4) ☗(25t) ⚓. At Lombardsijde, 800m NE, 🗙 ⌂ 🛒 ◎ bike hire.

VY-N, ♨ S & W of Novus Portus. ☎235232, www.vynieuwpoort. be info@vynieuwpoort.be 1000 + 𝗩 €1·90. ⏚16A €2·50p/d, ⚓ 🗙 ⌂ ◎ ◈ free wi-fi, ♨ (at fuel berth, see below) Ⓔ 🔋🔧🛠⚓⌂ ☗(50t) ⚓ free bikes.

KYCN (Royal Nieuwpoort YC). info@kycn.be www.kycn.be ☎234413, 440 + 75𝗩 €2·58 Jul/Aug, ⏚ €2·14/day. ⚓ inner end 𝗩 pontoon. 🗙 ⌂ 🛒 🔋 ⚓ 🔧 ◎ free wi-fi 🛠☗(25t) ⚓.

Fuel ⛽⚓ (H24) self service cr/debit cards, also ♨, available alongside S of VY-N on the E bank of the river, see inset. The river accesses the N Belgian canals. **Town** 🗙 ⌂ 🛒 🛉 ✉ Ⓑ ⇌ ✈ (Oostende).

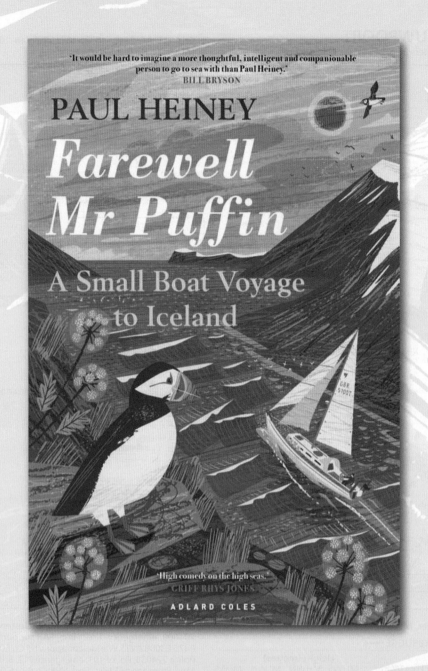

'It would be hard to imagine a more thoughtful,
intelligent and companionable person
to go to sea with than Paul Heiney.'
– *Bill Bryson*

transeurope
MARINAS

VISITORS BERTHING 50% DISCOUNT

The European marina network uniting over 80 marinas.

TransEurope Marinas cardholders benefit from a 50% visitor's berthing discount
in each associated marina for up to five days a year.
For a current list of members and further information, please visit
www.transeuropemarinas.com

UK ⌗
1. Bangor Marina
2. Rhu Marina
3. Troon Yacht Haven
4. Royal Quays Marina
5. Whitehaven Marina
6. Fleetwood Haven Marina
7. Liverpool Marina
8. Conwy Marina
9. Neyland Yacht Haven
10. Penarth Marina
11. Upton Marina
12. Portishead Marina
13. Mylor Yacht Harbour
14. Mayflower Marina
15. Dart Marina
16. Poole Quay Boat Haven
17. Buckler's Hard Yacht Harbour
18. Town Quay Marina
19. Universal Marina
20. Cowes Yacht Haven
21. Royal Clarence Marina
22. Emsworth Yacht Harbour
23. Birdham Pool Marina
24. Dover Marina
25. Gillingham Marina
26. Fambridge Yacht Haven
27. Tollesbury Marina
28. Fox's Marina
29. Brundall Bay Marina
30. Beaucette Marina

Germany ▬
1. Sonwik Marina
2. Ancora Marina
3. Marina Boltenhagen
4. Marina Wiek auf Rügen
5. Baltic Sea Resort
6. Naturhafen Krummin
7. Lagunenstadt Ueckermünde

France ▮
1. Dunkerque
2. Boulogne-sur-mer
3. Saint Valéry sur Somme
4. Dieppe
5. Saint Valery en Caux
6. Fécamp
7. Le Havre Plaisance
8. Port-Deauville
9. Dives-Cabourg-Houlgate
10. Ouistreham/Caen
11. Granville
12. Saint-Quay Port d'Armor
13. Perros-Guirec
14. Roscoff
15. Marinas de Brest
16. Douarnenez-Tréboul
17. Loctudy
18. Port la Forêt
19. Concarneau
20. Ports de Nantes

Spain ▬
1. Puerto Deportivo Gijón
2. Marina Combarro
3. Nauta Sanxenxo
4. Marina La Palma
5. Puerto Calero
6. Alcaidesa Marina
7. Pobla Marina

Belgium ▮
1. VNZ Blankenberge
2. VY Nieuwpoort

Netherlands ▬
1. Marina Den Oever
2. Jachthaven Waterland
3. Jachthaven Wetterwille
4. Marina Port Zélande
5. Jachthaven Biesbosch
6. Delta Marina Kortgene

Portugal ▬
1. Douro Marina
2. Marina de Portimão
3. Quinta do Lorde Marina

Italy ▮
1. Porto Romano
2. Venezia Certosa Marina
3. Marina del Cavallino

Ireland ▮
1. Malahide Marina

Croatia ▬
1. Marina Punat

Greece ⚏
1. Liniariá Marina
2. Kos Marina

3.1 North East England
Blakeney to Berwick-upon-Tweed

EMERGENCY 999
HMCG NATIONAL – 02392 552100
HMCG HUMBER – 01262 672317
HM CUSTOMS – 0845 010 9000
POLICE – 101   MEDICAL – 111

DISTANCE TABLE
Approximate distances in nautical miles are by the most direct route while avoiding dangers and allowing for TSS. Places in *Italics* are in adjoining areas; places in **bold** are in 0.34, Distances across the North Sea.

	1	2	3	4	5	6	7	8	9	10	11	12	13	14	15	16	17	18	19	20	21
1 *Lowestoft*	**1**																				
2 Blakeney	51	**2**																			
3 Wells-next-the-Sea	56	5	**3**																		
4 **King's Lynn**	92	42	37	**4**																	
5 Boston	90	39	34	34	**5**																
6 Spurn Lt Float	89	45	49	53	54	**6**															
7 **Grimsby**	101	57	61	65	66	12	**7**														
8 Hull	114	70	74	78	79	25	14	**8**													
9 Bridlington	121	79	83	87	83	35	44	58	**9**												
10 Scarborough	137	96	100	105	98	50	59	81	20	**10**											
11 Whitby	150	101	105	121	114	66	75	88	35	16	**11**										
12 River Tees (ent)	173	122	126	138	135	87	96	118	56	37	21	**12**									
13 **Hartlepool**	176	126	130	140	137	89	98	122	58	39	24	4	**13**								
14 Seaham	182	137	141	151	145	100	106	133	66	47	33	15	11	**14**							
15 Sunderland	187	142	146	156	149	105	110	138	70	51	36	20	16	5	**15**						
16 Tynemouth	190	149	153	163	154	112	115	145	75	56	41	27	23	12	7	**16**					
17 Blyth	197	156	160	171	162	120	123	153	83	64	49	35	31	20	15	8	**17**				
18 Amble	210	170	174	185	176	126	143	157	102	81	65	46	42	32	27	21	14	**18**			
19 Holy Island	232	191	195	196	198	148	166	180	126	104	88	68	65	54	50	44	37	22	**19**		
20 **Berwick-on-Tweed**	239	200	204	205	205	157	166	189	126	107	91	82	78	67	61	55	47	31	9	**20**	
21 *Eyemouth*	247	208	212	213	213	165	174	197	134	115	99	90	86	75	69	63	55	39	17	8	**21**

Magnetic Variation 0·1'W

See 4.1

BERWICK-ON-TWEED 3.21
HOLY ISLAND 3.20
AberdeenCG
Humber CG
Longstone
Farne Islands
Seahouses
Newton Haven & Beadnell Bay
Craster
Boulmer
AMBLE 3.19
Coquet Island
Newbiggin
Blyth Wind Farm
BLYTH 3.18
E Pier Head Lt
Tynemouth
RIVER TYNE/NORTH SHIELDS 3.17
SUNDERLAND 3.16
SEAHAM 3.15
Tees Bay Wind Farm
HARTLEPOOL 3.14
River Tees
Runswick Bay
WHITBY 3.13
IJmuiden

55°N   30'   2°W   1°W   00°   1°E   30'   30'   30'   30'

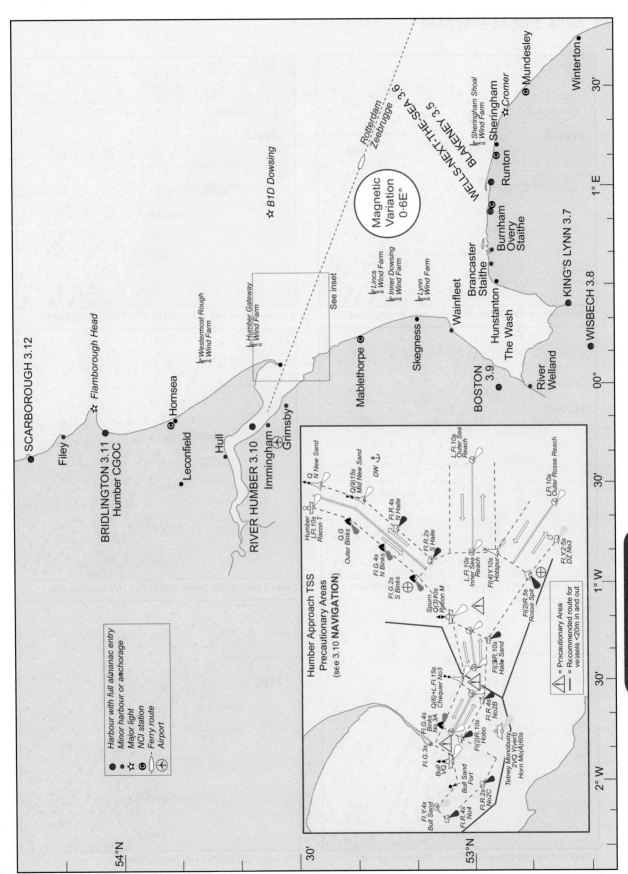

SCARBOROUGH 3.12

Filey

Flamborough Head

BRIDLINGTON 3.11
Humber CGOC

Hornsea

Leconfield

Hull

RIVER HUMBER 3.10

Immingham
Grimsby

Westermost Rough
Wind Farm

Humber Gateway
Wind Farm

See inset

☆ B1D Dowsing

Rotterdam
Zeebrugge

WELLS-NEXT-THE-SEA 3.6
BLAKENEY 3.5

Magnetic
Variation
0·6E°

Mundesley
Cromer
Sheringham
Runton
Sheringham Shoal
Wind Farm

Burnham
Overy
Staithe

Winterton

Lincs
Wind Farm
Inner Dowsing
Wind Farm
Lynn
Wind Farm

Brancaster
Staithe

Wainfleet
Hunstanton
The Wash

KING'S LYNN 3.7

WISBECH 3.8

Skegness

Mablethorpe

BOSTON
3.9

River
Welland

Humber Approach TSS
Precautionary Areas
(see 3.10 NAVIGATION)

Q N New Sand

Q(9)15s
Mid New Sand

DW ⚓

L.Fl.10s
Outer Sea
Reach

Humber
L.Fl.10s
Racon T

Outer Binks
Q.G

Fl.G.4s
N Binks

Fl.G.2s
S Binks

Spurn
Q(3)10s
Racon M

Fl.R.2s
S Haile

Fl.R.4s
N Haile

L.Fl.10s
Inner Sea
Reach

Fl(4)Y.10s
Hotspur

L.Fl.10s
Outer Rosse Reach

Fl.Y.2.5s
DZ No3

Fl(3)R.10s
Haile Sand

Fl(2)R.5s
Rosse Spit

Fl.G.4s
Binks
No 3A

Q(6)+L.Fl.15s
Chequer No3

Fl.G.3s

Fl(2)R.10s
Hobo

Fl.R.4s
No2B

Bull
VQ

Bull Sand
Fort

Tetney Monobuoy
2VQ.Y(vert)
Horn Mo(A)60s

Fl.Y.4s
Bull Sand

Fl.R.2s
No2C

Fl.R.4s
No4

△ = Precautionary Area

— = Recommended route for
vessels <20m in and out

Harbour with full almanac entry
Minor harbour or anchorage
NCI station
Major light
Ferry route
Airport

54°N
30'
53°N

2° W
1° W
30'
30'
00°
30'
1° E
30'

NE England

3.2 AREA 3 TIDAL STREAMS

5 Hours before HW Dover (0030 after HW Immingham)

4 Hours before HW Dover (0130 after HW Immingham)

3 Hours before HW Dover (0230 after HW Immingham)

2 Hours before HW Dover (0330 after HW Immingham)

1 Hour before HW Dover (0430 after HW Immingham)

HW Dover (0530 after HW Immingham)

Northward 4.2   Southward 1.2

1 Hour after HW Dover (0555 before HW Immingham)

2 Hours after HW Dover (0455 before HW Immingham)

3 Hours after HW Dover (0355 before HW Immingham)

4 Hours after HW Dover (0255 before HW Immingham)

5 Hours after HW Dover (0155 before HW Immingham)

6 Hours after HW Dover (0055 before HW Immingham)

NE England

3.3 LIGHTS, BUOYS AND WAYPOINTS

Bold print = light with a nominal range of 15M or more. CAPITALS = place or feature. *CAPITAL ITALICS* = light-vessel, light float or Lanby. *Italics* = Fog signal. ***Bold italics*** = Racon. Some marks/buoys are fitted with AIS (MMSI No); see relevant charts.

GREAT YARMOUTH TO THE WASH

(Direction of buoyage ⇧ South to North)
YARMOUTH and CAISTER ROADS/COCKLE GATEWAY
SW Scroby ▲ Fl G 2·5s; 52°35'·13N 01°46'·69E.
Scroby Elbow ▲ Fl (2) G 5s; *Bell*; 52°36'·55N 01°46'·26E.
Yarmouth Outfall ⌐ Q R; 52°37'·58N 01°45'·70E.
Mid Caister ⌐ Fl (2) R 5s; *Bell*; 52°38'·99N 01°45'·66E.
NW Scroby ▲ Fl (3) G 10s; 52°40'·36N 01°46'·31E.
N Caister ⌐ Fl (3) R 10s; 52°40'·77N 01°45'·65E.
Hemsby ⌐ Fl R 2·5s; 52°41'·80N 01°46'·00E.
N Scroby ↯ VQ; 52°41'·39N 01°46'·47E.
Cockle ↯ VQ (3) 5s; *Bell*; 52°44'·03N 01°43'·59E.

OFFSHORE ROUTE
Cross Sand ↯ L Fl 10s 5M; ***Racon (T) 10M***; 52°40'·33N 01°53'·70E.
Barley ↯ Q (6) + L Fl 15s 6M; 52°38'·76N 01°52'·90E.
E Cross Sand ⌐ Fl (4) R 15s; 52°40'·33N 01°53'·70E.
NE Cross Sand ↯ VQ (3) 5s; 52°44'·22N 01° 53'·80E.
Smith's Knoll ↯ Q (6) + L Fl 15s 7M; ***Racon (T) 10M***; 52°43'·52N 02°17'·89E.
S Winterton Ridge ↯ Q (6) + L Fl 15s; 52°47'·21N 02°03'·44E.
E Hammond Knoll ↯ Q (3) 10s; 52°52'·32N 01°58'·64E.
Hammond Knoll ↯ Q (9) 15s; 52°49'·68N 01°57'·54E.
Newarp ↯ L Fl 10s 7M; ***Racon (O) 10M***; 52°48'·37N 01°55'·69E; 992351118.
S Haisbro ↯ Q (6) + L Fl 15s; *Bell*; 52°50'·82N 01°48'·29E.
Mid Haisbro ▲ Fl (2) G 5s; 52°54'·22N 01°41'·59E.
N Haisbro ↯ Q; ***Racon (T) 10M***; 53°00'·22N 01°32'·29E; 992351031.
Happisburgh ☆ Fl (3) 30s 41m 14M; 52°49'·21N 01°32'·18E.

(Direction of buoyage ⇧ East to West)
CROMER
Cromer ☆ 52°55'·45N 01°19'·01E; Fl 5s 84m **21M**; W 8-sided twr; vis: 102°-307° H24; ***Racon (O) 25M***; 992351015.
Tayjack Wk ⌐ Fl R 2·5s; 52°57'·61N 01°15'·37E.
E Sheringham ↯ Q (3) 10s; 53°02'·21N 01°14'·84E.
W Sheringham ↯ Q (9) 15s; 53°02'·95N 01°06'·72E.

BLAKENEY
Blakeney Fairway ↯; 52°59'·22N 00°58'·53E.
Blakeney Overfalls ⌐ Fl (2) R 5s; *Bell*; 53°03'·01N 01°01'·37E.

WELLS-NEXT-THE-SEA/BRANCASTER STAITHE
Wells WCM ↯ Q(9) 15s; 52°59'·68N 00°50'·24E.
Bridgirdle ⌐ Fl R 2·5s; 53°01'·73N 00°43'·95E.

APPROACHES TO THE WASH
S Race ↯ Q (6) + L Fl 15s; *Bell*; 53°07'·81N 00°57'·34E.
E Docking ⌐ Fl R 2·5s; 53°09'·82N 00°50'·39E.
N Race ▲ Fl G 5s; *Bell*; 53°14'·98N 00°43'·87E.
N Docking ↯ Q; 53°14'·82N 00°41'·49E.
Scott Patch ↯ VQ (3) 5s; 53°11'·12N 00°36'·39E.
S Inner Dowsing ↯ Q (6) + L Fl 15s; *Bell*; 53°12'·12N 00°33'·69E.
Boygrift Tower ⌐ Fl (2) 10s 12m 5M; 53°17'·63N 00°19'·24E.
Burnham Flats ↯ Q (9) 15s; *Bell*; 53°07'·53N 00°34'·89E.
Lincs WF E ↯ Q (3) 10s; 53°07'·61N 00°31'·06E.

THE WASH
West Ridge ↯ Q (9) 15s; 53°19'·06N 00°44'·47E.
N Well ↯ L Fl 10s; *Whistle*; ***Racon (T) 10M***; 53°03'·02N 00°27'·87E.
↯ Fl(2) 10s; 53°01'·53N 00°25'·63E.
Z9 ↯ Fl(2) 6s; 52°59'·73N 00°22'·75E.
ROARING MIDDLE ⇌ L Fl 10s 7m 8M; 52°58'·64N 00°21'·08E.
Z6 ↯ Fl(2) 6s; 52°57'·52N 00°19'·17E.

KING'S LYNN
No 1 ▲ Fl G 3s; 52°56'·00N 00°21'·50E.
No 2 ⌐ Fl (2)R 6s; 52°55'·00N 00°21'·90E.

WISBECH CHANNEL/RIVER NENE
W2 ↯ Fl Y 6s; 52°54'·93N 00°16'·00E.
Nene Roads ↯ *Mo(A) 6s*; 52°53'·85N 01°15'·51E
East Knock ↯ VQ (3) 5s; 52°52'·14N 00°14'·69E.
Bob ⌐ LFl R 5s; 52°52'·05N 00°14'·74E.
Wisbech No 1 ▲ Fl G 3s; 52°53'·33N 00°13'·60E.
Tide Gauge DZ6 ↯; 52°52'·57N 00°13'·10E.
Beacons are moved as required.

FREEMAN CHANNEL
Boston No 1 ▲ Fl G 3s; 52°57'·84N 00°15'·03E.
Alpha ⌐ Fl R 3s; 52°57'·69N 00°15'·06E.
No 3 ▲ Fl G 6s; 52°57'·93N 00°15'·42E.
No 5 ▲ Fl G 3s; 52°58'·51N 00°12'·72E.
No 7 ▲ Fl G 6s; 52°58'·63N 00°11'·40E.
Delta ⌐ Fl R 6s; 52°58'·38N 00°11'·25E.

BOSTON LOWER ROAD
Echo ⌐ Fl R 3s; 52°58'·38N 00°10'·13E.
Foxtrot ⌐ Fl R 3s; 52°57'·60N 00°08'·94E.
Boston No 9 ▲ Fl G 3s; 52°57'·58N 00°08'·36E.
Black Buoy ⌐ Fl (2) R 6s; 52°56'·82N 00°07'·74E.
Tabs Head ↯ Q WG 4m 1M; R □ on W mast; vis: W shore-251°-G-shore; 52°56'·00N 00°04'·91E.

BOSTON, NEW CUT AND RIVER WITHAM
Ent N side, Dollypeg ↯ QG 4m 1M; B △; 52°56'·13N 00°05'·03E.
New Cut ↯ Fl G 3s; △ on pile; 52°55'·98N 00°04'·67E.
New Cut Ldg Lts 240°. Front, No 1, F 5m 5M; 52°55'·85N 00°04'·40E. Rear, 90m from front, F 8m 5M.

WELLAND CUT/RIVER WELLAND
SE side ↯ Iso R 2s; NW side Iso G 2s. Lts QR (to port) and QG (to stbd) mark the chan upstream; 52°55'·72E 00°04'·68E.

THE WASH TO THE RIVER HUMBER

(Direction of buoyage ⇧ South to North)
Dudgeon ↯ Q (9) 15s 7M; ***Racon (O) 10M***; 53°16'·62N 01°16'·90E.
E Dudgeon ↯ Q (3) 10s; 53°19'·72N 00°58'·69E.
W Ridge ↯ Q (9) 15s; 53°19'·04N 00°44'·50E.
Inner Dowsing ↯ Q (3) 10s 7M, ***Racon (T) 10M***; Horn 60s; 53°19'·10N 00°34'·80E.
Mid Outer Dowsing ▲ Fl (3) G 10s; 53°24'·82N 01°07'·79E.
N Outer Dowsing ↯ Q; ***Racon (T) 10M***; 53°33'·52N 00°59'·59E; 992351031.
B.1D Platform Dowsing ↯ 53°33'·68N 00°52'·63E; Fl (2) 10s 28m **22M**; Morse (U) R 15s 28m 3M; *Horn (2) 60s*.

RIVER HUMBER APPROACHES
Protector ⌐ Fl R 2·5s; 53°24'·84N 00°25'·12E.
DZ No 4 ↯ Fl Y 5s; 53°27'·15N 00°19'·06E.
DZ No 3 ↯ Fl Y 2·5s 53°29'·30N 00°19'·21E.
Rosse Spit ⌐ Fl (2) R 5s 53°30'·56N 00°16'·60E.
Outer Sand ↯ Q (3) 10s; 53°36'·41N 00°29'·39E; 992351119.
Haile Sand No 2 ⌐ Fl (3) R 10s; 53°32'·42N 00°13'·18E.
HUMBER LT FLOAT ⇌ L Fl G 10s 5M; ***Racon (T) 7M***; 53°38'·70N 00°21'·24E; AIS.
N Binks ▲ Fl G 4s; 53°36'·01N 00°18'·28E.
S Binks ▲ Fl G 2s 53°34'·74N 00°16'·55E.
SPURN ⇌ Q (3) 10s 10m 8M; ***Racon (M) 5M***; 53°33'·42N 00°14'·15E.
SE CHEQUER ⇌ VQ (6)+L Fl 10s 6m 6M; 53°33'·36N 00°12'·86E.
Chequer No 3 ↯ Q (6) + L Fl 15s; 53°33'·07N 00°10'·63E.
No 2B ⌐ Fl R 4s; 53°32'·33N 00°09'·10E.
TETNEY ⇌ 2 VQ Y (vert); *Horn Mo (A)60s*; QY on 290m floating hose; 53°32'·35N 00°06'·76E.

RIVER HUMBER/GRIMSBY/HULL
Binks No 3A ⚓ Fl G 4s; 53°33'·92N 00°07'·43E.
Spurn Pt ⚓ Fl G 3s 11m 5M; 53°34'·37N 00°06'·47E.
BULL ⚓ VQ 8m 6M; 53°33'·54N 00°05'·70E.
Bull Sand ⚓ Q R ; 53°34'·45N 00°03'·69E.
North Fort ⚓ Q; 53°33'·80N 00°04'·19E.
South Fort ⚓ Q (6) + L Fl 15s; 53°33'·65N 00°03'·96E.
Haile Sand Fort ⚓ Fl R 5s 21m 3M; 53°32'·07N 00°01'·99E.
Haile Chan No 4 ⚓ Fl R 4s; 53°33'·64N 00°02'·84E.
Middle No 7 VQ (6) + L Fl 10s; 53°35'·80N 00°01'·50E.
Sunk S8 ⚓ Fl G 1·5s; 53°37'·10N 00°02'·16E (992351275).
Grimsby Royal Dock ent E side ⚓ Fl (2) R 6s 10m 8M; Dn;
53°35'·08N 00°04'·04W.
Immingham Bulk Terminal ⚓ Dir Lt 291° Dir WRG 1s 17m 3M; vis:
288·5°-FG-289·5°-IsoG-290·5-FW-291·5-IsoR-292·5°-FR-295·5; on
bldg; 53°38'·41N 00°11'·97W (992351276).

RIVER HUMBER TO WHITBY
Canada & Giorgios Wreck ⚓ VQ (3) 5s; 53°42'·37N 00°07'·16E.
Albrough intake ⚓ Q R 17m 2M; 53°49'·01N 00°03'·38W.

BRIDLINGTON
SW Smithic ⚓ Q (9) 15s; 54°02'·41N 00°09'·21W.
N Pier Hd ⚓ Fl 2s 12m 9M; *Horn 60s;* (Tidal Lts) Fl R or Fl G;
54°04'·77N 00°11'·19W.
N Smithic ⚓ VQ; *Bell;* 54°06'·22N 00°03'·90W.
Flamborough Hd ☆ 54°06'·98N 00°04'·96W; Fl (4) 15s 65m
24M; W ○ twr; *Horn (2) 90s.*

FILEY/SCARBOROUGH/WHITBY
Filey Brigg ⚓ Q (3) 10s; *Bell;* 54°12'·74N 00°14'·60W.
Scarborough E Pier Hd ⚓ QG 8m 3M; 54°16'·88N 00°23'·36W.
Scarborough Pier ⚓ Iso 5s 17m 9M; W ○ twr; vis: 219°- 039°
(tide sigs); *Dia 60s;* 54°16'·91N 00°23'·40W.
Whitby ⚓ Q; *Bell;* 54°30'·33N 00°36'·58W.
Whitby High ☆ 54°28'·67N 00°34'·10W; Fl WR 5s 73m
18M,R16M; W 8-sided twr & dwellings; vis:128°-R-143°-W-
319°.
Whitby E Pier ⚓ Fl(2) R 4s 16m 5M; 54°29'·57N 00°36'·71W;
Twr.
Whitby E Pier Ext Hd ⚓ Q R 12m 5M; 54°29'·65N 00°36'·74W.
Whitby W Pier ⚓ Fl(2) G 4s 24m 5M; 54°29'·57N 00°36'·78W;
Twr.
Whitby W Pier Ext Hd ⚓ Q G 12m 5M; 54°29'·65N 00°36'·80W.

WHITBY TO THE RIVER TYNE
RUNSWICK/REDCAR
Salt Scar ⚓ 54°38'·12N 01°00'·12W VQ; *Bell.*
Luff Way Ldg Lts 197°. Front, on Esplanade, FR 8m 7M; vis:
182°-212°; 54°37'·10N 01°03'·71W. Rear, 115m from front, FR
12m 7M; vis: 182°-212°.
High Stone. Lade Way Ldg Lts 247°. Front, Oc R 2·5s 9m 7M;
54°37'·15N 01°03'·92W. Rear, 43m from front, Oc R 2·5s 11m
7M; vis: 232°-262°.

TEES APPROACHES/HARTLEPOOL
Tees Approach ⚓ Mo(A) 5s 8M; *Racon (B); Horn;* 54°40'·60N
01°04'·00W; AIS.
Bkwtr Hd S Gare ⚓ 54°38'·85N 01°08'·25W; Fl WR 12s 16m 10M;
W ○ twr; vis: 020°-W-240°-R-357°; Sig Stn.
Ldg Lts 210·1° Front, FR 18m 13M; 54°37'·22N 01°10'·20W.
Rear, 560m from front, FR 20m **16M.**
Longscar ⚓ Q (3) 10s; *Bell;* 54°40'·86N 01°09'·89W.
The Heugh ☆ 54°41'·79N 01°10'·56W; Fl (2) **WR** 10s 19m **19M;** vis:
309°-R-319°-W-190°; W twr.

Hartlepool Marina Lock Dir Lt 308° Dir Fl WRG2s 6m 3M; vis:
305·5°-G-307°-W-309°-R-310·5°; 54°41'·45N 01°11'·92W.

SEAHAM/SUNDERLAND
Seaham N Pier Hd ⚓ Fl G 10s 12m 5M; W col, B bands;
54°50'·26N 01°19'·26W.
Sunderland Roker Pier Hd ☆ 54°55'·28N 01°21'·15W; Fl 5s
25m **18M;** W □ twr, 3 R bands and cupola: vis: 211°- 357°;
Siren 20s.
Old N Pier Hd ⚓ QG 12m 8M; metal column; 54°55'·13N
01°21'·61W.
DZ ⚓ 54°57'·04N 01°18'·90W and ⚓ 54°58'·61N 01°19'·90W;
both Fl Y 2·5s.

TYNE ENTRANCE/NORTH SHIELDS
Ent North Pier Hd ☆ 55°00'·88N 01°24'·18W; Fl (3) 10s 26m
26M; Gy □ twr, W lantern; *Horn 10s.*
Herd Groyne Hd Dir Ldg Lt 249°, Oc 10s 14m **19M;** vis: 246·5°-
W-251·5°; R pile structure, R&W lantern. Same structure Oc RG
10s 13m, 11M; vis: 224°-G-246·5°, 251·5°-R-277°; sync with Dir lt
FR (unintens) 080°-224°. *Bell (1) 5s;* 55°00'·49N 01°25'·44W.

RIVER TYNE TO BERWICK-UPON-TWEED
CULLERCOATS and BLYTH
Cullercoats Ldg Lts 256°. Front, FR 27m 3M; 55°02'·06N
01°25'·91W. Rear, 38m from front, FR 35m 3M.
Blyth Ldg Lts 324°. Front ⚓, F Bu 11m 10M; 55°07'·42N 01°29'·82W.
Rear ⚓, 180m from front, F Bu 17m 10M. Both Or ⚓ on twr.
Blyth E Pier Hd ☆ 55°06'·98N 01°29'·21W; Fl(4) 10s 19m **21M,** W
twr; same structure FR 13m 13M, vis:152°-249°; Horn (3) 30s.
Met Mast ⚓; Mo(U)15s 17m 10M; 55°08'·78N 01°25'·25W; Aero
3 FR (107m), *Horn 30s.*

COQUET ISLAND, AMBLE and WARKWORTH
Coquet ☆ 55°20'·03N 01°32'·39W; Fl (3) WR 20s 25m **W19M,
R15M;** W □ twr, turreted parapet, lower half Gy; vis: 330°-R-
140°-W-163°-R-180°-W-330°; sector boundaries are indeter-
minate and may appear as Alt WR; *Horn 30s.*
Amble N Pier Head ⚓ Fl G 6s 12m 6M; 55°20'·39N
01°34'·25W.

SEAHOUSES, BAMBURGH and FARNE ISLANDS
N Sunderland ⚓ Fl R 2·5s; 55°34'·62N 01°37'·12W.
Bamburgh Black Rocks Point ☆ 55°36'·99N 01°43'·45W; Oc(2)
WRG 8s 12m **W14M,** R11M, G11M; W bldg; vis: 122°-G-165°-W-
175°-R-191°-W- 238°-R- 275°-W- 289°-G-300°.
Inner Farne ⚓ Fl (2) WR 15s 27m W10M, R7M; W ○ twr; vis:
119°- R - 280° - W -119°; 55°36'·92N 01°39'·35W.
Longstone ☆ W side 55°38'·62N 01°36'·65W; Fl 20s 23m **18M;**
R twr, W band; 992351127.
Swedman ⚓ Fl G 2·5s; 55°37'·65N 01°41'·63W.

HOLY ISLAND
Ridge ⚓ Q (3) 10s; 55°39'·70N 01°45'·97W.
Plough Rock ⚓ Q (9) 15s; 55°40'·24N 01°46'·00W.
Old Law E Bn ⚓ (Guile Pt) Oc WRG 6s 9m 4M; vis: 180·5°-G-258·5°-
W-261·5°-R-300°, 55°39'·49N 01°47'·59W; stone obelisk.
Heugh ⚓ Oc WRG 6s 24m 5M; vis: 135°-G-308°-W-311-R- shore;
55°40'·09N 01°47'·99W.
Plough Seat ⚓ QR; 55°40'·37N 01°44'·97W.
Goldstone ⚓ QG; 55°40'·25N 01°43'·64W.

BERWICK-UPON-TWEED
Bkwtr Hd ⚓ Fl 5s 15m 6M; vis: 201°-009°, (obscured 155°-201°);
W ○ twr, R cupola and base; FG (same twr) 8m 1M; vis 009°-
G-155°; 55°45'·88N 01°59'·06W.

NE England

149

3.4 PASSAGE INFORMATION

Admiralty Leisure Folios: 5614 Orford Ness to Whitby, 5615 Whitby to Berwick-upon-Tweed. **Bibliography:** *Forth, Tyne, Dogger, Humber – Blakeney to St Abbs –* (Imray/Irving) covers the southern part of this less frequented cruising ground. Northwards, use Royal Northumberland *YC's Sailing Directions Humber to Rattray Head*. The *North Sea (West) Pilot* (Admiralty NP54) covers the whole area.

OFFSHORE ENERGY INSTALLATIONS

See 3.14. Any craft going offshore in the N Sea will encounter wind farms and possibly oil or gas installations. These are shown on Admiralty charts, and the position of mobile rigs is updated in weekly NMs. At night, platforms show a white light, Fl Mo (U) 15s 15M. Secondary lts, Fl Mo (U) R 15s 2M, synchronised with the main lt, or W lts may mark projections. The usual fog signal is Horn Mo (U) 30s. See the Admiralty List of Lights and Fog Signals, Vol A.

Safety zones of radius 500m exist are around all permanent platforms, mobile rigs, and tanker loading moorings. Unauthorised vessels, including yachts, must not enter these except in emergency or due to stress of weather – Annual Summary of Admiralty Notices to Mariners No 20.

Increasing numbers of wind farms, both under construction and complete, are serviced by numerous fast work boats from Lowestoft, Gt Yarmouth, Wells, Wash and the Humber.

NORTH NORFOLK COAST

(AC 1503, 108) The coast of N Norfolk is unfriendly in bad weather, with no safe harbour accessible when there is any N in the wind. The harbours all dry, and seas soon build up in the entrances or over the bars, some of which are dangerous even in a moderate breeze on an ebb tide. In settled weather and moderate offshore winds it is a peaceful area to explore, particularly for boats which can take the ground. At Blakeney and Wells buoyed channels shift almost every year, so local advice is essential and may best be acquired in advance from the HM or harbour websites.

Haisborough Sand (buoyed) lies parallel to the Norfolk coast 8M off Happisburgh lt ho. Depths are less than 1m in many places, and dry 0.4m near the mid-point. The shoal is steep-to, on its NE side in particular, and there are tidal eddies. Even a moderate sea or swell breaks on the shallower parts. There are dangerous wrecks near the S end. Haisborough Tail and Hammond Knoll (with wk depth 1.6m) lie to the E of the S end of Haisborough Sand. Newarp lt F is 5M SE. Similar banks lie parallel to and up to 60M off the coast.

▶ *The streams follow the generally NW / SE direction of the coast and offshore channels. Further out the stream is some-what rotatory: when changing from SE-going to NW-going it sets SW, and when changing from NW-going to SE-going it sets NE, across the shoals. Close south of Haisborough Sand the SE-going stream begins at HW Immingham −0030 and the NW-going at HW Immingham +0515, Sp rates up to 2.5kn. A yacht may carry a fair tide from Gt Yarmouth to the Wash.* ◀

If proceeding directly from Cromer to the Humber, pass S of Sheringham Shoal (buoyed) and the wind farm close N. Head to the NE of Blakeney Overfalls (min depth 1m) and Docking Shoal, and then SW of Race Bank and adjacent wind farm so as to fetch Inner Dowsing lt (fog sig). Thence pass E of Protector Overfalls, and steer for Rosse Spit buoy at the SE entrance to the River Humber.

▶ *At Sheringham Shoal the ESE-going stream begins at HW Immingham −0225, and the WNW-going at +0430.* ◀

THE WASH

(AC 108,1200) The Wash is formed by the estuaries of the rivers Great Ouse, Nene, Welland and Witham; it is an area of shifting sands, most of which dry. Important features are the strong tidal streams, the low-lying shore, and the often poor vis. Watch the echo sounder carefully, buoys are often moved to accommodate changes in the channel.

▶ *Near North Well, the inward stream begins at HW Immingham −0430, and the outward at HW Immingham +0130, Sp rates about 2kn. The in-going stream is usually stronger than the out-going, but runs for less time. Prolonged NE winds frequently increase the rate and duration of the in-going stream and raise the water level at the head of the estuary. Do not attempt entry to the rivers too early on the flood, which runs hard in the rivers.* ◀

North Well SWM and Roaring Middle lt float are the keys to entering the Wash from N or E. From the E it is also possible to approach via a shallow route N of Stiffkey Overfalls and Bridgirdle PHM buoy; thence via Sledway and Woolpack PHM lt buoy to North Well and into Lynn Deeps. Near N end of Lynn Deeps there are overfalls over Lynn Knock at Sp tides. 3 x IDM mark the path of buried power transmission cables. Approach King's Lynn from No 1 light buoy, Fl G 3s, via Daseley Sled and well buoyed/lit channel. For R Nene (Wisbech) follow Old Lynn Channel and Wisbech Eye Channel to E Knock ECM which marks entrance to buoyed approach.

Boston and R Welland are reached via Freeman Channel, westward from Roaring Middle; or via Boston Deep, all lit. King's Lynn ⚓ is marked by Roaring Middle, Sunk and Seal Outer. ⚓ for Boston and Wisbech have AIS enhanced marks.

The NW shore of The Wash is fronted by mudflats extending 2–3M offshore and drying more than 4m; a bombing range is marked by Y beacons and buoys. Wainfleet Swatchway should only be used in good vis; the buoyed chan shifts constantly, and several shoals (charted depths unreliable) off Gibraltar Pt obstruct access to Boston Deep. In an emergency Wainfleet offers good shelter (dries).

Wisbech Cut provides access to the Fens Middle Levels, navigable by narrow boat and river cruisers. Dog in a Doublet Lock above Wisbech effectively limits sea-going vessels.

The Great Ouse is navigable as far as Ely 24M upstream. There is a lock half-way at Denver Sluice ☎(01366) 382340/VHF Ch 73, and low bridges beyond.

THE WASH TO THE RIVER HUMBER

(AC 108, 107) Inner Dowsing is a narrow N/S sandbank with a least depth of 1·2m, 8M offshore between Skegness and Mablethorpe. There are overfalls off the W side of the bank at the N end. Inner Dowsing ECM (Q(3) 10s, Racon T) is to the NE of the bank, S Inner Dowsing and Scott Patch indicate its southernmost extent. Inshore of the bank lie three wind farms: Lynn (27 turbines), Inner Dowsing (27 turbines) and Lincs (75 turbines) some lit Fl Y 5s and some by R Aero lts. The extremities of the wind farms are indicated by cardinal marks while under construction; when completed selected turbines are marked by lights and fog signals. 2 Wks lie inshore 3.5M NW of Lincs wind farm.

In the outer approaches to The Wash and R Humber there are many offlying banks, but few of them are of direct danger to yachts. The sea however breaks on some of them in bad weather, when they should be avoided. Fishing vessels may be encountered, and there are many oil/gas installations offshore.

RIVER HUMBER

(AC 104, 1188, 3497) The Humber is formed by the Ouse and the Trent, which meet 13M above Kingston-upon-Hull. The river is commercially important and gives access to these rivers and inland waterways; it also drains most of Yorkshire and the Midlands. Where the Humber estuary reaches the sea between Northcoates Pt and Spurn Hd it is 4M wide. A VTS scheme is in operation to regulate commercial shipping in the Humber, Ouse and Trent and provide full radar surveillance. Yachts are advised to monitor the appropriate Humber VTS frequency. Advice is at www.humber.com/Yachting_and_Leisure/Pleasure_Craft_Navigation/

Approaching from the S, a yacht should make good Rosse Spit and then Haile Sand No 2, both PHM lt buoys, before altering westward leading SW of Bull Channel.

If bound to/from the N, avoid The Binks, a shoal (dries 1·6m in places) extending 3M E from Spurn Hd, with a rough sea when wind is against tide. Depths offshore are irregular and subject to frequent change; it is best to cross the main channel at No 3 Chequer following the small vessel route and follow a line N of SE Chequer to close Spurn before heading NNE to pass inshore of the Humber Gateway wind farm (73 turbines). In poor weather extend offshore to S Binks SHM.

Haile Sand and Bull Sand Forts are both conspic to the SW of Spurn Head; beyond them it is advisable to keep just outside one of the buoyed chans, since shoals are liable to change. Hawke Channel (later Sunk) is the main dredged N approach. Bull Channel takes a middle course before merging with Haile Channnel, which favours the S side and Grimsby. There are good leisure facilities at Grimsby and Hull. Yachts may ⚓ inside Spurn Head to await favourable conditions.

▶ *Streams are strong, even fierce at Sp; local info suggests that they are stronger than shown in Tidal Streams based upon NP 251 (Admiralty Tidal Stream Atlas). 5ca S of Spurn Hd the flood sets NW from about HW Immingham –0520, Sp rate 3·5kn; the ebb sets SE from about HW Immingham, Sp rate 4kn. The worst seas are experienced in NW gales against a strong flood tide. 10M E of Spurn Hd the tidal streams are not affected by the river; relative to HW Immingham, the S-going stream begins at –0455, and the N-going at +0130. Nearer the entrance the direction of the S-going stream becomes more W'ly, and that of the N-going stream more E'ly.* ◀

RIVER HUMBER TO HARTLEPOOL

(AC 107, 121, 129, 134, 5615) NE of the Humber Estuary clear of the main channel lies Humber Gateway Wind Farm marked by 5 cardinal buoys and a 79m high met mast. Westermost Rough Wind Farm, with 35 turbines, some lit, lies 3M off Withernsea on the inshore route to Bridlington. A wreck hazardous to surface navigation lies in 8m, 2M off Tunstall.

Navigation is aided by the disused light house and prominent church spires/towers along the coast. Avoid a firing practice area inshore off the beach at Royston. Bridlington Bay (AC 1882) is clear of dangers apart from Smithic Shoals (marked by lit N and S cardinal buoys). These lie S of Flamborough Hd about 2½M off Bridlington; seas break on these shoals in strong N or E winds even at HW.

Flamborough Head is a steep, W cliff with conspic light house on summit. The light may be obscured by cliffs when close inshore. An old lt ho, also conspic, is 2½ca WNW.

▶ *Tides run hard around the Head which, in strong winds against a sp tide, is best avoided by 2M.* ◀

From here the coast runs NW, with no offshore dangers until Filey Brigg where rocky ledges extend 5ca ESE, marked by a lit ECM.⚓ in Filey B in N or offshore winds. NW of Filey Brigg beware Old Horse Rks and foul ground 5ca offshore; maintain this offing past Scarborough to Whitby High Lt. Off Whitby beware Whitby Rk and The Scar (dries in places) to the E of hbr, and Upgang Rks (dries in places) 1M to WNW; swell breaks heavily on all these rocks.

From Whitby to Hartlepool dangers lie no more than 1M offshore.Runswick Bay (AC 1612), 5M NW of Whitby, provides ⚓ in winds from S and W but is dangerous in onshore winds. 2½M further NW the little harbour of Staithes is suitable for yachts which can take the ground, but only in good weather and offshore winds.

Redcliff, dark red and 205m high, is a conspic feature of this coast which, along to Hunt Cliff, is prone to landslides and is fringed with rky ledges which dry for about 3ca off. There is a conspic radio mast 4ca SSE of Redcliff. Off Redcar and Coatham beware Salt Scar and West Scar, drying rky ledges lying 1–8ca offshore. Other ledges lie close SE and S of Salt Scar which has NCM lt buoy. Between R Tees and Hartlepool beware Long Scar, detached rky ledge (dries 2m) with extremity marked by ECM lt buoy. Tees and Hartlepool Bays are exposed to strong E/SE winds. The R Tees and Middlesbrough are highly industrialised. Tees Bay Wind Farm consists of 27 turbines (extremities Fl Y 5s 13m 5M) up to 1½M offshore SE of the Tees channel as far as West Scar.

NORTH SEA PASSAGES

See 0.34 for distances across the North Sea below for routes from Hartlepool. There is further information in Area 1 for the southern North Sea, in Area 4 for crossing to Norway and the Baltic and in Area 2 for crossings from the Frisian Islands, German Bight, Belgium and the Netherlands.

HARTLEPOOL TO SOUTHERN NETHERLANDS

(AC 2182A, 1191, 1190, 1503, 1408, 1610, 3371, 110) From abeam Whitby the passage can, theoretically, be made on one direct course, but this would conflict with oil/gas activities and platforms including Rough and Amethyst fields off Humber, Hewett off Cromer and very extensive fields further offshore.

Commercial, offshore support and fishing vessels may be met S of Flamborough Hd and particularly off NE Norfolk where it is advisable to follow an inshore track avoiding all wind farms. After passing Flamborough Head, N Outer Dowsing and Dudgeon cardinals leave Dudgeon Wind Farm (under construction with cardinal marks) and Haisborough Shoal to the E, and then either:

Proceed SSE inshore of Cross Sand to Outer Gabbard. Thence depart in a SE'ly direction to cross Nord Hinder TSS at right angles before heading for Roompotsluis via Middelbank and subsequent buoyed channel.

Or, set course on an ESE'ly heading from the vicinity of Smith's Knoll, so as to cross the N/S deep-water traffic routes to the East, altering SE towards Hoek van Holland, while keeping North of Maas Approaches TSS.

HARTLEPOOL TO THE GERMAN BIGHT

(AC 2182A, 1191, 266, 1405) Taking departure eastward from abeam Whitby High lt, skirt the SW Patch off Dogger Bank, clearing S of Katy Gas Field passing E Friesland wind farm and then N of German Bight W Approach TSS. Thence head for the Elbe or Helgoland. The latter may also serve as a convenient haven in order to adjust the passage for Elbe tides and streams, without greatly increasing passage distance.

▶ *Tidal streams are less than 1kn away from the coast and run E/W along much of the route.* ◀

HARTLEPOOL TO COQUET ISLAND

(AC 134, 152, 156, 5615) From The Heugh an offing of 1M clears all dangers until past Seaham and approaching Sunderland. White Stones, rocky shoals (depth 1·8m) lie 1·75M SSE of Roker Pier lt ho; Hendon Rk (depth 0·9m) lies 1·25M SE of the lt ho. 1M N of Sunderland is Whitburn Steel, a rocky ledge with less than 2m over it; a dangerous wreck (buoyed) lies 1ca SE of it.

The coast N of Tynemouth is foul, and on passage to Blyth it should be given an offing of 1M. St Mary's Island (with disused conspic lt ho) is 3·5M N of Tynemouth, joined to the mainland by a causeway. The tiny drying harbour of Seaton Sluice, 1M NW of St Mary's Island, is accessible only in offshore winds via a narrow entrance. A wind farm lies 3·5M off Blyth.

Proceeding N from Blyth, keep well seaward of The Sow and Pigs rocks, and set course to clear Newbiggin Pt and Beacon Pt by about 1M. Newbiggin church spire is prominent from N and S, and NW of Beacon Pt are conspic chys of aluminium smelter and power stn. 2M NNW of Beacon Pt is Snab Pt where rks extend 3ca seaward. Further offshore Cresswell Skeres, rocky patches with depth 3m, lie about 1·5M NNE of Snab Pt.

COQUET ISLAND TO FARNE ISLANDS

(AC 156) Coquet Is (lt, fog sig) lies about 5ca offshore at SE end of Alnmouth Bay, and nearly 1M NNE of Hauxley Pt, off which dangerous rks extend 6ca offshore, drying 1·9m. On passage, normally pass 1M E of Coquet Is in the W sector of the light. Coquet channel may be used in good vis by day; but it is only 2ca wide, not buoyed and has least depth of 0·9m near the centre. A wreck lies 3ca SE of the Island's southern tip in Coquet Channel on the boundary of the R/W sectors. In S or W winds, there are good ⚓s in Coquet Road, W and NW of the Island.

▶ *The stream runs strongly: S-going from HW Tyne –0515 and N-going from HW Tyne +0045.* ◀

Amble (Warkworth) Harbour entrance is about 1M West of Coquet Island, and 1·5M SE of Warkworth Castle (conspic). 4ca NE and ENE of the entrance is Pan Bush. This is a rocky shoal with least depth of 0·9m, on which dangerous seas can build in any swell. The bar has varying depths, down to less than 1m. The entrance is dangerous in strong winds from N/E when broken water may extend to Coquet Island. Once inside, the harbour is safe.

Between Coquet Is and the Farne Is, 19M to the North, keep at least 1M offshore to avoid various dangers. To seaward, Craster Skeres lie 5M East of Castle Point. Dicky Shad and Newton Skere lie 1·75M and 4·5M E of Beadnell Pt respectively. These are three rocky banks on which the sea breaks heavily in bad weather.

FARNE ISLANDS

(AC 111, 160) The coast between N Sunderland Pt (Snook) and Holy Island, 8M NW, has fine hill (Cheviots) scenery fronted by dunes and sandy beaches. The Farne Is and offlying shoals extend 4·5M offshore, and are a mini-cruising ground well worth visiting in good weather. The islands are a bird sanctuary, owned and operated by the National Trust, with large colonies of sea birds and grey seals. The R Northumberland YC's Sailing Directions (see 3.18) are useful; AC 111 is essential.

Inner Sound separates the islands from the mainland. In good conditions it is a better N/S route than keeping outside the whole group; but the stream runs at 3kn at Sp, and with strong wind against tide there is rough water. If course is set outside the Farne Islands, pass 1M East of Longstone (lit) to clear Crumstone Rk, Knivestone (dries 3·6m) and Whirl Rks (depth 0·6m) respectively 5 and 6ca NE of Longstone lt ho. The sea breaks on these rocks.

The islands, rocks and shoals are divided by Staple Sound, running NW/SE, into an inner and outer group. The former comprises Inner Farne, W and E Wideopens and Knock's Reef. Inner Farne is the innermost Is. Close NE The Kettle is an ⚓ sheltered except from NW. ⚓ out of the stream by The Bridges connecting Knock's Reef and West Wideopen. 1M NW of Inner Farne Is across Farne Sound, which runs NE/SW, lies the Megstone, a rock 5m high. Beware Swedman reef (dries 0·5m), marked by SHM buoy 4ca WSW of Megstone.

The outer group of Islands comprises Staple and Brownsman Islands, N and S Wamses, the Harcars and Longstone. There is an occasional ⚓ between Staple and Brownsman Island.

▶ *Piper Gut and Crafords Gut may be negotiated in calm weather and near HW, stemming the S-going stream.* ◀

HOLY ISLAND TO BERWICK

▶ *Near the Farne Is and Holy Is the SE-going stream begins at HW Tyne –0430, and the NW-going at HW Tyne +0130. Sp rates are about 2.5kn in Inner Sound, 4kn in Staple Sound and about 3·5kn 1M NE of Longstone, decreasing to seaward. There is an eddy S of Longstone on NW-going stream.* ◀

(AC 1612, 111, 160) Holy Is (or Lindisfarne) lies 6M WNW of Longstone, and is linked to mainland by a causeway covered at HW. There is a good ⚓ on S side (AC 1612) with conspic daymarks and directional lights. The castle and a white obelisk at Emmanuel Head are also conspicuous.

▶ *The stream runs strongly in and out of hbr; W-going from HW Tyne +0510, and E-going from HW Tyne –0045. E of Holy Is, Goldstone chan runs N/S between Goldstone Rk (dries) and SHM buoy on E side, and Plough Seat Reef/Plough Rk with PHM buoy (both dry) on the West side.* ◀

Berwick Bay has some offlying shoals. Berwick-upon-Tweed is easily visible against the low shoreline, which rises again to high cliffs further north. The harbour entrance is restricted by a shallow bar, which is dangerous in onshore winds.

HARBOURS ADJACENT to BLAKENEY and WELLS-NEXT-THE-SEA
BURNHAM OVERY STAITHE, Norfolk, **52°58´·95N 00°46´·55E** ✲⚓✿✿✿. AC 1190, 108. HW –0420 on Dover. See 3.7. Small drying hbr; ent chan has 0·3m MLWS. ⚓ off the Staithe only suitable in good weather. No lts. Scolt Hd is conspic to W and Gun Hill to E; Scolt Hd Island is conspic 3M long sandbank which affords some shelter. Chan varies constantly and buoys are moved to suit. Local knowledge advisable. Facilities: ⚓ ⚓ ⚓ ⚒ ⚒ ⚒.
Burnham Overy Staithe SC ☎(01328) 738348, ⚓ ⚓.
Burnham Market EC Wed; ⚒ ⚒ ⚒ ⚒ ✗ ⚒.

BRANCASTER STAITHE, Norfolk, **52°59´·02N 00°37´·65E** ✲⚓✿✿✿. AC 1190, 108. HW –0425 on Dover; as Burnham. Small drying hbr, dangerous to enter except by day in settled weather. Spd limit 6kn. Appr from due N. Conspic golf club house with lt, Fl 5s 8m 3M, is 0·5M S of chan ent and Fairway buoy. Beware wk shown on chart. Sandbanks shift; buoys changed to suit. Scolt Hd conspic to E. Local knowledge or Pilot advised. Possible ⚓ in The Hole. HM ☎(01485) 210638. Facilities: **Brancaster Staithe SC** ☎210249, ✗ ⚒; **Hunstanton SC** ☎(01485) 534705. Services: ⚒ ⚒ ⚒ ⚒ ⚒ ⚒.

3.5 BLAKENEY

Norfolk 52°59'·19N 00°57'·90E (ent shifts) ❀♦♦♧♧♧

CHARTS AC 1190, 108; Imray C29, C28, Y9

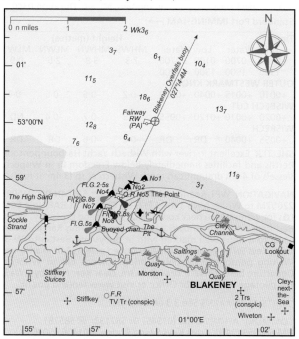

TIDES –0445 Dover; ML Cromer 2·8; Duration 0530; Zone 0 (UT)

Standard Port IMMINGHAM (→)

Times				Height (metres)			
High Water		Low Water		MHWS	MHWN	MLWN	MLWS
0100	0700	0100	0700	7·3	5·8	2·6	0·9
1300	1900	1300	1900				
Differences BLAKENEY BAR (approx 52°59'N 00°59'E)							
+0035	+0025	+0030	+0040	−1·6	−1·3	ND	ND
BLAKENEY (approx 52°57'N 01°01'E)							
+0115	+0055	ND	ND	−3·9	−3·8	ND	ND
BURNHAM OVERY STAITHE							
+0045	+0055	ND	ND	−5·0	−4·9	ND	ND
CROMER							
+0044	+0032	+0108	+0059	−2·3	−1·8	−0·7	0·0

SHELTER Very good but limited access over bar to shallow harbour. In fresh onshore winds conditions at the entrance deteriorate quickly, especially on the ebb. Moorings in The Pit dry out.

NAVIGATION WPT 53°00'·00N 00°59'·00E, approx 200°/8ca to RW SWM 52°59'·22N 00°58'·53E (2019) which is moved as required.

- Hjordis IDM Fl(2) 5s is a large dangerous wreck, close N of ent.
- The shallow bar shifts often. Access HW±2. Channel is marked by 8 SHM (Nos 1, 2, 3, S of Hjordis) and 3 PHM, which are lit and relaid each spring. Other marks are unlit. Speed limit 8kn.
- Strangers are best advised to follow local boats in. Pilotage is available from Blakeney Harbour Boatman's Association.

LIGHTS AND MARKS Blakeney and Langham churches (conspic), a chimney on the house on Blakeney Point neck, TV mast (R lts) approx 2M S of entrance.

COMMUNICATIONS (Code 01263) Dr 712461; Blakeney Harbour Boatman's Association – Neil Thompson mob 07929181138, Henry Archer 07786092405, Will Darby 07795 463943.

FACILITIES ⚓ ⚓ ⚓ (drying) may be rented, contact Charlie Ward.
Services ⚒ ✎ ⊞ △ ⚷ Blakeney Marine Services ☎0776944361; Neil Thompson Boats Ltd ☎741172.
Village ⓘ ⓘ ⓐ(garage ☎741456) ✉ ⛉ ✕ ⬚ ⇄ (Sheringham).

3.6 WELLS-NEXT-THE-SEA

Norfolk 52°59'·30N 00°49'·75E (ent shifts) ❀❀♦♦♦♧♧♧

CHARTS AC 1190, 108; Imray C29, C28, Y9

TIDES –0445 Dover; ML 1·2 Duration 0540

Standard Port IMMINGHAM (→)

Times				Height (metres)			
High Water		Low Water		MHWS	MHWN	MLWN	MLWS
0100	0700	0100	0700	7·3	5·8	2·6	0·9
1300	1900	1300	1900				
Differences WELLS BAR (approx 52°59'N 00°49'E)							
+0020	+0020	+0020	+0020	−1·3	−1·0	ND	ND
WELLS-NEXT-THE-SEA (approx 52°58'N 00°51'E)							
+0035	+0045	+0340	+0310	−3·8	−3·8	CD+	CD+
HUNSTANTON							
+0010	+0020	+0105	+0025	+0·1	−0·2	−0·1	0·0

NOTE: LW time differences at Wells are for the end of a LW stand which lasts about 4hrs at sp and about 5hrs at nps.

SHELTER Good, but entrance difficult in strong onshore winds. Outer Hbr for commercial wind farm tenders and survey vessels, but with HM prior permission, vessels >2m draught may shelter in adverse conditions. Limited access (max draught 3m at springs). Quay berths/pontoons at W end of Town Quay with 2m+ at LW.

NAVIGATION WPT WCM 52°59'·68N 00°50'·24E. Entry varies in depth and position; buoys moved to suit. Best attempted on the flood initially keeping to W side of chan to counter E-going tide; from WPT head to Y SPM keeping it close to port and then pass between lateral marks Nos 1 and 2. Obtain HM's advice, Hbr Launch often available to escort visitors into hbr and up to Quay. Spd limits: No 6 buoy to Quay 8kn; above this 4kn.

See www.portofwells.co.uk for navigation video.

LIGHTS AND MARKS From WCM Q (9) 15s the channel is well marked by lateral buoys, all Fl.3s, R to port, G to stbd. The lifeboat house (W with R roof) at N end of harbour is conspicuous.

COMMUNICATIONS (Code 01328) HM 711646, mob 07775 507284.

Call 'Wells Harbour' Ch **12** 16 before entering, listens HW–2 to HW+2 and when vessels expected.

FACILITIES Main Quay ⚓ on pontoons or quay, £24-£30/night; ⚡ ⛽ ⓦⓒ ⊞ ⚓ ⚡(9t) ⚓(25t mob). **E Quay** ⚓ (£12/craft/day), ⚒ ⚓.
Services ⚒ ✎ ⊞ Ⓔ ACA △ ⚓ LB. **Wells SC** ☎710622, ⚓ ⬚.
Town ⓘ ⓘ (Hbr fuelling stn HW-2 to HW+3; up to 14,000 ltrs), ⓐ ⓘ ⛒ ✕ ⬚ ✉ ⑧ ⇄ (bus to Norwich/King's Lynn), ✈ (Norwich).

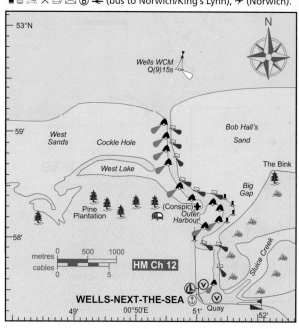

3.7 KING'S LYNN

Norfolk **52°49´·72N 00°21´·14E** (W Stones Bn) ✲✲✲✿✿✿

CHARTS AC 1190, 108, 1200, 5614. Imray C29, Y9

TIDES –0443 Dover, +0030 Immingham; ML 3·6; Duration 0340

Standard Port IMMINGHAM (→)

Times				Height (metres)			
High Water		Low Water		MHWS	MHWN	MLWN	MLWS
0100	0700	0100	0700	7·3	5·8	2·6	0·9
1300	1900	1300	1900				
Differences KING'S LYNN							
+0030	+0030	+0305	+0140	–0·5	–0·8	–0·8	+0·1
WEST STONES							
+0025	+0025	+0115	+0040	–0·3	–0·4	–0·3	+0·2

SHELTER Port is well sheltered; entry only recommended HW–3½. A busy commercial and fishing port. 7 ♥ pontoons on S quay. River moorings available from local clubs; keep clear of FV moorings.

NAVIGATION WPT No 1 SHM, Fl G 3s, 52° 56'.00N 00° 21'.25E follow Daseley Sled and well buoyed/lit chan to King's Lynn. Upstream to Denver Sluice (ent to inland routes) 6 bridges span river, min clearance 9·15m less ht of tide above dock sill at King's Lynn. Allow 1½hrs for passage. Sandbanks regularly shift and extend several miles into the Wash; buoyage is altered accordingly. Contact HM (www.kingslynnport.co.uk) in advance or www.sailthewash.com.

LIGHTS AND MARKS See 3.3 and chartlet.

COMMUNICATIONS Code (01553) HM 0773411; Docks 691555. *Kings Lynn Hbr Radio* Ch **14** 11 (M-F: 0800-1730 LT. Other times: HW –4 to HW+1) (ABP) Ch **14** 16 11 (HW–2½ to HW).

FACILITIES 6 ⌒ £42 (<9m/48hrs), ⚓ ▲ ✕ ⚒ Ⓔ ⌂(32t) ⚓. **Town** ⌂ ⌂ ⌂ ⊠ Ⓑ ⚒ ✕ ⌂ ⇌ ✈(Norwich). **Ely Marina** 24M up the Great Ouse River, ☎(01353) 664622, ▲ ▬ ⚓ ▲ ✕ ✎ Ⓔ ⌂(10t) ⚓.

3.8 WISBECH

Cambridgeshire **52°40´·02N 00°09´·55E** ✲✲✿✿✿

CHARTS AC 1190, 108, 1200, 5614. Imray C29, Y9

TIDES –0443 Dover, +0030 Immingham; ML 3·6; Duration 0340

Standard Port IMMINGHAM (→)

Times				Height (metres)			
High Water		Low Water		MHWS	MHWN	MLWN	MLWS
0100	0700	0100	0700	7·3	5·8	2·6	0·9
1300	1900	1300	1900				
OUTER WESTMARK KNOCK							
+0010	+0015	+0040	+0020	–0·2	–0·5	–0·6	–0·4
WISBECH CUT							
+0020	+0010	+0120	+0055	–0·3	–0·7	–0·4	ND
WISBECH							
+0055	+0040	DR	DR	–0·2	–0·6	DR	DR

SHELTER Excellent in river with Wisbech Yacht Harbour pontoon berths and facilities immediately below Freedom Br in Wisbech. Vessels of 4·8m draught can reach Wisbech at sp (3·4m at nps).

NAVIGATION WPT Roaring Middle Lt Flt 52° 58'.64N 00° 21'.08E 220°/7M to Wisbech No 1 SHM Fl G 5s. Call HM at RAF No 4 ECM (⚓s for waiting) to check commercial traffic and Cross Keys Sw Br. Red flags and lights shown when Holbeach Firing Range in use. Chan to R Nene well marked with lit buoys/bns. Best ent HW–3. Cross Keys Sw Br manned HW±4 if booked at least 24H in advance. Waiting pontoon 0.5M below bridge thence 6M to Wisbech. Departure best at HW; if draught >3m, clear Kerr NCM by HW+3. For pilotage notes ☎ Hbr Office or visit www.fenland.gov.uk.

LIGHTS AND MARKS See 3.3 and chartlet.

COMMUNICATIONS Code (01945) Dr 582133; Ⓗ 585781; HM 588059 (24H); Cross Keys Swing Bridge ☎01406 350364. HM *Wisbech Harbour* Ch **09** call HM and Cross Keys Sw Br HW±3.

FACILITIES Yacht Hbr (102⌒+15♥) £1, min charge £5, ⚓ ⌂ ✎ Ⓔ ▲(barge). **Town** ⌂ ▲ ⚓ ⚒ ✕ ⌂.

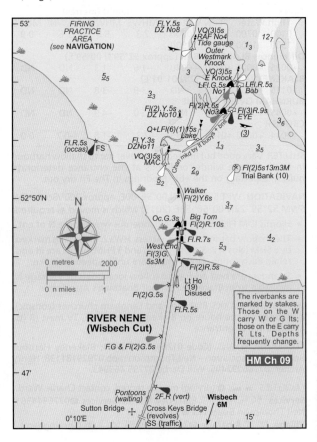

3.9 BOSTON

Lincs **52°56'·00N 00°04'·92E** (Tabs Head bn) ❀❀♒♒♒♒♒

CHARTS AC 108, 1200, 5614; Imray C29, Y9

TIDES –0415 Dover; ML 3·3; Duration Flood 0500, Ebb 0700

Standard Port IMMINGHAM (→)

Times				Height (metres)			
High Water		Low Water		MHWS	MHWN	MLWN	MLWS
0100	0700	0100	0700	7·3	5·8	2·6	0·9
1300	1900	1300	1900				
Differences BOSTON							
0000	+0010	+0140	+0050	–0·5	–1·0	–0·9	–0·5
TABS HEAD (WELLAND RIVER)							
0000	+0005	+0125	+0020	+0·2	–0·2	–0·2	–0·2
SKEGNESS							
+0010	+0015	+0030	+0020	–0·4	–0·5	–0·1	0·0
INNER DOWSING LIGHT TOWER							
0000	0000	+0010	+0010	–0·9	–0·7	–0·1	+0·3

SHELTER Very good. Except in emergency, berthing in the Dock is prohib without HM permission. Yachts secure just above Dock ent and see HM. The port is administered by Port of Boston Ltd.

Yachts capable of lowering masts can pass through the Grand Sluice (*24hrs notice required*) into fresh water. Sluice 16m x 9m and opens twice a tide at approx HW±2. It leads into the R Witham Navigation which goes 31M to Lincoln. Marina is to stbd immediately beyond the sluice. British Waterways have 50 berths, with ⚓ and ⬲, beyond Grand Sluice.

NAVIGATION WPT Boston Rds SWM lt buoy, 52°57'·61N 00°16'·29E, 282°/0·75M to Freeman Chan ent. Thence Bar Chan is well marked, but liable to change. SW of Clay Hole a new chan has formed which dries 0.6m at entr; it is marked by SHM lt buoys Nos 11N, 13N, and 15. Tabs Head marks the ent to the river; it should be passed not earlier than HW–3 to enable the Grand Sluice to be reached before the start of the ebb. Beware rocky bottom within 100m of the Sluice. On reaching Boston Dock, masts should be lowered to negotiate swing bridge (cannot always be opened) and three fixed bridges. Chan through town is unnavigable at LW.

LIGHTS AND MARKS St Boltoph's ch tr (the Boston Stump) is conspic from afar. New Cut and R Witham are marked by bns with topmarks. FW lts mark ldg lines: three pairs going upstream and six pairs going downstream.

COMMUNICATIONS (Code 01205) Ⓗ 364801. Dock office 365571 (H24 & emergency); HM 362328; Grand Sluice Control 364864 (not always manned but has answerphone) mob 07712 010920.

All vessels between No 9 buoy and Grand Sluice must listen Ch 12 (also advisable to maintain watch while in local tidal waters). Call: *Boston Port Control* VHF Ch 12 (HW –2½ to HW +1½ when commercial shipping is moving). Ch 11 used by dock staff as required. *Grand Sluice* Ch 74.

FACILITIES Boston Gateway Marina ☎07480525230, (48⬲+❶) £10/night any size inc ⬲ ⚓ ⬲ in dock (see HM).

Grand Sluice 🚾/▮ᴾ; **BWB** moorings: 1st night free, then £5·00.
Services ⬲ ⚒ ⚒ Ⓔ.
Town Thurs; ✉ Ⓑ ⛽ ✕ ⬲ ⇌ ✈(Humberside).

ADJACENT HARBOURS

RIVER WELLAND, Lincolnshire, **52°56'·00N 00°04'·92E** (Tabs Head bn). AC 1190, 1200. At Welland Cut HW –0440 on Dover; ML 0·3m; Duration 0520. See 3.9. At Tabs Head bn HW ±3, ent Welland Cut which is defined by training walls and lt bns. Beware sp flood of up to 5kn. Berth 6M up at **Fosdyke Yacht Haven** ☎01205 260240. (50⬲ + 6❶ 2m depth); ⬲ ⚓ 🚾/▮ᴾ by prior arrangement, ⚒ ▮ (50t) – only one between R Humber & Lowestoft ✕ ⬲.

WAINFLEET, Lincolnshire, **53°04'·79N 00°19'·89E** (chan ent). AC 108. Skegness HW +0500 on Dover. See 3.9 (Skegness). ML 4·0m; Duration 0600. Shelter good. Recommended max boat length 10m, draught 1·5m. Lit PHM indicates entrance to drying channel close S of Gibraltar Point. Chan through saltings marked by buoys and bns with lateral topmarks but no lts. Enter HW ±1½. Facilities: ▲ ⬲ (larger boats at fishing jetties, smaller at YC) ⚓ at YC ⬲.
Town All facilities at Skegness (3½ miles).

Skegness YC skegnessyachtclub.co.uk ☎0779 941856 (Commodore) on the R Steeping inside Gibraltar Pt has a membership of about 65 with a small clubhouse. ▲⬲⚓ at ⬲ ⬲ ⚓ 🚾 ▮ᴾ.

NE England

IMMINGHAM

MEAN SPRING
AND NEAP CURVES

MEAN RANGES
Springs 6.4m
Neaps 3.2m

An intriguing place to sail, with more destinations than you might think...

Something for every leisure sailor and their crews

www.sailthewash.co.uk

STANDARD TIME (UT)
For Summer Time add ONE hour in **non-shaded areas**

IMMINGHAM   LAT 53°38′N   LONG 0°11′W
TIMES AND HEIGHTS OF HIGH AND LOW WATERS

Dates in red are **SPRINGS**
Dates in blue are **NEAPS**

YEAR 2022

JANUARY
Time	m		Time	m
1 0403	6.9		**16** 0451	6.3
1033	1.4		1101	2.0
SA 1640	6.9		SU 1711	6.6
2300	1.5		2334	1.8
2 0502	7.1		**17** 0532	6.4
1128	1.3		1143	1.8
SU 1729	7.1		M 1748	6.7
● 2357	1.1		○	
3 0558	7.2		**18** 0015	1.6
1219	1.2		0611	6.6
M 1816	7.3		TU 1221	1.8
			1824	6.9
4 0050	0.9		**19** 0055	1.5
0653	7.3		0649	6.6
TU 1307	1.2		W 1257	1.7
1902	7.4		1859	6.9
5 0140	0.8		**20** 0131	1.4
0744	7.2		0726	6.7
W 1353	1.3		TH 1330	1.7
1947	7.4		1932	6.9
6 0228	0.8		**21** 0206	1.4
0833	7.1		0802	6.7
TH 1436	1.5		F 1402	1.7
2030	7.3		2004	6.9
7 0314	1.0		**22** 0239	1.4
0922	6.8		0838	6.6
F 1518	1.7		SA 1436	1.7
2115	7.0		2036	6.9
8 0400	1.3		**23** 0313	1.5
1012	6.4		0914	6.5
SA 1600	2.1		SU 1513	1.8
2203	6.7		2113	6.8
9 0445	1.7		**24** 0351	1.6
1104	6.1		0955	6.3
SU 1644	2.4		M 1554	2.0
☽ 2257	6.4		2157	6.7
10 0534	2.0		**25** 0436	1.7
1159	5.9		1043	6.1
M 1735	2.7		TU 1643	2.2
2357	6.1		☽ 2250	6.5
11 0627	2.3		**26** 0532	1.9
1257	5.7		1144	5.9
TU 1836	2.8		W 1746	2.4
			2355	6.3
12 0102	5.9		**27** 0641	2.1
0728	2.5		1300	5.9
W 1355	5.7		TH 1903	2.5
1950	2.8			
13 0208	5.9		**28** 0116	6.1
0831	2.5		0759	2.2
TH 1453	5.8		F 1418	6.0
2104	2.6		2028	2.4
14 0310	6.0		**29** 0243	6.2
0928	2.4		0914	2.0
F 1546	6.1		SA 1527	6.2
2201	2.3		2147	2.0
15 0404	6.1		**30** 0359	6.5
1017	2.2		1019	1.8
SA 1631	6.3		SU 1627	6.6
2250	2.0		2254	1.6
			31 0505	6.8
			1117	1.5
			M 1720	7.0
			2352	1.1

FEBRUARY
Time	m		Time	m
1 0602	7.0		**16** 0000	1.5
1209	1.3		0555	6.6
TU 1807	7.2		W 1207	1.7
●			○ 1804	6.9
2 0044	0.8		**17** 0040	1.3
0653	7.2		0632	6.7
W 1256	1.2		TH 1243	1.6
1852	7.4		1840	7.0
3 0132	0.6		**18** 0118	1.1
0738	7.2		0708	6.8
TH 1340	1.1		F 1317	1.5
1934	7.5		1913	7.1
4 0215	0.6		**19** 0152	1.0
0819	7.1		0742	6.9
F 1419	1.2		SA 1349	1.4
2014	7.4		1946	7.2
5 0255	0.8		**20** 0223	1.0
0857	6.9		0815	6.9
SA 1455	1.4		SU 1421	1.4
2052	7.3		2018	7.2
6 0330	1.1		**21** 0254	1.1
0933	6.6		0849	6.8
SU 1529	1.7		M 1455	1.4
2130	6.9		2053	7.1
7 0403	1.5		**22** 0326	1.3
1009	6.2		0925	6.6
M 1602	2.0		TU 1531	1.6
2210	6.6		2135	6.9
8 0437	2.0		**23** 0404	1.6
1049	5.9		1008	6.3
TU 1641	2.4		W 1614	1.9
☽ 2257	6.1		☽ 2224	6.5
9 0518	2.4		**24** 0454	2.0
1140	5.6		1103	6.0
W 1730	2.7		TH 1713	2.3
2359	5.7		2330	6.1
10 0613	2.7		**25** 0606	2.4
1250	5.4		1220	5.7
TH 1835	2.9		F 1837	2.5
11 0118	5.5		**26** 0102	5.8
0724	2.9		0739	2.6
F 1404	5.5		SA 1354	5.7
2001	2.9		2019	2.5
12 0237	5.5		**27** 0249	5.9
0845	2.8		0905	2.4
SA 1511	5.7		SU 1515	6.0
2135	2.6		2146	2.0
13 0343	5.8		**28** 0408	6.3
0952	2.5		1013	2.0
SU 1605	6.1		M 1617	6.5
2231	2.2		2251	1.4
14 0435	6.1			
1043	2.2			
M 1649	6.4			
2318	1.8			
15 0517	6.3			
1127	1.9			
TU 1728	6.7			

MARCH
Time	m		Time	m
1 0509	6.7		**16** 0454	6.4
1108	1.6		1105	1.9
TU 1708	6.9		W 1700	6.6
2345	1.0		2336	1.4
2 0558	7.0		**17** 0532	6.6
1157	1.3		1145	1.6
W 1753	7.2		TH 1737	6.9
●				
3 0032	0.6		**18** 0016	1.1
0641	7.2		0608	6.9
TH 1241	1.1		F 1221	1.4
1836	7.4		○ 1813	7.1
4 0115	0.5		**19** 0054	0.9
0719	7.2		0643	7.0
F 1321	1.0		SA 1257	1.2
1915	7.5		1848	7.3
5 0153	0.6		**20** 0129	0.8
0753	7.1		0717	7.1
SA 1357	1.1		SU 1331	1.1
1951	7.5		1923	7.4
6 0227	0.8		**21** 0201	0.8
0823	6.9		0750	7.1
SU 1429	1.2		M 1404	1.1
2025	7.3		1958	7.4
7 0255	1.1		**22** 0233	0.9
0851	6.7		0823	7.0
M 1457	1.5		TU 1438	1.2
2057	7.0		2036	7.3
8 0321	1.5		**23** 0305	1.2
0916	6.4		0900	6.8
TU 1525	1.8		W 1515	1.4
2129	6.6		2119	6.9
9 0349	1.9		**24** 0342	1.6
0945	6.1		0943	6.4
W 1558	2.1		TH 1559	1.8
2207	6.1		2211	6.4
10 0424	2.4		**25** 0432	2.2
1025	5.7		1038	6.0
TH 1642	2.5		F 1701	2.2
☽ 2259	5.6		☽ 2323	5.9
11 0515	2.8		**26** 0549	2.7
1127	5.4		1159	5.6
F 1745	2.9		SA 1834	2.5
12 0026	5.3		**27** 0117	5.6
0628	3.1		0731	2.8
SA 1313	5.3		SU 1342	5.6
1908	3.0		2022	2.3
13 0207	5.3		**28** 0258	5.9
0759	3.1		0858	2.5
SU 1436	5.5		M 1502	6.0
2103	2.7		2141	1.8
14 0319	5.6		**29** 0408	6.4
0928	2.7		1001	2.0
M 1536	5.9		TU 1601	6.5
2207	2.2		2238	1.2
15 0412	6.0		**30** 0459	6.8
1022	2.3		1051	1.6
TU 1621	6.3		W 1649	6.9
2254	1.8		2326	0.9
			31 0541	7.0
			1137	1.3
			TH 1732	7.2

APRIL
Time	m		Time	m
1 0009	0.7		**16** 0537	7.0
0618	7.1		1152	1.3
F 1218	1.1		SA 1742	7.2
● 1812	7.3		○	
2 0048	0.6		**17** 0022	0.8
0651	7.1		0614	7.1
SA 1256	1.0		SU 1231	1.1
1850	7.4		1821	7.4
3 0123	0.8		**18** 0101	0.7
0721	7.0		0650	7.2
SU 1331	1.0		M 1310	0.9
1925	7.3		1901	7.5
4 0154	1.0		**19** 0137	0.7
0748	6.9		0725	7.2
M 1401	1.2		TU 1348	0.9
1958	7.1		1942	7.5
5 0220	1.3		**20** 0213	0.9
0812	6.8		0802	7.1
TU 1428	1.4		W 1427	1.0
2027	6.8		2025	7.2
6 0245	1.6		**21** 0250	1.3
0836	6.5		0842	6.9
W 1456	1.7		TH 1509	1.3
2058	6.5		2113	6.8
7 0311	1.9		**22** 0331	1.7
0904	6.3		0928	6.5
TH 1527	2.0		F 1559	1.7
2133	6.0		2211	6.3
8 0343	2.3		**23** 0426	2.3
0939	5.9		1026	6.0
F 1609	2.4		SA 1709	2.1
2220	5.6		☽ 2336	5.8
9 0430	2.8		**24** 0545	2.7
1030	5.5		1150	5.7
SA 1711	2.7		SU 1840	2.2
☽ 2341	5.2			
10 0541	3.1		**25** 0124	5.7
1212	5.2		0717	2.8
SU 1831	2.8		M 1325	5.8
			2010	2.0
11 0130	5.2		**26** 0246	6.0
0712	3.1		0836	2.5
M 1353	5.4		TU 1438	6.1
2006	2.6		2118	1.6
12 0245	5.5		**27** 0349	6.4
0844	2.8		0935	2.1
TU 1456	5.8		W 1536	6.5
2125	2.2		2211	1.2
13 0339	6.0		**28** 0435	6.7
0945	2.4		1025	1.7
W 1543	6.2		TH 1623	6.8
2216	1.7		2257	1.0
14 0422	6.4		**29** 0514	6.9
1030	2.0		1109	1.4
TH 1624	6.6		F 1706	7.0
2301	1.3		2339	0.9
15 0500	6.7		**30** 0547	6.9
1112	1.6		1151	1.2
F 1703	6.9		SA 1746	7.1
2343	1.0		●	

NE England

Chart Datum: 3·90 metres below Ordnance Datum (Newlyn). HAT is 8·0 metres above Chart Datum.

》》 **FREE** monthly updates. Register at 《《
www.reedsnauticalalmanac.co.uk

157

STANDARD TIME (UT)
For Summer Time add ONE hour in **non-shaded areas**

IMMINGHAM   LAT 53°38'N   LONG 0°11'W
TIMES AND HEIGHTS OF HIGH AND LOW WATERS

Dates in **red** are SPRINGS
Dates in blue are NEAPS

YEAR 2022

MAY

Time	m	Time	m
1 0016	1.0	**16** 0545	7.1
0619	6.9	1206	1.1
SU 1229	1.2	M 1757	7.4
1824	7.1	○	
2 0050	1.1	**17** 0034	0.8
0648	6.9	0626	7.3
M 1304	1.2	TU 1251	0.9
1900	7.0	1844	7.4
3 0121	1.2	**18** 0116	0.8
0716	6.9	0706	7.3
TU 1336	1.3	W 1336	0.8
1933	6.8	1931	7.3
4 0149	1.4	**19** 0158	1.0
0741	6.8	0747	7.2
W 1405	1.4	TH 1421	0.9
2004	6.6	2020	7.1
5 0215	1.7	**20** 0241	1.3
0807	6.6	0831	7.0
TH 1434	1.7	F 1510	1.1
2036	6.3	2114	6.7
6 0243	2.0	**21** 0328	1.8
0837	6.4	0921	6.6
F 1506	1.9	SA 1606	1.4
2113	6.0	2219	6.3
7 0316	2.3	**22** 0423	2.2
0912	6.0	1021	6.3
SA 1549	2.2	SU 1713	1.7
2159	5.6	☽ 2344	6.0
8 0401	2.6	**23** 0532	2.5
0959	5.7	1138	6.1
SU 1647	2.5	M 1827	1.8
2308	5.4		
9 0504	2.9	**24** 0103	5.9
1115	5.4	0649	2.6
M 1800	2.6	TU 1256	6.1
☾		1940	1.7
10 0041	5.3	**25** 0213	6.1
0623	3.0	0800	2.5
TU 1253	5.5	W 1404	6.2
1916	2.4	2042	1.6
11 0156	5.6	**26** 0312	6.3
0742	2.8	0901	2.2
W 1402	5.8	TH 1502	6.4
2028	2.1	2135	1.5
12 0254	6.0	**27** 0400	6.4
0850	2.5	0953	1.9
TH 1456	6.1	F 1553	6.6
2127	1.7	2222	1.4
13 0342	6.3	**28** 0439	6.6
0944	2.1	1040	1.7
F 1543	6.5	SA 1638	6.7
2218	1.3	2304	1.4
14 0425	6.7	**29** 0514	6.7
1033	1.7	1123	1.5
SA 1627	6.6	SU 1720	6.7
2305	1.1	2343	1.4
15 0505	6.9	**30** 0547	6.7
1120	1.3	1204	1.4
SU 1712	7.2	M 1800	6.7
2350	0.9	●	
		31 0019	1.5
		0620	6.8
		TU 1241	1.4
		1838	6.7

JUNE

Time	m	Time	m
1 0053	1.5	**16** 0100	1.0
0650	6.8	0653	7.3
W 1315	1.4	TH 1329	0.8
1914	6.6	1929	7.2
2 0124	1.6	**17** 0147	1.1
0720	6.7	0739	7.3
TH 1348	1.5	F 1419	0.8
1948	6.5	2022	7.1
3 0154	1.8	**18** 0234	1.3
0751	6.6	0825	7.1
F 1421	1.7	SA 1510	0.9
2023	6.3	2117	6.8
4 0224	2.0	**19** 0321	1.6
0823	6.5	0915	6.9
SA 1455	1.9	SU 1604	1.1
2101	6.1	2218	6.5
5 0258	2.2	**20** 0412	1.9
0858	6.2	1010	6.7
SU 1536	2.0	M 1700	1.3
2145	5.9	2322	6.3
6 0340	2.4	**21** 0507	2.2
0941	6.0	1113	6.4
M 1627	2.1	TU 1759	1.6
2241	5.7	☽	
7 0433	2.6	**22** 0024	6.1
1038	5.8	0609	2.4
TU 1727	2.2	W 1218	6.3
☽ 2349	5.6	1859	1.8
8 0536	2.7	**23** 0125	6.0
1149	5.8	0714	2.5
W 1831	2.1	TH 1322	6.2
		1959	1.9
9 0059	5.7	**24** 0222	6.0
0646	2.7	0819	2.4
TH 1304	5.9	F 1423	6.2
1935	2.0	2055	1.9
10 0202	5.9	**25** 0315	6.1
0754	2.5	0919	2.2
F 1404	6.2	SA 1520	6.2
2037	1.7	2145	1.9
11 0258	6.2	**26** 0401	6.2
0858	2.2	1011	2.0
SA 1501	6.5	SU 1612	6.3
2136	1.5	2231	1.9
12 0349	6.5	**27** 0442	6.4
0957	1.8	1058	1.8
SU 1556	6.8	M 1659	6.4
2231	1.3	2314	1.8
13 0436	6.8	**28** 0520	6.6
1052	1.5	1142	1.7
M 1649	7.0	TU 1742	6.4
2323	1.1	2354	1.8
14 0522	7.0	**29** 0556	6.7
1146	1.2	1224	1.6
TU 1742	7.2	W 1821	6.5
○		●	
15 0012	1.0	**30** 0031	1.8
0608	7.2	0631	6.8
W 1238	0.9	TH 1302	1.5
1836	7.3	1859	6.5

JULY

Time	m	Time	m
1 0106	1.8	**16** 0138	1.1
0705	6.8	0731	7.4
F 1339	1.5	SA 1414	0.5
1935	6.5	2021	7.2
2 0139	1.8	**17** 0223	1.2
0739	6.7	0816	7.4
SA 1414	1.6	SU 1501	0.6
2012	6.4	2108	7.0
3 0211	1.9	**18** 0307	1.4
0812	6.6	0901	7.3
SU 1448	1.6	M 1547	0.8
2049	6.3	2156	6.7
4 0244	2.0	**19** 0349	1.7
0846	6.5	0948	7.0
M 1524	1.7	TU 1632	1.2
2128	6.2	2244	6.4
5 0321	2.1	**20** 0432	2.0
0923	6.4	1038	6.7
TU 1605	1.8	W 1718	1.6
2211	6.1	☽ 2335	6.1
6 0404	2.2	**21** 0519	2.3
1007	6.3	1134	6.3
W 1652	1.9	TH 1806	1.9
2302	5.9		
7 0456	2.4	**22** 0029	5.8
1101	6.2	0614	2.6
TH 1746	1.9	F 1236	6.0
●		1903	2.3
8 0001	5.9	**23** 0127	5.7
0557	2.5	0723	2.7
F 1203	6.2	SA 1342	5.9
1848	2.0	2007	2.5
9 0109	5.9	**24** 0227	5.8
0706	2.5	0842	2.6
SA 1314	6.2	SU 1449	5.8
1955	1.9	2109	2.5
10 0216	6.1	**25** 0324	5.9
0818	2.3	0947	2.4
SU 1427	6.3	M 1550	6.0
2102	1.8	2204	2.3
11 0318	6.3	**26** 0414	6.2
0929	2.0	1040	2.1
M 1535	6.5	TU 1643	6.1
2206	1.6	2251	2.1
12 0414	6.6	**27** 0458	6.5
1034	1.6	1126	1.8
TU 1639	6.8	W 1728	6.3
2304	1.4	2335	2.0
13 0507	6.9	**28** 0536	6.7
1135	1.3	1210	1.6
W 1740	7.0	TH 1807	6.4
○ 2359	1.3	●	
14 0557	7.1	**29** 0016	1.8
1232	0.9	0613	6.8
TH 1837	7.2	F 1250	1.4
		1844	6.5
15 0050	1.1	**30** 0053	1.8
0645	7.3	0649	6.9
F 1324	0.7	SA 1328	1.4
1931	7.3	1919	6.6
		31 0127	1.7
		0723	6.9
		SU 1403	1.3
		1954	6.6

AUGUST

Time	m	Time	m
1 0158	1.7	**16** 0244	1.2
0756	6.9	0838	7.5
M 1435	1.4	TU 1519	0.6
2029	6.6	2120	6.9
2 0228	1.8	**17** 0319	1.5
0828	6.8	0918	7.2
TU 1506	1.4	W 1554	1.3
2103	6.5	2157	6.5
3 0300	1.9	**18** 0353	1.6
0900	6.8	0959	6.8
W 1537	1.5	TH 1627	1.8
2138	6.4	2236	6.1
4 0336	1.9	**19** 0429	2.2
0938	6.7	1046	6.3
TH 1614	1.7	F 1704	2.3
2219	6.2	☽ 2324	5.8
5 0419	2.1	**20** 0514	2.6
1025	6.5	1146	5.8
F 1702	1.9	SA 1753	2.7
☽ 2311	6.0		
6 0514	2.4	**21** 0028	5.5
1123	6.2	0616	2.9
SA 1804	2.2	SU 1301	5.6
		1902	3.0
7 0018	5.8	**22** 0141	5.5
0627	2.5	0752	3.0
SU 1238	6.1	M 1421	5.5
1921	2.3	2034	2.9
8 0141	5.8	**23** 0251	5.7
0751	2.5	0930	2.6
M 1410	6.1	TU 1532	5.7
2041	2.2	2144	2.7
9 0257	6.1	**24** 0349	6.1
0916	2.2	1024	2.2
TU 1534	6.1	W 1627	6.1
2153	2.0	2234	2.3
10 0402	6.5	**25** 0435	6.4
1029	1.7	1109	1.8
W 1643	6.7	TH 1710	6.3
2255	1.7	2318	2.0
11 0457	6.9	**26** 0514	6.7
1131	1.2	1151	1.5
TH 1743	7.0	F 1747	6.6
2349	1.4	2359	1.8
12 0546	7.2	**27** 0550	6.9
1225	0.8	1231	1.3
F 1835	7.2	SA 1822	6.7
○		●	
13 0038	1.2	**28** 0035	1.7
0633	7.5	0626	7.0
SA 1314	0.5	SU 1308	1.2
1922	7.3	1856	6.8
14 0124	1.1	**29** 0108	1.6
0716	7.6	0700	7.1
SU 1359	0.4	M 1342	1.1
2005	7.3	1930	6.9
15 0205	1.1	**30** 0138	1.5
0758	7.6	0732	7.2
M 1441	0.5	TU 1412	1.1
2043	7.1	2002	6.9
		31 0207	1.5
		0803	7.2
		W 1440	1.2
		2033	6.8

Chart Datum: 3·90 metres below Ordnance Datum (Newlyn). HAT is 8·0 metres above Chart Datum.

》》 **FREE** monthly updates. Register at 《
www.reedsnauticalalmanac.co.uk

STANDARD TIME (UT)
For Summer Time add ONE hour in **non-shaded areas**

IMMINGHAM LAT 53°38'N LONG 0°11'W
TIMES AND HEIGHTS OF HIGH AND LOW WATERS

Dates in red are SPRINGS
Dates in blue are NEAPS

YEAR 2022

SEPTEMBER

#	Time	m	#	Time	m
1 TH	0238 / 0835 / 1508 / 2105	1.6 / 7.1 / 1.4 / 6.7	**16** F	0314 / 0920 / 1537 / 2136	1.8 / 6.7 / 1.9 / 6.3
2 F	0310 / 0912 / 1540 / 2143	1.7 / 6.9 / 1.7 / 6.4	**17** SA	0346 / 0959 / 1609 / 2213 ◑	2.2 / 6.2 / 2.4 / 5.9
3 SA ◐	0350 / 0958 / 1623 / 2232	2.0 / 6.6 / 2.0 / 6.1	**18** SU	0427 / 1053 / 1656 / 2315	2.6 / 5.7 / 2.9 / 5.5
4 SU	0442 / 1058 / 1727 / 2341	2.3 / 6.1 / 2.5 / 5.8	**19** M	0528 / 1222 / 1806	2.9 / 5.3 / 3.2
5 M	0602 / 1225 / 1900	2.6 / 5.8 / 2.7	**20** TU	0057 / 0656 / 1355 / 1950	5.4 / 3.1 / 5.3 / 3.2
6 TU	0118 / 0742 / 1417 / 2034	5.7 / 2.6 / 5.9 / 2.6	**21** W	0219 / 0907 / 1507 / 2122	5.6 / 2.7 / 5.7 / 2.9
7 W	0246 / 0918 / 1542 / 2148	6.0 / 2.2 / 6.3 / 2.2	**22** TH	0320 / 0959 / 1602 / 2212	6.0 / 2.2 / 6.1 / 2.4
8 TH	0351 / 1027 / 1644 / 2245	6.5 / 1.6 / 6.7 / 1.8	**23** F	0406 / 1042 / 1644 / 2254	6.4 / 1.8 / 6.4 / 2.1
9 F	0444 / 1122 / 1736 / 2335	7.0 / 1.0 / 7.1 / 1.4	**24** SA	0445 / 1122 / 1719 / 2332	6.7 / 1.4 / 6.7 / 1.8
10 SA ○	0529 / 1210 / 1820	7.3 / 0.6 / 7.3	**25** SU ●	0520 / 1201 / 1753	7.0 / 1.2 / 6.9
11 SU	0020 / 0613 / 1255 / 1900	1.1 / 7.6 / 0.4 / 7.4	**26** M	0008 / 0556 / 1238 / 1827	1.6 / 7.1 / 1.0 / 7.0
12 M	0102 / 0653 / 1335 / 1936	1.0 / 7.7 / 0.4 / 7.3	**27** TU	0041 / 0630 / 1312 / 1900	1.5 / 7.3 / 1.0 / 7.1
13 TU	0141 / 0732 / 1411 / 2009	1.0 / 7.7 / 0.7 / 7.2	**28** W	0113 / 0704 / 1343 / 1931	1.4 / 7.4 / 1.0 / 7.1
14 W	0215 / 0809 / 1443 / 2039	1.2 / 7.5 / 1.0 / 6.9	**29** TH	0144 / 0738 / 1412 / 2003	1.4 / 7.4 / 1.2 / 7.0
15 TH	0246 / 0845 / 1510 / 2107	1.4 / 7.2 / 1.5 / 6.6	**30** F	0217 / 0813 / 1441 / 2036	1.4 / 7.2 / 1.4 / 6.8

OCTOBER

#	Time	m	#	Time	m
1 SA	0251 / 0854 / 1515 / 2115	1.6 / 6.9 / 1.8 / 6.5	**16** SU	0313 / 0923 / 1527 / 2125	2.1 / 6.2 / 2.5 / 6.1
2 SU	0331 / 0942 / 1559 / 2205	1.9 / 6.5 / 2.3 / 6.1	**17** M ◑	0353 / 1012 / 1611 / 2215	2.5 / 5.7 / 2.9 / 5.7
3 M ◐	0429 / 1050 / 1708 / 2319	2.3 / 6.0 / 2.8 / 5.7	**18** TU	0453 / 1138 / 1718	2.9 / 5.3 / 3.3
4 TU	0558 / 1239 / 1851	2.6 / 5.7 / 3.0	**19** W	0000 / 0617 / 1318 / 1852	5.4 / 3.0 / 5.3 / 3.4
5 W	0105 / 0746 / 1424 / 2026	5.7 / 2.5 / 5.9 / 2.7	**20** TH	0136 / 0810 / 1430 / 2037	5.5 / 2.8 / 5.6 / 3.0
6 TH	0231 / 0912 / 1537 / 2134	6.1 / 1.9 / 6.4 / 2.3	**21** F	0240 / 0917 / 1525 / 2134	5.9 / 2.3 / 6.0 / 2.6
7 F	0333 / 1012 / 1632 / 2226	6.6 / 1.4 / 6.8 / 1.8	**22** SA	0327 / 1002 / 1607 / 2217	6.3 / 1.8 / 6.4 / 2.2
8 SA	0422 / 1101 / 1716 / 2312	7.0 / 0.9 / 7.1 / 1.4	**23** SU	0407 / 1044 / 1644 / 2255	6.6 / 1.5 / 6.7 / 1.9
9 SU ○	0506 / 1146 / 1755 / 2356	7.4 / 0.7 / 7.3 / 1.2	**24** M	0444 / 1124 / 1719 / 2333	6.9 / 1.2 / 7.0 / 1.6
10 M	0547 / 1227 / 1829	7.6 / 0.6 / 7.3	**25** TU ●	0521 / 1202 / 1754	7.2 / 1.1 / 7.1
11 TU	0036 / 0627 / 1304 / 1902	1.1 / 7.6 / 0.7 / 7.3	**26** W	0010 / 0559 / 1238 / 1829	1.4 / 7.4 / 1.0 / 7.2
12 W	0113 / 0705 / 1337 / 1932	1.1 / 7.5 / 1.0 / 7.1	**27** TH	0046 / 0638 / 1313 / 1903	1.3 / 7.4 / 1.0 / 7.3
13 TH	0145 / 0741 / 1405 / 2000	1.2 / 7.3 / 1.3 / 7.0	**28** F	0123 / 0717 / 1347 / 1938	1.2 / 7.4 / 1.2 / 7.2
14 F	0214 / 0814 / 1431 / 2025	1.5 / 7.0 / 1.6 / 6.7	**29** SA	0201 / 0759 / 1423 / 2016	1.3 / 7.2 / 1.4 / 7.0
15 SA	0242 / 0847 / 1456 / 2051	1.7 / 6.6 / 2.0 / 6.4	**30** SU	0241 / 0845 / 1502 / 2059	1.5 / 6.9 / 1.9 / 6.7
			31 M	0329 / 0940 / 1551 / 2152	1.8 / 6.4 / 2.4 / 6.3

NOVEMBER

#	Time	m	#	Time	m
1 TU ◐	0434 / 1057 / 1703 / 2308	2.2 / 5.9 / 2.8 / 5.9	**16** W ◑	0426 / 1054 / 1637 / 2253	2.6 / 5.5 / 3.1 / 5.6
2 W	0601 / 1245 / 1836	2.3 / 5.8 / 3.0	**17** TH	0538 / 1222 / 1753	2.7 / 5.4 / 3.2
3 TH	0046 / 0734 / 1408 / 2000	5.9 / 2.2 / 6.0 / 2.7	**18** F	0031 / 0657 / 1335 / 1916	5.6 / 2.6 / 5.6 / 3.1
4 F	0204 / 0847 / 1515 / 2105	6.2 / 1.8 / 6.4 / 2.3	**19** SA	0141 / 0809 / 1433 / 2028	5.8 / 2.3 / 5.9 / 2.8
5 SA	0305 / 0943 / 1606 / 2158	6.6 / 1.4 / 6.8 / 1.9	**20** SU	0236 / 0907 / 1522 / 2123	6.1 / 2.0 / 6.3 / 2.4
6 SU	0355 / 1031 / 1648 / 2244	7.0 / 1.1 / 7.0 / 1.6	**21** M	0322 / 0956 / 1604 / 2211	6.5 / 1.6 / 6.6 / 2.0
7 M	0439 / 1114 / 1724 / 2328	7.2 / 1.0 / 7.1 / 1.4	**22** TU	0406 / 1041 / 1644 / 2256	6.8 / 1.4 / 6.9 / 1.7
8 TU	0521 / 1154 / 1757 ○	7.3 / 1.0 / 7.1	**23** W ●	0449 / 1125 / 1723 / 2340	7.1 / 1.2 / 7.1 / 1.4
9 W	0008 / 0602 / 1230 / 1830	1.3 / 7.3 / 1.2 / 7.1	**24** TH	0533 / 1207 / 1802	7.3 / 1.1 / 7.2
10 TH	0045 / 0640 / 1302 / 1900	1.3 / 7.3 / 1.3 / 7.1	**25** F	0024 / 0618 / 1248 / 1842	1.2 / 7.4 / 1.1 / 7.3
11 F	0119 / 0716 / 1332 / 1928	1.4 / 7.0 / 1.5 / 7.0	**26** SA	0108 / 0705 / 1330 / 1922	1.1 / 7.3 / 1.2 / 7.3
12 SA	0149 / 0750 / 1359 / 1955	1.5 / 6.8 / 1.8 / 6.8	**27** SU	0153 / 0753 / 1412 / 2005	1.1 / 7.2 / 1.5 / 7.1
13 SU	0218 / 0824 / 1426 / 2024	1.7 / 6.5 / 2.1 / 6.6	**28** M	0241 / 0844 / 1457 / 2051	1.3 / 6.9 / 1.8 / 6.9
14 M	0250 / 0901 / 1459 / 2057	2.0 / 6.1 / 2.4 / 6.3	**29** TU	0334 / 0944 / 1549 / 2146	1.6 / 6.5 / 2.2 / 6.6
15 TU	0331 / 0947 / 1540 / 2142	2.3 / 5.8 / 2.7 / 5.9	**30** W ◐	0437 / 1100 / 1652 / 2255	1.8 / 6.2 / 2.6 / 6.3

DECEMBER

#	Time	m	#	Time	m
1 TH	0549 / 1222 / 1806	1.9 / 6.0 / 2.7	**16** F ◑	0457 / 1118 / 1700 / 2313	2.4 / 5.7 / 2.9 / 5.9
2 F	0015 / 0702 / 1332 / 1921	6.2 / 1.9 / 6.1 / 2.7	**17** SA	0559 / 1227 / 1807	2.4 / 5.7 / 2.9
3 SA	0126 / 0809 / 1435 / 2027	6.3 / 1.8 / 6.3 / 2.4	**18** SU	0025 / 0704 / 1331 / 1918	5.9 / 2.3 / 5.8 / 2.8
4 SU	0229 / 0906 / 1529 / 2125	6.5 / 1.7 / 6.5 / 2.1	**19** M	0132 / 0807 / 1430 / 2025	6.0 / 2.1 / 6.0 / 2.5
5 M	0324 / 0956 / 1613 / 2215	6.7 / 1.6 / 6.6 / 1.9	**20** TU	0233 / 0907 / 1523 / 2126	6.3 / 1.9 / 6.3 / 2.2
6 TU	0413 / 1041 / 1652 / 2301	6.8 / 1.5 / 6.8 / 1.7	**21** W	0329 / 1002 / 1612 / 2223	6.6 / 1.6 / 6.6 / 1.8
7 W	0458 / 1122 / 1728 / 2344	6.9 / 1.5 / 6.9 / 1.5	**22** TH	0423 / 1054 / 1658 / 2317	6.9 / 1.4 / 6.9 / 1.5
8 TH ○	0541 / 1200 / 1802	6.9 / 1.6 / 6.9	**23** F ●	0516 / 1144 / 1743	7.1 / 1.3 / 7.1
9 F	0023 / 0621 / 1234 / 1836	1.5 / 6.8 / 1.6 / 7.0	**24** SA	0009 / 0609 / 1232 / 1829	1.2 / 7.2 / 1.2 / 7.3
10 SA	0100 / 0659 / 1306 / 1907	1.5 / 6.7 / 1.7 / 6.9	**25** SU	0101 / 0701 / 1319 / 1913	1.0 / 7.3 / 1.2 / 7.4
11 SU	0133 / 0734 / 1337 / 1938	1.6 / 6.6 / 1.9 / 6.8	**26** M	0151 / 0753 / 1405 / 1958	0.9 / 7.2 / 1.3 / 7.3
12 M	0205 / 0809 / 1407 / 2009	1.7 / 6.4 / 2.0 / 6.7	**27** TU	0241 / 0846 / 1451 / 2045	0.9 / 7.0 / 1.5 / 7.2
13 TU	0239 / 0846 / 1440 / 2042	1.9 / 6.2 / 2.2 / 6.4	**28** W	0332 / 0941 / 1539 / 2136	1.0 / 6.7 / 1.8 / 7.0
14 W	0316 / 0927 / 1517 / 2121	2.0 / 6.0 / 2.4 / 6.2	**29** TH	0425 / 1041 / 1630 / 2233	1.3 / 6.4 / 2.1 / 6.7
15 TH	0402 / 1016 / 1603 / 2210	2.2 / 5.8 / 2.7 / 5.9	**30** F ◐	0521 / 1143 / 1727 / 2336	1.6 / 6.2 / 2.4 / 6.5
			31 SA	0620 / 1244 / 1830	1.8 / 6.0 / 2.6

Chart Datum: 3·90 metres below Ordnance Datum (Newlyn). HAT is 8·0 metres above Chart Datum.

NE England

>> FREE monthly updates. Register at <<
www.reedsnauticalalmanac.co.uk

159

3.10   RIVER HUMBER

S bank: NE and N Lincolnshire. N bank: E Riding of Yorks and City of Kingston-upon-Hull.
Hull marina: **53°44'·24N 00°20'·15W** ❀❀◊◊◊ ✿✿✿

CHARTS AC 1190, 107, 104, 1188, 3496, 3497, 5614; Imray C29; ABP

TIDES –0510 Immingham, –0452 Hull, Dover; ML 4·1; Duration 0555
Standard Port IMMINGHAM (◀—)

Times				Height (metres)			
High Water		Low Water		MHWS	MHWN	MLWN	MLWS
0100	0700	0100	0700	7·3	5·8	2·6	0·9
1300	1900	1300	1900				
Differences BULL SAND FORT							
–0020	–0030	–0035	–0015	–0·4	–0·3	+0·1	+0·2
GRIMSBY							
–0012	–0014	–0015	–0013	–0·3	–0·2	+0·1	+0·4
HULL (ALBERT DOCK)							
+0019	+0019	+0033	+0027	+0·3	+0·1	–0·1	–0·2
HUMBER BRIDGE							
+0027	+0022	+0049	+0039	–0·1	–0·4	–0·7	–0·6
BURTON STATHER (R Trent)*							
+0105	+0050	+0240	+0205	–2·0	–2·7	–2·2	–1·1
KEADBY (R Trent)*							
+0135	+0120	+0425	+0410	–2·8	–3·3	–2·3	–0·9
BLACKTOFT (R Ouse)†							
+0100	+0055	+0325	+0255	–1·6	–1·8	–2·2	–1·1
GOOLE (R Ouse)†							
+0130	+0115	+0355	+0350	–1·6	–2·1	–1·9	–0·6

* Normal river level at Burton Stather is about 0·1m below CD, and at Keadby 0·1m to 0·2m below CD.

† Heights of LW can increase by up to 0·3m at Blacktoft and 0·6m at Goole when river in spate. HW hts are little affected.

SHELTER R Humber is the estuary of the rivers Ouse and Trent. The estuary has strong tidal streams: a strong NW'ly against a spring flood of 3-4kn causes a short steep sea, as does a SE'ly over the ebb stream. Off Hull Marina it can be very choppy with fresh winds over spring tidal streams.

Anchorages Inside Spurn Hd only with winds from NE to ESE, or close off Haile Sand Fort in fair weather. In S to W winds there is a good ⚓ off the SW bank 8ca above N Killingholme Oil jetty, well out of main chan. In N'lies ⚓ off Hawkin's Pt, N of S9 buoy.

Marinas at Hull, S Ferriby and the docks at Goole are all entered by lock access HW±3. At Grimsby lock best to await levels at HW±2. Otherwise £10 lock fee. Gates may shut at extreme HW Sp. Immingham should only be used in emergency. S Ferriby should not be attempted without up-to-date ABP charts for the ever-changing buoyed chan above Hull. Waiting pontoon at S Ferriby.

Do not attempt entry to Winteringham or Brough Havens without contacting Humber Yawl Club for details of approach channel and mooring availability. Both dry to soft mud. Winteringham is prone to heavy silting, but is dredged.

NAVIGATION Note TSS on chartlet 3.1, AC 107 and at: www. humber.com/Yachting_and_Leisure/Pleasure_Craft_Navigation
From S, WPT 53°30'·50N 00°16'·50E, 1ca SW of Rosse Spit PHM buoy, Fl (2) R 5s. Thence pass S of Haile Sand No 2, then via No 2B, Tetney monobuoy and No 2C into Haile Channel.

From N, WPT 53°34'·74N 00°16'·55E, S Binks SHM buoy, Fl G 2s. Thence passing N of Spurn Lt Float, SE Chequer to Chequer No 3 crossing to S of Bull Channel at this point. This avoids strong tidal streams off Spurn Hd. Best arrival at LW. Sp tides are fierce: 4·4kn ebb off Spurn Head and Immingham. There is a big ship ⚓ S of Spurn Hd. Keep clear of large commercial vessels using Hawke (8·4m) and Sunk (8·8m) Chans; these are marked by S1-S9 SHM buoys, all Fl G 1·5s (S8 is a SHM bn, Fl G 1·5s with tide gauge); and by P2-P9 PHM buoys, all Fl R 1·5s. Foul Holme Chan (SHM buoys FH1 to FH9) off Immingham is recommended for small craft.

For **Grimsby,** the lock into Fish Docks is 255°/1·35M from Lower Burcom No 6 Lt Float, Fl R 4s. The jetty off the W entrance to Royal Dock has been extended further into Grimsby Road. Many offshore energy service cats use the port travelling at up to 28kn.

Alexander Dock accessed through Royal Dock. Lock opens from HW-3.5 to HW+2.5 with free flow from HW–1.5 until just before HW.

Off Kingston-upon-Hull a tidal eddy and streams can be rotatory: the flood makes W up Hull Roads for ¾hr whilst the ebb is already running downriver over Skitter Sand on the opposite bank (reaches 2½kn at sp). Humber Bridge (conspic) has 29m clearance.

LIGHTS AND MARKS The Humber is well marked. At Grimsby a conspic tr (94m with 'minaret' on top) is 300m W of Fish Dock lock. IPTS at Grimsby, Killingholme, Hull and Goole. A number of jetties with F lts have additional FL lts shown in fog.

COMMUNICATIONS (Codes: Grimsby 01472; Hull 01482) HUMBER HM 01482 327171; see also: www.humber.com

Advise VTS Humber on Ch 14 (or ☎01482 212191) position and intentions on appr from seaward of Clee Ness lt float; listen on Ch 14 / 12 when West of the float and Ch 15 upstream from the Humber Bridge to Gainsborough (R Trent) and Goole (R Ouse).

☲, nav & tidal information is broadcast on Ch 12/14 every odd H+03; more info, including height of tide, is available on request.

GRIMSBY Port Director 327171, Assistant Dock Master 263509.

HULL Lock ☎330508; ⊜ 782107.

Other VHF stns: Grimsby Docks Radio Ch 74 (H24) 18 79 call Humber Fishdock Island for lock keeper or Meridian Quay.

Immingham Docks Radio Ch 19 68 (H24).

Hull Port Ops: Drypool Radio Ch 22 (–2 HW +1; Sat 0900-1100 LT).

Hull Marina Ch M 80 (H24); Albert Dock Radio Ch 09.

Ferriby Sluice (Ancholme Lock) Ch 74. Humber YC, Ch M (racing).

Goole Docks Radio Ch 14 (H24) 09 19.

Boothferry Bridge Ch 09 (H24). Selby Railway and Toll Bridges Ch 09. Br Waterways locks Ch 74.

Brough and Winteringham Havens, Humber Yawl Club Ch M.

FACILITIES

Humber Mouth YC ☎(01472) 812063, M drying at Tetney Haven. Humber Cruising Association.

GRIMSBY NE Lincs (01472) Fish Docks Lock access (R/G tfc lts) HW±3 £10 locking fee for Ⓥ, both gates open for free flow HW±2, enter free of charge with authorisation by Fish Dock Island, Ch 74. Gates may close at extreme HW springs to prevent flooding.

Meridian Quay Marina www.hcagrimsby.co.uk ☎(01472) 268424, mob 07415 209659, Ch 74. ⌫+30 Ⓥ, £2·10 inc ⎗, ▢, ▮ ⚒ ✎ ⌨ ☏ ▣(35t) ⌿ wi-fi.

Grimsby and Cleethorpes YC www.gcyc.co.uk ☎(01482) 356678; enter via Royal Dock, avoiding the extended piers enclosing tidal basin to N and W, limited 50⌫; ⚓ ⚓ ▢ ✕ ⌿. Town All facilities.

Hull Marina ⚓ www.bwml.co.uk/hull_marina ☎(01482) 609960; (312+20Ⓥ £3·10) access HW±3 via lock (width 8·5m) 150m to the E. 1 Apr–31 Oct H24, 1 Nov-31 Mar 0700-2100 – otherwise 24hrs notice. No shelter from W through S to E when waiting outside lock in river especially in strong W winds or if marina shut. The pontoon in basin for craft awaiting lock in dries, do not settle into the mud. Marina office open 0900-1700 daily; ▣⚓▮⚒♣✕✎ ☏⌀▣(50t) ⌿(2t) ⚓ ACA. City All facilities.

Ferries: Rotterdam/Zeebrugge daily; 10hrs; www.poferries.com.

South Ferriby Marina N Lincs. southferribymarina.com ☎(01652) 635620; access HW±3, 100+20Ⓥ £10/craft<10m<+£1/m max LOA 12m. Lock fee £7. VHF 80; ⚓ ⎗ ▮ ⚓ ▣(20t). Village ⌿ ⌿.

S Ferriby Lock ☎01652 635219. River Authority Ⓥ berths £8/48hrs. Lock Fee £7 (70ft LOA, 18ft beam, 6ft draught); ⚓. VHF 74: 0730-1600.

Humber Yawl Club has two facilities: Brough Haven E Riding, ☎(01482) 667224, entry HW±1½; Ch 37/M1 limited ⌫; ▬ ⚓ ⌿.

Winteringham Haven N Lincs ☎(01724) 734452. Limited access; Ch 37/M1. ▣(10t) ⌧.

GOOLE Take the flood up the R Humber, follow the buoyed channel past Hull, Brough and when approaching Trent Falls Apex alter course to stbd and follow the R Ouse to Goole. Situated off the Aire and Calder Navigation and accessed via the commercial lock for Goole Docks (Ch 14) are two havens, limited ♥.

Goole Boathouse ☎(01405) 763985 ⚓£5<64ft, max draught 1·5m.
Viking Marina www.vikingmarine.com ☎(01405) 765737, ⚓ £8·00/boat/nt, <80' LOA, 20' beam, 9' draught; ⚓ 🔧 🚿 🛢 🔥 ⚒ ⚓ 🏪(18t) 🅿.

NABURN follow R Ouse, 4M S of York and 80M above Spurn Pt; **Naburn Marina** ☎(01904) 621021; 300+50♥ max draught 1m £3·15 (min £21) 🔧 🔌 (£2·00) 🚾/🚿 🛢 ♨ 🔥 ⚒ ⚓ 🏪(16t) 🅿 ✕.

3.11 BRIDLINGTON

E Riding of Yorkshire 54°04'·78N 00°11'·21W ✦✦♦♦✿✿

CHARTS AC 1191, 1190, 129, 121, 1882, 5614; Imray C29

TIDES +0553 Dover; ML 3·6; Duration 0610

Standard Port RIVER TEES (→)

Times				Height (metres)			
High Water		Low Water		MHWS	MHWN	MLWN	MLWS
0000	0600	0000	0600	5·5	4·3	2·0	0·9
1200	1800	1200	1800				
Differences BRIDLINGTON							
+0100	+0050	+0055	+0050	+0·6	+0·4	+0·3	+0·2
FILEY BAY							
+0042	+0042	+0047	+0034	+0·3	+0·6	+0·4	+0·1

SHELTER Good, except in E, SE and S winds. Hbr dries completely to soft black mud. Berth on S pier or near HM's Office as directed. Dredged 2017, but ♥berth availability limited by FV activity.

NAVIGATION WPT SW Smithic WCM, Q (9) 15s, 54°02'·41N 00°09'·21W, 333°/2·6M to ent. Close-in appr is with N pier hd lt on brg 002° to keep W of drying patch (The Canch). Beware bar.

LIGHTS AND MARKS Hbr is 4M WSW of Flamborough Hd lt, Fl (4) 15s 65m 24M. Y racing marks are laid in the Bay, Apr–Oct. Tidal sigs, by day from S pier: R flag = >2·7m in hbr; No flag = < 2·7m. At night from N pier: Fl ● = >2·7m in hbr; Fl ● = < 2·7m.

COMMUNICATIONS (Code 01262) HM 670148/9, mob 0860 275150. Call on VHF Ch 16, then Ch **12** for working.

FACILITIES S Pier ⚓ £2.80/m²/week or £20/yacht <3 days, 🔧 ⚓ see HM, ⚓ ⚓(500227), ⚓(3t) 🅿(75t); **Royal Yorks YC** ☎672041 🔧🔌✕🅿.
Town 🏪 🔧 ⚓ 🅿 🏧 ✉ ⓑ 🛒 ✕ 🖥 ⚡ ✈(Humberside).

ADJACENT ANCHORAGE (7M SE of Scarborough)

FILEY, N Yorkshire, 54°12'·80N 00°16'·20W, AC 1882, 129. HW +0532 on Dover; ML 3·5m; Duration 0605. See 3.11. Good ⚓ in winds from S to NNE in 4–5m on hard sand. Lt on cliff above CG Stn, G metal column, FR 31m 1M vis 272°-308°. Filey Brigg, a natural bkwtr, is marked by ECM buoy, Q(3)10s, Bell. Beware Old Horse Rks, 2M WNW of Filey Brigg, foul ground extending ½M offshore. An unmarked Historic Wreck (see 0.32) lies at 54°11'·51N 00°13'·48W. Facilities: 🔧 ✉ ⓑ 🛢 ✕ 🖥 🅷 ☎(01723) 68111 ⚡.

3.12 SCARBOROUGH

N. Yorkshire **54°16'·88N 00°23'·36W** ❀✦♦♦♦❁❁❁

CHARTS AC 1191, 129, 1612, 5614; Imray C29

TIDES +0527 Dover; ML 3·5; Duration 0615

Standard Port RIVER TEES (→)

Times				Height (metres)			
High Water		Low Water		MHWS	MHWN	MLWN	MLWS
0000	0600	0000	0600	5·5	4·3	2·0	0·9
1200	1800	1200	1800				
Differences SCARBOROUGH							
+0040	+0040	+0030	+0030	+0·2	+0·3	+0·3	0·0

SHELTER Good in Outer Harbour (dries) for local residents, access via narrow (10m) entrance by East pier, but not in strong E/SE'lies. In winter months. Outer Harbour access is via the drawbridge.
Ⓥ� on SE side of pontoons in Inner Harbour. Berths have 2m alongside pontoon, but bottom shelves rapidly beyond one boat's breadth from pontoons limiting access to approx HW ±2hrs.

NAVIGATION WPT 54°16'·50N 00°22'·00W, 302°/0·83M to E pier lt. Appr from the E to avoid Ramsdale Scar, rky shoal 0·9m. Keep careful watch for salmon nets E and SE of ent. Beware rks extending approx 20m SW of E pier head. Give Castle Headland close N of hbr a wide berth due to coastal defences. Min depths in approach and entrance to Inner Harbour approx 0·1m. Best water to starboard side of entrance (inbound).

LIGHTS AND MARKS Lt ho (conspic), Iso 5s, Dia 60s, on Vincent Pier is shown by night or B ● by day when there is more than 3·7m over bar in entrance. A Y SPM Fl Y 4s, 110° E pier 1·8M marks the end of an outfall; another, N of the harbour 0·7NM NE of Scalby Ness, is marked by a PHM Fl R 5s. Scarborough YC sets lit Y SPM. Other lts as shown on chartlet.

COMMUNICATIONS (Code 01723) Ⓗ 368111. Port Control 373877. Call *Scarborough Port Control* VHF Ch **12** 16 (H24). Watchkeeper will offer guidance to approaching visitors.

FACILITIES HM www.scarboroughbc.gov.uk ☎373530 (HO); ⌂ £14/night, inner harbour pontoon berth £2·64 min charge £21·12, ▲ ⚓ ⟲(4t) ▬ (£11·50).
Scarborough YC www.syc.org.uk ☎373821, ▲ ▬ ⌂⚓✎ ⒸⒹ.
Services ✎ ⒸⒹ ✂ Ⓛ Ⓔ.
Town ⌂⌂⌂ ✉ Ⓑ ▦ ✕ ▭ ⇌ ✈(Humberside).

ADJACENT ANCHORAGE (5M WNW of Whitby)
RUNSWICK BAY, N Yorkshire, **54°32'·11N 00°44'·20W.** AC 1612. HW +0505 on Dover: Differences on R Tees are approx as Whitby; ML 3·1m; Duration 0605. Good shelter in all winds from SSE thru W to NW. Enter bay at 225° keeping clear of many rks at base of cliffs. Two W posts (2FY by night when required by lifeboat) 18m apart are ldg marks 270° to LB ho and can be used to lead into ⚓. Good holding in 6m to 9m in middle of bay. Facilities: **Runswick Bay Rescue Boat Station** ☎(01947) 840965. **Village** ▦✕⌂.

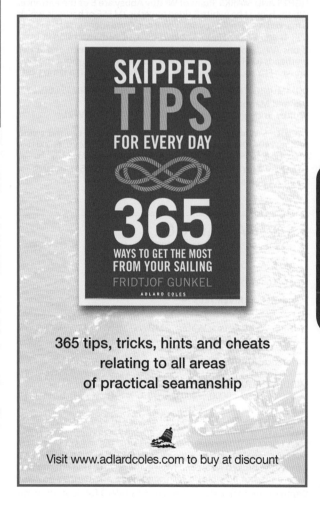

SKIPPER TIPS FOR EVERY DAY

365 WAYS TO GET THE MOST FROM YOUR SAILING

FRIDTJOF GUNKEL

ADLARD COLES

365 tips, tricks, hints and cheats relating to all areas of practical seamanship

Visit www.adlardcoles.com to buy at discount

3.13 WHITBY

N. Yorkshire 54°29'·65N 00°36'·78W ❀❀⚓⚓⚓⚓❀❀❀

CHARTS AC 129, 134, 1612, 5614, 5615; Imray C29, C24

TIDES +0500 Dover; ML 3·3; Duration 0605

Standard Port RIVER TEES (➡)

Times				Height (metres)			
High Water		Low Water		MHWS	MHWN	MLWN	MLWS
0000	0600	0000	0600	5·5	4·3	2·0	0·9
1200	1800	1200	1800				
Differences WHITBY							
+0020	+0020	+0018	+0017	+0·1	+0·1	+0·2	+0·1

SHELTER Good, except in lower hbr in strong NW to NE winds.

NAVIGATION WPT 54°30'·21N 00°36'·96W, 169°/0·57M to ent. In N-NE gales seas break in the approach, which is dangerous.

• From the SE beware Whitby Rk; leave Whitby NCM to port.
• Beware strong set to E from HW −2 to HW, when nearing piers.

Vessels >37m LOA must embark pilot and sailing vessels are to use auxiliary power if so equipped. Min depth in entr approx 1·0m.

Swing Bridge opens on request HW±2 every H and H+30.

F ● = open; FR ● = shut. Wait on pontoon at Fish Pier if necessary. If alongside Fish Quay or FVs, craft must not be left unattended. Priority: 1. Commercial vessels with pilot embarked (keep clear); 2. Large vessels; 3. Inbound vessels; 4. When both bridge sections are open 2-way traffic in single file keeping to stbd. Establish comms with Whitby Bridge Ch **11** prior to transit.

LIGHTS AND MARKS Ruins of Whitby Abbey are E of the entrance. Whitby High Lt ho (white 8-sided tower) is 2M ESE of harbour, which is marked on each side by 5m high R and G wooden towers. E Pier Fl (2)R 4s and W Pier Fl(2)G 4s 24m lt ho, sync with extension lights.
2 bns (W △, and W ○ with B stripe) seen between the outer pierheads (Q Fl R and Q Fl G) lead 169° into hbr. At night the Fwd bn sync Fl Y 4s, aligns with a lt sync Fl Y 4s (46m) on a lamp post.

COMMUNICATIONS (Code 01947) Dr 820888.HM 602354/602272. Hbr and Marina VHF Ch **11** 16 12 (H24).
Whitby Bridge Ch **11** (listens on Ch 16 HW−2 to HW+2).

FACILITIES Whitby Marina (dredged 1.5m) is 2ca beyond swing bridge; 240+10♥ at seaward end of long pontoon £2.20; ☎600165. ⛽⚓ 🏠⛴✕⚓♨⛴⚓🛒⛽. ACA. **Whitby YC** ☎603623 ⚓⛽⛴.
Fish Quay ⚓(in commercial quantities only, ☎602255) ⛴(1t).
Town All domestic facilities, ✕⛴⚋✈(Teesside).

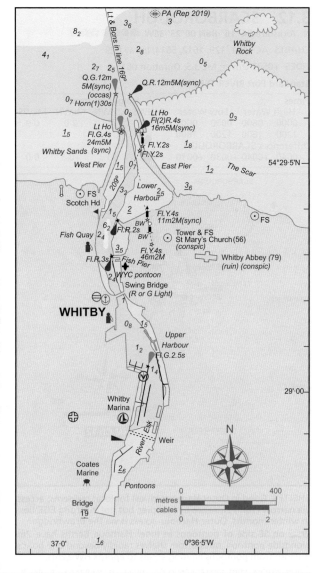

3.14 HARTLEPOOL

Hartlepool 54°41'·26N 01°11'·90W (West Hbr ent) ❀❀⚓⚓⚓❀❀

CHARTS AC 152, 2567, 2566, 5615; Imray C24

TIDES +0437 Dover; ML 3·0; Duration 0600

Standard Port RIVER TEES (⬅)

Times				Height (metres)			
High Water		Low Water		MHWS	MHWN	MLWN	MLWS
0000	0600	0000	0600	5·5	4·3	2·0	0·9
1200	1800	1200	1800				
Differences HARTLEPOOL							
−0004	−0004	−0006	−0006	−0·1	−0·1	−0·2	−0·1
MIDDLESBROUGH							
0000	+0002	0000	−0003	+0·1	+0·2	+0·1	−0·1

SHELTER Excellent in marina (5m) 4Ca SW of port.

NAVIGATION WPT 54°40'·86N 01°09'·90W, Longscar ECM buoy, 295°/1·06M to W Hbr ent. (For Victoria Hbr, 308°/0·65M to Nos 1/2 buoys.) From S, beware Longscar Rks, 4ca WSW of WPT. Strong E/SE winds raise broken water and swell in the bay, making ent channel hazardous, but possible. In such conditions, ask marina's advice.

Depth in app chan to lock limits entry to HW±3 for boats drawing

>1.5m, check with HM. Beware fierce eddy outside lock on opening which catches the unwary, but subsides. Speed limit 4kn in W Hbr.

LIGHTS AND MARKS Tees Appr (54°40'·60N 01°04'·00W) Mo(A) 5s 8M, Horn, is 2M E of Longscar ECM, Q(3), bell, which lies off the entrance. Steetly Works chimney, 1·4M NW of marina entrance, and St Hilda's Church tower on The Heugh, are both prominent. Ldg Dir lt Iso WRG 324° leads to commercial port by buoyed chan. Dir lt Fl WRG leads 308° to marina lock, between W Hbr outer piers, Oc R / Oc G, and inner piers, FR and FG; bright street lts on S pier.
Lock sigs: ● = Proceed; ● = Wait; ● ● = Lock closed.
Dir lt, Iso WRG, leads 325° via lit buoyed chan to Victoria Hbr.

COMMUNICATIONS (Code 01429) Dr 272679; Tees Port Authority (01642) 277205; *Tees Port Control* info Ch 14, 22 (H24).
Marina/Lock Ch **M**, 80. *Hartlepool Dock Radio* Ch 12 (ship berthing).

FACILITIES Hartlepool Marina www.hartlepool-marina.com ☎865744 Access chan dredged to CD and lock(max beam 8.5m), (HW±3), (H24). 500+100♥ £2.16, ⛽⚓⚓(H24) ⚓ LPG ✕⛴♨🛒⚓⛴ (40/300t) ⛴ (13t).
Victoria Hbr (commercial dock only) H24. Call *Tees Port Control*.
Tees & Hartlepool YC ☎233423, ⛽⛴.
Town 🏠🏠✉Ⓑ🍽(H24) ✕⛴⚋✈(Teesside).

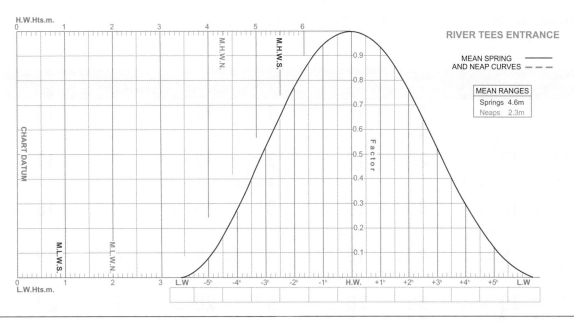

RIVER TEES ENTRANCE

MEAN SPRING ———
AND NEAP CURVES ─ ─ ─

MEAN RANGES
Springs 4.6m
Neaps 2.3m

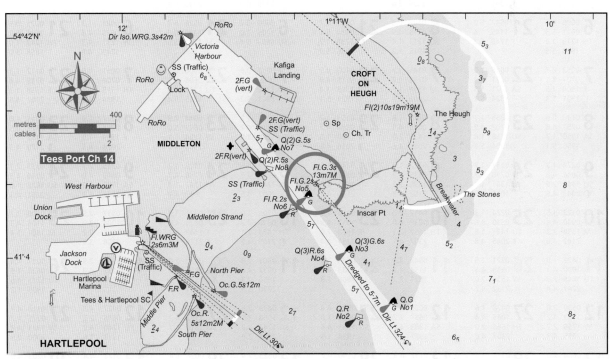

Tees Port Ch 14

ADJACENT PORT (3M SSE of Hartlepool)
RIVER TEES/MIDDLESBROUGH, Middlesbrough/Stockton, **54°38'·94N 01°08'·48W**. ⚓⚓🌊🔱. AC 152, 2567, 2566; Imray C29; OS 93. HW +0450 Dover; Standard Port River Tees. ML 3·1; duration 0605.

SHELTER Entry to R Tees is not recommended for small craft in heavy weather, especially in strong winds from NE to SE.

NAVIGATION R Tees and Middlesbrough are a major industrial area. Tees Bay wind farm, is up to 1½M offshore SE of the Tees channel as far as West Scar.

LIGHTS AND MARKS Tees Approach SWM, Mo(A) 5s 8M, Horn 5s, Racon, is 055°/3·0M from S Gare bkwtr. Running on FR Ldg lts

210° (framework towers). The channel is well buoyed from the Fairway buoy to beyond Middlesbrough. At Old CG stn a Q lt, or 3 ● (vert), = no entry.

COMMUNICATIONS Call: *Tees Port Control* VHF Ch **14** 22 16 12 (H24). Monitor Ch 14; also info Ch 14 22. *Tees Barrage Radio* Ch M (37). HM ☎(01642) 277201.

FACILITIES South Gare Marine Club ☎491039(occas) ⚓⚓⚓.
Castlegate Marine Club ☎583299, ⚓⚓⚓⚓⚓.
Tees Motor Boat Club ⚓.
City All domestic facilities, ⇌ ✈.

STANDARD TIME (UT)
For Summer Time add ONE hour in **non-shaded areas**

RIVER TEES   LAT 54°38'N   LONG 1°09'W
TIMES AND HEIGHTS OF HIGH AND LOW WATERS

Dates in red are **SPRINGS**
Dates in blue are **NEAPS**

YEAR 2022

JANUARY

Time	m	Time	m
1 0142 SA 0813 1413 2039	5.2 1.1 5.2 1.1	**16** 0239 SU 0851 1458 2116	4.7 1.7 4.9 1.4
2 0240 SU 0907 1504 ●2134	5.3 1.0 5.4 0.9	**17** 0320 M 0928 1533 ○2154	4.8 1.6 5.0 1.3
3 0335 M 0958 1553 2226	5.5 0.9 5.5 0.7	**18** 0357 TU 1002 1606 2230	4.9 1.5 5.1 1.1
4 0428 TU 1047 1641 2317	5.5 1.0 5.6 0.6	**19** 0432 W 1036 1638 2305	5.0 1.4 5.2 1.1
5 0520 W 1134 1727 2341	5.4 1.1 5.6 1.0	**20** 0507 TH 1110 1712	5.0 1.4 5.2
6 0005 0611 TH 1219 1814	0.6 5.3 1.2 5.5	**21** 0542 1145 F 1746	5.0 1.4 5.2
7 0052 0701 F 1304 1901	0.7 5.1 1.5 5.3	**22** 0016 0621 SA 1221 1824	1.0 4.9 1.5 5.1
8 0139 0751 SA 1350 1950	0.9 4.8 1.7 5.1	**23** 0055 0702 SU 1258 1904	1.1 4.9 1.6 5.1
9 0228 0844 SU 1440 ☽2043	1.2 4.6 2.0 4.8	**24** 0137 0748 M 1341 1950	1.2 4.7 1.7 4.9
10 0322 0940 M 1538 2142	1.5 4.4 2.2 4.6	**25** 0224 0840 TU 1431 ☾2045	1.3 4.6 1.8 4.8
11 0422 1040 TU 1645 2247	1.8 4.3 2.3 4.4	**26** 0321 0939 W 1536 2152	1.5 4.5 2.0 4.7
12 0530 1143 W 1755 2355	2.0 4.2 2.2 4.3	**27** 0428 1045 TH 1654 2307	1.6 4.4 2.0 4.6
13 0634 1244 TH 1858	2.0 4.4 2.1	**28** 0543 1154 F 1814	1.7 4.5 1.8
14 0058 0727 F 1335 1950	4.4 1.9 4.5 1.8	**29** 0023 0658 SA 1301 1931	4.7 1.6 4.7 1.5
15 0153 0812 SA 1419 2035	4.5 1.8 4.7 1.6	**30** 0136 0805 SU 1403 2036	4.9 1.4 5.0 1.2
		31 0239 0901 M 1457 2132	5.1 1.2 5.2 0.8

FEBRUARY

Time	m	Time	m
1 0333 0952 TU 1545 ●2222	5.3 1.0 5.4 0.6	**16** 0341 0948 W 1548 ○2213	4.9 1.4 5.1 0.9
2 0423 1038 W 1630 2308	5.4 1.0 5.6 0.4	**17** 0414 1021 TH 1620 2247	5.0 1.2 5.3 0.8
3 0508 1120 TH 1712 2350	5.4 1.0 5.6 0.4	**18** 0447 1054 F 1651 2321	5.1 1.1 5.3 0.7
4 0552 1200 F 1753	5.3 1.0 5.6	**19** 0520 1127 SA 1723 2355	5.2 1.1 5.4 0.7
5 0029 0634 SA 1236 1834	0.6 5.2 1.2 5.4	**20** 0555 1201 SU 1757	5.2 1.1 5.4
6 0107 0715 SU 1313 1915	0.8 4.9 1.4 5.2	**21** 0031 0634 M 1235 1836	0.7 5.1 1.2 5.3
7 0145 0757 M 1351 2000	1.2 4.7 1.7 4.9	**22** 0109 0715 TU 1313 1921	0.9 4.9 1.4 5.1
8 0225 0843 TU 1435 ☽2051	1.6 4.4 2.0 4.6	**23** 0153 0804 W 1400 ☾2016	1.2 4.7 1.6 4.8
9 0312 0935 W 1535 2153	1.9 4.2 2.2 4.3	**24** 0245 0902 TH 1501 2126	1.5 4.4 1.8 4.5
10 0417 1039 TH 1657 2307	2.2 4.0 2.3 4.1	**25** 0356 1013 F 1628 2251	1.8 4.3 2.0 4.4
11 0542 1153 F 1821	2.3 4.3 2.2	**26** 0524 1133 SA 1808	2.0 4.3 1.9
12 0025 0657 SA 1303 1927	4.1 2.2 4.3 2.0	**27** 0022 0654 SU 1253 1934	4.4 1.8 4.5 1.5
13 0132 0751 SU 1357 2017	4.3 2.0 4.5 1.7	**28** 0140 0802 M 1358 2036	4.7 1.6 4.8 1.1
14 0223 0835 M 1439 2059	4.5 1.8 4.7 1.4		
15 0304 0913 TU 1515 2138	4.7 1.6 4.9 1.1		

MARCH

Time	m	Time	m
1 0239 0854 TU 1449 2126	5.0 1.3 5.2 0.7	**16** 0239 0849 W 1447 2112	4.7 1.5 4.9 1.0
2 0326 0940 W 1534 ●2210	5.2 1.1 5.4 0.4	**17** 0314 0924 TH 1520 2148	5.0 1.3 5.1 0.7
3 0409 1021 TH 1613 2250	5.4 0.9 5.6 0.3	**18** 0347 0958 F 1552 ○2222	5.1 1.1 5.3 0.5
4 0448 1058 F 1651 2326	5.4 0.9 5.6 0.4	**19** 0419 1031 SA 1624 2255	5.3 0.9 5.5 0.4
5 0525 1133 SA 1726 2359	5.3 0.9 5.6 0.6	**20** 0453 1104 SU 1657 2330	5.3 0.8 5.6 0.4
6 0600 1205 SU 1803	5.2 1.0 5.4	**21** 0528 1138 M 1734	5.3 0.8 5.5
7 0030 0635 M 1236 1841	0.8 5.0 1.2 5.2	**22** 0006 0606 TU 1213 1815	0.6 5.2 0.9 5.4
8 0101 0710 TU 1309 1921	1.2 4.7 1.5 4.9	**23** 0044 0647 W 1254 1903	0.8 5.0 1.1 5.1
9 0132 0749 W 1346 2007	1.6 4.5 1.8 4.5	**24** 0128 0736 TH 1342 2002	1.2 4.7 1.4 4.7
10 0209 0836 TH 1434 ☽2105	1.9 4.2 2.1 4.2	**25** 0221 0835 F 1447 ☾2118	1.7 4.4 1.7 4.4
11 0301 0937 F 1556 2220	2.3 4.0 2.3 3.9	**26** 0338 0952 SA 1625 2251	2.0 4.2 1.9 4.2
12 0439 1058 SA 1742 2351	2.5 3.9 2.3 3.9	**27** 0520 1122 SU 1814	2.1 4.2 1.7
13 0623 1225 SU 1858	2.4 4.0 2.0	**28** 0028 0650 M 1246 1930	4.4 1.9 4.5 1.3
14 0107 0725 M 1327 1951	4.1 2.1 4.3 1.7	**29** 0137 0750 TU 1346 2024	4.7 1.6 4.8 0.9
15 0159 0811 TU 1411 2034	4.4 1.8 4.6 1.3	**30** 0228 0838 W 1433 2109	5.0 1.3 5.2 0.6
		31 0310 0919 TH 1514 2148	5.2 1.1 5.4 0.5

APRIL

Time	m	Time	m
1 0347 0956 F 1550 ●2223	5.3 0.9 5.5 0.5	**16** 0313 0927 SA 1519 ○2151	5.2 1.0 5.4 0.4
2 0422 1031 SA 1624 2255	5.3 0.9 5.5 0.6	**17** 0348 1003 SU 1555 2228	5.4 0.8 5.6 0.3
3 0454 1103 SU 1658 2325	5.2 0.9 5.4 0.7	**18** 0424 1040 M 1634 2305	5.4 0.7 5.6 0.4
4 0525 1134 M 1733 2354	5.1 0.9 5.3 1.0	**19** 0502 1118 TU 1716 2344	5.4 0.7 5.6 0.6
5 0556 1205 TU 1809	5.0 1.1 5.1	**20** 0543 1159 W 1804	5.3 0.8 5.3
6 0021 0629 W 1237 1849	1.3 4.8 1.3 4.8	**21** 0025 0628 TH 1243 1858	0.9 5.1 1.0 5.0
7 0051 0706 TH 1313 1934	1.6 4.6 1.6 4.5	**22** 0112 0719 F 1338 2002	1.3 4.8 1.3 4.6
8 0127 0751 F 1359 2028	1.9 4.3 1.9 4.1	**23** 0211 0821 SA 1452 ☾2120	1.8 4.5 1.6 4.3
9 0215 0849 SA 1509 ☽2138	2.3 4.0 2.2 3.9	**24** 0333 0940 SU 1628 2251	2.1 4.3 1.6 4.3
10 0337 1004 SU 1655 2308	2.5 3.9 2.2 3.9	**25** 0508 1108 M 1801	2.2 4.3 1.4
11 0536 1132 M 1817	2.5 4.0 1.9	**26** 0017 0628 TU 1225 1909	4.2 1.9 4.6 1.2
12 0027 0646 TU 1240 1913	4.1 2.2 4.2 1.6	**27** 0118 0725 W 1323 2000	4.7 1.7 4.8 0.9
13 0121 0734 W 1328 1958	4.4 1.9 4.6 1.2	**28** 0205 0811 TH 1409 2043	4.9 1.4 5.1 0.8
14 0202 0814 TH 1408 2037	4.7 1.5 4.9 0.9	**29** 0245 0852 F 1448 2120	5.1 1.2 5.2 0.7
15 0238 0851 F 1444 2114	5.0 1.2 5.2 0.6	**30** 0320 0928 SA 1524 ●2153	5.1 1.0 5.3 0.7

Chart Datum: 2·85 metres below Ordnance Datum (Newlyn). HAT is 6·1 metres above Chart Datum.

>> **FREE** monthly updates. Register at <<
www.reedsnauticalalmanac.co.uk

STANDARD TIME (UT)
For Summer Time add ONE hour in **non-shaded areas**

RIVER TEES LAT 54°38′N LONG 1°09′W
TIMES AND HEIGHTS OF HIGH AND LOW WATERS

Dates in red are **SPRINGS**
Dates in blue are NEAPS

YEAR 2022

MAY

Time	m	Time	m
1 0353	5.2	**16** 0318	5.3
1002	1.0	0937	0.8
SU 1558	5.3	M 1532	5.5
2223	0.8	○ 2203	0.5
2 0423	5.1	**17** 0359	5.4
1035	0.9	1020	0.6
M 1633	5.2	TU 1618	5.6
2253	1.0	2245	0.5
3 0452	5.1	**18** 0442	5.4
1107	1.0	1104	0.6
TU 1708	5.1	W 1708	5.5
2321	1.2	2329	0.7
4 0523	5.0	**19** 0527	5.3
1140	1.1	1152	0.7
W 1744	4.9	TH 1801	5.3
2350	1.4		
5 0556	4.8	**20** 0015	1.0
1214	1.3	0616	5.1
TH 1824	4.7	F 1243	0.9
		1859	4.9
6 0022	1.6	**21** 0107	1.4
0635	4.6	0710	4.9
F 1252	1.5	SA 1343	1.1
1909	4.4	2003	4.7
7 0100	1.9	**22** 0208	1.8
0720	4.4	0812	4.7
SA 1338	1.8	SU 1453	1.3
2001	4.2	◑ 2115	4.5
8 0148	2.2	**23** 0321	2.0
0815	4.2	0924	4.5
SU 1440	2.0	M 1611	1.4
2103	4.0	2231	4.4
9 0257	2.4	**24** 0438	2.1
0920	4.1	1041	4.5
M 1603	2.0	TU 1728	1.3
◑ 2217	4.0	2345	4.5
10 0434	2.4	**25** 0550	2.0
1034	4.1	1152	4.6
TU 1720	1.8	W 1833	1.2
2330	4.1		
11 0548	2.2	**26** 0045	4.6
1142	4.3	0650	1.8
W 1821	1.6	TH 1250	4.8
		1927	1.1
12 0029	4.4	**27** 0134	4.7
0644	1.9	0739	1.6
TH 1236	4.6	F 1339	4.9
1911	1.2	2011	1.1
13 0116	4.7	**28** 0215	4.9
0730	1.6	0822	1.4
F 1323	4.9	SA 1421	5.0
1956	0.9	2049	1.1
14 0157	5.0	**29** 0252	4.9
0813	1.3	0901	1.2
SA 1406	5.2	SU 1500	5.0
2038	0.7	2123	1.1
15 0238	5.2	**30** 0325	5.0
0855	1.0	0937	1.1
SU 1448	5.4	M 1537	5.0
2120	0.5	● 2155	1.2
		31 0357	5.0
		1012	1.1
		TU 1613	5.0
		2226	1.3

JUNE

Time	m	Time	m
1 0427	5.0	**16** 0428	5.4
1047	1.1	1059	0.6
W 1650	4.9	TH 1704	5.4
2256	1.3	2322	0.9
2 0459	5.0	**17** 0517	5.4
1122	1.2	1151	0.6
TH 1727	4.8	F 1759	5.3
2328	1.5		
3 0534	4.9	**18** 0011	1.1
1159	1.3	0607	5.3
F 1807	4.7	SA 1244	0.7
		1855	5.1
4 0003	1.6	**19** 0102	1.3
0613	4.8	0700	5.2
SA 1238	1.4	SU 1339	0.8
1850	4.5	1953	4.9
5 0042	1.8	**20** 0156	1.6
0657	4.6	0756	5.0
SU 1322	1.6	M 1437	1.0
1938	4.4	2053	4.7
6 0128	2.0	**21** 0255	1.8
0746	4.5	0857	4.8
M 1415	1.7	TU 1539	1.2
2032	4.3	◑ 2155	4.5
7 0225	2.2	**22** 0358	2.0
0842	4.4	1002	4.7
TU 1516	1.7	W 1644	1.4
◑ 2132	4.2	2300	4.4
8 0335	2.2	**23** 0504	2.0
0944	4.3	1108	4.6
W 1621	1.7	TH 1749	1.5
2234	4.3		
9 0446	2.1	**24** 0002	4.4
1047	4.4	0608	1.9
TH 1723	1.5	F 1211	4.6
2334	4.4	1848	1.5
10 0548	1.9	**25** 0057	4.5
1146	4.6	0705	1.8
F 1821	1.3	SA 1308	4.7
		1937	1.5
11 0029	4.6	**26** 0144	4.6
0644	1.7	0754	1.6
SA 1241	4.9	SU 1357	4.7
1915	1.1	2020	1.5
12 0119	4.9	**27** 0226	4.8
0736	1.4	0838	1.5
SU 1334	5.1	M 1442	4.8
2006	0.9	2058	1.5
13 0207	5.1	**28** 0303	4.9
0827	1.1	0918	1.3
M 1425	5.3	TU 1522	4.8
2055	0.8	2134	1.5
14 0254	5.3	**29** 0338	5.0
0917	0.9	0956	1.2
TU 1517	5.4	W 1600	4.9
○ 2145	0.7	● 2207	1.5
15 0341	5.4	**30** 0410	5.0
1007	0.7	1033	1.2
W 1610	5.5	TH 1637	4.9
2233	0.8	2240	1.5

JULY

Time	m	Time	m
1 0443	5.0	**16** 0507	5.6
1109	1.2	1146	0.4
F 1713	4.8	SA 1749	5.4
2314	1.5		
2 0517	5.0	**17** 0001	1.0
1146	1.2	0554	5.6
SA 1750	4.8	SU 1233	0.4
2350	1.6	1840	5.3
3 0554	4.9	**18** 0046	1.2
1223	1.3	0641	5.5
SU 1830	4.7	M 1320	0.6
		1929	5.1
4 0027	1.7	**19** 0132	1.4
0634	4.8	0730	5.3
M 1303	1.3	TU 1408	0.9
1913	4.6	2019	4.8
5 0108	1.8	**20** 0219	1.6
0717	4.8	0821	5.0
TU 1347	1.4	W 1458	1.3
2000	4.5	◑ 2111	4.6
6 0153	1.9	**21** 0312	1.9
0804	4.7	0918	4.7
W 1436	1.5	TH 1554	1.6
2051	4.5	2208	4.3
7 0246	2.0	**22** 0413	2.1
0858	4.6	1021	4.5
TH 1532	1.5	F 1657	1.9
◑ 2148	4.4	2310	4.2
8 0349	2.0	**23** 0523	2.1
0959	4.6	1130	4.4
F 1634	1.5	SA 1805	2.0
2248	4.4		
9 0457	2.0	**24** 0015	4.3
1104	4.7	0632	2.0
SA 1738	1.5	SU 1239	4.4
2349	4.5	1907	2.0
10 0604	1.8	**25** 0114	4.4
1209	4.8	0731	1.8
SU 1841	1.4	M 1338	4.5
		1957	1.9
11 0048	4.7	**26** 0204	4.6
0708	1.5	0820	1.6
M 1313	5.0	TU 1427	4.6
1943	1.2	2040	1.8
12 0145	4.9	**27** 0246	4.8
0809	1.2	0903	1.4
TU 1414	5.2	W 1510	4.8
2041	1.1	2118	1.6
13 0239	5.2	**28** 0323	4.9
0908	0.9	0942	1.3
W 1511	5.3	TH 1548	4.9
○ 2135	1.0	● 2154	1.5
14 0330	5.4	**29** 0356	5.1
1003	0.7	1019	1.1
TH 1606	5.5	F 1623	4.9
2226	0.9	2227	1.4
15 0419	5.5	**30** 0428	5.1
1056	0.5	1054	1.1
F 1659	5.5	SA 1657	5.0
2315	0.9	2300	1.4
		31 0500	5.2
		1128	1.0
		SU 1730	5.0
		2334	1.4

AUGUST

Time	m	Time	m
1 0532	5.2	**16** 0020	1.0
1203	1.0	0614	5.6
M 1805	5.0	TU 1251	0.6
		1856	5.2
2 0007	1.4	**17** 0058	1.2
0607	5.1	0657	5.4
TU 1238	1.1	W 1330	0.8
1844	4.9	1938	4.9
3 0043	1.5	**18** 0137	1.5
0644	5.1	0742	5.1
W 1317	1.2	TH 1411	1.4
1925	4.8	2023	4.6
4 0121	1.6	**19** 0221	1.8
0725	5.0	0833	4.7
TH 1400	1.3	F 1457	1.8
2012	4.6	◐ 2114	4.3
5 0205	1.8	**20** 0318	2.1
0816	4.8	0935	4.4
F 1451	1.5	SA 1559	2.2
◐ 2106	4.5	2216	4.1
6 0301	1.9	**21** 0437	2.3
0918	4.7	1050	4.2
SA 1553	1.7	SU 1721	2.4
2209	4.4	2331	4.1
7 0415	2.0	**22** 0603	2.2
1032	4.6	1213	4.2
SU 1706	1.8	M 1839	2.3
2318	4.4		
8 0537	1.9	**23** 0045	4.3
1151	4.6	0711	2.0
M 1822	1.7	TU 1321	4.3
		1937	2.1
9 0028	4.6	**24** 0142	4.5
0657	1.6	0803	1.7
TU 1306	4.8	W 1412	4.6
1934	1.5	2022	1.9
10 0133	4.8	**25** 0226	4.8
0806	1.3	0845	1.4
W 1412	5.1	TH 1453	4.8
2035	1.3	2100	1.5
11 0230	5.2	**26** 0303	5.0
0905	0.9	0923	1.1
TH 1509	5.3	F 1529	5.0
2128	1.1	2135	1.5
12 0321	5.4	**27** 0336	5.1
0958	0.6	0959	1.0
F 1559	5.5	SA 1601	5.1
○ 2216	0.9	● 2208	1.3
13 0407	5.6	**28** 0406	5.3
1046	0.3	1032	0.9
SA 1646	5.6	SU 1632	5.2
2300	0.9	2240	1.2
14 0450	5.7	**29** 0435	5.3
1130	0.3	1104	0.8
SU 1730	5.5	M 1703	5.2
2342	0.9	2311	1.2
15 0532	5.7	**30** 0505	5.4
1211	0.4	1136	0.8
M 1813	5.4	TU 1736	5.2
		2343	1.2
		31 0537	5.4
		1210	0.9
		W 1811	5.1

Chart Datum: 2·85 metres below Ordnance Datum (Newlyn). HAT is 6·1 metres above Chart Datum.

》》**FREE** monthly updates. Register at 《
www.reedsnauticalalmanac.co.uk

NE England

167

For Summer Time add ONE hour in **non-shaded areas**

RIVER TEES LAT 54°38'N LONG 1°09'W
TIMES AND HEIGHTS OF HIGH AND LOW WATERS

Dates in **red** are **SPRINGS**
Dates in blue are NEAPS

YEAR 2022

SEPTEMBER

#	Time	m	#	Time	m
1 TH	0015 / 0612 / 1246 / 1850	1.3 / 5.3 / 1.0 / 5.0	16 F	0057 / 0705 / 1321 / 1934	1.4 / 5.0 / 1.6 / 4.6
2 F	0051 / 0653 / 1327 / 1935	1.4 / 5.1 / 1.3 / 4.8	17 SA	0136 / 0752 / 1358 / 2019	1.7 / 4.6 / 2.0 / 4.4
3 SA	0133 / 0744 / 1416 / 2029	1.6 / 4.9 / 1.6 / 4.5	18 SU	0226 / 0851 / 1451 / 2120	2.1 / 4.3 / 2.4 / 4.1
4 SU	0229 / 0851 / 1520 / 2137	1.9 / 4.6 / 1.9 / 4.3	19 M	0350 / 1011 / 1632 / 2242	2.3 / 4.0 / 2.6 / 4.0
5 M	0350 / 1017 / 1647 / 2256	2.0 / 4.4 / 2.1 / 4.3	20 TU	0532 / 1144 / 1810	2.3 / 4.0 / 2.5
6 TU	0531 / 1149 / 1818	2.0 / 4.5 / 2.0	21 W	0010 / 0645 / 1258 / 1911	4.2 / 2.0 / 4.3 / 2.3
7 W	0017 / 0700 / 1311 / 1931	4.5 / 1.6 / 4.7 / 1.7	22 TH	0113 / 0737 / 1347 / 1956	4.4 / 1.7 / 4.6 / 2.0
8 TH	0127 / 0805 / 1411 / 2027	4.8 / 1.1 / 5.1 / 1.4	23 F	0157 / 0819 / 1427 / 2034	4.7 / 1.4 / 4.8 / 1.7
9 F	0221 / 0858 / 1500 / 2115	5.2 / 0.7 / 5.4 / 1.1	24 SA	0234 / 0856 / 1501 / 2108	5.0 / 1.1 / 5.1 / 1.4
10 SA	0307 / 0944 / 1544 / 2158	5.5 / 0.5 / 5.5 / 0.9	25 SU	0306 / 0930 / 1531 / 2141	5.2 / 0.9 / 5.2 / 1.2
11 SU	0348 / 1026 / 1625 / 2237	5.7 / 0.3 / 5.6 / 0.8	26 M	0336 / 1002 / 1601 / 2212	5.4 / 0.7 / 5.3 / 1.1
12 M	0427 / 1105 / 1704 / 2314	5.8 / 0.3 / 5.5 / 0.9	27 TU	0405 / 1035 / 1632 / 2244	5.5 / 0.7 / 5.4 / 1.0
13 TU	0505 / 1141 / 1741 / 2349	5.8 / 0.5 / 5.4	28 W	0436 / 1107 / 1705 / 2317	5.6 / 0.7 / 5.4 / 1.0
14 W	0543 / 1215 / 1817	5.6 / 0.8 / 5.2	29 TH	0509 / 1142 / 1741 / 2352	5.5 / 0.8 / 5.3 / 1.1
15 TH	0023 / 0623 / 1247 / 1854	1.2 / 5.4 / 1.2 / 4.9	30 F	0548 / 1219 / 1820	5.4 / 1.0 / 5.1

OCTOBER

#	Time	m	#	Time	m
1 SA	0029 / 0634 / 1300 / 1906	1.3 / 5.2 / 1.4 / 4.9	16 SU	0102 / 0719 / 1312 / 1935	1.7 / 4.6 / 2.1 / 4.5
2 SU	0114 / 0730 / 1350 / 2002	1.5 / 4.8 / 1.8 / 4.6	17 M	0149 / 0815 / 1400 / 2031	2.0 / 4.4 / 2.4 / 4.2
3 M	0214 / 0844 / 1501 / 2115	1.8 / 4.5 / 2.1 / 4.3	18 TU	0304 / 0929 / 1528 / 2147	2.3 / 4.0 / 2.7 / 4.1
4 TU	0347 / 1016 / 1641 / 2243	2.0 / 4.3 / 2.3 / 4.3	19 W	0448 / 1102 / 1724 / 2318	2.3 / 4.0 / 2.6 / 4.1
5 W	0536 / 1155 / 1814	1.8 / 4.5 / 2.1	20 TH	0605 / 1219 / 1832	2.0 / 4.2 / 2.4
6 TH	0009 / 0656 / 1308 / 1919	4.6 / 1.4 / 4.8 / 1.8	21 F	0027 / 0659 / 1310 / 1919	4.4 / 1.7 / 4.5 / 2.0
7 F	0114 / 0753 / 1400 / 2009	4.9 / 1.0 / 5.1 / 1.4	22 SA	0115 / 0742 / 1350 / 1958	4.7 / 1.4 / 4.8 / 1.7
8 SA	0204 / 0840 / 1443 / 2053	5.3 / 0.7 / 5.4 / 1.2	23 SU	0153 / 0820 / 1424 / 2033	4.9 / 1.1 / 5.1 / 1.5
9 SU	0247 / 0922 / 1523 / 2133	5.5 / 0.5 / 5.5 / 1.0	24 M	0228 / 0855 / 1456 / 2108	5.2 / 0.9 / 5.3 / 1.2
10 M	0325 / 1000 / 1559 / 2210	5.7 / 0.5 / 5.5 / 0.9	25 TU	0301 / 0929 / 1528 / 2143	5.4 / 0.7 / 5.4 / 1.0
11 TU	0401 / 1034 / 1634 / 2244	5.7 / 0.6 / 5.5 / 0.9	26 W	0335 / 1004 / 1602 / 2218	5.5 / 0.6 / 5.5 / 0.9
12 W	0437 / 1107 / 1707 / 2318	5.6 / 0.8 / 5.4 / 1.0	27 TH	0411 / 1040 / 1638 / 2255	5.6 / 0.7 / 5.5 / 0.9
13 TH	0514 / 1138 / 1739 / 2351	5.5 / 1.0 / 5.2 / 1.2	28 F	0451 / 1118 / 1717 / 2334	5.6 / 0.8 / 5.4 / 1.0
14 F	0552 / 1207 / 1813	5.2 / 1.4 / 5.0	29 SA	0535 / 1158 / 1759	5.5 / 1.1 / 5.2
15 SA	0025 / 0633 / 1237 / 1851	1.4 / 4.9 / 1.7 / 4.7	30 SU	0017 / 0628 / 1243 / 1849	1.1 / 5.1 / 1.5 / 5.0
			31 M	0109 / 0730 / 1338 / 1948	1.4 / 4.8 / 1.9 / 4.7

NOVEMBER

#	Time	m	#	Time	m
1 TU	0217 / 0846 / 1455 / 2101	1.6 / 4.5 / 2.2 / 4.5	16 W	0226 / 0848 / 1434 / 2059	2.1 / 4.1 / 2.5 / 4.2
2 W	0349 / 1015 / 1629 / 2226	1.7 / 4.4 / 2.3 / 4.5	17 TH	0346 / 1002 / 1612 / 2212	2.1 / 4.1 / 2.6 / 4.2
3 TH	0523 / 1143 / 1751 / 2347	1.6 / 4.5 / 2.1 / 4.7	18 F	0504 / 1116 / 1729 / 2322	2.0 / 4.2 / 2.4 / 4.3
4 F	0635 / 1249 / 1853	1.3 / 4.8 / 1.8	19 SA	0605 / 1215 / 1826	1.8 / 4.4 / 2.2
5 SA	0050 / 0730 / 1338 / 1944	4.9 / 1.0 / 5.1 / 1.6	20 SU	0018 / 0654 / 1300 / 1912	4.6 / 1.5 / 4.7 / 1.9
6 SU	0140 / 0815 / 1420 / 2027	5.2 / 0.8 / 5.2 / 1.3	21 M	0105 / 0737 / 1340 / 1954	4.8 / 1.2 / 5.0 / 1.6
7 M	0223 / 0855 / 1457 / 2106	5.4 / 0.8 / 5.3 / 1.1	22 TU	0147 / 0817 / 1418 / 2035	5.1 / 1.0 / 5.2 / 1.3
8 TU	0301 / 0931 / 1532 / 2143	5.4 / 0.8 / 5.4 / 1.1	23 W	0229 / 0857 / 1457 / 2116	5.3 / 0.8 / 5.4 / 1.1
9 W	0338 / 1004 / 1605 / 2218	5.4 / 0.9 / 5.3 / 1.0	24 TH	0311 / 0938 / 1536 / 2158	5.5 / 0.8 / 5.5 / 0.9
10 TH	0414 / 1036 / 1636 / 2252	5.4 / 1.1 / 5.3 / 1.1	25 F	0355 / 1019 / 1618 / 2241	5.5 / 0.8 / 5.5 / 0.8
11 F	0451 / 1105 / 1707 / 2327	5.2 / 1.3 / 5.2 / 1.2	26 SA	0442 / 1102 / 1701 / 2327	5.5 / 0.9 / 5.4 / 0.8
12 SA	0529 / 1135 / 1741	5.0 / 1.5 / 5.0	27 SU	0533 / 1148 / 1748	5.3 / 1.2 / 5.3
13 SU	0002 / 0610 / 1206 / 1820	1.4 / 4.8 / 1.8 / 4.8	28 M	0017 / 0630 / 1237 / 1840	0.9 / 5.1 / 1.5 / 5.1
14 M	0041 / 0655 / 1243 / 1904	1.6 / 4.6 / 2.0 / 4.6	29 TU	0113 / 0732 / 1335 / 1938	1.1 / 4.9 / 1.8 / 4.9
15 TU	0126 / 0746 / 1329 / 1956	1.8 / 4.3 / 2.3 / 4.4	30 W	0219 / 0840 / 1444 / 2045	1.3 / 4.6 / 2.1 / 4.8

DECEMBER

#	Time	m	#	Time	m
1 TH	0332 / 0954 / 1559 / 2158	1.4 / 4.5 / 2.2 / 4.7	16 F	0248 / 0907 / 1500 / 2115	1.8 / 4.3 / 2.4 / 4.4
2 F	0449 / 1109 / 1713 / 2311	1.4 / 4.6 / 2.1 / 4.7	17 SA	0351 / 1008 / 1612 / 2217	1.9 / 4.3 / 2.4 / 4.4
3 SA	0559 / 1215 / 1818	1.3 / 4.7 / 1.9	18 SU	0455 / 1109 / 1720 / 2318	1.8 / 4.4 / 2.2 / 4.5
4 SU	0016 / 0658 / 1307 / 1913	4.8 / 1.3 / 4.8 / 1.7	19 M	0556 / 1205 / 1819	1.6 / 4.6 / 2.0
5 M	0112 / 0746 / 1353 / 2001	5.0 / 1.2 / 5.0 / 1.5	20 TU	0016 / 0651 / 1257 / 1914	4.7 / 1.4 / 4.8 / 1.7
6 TU	0159 / 0828 / 1433 / 2043	5.0 / 1.2 / 5.1 / 1.4	21 W	0111 / 0743 / 1345 / 2005	4.9 / 1.2 / 5.0 / 1.4
7 W	0242 / 0905 / 1509 / 2122	5.1 / 1.2 / 5.1 / 1.3	22 TH	0204 / 0832 / 1432 / 2056	5.1 / 1.2 / 5.2 / 1.1
8 TH	0321 / 0940 / 1542 / 2159	5.1 / 1.3 / 5.2 / 1.2	23 F	0256 / 0920 / 1518 / 2146	5.3 / 1.0 / 5.4 / 0.9
9 F	0359 / 1012 / 1614 / 2235	5.1 / 1.4 / 5.2 / 1.2	24 SA	0347 / 1008 / 1605 / 2236	5.4 / 1.0 / 5.5 / 0.7
10 SA	0437 / 1043 / 1646 / 2312	5.0 / 1.5 / 5.1 / 1.2	25 SU	0440 / 1056 / 1652 / 2327	5.5 / 1.0 / 5.5 / 0.6
11 SU	0514 / 1114 / 1720 / 2348	4.9 / 1.6 / 5.1 / 1.3	26 M	0533 / 1145 / 1741	5.4 / 1.1 / 5.5
12 M	0553 / 1148 / 1758	4.8 / 1.7 / 5.0	27 TU	0017 / 0627 / 1233 / 1831	0.6 / 5.3 / 1.3 / 5.4
13 TU	0025 / 0635 / 1224 / 1840	1.5 / 4.6 / 1.9 / 4.8	28 W	0109 / 0722 / 1324 / 1924	0.7 / 5.1 / 1.5 / 5.3
14 W	0107 / 0720 / 1307 / 1926	1.6 / 4.5 / 2.1 / 4.6	29 TH	0204 / 0819 / 1419 / 2020	0.9 / 4.9 / 1.8 / 5.1
15 TH	0153 / 0811 / 1358 / 2017	1.7 / 4.4 / 2.3 / 4.5	30 F	0301 / 0919 / 1519 / 2121	1.2 / 4.6 / 2.0 / 4.7
			31 SA	0404 / 1023 / 1625 / 2227	1.4 / 4.5 / 2.1 / 4.7

Chart Datum: 2·85 metres below Ordnance Datum (Newlyn). HAT is 6·1 metres above Chart Datum.

3.15 SEAHAM

Durham 54°50'·24N 01°19'·28W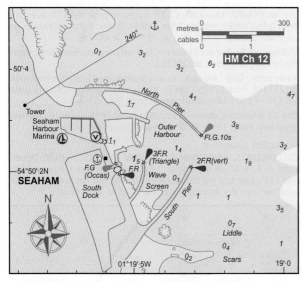

CHARTS AC 152, 1627, 5615; Imray C24

TIDES +0435 Dover; ML 3·0; Duration 0600

Standard Port RIVER TEES (←)

Times				Height (metres)			
High Water		Low Water		MHWS	MHWN	MLWN	MLWS
0000	0600	0000	0600	5·5	4·3	2·0	0·9
1200	1800	1200	1800				
Differences SEAHAM							
–0015	–0015	–0015	–0015	–0·3	–0·2	0·0	–0·2

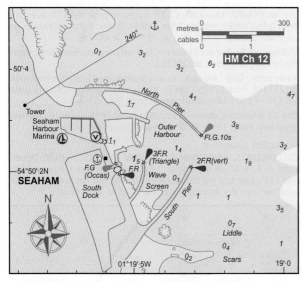

SHELTER Small craft berth in North Dock marina with an automatic gate opening HW ± 3 maintaining 1.5m min depth near entrance. 4 Ⓥ to starboard on entry up to 1·9m draught. Yachts should confirm availability/suitability of berth with HM. South Dock is not usually available to non-commercial vessels. Speed limit 5kn. ⚓ 2½ca offshore with clock twr in transit 240° with St John's ✠ twr.

NAVIGATION WPT 54°50'·36N 01°18'·60W (off chartlet), 256°/ 0·40M to N breakwater lighthouse. Shoals and rocks to S of S breakwater (Liddle Scars). Outer harbour is shallow, min depth 1.2m, and the harbour can be subject to considerable swell; entrance should not be attempted in strong onshore winds. The N Dock lies to the right of S Dock gates, the appr chan leading between small drying basins. Automatic gate opens/shuts when height of tide 2.5m above CD (approx HW ±3½).

LIGHTS AND MARKS No leading lights, but harbour is easily identified by lighthouse (W with B bands) on N pier, Fl G 10s 12m 5M. FS at NE corner of S dock on with N lighthouse leads in 256° clear of Tangle Rocks. 3FR lts on wave screen are in form of a △.

Traffic sigs at S Dock: ● = Vessels enter: ● = Vessels leave.

Traffic sigs at N Dock gate: 3 ● (vert) = shut : 3 ● (vert) = open.

COMMUNICATIONS (Code 0191) CGOC (01262) 672317; Police 101; Dr 5812332. HM 07801 215236.

VHF Ch **12** 16 06 0800–1700 (Mon-Fri), *Seaham Marina* Ch 80.

FACILITIES N Dock Marina ☎581 8998; 78 ⌣ inc 4Ⓥ up to 10m. **S Dock** (Seaham Hbr Dock Co) ☎516 1700, ⚓ ⌂(40t).
Town (½M) and available out of town (about 5M). ✉ Ⓑ 🍴 ✕ 🛒 ⇌ ✈(Teesside or Newcastle).

3.16 SUNDERLAND

Tyne and Wear 54°55'·23N 01°21'·15W

CHARTS AC 152, 1627, 5615; Imray C24

TIDES +0430 Dover; ML 2·9; Duration 0600; Zone 0 (UT)

Standard Port RIVER TEES (←)

Times				Height (metres)			
High Water		Low Water		MHWS	MHWN	MLWN	MLWS
0000	0600	0000	0600	5·5	4·3	2·0	0·9
1200	1800	1200	1800				
Differences SUNDERLAND							
–0017	–0017	–0016	–0016	–0·2	–0·1	0·0	0·0

SHELTER Very good, but strong Easterlies cause heavy swell in entrance and outer harbour. Marina is protected by a fixed breakwater; access H24.

NAVIGATION WPT 54°55'·21N 01°20'·10W, 278°/0·61M to Roker Pier lt. Beware wreck at Whitburn Steel, about 1M N of entrance, and Hendon Rk (0·9m), 1·2M SE of harbour entrance.

Appr to marina ent is marked by SHM dolphin, Fl G 5s, and E jetty, Fl (2) G 10s. Close (4m) SSW of end of pontoon ⚓ beware substantial obst'n (1·6m) in surrounding depth 2·1m, see chartlet.

LIGHTS AND MARKS 3 Fl ● at Pilot Stn (Old N Pier) = danger in harbour; no entry/departure.

COMMUNICATIONS (Code 0191) CGOC (01262) 672317; ⊖ (0191) 257 9441; Police 101; 🏥 565 6256. HM 567 2626 (HO), 567 0161 (OT).

Sunderland Marina Ch ☎ 80. Port VHF Ch **14** (H24); tide and visibility reports on request.

FACILITIES Sunderland Marina www.sunmac.org.uk1 ☎ 5144721. 20⌣ pontoon berths in 2·1m, max LOA 13m; and 110 ⚓. Ⓥ (if available) £2·40/m; half-tide shelf £12/day, 🔧 ⚓ ⛽(H24) ⚓.
Sunderland YC ☎ 5675133, ⚓ (dinghy) ⌣⚓⌂.
Wear Boating Association ☎5675313, ⌣.
Services 🔧 ⚓ △ ⚓.
Town 🏧 🛢 ✉ Ⓑ 🍴 🛒 ✕ 🛒 ⇌ ✈(Newcastle).

3.17 RIVER TYNE/NORTH SHIELDS

Tyne and Wear 55°00'·89N 01°24'·10W ✿❀❄❄❄❄✿✿

CHARTS AC 152, 1191, 1934, 5615; Imray C24

TIDES +0430 Dover; ML 3·0; Duration 0604

Standard Port NORTH SHIELDS (→)

Times				Height (metres)			
High Water		Low Water		MHWS	MHWN	MLWN	MLWS
0200	0800	0100	0800	5·0	3·9	1·8	0·7
1400	2000	1300	2000				
Differences NEWCASTLE-UPON-TYNE							
+0003	+0003	+0008	+0008	+0·3	+0·2	+0·1	+0·1

SHELTER Good in all weather. Access H24, but in strong E and NE winds appr may be difficult for smaller craft due to much backwash off the piers. Confused seas can build at the ent in severe weather, and a large steep swell can break dangerously when meeting an ebb tide up to half a mile inside the harbour. In emergency or as a refuge yachts may berth on Fish Quay; contact HM.

NAVIGATION WPT 55°01'·00N 01°23'·00W, 250°/0·7M to hbr ent, recommended route in Ldg lt Oc W sector. Outbound keep S of hbr ent centreline. From S, no dangers. From N, beware Bellhues Rk (approx 1M N of hbr and ¾M offshore); give N pier a wide berth. Dredged chan in Lower Hbr is buoyed. 6kn speed limit in the river west of Herd Groyne Lt Ho. In river proceed under power keeping to the starboard side; if <20m or under sail conform to Colreg Rule 9 – do not impede large vessels. Millennium Br air draft is 4.5m when closed, the clearance for all bridges is 25m when it is open.

LIGHTS AND MARKS See 3.3 and chartlet. W Lt LFl 10s shows from centre span of the Millennium Bridge when fully open.

COMMUNICATIONS (Code 0191) CGOC (01262) 672317; 📡2326453; Police 101; Ⓗ (Tynemouth) 2596660; Ⓗ (Newcastle) 2325131. HM 2570407; Tyne VTS 2572080.

Tyne VTS Ch **12**, 11 (H24) call on arrival and prior to departure. Marinas: Royal Quays Ch 80. St Peter's Ch 80 M.

FACILITIES A conservancy fee (£10) may be levied by the Port Authority on all visiting craft. Craft waiting to enter the marinas should do so outside the fairway.

Royal Quays Marina ⚓ 54°59'·79N 01°26'·84W royalquays@boatfolk. co.uk ☎2728282 2M upriver from pierheads (Albert Edward Dock); 302 ◯ inc ♥, £2·30 7·9m depth. Lock (42½m x 7½m) departures H / H+30; arrivals H+15 / H+45, or on request when quiet. Waiting pontoon outside lock. ⚓ ◻ 🅿 ⛽(H24) ⬚ ⊡ 🛒 🛒(30t) 🍴🍺.

St Peter's Marina 54°57'·94N 01°34'·35W, 8M upriver, and 1M E of city. ☎2654472; 140+20♥, £2.27. Access approx HW±3½ over sill, dries 0·8m, which retains 2·5m within. Traffic lights at ent. 🅿 on pontoon outside ent in 2m. ⚓ ◻ 🔧⚓ 🛒 ACA, Ⓔ.

Millennium Bridge in city centre, limited pontoon berthing below the bridge; pre-book ☎2211363.

Newcastle City Marina enquiries@newcastlecitymarina.co.uk ☎2211348, mob 07435 788426; Boats <26m: price on sliding scale 5m £10 → £30 >14m, short stay (< 5hrs) free. ⬚🅿 ⚓.

City All amenities, ≥ (Newcastle/S Shields), ✈ (Newcastle). **Ferries**: Ijmuiden; daily; 16hrs; DFDS (www.dfdsseaways.co.uk).

ADJACENT HARBOUR

CULLERCOATS, 55°02'·08N 01°25'·81W. AC 1191. +0430 Dover. Tides as 3.16. Small drying hbr 1·6M N of R Tyne ent. Appr on ldg line 256°, two bns (FR lts), between drying rks. An occasional fair weather ⚓ or dry against S pier. Facilities at Tynemouth.

RIVER TYNE/NORTH SHIELDS   LAT 55°00'N   LONG 1°26'W

STANDARD TIME (UT)
For Summer Time add ONE hour in **non-shaded areas**

TIMES AND HEIGHTS OF HIGH AND LOW WATERS

Dates in red are **SPRINGS**
Dates in blue are NEAPS

YEAR **2022**

JANUARY

Day	Time	m	Day	Time	m
1 SA	0130 / 0801 / 1402 / 2027	4.9 / 1.0 / 4.9 / 1.1	**16** SU	0231 / 0841 / 1448 / 2108	4.4 / 1.6 / 4.6 / 1.4
2 SU ●	0227 / 0854 / 1450 / 2121	5.1 / 0.9 / 5.1 / 0.8	**17** M ○	0310 / 0917 / 1522 / 2145	4.6 / 1.5 / 4.7 / 1.2
3 M	0320 / 0944 / 1537 / 2213	5.2 / 0.9 / 5.2 / 0.6	**18** TU	0345 / 0951 / 1555 / 2220	4.6 / 1.4 / 4.8 / 1.1
4 TU	0413 / 1032 / 1623 / 2304	5.2 / 1.0 / 5.3 / 0.7	**19** W	0420 / 1024 / 1627 / 2255	4.7 / 1.3 / 4.9 / 1.0
5 W	0504 / 1119 / 1709 / 2353	5.2 / 1.1 / 5.2 / 0.6	**20** TH	0454 / 1057 / 1659 / 2330	4.7 / 1.3 / 4.9 / 0.9
6 TH	0555 / 1203 / 1757	5.0 / 1.2 / 5.1	**21** F	0529 / 1131 / 1733	4.7 / 1.3 / 4.9
7 F	0041 / 0647 / 1247 / 1846	0.7 / 4.8 / 1.4 / 5.0	**22** SA	0006 / 0606 / 1205 / 1809	0.9 / 4.7 / 1.4 / 4.9
8 SA	0129 / 0739 / 1332 / 1938	0.9 / 4.5 / 1.7 / 4.8	**23** SU	0044 / 0645 / 1241 / 1849	1.0 / 4.6 / 1.5 / 4.8
9 SU ◑	0219 / 0832 / 1423 / 2033	1.2 / 4.3 / 1.9 / 4.6	**24** M	0125 / 0729 / 1322 / 1934	1.1 / 4.5 / 1.6 / 4.7
10 M	0313 / 0928 / 1522 / 2133	1.5 / 4.1 / 2.1 / 4.3	**25** TU ◑	0211 / 0820 / 1412 / 2028	1.2 / 4.3 / 1.7 / 4.6
11 TU	0412 / 1029 / 1632 / 2239	1.7 / 4.0 / 2.1 / 4.2	**26** W	0307 / 0920 / 1517 / 2134	1.4 / 4.2 / 1.9 / 4.4
12 W	0516 / 1134 / 1744 / 2349	1.8 / 4.0 / 2.1 / 4.1	**27** TH	0416 / 1029 / 1640 / 2252	1.5 / 4.2 / 1.9 / 4.4
13 TH	0619 / 1235 / 1850	1.9 / 4.0 / 2.0	**28** F	0532 / 1143 / 1803	1.6 / 4.3 / 1.8
14 F	0053 / 0715 / 1326 / 1944	4.2 / 1.8 / 4.3 / 1.8	**29** SA	0013 / 0646 / 1252 / 1919	4.4 / 1.5 / 4.4 / 1.5
15 SA	0146 / 0801 / 1410 / 2029	4.3 / 1.7 / 4.5 / 1.6	**30** SU	0126 / 0752 / 1351 / 2024	4.6 / 1.3 / 4.7 / 1.1
			31 M	0226 / 0848 / 1442 / 2119	4.9 / 1.2 / 4.9 / 0.8

FEBRUARY

Day	Time	m	Day	Time	m
1 TU ●	0319 / 0938 / 1528 / 2209	5.1 / 1.0 / 5.2 / 0.5	**16** W ○	0328 / 0936 / 1536 / 2202	4.6 / 1.3 / 4.8 / 0.9
2 W	0407 / 1023 / 1612 / 2255	5.1 / 0.9 / 5.3 / 0.4	**17** TH	0400 / 1008 / 1607 / 2236	4.8 / 1.1 / 5.0 / 0.7
3 TH	0453 / 1104 / 1654 / 2338	5.1 / 0.9 / 5.3 / 0.4	**18** F	0433 / 1040 / 1638 / 2310	4.9 / 1.0 / 5.1 / 0.6
4 F	0536 / 1143 / 1736	5.0 / 1.0 / 5.3	**19** SA	0506 / 1113 / 1710 / 2345	4.9 / 1.0 / 5.1 / 0.6
5 SA	0017 / 0619 / 1219 / 1818	0.6 / 4.8 / 1.2 / 5.1	**20** SU	0540 / 1145 / 1745	4.8 / 1.0 / 5.1
6 SU	0056 / 0700 / 1255 / 1901	0.8 / 4.6 / 1.4 / 4.9	**21** M	0020 / 0618 / 1219 / 1824	0.7 / 4.8 / 1.1 / 5.0
7 M	0133 / 0743 / 1333 / 1946	1.1 / 4.3 / 1.6 / 4.6	**22** TU	0057 / 0658 / 1257 / 1908	0.9 / 4.6 / 1.3 / 4.8
8 TU ◑	0214 / 0829 / 1418 / 2038	1.5 / 4.1 / 1.9 / 4.3	**23** W ◑	0139 / 0745 / 1343 / 2001	1.1 / 4.4 / 1.5 / 4.6
9 W	0302 / 0924 / 1520 / 2141	1.8 / 3.9 / 2.1 / 4.0	**24** TH	0232 / 0843 / 1445 / 2110	1.4 / 4.2 / 1.7 / 4.3
10 TH	0406 / 1030 / 1644 / 2259	2.0 / 3.8 / 2.2 / 3.9	**25** F	0344 / 0957 / 1616 / 2239	1.7 / 4.1 / 1.9 / 4.2
11 F	0526 / 1149 / 1813	2.2 / 3.8 / 2.1	**26** SA	0515 / 1122 / 1756	1.8 / 4.1 / 1.7
12 SA	0023 / 0645 / 1257 / 1923	3.9 / 2.1 / 4.0 / 1.9	**27** SU	0014 / 0642 / 1242 / 1920	4.2 / 1.7 / 4.3 / 1,4
13 SU	0128 / 0742 / 1349 / 2012	4.1 / 1.9 / 4.2 / 1.6	**28** M	0129 / 0749 / 1344 / 2022	4.5 / 1.5 / 4.6 / 1.0
14 M	0216 / 0826 / 1429 / 2052	4.3 / 1.7 / 4.5 / 1.3			
15 TU	0254 / 0903 / 1504 / 2128	4.5 / 1.5 / 4.7 / 1.1			

MARCH

Day	Time	m	Day	Time	m
1 TU	0226 / 0842 / 1433 / 2112	4.8 / 1.2 / 4.9 / 0.6	**16** W	0228 / 0840 / 1436 / 2102	4.4 / 1.4 / 4.6 / 1.0
2 W ●	0312 / 0926 / 1516 / 2157	5.0 / 1.0 / 5.1 / 0.4	**17** TH	0301 / 0913 / 1508 / 2136	4.7 / 1.2 / 4.8 / 0.7
3 TH	0354 / 1006 / 1556 / 2237	5.1 / 0.9 / 5.3 / 0.3	**18** F ○	0333 / 0945 / 1539 / 2210	4.8 / 1.0 / 5.0 / 0.5
4 F	0432 / 1043 / 1633 / 2313	5.1 / 0.8 / 5.3 / 0.4	**19** SA	0405 / 1017 / 1611 / 2245	5.0 / 0.8 / 5.2 / 0.4
5 SA	0509 / 1117 / 1710 / 2347	5.0 / 0.8 / 5.2 / 0.5	**20** SU	0439 / 1050 / 1645 / 2320	5.0 / 0.8 / 5.2 / 0.4
6 SU	0544 / 1149 / 1747	4.8 / 1.0 / 5.1	**21** M	0513 / 1124 / 1722 / 2355	5.0 / 0.8 / 5.2 / 0.6
7 M	0018 / 0620 / 1220 / 1825	0.8 / 4.6 / 1.1 / 4.9	**22** TU	0551 / 1200 / 1803	4.9 / 0.9 / 5.1
8 TU	0049 / 0655 / 1253 / 1906	1.1 / 4.4 / 1.4 / 4.6	**23** W	0032 / 0632 / 1239 / 1851	0.8 / 4.7 / 1.1 / 4.8
9 W	0122 / 0735 / 1332 / 1952	1.5 / 4.2 / 1.7 / 4.2	**24** TH	0115 / 0720 / 1329 / 1950	1.2 / 4.5 / 1.3 / 4.5
10 TH ◑	0202 / 0823 / 1424 / 2052	1.8 / 4.0 / 1.9 / 3.9	**25** F ◑	0210 / 0820 / 1437 / 2107	1.6 / 4.2 / 1.6 / 4.2
11 F	0259 / 0927 / 1544 / 2211	2.1 / 3.8 / 2.2 / 3.7	**26** SA	0330 / 0938 / 1615 / 2244	1.9 / 4.0 / 1.7 / 4.0
12 SA	0430 / 1051 / 1729 / 2347	2.3 / 3.7 / 2.2 / 3.7	**27** SU	0511 / 1111 / 1758	2.0 / 4.0 / 1.5
13 SU	0611 / 1219 / 1852	2.3 / 3.8 / 1.9	**28** M	0017 / 0638 / 1232 / 1915	4.2 / 1.8 / 4.2 / 1.2
14 M	0102 / 0719 / 1319 / 1946	3.9 / 2.0 / 4.1 / 1.6	**29** TU	0124 / 0739 / 1331 / 2010	4.5 / 1.5 / 4.6 / 0.8
15 TU	0151 / 0803 / 1401 / 2026	4.2 / 1.7 / 4.3 / 1.3	**30** W	0215 / 0826 / 1418 / 2056	4.7 / 1.2 / 4.8 / 0.6
			31 TH	0256 / 0907 / 1457 / 2135	4.9 / 1.0 / 5.0 / 0.4

APRIL

Day	Time	m	Day	Time	m
1 F ●	0332 / 0943 / 1533 / 2211	5.0 / 0.8 / 5.2 / 0.4	**16** SA ○	0301 / 0915 / 1507 / 2139	4.9 / 0.9 / 5.1 / 0.4
2 SA	0406 / 1017 / 1609 / 2243	5.0 / 0.8 / 5.2 / 0.5	**17** SU	0335 / 0950 / 1543 / 2217	5.0 / 0.7 / 5.2 / 0.3
3 SU	0438 / 1049 / 1644 / 2313	4.9 / 0.8 / 5.1 / 0.7	**18** M	0411 / 1027 / 1622 / 2254	5.1 / 0.6 / 5.3 / 0.4
4 M	0510 / 1120 / 1719 / 2342	4.8 / 0.9 / 5.0 / 0.9	**19** TU	0448 / 1105 / 1704 / 2333	5.1 / 0.6 / 5.2 / 0.6
5 TU	0542 / 1152 / 1755	4.7 / 1.1 / 4.7	**20** W	0528 / 1147 / 1751	5.0 / 0.7 / 5.0
6 W	0010 / 0616 / 1224 / 1835	1.2 / 4.5 / 1.3 / 4.5	**21** TH	0015 / 0613 / 1233 / 1846	0.9 / 4.8 / 0.9 / 4.8
7 TH	0041 / 0652 / 1302 / 1920	1.5 / 4.3 / 1.5 / 4.2	**22** F	0102 / 0705 / 1329 / 1952	1.3 / 4.5 / 1.2 / 4.4
8 F	0118 / 0736 / 1350 / 2017	1.8 / 4.0 / 1.8 / 3.9	**23** SA ◑	0203 / 0808 / 1443 / 2113	1.7 / 4.3 / 1.4 / 4.2
9 SA	0210 / 0835 / 1500 / 2131	2.1 / 3.8 / 2.0 / 3.7	**24** SU	0327 / 0929 / 1618 / 2242	2.0 / 4.1 / 1.5 / 4.1
10 SU ◑	0334 / 0955 / 1637 / 2259	2.4 / 3.7 / 2.1 / 3.7	**25** M	0502 / 1056 / 1747	2.0 / 4.1 / 1.3
11 M	0523 / 1124 / 1804	2.3 / 3.8 / 1.8	**26** TU	0004 / 0619 / 1211 / 1855	4.2 / 1.8 / 4.3 / 1.1
12 TU	0018 / 0638 / 1232 / 1904	3.9 / 2.1 / 4.0 / 1.5	**27** W	0105 / 0716 / 1309 / 1947	4.4 / 1.5 / 4.6 / 0.9
13 W	0111 / 0726 / 1320 / 1947	4.1 / 1.7 / 4.3 / 1.2	**28** TH	0152 / 0801 / 1354 / 2030	4.6 / 1.3 / 4.8 / 0.7
14 TH	0151 / 0805 / 1358 / 2026	4.4 / 1.4 / 4.6 / 0.9	**29** F	0230 / 0841 / 1433 / 2107	4.7 / 1.1 / 4.9 / 0.7
15 F	0226 / 0840 / 1432 / 2103	4.7 / 1.2 / 4.8 / 0.6	**30** SA ●	0305 / 0916 / 1509 / 2140	4.8 / 0.9 / 5.0 / 0.7

Chart Datum: 2·60 metres below Ordnance Datum (Newlyn). HAT is 5·7 metres above Chart Datum.

NE England

》 FREE monthly updates. Register at 《
www.reedsnauticalalmanac.co.uk

171

<table>
<tr><td>

STANDARD TIME (UT)
For Summer Time add ONE
hour in **non-shaded areas**

</td><td>

RIVER TYNE/NORTH SHIELDS LAT 55°00′N LONG 1°26′W
TIMES AND HEIGHTS OF HIGH AND LOW WATERS

</td><td>

Dates in **red** are **SPRINGS**
Dates in blue are NEAPS

YEAR **2022**

</td></tr>
</table>

MAY

Time	m	Time	m
1 0337 4.9 / 0950 0.9 / SU 1544 5.0 / 2211 0.8		**16** 0306 5.0 / 0925 0.7 / M 1519 5.2 / ○ 2151 0.5	
2 0409 4.8 / 1024 0.9 / M 1620 4.9 / 2241 0.9		**17** 0345 5.1 / 1008 0.6 / TU 1605 5.2 / 2234 0.6	
3 0440 4.8 / 1056 0.9 / TU 1656 4.8 / 2310 1.1		**18** 0427 5.1 / 1053 0.6 / W 1654 5.2 / 2318 0.8	
4 0512 4.7 / 1129 1.1 / W 1733 4.6 / 2340 1.3		**19** 0512 5.0 / 1141 0.6 / TH 1747 5.0	
5 0545 4.5 / 1204 1.2 / TH 1813 4.4		**20** 0005 1.0 / 0601 4.9 / F 1233 0.8 / 1847 4.7	
6 0012 1.6 / 0623 4.4 / F 1242 1.4 / 1858 4.2		**21** 0057 1.4 / 0656 4.7 / SA 1333 1.0 / 1953 4.5	
7 0049 1.8 / 0706 4.2 / SA 1329 1.6 / 1951 3.9		**22** 0158 1.7 / 0800 4.5 / SU 1445 1.1 / ◗ 2106 4.3	
8 0138 2.1 / 0800 4.0 / SU 1430 1.8 / 2055 3.8		**23** 0314 1.9 / 0913 4.3 / M 1603 1.2 / 2221 4.2	
9 0247 2.3 / 0908 3.8 / M 1547 1.8 / ◑ 2208 3.8		**24** 0433 1.9 / 1028 4.3 / TU 1718 1.2 / 2333 4.2	
10 0419 2.3 / 1023 3.9 / TU 1705 1.7 / 2320 3.9		**25** 0542 1.8 / 1138 4.4 / W 1822 1.1	
11 0538 2.1 / 1132 4.0 / W 1808 1.5		**26** 0032 4.3 / 0641 1.6 / TH 1237 4.5 / 1915 1.1	
12 0019 4.1 / 0635 1.8 / TH 1227 4.3 / 1859 1.4		**27** 0120 4.5 / 0730 1.4 / F 1326 4.6 / 1958 1.0	
13 0106 4.4 / 0720 1.5 / F 1313 4.5 / 1944 0.9		**28** 0201 4.6 / 0812 1.3 / SA 1408 4.7 / 2036 1.0	
14 0148 4.7 / 0802 1.2 / SA 1355 4.8 / 2026 0.7		**29** 0237 4.7 / 0851 1.1 / SU 1447 4.7 / 2110 1.0	
15 0227 4.9 / 0843 1.0 / SU 1436 5.0 / 2108 0.5		**30** 0311 4.7 / 0928 1.1 / M 1525 4.7 / ● 2142 1.1	
		31 0345 4.8 / 1003 1.0 / TU 1602 4.7 / 2214 1.2	

JUNE

Time	m	Time	m
1 0417 4.7 / 1038 1.0 / W 1640 4.6 / 2246 1.3		**16** 0413 5.1 / 1047 0.5 / TH 1649 5.1 / 2309 0.9	
2 0450 4.7 / 1113 1.1 / TH 1717 4.5 / 2318 1.4		**17** 0500 5.1 / 1139 0.5 / F 1744 5.0 / 2358 1.1	
3 0524 4.6 / 1149 1.2 / F 1756 4.4 / 2352 1.5		**18** 0551 5.0 / 1232 0.6 / SA 1842 4.8	
4 0601 4.5 / 1228 1.3 / SA 1839 4.2		**19** 0048 1.3 / 0645 4.9 / SU 1328 0.7 / 1942 4.6	
5 0030 1.7 / 0643 4.4 / SU 1312 1.4 / 1926 4.1		**20** 0143 1.5 / 0744 4.7 / M 1428 0.9 / 2043 4.4	
6 0114 1.9 / 0731 4.2 / M 1403 1.5 / 2020 4.0		**21** 0243 1.7 / 0846 4.6 / TU 1531 1.1 / ◗ 2145 4.2	
7 0209 2.0 / 0826 4.1 / TU 1503 1.6 / ◗ 2120 3.9		**22** 0348 1.8 / 0951 4.4 / W 1635 1.3 / 2249 4.2	
8 0316 2.1 / 0928 4.1 / W 1608 1.5 / 2223 4.0		**23** 0455 1.9 / 1056 4.3 / TH 1737 1.4 / 2350 4.2	
9 0430 2.0 / 1031 4.2 / TH 1712 1.4 / 2324 4.1		**24** 0559 1.8 / 1200 4.3 / F 1834 1.4	
10 0536 1.8 / 1132 4.3 / F 1809 1.2		**25** 0044 4.3 / 0657 1.7 / SA 1257 4.4 / 1924 1.4	
11 0020 4.4 / 0633 1.6 / SA 1229 4.5 / 1903 1.0		**26** 0131 4.4 / 0747 1.5 / SU 1346 4.4 / 2007 1.4	
12 0110 4.6 / 0725 1.3 / SU 1322 4.8 / 1954 0.8		**27** 0213 4.5 / 0831 1.4 / M 1431 4.5 / 2045 1.4	
13 0157 4.8 / 0816 1.1 / M 1413 5.0 / 2043 0.7		**28** 0251 4.6 / 0911 1.2 / TU 1512 4.5 / 2121 1.3	
14 0242 5.0 / 0906 0.8 / TU 1504 5.1 / ○ 2132 0.7		**29** 0326 4.7 / 0948 1.1 / W 1550 4.6 / ● 2155 1.3	
15 0327 5.1 / 0956 0.6 / W 1556 5.2 / 2220 0.7		**30** 0400 4.7 / 1024 1.1 / TH 1626 4.6 / 2229 1.3	

JULY

Time	m	Time	m
1 0433 4.7 / 1100 1.0 / F 1702 4.6 / 2302 1.4		**16** 0449 5.3 / 1132 0.3 / SA 1734 5.1 / 2345 1.0	
2 0507 4.7 / 1135 1.0 / SA 1739 4.5 / 2336 1.4		**17** 0537 5.2 / 1221 0.4 / SU 1825 4.9	
3 0543 4.7 / 1213 1.1 / SU 1817 4.4		**18** 0029 1.1 / 0626 5.1 / M 1308 0.6 / 1916 4.7	
4 0012 1.5 / 0621 4.6 / M 1252 1.2 / 1859 4.3		**19** 0114 1.3 / 0716 4.9 / TU 1357 0.8 / 2007 4.5	
5 0051 1.6 / 0701 4.5 / TU 1335 1.2 / 1943 4.2		**20** 0201 1.5 / 0809 4.7 / W 1447 1.1 / ◗ 2100 4.2	
6 0134 1.7 / 0747 4.4 / W 1422 1.3 / 2034 4.2		**21** 0255 1.8 / 0907 4.5 / TH 1542 1.4 / 2158 4.1	
7 0225 1.8 / 0839 4.4 / TH 1517 1.4 / ◗ 2131 4.1		**22** 0359 1.9 / 1010 4.2 / F 1644 1.7 / 2301 4.0	
8 0328 1.9 / 0939 4.3 / F 1620 1.4 / 2233 4.2		**23** 0512 2.0 / 1120 4.1 / SA 1749 1.8	
9 0440 1.9 / 1045 4.4 / SA 1725 1.4 / 2337 4.3		**24** 0006 4.1 / 0625 1.9 / SU 1230 4.1 / 1853 1.8	
10 0551 1.7 / 1154 4.5 / SU 1829 1.3		**25** 0104 4.2 / 0726 1.7 / M 1330 4.2 / 1945 1.7	
11 0038 4.5 / 0657 1.5 / M 1301 4.6 / 1930 1.1		**26** 0153 4.4 / 0816 1.5 / TU 1418 4.3 / 2028 1.6	
12 0134 4.7 / 0759 1.2 / TU 1402 4.8 / 2027 1.0		**27** 0234 4.5 / 0857 1.3 / W 1500 4.5 / 2106 1.5	
13 0226 4.9 / 0856 0.8 / W 1458 5.0 / ○ 2121 0.9		**28** 0310 4.7 / 0935 1.1 / TH 1536 4.6 / ● 2141 1.4	
14 0314 5.1 / 0951 0.6 / TH 1551 5.2 / 2211 0.9		**29** 0343 4.8 / 1009 1.0 / F 1610 4.6 / 2214 1.3	
15 0402 5.2 / 1042 0.4 / F 1643 5.2 / 2259 0.9		**30** 0415 4.8 / 1043 0.9 / SA 1643 4.7 / 2246 1.3	
		31 0447 4.9 / 1117 0.9 / SU 1716 4.7 / 2318 1.2	

AUGUST

Time	m	Time	m
1 0520 4.9 / 1152 0.9 / M 1751 4.6 / 2351 1.3		**16** 0002 1.0 / 0558 5.3 / TU 1238 0.5 / 1841 4.8	
2 0553 4.9 / 1227 0.9 / TU 1827 4.6		**17** 0040 1.2 / 0642 5.0 / W 1316 0.9 / 1924 4.5	
3 0024 1.4 / 0630 4.8 / W 1304 1.0 / 1907 4.5		**18** 0119 1.4 / 0728 4.7 / TH 1356 1.3 / 2010 4.3	
4 0102 1.5 / 0711 4.7 / TH 1345 1.2 / 1952 4.4		**19** 0203 1.7 / 0820 4.4 / F 1443 1.7 / ◗ 2103 4.1	
5 0146 1.6 / 0759 4.6 / F 1434 1.3 / ◗ 2046 4.3		**20** 0302 2.0 / 0922 4.1 / SA 1543 2.0 / 2207 3.9	
6 0242 1.8 / 0859 4.4 / SA 1536 1.5 / 2150 4.2		**21** 0422 2.1 / 1039 3.9 / SU 1702 2.2 / 2324 3.9	
7 0357 1.9 / 1013 4.3 / SU 1652 1.6 / 2303 4.2		**22** 0554 2.1 / 1206 3.9 / M 1825 2.1	
8 0524 1.8 / 1136 4.3 / M 1809 1.6		**23** 0036 4.1 / 0708 1.9 / TU 1314 4.1 / 1927 2.0	
9 0017 4.3 / 0645 1.5 / TU 1255 4.5 / 1920 1.4		**24** 0132 4.3 / 0759 1.6 / W 1403 4.3 / 2012 1.8	
10 0121 4.6 / 0754 1.2 / W 1400 4.8 / 2021 1.2		**25** 0214 4.5 / 0839 1.3 / TH 1442 4.5 / 2049 1.6	
11 0216 4.9 / 0853 0.8 / TH 1455 5.0 / 2113 1.0		**26** 0250 4.7 / 0915 1.1 / F 1515 4.6 / 2122 1.4	
12 0304 5.1 / 0944 0.5 / F 1544 5.2 / ○ 2200 0.9		**27** 0321 4.9 / 0948 0.9 / SA 1547 4.8 / ● 2153 1.2	
13 0348 5.3 / 1032 0.2 / SA 1630 5.2 / 2243 0.8		**28** 0351 5.0 / 1020 0.7 / SU 1617 4.9 / 2224 1.1	
14 0432 5.4 / 1116 0.2 / SU 1715 5.2 / 2324 0.9		**29** 0421 5.1 / 1052 0.7 / M 1649 4.9 / 2255 1.1	
15 0515 5.4 / 1158 0.3 / M 1758 5.0		**30** 0452 5.1 / 1125 0.7 / TU 1721 4.9 / 2326 1.1	
		31 0524 5.1 / 1159 0.7 / W 1755 4.8 / 2359 1.2	

Chart Datum: 2·60 metres below Ordnance Datum (Newlyn). HAT is 5·7 metres above Chart Datum.

》》**FREE** monthly updates. Register at 《
www.reedsnauticalalmanac.co.uk

172

STANDARD TIME (UT)
For Summer Time add ONE hour in **non-shaded areas**

RIVER TYNE/NORTH SHIELDS   LAT 55°00'N   LONG 1°26'W

TIMES AND HEIGHTS OF HIGH AND LOW WATERS

Dates in red are **SPRINGS**
Dates in blue are **NEAPS**

YEAR 2022

SEPTEMBER

Time	m	Time	m
1 0600	5.0	**16** 0041	1.4
1233	0.9	0650	4.7
TH 1833	4.7	F 1307	1.5
		1918	4.4
2 0034	1.3	**17** 0121	1.7
0642	4.9	0738	4.3
F 1311	1.1	SA 1346	1.9
1916	4.5	◑ 2007	4.1
3 0116	1.5	**18** 0213	2.0
0731	4.6	0839	4.0
SA 1358	1.4	SU 1442	2.2
◐ 2010	4.3	2111	3.9
4 0213	1.7	**19** 0332	2.2
0835	4.4	0959	3.8
SU 1504	1.7	M 1611	2.4
2118	4.2	2234	3.8
5 0335	1.9	**20** 0518	2.2
1000	4.2	1135	3.8
M 1633	1.9	TU 1756	2.4
2242	4.1		
6 0517	1.8	**21** 0001	4.0
1137	4.2	0641	1.9
TU 1804	1.9	W 1249	4.0
		1904	2.1
7 0006	4.3	**22** 0102	4.2
0646	1.5	0732	1.6
W 1258	4.5	TH 1338	4.3
1918	1.4	1948	1.8
8 0113	4.6	**23** 0145	4.5
0752	1.0	0811	1.3
TH 1358	4.8	F 1415	4.5
2013	1.3	2024	1.6
9 0205	4.9	**24** 0220	4.7
0844	0.7	0846	1.0
F 1446	5.1	SA 1446	4.7
2100	1.1	2056	1.3
10 0249	5.2	**25** 0251	4.9
0930	0.4	0918	0.8
SA 1529	5.2	SU 1517	4.9
○ 2142	0.9	● 2126	1.1
11 0330	5.4	**26** 0321	5.1
1012	0.2	0950	0.7
SU 1609	5.2	M 1547	5.0
2220	0.8	2157	1.0
12 0409	5.5	**27** 0351	5.2
1051	0.3	1023	0.6
M 1647	5.2	TU 1618	5.1
2257	0.8	2229	0.9
13 0448	5.4	**28** 0423	5.3
1128	0.4	1056	0.6
TU 1724	5.0	W 1651	5.1
2332	0.9	2301	0.9
14 0527	5.3	**29** 0458	5.2
1201	0.7	1130	0.7
W 1800	4.8	TH 1725	5.0
		2336	1.0
15 0005	1.1	**30** 0537	5.1
0607	5.0	1205	0.9
TH 1233	1.1	F 1804	4.8
1838	4.6		

OCTOBER

Time	m	Time	m
1 0014	1.2	**16** 0049	1.6
0622	4.9	0706	4.3
SA 1245	1.3	SU 1301	2.0
1850	4.6	1920	4.2
2 0100	1.4	**17** 0139	1.9
0717	4.6	0804	4.0
SU 1336	1.6	M 1351	2.3
1945	4.4	◑ 2020	4.0
3 0204	1.7	**18** 0249	2.1
0830	4.3	0919	3.8
M 1449	2.0	TU 1514	2.5
◐ 2100	4.2	2140	3.9
4 0335	1.8	**19** 0426	2.2
1005	4.1	1046	3.8
TU 1630	2.1	W 1707	2.5
2231	4.1	2307	3.9
5 0520	1.7	**20** 0552	2.0
1141	4.3	1205	4.0
W 1801	2.0	TH 1822	2.3
2357	4.3		
6 0641	1.3	**21** 0016	4.1
1254	4.6	0649	1.7
TH 1907	1.7	F 1258	4.2
		1910	1.9
7 0100	4.7	**22** 0104	4.4
0740	0.9	0732	1.4
F 1346	4.8	SA 1337	4.5
1957	1.4	1948	1.7
8 0149	5.0	**23** 0142	4.7
0827	0.6	0808	1.1
SA 1429	5.0	SU 1411	4.8
2040	1.1	2022	1.4
9 0230	5.2	**24** 0215	4.9
0909	0.5	0843	0.8
SU 1507	5.2	M 1443	5.0
○ 2118	0.9	2055	1.2
10 0308	5.4	**25** 0248	5.1
0947	0.4	0917	0.7
M 1542	5.2	TU 1515	5.1
2154	0.8	● 2128	1.0
11 0344	5.4	**26** 0322	5.3
1021	0.5	0952	0.6
TU 1616	5.1	W 1548	5.2
2229	0.9	2204	0.9
12 0421	5.3	**27** 0358	5.3
1054	0.7	1028	0.6
W 1650	5.0	TH 1623	5.2
2303	1.0	2241	0.9
13 0459	5.1	**28** 0438	5.3
1124	1.0	1106	0.8
TH 1723	4.9	F 1701	5.1
2336	1.1	2320	1.0
14 0538	4.9	**29** 0523	5.1
1154	1.3	1146	1.1
F 1758	4.7	SA 1744	4.9
15 0010	1.4	**30** 0005	1.1
0619	4.6	0615	4.9
SA 1225	1.6	SU 1231	1.4
1836	4.5	1833	4.7
		31 0059	1.3
		0717	4.6
		M 1327	1.8
		1933	4.5

NOVEMBER

Time	m	Time	m
1 0208	1.5	**16** 0214	1.9
0835	4.3	0838	3.9
TU 1445	2.1	W 1422	2.4
◑ 2049	4.3	◐ 2048	4.0
2 0339	1.6	**17** 0328	2.0
1004	4.2	0949	3.8
W 1621	2.2	TH 1553	2.5
2216	4.3	2202	4.0
3 0509	1.5	**18** 0446	1.9
1128	4.3	1101	3.9
TH 1742	2.0	F 1716	2.3
2335	4.5	2312	4.1
4 0621	1.2	**19** 0550	1.7
1234	4.6	1202	4.2
F 1843	1.7	SA 1815	2.1
5 0037	4.7	**20** 0009	4.3
0717	1.0	0641	1.5
SA 1324	4.8	SU 1249	4.4
1933	1.5	1902	1.8
6 0126	4.9	**21** 0055	4.6
0803	0.8	0725	1.2
SU 1405	4.9	M 1330	4.7
2015	1.3	1943	1.5
7 0207	5.1	**22** 0136	4.8
0843	0.8	0805	1.0
M 1442	5.0	TU 1408	4.9
2053	1.1	2022	1.3
8 0246	5.2	**23** 0216	5.0
0918	0.8	0845	0.8
TU 1516	5.1	W 1445	5.1
○ 2130	1.0	● 2102	1.1
9 0323	5.2	**24** 0257	5.2
0951	0.9	0926	0.8
W 1549	5.1	TH 1523	5.2
2205	1.0	2144	0.9
10 0400	5.1	**25** 0341	5.3
1023	1.0	1008	0.8
TH 1621	5.0	F 1603	5.2
2240	1.1	2228	0.8
11 0438	5.0	**26** 0428	5.2
1101	1.3	1051	0.9
F 1654	4.9	SA 1645	5.1
2315	1.2	2315	0.8
12 0517	4.8	**27** 0518	5.1
1123	1.5	1136	1.2
SA 1728	4.7	SU 1732	5.0
2350	1.4		
13 0557	4.5	**28** 0005	0.9
1155	1.7	0615	4.9
SU 1805	4.6	M 1226	1.5
		1824	4.9
14 0029	1.6	**29** 0103	1.1
0643	4.3	0718	4.7
M 1231	2.0	TU 1323	1.8
1848	4.6	1924	4.7
15 0115	1.8	**30** 0209	1.2
0735	4.1	0829	4.4
TU 1318	2.2	W 1432	2.0
1941	4.2	◐ 2034	4.5

DECEMBER

Time	m	Time	m
1 0325	1.3	**16** 0237	1.7
0943	4.3	0854	4.0
TH 1551	2.1	F 1441	2.2
2149	4.5	◐ 2059	4.2
2 0440	1.3	**17** 0340	1.8
1056	4.3	0955	4.0
F 1704	2.0	SA 1554	2.3
2301	4.5	2202	4.2
3 0547	1.3	**18** 0444	1.7
1200	4.4	1057	4.1
SA 1808	1.9	SU 1706	2.2
		2305	4.3
4 0005	4.6	**19** 0544	1.6
0646	1.2	1156	4.3
SU 1253	4.5	M 1808	1.9
1903	1.7		
5 0059	4.8	**20** 0004	4.4
0734	1.2	0640	1.4
M 1338	4.7	TU 1248	4.5
1950	1.5	1903	1.7
6 0146	4.8	**21** 0100	4.7
0815	1.2	0731	1.2
TU 1418	4.8	W 1336	4.7
2032	1.3	1954	1.4
7 0228	4.9	**22** 0152	4.9
0852	1.2	0820	1.1
W 1454	4.9	TH 1421	4.9
2111	1.2	2043	1.1
8 0308	4.9	**23** 0243	5.1
0926	1.2	0908	1.0
TH 1528	4.9	F 1505	5.1
○ 2149	1.2	● 2133	0.9
9 0347	4.8	**24** 0333	5.2
0959	1.3	0956	0.9
F 1602	4.9	SA 1550	5.2
2225	1.2	2223	0.7
10 0425	4.8	**25** 0424	5.2
1032	1.4	1043	1.0
SA 1635	4.9	SU 1635	5.2
2301	1.2	2314	0.6
11 0503	4.7	**26** 0516	5.2
1103	1.5	1131	1.1
SU 1709	4.8	M 1723	5.2
2336	1.3		
12 0541	4.5	**27** 0005	0.6
1136	1.7	0611	5.0
M 1745	4.7	TU 1219	1.3
		1814	5.1
13 0014	1.4	**28** 0058	0.7
0623	4.4	0708	4.8
TU 1212	1.8	W 1309	1.5
1825	4.6	1909	5.0
14 0055	1.5	**29** 0154	0.9
0707	4.2	0807	4.6
W 1252	2.0	TH 1404	1.7
1909	4.4	2008	4.8
15 0142	1.6	**30** 0254	1.1
0757	4.1	0908	4.4
TH 1341	2.1	F 1506	1.9
2001	4.3	◑ 2111	4.6
		31 0357	1.3
		1011	4.2
		SA 1614	2.0
		2218	4.5

Chart Datum: 2·60 metres below Ordnance Datum (Newlyn). HAT is 5·7 metres above Chart Datum.

NE England

》》 **FREE** monthly updates. Register at 《
www.reedsnauticalalmanac.co.uk

173

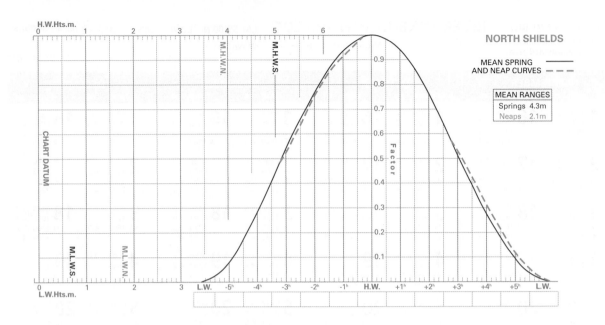

NORTH SHIELDS

MEAN SPRING ——————
AND NEAP CURVES – – – –

MEAN RANGES
Springs 4.3m
Neaps 2.1m

H.W.Hts.m.

CHART DATUM

M.H.W.N.

M.H.W.S.

M.L.W.S.

M.L.W.N.

Factor

L.W. -5ʰ -4ʰ -3ʰ -2ʰ -1ʰ H.W. +1ʰ +2ʰ +3ʰ +4ʰ +5ʰ L.W.

L.W.Hts.m.

3.18   BLYTH

Northumberland 55°06′·98N 01° 29′·27W ❄❄❄❄❄🌢🌢❀❀❀

CHARTS AC 152, 156, 1626, 5615; Imray C24

TIDES +0430 Dover; ML 2·8; Duration 0558

Standard Port NORTH SHIELDS (←—)

Times				Height (metres)			
High Water		Low Water		MHWS	MHWN	MLWN	MLWS
0200	0800	0100	0800	5·0	3·9	1·8	0·7
1400	2000	1300	2000				
Differences *BLYTH*							
+0005	−0007	−0001	+0009	0·0	0·0	−0·1	+0·1

SHELTER Very good. Access H24 but at LW in strong SE winds, seas break across entrance.

NAVIGATION WPT 55°06′·57N 01°28′·74W, 324°/0·5M to harbour entrance. From N, beware The Pigs, The Sow and Seaton Sea Rks. A wind farm with a met mast is 3M offshore and 2 wind turbines on North Spit (1·2M N of hbr ent) centred on 55°08′·16N 01°29′·41W. No dangers from S. See RNYC Sailing Directions, from RNYC, House Yacht Tyne, S Hbr, Blyth NE24 3PB (website below).

LIGHTS AND MARKS Blyth E Pier Hd, W twr on S end. Outer ldg lts 324°, Or ◊ on framework trs. Inner ldg lts 338°, front W 6-sided tr; rear W △ on mast. See chartlet and 3.3 for lt details.

COMMUNICATIONS (Code 01670) Police 101. Port Ops 357025, Call *Blyth Hbr Control* Ch **12** 11 (H24) for clearance to enter/ leave.

FACILITIES R Northumberland YC www.rnyc.org.uk ☎353636. In SE part of South Hbr, E side of Middle Jetty, Ⓥ berth on N side of RNYC pontoons in 4·4m least depth. 123 ⌇ £2·50, min £17; 🛢 ⛽ (20t) 🅿(1½t for trailer sailers) @ 🖥 ⚒ (www.millermarine.co.uk).

South Hbr ☎352678, ⚓ 🅿(50t).

Town 🛒 🛍 🛢 ✉ Ⓑ ⚒ ✕ 🍴 bus to Newcastle ⇌ ✈.

ADJACENT ANCHORAGE
NEWBIGGIN, Northumberland, **55°10′·75N 01°30′·10W**. AC 156. Tides approx as for Blyth, 3·5M to the S. Temp, fair weather ⚓ in about 4m in centre of the bay, off the conspic sculptures on the breakwater; sheltered from SW to N winds. Caution: offlying rky

F.Bu
Ldg Lts
2F.R(vert)
Ramp
Or ◊
F.Bu.
17m10M
F.Bu.
11m10M
Or ◊
Fl.R.4s
Workshop Quay
Fl.R.6s (vert)
North Quay
Inner West Pier
8.5m
South Harbour
West Quay
7.3m
Middle Jetty
RoRo
RNYC Mast
BLYTH
55°7′N
South Beach
metres
cables
0 400
HM Ch 12
01°29·8′W
Fl.G.3s
East Pier
2F.G (vert)
2F.R (vert)
Fl.G.6s
Mast
Outer West Pier
Wave Trap
Fl.R.6s
2F.R(vert)8M
The Pigs (dries 1.1m)
The Sow
Seaton Sea Rocks
Wk
Wave Trap
Beacon Bushes
324°
Fl(4)10s19m21M
F.R.13m13M
Horn(3)30s
Dredged to 8.5m
29·5′

ledges to N and S. Conspic church on N side of bay; bkwtr lt Fl G 10s 4M. Facilities: **SC** (dinghies).
Town 🛒 ✕ 🍴.

3.19 AMBLE

Northumberland 55°20'·37N 01°34'·25W ❀❀❀♦♦♦❀❀

CHARTS AC 156, 1627, 5615; Imray C24

TIDES +0412 Dover; ML 3·1; Duration 0606

Standard Port NORTH SHIELDS (◀——)

Times				Height (metres)			
High Water		Low Water		MHWS	MHWN	MLWN	MLWS
0200	0800	0100	0800	5·0	3·9	1·8	0·7
1400	2000	1300	2000				
Differences AMBLE							
–0013	–0013	–0016	–0020	0·0	0·0	+0·1	+0·1
COQUET ISLAND							
–0010	–0010	–0020	–0020	+0·1	+0·1	0·0	+0·1

SHELTER The Hbr (alias Warkworth Hbr) is safe in all winds. But ent is dangerous in strong N to E winds or in swell, when heavy seas break on Pan Bush shoal and on the bar at hbr ent, where least depth is 0·8m. ⚓ in Coquet Road or NNE of North Pier.

NAVIGATION WPT 55°21'·00N 01°33'·10W, 225° to hbr ent, 0·9M. Ent recommended from NE, passing N and W of Pan Bush. The S-going stream sets strongly across ent. Once inside the N bkwtr, beware drying banks to stbd, ie on N side of channel; keep close (15m) to S quays. 4kn speed limit in hbr.

- In NE'ly gales broken water can extend to Coquet Island, keep E of island and go to Blyth where appr/ent may be safer.
- Coquet Chan (min depth 0·3m) is not buoyed and is only advised with caution, by day, in good vis/weather, slight sea state and with adequate rise of tide, ie HW–2.

LIGHTS AND MARKS Coquet Island lt ho, (conspic) W□tr, turreted parapet, lower half grey; horn 30s. See chartlet and 3.3.

COMMUNICATIONS (Code 01665) HM 710306; CGOC (01262) 672317; local CG 710575; Police 101; Ⓗ (01670) 521212. *Amble Marina* Ch 80 (7/7, 0900-1700). HM Ch 16, works Ch 14 (Mon-Fri 0900-1700 LT). Coquet YC Ch M (occas).

FACILITIES Amble Marina marina@ amble.co.uk ☎712168, is about 5ca from hbr ent. Tidal gauge shows depth over sill, 0·8m above CD; access between PHM buoy and old jetty, both unlit. Pontoons are 'A' to 'F' from sill; ❷ berth on 'B' initially. 200 ⚓+40 ❷, £2·50. 🛒🔧🛟⚓♨✕⚓Ⓔ♨⛽🚿✕⚓ Hbr 🛟⚓.
Coquet YC ☎711179, 🔧🛒🏪⚓♨.
Town ✉🛒✕🏪🚉 (Alnmouth), ✈ (Newcastle).

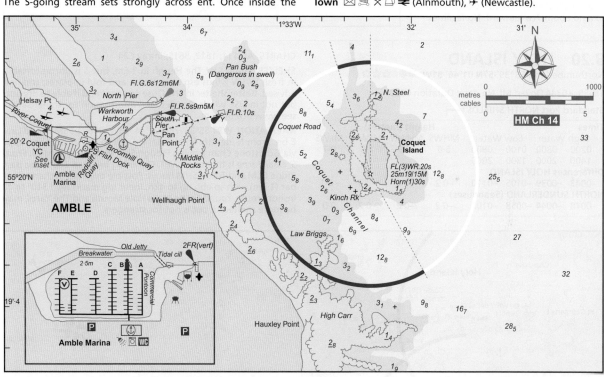

HBRS AND ANCHORAGES BETWEEN AMBLE AND HOLY ISLAND

BOULMER, Northumberland, **55°25'·00N 01°33'·90W**. AC 156. Tides approx as for Amble, 4·6M to the S. A small haven almost enclosed by N and S Rheins, rky ledges either side of the narrow (30m) ent, Marmouth; only advised in settled offshore weather. 2 FW bns (lit when req'd by LB or FVs) lead approx 257° through the ent, leaving close to stbd a bn on N Rheins. ⚓ just inside in about 1·5m or dry out on sand at the N end. Few facilities: ✉🏪 in village. Alnwick is 4M inland.

CRASTER, Northumberland, **55°28'·40N 01°35'·30W**. AC 156. Tidal differences: interpolate between Amble (3.19) and N Sunderland (3.20). Strictly a fair weather ⚓ in offshore winds, 1M S of the conspic Dunstanburgh Castle (ru). The ent, 40m wide, is N of Muckle Carr and S of Little Carr which partly covers and has a bn on its S end. ⚓ in about 3·5m just inshore of these 2 rocky outcrops; or berth at the E pier on rk/sand inside the tiny drying hbr. Facilities: 🛒✕🏪.

NEWTON HAVEN and BEADNELL BAY, Northumberland, **55°30'·90N 01° 36'·70W**. AC 156. HW +0342 on Dover; Tidal differences: interpolate between Amble (3.19) and N Sunderland (3.20). ML 2·6m; Duration 0625. Safe attractive ⚓ in winds from NNW to SE via S but susceptible to swell. Ent to S of Newton PHM buoy and Newton Pt. Beware Fills Rks. ⚓ between Fills Rks and Low Newton by the Sea in 4/5m. No lts, marks or facilities except pub. Further ⚓ S of Beadnell Pt (1M N of Newton Pt) in 4–6m off small fishing hbr. Beadnell SC. Village 0·5M.

SEAHOUSES (N Sunderland), Northumberland, **55°35'·04N 01°38'·91W**. AC 1612. HW +0340 on Dover; Duration 0618. See 3.20. Good shelter except in onshore winds when swell makes outer hbr very uncomfortable. Inner hbr berths (0·7m) but usually full of FVs. Beware The Tumblers (rks) to the W of ent and rks NE from bwtr. Bwtr hd Fl R 2·5s 6mNW pier hd FG 11m 3M; vis 159°-294°, W tr; traffic sigs; Siren 90s if vessels expected. If dangerous to enter, ● is shown over the FG lt (or R flag over a Bu flag) on NW pier hd.

ADJACENT ISLANDS

FARNE ISLANDS, Northumberland, **55°37'·15N 01°39'·37W.** AC 160, 156, 111. HW +0345 on Dover; ML 2·6m; Duration 0630. See 3.20. The islands are a NT nature reserve in a beautiful area; they should only be attempted in good weather. Landing is only allowed on Farne Is, Staple Is and Longstone. In the inner group, ⚓ in The Kettle on the NE side of Inner Farne; near the Bridges (connecting Knocks Reef to West Wideopen); or to the S of West Wideopen. In the outer group, ⚓ in Pinnacle Haven (between Staple Is/Brownsman). Beware turbulence over Knivestone and Whirl Rks and eddy S of Longstone during NW tidal streams. Lts and marks: Black Rocks Pt, Oc (2) WRG 8s 12m 14/11M;122°-G-165°-W-175°-R-191°-W-238°-R-275°-W-289°-G-300°. Bamburgh Castle is conspic 6ca to the SE. Farne Is lt ho at SW Pt, Fl (2) WR 15s 27m 8/6M; W○ tr; 119°-R-280°-W-119°. Longstone Fl 20s 23m 24M, R tr with W band (conspic), temp'ly replaced by Light vessel Fl(2) 20s15M (2015). Caution: reefs extend about 7ca seaward. No facilities.

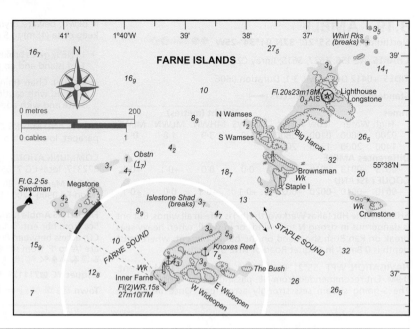

3.20 HOLY ISLAND

Northumberland 55°39'·57N 01°46'·81W ❀❀⚓❀❀❀

TIDES +0344 Dover; ML No data; Duration 0630

Standard Port NORTH SHIELDS (◀—)

Times				Height (metres)			
High Water		Low Water		MHWS	MHWN	MLWN	MLWS
0200	0800	0100	0800	5·0	3·9	1·8	0·7
1400	2000	1300	2000				
Differences HOLY ISLAND							
−0043	−0039	−0105	−0110	−0·2	−0·2	−0·3	−0·1
NORTH SUNDERLAND (Seahouses)							
−0048	−0044	−0058	−0102	−0·2	−0·2	−0·2	0·0

CHARTS AC 111, 1612, 5615; Imray C24

SHELTER Good S of The Heugh in 3-6m, but ⚓ is uncomfortable in fresh W/SW winds esp at sp flood, and foul in places; trip-line advised. Better shelter in The Ouse on sand/mud if able to dry out; but not in S/SE winds. For detailed information for trailer sailers see www.dca.uk.com.

NAVIGATION WPT 55°39'·76N 01°44'·88W, 260°/1·55M to Old Law E bn. From N identify Emmanuel Hd, conspic W △ bn, then appr via Goldstone Chan leaving Plough Seat PHM buoy to stbd. From S, clear Farne Is thence to WPT. Outer ldg bns lead 260° close past Ridge ECM and Triton SHM buoys. Possible overfalls in chan across bar (1·6m) with sp ebb up to 4kn. Inner ldg marks lead 310° to ⚓. Inshore route, round Castle Pt via Hole Mouth and The Yares, may be more sheltered, but is not for strangers.

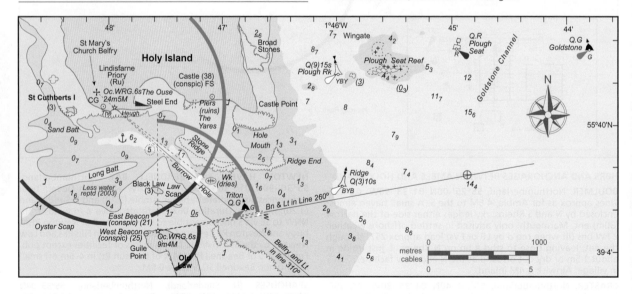

LIGHTS AND MARKS See 3.3 and chartlet. Outer leading marks/lts are Old Law beacons (conspic), 2 reddish obelisks 21/25m on 260°; E beacon has directional light, Oc WRG 6s. Inner leading marks/ lights are The Heugh tower, B △, on with St Mary's church belfry 310°. The Heugh has directional light, Oc WRG 6s. Directional lights Oc WRG are aligned on 260° and 309·5° respectively.

COMMUNICATIONS (Code 01289) HM 389248.

FACILITIES Limited. ⚓ (contact HM prior to launching) £5.00, ⚓ on village green, ✕ 🍴 limited 🛒 🅿 📞 from Beal (5M); bus (occas) to Berwick. Note Lindisfarne is ancient name; Benedictine Abbey (ruins) and Castle (NT) are worth visiting. Causeway to mainland, covers at HW, is usable approx HW+3½ to HW–2.

NATIONAL NATURE RESERVE (Holy Island) A National Nature Reserve (NNR) extends from Budle Bay (**55°37´N 01°45´W**, close to Black Rocks Point lt ho) along the coast to Cheswick Black Rocks, 3M SE of Berwick-upon-Tweed. The NNR extends seaward from the HW shoreline to the drying line; it includes Holy Island and the adjacent islets.

Visiting craft are asked to respect two constraints:

- Landing is prohibited on the small island of Black Law (55°39´·68N 01°47´·50W) from April to August inclusive.
- Boats should not be landed or recovered anywhere in the NNR except at the designated and buoyed watersports zone on the SE side of Budle Bay.

3.21 BERWICK-UPON-TWEED

Northumberland 55°45´·87N 01°59´·05W ✿✿⚓⚓✿✿

CHARTS AC 111, 160, 1612, 5615; Imray C24

TIDES +0348 Dover; ML 2·5; Duration 0620

Standard Port NORTH SHIELDS (←)

Times				Height (metres)			
High Water		Low Water		MHWS	MHWN	MLWN	MLWS
0200	0800	0100	0800	5·0	3·9	1·8	0·7
1400	2000	1300	2000				
Differences BERWICK-UPON-TWEED							
–0053	–0053	–0109	–0109	–0·3	–0·1	–0·5	–0·1

SHELTER Good shelter or ⚓ except in strong E/SE winds. ⚓ on floating pontoon (1.4m below CD) to S side in Tweed Dock (no dock gates) which is primarily used by commercial shipping. If possible contact HM beforehand to avoid disappointment. Alternative temporary ⚓ possible at W end of Fish Jetty (1·2m).

NAVIGATION WPT 55°45´·62N 01°58´·0W, 294°/0·65M to bkwtr lt ho.

- Onshore winds and ebb tides cause very confused seas over the bar, minimum depth 0·6m. From HW–2 to HW+1 strong flood tide sets S across the entrance; keep well up to breakwater.
- The sands at the mouth of the Tweed shift so frequently that local knowledge is essential to enter the harbour.

Town Hall Spire and Lt ho in line at 294°. Keep close to breakwater to avoid Sandstell Point. When past PHM and S of Crabwater Rk, keep Spittal Bns (Or ▽ on B Or Bn) in line brg 207°; best water may be further W. Berwick Br (first/lowest) has about 3m clearance.

LIGHTS AND MARKS See 3.3 and chartlet.

COMMUNICATIONS (Code 01289) Dr 307484. HM mob 07931 710156.

VHF Ch 12 16 (0800-1700).

FACILITIES Tweed Dock ⚓ £8 ⚓ ⚓ ⚓ 🏴 🛒 ✕ ⚒ 🅿 ⛽ 🔺(3t) Mob. **Town** 🅿 📮 ✉ Ⓑ 🛒 ✕ 🍴 ⇌ and ✈ (Newcastle or Edinburgh).

EXPLORE
WITHOUT LIMITS

East Scotland

Eyemouth to Shetland Islands

SE Scotland

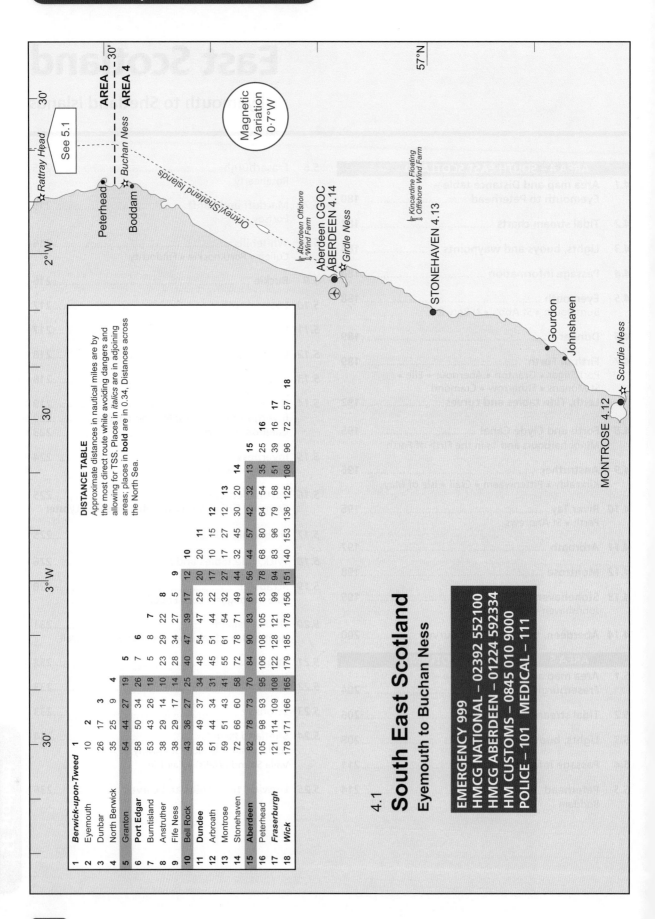

4.1

South East Scotland
Eyemouth to Buchan Ness

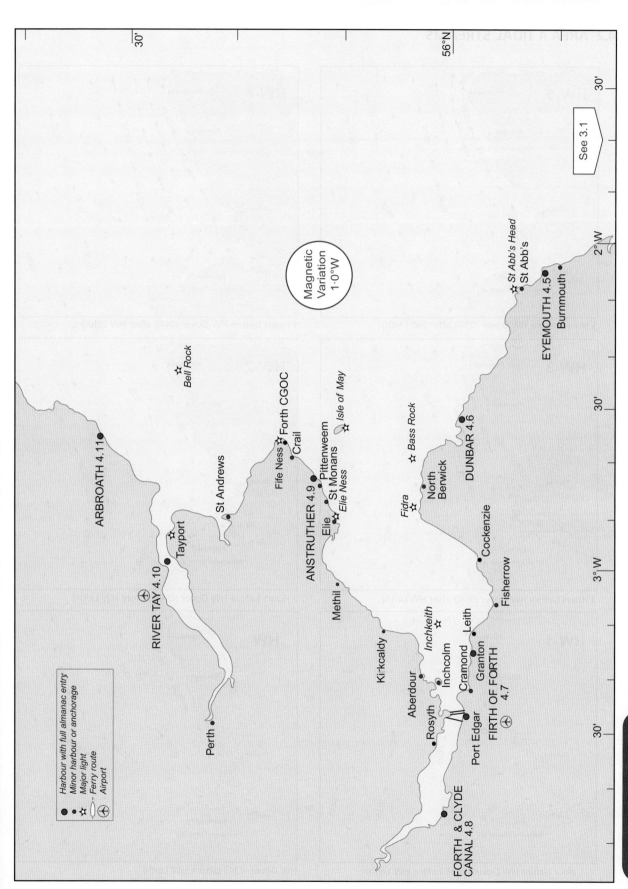

Magnetic Variation 1·0°W

See 3.1

Harbour with full almanac entry
Minor harbour or anchorage
Major light
Ferry route
Airport

ARBROATH 4.11

Bell Rock

Tayport

RIVER TAY 4.10

Perth

St Andrews

Fife Ness ✩ Forth CGOC
Crail

Isle of May

ANSTRUTHER 4.9
Pittenweem
Elie St Monans
Elie Ness

Methil

Bass Rock

Fidra

North Berwick

DUNBAR 4.6

Kirkcaldy

Aberdour

Inchkeith

Rosyth
Inchcolm
Cramond
Port Edgar   Granton   Leith
FIRTH OF FORTH 4.7

Cockenzie

Fisherrow

FORTH & CLYDE CANAL 4.8

St Abb's Head
St Abb's

EYEMOUTH 4.5
Burnmouth

SE Scotland

4.2 AREA 4 TIDAL STREAMS

5 Hours before HW Dover (0340 after HW Leith)

4 Hours before HW Dover (0440 after HW Leith)

3 Hours before HW Dover (0540 after HW Leith)

2 Hours before HW Dover (0545 before HW Leith)

1 Hour before HW Dover (0445 before HW Leith)

HW Dover (0345 before HW Leith)

Northward 5.2   Southward 3.2

1 Hour after HW Dover (0245 before HW Leith)

2 Hours after HW Dover (0145 before HW Leith)

3 Hours after HW Dover (0045 before HW Leith)

4 Hours after HW Dover (0015 after HW Leith)

5 Hours after HW Dover (0115 after HW Leith)

6 Hours after HW Dover (0215 after HW Leith)

SE Scotland

4.3 LIGHTS, BUOYS AND WAYPOINTS

Bold print = light with a nominal range of 15M or more. CAPITALS = place or feature. *CAPITAL ITALICS* = light-vessel, light float or Lanby. *Italics* = Fog signal. ***Bold italics*** = Racon. Some marks/buoys are fitted with AIS (<u>MMSI No</u>); see relevant charts.

BERWICK-UPON-TWEED TO BASS ROCK
BURNMOUTH
Ldg lts 241°. Front, FR 29m 4M; 55°50'·53N 02°04'·25W. Rear, 45m from front, FR 35m 4M. Both on W posts (unclear by day).

EYEMOUTH
Blind Buss ↙ Q; 55°52'·80N 02°05'·25E.
Ldg Lts 174°. Front, W Bkwtr Hd ⚓, FG 9m 6M; 55°52'·47N 02°05'·29W. Rear, elbow 55m from front, FG 10m 6M.

ST ABBS to DUNBAR and BASS ROCK
St Abbs Hd ☆ 55°54'·96N 02°08'·29W; Fl 10s 68m **18M**; W twr; ***Racon (T) 18M***.
Barns Ness Tower (Lt ho disused 36m); 55°59'·22N 02°26'·76W.
Torness Pwr Stn Ldg Lts 215°. Front, Iso G 4s 6m 6M; W □ with B vert stripe on plinth; 55°58'·27N 02°24'·86W. Rear, Iso G 4s 22m 3M; W □ with B vert stripe on post; sync with front.
Dunbar Hbr Ldg Lts (Bayswell Hill) 198°. Front, Oc G 6s 15m 3M; 3 Or △ on col; 56°00'·26N 02°31'·21W. Rear, Oc G 6s 22m 3M; 3 Or ▽; sync with front; both lts 188°-G(intens)-208°.
S Carr ↙ Q; 56°03'·60N 02°37'·65W.
Bass Rock, S side, ⚓ Fl (3) 20s 46m 10M; W twr; vis: 241°-107°; 56°04'·61N 02°38'·48W.

FIRTH OF FORTH AND SOUTH SHORE
(Direction of buoyage East to West)
NORTH BERWICK
Outfall ↙ Fl Y; 56°04'·29N 02°40'·89W.

Fidra ☆ 56°04'·39N 02°47'·13W; Fl(4) 30s 34m **15M**; W twr; obsc by Bass Rock, Craig Leith and Lamb Island.

PORT SETON, COCKENZIE, FISHERROW and S CHANNEL
Port Seton, E Pier Hd ⚓ Iso WR 4s 10m W9M, R6M; vis: shore-R-105°-W-225°-R-shore; *Bell (occas)*; 55°58'·40N 02°57'·23W.
Fisherrow E Pier Hd ⚓ Oc 6s 5m 6M; 55°56'·79N 03°04'·11W.
Narrow Deep ⬢ Fl(2) R 10s; 56°01'·46N 03°04'·59W.
Herwit ▲ Fl(3) G 10s; 56°01'·05N 03°06'·52W.
North Craig ↙ Q(3) 10s; 56°01'·02N 03°03'·52W.
Craigh Waugh ↙ Fl(2) 10s; 56°00'·26N 03°04'·47W.
Diffuser Hds (Outer) ↙ Q; 55°59'·81N 03°07'·84W.
Diffuser Hds (Inner) ↙ Q(6) + LFl 15s; 55°59'·38N 03°08'·02W.

LEITH and GRANTON
Leith Approach ⬢ Fl R 3s; 55°59'·95N 03°11'·51W.
East Bkwtr Hd ⚓ Iso R 4s 7m 9M; 55°59'·48N 03°10'·94W.
Granton E Pier Hd ⚓ Fl R 2s 5m 6M; 55°59'·28N 03°13'·27W.

NORTH CHANNEL and MIDDLE BANK
Inchkeith Fairway ⬢ Iso 2s; ***Racon (T) 5M***; 56°03'·49N 03°00'·10W.
No 1 ▲ Fl G 9s; 56°03'·22N 03°03'·71W.
No 2 ⬢ Fl R 9s; 56°02'·90N 03°03'·72W.
No 3 ▲ Fl G 6s; 56°03'·22N 03°06'·10W.
No 4 ⬢ Fl R 6s; 56°02'·89N 03°06'·11W.
No 5 ▲ Fl G 3s; 56°03'·18N 03°07'·88W.
No 6 ⬢ Fl R 3s; 56°03'·05N 03°08'·44W.
No 8 ⬢ Fl R 9s 56°02'·95N 03°09'·62W.
Inchkeith ⚓ 56°02'·01N 03°08'·17W; Fl 15s 67m 14M; stone twr.
Pallas Rock ↙ VQ (9) 10s 56°01'·50N 03°09'·30W.
East Gunnet ↙ Q (3) 10s 56°01'·41N 03°10'·38W.
West Gunnet ↙ Q (9) 15s 56°01'·34N 03°11'·06W.
No 7 ▲ QG; ***Racon (T) 5M***; 56°02'·80N 03°10'·97W.
No 9 ▲ Fl G 6s; 56°02'·32N 03°13'·48W.

No 10 ⬢ Fl R 6s; 56°02'·07N 03°13'·32W.
No 11 ▲ Fl G 3s 56°02'·08N 03°15'·26W.
No 12 ⬢ Fl R 3s; 56°01'·78N 03°15'·15W.
No 13 ▲ Fl G 9s; 56°01'·77N 03°16'·94W.
No 14 ⬢ Q R; 56°01'·51N 03°16'·90W.
Oxcars ⚓ Fl (2) WR 7s 16m W13M, R12M; W twr, R band; vis: 072°-W-087°- R-196°-W-313°-R-072°; 56°01'·36N 03°16'·84W.
Inchcolm E Pt ⚓ Fl (3) 15s 20m 10M; Gy twr; part obsc by land 075°-145·5°; 56°01'·72N 03°17'·83W.
No 15 ▲ Fl G 6s; 56°01'·39N 03°18'·95W.

MORTIMER'S DEEP
Hawkcraig Point Ldg Lts 292°. Front, Iso 5s 12m 14M; W twr; vis: 282°-302°; 56°03'·03N 03°17'·07W. Rear, 96m from front, Iso 5s 16m 14M; W twr; vis: 282°-302°.
Inchcolm S Lts in line 066°. Front, 84m from rear, Q 7m 7M; W twr; vis: 062·5°-082·5°; 56°01'·78N 03°18'·28W. Common Rear, Iso 5s 11m 7M; W twr; vis: 062·5°-082·5°; 56°01'·80N 03°18'·13W. N Lts in line 076·7°. Front, 80m from rear, Q 7m 7M; W twr; vis: 062·5°-082·5°.

APPROACHES TO FORTH BRIDGES
No 17 ▲ Fl G 3s; 56°01'·23N 03°19'·84W.
No 16 ⬢ Fl R 3s; 56°00'·87N 03°19'·60W.
No 19 ▲ Fl G 9s; 56°00'·71N 03°22'·47W.
Rosyth Chan centreline ⚓ Iso 4s 56m 8M; 56°00'·44N 03°24'·64W.
Central Twr (Beamer Rk) ⚓ Iso 2s 7m 9M; 56°00'·29N 03°24'·75W.
Forth Chan centreline ⚓ Iso 8s 56m 8M; 56°00'·12N 03°24'·85W.

PORT EDGAR
W Bkwtr Hd ⚓ Fl R 4s 4m 8M; 55°59'·86N 03°24'·78W. W blockhouse.

FIRTH OF FORTH – NORTH SHORE (INWARD)
BURNTISLAND
W Pier Outer Hd ⚓ Fl (2) R 6s 7m; W twr; 56°03'·22N 03°14'·26W.
E Pier Outer Hd ⚓ Fl (2) G 6s 7m 5M; 56°03'·24N 03°14'·17W.

ABERDOUR, BRAEFOOT BAY and INCHCOLM
Hawkcraig Pt ⚓ (see **MORTIMER'S DEEP** above).
Braefoot Bay Terminal, W Jetty. Ldg Lts 247·3°. **Front**, Fl 3s 6m **15M**; W △ on E dolphin; vis: 237·2°-257·2°; 56°02'·16N 03°18'·71W; 4 dolphins with 2 FG (vert). **Rear**, 88m from front, Fl 3s 12m **15M**; W ▽ on appr gangway; vis: 237·2°-257·2°; sync with front.

INVERKEITHING BAY
St David's ↙ Fl G 5s 3m 7M; Or □, on pile; 56°01'·37N 03°22'·29W.
Channel ▲ QG; 56°01'·43N 03°23'·02W.

ROSYTH
No 2 ↙ Q (3) 10s; 56°00'·69N 03°25'·18W.
Main Chan Dir lt 323·5°. Bn 'A' Oc WRG 7m 4M; R □ on W post with R bands; vis: 318°-G-321°-321°-W-326°-R-328° (H24); 56°01'·19N 03°25'·61W.
Dir lt 115°, Bn 'C' Oc WRG 6s 7m 4M; W ▽ on W Bn; vis: 110°- R -113° W -116·5° - G -120°; 56°00'·61N 03°24'·25W.
S Arm Jetty Hd ⚓ L Fl (2) WR 12s 5m W9M; R6M; vis: 010°-W-280°-R-010°; 56°01'·09N 03°26'·58W.

RIVER FORTH
ROSYTH to GRANGEMOUTH
Dhu Craig ▲ Fl G 5s; 56°00'·74N 03°27'·23W.
Blackness ⬢ QR; 56°01'·06N 03°30'·30W.
Tancred Bank ⬢ Fl (2) R 10s; 56°01'·58N 03°31'·91W.
Dods Bank ⬢ Fl R 3s; 56°02'·03N 03°34'·07W.
Bo'ness ⬢ Fl R 10s; 56°02'·23N 03°35'·38W.
Torry ⚓ Fl G 10s 5m 7M; G ○ structure; 56°02'·46N 03°35'·28W.
Bo'ness Bcns ⬔ 2 QR 3m 2M; 56°01'·85N 03°36'·22W.
Bo'ness Hbr ⌃; 56°01'·26N 03°36'·46W.

GRANGEMOUTH

Grangemouth App No 1 ⚓ Fl (3) 10s 4m 6M;56°02'·12N 03°38'·10W.
Hen & Chickens ⬥ Fl (3) G 10s; 56°02'·35N 03°38'·08W.

FIRTH OF FORTH – NORTH SHORE (OUTWARD)

KIRKCALDY and METHIL

Kirkcaldy W Pier Hd ⚡ Fl R 5s 7m 3M; 56°06'·80N 03°08'·97W.
Kirkcaldy E Pier Hd ⚡ Fl G 5s 12m 3M; 56°06'·78N 03°08'·90W.
Methil Outer Pier Hd ⚡ Oc G 6s 8m 5M; W twr; vis: 280°-100°; 56°10'·76N 03°00'·48W.

ELIE and ST MONANS

Elie Ness ☆ 56°11'·04N 02°48'·77W; Fl 6s 15m **17M**; W twr.
St Monans Bwtr Hd ⚡ Fl G 3s 3m 4M; 56°12'·19N 02°45'·94W.
St Monans Inner Lt ⚡ Iso 4s 3m 4M; 56°12'·29N 02°45'·95W.

PITTENWEEM and ANSTRUTHER EASTER

Pittenweem, Ldg Lts 037° Middle Pier Hd. Front, FR 4m 5M. Rear, FR 8m 5M. Both Gy Cols, Or stripes; 56°12'·69N 02°43'·69W.
Pittenweem, E Bkwtr Hd ⚡ Fl (2) RG 5s 9m R9M, G6M; vis: 265°-R-345°-G-055°; 56°12'·63N 02°43'·74W.
Anstruther, Ldg Lts 019°. Front FG 7m 4M; 56°13'·28N 02°41'·76W. Rear, 38m from front, FG 11m 4M (both W masts).

MAY I, CRAIL, ST ANDREWS and FIFE NESS to MONTROSE

Isle of May ☆ 56°11'·12N 02°33'·46W(Summit); Fl (2) 15s 73m **22M**; □ twr on stone dwelling.
Crail, Ldg Lts 295°. Front, FR 24m 6M (not lit when hbr closed); 56°15'·46N 02°37'·84W. Rear, 30m from front, FR 30m 6M.
Fife Ness ☆ 56°16'·74N 02°35'·19W; Iso WR 10s 12m **W15M**, R12M; W bldg; vis: 143°-W-197°-R-217°-W-023°; 002320798.
N Carr ⚓ Q (3) 10s 3m 5M; 56°18'·05N 02°32'·94W.
St Andrews ⚡ 56°20'·38N 02°47'·07W; Dir lt 277·5; Iso WRG 2s 17m 9M; vis: 272°-G-276°-AlWG-277°-W-278°-AlWR-279°-R-283°.
St Andrews N Bkwtr Bn ⚡ Fl G 3M 56°20'·36N 02°46'·77W.

Bell Rk ☆ 56°26'·08N 02°23'·21W; Fl 5s 28m **18M**; *Racon (M) 18M.*
Met Mast ⚡ Mo(U) 15s 22m 10M; Aero FR (116m), Horn Mo(U) 30s; 56°26'·40N 02°14'·49W; 992351153.

RIVER TAY, TAYPORT, DUNDEE and PERTH

Tay Fairway ⦿ L Fl 10s; *Bell;* 56°28'·45N 02°36'·60W.
Middle ⬥ Fl G 3s; 56°28'·08N 02°38'·47W.
Middle ⬮ Fl (2) R 6s 56°27'·87N 02°37'·95W.
Abertay N ⚓ Q (3) 10s; 56°27'·61N 02°40'·75W.
Abertay S (Elbow) ⬮ Fl R 6s 56°27'·18N 02°39'·63W.

Tayport High Lt ⚡ Dir lt 268·25°; WRG 3s 23m WRG14M; vis: 266°-IsoG-267·5°-VQG-268°-IsoW-268·5°-VQR-269°-IsoR-271°; W twr, 56°27'·17N 02°53'·94W.

ARBROATH

Ldg lts 299·2°. Front , FR 7m 5M; W col; 56°33'·29N 02°35'·16W. Rear, 50m from front, FR 13m 5M; W col.

MONTROSE

Scurdie Ness ☆ 56°42'·10N 02°26'·24W; Fl (3) 20s 38m **20M**; W twr; *Racon (T) 14-16M.*
Outer Ldg Lts 271·5°; Front, FR 11m 5M; W twin pillars, R bands; 56°42'·21N 02°27'·41W; Rear, 272m from front, FR 18m 5M; W twr, R cupola.
Inner Ldg Lts 265°; Front FG 21m 5M; Rear FG 33m 5M.

MONTROSE TO RATTRAY HEAD

JOHNSHAVEN and GOURDON HARBOUR

Johnshaven, Ldg Lts 316°. Front, FR 5m; 56°47'·62N 02°20'·26W. Rear, 85m from front, FG 20m; shows R when unsafe to ent hbr.
Gourdon Hbr, Ldg Lts 358°. Front, FR 5m 5M; W twr; shows G when unsafe to enter; *Siren (2) 60s (occas);* 56°49'·69N 02°17'·24W. Rear, 120m from front, FR 30m 5M; W twr.
Gourdon E B'water ⚡ Q 3m 3M; 49°57'·60N 02°17'·19W.
Todhead Lighthouse (disused), white tower, 13m.

STONEHAVEN to GIRDLE NESS

Outer Pier Hd ⚡ Iso WRG 4s 7m 5M; vis: 214°-G-246°-W-268°-R-280°; 56°57'·59N 02°12'·00W.
Girdle Ness ☆ Fl (2) 20s 56m **22M**; obsc by Greg Ness when brg > 020°; *Racon (G) 25M;* 57°08'·34N 02°02'·91W.

ABERDEEN

Fairway ⦿ Mo (A) 5s; *Racon (T) 7M;* 57°09'·31N 02°01'·95W.
Torry Ldg lts 237·2°, Front FR or G 14m 5M; R when ent safe, FG when dangerous to navigate; W twr; 57°08'·38N 02°04'·50W. Rear, 220m from front, FR or G 19m 5M; R when ent safe, FG when dangerous to navigate; W twr; 57°08'·31N 02°04'·68W.
Aberdeen Harbour Ent ⚡ 57°08'·38N 02°04'·48W; Dir lt 237·2° Fl WRG 1s 7m 9M; metal post; vis: 235·2°-QG-236·2°-AlQGW-236·7°-QW-237·7°-AlQRW-238·2°-QR-239·2°.
S Bkwtr Hd ⚡ Fl (3) R 8s 23m 7M; 57°08'·69N 02°03'·34W.
N Pier Hd ⚡ Iso G 4s 11m 10M; W twr; 57°08'·74N 02°03'·69W. In fog FY 10m (same twr) vis: 136°-336°; Bell (3) 12s.
S Skates Nose Jetty Hd ⚡ Q R 4m 4M; 57°08'·49N 02°04'·06W.
Abercrombie Jetty Hd ⚡ Oc G 4s 5m 4M; 57°08'·53N 02°04'·15W.

SE Scotland

4.4 PASSAGE INFORMATION

Admiralty Leisure Folios 5615 and 5617 cover the area from Eyemouth to Peterhead. **Bibliography:** *North and East Scotland – Farne Islands to Cape Wrath –* (Lawrence/Imray), the Royal Northumberland *YC's Sailing Directions Humber to Rattray Head* and *Forth Yacht Clubs Association Pilot Handbook* for the the Firth of Forth. The *North Sea (West) Pilot* (Admiralty NP54) covers the entire area.

BERWICK-UPON-TWEED TO BASS ROCK

(AC 160,175) From Berwick-upon-Tweed to the Firth of Forth there is no good harbour which can be approached with safety in strong onshore winds. If on passage with strong winds from N or E, plan accordingly and keep well to seaward. In late spring/early summer, fog (haar) is likely in onshore winds.

The coast North from Berwick is rocky with cliffs rising in height to Burnmouth, then diminishing gradually to Eyemouth. Keep 5ca offshore to clear outlying rocks. Burnmouth, although small, has more berths than Eyemouth, which is a crowded fishing harbour. St Abb's Hd (Fl 10s 68m 26M) is a bold, steep headland, 92m high, with no offlying dangers and a temp ⚓ in offshore winds in Coldingham Bay close South.

► *The stream runs strongly round the Head, causing turbulence with wind against tide; this can be largely avoided by keeping close inshore. The ESE-going stream begins at HW Leith –0345, and the WNW-going at HW Leith +0240.* ◄

There is a good ⚓ in Pettico Wick, on NW side of St Abb's Hd, in S'ly winds, but it is dangerous if the wind shifts onshore. Between St Abb's Hd and Fast Castle Hd, 3M WNW, there are no offlying dangers and some 8M further NW, is the attractive little harbour of Cove. This dries and should only be approached in ideal conditions.

Torness Power Station (conspic, lt on bkwtr) and 2 SPM Fl(5) Y 20s 5ca off Chapel Pt lie 1·75M SE of Barns Ness (lt ho disused); Fringed with rocks tidal streams are similar to St Abb's Hd. Conspic chys (119m) are 7½ca WSW inland of Barns Ness. Between here and Dunbar keep at least 2½ca offshore to clear rocky patches. Sicar Rk (7·9m) lies about 1·25M ENE of Dunbar, and seas break on it in onshore gales.

The direct course from Dunbar to Bass Rk (Fl(3) 20s 46m 10M) is clear of all dangers; inshore of this line beware Wildfire Rks (dry) on the NW side of Bellhaven Bay. In offshore winds there is a temp'y ⚓ in Scoughall Road. 1M ESE of Gin Head, Carr bn (stone twr surmounted by ✠) marks the N end of Great Carr, a ledge of rocks, nearly covering at HW. Drying rock ledges extend 3ca offshore as far as 1M SE of Great Carr. Keep at least 5ca off Carr bn in strong onshore winds. Tantallon Castle (ruins) is on the cliff edge 1M West of Great Carr. Bass Rk (lit) lies 1·25M NNE of Gin Head, and is a sheer, conspic rk (115m) with no offlying dangers; landing is difficult due to swell.

FIRTH OF FORTH (SOUTH SHORE)

(AC 734, 735) Westward of Bass Rk, Craigleith (51m), Lamb Is (24m) and Fidra (31m) lie 5ca or more offshore, while the coast is generally foul. Craigleith is steep-to, and temporary ⚓ can be found on SE and SW sides; if passing inshore of it keep well to N side of chan. N Berwick harbour (dries) lies S of Craigleith, but is unsafe in onshore winds. Between Craigleith and Lamb Is, beware drying rocks up to 3ca from land. Lamb Is (1·5M WNW of N Berwick) has a rocky ledge extending 2½ca SW. Fidra Is (Fl(4) 30s 34m 15M) is a bird reserve, nearly connected to the shore by rocky ledges, and should be passed to the N; passage and ⚓ on S side are tricky. ⚓ on E or W sides, depending on wind, only in good weather.

To the East of Fidra some shelter can be found in SE winds in Aberlady and Gosford Bays. The best ⚓ is SW of Craigielaw Pt. Port Seton is a drying fishing hbr 7½ca E of Cockenzie (dries); entry is not advisable in strong onshore winds; beware Corsik Rk 400m to the East. No attractions except boatyard.

There are no dangers on the direct course from Fidra to Inchkeith (Fl 15s 67m 14M), which stands between the buoyed deep water channels. Rocks extend 7½ca SE from Inchkeith, and for 5ca off the West side where there is a small harbour below the lt ho; landing is forbidden without permission. N Craig and Craig Waugh (least depth 0·2m) are buoyed shoals 2·5M SE from Inchkeith lt.

►*In N Chan, close to Inchkeith the W-going (flood) stream begins about HW Leith –0530, and the E-going at HW Leith +0030, Sp rates about 1kn. The streams gather strength towards the Forth Bridges, where they reach 2·25kn and there may be turbulence.*◄

Leith is wholly commercial; Granton has moorings (E hbr); Port Edgar is a major yacht hbr close W of Forth Road Bridge. Hound Point oil terminal is an 'island-jetty' almost in mid-stream, connected to the shore by underwater pipeline (⚓). Yachts may pass the terminal on either side at least 30m off keeping well clear of manoeuvring ships.

CROSSING THE FIRTH OF FORTH

►*Tidal streams are quite weak in the outer part of the Firth, apart from the stream in the Tay, which attains 5kn in most places. Coastwise tidal streams between Fife Ness and Arbroath are weak.*◄

FLOOD
Firths of Forth & Tay

(d) 2.5k
(c) 1.0k
(b) 1.0k
(a) 4.5k

(a)	Leith –0530 to Leith +0015
(b)	Leith –0500 to Leith +0030
(c)	Leith –0430 to Leith +0130
(d)	Leith –0540 to Leith +0100

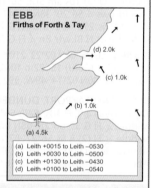

EBB
Firths of Forth & Tay

(d) 2.0k
(c) 1.0k
(b) 1.0k
(a) 4.5k

(a)	Leith +0015 to Leith –0530
(b)	Leith +0030 to Leith –0500
(c)	Leith +0130 to Leith –0430
(d)	Leith +0100 to Leith –0540

Northbound. *Leave before HW (Dover +0400) to be at N Carr at Dover +0600. Bound from Forth to Tay aim to arrive at Abertay By at LW slack (Dover –0200).*

Southbound. *Leave before LW (Dover -0200) to be at Bass Rk at HW Dover. If bound from Tay to Forth, leave late in ebb to pick up early flood off St Andrews to N Carr and into Forth.*

RIVER FORTH TO KINCARDINE

(AC 736, 737, 738) The main shipping channel under the span of the rail bridge N of Inchgarvie is busy with commercial traffic for Grangemouth and Rosyth. W of Beamer Rk, which supports the Queensferry Crossing the Firth widens as far as Bo'ness (small drying hbr) on the S shore where the channel narrows between drying mudbanks.

The Queensferry Crossing is W of the Forth Road Bridge with 3 pillars, one on Beamer Rk and two clear of the main navigable routes. The North span gives access to Rosyth while the South span allows traffic to pass upstream to Grangemouth. Forth and Tay Navigation Service broadcast information and vessels should maintain a listening watch on VHF Ch 71.

Charlestown (N bank) dries, but is a secure harbour. Grangemouth is industrially conspicuous. Beware of gas carriers, tankers and other cargo vessels; there are no facilities for yachts. Few yachts go beyond Kincardine swing bridge, clearance 7·8m, which is no longer opened. Clackmannanshire Bridge, clearance 7·6m, is about 4ca further upriver.

FIRTH OF FORTH (NORTH SHORE)

(AC 734, 190) From Burntisland the N shore of Firth of Forth leads E to Kinghorn Ness. 1M SSW of which Blae Rock (SHM) has least depth of 4·1m, and seas break on it in E gales.

▶ *Rost Bank lies halfway between Kinghorn Ness and Inchkeith, with tide rips at Sp tides or in strong winds.* ◀

From Kinghorn Ness to Kirkcaldy, drying rocks lie up to 3ca offshore. Yachts can enter Kirkcaldy Harbour (commercial) inner dock near HW by arrangement; entry is dangerous in strong E'lies, when seas break a long way out.

From Kirkcaldy to Methil the only dangers over 2ca offshore are The Rockheads, marked by 2 SHM, 4ca SE of Dysart. Largo Bay is an ⚓, well sheltered from N and E, but avoid gaspipes on the E side. Close SW of Elie Ness, beware the W Vows (dries) and E Vows (dries, bn). There is an ⚓ close W of Elie Ness (4.7). Ox Rock (dries 2m) lies 5ca ENE of Elie Ness, and 2½ca offshore; otherwise there are no dangers more than 2ca offshore to St Monance. In bad weather seas break on Shield Rk 4ca off Pittenweem. From Anstruther to Crail and Fife Ness keep 3ca offshore to clear Caiplie Rk and other dangers.

May Island (Fl(2) 15s 73m 22M) lies about 5M S of Fife Ness; its shores are bold except at NW end where rks extend 1ca off. In good weather it is possible to land ⚓ near N end at E or W Tarbert, on lee side according to winds. Lt ho boats use Kirkhaven, close SE of the lt ho.

FIRTH OF FORTH TO NORWAY AND THE BALTIC

(AC 2182B, 2182C) Heading ENE'ly from the Firth of Forth the main hazards result from offshore industrial activities and their associated traffic. Rig movements and other activities are published in Notices to Mariners, but it is wise to avoid the gas and oil fields stay 500m beyond any installations.

There are TSS to be avoided off the S and SW coast of Norway. Strong currents and steep seas may be experienced in the approaches to the Skagerrak.

FIFE NESS TO MONTROSE

(AC 190) Fife Ness is fringed by rocky ledges, and a reef extends 1M NE to N Carr Rk (dries 1·4m, marked by bn). In strong onshore winds keep to seaward of N Carr ECM lit buoy. From here keep 5ca offshore to clear dangers entering St Andrews Bay ⚓; the little harbour dries, and should not be approached in onshore winds.

Northward from Firth of Forth to Rattray Head the coast is mostly rocky and steep-to, and there are no out-lying dangers within 2M of the coast except off the River Tay and Bell Rock. In an onshore blow there are few safe havens; yachts and crews need to be fully prepared for offshore cruising.

Approach the **River Tay** (AC 1481) from Fairway SWM to the NE; it is dangerous to cut corners from the S. Abertay Sands extend nearly 4M East of Tentsmuir Point on the S side of the buoyed channel. Elbow shoal extends eastward. The Bar, NE of Abertay buoy, is dangerous in heavy weather, particularly in strong onshore wind or swell. On the N side of the chan Gaa Sands, run 1¾M E from Buddon Ness, marked by Abertay ECM (Racon). Passage across Abertay and Gaa Sands is very dangerous. The estuary is shallow, with shifting sandbanks. Tayport (drying) is a sheltered haven in the Tay.

▶ *2M E of Bell Rk the S-going stream begins HW Aberdeen –0220, and the N-going at HW Aberdeen +0405, Sp rates 1kn. W of Bell Rock the streams begin earlier.* ◀

Bell Rk (Fl 5s 28m 18M, Racon(M)) is 11½M E of Buddon Ness.

▶ *S of Buddon Ness the W-going (flood) stream begins at HW Aberdeen –0400, and the E-going at HW Aberdeen +0230, Sp rates 2kn.* ◀

N from Buddon Ness the coast is sandy. 1·25M SW of Arbroath beware Elliot Horses, rock patches extending 5ca offshore with a min depth 1·9m. Between Whiting Ness and Scurdie Ness, 9·5M NNE, the coast is clear of out-lying dangers, but is mostly fringed with drying rocks up to 1ca offshore. In offshore winds there is a temp ⚓ in SW of Lunan B, off Ethie Haven. Scurdie Ness (Fl(3) 20s 38m 23M) conspic, S of Montrose guards Scurdie Rks (dry) extending 2ca E of the Ness. On N side of the chan Annat Bank dries up to 5ca E of the shore.

▶ *The flood begins at HW Aberdeen –0500, and the ebb at HW Aberdeen +0115; both streams are very strong, up to 7kn at Sp. The entrance is dangerous in strong onshore winds, with breakers extending to Scurdie Ness on the ebb. If marginal the last quarter of the flood is best window.* ◀

MONTROSE TO BUCHAN NESS

(AC 210) 5M N of Montrose is Milton Ness, where there is an ⚓ on the S side in N winds. Johnshaven, 2M NE, is a small harbour (dries) with a tight entrance. It should not be approached with onshore wind or swell. 5ca NE, off Brotherton Castle, drying rks extend 4ca offshore. Gourdon has a small harbour (mostly dries) approached on leading line between rocky ledges; with storm gates to inner basin. Outside rocks extend both sides of the entrance, and the sea breaks heavily in strong E'ly winds. Keep a sharp lookout for lobster pot dan buoys between Montrose and Stonehaven.

North to Inverbervie the coast is fringed with rocky ledges up to 2ca offshore. Just N of Todhead Pt is Catterline, a small bay which forms a natural ⚓ in W winds, but is open to E. Downie Pt, SE of Stonehaven, should be rounded 1ca off. The Bay is lined by rocky ledges up to 2ca from shore and exposed to the E; ⚓ 6ca E of Bay Hotel or berth afloat in outer harbour.

From Garron Pt to Girdle Ness (Fl(2) 20s 56m 22M) the coast is steep-to. Nets may be met off headlands in season. Craigmaroinn and Seal Craig are reefs 3ca SE of Portlethen, a fishing village with landing sheltered by rocks. Kincardine wind farm lies 8M off Findon Ness. Cove Bay has a very small fishing harbour; ⚓ off in good weather; Mutton Rk (dries 2·1m) lies 1½ca offshore. From Cove to Girdle Ness keep 5ca offshore, avoiding Hasman Rks (dry 3·4m) 1ca off Altens. Greg Ness and Girdle Ness, at SE corner of Aberdeen Bay, are fringed by rks drying 2ca SE of lt ho. Girdlestone is a rocky patch, depth<2m, ENE of the lt.

▶ *Off Girdle Ness the S-going stream begins at HW Aberdeen -0430, and the N-going at HW Aberdeen +0130, Sp rates 2·5kn. A race forms on S-going stream.* ◀

(AC 213) Few dangers lie between Aberdeen and Buchan Ness. Black Dog firing range 4½M N of Aberdeen is marked by SPM; the seaward buoy Fl(5)Y 20s (AIS), is within the Aberdeen Offshore wind farm (11 turbines). Drums Links 4¼M further North, is not buoyed; red flags/lights are shown when firing.

R Ythan, 1·75M SSW of Hackley Hd, is navigable by small craft, but channel shifts constantly. 3M North is the very small harbour of Collieston (mostly dries), only accessible in fine weather. 4¾M NNE of Hackley Head The Skares, rocks (marked by lit PHM) extend 3½ca from South arm of Cruden Bay, where there is a temp'y ⚓ in offshore winds. On N side of Cruden B is Port Erroll (dries 2·5m).

4.5 EYEMOUTH

Borders **55°52´·52N 02°05´·29W** ❀❀☆◊◊✿✿✿

CHARTS AC 160, 1612, 5615; Imray C24

TIDES +0330 Dover; ML No data; Duration 0610

Standard Port LEITH (→)

Times				Height (metres)			
High Water		Low Water		MHWS	MHWN	MLWN	MLWS
0300	0900	0300	0900	5·2	4·1	2·0	0·9
1500	2100	1500	2100				
Differences EYEMOUTH							
−0005	+0007	+0012	+0008	−0·4	−0·3	0·0	+0·1

SHELTER Good but for uncomfortable surge in N over F5. Busy FV hbr which encourages yachtsmen. Berth as directed by HM:
- On Middle Quay (100m pontoon), depth 0.9m on gravel bed.
- ⚓ in bay only in offshore winds.

NAVIGATION WPT 55°52´·80N 02°05´·34W, 174°/3ca to E bkwtr lt.

- Appr from N of Hurkars avoiding Blind Buss, depth 1·2m.
- From the S, approach on 250° midway between Hurkars and Hettle Scar (no ldg marks).
- Contact HM Ch 12 (mob 07885 742505) for depth/latest info.
- Entry should not be attempted in strong N to E winds.
- F.R ⬤ (occas) or R flag indicates unsafe to enter bay or hbr.

Entrance is 17m wide; maintained depth 3m may be reduced by frequent sand movement and silting. E of E pier inwards CD reduces to 1m. Depth 0.8m on ❷ pontoon but very shallow by RNLI office. Inbound keep to W side of chan until past lift bridge. Contact HM for latest depth information.

LIGHTS AND MARKS St Abbs Hd lt ho Fl 10s 68m 26M is 3M NW. Ldg lts 174° both FG 9/10m 6M, orange columns on W pier.

COMMUNICATIONS (Code 01890) Dr 750599, Ⓗ (0131) 536 1000. HM 750223, Mobile 07885 742505.
VHF Ch 16 12 (HO). Listen to VHF Ch 6 for FV movements.

FACILITIES Hbr www.eyemouth-harbour.co.uk ⚓ ♨. For 10m LOA £19·00 (quay), £23·80 (pontoon) discount >3 nts. ⚓ �⌦ Ⓞ �llⓌ ⛴ (at harbour bldg). ✕ ⚒ Ⓑ Ⓔ ♨ ⌇(12t mob) wi-fi.

Town LB, ⛽ ⓐ ⚒ ✕ ⬜ ⊠ Ⓞ ▮ Ⓑ. ⇌ (bus to Berwick-on-Tweed and Edinburgh), ✈ (Edinburgh).

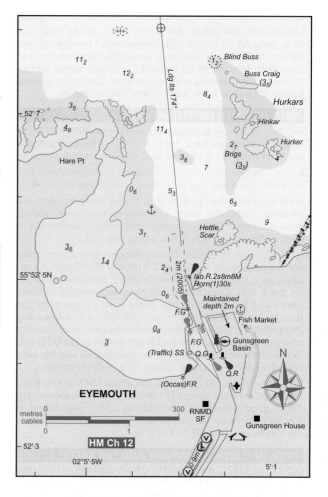

ADJACENT HARBOURS – EYEMOUTH

BURNMOUTH, Borders, **55°50´·61N 02°04´·10W**. AC 160. HW +0315 on Dover, −0025 on Leith; Duration 0615. Use Eyemouth tides 4.5. From S beware Quarry Shoal Rks; and E and W Carrs from N. 2 W posts (unclear by day, FR 29/35m 4M) 45m apart, lead 253° to close N of the hbr; as hbr mouth opens, enter on about 185° with outer hbr ent in line with 2FG (vert). Min depth at ent at LWS is 0·6m. Shelter is good especially in inner hbr (dries). With onshore winds, swell makes outer hbr uncomfortable. HM (018907) 81283 (home). Facilities: ♨ £10 (all LOA), ⚓ limited ⚒.

ST ABB'S, Borders, **55°54´·10N 02°07´·74W**. AC 175. HW +0330 on Dover, −0017 on Leith; HW −0·6m on Leith; Duration 0605. Ldg line (about 228°) S face of Maw Carr on village hall (conspic R roof) leads SW until the hbr ent opens to port and the 2nd ldg line (about 176°) can be seen 2FR 2/4m 1M, or Y LB ho visible through ent. On E side of ent chan, beware Hog's Nose and on W side the Maw Carr. Shelter good. In strong onshore winds outer hbr suffers from waves breaking over E pier. Inner hbr (dries) is best but often full of FVs. HM (0775 1136758) directs visitors. Facilities: ♨ £15 (all LOA) ⚓ (launching £15), ⚓ ⏌⌦ at quay, ⊠ ⚒ ✕ more facilities & ⬜ at Coldingham.

ADJACENT HARBOUR – DUNBAR

NORTH BERWICK, East Lothian, **56°03´·74N 02°43´·04W**. AC 734. Fidra HW +0344 on Dover; ML 3·0m; Duration 0625. See 4.6 Fidra. Shelter good with winds from S to W but dangerous with onshore winds. Very small drying harbour with entrance 8m wide. Max LOA normally 30´; LOA >40´ only in emergency. From E or W, from position 0·25M S of Craigleith, steer S for Plattock Rks, thence SSW 40m off harbour wall (beware Maiden Rocks to the W) before turning 180° to port into hbr. Galloway Pier extends N from hbr wall.

Bkwtr light F R 7m 3M and FG 6m 3M (about 1ca S) in transit 188° (2 F R (vert) when harbour closed). Facilities: ⚓⚓ on pier, ♨ £15, HM www.nbharbour.org.uk ☎(01620) 893333, mob 0777 6467373.

East Lothian YC ☎(01620) 892698, ⚓ Ⓞs ⬜.

Town ⛽ ⛽ ▮ ⊠ Ⓑ ⚒ ⇌ and bus Edinburgh.

4.6 DUNBAR

East Lothian 56°00'·39N 02°31'·09W ✿✿◊◊◊ ✿✿✿

CHARTS AC 175, 734, 5615; Imray C24, C23, C27

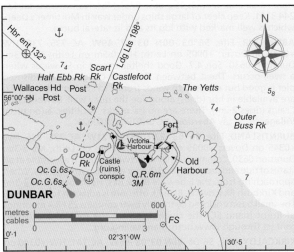

TIDES +0330 Dover; ML 3·0; Duration 0600

Standard Port LEITH (→)

Times				Height (metres)			
High Water		Low Water		MHWS	MHWN	MLWN	MLWS
0300	0900	0300	0900	5·6	4·4	2·0	0·8
1500	2100	1500	2100				
Differences DUNBAR							
−0005	+0003	+0003	−0003	−0·3	−0·3	0·0	+0·1
FIDRA							
−0001	0000	−0002	+0001	−0·2	−0·2	0·0	0·0

SHELTER Outer (Victoria) Hbr is subject to surge in strong NW to NE winds. N side dries; ❷ berth signed by rubber ladder on W wall beneath castle, dries approx HW±2. Contact HM. Keep steps clear. Inner (Old or Cromwell) Hbr dries and is safe in strong onshore conditions; enter under bridge, lifted by HM on request.

NAVIGATION WPT 56°00'·60N 02°31'·49W, 132°/3ca to hbr ent, preferable entry in marginal conditions.

- Entry is dangerous in heavy onshore swell with no access in strong winds from NW to E.
- Beware Wallace's Head Rock, Half Ebb Rock (2₁m), 1½ca from ent. and Outer Buss 4ca E of ent.
- Min depth at ent 0·5m, but may be much less in abnormal circumstances.
- Keep to port on entry to avoid rockfall off castle.

LIGHTS AND MARKS Church and Castle ruin both conspic. From NE, ldg lts, Oc G 6s 15/22m 3M, synch, intens 188°-208°, 2 W △ on Or cols, lead 198° through the outer rks to the Roads; thence narrow ent opens with QR brg 132°. From NW, appr on brg 132° between bns on Wallaces Head and Half Ebb Rk.

COMMUNICATIONS (01368) Dr 863704; Ⓗ (0131) 536 1000; HM mob 07958 754858, Dep HM 07583 463991.

FACILITIES www.dunbarharbourtrust.co.uk **Quay** ⟼ (launch £10) ⊜ £16 (£20 >12m LOA), ⚓ ⛟.

N Wall ⊜; **Inner Hbr** ⚓ ⟼ ⊜.

Town ⚑ 🏕 🏪 ⚒ ⊗ ✉ Ⓑ 🛒 ✕ 🏠 ⇌ ✈ Edinburgh.

4.7 FIRTH OF FORTH

E and W Lothian/City of Edinburgh/Fife

CHARTS AC 734, 735, 736, 737, 741, 5615; Imray C23, C27

TIDES +0350 (Granton) Dover; ML 3·3; Duration 0620

Standard Port LEITH (→)

Times				Height (metres)			
High Water		Low Water		MHWS	MHWN	MLWN	MLWS
0300	0900	0300	0900	5·6	4·4	2·0	0·8
1500	2100	1500	2100				
Differences COCKENZIE							
−0007	−0015	−0013	−0005	−0·2	0·0	ND	ND
GRANTON: Same as LEITH							

SHELTER Port Edgar offers good shelter, but strong surge at LW esp in E winds. Silting in centre of entrance and close to wavebreak. Granton mostly dries but is open to violent swell in N'lies. Pontoons on E side of Middle Pier in about 2m and RFYC welcomes visitors. Pilot launches berth at seaward end. Leith is purely commercial. Rosyth should only be used in emergency. Forth Navigation Service controls Firth of Forth, Granton Hbr and all commercial docks.

NAVIGATION Port Edgar 56°N 03°24'·3W, 244°/3ca to W bkwtr. Do not enter E of wavebreak, beware of shallows at W end; 3kn sp limit. Granton WPT 56°00'·00N 03°13'·31W, 180°/0·72M to entry.

- Beware Hound Pt terminal 12kn speed limit W of Rlwy Bridge.
- N shore, no vessel may enter Mortimer's Deep (Braefoot gas terminal) without approval from Forth Navigation Service.
- Protected chan runs from Nos 13 & 14 buoys (NNW of Oxcars) under the bridges (N of Inch Garvie and Beamer Rk), to Rosyth. When activated by Forth Ports, vessels must clear the channel.
- Caution: strong tidal streams.

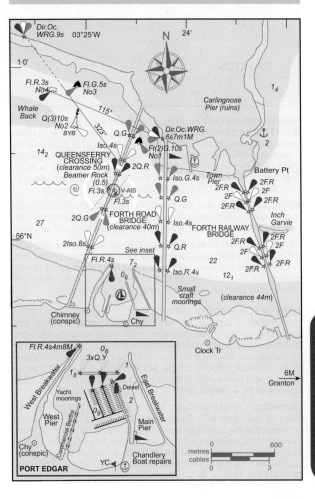

LIGHTS AND MARKS See 4.3 and chartlets.

COMMUNICATIONS (Code 0131) Ⓗ Edinburgh Royal Infirmary 2292477; Forth and Tay Navigation Service (01324) 498584; QHM Rosyth (01383) 425050. HMNB CLYDE (01436) 674321 ext 3206, for naval activity off Scotland; Forth Yacht Clubs Ass'n 5523452.

Call *Forth Navigation* (at Grangemouth) Ch **71** (calling and info, H24) 16; **20** 12 will be used if necessary. Leith Hbr Radio Ch 12.

FACILITIES

GRANTON Extensive development is taking place in NW of W Hbr. Entry prohibited when R flag with W diagonal cross flown (or ●) on mast at middle pier hd. HM via Leith ☎555 8866, Call *Boswell* Ch M ⚓ ⬎; **Royal Forth YC** ☎552 3006, ⚓ ⬎ ⬎ ⬎(5t) ⬚; **Forth Corinthian YC** ☎552 5939, ⚓ ⬎ ⬎ ✕ ⬚.
Town 🏪 🛒 🛢 ✉ Ⓑ 🛒 ✕ ⬚ ⇌ ✈ (buses to Edinburgh).

SOUTH QUEENSFERRY Port Edgar Marina ④ www.portedgar.co.uk ☎3313330 Access H24 but floating b'water exposes berths in N'lies; boats are beam on and roll with pulpits vulnerable against piles. S pontoon offers most shelter. Comms call Ch M **80** (Apr-Sept 0900-1930; Oct-Mar 0900-1630 LT). (301 ⬚ +8Ⓥ) £3·00, ⚓ ⬎ ⚓ 🛢 ⚓ ✕ ✎ 🏪 Ⓔ ⚠(5t) N end of main pier, 🛢 @; Port Edgar YC ✕ ⬚. **Town** 🏪 🛒 ✕ ⬚ ✉ Ⓑ ⇌ (Dalmeny), ✈ Edinburgh.

ROSYTH Dockyard and ferry port; no facilities for yachts except in emergency. Comms call *QHM* Ch 74 13 73 (Mon-Fri: 0730-1700) Ferries: Zeebrugge; 3/wk; 17hrs; Superfast (www.superfast.com).

GRANGEMOUTH HM ☎01324 498566 (H24); Port Office ☎498597 (HO). VHF Ch **14** 16, H24. Commercial port. An enclosed dock, ships in the appr to the locks are constrained by their draught. Yachts making for the R Carron should take care to remain clear. LPG carriers may be expected at the new gas storage terminal.

FIRTH OF FORTH SOUTH SHORE

FISHERROW, E Lothian, **55°56'·79N 03°04'·09W**. AC 734, 735. HW +0345 on Dover, −0005 on Leith; HW −0·1m on Leith; ML 3·0m; Duration 0620. Shelter good except in NW winds when appr can be dangerous. Mainly a pleasure craft hbr, it dries 5ca offshore. High-rise block (38m) is conspic 9ca W of hbr. E pier lt, Oc 6s 5m 6M on metal framework tr. Berth on E pier. HM ☎(0131) 665 5900; **Fisherrow YC** ⚓. **Town** 🛒 🏪 🛒 from garage, ⚠ ✉ Ⓑ ✕ ⬚.

CRAMOND, City of Edinburgh, **55°59'·80N 03°17'·49W**. AC 736. Tides as Leith (see 4.7). Cramond Island, approx 1M offshore, is connected to the S shore of the Firth by a drying causeway. A chan, virtually dries, marked by 7 SHM posts, leads W of Cramond Island to Cramond hbr at the mouth of R Almond, conspic white houses. ⬚ free or ⚓ off the Is. Seek local advice from: **Cramond Boat Club** ☎(0131) 336 1356 ⚓ ⚓ ⬚. **Village** 🛒 ✕ ⬚ Bus.

FIRTH OF FORTH NORTH SHORE

INCHCOLM, Fife, **56°01'·85N 03°17'·89W**. AC 736. Tides see 4.7. Best ⚓ in 4m, N of abbey (conspic); appr from NW or ESE, to land at pier close E (small fee). Meaduslue Rks (dry) on N side. Ends of island foul. At SE end, lt Fl (3) 15s, obsc 075°-145°. No facilities. ☎0131 244 3101. Keep clear of large ships under way in Mortimer's Deep, which is well marked with ldg lts and lit lateral buoys.

ABERDOUR, Fife, **56°03'·00N 03°17'·49W**. AC 735, 736. HW +0345 on Dover; +0005 on Leith; HW 0·5m on Leith; ML 3·3m; Duration 0630. See 4.7. Good shelter except in SE winds when a swell occurs. The ⚓ between The Little Craigs and the disused pier is good but exposed to winds from E to SW. Temp berths, £7, are available in hbr (dries) alongside the quay wall. Beware Little Craigs (dries 2·2m). There are no lts/ marks. Facilities: ⚓(on pier). **Village** 🛒 ✕ ⬚. **Aberdour BC** ☎(01383) 860029.

BURNTISLAND, Fife, **56°03'·22N 03°14'·21W**. AC 735, 736. HW +0345 on Dover; +0005 on Leith; HW 0·5m on Leith; ML 3·3m; Duration 0630. Commercial hbr with two basins it is accessible at all states of tide and provides good shelter except in strong S'lies. When approaching from the E beware Black Rks, Heuchboy (dries 2·3m) and Kirkbush Rk (covers). Blae Rk offshore is adjacent to No 7 SHM. The small basin enclosed by the E'ly bwtr contains 25 F&A moorings of Burnt Island SC. The clubhouse is at the root of the bkwtr, contact through www.burntislandsailing.org.

KIRKCALDY, Fife, **56°06'·80N 03°08'·96W**. AC 741. HW +0340 on Dover, −0005 on Leith; HW −0·1m on Leith; ML 3·2m; Duration 0620. See 4.9. Hbr has outer and inner basin with good shelter; an emergency refuge except in strong E winds. Dredged in 2015 for flour mill and commercial aggregate tfc, with some local FVs. Charted depths are likely to have changed. Outer piers lit Fl G 5s /Fl R 5s respectively. W pier is high concrete wall and care needed at the ⬎. Small craft should contact Forth Ports Authority ☎01383 421800, Forth Navigation (H24) Ch 71.

METHIL, Fife, **56°10'·75N 03°00'·55W**. AC 734,741. HW +0330 Dover; −0020 and −0·1 on Leith; ML 3m; Duration 0615. Commercial activity greatly reduced; infrastructure limited. Access at all states of the tide and provides shelter from E'lies. Ent is difficult in strong E and SE winds until within lee of bwtr. In bad weather seas can pile up in the shallow appr esp on a shallow bar which forms to seaward of the bwtr lt. The Fife Energy Park has a buoyed area and wind turbine on the foreshore W of the dock entrance. This is lit on each side by 2 F R (vert) and 2 F G (vert). Dock ☎(01333) 426725. Berthing with permission at Methil Boat Club ☎(01333) 421110.

ELIE, Fife, **56°11'·20N 02°49'·29W**. AC 734. HW +0325 on Dover, −0015 on Leith; HW −0·1m on Leith; ML 3·0m; Duration 0620; Elie B provides good shelter from N winds but local knowledge is needed. Hbr dries; 3 waiting buoys available. Beware ledge off end of pier which dries. From E beware Ox Rk (dries 1m) 5M ENE of Elie Ness; from W beware rks off Chapel Ness, W Vows, E Vows (surmounted by cage bn) and Thill Rk, marked by PHM buoy. Lt: Elie Ness Fl 6s 15m 17M, W tr. HM (01333) 330219; ⬚ (3) drying £10/night, ⚓ ⬎ ⚓ ⠇ 🛢. SC. Police 08456 005702. Dr ☎330302. Services: 🛢(tanker) 🛢 🛢. Elie and Earlsferry: ✉ Ⓑ 🛒 ✕ ⬚.

ST MONANS, Fife, **56°12'·25 N 02°45'·94W**. AC 734. HW +0335 on Dover, −0020 on Leith; HW −0·1m on Leith; ML 3·0m; Duration 0620. Shelter good except in strong SE to SW winds when scend occurs in the hbr (dries). Berth alongside E pier until contact with HM. From NE keep at least 2½ca from coast. Bkwtr hd Oc WRG 6s 5m 7/4M; E pier hd 2 FG (vert) 6m 4M. W pier hd 2 FR (vert) 6m 4M. Facilities: HM ☎07930 869538 (part time) if no reply, 01333 310836 (Anstruther HM assists); ⬚ (example for 10m LOA) £17.20 then £8.60/day thereafter, ⚓ ⠇, 🛢; Services: 🛢(tanker ☎730622) 🛢 ⠇. Police ☎08456 005702. Village ✉ Ⓑ 🛒 ✕ ⬚.

PITTENWEEM, Fife, **56°12'·60N 02°43'·79W**. AC 734. HW +0325 Dover, −0015 and −0·1m on Leith; ML 3m; Duration 0620. Busy fishing hbr, dredged 1-2m, access all tides, but seek advice before entering at LW springs. Yachts not encouraged; contact HM for berth at W end of inner hbr, but only for emergency use. Outer hbr dries to rock; is only suitable for temp stop in calm weather. Appr 037° on ldg marks/lts, W cols, both FR 3/8m 5M. Rks to port marked by bn, Fl R 4s 3m 2M, and 3 unlit bns. VHF Ch 11 (0700-2100 Mon-Fri) or Forth CG Ch 16 (other times). HM ☎(01333) 312591. Facilities: ⚓ 🛢 🛢(tanker: ☎730622) 🛢 🛒 ⬚.

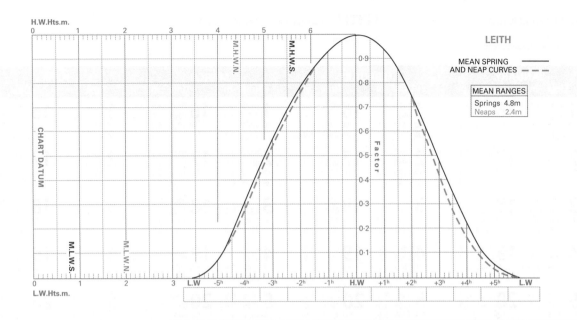

LEITH

MEAN SPRING ⎯⎯⎯⎯
AND NEAP CURVES ⎯ ⎯ ⎯

MEAN RANGES
Springs 4.8m
Neaps 2.4m

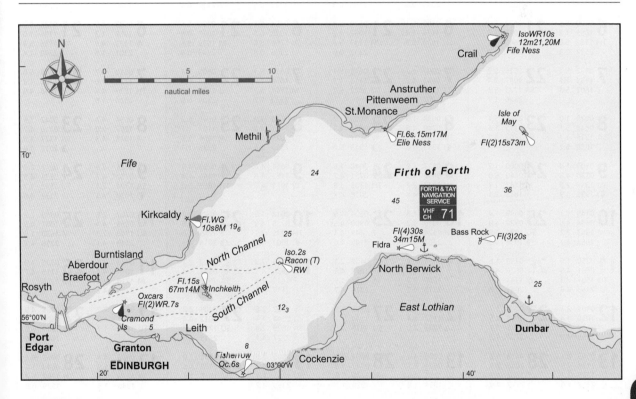

OFFSHORE ISLAND

ISLE OF MAY, Fife, 56°11´·40N 02°33´·69W. AC 734. HW +0325 on Dover, –0025 on Leith. In settled weather and wind dependent ⚓ at E or W Tarbert in 4m; landing at Altarstanes. Near the SE tip there is a tiny hbr at Kirkhaven (where restrictions may apply). Narrow, rky ent; mooing fore-and-aft to rings in rks, in about 1-1·5m. Beware Norman Rk to N of Island, and Maiden Hair Rk to S. Warden in residence Easter to late October when visitor centre opens 1000-1730 BST. Call on VHF Ch 16 or **6**, or on first landing.

The island is a National Nature Reserve managed by Scottish National Heritage (☎01334 654038).

Sensitive seasons: (a) breeding birds Apr to Sep; (b) breeding seals Oct to Jan; (c) moulting seals Jan to Mar. Land only at Alterstanes or Kirkhaven. Avoid marked areas to minimise disturbance to wildlife and ongoing conservation experiments.

No overnight accommodation or camping.

STANDARD TIME (UT)
For Summer Time add ONE hour in **non-shaded areas**

LEITH LAT 55°59'N LONG 3°11'W
TIMES AND HEIGHTS OF HIGH AND LOW WATERS

Dates in red are **SPRINGS**
Dates in blue are **NEAPS**

YEAR **2022**

JANUARY

Day	Time	m	Time	m	Day	Time	m	Time	m
1 SA	0041	5.4			16 SU	0140	4.8		
	0651	1.2				0719	1.7		
	1308	5.4				1358	5.0		
	1913	1.1				1946	1.5		
2 SU	0136	5.6			17 M	0218	5.0		
	0747	1.0				0754	1.6		
	1357	5.6				1434	5.1		
	●2013	0.9				○2023	1.3		
3 M	0228	5.8			18 TU	0254	5.1		
	0840	0.9				0830	1.4		
	1446	5.7				1508	5.2		
	2109	0.6				2100	1.1		
4 TU	0319	5.8			19 W	0328	5.2		
	0929	0.9				0905	1.4		
	1534	5.7				1541	5.3		
	2202	0.5				2137	1.0		
5 W	0410	5.8			20 TH	0402	5.2		
	1016	1.0				0941	1.3		
	1623	5.7				1614	5.3		
	2251	0.6				2214	1.0		
6 TH	0500	5.6			21 F	0438	5.2		
	1059	1.2				1016	1.3		
	1712	5.6				1648	5.3		
	2337	0.8				2251	1.0		
7 F	0552	5.4			22 SA	0516	5.2		
	1139	1.5				1047	1.4		
	1803	5.4				1723	5.2		
						2326	1.1		
8 SA	0020	1.0			23 SU	0556	5.1		
	0644	5.1				1115	1.5		
	1215	1.7				1802	5.2		
	1858	5.2							
9 SU	0103	1.4			24 M	0000	1.2		
	0738	4.8				0640	5.0		
	1257	2.0				1147	1.7		
	◐1955	4.9				1846	5.1		
10 M	0149	1.7			25 TU	0039	1.4		
	0834	4.6				0729	4.8		
	1353	2.2				1234	1.8		
	2053	4.7				◐1938	4.9		
11 TU	0250	1.9			26 W	0130	1.6		
	0931	4.5				0826	4.7		
	1507	2.3				1343	2.0		
	2153	4.6				2043	4.8		
12 W	0403	2.1			27 TH	0243	1.7		
	1030	4.4				0934	4.6		
	1621	2.3				1519	2.1		
	2255	4.5				2204	4.7		
13 TH	0508	2.1			28 F	0418	1.8		
	1133	4.5				1046	4.7		
	1725	2.1				1652	1.9		
	2358	4.6				2322	4.9		
14 F	0559	2.0			29 SA	0538	1.7		
	1231	4.7				1155	4.9		
	1820	1.9				1807	1.6		
15 SA	0054	4.7			30 SU	0032	5.1		
	0642	1.9				0645	1.5		
	1318	4.9				1256	5.1		
	1906	1.7				1915	1.2		
					31 M	0131	5.4		
						0742	1.2		
						1349	5.4		
						2015	0.8		

FEBRUARY

Day	Time	m	Day	Time	m
1 TU	0223	5.6	16 W	0236	5.1
	0833	1.0		0817	1.4
	1437	5.6		1451	5.3
	●2107	0.5		○2047	1.0
2 W	0311	5.7	17 TH	0309	5.3
	0918	0.9		0853	1.2
	1523	5.8		1523	5.4
	2153	0.4		2124	0.8
3 TH	0357	5.7	18 F	0342	5.4
	1000	0.9		0928	1.0
	1608	5.8		1554	5.5
	2235	0.4		2200	0.6
4 F	0441	5.6	19 SA	0416	5.4
	1038	1.0		1002	1.0
	1652	5.7		1627	5.5
	2313	0.6		2235	0.6
5 SA	0525	5.4	20 SU	0452	5.4
	1109	1.1		1030	1.0
	1736	5.5		1701	5.5
	2345	0.9		2306	0.8
6 SU	0609	5.1	21 M	0530	5.3
	1134	1.4		1052	1.2
	1820	5.3		1739	5.4
				2332	0.9
7 M	0007	1.2	22 TU	0611	5.1
	0653	4.8		1119	1.3
	1202	1.7		1822	5.1
	1907	5.0			
8 TU	0034	1.6	23 W	0002	1.2
	0740	4.6		0657	4.9
	1245	2.0		1201	1.6
	◐1959	4.6		◑1913	5.0
9 W	0117	1.9	24 TH	0048	1.6
	0832	4.3		0751	4.7
	1347	2.2		1303	1.8
	2058	4.4		2018	4.7
10 TH	0223	2.3	25 F	0204	1.9
	0930	4.2		0900	4.5
	1524	2.4		1449	2.1
	2202	4.2		2146	4.6
11 F	0411	2.4	26 SA	0407	2.1
	1036	4.2		1023	4.5
	1656	2.3		1652	1.9
	2316	4.2		2316	4.7
12 SA	0530	2.3	27 SU	0537	1.9
	1152	4.4		1144	4.7
	1803	2.0		1815	1.5
13 SU	0030	4.4	28 M	0031	5.0
	0624	2.1		0643	1.6
	1255	4.6		1249	5.0
	1854	1.8		1920	1.1
14 M	0122	4.7			
	0705	1.8			
	1340	4.9			
	1935	1.5			
15 TU	0202	4.9			
	0742	1.6			
	1417	5.1			
	2012	1.2			

MARCH

Day	Time	m	Day	Time	m
1 TU	0128	5.3	16 W	0135	4.9
	0735	1.3		0723	1.6
	1341	5.3		1350	5.0
	2011	0.7		1951	1.1
2 W	0215	5.5	17 TH	0210	5.1
	0819	1.0		0757	1.2
	1425	5.6		1424	5.3
	●2055	0.4		2026	0.8
3 TH	0257	5.6	18 F	0243	5.3
	0900	0.8		0832	1.0
	1506	5.7		1456	5.5
	2135	0.3		○2102	0.5
4 F	0337	5.6	19 SA	0316	5.5
	0937	0.7		0907	0.8
	1547	5.8		1528	5.6
	2211	0.3		2138	0.4
5 SA	0416	5.5	20 SU	0350	5.6
	1010	0.8		0941	0.7
	1627	5.7		1602	5.7
	2243	0.5		2212	0.4
6 SU	0454	5.4	21 M	0426	5.5
	1038	0.9		1010	0.8
	1706	5.5		1639	5.6
	2306	0.8		2243	0.6
7 M	0532	5.1	22 TU	0505	5.4
	1058	1.2		1033	0.9
	1744	5.2		1720	5.5
	2320	1.2		2308	0.9
8 TU	0610	4.9	23 W	0546	5.2
	1121	1.4		1102	1.1
	1825	4.9		1806	5.3
	2343	1.5		2338	1.3
9 W	0651	4.6	24 TH	0632	4.9
	1155	1.8		1146	1.4
	1911	4.6		1859	5.0
10 TH	0018	1.9	25 F	0029	1.7
	0738	4.3		0727	4.6
	1245	2.1		1255	1.8
	◐2007	4.3		◑2010	4.6
11 F	0115	2.3	26 SA	0203	2.1
	0836	4.1		0842	4.4
	1413	2.4		1508	2.0
	2113	4.1		2143	4.5
12 SA	0302	2.6	27 SU	0409	2.2
	0944	4.1		1012	4.4
	1629	2.4		1701	1.7
	2227	4.1		2313	4.6
13 SU	0505	2.5	28 M	0531	2.0
	1103	4.2		1135	4.6
	1745	2.1		1815	1.3
	2355	4.2			
14 M	0604	2.2	29 TU	0025	4.9
	1222	4.4		0630	1.6
	1835	1.7		1237	5.0
				1911	1.0
15 TU	0055	4.6	30 W	0117	5.2
	0647	1.9		0716	1.3
	1312	4.7		1325	5.3
	1916	1.4		1955	0.7
			31 TH	0159	5.4
				0756	1.0
				1406	5.5
				2033	0.5

APRIL

Day	Time	m	Day	Time	m
1 F	0236	5.5	16 SA	0210	5.4
	0834	0.8		0802	0.9
	1445	5.6		1424	5.5
	●2109	0.4		○2032	0.5
2 SA	0312	5.5	17 SU	0246	5.6
	0909	0.7		0839	0.7
	1523	5.6		1500	5.7
	2141	0.5		2110	0.4
3 SU	0348	5.4	18 M	0323	5.6
	0942	0.7		0916	0.6
	1600	5.5		1538	5.8
	2208	0.7		2148	0.4
4 M	0423	5.3	19 TU	0401	5.6
	1009	0.9		0953	0.6
	1637	5.4		1620	5.7
	2227	1.0		2224	0.7
5 TU	0458	5.1	20 W	0442	5.5
	1029	1.1		1027	0.8
	1714	5.1		1706	5.6
	2240	1.3		2259	1.0
6 W	0533	4.9	21 TH	0526	5.3
	1050	1.3		1106	1.0
	1753	4.9		1756	5.3
	2301	1.6		2340	1.4
7 TH	0610	4.7	22 F	0615	5.0
	1120	1.6		1202	1.3
	1836	4.6		1856	4.9
	2334	1.9			
8 F	0654	4.4	23 SA	0042	1.9
	1207	2.0		0716	4.7
	1928	4.3		1327	1.6
				◑2012	4.6
9 SA	0025	2.3	24 SU	0217	2.2
	0750	4.2		0836	4.5
	1324	2.3		1522	1.7
	◑2030	4.1		2137	4.6
10 SU	0202	2.6	25 M	0355	2.2
	0858	4.1		1001	4.5
	1540	2.3		1650	1.5
	2140	4.1		2258	4.7
11 M	0426	2.5	26 TU	0505	1.9
	1014	4.1		1115	4.7
	1710	2.0		1755	1.2
	2258	4.2			
12 TU	0528	2.2	27 W	0005	4.9
	1131	4.3		0600	1.7
	1759	1.7		1215	5.0
				1847	1.0
13 W	0008	4.5	28 TH	0055	5.1
	0612	1.9		0646	1.4
	1229	4.7		1302	5.2
	1840	1.3		1929	0.8
14 TH	0055	4.8	29 F	0135	5.3
	0649	1.5		0726	1.1
	1312	5.0		1343	5.3
	1918	1.0		2005	0.7
15 F	0134	5.2	30 SA	0212	5.3
	0725	1.2		0804	0.9
	1349	5.3		1421	5.4
	1954	0.7		●2037	0.7

Chart Datum: 2·90 metres below Ordnance Datum (Newlyn). HAT is 6·3 metres above Chart Datum.

STANDARD TIME (UT)
For Summer Time add ONE hour in **non-shaded areas**

LEITH   LAT 55°59'N   LONG 3°11'W
TIMES AND HEIGHTS OF HIGH AND LOW WATERS

Dates in red are **SPRINGS**
Dates in blue are NEAPS

YEAR 2022

MAY

Day	Time m	Time m	Time m	Time m
1 SU	0247 5.3	0840 0.8	1459 5.4	2107 0.8
2 M	0321 5.3	0914 0.8	1536 5.3	2132 0.9
3 TU	0355 5.2	0944 1.0	1613 5.2	2152 1.2
4 W	0428 5.1	1009 1.1	1650 5.0	2211 1.4
5 TH	0502 4.9	1034 1.3	1728 4.8	2236 1.6
6 F	0539 4.7	1106 1.5	1810 4.6	2310 1.9
7 SA	0621 4.5	1152 1.8	1858 4.4	
8 SU	0000 2.2	0712 4.3	1257 2.0	1953 4.3
9 M	0121 2.5	0815 4.2	1421 2.1	2057 4.2
10 TU	0310 2.5	0926 4.2	1607 1.9	2205 4.3
11 W	0432 2.2	1036 4.4	1706 1.6	2311 4.5
12 TH	0523 1.9	1137 4.6	1752 1.3	
13 F	0007 4.8	0606 1.6	1227 5.0	1834 1.0
14 SA	0054 5.1	0647 1.3	1311 5.3	1916 0.8
15 SU	0136 5.4	0728 1.0	1352 5.5	1959 0.6
16 M	0216 5.5	0811 0.7	1435 5.7	2043 0.5
17 TU	0257 5.6	0857 0.6	1519 5.8	2128 0.6
18 W	0340 5.6	0945 0.6	1607 5.7	2213 0.8
19 TH	0425 5.5	1034 0.7	1657 5.6	2300 1.1
20 F	0513 5.3	1126 0.9	1752 5.3	2350 1.5
21 SA	0607 5.1	1225 1.1	1854 5.0	
22 SU	0049 1.8	0711 4.9	1338 1.3	2005 4.8
23 M	0203 2.0	0826 4.7	1503 1.4	2118 4.7
24 TU	0320 2.1	0939 4.7	1618 1.4	2228 4.7
25 W	0425 1.9	1045 4.8	1721 1.3	2331 4.8
26 TH	0519 1.7	1144 4.9	1813 1.2	
27 F	0023 4.9	0608 1.5	1234 5.0	1856 1.2
28 SA	0107 5.0	0652 1.3	1319 5.1	1930 1.1
29 SU	0146 5.1	0734 1.2	1400 5.2	2002 1.1
30 M	0223 5.2	0813 1.1	1439 5.2	2031 1.1
31 TU	0258 5.2	0849 1.0	1516 5.1	2059 1.2

JUNE

Day	Time m	Time m	Time m	Time m
1 W	0331 5.1	0922 1.1	1553 5.1	2127 1.3
2 TH	0405 5.1	0953 1.2	1629 5.0	2155 1.5
3 F	0439 5.0	1025 1.3	1707 4.9	2226 1.6
4 SA	0516 4.8	1101 1.4	1747 4.8	2302 1.8
5 SU	0557 4.7	1144 1.6	1832 4.6	2347 2.0
6 M	0642 4.6	1235 1.7	1921 4.5	
7 TU	0047 2.2	0736 4.5	1336 1.8	2017 4.4
8 W	0203 2.3	0837 4.4	1449 1.8	2119 4.5
9 TH	0323 2.2	0943 4.5	1600 1.6	2222 4.6
10 F	0427 2.0	1046 4.7	1659 1.4	2322 4.8
11 SA	0520 1.7	1144 4.9	1750 1.2	
12 SU	0015 5.1	0609 1.4	1237 5.2	1841 1.0
13 M	0105 5.3	0659 1.1	1327 5.4	1932 0.8
14 TU	0151 5.5	0751 0.8	1417 5.6	2024 0.8
15 W	0237 5.6	0847 0.6	1507 5.7	2116 0.8
16 TH	0324 5.6	0943 0.5	1558 5.7	2207 0.9
17 F	0412 5.6	1036 0.5	1650 5.6	2256 1.1
18 SA	0503 5.5	1129 0.6	1745 5.4	2344 1.3
19 SU	0558 5.3	1223 0.8	1843 5.2	
20 M	0034 1.6	0658 5.1	1320 1.1	1945 5.0
21 TU	0130 1.8	0803 5.0	1423 1.3	2047 4.8
22 W	0231 2.0	0906 4.9	1530 1.5	2148 4.7
23 TH	0335 2.0	1008 4.8	1633 1.6	2248 4.6
24 F	0435 1.9	1107 4.8	1729 1.6	2346 4.7
25 SA	0531 1.8	1204 4.8	1815 1.6	
26 SU	0037 4.8	0623 1.6	1256 4.8	1854 1.5
27 M	0122 4.9	0709 1.4	1342 4.9	1928 1.5
28 TU	0202 5.0	0751 1.3	1423 5.0	2002 1.4
29 W	0239 5.1	0829 1.2	1500 5.0	2035 1.4
30 TH	0314 5.1	0904 1.1	1535 5.0	2108 1.4

JULY

Day	Time m	Time m	Time m	Time m
1 F	0347 5.1	0939 1.1	1611 5.0	2142 1.4
2 SA	0422 5.1	1015 1.1	1647 5.0	2217 1.5
3 SU	0457 5.0	1052 1.2	1725 4.9	2253 1.6
4 M	0535 4.9	1131 1.3	1806 4.9	2329 1.7
5 TU	0614 4.9	1212 1.4	1850 4.8	
6 W	0009 1.9	0659 4.8	1257 1.5	1940 4.7
7 TH	0101 2.0	0750 4.7	1351 1.6	2035 4.6
8 F	0211 2.1	0850 4.7	1455 1.6	2137 4.6
9 SA	0328 2.0	0959 4.7	1608 1.6	2241 4.7
10 SU	0439 1.8	1109 4.8	1717 1.4	2343 4.9
11 M	0543 1.6	1213 5.1	1819 1.3	
12 TU	0041 5.1	0644 1.2	1312 5.3	1918 1.1
13 W	0134 5.4	0746 0.9	1406 5.6	2015 1.0
14 TH	0223 5.6	0846 0.6	1458 5.7	2108 0.9
15 F	0312 5.7	0940 0.4	1548 5.8	2157 0.9
16 SA	0401 5.7	1031 0.3	1638 5.7	2242 0.9
17 SU	0450 5.7	1118 0.4	1728 5.5	2325 1.1
18 M	0540 5.6	1203 0.6	1820 5.3	
19 TU	0005 1.3	0633 5.4	1245 0.9	1913 5.0
20 W	0044 1.6	0728 5.1	1328 1.3	2007 4.8
21 TH	0131 1.9	0826 4.9	1417 1.7	2102 4.6
22 F	0234 2.1	0925 4.7	1524 1.9	2200 4.5
23 SA	0350 2.1	1027 4.5	1637 2.0	2302 4.5
24 SU	0502 2.0	1133 4.5	1737 2.0	
25 M	0005 4.6	0603 1.9	1235 4.6	1825 1.9
26 TU	0100 4.8	0653 1.7	1327 4.7	1905 1.8
27 W	0145 4.9	0736 1.4	1409 4.9	1941 1.6
28 TH	0223 5.1	0814 1.2	1445 5.0	2017 1.5
29 F	0258 5.2	0849 1.1	1518 5.1	2052 1.4
30 SA	0331 5.2	0925 0.9	1551 5.2	2128 1.3
31 SU	0403 5.3	1001 0.9	1625 5.2	2203 1.3

AUGUST

Day	Time m	Time m	Time m	Time m
1 M	0436 5.3	1037 0.9	1701 5.2	2236 1.3
2 TU	0510 5.2	1111 1.0	1739 5.1	2303 1.4
3 W	0546 5.1	1143 1.1	1819 5.0	2330 1.6
4 TH	0626 5.0	1215 1.3	1904 4.9	
5 F	0007 1.7	0712 4.9	1257 1.5	1955 4.7
6 SA	0104 1.9	0809 4.8	1359 1.7	2056 4.6
7 SU	0229 2.0	0923 4.7	1529 1.8	2208 4.6
8 M	0414 2.0	1046 4.7	1702 1.8	2320 4.8
9 TU	0536 1.7	1202 5.0	1813 1.6	
10 W	0026 5.0	0646 1.3	1306 5.3	1914 1.3
11 TH	0123 5.3	0748 0.8	1359 5.6	2007 1.1
12 F	0212 5.6	0842 0.5	1448 5.8	2035 0.8
13 SA	0258 5.8	0930 0.2	1533 5.8	2139 0.7
14 SU	0343 5.9	1014 0.1	1618 5.8	2220 0.8
15 M	0428 5.9	1055 0.3	1703 5.6	2257 0.9
16 TU	0514 5.7	1132 0.6	1748 5.3	2328 1.2
17 W	0600 5.5	1202 1.0	1833 5.0	2356 1.5
18 TH	0647 5.1	1226 1.4	1921 4.8	
19 F	0032 1.8	0741 4.8	1300 1.8	2013 4.5
20 SA	0129 2.1	0839 4.5	1359 2.2	2110 4.3
21 SU	0300 2.3	0944 4.3	1544 2.4	2214 4.3
22 M	0441 2.3	1057 4.3	1712 2.3	2329 4.4
23 TU	0552 2.0	1216 4.4	1808 2.2	
24 W	0038 4.6	0644 1.7	1311 4.7	1850 1.9
25 TH	0126 4.9	0725 1.4	1351 4.9	1926 1.7
26 F	0203 5.1	0759 1.2	1424 5.1	2000 1.4
27 SA	0236 5.3	0832 1.0	1455 5.2	2035 1.2
28 SU	0308 5.4	0906 0.8	1527 5.3	2109 1.1
29 M	0339 5.5	0941 0.7	1559 5.4	2143 1.0
30 TU	0410 5.5	1014 0.7	1634 5.4	2212 1.1
31 W	0443 5.5	1044 0.8	1710 5.3	2233 1.2

Chart Datum: 2·90 metres below Ordnance Datum (Newlyn). HAT is 6·3 metres above Chart Datum.

SE Scotland

》》 **FREE** monthly updates. Register at 《
www.reedsnauticalalmanac.co.uk

193

Leith tides – Forth and Clyde Canal

LEITH LAT 55°59′N LONG 3°11′W
TIMES AND HEIGHTS OF HIGH AND LOW WATERS

Dates in red are SPRINGS
Dates in blue are NEAPS

YEAR **2022**

SEPTEMBER

Day	Time m		Day	Time m
1 TH	0518 5.4 / 1108 1.0 / 1749 5.2 / 2256 1.3		**16** F	0609 5.1 / 1129 1.5 / 1836 4.8 / 2343 1.8
2 F	0559 5.2 / 1133 1.2 / 1832 5.0 / 2332 1.5		**17** SA ◐	0658 4.7 / 1201 2.0 / 1924 4.5
3 SA ◑	0646 5.0 / 1213 1.5 / 1921 4.8		**18** SU	0033 2.1 / 0755 4.4 / 1255 2.4 / 2022 4.3
4 SU	0026 1.8 / 0745 4.8 / 1320 1.9 / 2024 4.6		**19** M	0201 2.4 / 0900 4.2 / 1439 2.7 / 2129 4.2
5 M	0202 2.1 / 0906 4.6 / 1521 2.2 / 2145 4.5		**20** TU	0425 2.4 / 1014 4.1 / 1651 2.6 / 2246 4.3
6 TU	0418 2.0 / 1038 4.6 / 1703 2.0 / 2308 4.7		**21** W	0537 2.1 / 1144 4.3 / 1749 2.3
7 W	0544 1.6 / 1159 4.9 / 1811 1.7		**22** TH	0004 4.5 / 0625 1.7 / 1244 4.6 / 1830 2.0
8 TH	0017 5.0 / 0650 1.1 / 1300 5.3 / 1905 1.4		**23** F	0055 4.8 / 0702 1.4 / 1322 4.9 / 1904 1.7
9 F	0111 5.4 / 0743 0.7 / 1349 5.6 / 1952 1.1		**24** SA	0133 5.1 / 0735 1.1 / 1355 5.2 / 1937 1.4
10 SA ○	0157 5.7 / 0829 0.4 / 1432 5.8 / 2034 0.8		**25** SU ●	0206 5.3 / 0807 0.9 / 1426 5.4 / 2010 1.1
11 SU	0239 5.9 / 0911 0.2 / 1512 5.8 / 2115 0.7		**26** M	0238 5.5 / 0840 0.7 / 1457 5.5 / 2044 1.0
12 M	0320 5.9 / 0950 0.2 / 1553 5.7 / 2152 0.7		**27** TU	0309 5.6 / 0913 0.6 / 1530 5.6 / 2116 0.9
13 TU	0402 5.9 / 1025 0.4 / 1633 5.6 / 2225 0.9		**28** W	0341 5.6 / 0945 0.6 / 1605 5.6 / 2144 0.9
14 W	0444 5.7 / 1054 0.7 / 1713 5.3 / 2250 1.1		**29** TH	0417 5.6 / 1014 0.7 / 1641 5.4 / 2207 1.0
15 TH	0526 5.4 / 1112 1.1 / 1753 5.0 / 2312 1.4		**30** F	0456 5.5 / 1036 1.0 / 1721 5.3 / 2234 1.2

OCTOBER

Day	Time m		Day	Time m
1 SA	0540 5.3 / 1103 1.3 / 1805 5.1 / 2314 1.5		**16** SU	0623 4.7 / 1116 2.1 / 1840 4.6 / 2355 2.1
2 SU	0631 5.0 / 1148 1.8 / 1857 4.8		**17** M ◐	0716 4.4 / 1206 2.4 / 1936 4.3
3 M ◑	0016 1.8 / 0736 4.7 / 1317 2.2 / 2005 4.6		**18** TU	0110 2.3 / 0818 4.2 / 1337 2.8 / 2044 4.2
4 TU	0225 2.1 / 0904 4.6 / 1529 2.4 / 2134 4.5		**19** W	0346 2.4 / 0926 4.1 / 1610 2.7 / 2158 4.3
5 W	0427 1.9 / 1035 4.7 / 1657 2.1 / 2258 4.7		**20** TH	0500 2.1 / 1043 4.3 / 1712 2.4 / 2312 4.5
6 TH	0542 1.4 / 1152 5.0 / 1757 1.8		**21** F	0547 1.8 / 1154 4.6 / 1754 2.1
7 F	0004 5.1 / 0640 1.0 / 1248 5.3 / 1846 1.4		**22** SA	0010 4.8 / 0625 1.5 / 1239 4.9 / 1830 1.7
8 SA	0054 5.4 / 0726 0.7 / 1332 5.6 / 1928 1.1		**23** SU	0053 5.1 / 0659 1.2 / 1316 5.2 / 1905 1.4
9 SU ○	0137 5.7 / 0807 0.5 / 1410 5.7 / 2008 0.9		**24** M	0129 5.3 / 0732 0.9 / 1351 5.4 / 1939 1.2
10 M	0217 5.8 / 0845 0.4 / 1447 5.7 / 2046 0.8		**25** TU ●	0204 5.5 / 0806 0.7 / 1426 5.6 / 2014 1.0
11 TU	0256 5.8 / 0920 0.5 / 1525 5.6 / 2123 0.8		**26** W	0239 5.7 / 0841 0.6 / 1501 5.7 / 2048 0.9
12 W	0336 5.7 / 0951 0.7 / 1602 5.5 / 2154 0.9		**27** TH	0316 5.7 / 0916 0.7 / 1538 5.7 / 2123 0.9
13 TH	0416 5.5 / 1013 1.0 / 1640 5.3 / 2218 1.2		**28** F	0356 5.7 / 0950 0.8 / 1617 5.6 / 2156 1.0
14 F	0456 5.3 / 1025 1.3 / 1716 5.1 / 2239 1.4		**29** SA	0440 5.6 / 1022 1.1 / 1659 5.4 / 2234 1.2
15 SA	0538 5.0 / 1044 1.7 / 1755 4.8 / 2308 1.7		**30** SU	0529 5.4 / 1100 1.5 / 1746 5.1 / 2328 1.5
			31 M	0625 5.1 / 1202 2.0 / 1842 4.9

NOVEMBER

Day	Time m		Day	Time m
1 TU ●	0052 1.7 / 0735 4.8 / 1335 2.3 / 1956 4.7		**16** W ◑	0036 2.1 / 0738 4.3 / 1250 2.6 / 1958 4.4
2 W	0239 1.8 / 0859 4.7 / 1515 2.3 / 2123 4.7		**17** TH	0157 2.2 / 0839 4.3 / 1436 2.7 / 2107 4.3
3 TH	0414 1.6 / 1021 5.0 / 1631 2.1 / 2239 4.9		**18** F	0351 2.1 / 0945 4.3 / 1611 2.5 / 2214 4.5
4 F	0522 1.3 / 1131 5.0 / 1728 1.8 / 2341 5.1		**19** SA	0450 1.9 / 1050 4.5 / 1704 2.2 / 2315 4.7
5 SA	0616 1.1 / 1225 5.2 / 1816 1.5		**20** SU	0535 1.6 / 1146 4.8 / 1747 1.9
6 SU	0031 5.4 / 0702 0.9 / 1308 5.4 / 1859 1.3		**21** M	0006 5.0 / 0615 1.3 / 1233 5.1 / 1827 1.6
7 M	0115 5.5 / 0740 0.8 / 1346 5.5 / 1939 1.1		**22** TU	0050 5.2 / 0653 1.1 / 1316 5.4 / 1905 1.3
8 TU ○	0155 5.6 / 0815 0.8 / 1423 5.5 / 2019 1.0		**23** W ●	0132 5.5 / 0732 0.9 / 1355 5.5 / 1945 1.1
9 W	0235 5.6 / 0847 0.9 / 1500 5.5 / 2056 1.1		**24** TH	0214 5.6 / 0812 0.8 / 1435 5.7 / 2028 0.9
10 TH	0315 5.5 / 0915 1.0 / 1536 5.4 / 2129 1.1		**25** F	0256 5.7 / 0855 0.8 / 1515 5.7 / 2114 0.8
11 F	0354 5.4 / 0936 1.3 / 1611 5.3 / 2156 1.2		**26** SA	0342 5.7 / 0940 1.0 / 1559 5.6 / 2204 0.9
12 SA	0433 5.2 / 0954 1.5 / 1646 5.1 / 2221 1.4		**27** SU	0430 5.6 / 1028 1.2 / 1645 5.5 / 2257 1.0
13 SU	0513 4.9 / 1019 1.8 / 1722 4.9 / 2253 1.7		**28** M	0523 5.4 / 1119 1.6 / 1736 5.3 / 2355 1.2
14 M	0555 4.7 / 1053 2.0 / 1804 4.7 / 2337 1.9		**29** TU	0621 5.2 / 1216 1.9 / 1834 5.1
15 TU	0643 4.5 / 1139 2.3 / 1856 4.5		**30** W ◑	0102 1.4 / 0728 5.0 / 1324 2.1 / 1946 4.9

DECEMBER

Day	Time m		Day	Time m
1 TH	0220 1.5 / 0842 4.8 / 1439 2.2 / 2102 4.9		**16** F ◑	0105 1.9 / 0754 4.5 / 1318 2.4 / 2010 4.5
2 F	0339 1.5 / 0952 4.8 / 1549 2.1 / 2210 4.9		**17** SA	0212 2.0 / 0852 4.4 / 1441 2.4 / 2114 4.5
3 SA	0446 1.4 / 1057 4.9 / 1649 1.9 / 2311 5.0		**18** SU	0327 1.9 / 0954 4.5 / 1557 2.3 / 2219 4.6
4 SU	0544 1.4 / 1154 5.0 / 1742 1.7		**19** M	0433 1.7 / 1055 4.7 / 1656 2.1 / 2319 4.8
5 M	0005 5.1 / 0632 1.3 / 1242 5.1 / 1830 1.5		**20** TU	0527 1.5 / 1152 4.9 / 1747 1.8
6 TU	0054 5.2 / 0711 1.3 / 1324 5.2 / 1915 1.3		**21** W	0015 5.1 / 0617 1.3 / 1243 5.2 / 1836 1.5
7 W	0138 5.3 / 0744 1.3 / 1403 5.3 / 1957 1.2		**22** TH	0107 5.3 / 0706 1.2 / 1330 5.4 / 1927 1.2
8 TH ○	0220 5.3 / 0815 1.3 / 1440 5.3 / 2035 1.2		**23** F ●	0156 5.3 / 0756 1.1 / 1415 5.6 / 2020 0.9
9 F	0300 5.3 / 0844 1.4 / 1516 5.3 / 2109 1.2		**24** SA	0244 5.7 / 0847 1.0 / 1500 5.7 / 2115 0.7
10 SA	0338 5.2 / 0911 1.5 / 1550 5.2 / 2140 1.3		**25** SU	0333 5.8 / 0938 1.0 / 1547 5.7 / 2209 0.6
11 SU	0414 5.1 / 0938 1.6 / 1624 5.1 / 2211 1.3		**26** M	0423 5.7 / 1028 1.1 / 1635 5.7 / 2302 0.7
12 M	0452 5.0 / 1009 1.7 / 1659 5.0 / 2245 1.5		**27** TU	0515 5.6 / 1116 1.3 / 1726 5.5 / 2354 0.8
13 TU	0531 4.9 / 1043 1.9 / 1738 4.9 / 2324 1.6		**28** W	0610 5.4 / 1204 1.5 / 1821 5.4
14 W	0614 4.7 / 1123 2.1 / 1822 4.7		**29** TH	0046 1.0 / 0709 5.1 / 1253 1.8 / 1923 5.2
15 TH	0010 1.8 / 0701 4.6 / 1212 2.3 / 1913 4.6		**30** F ◐	0143 1.3 / 0811 4.9 / 1349 2.0 / 2029 5.0
			31 SA	0246 1.5 / 0914 4.7 / 1454 2.1 / 2134 4.9

Chart Datum: 2·90 metres below Ordnance Datum (Newlyn). HAT is 6·3 metres above Chart Datum.

FREE monthly updates. Register at
www.reedsnauticalalmanac.co.uk

4.8 FORTH AND CLYDE CANAL

Lowland Carron River Ent. **51°02'·30N 03°41'·46W** ❀♢♢♧♧

These notes are for the convenience of those entering the canal at Grangemouth. The eastern extension by-passes low bridges and gives access to the Forth via R Carron through either Carron or Helix locks, which handle boats of different sizes in daylight 0800–2000. The two legs join at Kelpies Lock 1a.

CHARTS AC 737, 741, 5615; Imray C27; *The Skipper's Guide* Forth & Clyde and Union Canal essential. Obtain from, Lowland Canals Office, Canal House, Applecross Street, Glasgow, G4 9SP. ☎(0141) 332 6936, www.scottishcanals.co.uk or www.waterscape.com.

TIDES Carron River +0325 Dover, 0030 Leith.
Helix 1 lock - HW–4 - HW+2½; Carron lock - HW–4 - HW+1½.

SHELTER Temporary berthing at Grangemouth YC or at nearby Refuge Posts. Pontoon outside Helix and Carron sea locks. Temp'y ⚓s close WNW of Carron PHM and close SSW of Carron Bn SHM.

NAVIGATION R Carron entrance approached from Grangemouth Roads via Small Craft Recommended Track. River dries at LW.

- Canal passage has to be booked in advance, ☎07810 0794468. Masts must be unstepped before proceeding above sea lock 1.
- Helix 1 lock – 20m long, 5m beam, 1.8m depth, 3m air draught. Carron lock – 6m beam. Kerse Rd Bridge is 5m above river bed, which at is highest pt is 2.3m above CD; it is equipped with air draught gauges calibrated for the canal dimensions. Add 0.1m/4in to draught for freshwater.
- Mast craneage at Bowling, Helix Lock (500kg), Grangemouth YC and Port Edgar for larger yachts.

- The canal is about 30M long with 39 locks. Allow a minimum of 21 hours underway for a passage to Bowling Sea Lock. Transit of the canal can be achieved in 2 days by reaching the Summit Pound at Lock 20, Wyndford, on the first day.
- Vessels should have a reliable engine and be capable of a minimum speed through the water of 4kn against adverse conditions. Ebb tide attains rates of up to 6kn in R Carron after heavy rainfall. 4mph speed limit throughout the canal.
- Access via Falkirk Wheel to Union Canal and Edinburgh, refer to *Scottish Canals Skipper's Guide*.
- The canal is occasionally closed at short notice for safety works check www.scottishcanals.co.uk for notices.

LOCKS Carron Sea Lock and Bowling Sea Lock are operated by canal staff. Locks operate over long 4-day weekends with 10-day passage licence bridging 2 adjacent operating periods, including access to the Falkirk Wheel, Union Canal and Edinburgh.

LIGHTS AND MARKS Carron River channel is marked by lighted By PHM and Bn SHM and unlit By(s) PHM and SHM. Bkwtr/Training Bank to W and N of channel marked with Bn(s) and Bol(s).

BOAT SAFETY SCHEME *The Skipper's Guide* refers. At Carron Sea Lock transient/visiting craft staying no more than 28 days will be subject to a Boat Safety Check of gas and fuel systems. Also required to complete a boat condition declaration and provide evidence of insurance for £1 million third party liability.

COMMUNICATIONS Carron Sea Lock (01324) 483034/07810 794468. *Carron Sea Lock* VHF Ch **74**.

FACILITIES Carron Sea Lock ⚓ P 🚾 🏚 ⚓. **Falkirk Wheel (on Forth & Clyde)** ⚓ 🏚 🚾 ⚓. For details refer to *The Skipper's Guide*.

Anstruther – Arbroath

4.9 ANSTRUTHER

Fife 56°13'·15N 02°41'·82W ✿✿♦♦♦✿✿✿

CHARTS AC 175, 734, 5615; Imray C24, C23, C27

TIDES +0315 Dover; ML 3·1; Duration 0620

Standard Port LEITH (←)

Times				Height (metres)			
High Water		Low Water		MHWS	MHWN	MLWN	MLWS
0300	0900	0300	0900	5·6	4·4	2·0	0·8
1500	2100	1500	2100				
Differences ANSTRUTHER EASTER							
−0018	−0012	−0006	−0008	−0.3	−0.2	0·0	0·0

SHELTER Good, but dangerous to enter in strong E to S winds. Hbr dries, soft mud. Pontoon berths for bilge keel craft only.

NAVIGATION WPT 56°12'·59N 02°42'·20W, 019° to ent, 0·60M. Beware FVs and creels in the area. Do not go N of W Pier Lt due to rks extending N and W across the mouth of Dreel Burn.

LIGHTS AND MARKS Conspic tr on W pier. Ldg lts 019°, both FG 7/11m 4M. Pier lts as chartlet. Horn (3) 60s in conspic tr.

COMMUNICATIONS (Code 01333) Dr 310352; ⊞ St Andrews 01334 472327, Kirkaldy 01592 643355; HM 312591 (HO).
Anstruther Hbr VHF Ch 11 16 (HO) or Forth CG 16 (OT).

FACILITIES Harbour: wall ⌂22+8❷ <10m LOA: entry £16·00 then £8/day; pontoons (no fin keels, 100+8❷ check availability with HM) 1st night £23·90, then £13·70 per day; ▬ ⚓ ⬦ ⚒ ⬥ 0800-2100; **Services** ⬧(tanker ☎730622) ⬧ ⬧ Ⓔ (☎311459) ACA.

Town ⬧ ⬧ △ (☎01383 622444), SC (08456 0057023492) ✉ Ⓑ ⬧ ✕ ⬧ ⇌ (bus Cupar or Leuchars) ✈ (Edinburgh/Dundee).

ADJACENT HARBOURS AND ANCHORAGE

CRAIL, Fife, **56°15'·35N 02°37'·29W.** AC 175. HW +0320 on Dover, −0020 on Leith; HW −0·2m on Leith; ML 3·0m; Duration 0615. Good shelter for boats able to take the ground, but limited manoeuvring area. Appr between S pier and bn on rks to S following ldg line 295°, two W concrete pillars with FR lts, 24/30m 6M. Turn 150° to stbd for ent. Call Forth CG before entering. Beware FVs and creel ends. HM ☎07540 672809 (part-time, Mon-Fri). Facilities: ⌂, entry £16·00/craft then £8/day, ⬦ ⚓ ⬥ ▬. **Village** ✉ Ⓑ ⬧ ✕ ⬧.

ST ANDREWS, Fife, **56°20'·32N 02°46'·79W.** AC 190. HW −0015 Leith. Small drying hbr 7M S of Tay Estuary /8M NW of Fife Ness. In strong onshore winds breaking seas render appr/ent impossible. Appr near HW on 270°, N bkwtr bn in transit with cathedral twr; Dir Iso WRG 2s (277·5°) on lookout bldg. Recce by dinghy is useful. Best water is about 10m S of the bkwtr; 8m wide ent to inner hbr (drying 2·5m) has lock gates, usually open, and sliding footbridge, which opens on req to HM (07506 409792 – call in advance) or berth temp'ly on W side. Gates shut on some HW Sp to hold back water. Facilities: ⚓ SC; all amenities of university town, inc golf course.

4.10 RIVER TAY

Fife/Angus Tayport **(56°27'·10N 02°52'·87W)** ✿✿♦♦♦✿✿

CHARTS AC 190, 1481, 5617; Imray C23

TIDES +0401 (Dundee) Dover; ML 3·1; Duration 0610

Standard Port ABERDEEN (→)

Times				Height (metres)			
High Water		Low Water		MHWS	MHWN	MLWN	MLWS
0000	0600	0100	0700	4·3	3·4	1·6	0·6
1200	1800	1300	1900				
Differences BAR							
+0100	+0100	+0050	+0110	+0.9	+0.8	+0.3	+0.1
DUNDEE							
+0140	*+0120*	*+0055*	*+0145*	*+1·2*	*+1·0*	*+0·5*	*+0·4*
NEWBURGH							
+0215	+0200	+0250	+0335	−0·2	−0·4	−1·1	−0·5
PERTH							
+0220	+0225	+0510	+0530	−0·9	−1·4	−1·2	−0·3

NOTE: At Perth LW time differences give the start of the rise, following a LW stand of about 4hrs.

SHELTER Good in Tay Estuary, but entrance is dangerous in strong E/SE winds or onshore swell. **Tayport** dredged to 0.6m below CD, best for yachts on passage; keels sink into soft mud; ⚓ on S side. **Dundee** – commercial port. Possible ⚓ at Royal Tay YC or ⚓ off. The city is exposed/landing difficult. Good shelter at Woodhaven and ❷s from Wormit BC. There are other ⚓s upriver at Balmerino, Newburgh and Inchyra. Upriver 4M below Perth ⚓ in scenic mouth of R Earn crossing bar at half/full tide.

NAVIGATION WPT Tay Fairway SWM buoy, 56°28'·30N 02°36'·60W, 239°/1M to Middle Bar buoys. Chan is well buoyed, least depth 5·2m. Keep N of Larick, a conspic disused lt bn.

Beware strong tidal streams. No passage across Abertay or Gaa Sands; charted depths are unreliable.

LIGHTS AND MARKS See 4.3 and chartlet. 'Abertay' ECM buoy (Racon), at E end of Gaa Sands is a clear visual mark.

Virtual aids to navigation (V-AIS) lateral marks numbered LS1-LS10 bound the chan north of Tentsmuir Pt leading to Tayport.

COMMUNICATIONS (Code 01382) Forth and Tay Navigation Service (01324) 498584; HM (Dundee) 224121; HM (Perth) (01738) 624056. Dr 221976; ⊕ 660111.
Forth & Tay Navigation Service VHF Ch **71**; *Dundee Hbr Radio* VHF Ch **12** 16 (H24); nav warnings, weather, vis and tides on request. Royal Tay YC, Ch M.

FACILITIES

N BANK: Royal Tay YC (Broughty Ferry) ☎477516, ❷s free, ✕ ⬧.
Services ⚓ ⬥ ✕ ⬧ ⬦(2t) ⬧ ACA.
Dundee City ⬧ ⬧ ✉ Ⓑ ⬧ ⬧ ✕ ⬧ ⇌ ✈.

Tayport Hbr Tayport Hbr Trust, (phil.tayportharbour@gmail.com) Berthing Master 553799; Access HW±4, ent chan dredged 0.8m below CD. SWM at edge of chan 100m from hbr; ldg marks (185°) R △ on slipway and post. R/Wpost, lit FL R 5s on East wall. W Inner wall G/W post, lit Fl G 5s. Ent walls painted W for better visibility. ⌂ (88 + 7❷ on walls) £18/day; ▬ ⬥ ⚓ ⬦ ⬧ ⬥ ✉ Ⓑ ⬧ ✕(hbr cafe) ⬧(Bell Rock Tavern) bus to St Andrews/Dundee for ⇌.
Wormit Boating Club ☎541400 ❷s free, ▬ ⬥ ⚓ ⬥.

ADJACENT HARBOURS

PERTH, Perth & Kinross, **56°22'·89N 03°25'·74W.** AC 1481; OS 53, 58. Tides, see 4.11. FYCA Pilot Handbook needed. Leave Tay Rly bridge about HW Dundee −2 to carry the tide for 16·5M to Perth. Keep clear of coasters which travel at speed and are constrained by their draught. Lit chan favours S bank for 9M to Newburgh. ⚓ to N of chan at W of town in 2m, use piers with caution, ▬. Care is required due to mudbanks mid-stream; keep S of Mugdrum Is. Upriver, power cables clearance 33m and Friarton Bridge 26m. Keep S of Willow Is, past gasworks to Hbr on W bank. Hbr has approx 1·5m. See HM, ☎(01738) 624056, for berth. VHF Ch 09 16. ⚓ ⬧ ⬧ all city amenities, ⇌ ✈.

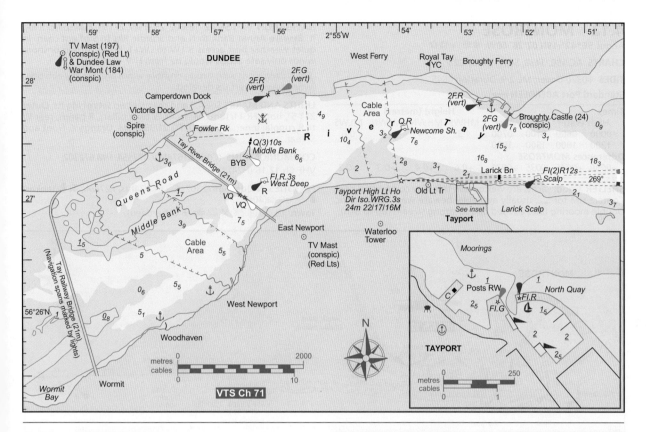

VTS Ch 71

4.11 ARBROATH

Angus 56°33'·22N 02°34'·99W ✿✿◊◊✿✿

CHARTS AC 190, 1438, 5617; Imray C23

TIDES +0317 Dover; ML 2·9; Duration 0620

Standard Port ABERDEEN (→)

Times				Height (metres)			
High Water		Low Water		MHWS	MHWN	MLWN	MLWS
0000	0600	0100	0700	4·3	3·4	1·6	0·6
1200	1800	1300	1900				
Differences ARBROATH							
+0056	+0037	+0034	+0055	+1·0	+0·8	+0·4	+0·2

SHELTER Good, especially in Inner Basin with lock gates, afloat pontoon berths with 2.5m depth maintained. Ent can be dangerous in moderate SE swell. Inside the entrance, turn to starboard and then to starboard again. HM manned 0700-2000 (Apr-Sep), 0700-1800 (Oct-Mar), during which time lock opens approx HW±3.

NAVIGATION WPT 56°32'·98N 02°34'·21W, 299°/0·5M to ent.

Entry should not be attempted LW±2½. Beware Knuckle Rocks to starboard and Cheek Bush Rocks to port on entering.

LIGHTS AND MARKS Ldg lts 299°, both FR 7/13m 5M, or twin trs of St Thomas' ⌖ visible between N pier lt ho and W bkwtr bn. Hbr entry sigs: Fl G 3s on E pier = Entry safe. Same lt shows FR when hbr closed, entry dangerous. Siren (3) 60s at E pier lt is occas, for FVs.

COMMUNICATIONS (Code 01241) Infirmary 872584, Dr 876836. HM 872166; harbourmaster@angus.gov.uk.

Arbroath Harbour VHF Ch **11**.

FACILITIES Inner Basin 59� inc ❶ £25/craft for Inner Basin, £17/craft for Pier; 🚻 🛒 ⚓ 🛢 Ⓔ 🚻 (25t).
Pier ⚓🔧⛽ ⌇£13/craft, 🛢 🔲 ⚓(Oil Pier) ⌇(8t).
Town 🏨🍴🛒 ✉ Ⓑ ✕ 🚇 ⇌ ✈ (Dundee).

HM Ch 11

4.12 MONTROSE

Angus 56°42'·19N 02°26'·60W ❀❀⚓⚓❀❀

CHARTS AC 190, 1438, 5617; Imray C23

TIDES +0320 Dover; ML 2·9; Duration 0645

Standard Port ABERDEEN (→)

Times				Height (metres)			
High Water		Low Water		MHWS	MHWN	MLWN	MLWS
0000	0600	0100	0700	4·3	3·4	1·6	0·6
1200	1800	1300	1900				
Differences *MONTROSE*							
+0050	+0045	+0035	+0030	+0·6	+0·4	+0·3	+0·2

SHELTER Good; yachts are welcome in this busy commercial port. Contact HM for ⚓, usually available, beware wash from traffic. Double mooring lines advised due to strong stream (up to 6kn).

NAVIGATION WPT 56°42'·18N 02°25'·11W, 271°/1·25M to front ldg lt. Beware Annat Bank to N and Scurdie Rks to S of ent chan. In quiet weather best access is LW to LW+1, but in strong onshore winds only safe access would be from HW –2 to HW.

Ent is dangerous with strong onshore winds against any ebb tide when heavy overfalls develop.

LIGHTS AND MARKS See 4.3 and chartlet two sets of ldg lts: Outer 271·5°, both FR 11/18m 5M, front W twin pillars, R bands; rear W tr, R cupola. Inner 265°, both FG 21/33m 5M, Orange △ front and ▽ rear.

COMMUNICATIONS (Code 01674) Dr 672554. HM 672302. VHF Ch 12 16 (H24).

FACILITIES N Quay ☎672302, ⚓ £11/24hrs, £27/wk; ⚓ ⬛(tanker) ⬛ ⚒ ⬛ ⬛(40t) ⬛. Town ⬛ ⊠ Ⓑ 🛒 ✕ ⬛ ⇌ ✈ (Aberdeen).

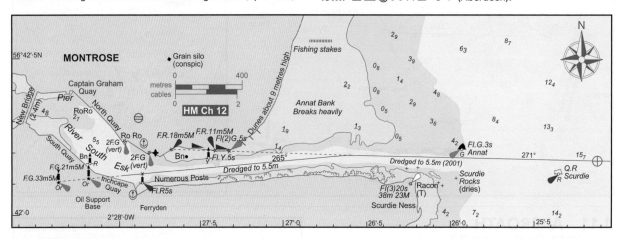

HARBOURS NORTH OF MONTROSE

JOHNSHAVEN, Aberdeenshire, 56°47'·60N 02°20'·07W. AC 210. HW +0245 on Dover; +0045 and +0·4m on Aberdeen; ML 2·7m. Duration 0626. Very small attractive drying hbr 6·5M N of Montrose.

Entry impossible in strong onshore winds. Even in calm weather swell is a problem inside the hbr. Exercise great caution.

Appr from 5ca SE at near HW. Conspic W shed at N end of hbr. Ldg marks/lts on 316°: front, R structure with FR 5m; rear G structure, 20m up the hill and 85m from front, with FG (FR when unsafe). Transit leads between rky ledges to narrow (20m) ent. Turn 90° port into Inner Basin (dries 2·5m). Berth on outer wall or secure to mooring chains, rigged NE/SW. Stonehaven HM ☎(01569) 762741. Facilities: ⬛ ⚓ £20/night, ⬛ ⚓ ⚒ ⬛(5t) ⊠ 🛒 ✕ ⬛. Bus to Montrose/Aberdeen.

GOURDON, Aberdeenshire, 56°49'·49N 02°17'·21W. AC 210. HW +0240 on Dover; +0035 and +0·4m on Aberdeen; ML 2·7m; Duration 0620. Shelter good in inner W hbr (dries to 2m) protected by storm gates; access from about mid-flood. E (or Gutty) hbr is rocky, with difficult access. Bn marks rock ledges extending 200m S from W pier. **Dangerous rk dries on ldg line** 1½ca S of pier head. Ldg marks/lts 358°, both FR 5/30m 5M, 2 W trs; front lt shows G when not safe to enter. E bkwtr hd Q 3m 7M. W pier hd Fl WRG 3s 5m 9/7M, vis 180°-G-344°-W-354°-R-180°. Essential to keep in W sector until R Ldg Lts are aligned. HM ☎(01569) 762741 (part-time, same as 4.13). Facilities: ⚓ ⬛ ⚓ ⬛ ⚒ 🛒 ✕ ⬛.

For details of 'Rover Ticket' see 5.4.

4.13 STONEHAVEN

Aberdeenshire 56°57'·57N 02°12'·02W ❀❀❀❀◊✿✿

CHARTS AC 210, 1438, 5617; Imray C23

TIDES +0235 Dover; ML 2·6; Duration 0620

Standard Port ABERDEEN (⟶)

Times				Height (metres)			
High Water		Low Water		MHWS	MHWN	MLWN	MLWS
0000	0600	0100	0700	4·3	3·4	1·6	0·6
1200	1800	1300	1900				
Differences STONEHAVEN							
+0013	+0008	+0013	+0009	+0·2	+0·2	+0·1	0·0

SHELTER Good, especially from offshore winds. Berth in Outer harbour on W side of breakwater (3m to 2m) or N wall; sandbank forms with varying depths (not <0.6m to date) in middle to W side. Or ⚓ outside in fair weather.

NAVIGATION WPT 56°57'·69N 02°11'·11W, 258°/0·5M to bkwtr lt. Give Downie Pt a wide berth. *Do not enter in strong onshore winds.* Inner hbr dries 3̲·4m and in bad weather is closed, indicated by FG(occas) lt as shown. Do not go S of leading line, to clear rocks close E of inner harbour wall. Harbour speed limit 3kn.

LIGHTS AND MARKS N pier Iso WRG 4s 7m 5M; appr in W sector, 246°-268°. Inner hbr ldg lts 273° only apply to inner hbr: front FW 6m 5M; rear FR 8m 5M. FG on SE pier is shown when inner hbr is closed by boom in bad weather. Conspic monument on hill top to S of hbr. Wave Buoy (temp'y) 5ca NE of B'water lt in G sector.

COMMUNICATIONS (Code 01569) Dr 762945; HM (part-time) 762741, Mobile 07741050210.

VHF Ch 11.

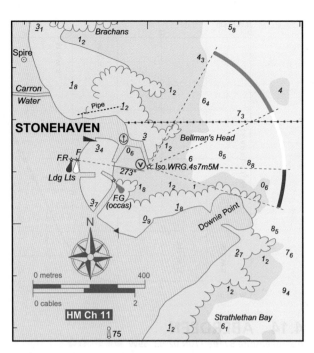

STONEHAVEN

HM Ch 11

Brachans
Spire
Carron Water
Bellman's Head
Iso.WRG.4s7m5M
273°
Ldg Lts
FG (occas)
Downie Point
Strathlethan Bay

FACILITIES ⚓ ⚓🔧⚓ ⚓ (£20) ⚲ £20/night ⚓ ⬦ WC/🚿 ♿ 🛟(1½t) 🛢(tanker, Fri early am). **Aberdeen & Stonehaven SC** 🛥 🏠. **Town** 🅿🛒🍴✕🏠🏨✉Ⓑ🚆✈ (Aberdeen). *For details of a 'Rover Ticket' see 5.4.*

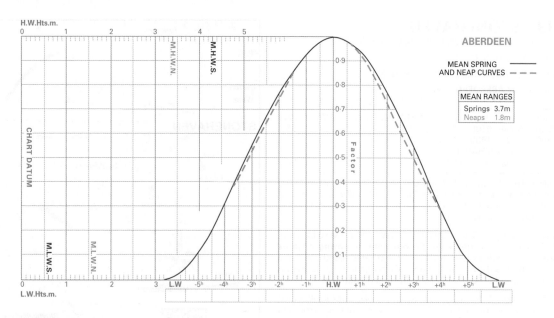

ABERDEEN

MEAN SPRING
AND NEAP CURVES

MEAN RANGES	
Springs	3.7m
Neaps	1.8m

4.14 ABERDEEN

Aberdeenshire 57°08'·70N 02°03'·59W ✿✿✿✿✿✿✿

CHARTS AC 210, 1446, 5617; Imray C23

TIDES +0231 Dover; ML 2·5; Duration 0620

SHELTER Good in hbr; open at all tides, but do not enter in strong NE/ESE winds. Call Aberdeen VTS when 3M off for permission to enter VTS area and berthing availability.

Yachts are not encouraged in this busy commercial port, but occasionally lie in Albert Basin either on floating linkspan or pontoon at western end as directed by HM.

⚓ in Aberdeen Bay gives some shelter from S and W winds. Peterhead is 25M to N; Stonehaven is 13M S. A new South Harbour is under construction in Nigg Bay – avoid

NAVIGATION WPT Fairway SWM buoy, Mo (A) 5s, Racon, 57°09'·31N

02°01'·96W, 236°/1M to harbour entrance. Wind farm lies 4½ N. Give Girdle Ness a berth of at least ¼M (more in bad weather). Do not pass close to pier hds. Strong tidal streams and, with river in spate, overfalls. Maintained depth 6m with 7m on ldg line.

LIGHTS AND MARKS Dir lt 237·2° Fl WRG 1s 7m 9M. Ldg lts FR 237·2° 5M (FG when unsafe). Traffic sigs at root of N pier:

🔴	=	Entry prohib
🔴 (vert)	=	Dep prohib
🔴 & 🔴	=	Port closed

COMMUNICATIONS (Code 01224) ⚓ 722334, HM 59700. Aberdeen VTS 597000; VHF Ch **12** 16 (H24).

FACILITIES Services 🛢 £18/craft for up to 5 days, ⚓ 🔌 Ⓔ ACA. **City** all amenities, 🚌 ✈. **Ferries** Kirkwall and Lerwick (www. northlinkferries.co.uk).

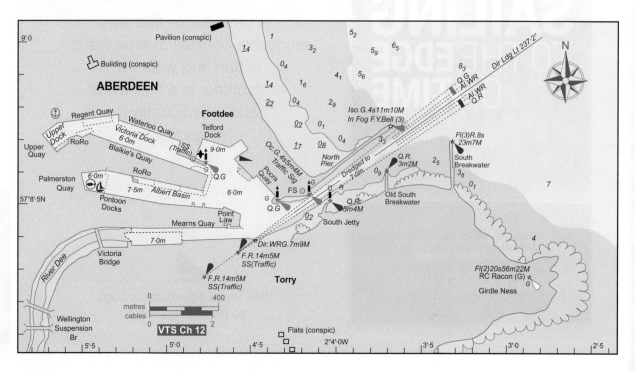

STANDARD TIME (UT)
For Summer Time add ONE hour in **non-shaded areas**

ABERDEEN   LAT 57°09'N   LONG 2°04'W
TIMES AND HEIGHTS OF HIGH AND LOW WATERS

Dates in red are **SPRINGS**
Dates in blue are NEAPS

YEAR **2022**

JANUARY

Day	Time	m		Day	Time	m
1 SA	0537 / 1156 / 1804	1.0 / 4.2 / 1.0		**16** SU	0023 / 0620 / 1240 / 1846	3.8 / 1.5 / 3.9 / 1.3
2 SU	0021 / 0630 / 1243 / ●1857	4.3 / 0.9 / 4.4 / 0.8		**17** M	0103 / 0655 / 1314 / ○1921	3.9 / 1.4 / 4.0 / 1.1
3 M	0114 / 0719 / 1329 / 1947	4.4 / 0.9 / 4.5 / 0.6		**18** TU	0139 / 0728 / 1347 / 1956	3.9 / 1.3 / 4.1 / 1.0
4 TU	0207 / 0806 / 1416 / 2037	4.5 / 0.9 / 4.5 / 0.5		**19** W	0213 / 0801 / 1419 / 2030	4.0 / 1.2 / 4.2 / 0.9
5 W	0259 / 0853 / 1503 / 2126	4.4 / 1.0 / 4.5 / 0.5		**20** TH	0248 / 0834 / 1451 / 2106	4.0 / 1.2 / 4.2 / 0.9
6 TH	0350 / 0938 / 1551 / 2216	4.3 / 1.2 / 4.4 / 0.7		**21** F	0323 / 0908 / 1525 / 2142	4.0 / 1.2 / 4.2 / 0.9
7 F	0442 / 1024 / 1641 / 2306	4.1 / 1.3 / 4.2 / 0.9		**22** SA	0400 / 0943 / 1601 / 2220	3.9 / 1.3 / 4.1 / 0.9
8 SA	0534 / 1112 / 1733 / 2357	3.9 / 1.5 / 4.1 / 1.1		**23** SU	0440 / 1020 / 1641 / 2301	3.8 / 1.3 / 4.1 / 1.0
9 SU	0627 / 1204 / 1828 ☽	3.7 / 1.7 / 3.9		**24** M	0524 / 1103 / 1727 / 2349	3.8 / 1.4 / 4.0 / 1.1
10 M	0050 / 0724 / 1302 / 1927	1.3 / 3.5 / 1.8 / 3.7		**25** TU	0616 / 1155 / 1823 ◐	3.7 / 1.6 / 3.9
11 TU	0149 / 0826 / 1409 / 2034	1.5 / 3.4 / 1.9 / 3.5		**26** W	0046 / 0717 / 1302 / 1931	1.3 / 3.6 / 1.7 / 3.8
12 W	0256 / 0932 / 1526 / 2145	1.7 / 3.4 / 1.9 / 3.5		**27** TH	0153 / 0825 / 1420 / 2047	1.4 / 3.6 / 1.7 / 3.7
13 TH	0405 / 1031 / 1634 / 2248	1.7 / 3.5 / 1.8 / 3.6		**28** F	0308 / 0937 / 1543 / 2207	1.4 / 3.6 / 1.6 / 3.8
14 F	0458 / 1121 / 1725 / 2340	1.6 / 3.7 / 1.6 / 3.7		**29** SA	0425 / 1045 / 1659 / 2320	1.4 / 3.8 / 1.3 / 4.0
15 SA	0541 / 1203 / 1807	1.6 / 3.8 / 1.4		**30** SU	0530 / 1144 / 1800	1.2 / 4.0 / 1.0
				31 M	0020 / 0624 / 1234 / 1853	4.2 / 1.1 / 4.2 / 0.7

FEBRUARY

Day	Time	m		Day	Time	m
1 TU	0113 / 0712 / 1321 / ●1942	4.3 / 1.0 / 4.4 / 0.5		**16** W	0122 / 0711 / 1329 / ○1937	3.9 / 1.2 / 4.1 / 0.8
2 W	0201 / 0756 / 1405 / 2027	4.4 / 0.9 / 4.4 / 0.4		**17** TH	0155 / 0744 / 1400 / 2011	4.0 / 1.1 / 4.2 / 0.7
3 TH	0247 / 0837 / 1447 / 2111	4.4 / 0.9 / 4.5 / 0.4		**18** F	0227 / 0816 / 1431 / 2045	4.1 / 1.0 / 4.3 / 0.6
4 F	0330 / 0917 / 1529 / 2152	4.2 / 1.0 / 4.5 / 0.5		**19** SA	0300 / 0848 / 1504 / 2119	4.1 / 0.9 / 4.3 / 0.6
5 SA	0412 / 0955 / 1612 / 2232	4.1 / 1.1 / 4.3 / 0.8		**20** SU	0334 / 0921 / 1539 / 2154	4.1 / 1.0 / 4.3 / 0.7
6 SU	0455 / 1033 / 1655 / 2311	3.9 / 1.2 / 4.1 / 1.0		**21** M	0411 / 0956 / 1617 / 2232	4.0 / 1.0 / 4.2 / 0.8
7 M	0538 / 1114 / 1740 / 2354	3.7 / 1.4 / 3.9 / 1.3		**22** TU	0452 / 1035 / 1702 / 2316	3.9 / 1.2 / 4.1 / 1.0
8 TU	0625 / 1202 / 1833 ◐	3.5 / 1.7 / 3.6		**23** W	0540 / 1123 / 1756 ◐	3.7 / 1.3 / 3.9
9 W	0043 / 0720 / 1304 / 1936	1.6 / 3.3 / 1.9 / 3.4		**24** TH	0010 / 0640 / 1229 / 1908	1.3 / 3.6 / 1.5 / 3.7
10 TH	0145 / 0827 / 1425 / 2054	1.8 / 3.3 / 2.0 / 3.3		**25** F	0123 / 0753 / 1356 / 2034	1.5 / 3.4 / 1.6 / 3.5
11 F	0310 / 0944 / 1603 / 2218	1.9 / 3.3 / 1.9 / 3.3		**26** SA	0252 / 0915 / 1538 / 2207	1.6 / 3.5 / 1.5 / 3.6
12 SA	0433 / 1051 / 1706 / 2322	1.9 / 3.4 / 1.7 / 3.4		**27** SU	0423 / 1034 / 1659 / 2323	1.6 / 3.6 / 1.2 / 3.8
13 SU	0524 / 1141 / 1751	1.7 / 3.6 / 1.5		**28** M	0527 / 1137 / 1757	1.4 / 3.9 / 0.9
14 M	0009 / 0604 / 1221 / 1829	3.6 / 1.6 / 3.8 / 1.2				
15 TU	0048 / 0639 / 1256 / 1903	3.8 / 1.4 / 4.0 / 1.0				

MARCH

Day	Time	m		Day	Time	m
1 TU	0019 / 0617 / 1226 / 1846	4.0 / 1.1 / 4.1 / 0.6		**16** W	0023 / 0615 / 1229 / 1837	3.7 / 1.3 / 3.9 / 0.9
2 W	0106 / 0700 / 1309 / ●1930	4.2 / 1.0 / 4.3 / 0.4		**17** TH	0056 / 0647 / 1302 / 1910	3.9 / 1.1 / 4.1 / 0.7
3 TH	0147 / 0739 / 1348 / 2009	4.3 / 0.8 / 4.5 / 0.3		**18** F	0128 / 0719 / 1333 / ○1944	4.1 / 0.9 / 4.2 / 0.5
4 F	0226 / 0816 / 1426 / 2046	4.3 / 0.8 / 4.5 / 0.4		**19** SA	0200 / 0752 / 1406 / 2018	4.2 / 0.8 / 4.4 / 0.4
5 SA	0302 / 0851 / 1502 / 2121	4.2 / 0.8 / 4.4 / 0.5		**20** SU	0233 / 0825 / 1440 / 2053	4.2 / 0.7 / 4.4 / 0.4
6 SU	0338 / 0924 / 1541 / 2154	4.1 / 0.9 / 4.3 / 0.5		**21** M	0308 / 0859 / 1517 / 2128	4.2 / 0.7 / 4.4 / 0.5
7 M	0413 / 0958 / 1618 / 2226	3.9 / 1.0 / 4.1 / 1.0		**22** TU	0345 / 0935 / 1558 / 2207	4.1 / 0.8 / 4.3 / 0.8
8 TU	0449 / 1033 / 1659 / 2301	3.7 / 1.2 / 3.8 / 1.3		**23** W	0425 / 1016 / 1646 / 2251	4.0 / 1.0 / 4.1 / 1.1
9 W	0529 / 1114 / 1747 / 2343	3.5 / 1.5 / 3.5 / 1.6		**24** TH	0513 / 1107 / 1745 / 2350	3.7 / 1.2 / 3.8 / 1.4
10 TH	0619 / 1208 / 1848 ◐	3.3 / 1.7 / 3.3		**25** F	0614 / 1219 / 1904	3.5 / 1.4 / 3.5
11 F	0041 / 0724 / 1328 / 2006	1.9 / 3.2 / 1.9 / 3.1		**26** SA	0109 / 0733 / 1355 / 2036	1.7 / 3.4 / 1.5 / 3.4
12 SA	0210 / 0845 / 1521 / 2142	2.1 / 3.1 / 1.9 / 3.1		**27** SU	0251 / 0902 / 1541 / 2213	1.8 / 3.4 / 1.4 / 3.6
13 SU	0404 / 1012 / 1640 / 2257	2.0 / 3.2 / 1.7 / 3.3		**28** M	0418 / 1025 / 1653 / 2320	1.6 / 3.6 / 1.1 / 3.8
14 M	0502 / 1112 / 1726 / 2346	1.8 / 3.4 / 1.4 / 3.5		**29** TU	0516 / 1124 / 1745	1.4 / 3.8 / 0.8
15 TU	0541 / 1155 / 1803	1.6 / 3.7 / 1.1		**30** W	0009 / 0602 / 1210 / 1830	4.0 / 1.1 / 4.1 / 0.6
				31 TH	0049 / 0641 / 1250 / 1909	4.1 / 0.9 / 4.2 / 0.4

APRIL

Day	Time	m		Day	Time	m
1 F	0125 / 0717 / 1326 / ●1944	4.2 / 0.8 / 4.3 / 0.4		**16** SA	0056 / 0650 / 1302 / ○1913	4.1 / 0.8 / 4.2 / 0.4
2 SA	0159 / 0756 / 1402 / 2017	4.2 / 0.7 / 4.4 / 0.5		**17** SU	0130 / 0725 / 1339 / 1950	4.2 / 0.7 / 4.4 / 0.3
3 SU	0231 / 0824 / 1437 / 2048	4.1 / 0.7 / 4.3 / 0.6		**18** M	0205 / 0801 / 1418 / 2027	4.3 / 0.6 / 4.4 / 0.4
4 M	0303 / 0856 / 1512 / 2117	4.0 / 0.8 / 4.1 / 0.8		**19** TU	0242 / 0839 / 1500 / 2106	4.3 / 0.6 / 4.4 / 0.6
5 TU	0335 / 0928 / 1549 / 2147	3.9 / 1.0 / 4.0 / 1.1		**20** W	0322 / 0921 / 1546 / 2149	4.2 / 0.7 / 4.2 / 0.8
6 W	0408 / 1002 / 1628 / 2219	3.8 / 1.1 / 3.7 / 1.4		**21** TH	0405 / 1009 / 1640 / 2239	4.0 / 0.8 / 4.0 / 1.2
7 TH	0444 / 1041 / 1714 / 2257	3.6 / 1.4 / 3.5 / 1.6		**22** F	0457 / 1108 / 1748 / 2343	3.8 / 1.1 / 3.7 / 1.5
8 F	0529 / 1131 / 1814 / 2351	3.4 / 1.6 / 3.3 / 1.9		**23** SA	0603 / 1225 / 1907 ◐	3.6 / 1.2 / 3.5
9 SA	0632 / 1244 / 1927 ☽	3.2 / 1.8 / 3.1		**24** SU	0106 / 0722 / 1358 / 2036	1.8 / 3.4 / 1.3 / 3.5
10 SU	0117 / 0750 / 1422 / 2053	2.1 / 3.1 / 1.8 / 3.1		**25** M	0241 / 0846 / 1529 / 2201	1.8 / 3.5 / 1.2 / 3.6
11 M	0310 / 0915 / 1555 / 2215	2.1 / 3.2 / 1.6 / 3.3		**26** TU	0358 / 1004 / 1634 / 2301	1.6 / 3.6 / 1.0 / 3.7
12 TU	0424 / 1027 / 1647 / 2308	1.8 / 3.3 / 1.3 / 3.5		**27** W	0453 / 1102 / 1723 / 2347	1.4 / 3.8 / 0.8 / 3.9
13 W	0506 / 1115 / 1726 / 2348	1.6 / 3.6 / 1.1 / 3.7		**28** TH	0537 / 1148 / 1805	1.2 / 4.0 / 0.7
14 TH	0542 / 1153 / 1802	1.3 / 3.8 / 0.8		**29** F	0025 / 0616 / 1226 / 1842	4.0 / 1.0 / 4.1 / 0.6
15 F	0022 / 0616 / 1228 / 1837	3.9 / 1.0 / 4.0 / 0.6		**30** SA	0058 / 0652 / 1303 / ●1915	4.0 / 0.9 / 4.2 / 0.6

Chart Datum: 2·25 metres below Ordnance Datum (Newlyn). HAT is 4·8 metres above Chart Datum.

SE Scotland

≫ **FREE** monthly updates. Register at ≪
www.reedsnauticalalmanac.co.uk

201

STANDARD TIME (UT)
For Summer Time add ONE hour in **non-shaded areas**

ABERDEEN LAT 57°09′N LONG 2°04′W
TIMES AND HEIGHTS OF HIGH AND LOW WATERS

Dates in red are **SPRINGS**
Dates in blue are **NEAPS**

YEAR 2022

MAY

Day	Time	m	Time	m	Time	m	Time	m
1 SU	0130	4.1	0726	0.8	1338	4.2	1946	0.7
2 M	0202	4.1	0800	0.8	1414	4.1	2017	0.8
3 TU	0233	4.0	0833	0.9	1449	4.0	2047	0.8
4 W	0304	3.9	0906	1.0	1526	3.8	2117	1.2
5 TH	0337	3.8	0941	1.0	1606	3.7	2150	1.4
6 F	0413	3.7	1020	1.3	1652	3.5	2229	1.6
7 SA	0456	3.5	1109	1.4	1748	3.3	2319	1.8
8 SU	0553	3.3	1211	1.6	1853	3.2		
9 M	0031	2.0	0704	3.2	1330	1.6	◑2003	3.2
10 TU	0202	2.0	0816	3.2	1448	1.5	2115	3.3
11 W	0320	1.8	0925	3.3	1551	1.3	2217	3.5
12 TH	0416	1.6	1023	3.5	1639	1.1	2304	3.7
13 F	0459	1.3	1110	3.8	1721	1.1	2344	3.9
14 SA	0539	1.1	1152	4.0	1802	0.6		
15 SU	0022	4.1	1233	4.2	1843	0.5		
16 M	0101	4.2	0700	0.7	1316	4.4	○1924	0.4
17 TU	0140	4.3	0742	0.6	1400	4.4	2007	0.5
18 W	0221	4.3	0827	0.5	1449	4.3	2052	0.7
19 TH	0305	4.2	0916	0.6	1541	4.2	2140	1.0
20 F	0353	4.1	1010	0.7	1642	4.0	2235	1.3
21 SA	0449	3.9	1113	0.9	1749	3.8	2339	1.5
22 SU	0555	3.7	1225	1.0	1900	3.6	◑	
23 M	0052	1.7	0706	3.6	1341	1.1	2016	3.5
24 TU	0209	1.7	0820	3.6	1457	1.1	2130	3.6
25 W	0321	1.6	0932	3.6	1602	1.0	2230	3.6
26 TH	0420	1.5	1032	3.7	1653	1.0	2317	3.7
27 F	0508	1.3	1120	3.8	1735	0.9	2356	3.8
28 SA	0550	1.1	1203	3.9	1813	0.9		
29 SU	0031	3.9	0629	1.0	1241	3.9	1847	0.9
30 M	0105	4.0	0705	0.9	1319	3.9	●1920	1.0
31 TU	0137	4.0	0741	0.9	1356	3.9	1952	1.1

JUNE

Day	Time	m	Time	m	Time	m	Time	m
1 W	0209	4.0	0816	0.9	1433	3.9	2024	1.2
2 TH	0242	3.9	0913	1.0	1511	3.8	2057	1.3
3 F	0315	3.9	0927	1.1	1550	3.7	2132	1.4
4 SA	0352	3.8	1006	1.1	1634	3.5	2211	1.5
5 SU	0433	3.6	1051	1.3	1723	3.4	2256	1.7
6 M	0523	3.5	1143	1.3	1818	3.3	2352	1.8
7 TU	0621	3.4	1244	1.4	1916	3.3		
8 W	0101	1.8	0724	3.4	1348	1.4	2018	3.4
9 TH	0212	1.8	0826	3.5	1450	1.2	2119	3.5
10 F	0316	1.6	0927	3.6	1547	1.1	2216	3.7
11 SA	0413	1.4	1026	3.8	1640	0.9	2306	3.9
12 SU	0504	1.2	1119	4.0	1730	0.8	2352	4.0
13 M	0553	1.0	1210	4.2	1818	0.7		
14 TU	0036	4.2	0642	0.7	1300	4.3	○1907	0.7
15 W	0121	4.3	0731	0.6	1351	4.4	1955	0.7
16 TH	0206	4.3	0822	0.5	1444	4.3	2044	0.8
17 F	0253	4.3	0914	0.5	1539	4.2	2134	1.0
18 SA	0344	4.2	1008	0.5	1638	4.1	2226	1.2
19 SU	0439	4.1	1106	0.7	1737	3.9	2322	1.4
20 M	0538	4.0	1206	0.8	1837	3.7		
21 TU	0022	1.5	0639	3.8	1308	1.0	◑1940	3.6
22 W	0125	1.6	0743	3.7	1412	1.1	2045	3.5
23 TH	0232	1.7	0850	3.6	1518	1.2	2148	3.5
24 F	0339	1.6	0955	3.6	1617	1.3	2241	3.6
25 SA	0438	1.5	1052	3.6	1705	1.3	2327	3.7
26 SU	0527	1.3	1141	3.7	1747	1.3		
27 M	0007	3.8	0610	1.2	1225	3.7	1825	1.2
28 TU	0044	3.9	0649	1.1	1305	3.8	1901	1.2
29 W	0119	3.9	0727	1.0	1344	3.8	●1935	1.2
30 TH	0153	4.0	0802	1.0	1421	3.8	2008	1.2

JULY

Day	Time	m	Time	m	Time	m	Time	m
1 F	0226	4.0	0837	0.9	1457	3.8	2042	1.3
2 SA	0259	4.0	0913	1.0	1534	3.8	2116	1.3
3 SU	0334	3.9	0950	1.0	1613	3.7	2152	1.4
4 M	0412	3.8	1030	1.0	1655	3.6	2232	1.5
5 TU	0453	3.8	1113	1.1	1741	3.5	2316	1.5
6 W	0541	3.7	1202	1.2	1832	3.5		
7 TH	0009	1.6	0636	3.6	1257	1.2	●1929	3.5
8 F	0114	1.7	0736	3.6	1358	1.2	2029	3.5
9 SA	0222	1.6	0842	3.6	1502	1.2	2133	3.6
10 SU	0331	1.5	0950	3.7	1607	1.1	2234	3.8
11 M	0437	1.3	1057	3.9	1709	1.0	2329	3.9
12 TU	0538	1.0	1158	4.1	1805	0.9		
13 W	0019	4.1	0634	0.8	1253	4.2	○1857	0.9
14 TH	0108	4.3	0726	0.5	1346	4.3	1946	0.8
15 F	0155	4.4	0817	0.4	1438	4.4	2034	0.8
16 SA	0242	4.4	0907	0.3	1530	4.3	2120	0.9
17 SU	0330	4.4	0956	0.4	1620	4.1	2206	1.0
18 M	0419	4.3	1045	0.5	1711	4.0	2253	1.2
19 TU	0510	4.2	1134	0.8	1802	3.8	2342	1.4
20 W	0603	4.0	1225	1.0	1855	3.6	◑	
21 TH	0036	1.6	0701	3.7	1319	1.3	1954	3.4
22 F	0138	1.7	0804	3.6	1421	1.5	2058	3.4
23 SA	0252	1.8	0916	3.4	1534	1.6	2202	3.4
24 SU	0410	1.7	1026	3.4	1638	1.6	2259	3.6
25 M	0509	1.5	1125	3.5	1727	1.6	2346	3.7
26 TU	0555	1.4	1213	3.6	1808	1.5		
27 W	0027	3.8	0635	1.2	1254	3.7	1845	1.4
28 TH	0103	3.9	0712	1.0	1331	3.8	●1919	1.3
29 F	0137	4.0	0746	0.9	1405	3.9	1951	1.2
30 SA	0209	4.1	0820	0.8	1439	3.9	2024	1.1
31 SU	0241	4.1	0854	0.8	1512	3.9	2056	1.1

AUGUST

Day	Time	m	Time	m	Time	m	Time	m
1 M	0313	4.1	0928	0.8	1547	3.9	2129	1.2
2 TU	0347	4.1	1004	0.8	1623	3.8	2204	1.2
3 W	0424	4.0	1041	0.9	1703	3.7	2242	1.3
4 TH	0505	3.9	1122	1.0	1749	3.7	2328	1.5
5 F	0555	3.8	1213	1.2	1844	3.6	◐	
6 SA	0026	1.6	0657	3.7	1315	1.3	1948	3.5
7 SU	0141	1.7	0811	3.6	1428	1.4	2059	3.5
8 M	0304	1.6	0931	3.6	1548	1.4	2211	3.7
9 TU	0427	1.4	1050	3.8	1701	1.3	2315	3.9
10 W	0534	1.1	1155	4.0	1759	1.1		
11 TH	0009	4.1	0629	0.7	1250	4.2	1849	1.0
12 F	0057	4.3	0719	0.4	1339	4.4	○1935	0.9
13 SA	0142	4.5	0805	0.3	1425	4.4	2017	0.8
14 SU	0225	4.6	0850	0.2	1509	4.3	2058	0.8
15 M	0308	4.6	0932	0.3	1552	4.2	2138	0.9
16 TU	0352	4.4	1013	0.5	1635	4.0	2217	1.1
17 W	0436	4.2	1054	0.8	1719	3.8	2259	1.3
18 TH	0523	4.0	1136	1.2	1806	3.6	2347	1.5
19 F	0616	3.7	1224	1.5	1900	3.4		
20 SA	0046	1.7	0719	3.5	1323	1.8	2004	3.3
21 SU	0204	1.9	0835	3.3	1444	1.9	2119	3.3
22 M	0346	1.8	1002	3.3	1615	1.9	2230	3.5
23 TU	0453	1.6	1109	3.4	1710	1.8	2324	3.6
24 W	0539	1.4	1158	3.6	1751	1.6		
25 TH	0006	3.8	0617	1.2	1237	3.8	1827	1.4
26 F	0042	4.0	0652	1.0	1311	3.9	1859	1.3
27 SA	0115	4.1	0724	0.8	1342	4.0	●1930	1.1
28 SU	0145	4.2	0756	0.7	1413	4.1	2001	1.0
29 M	0215	4.3	0828	0.6	1444	4.1	2032	0.9
30 TU	0247	4.3	0901	0.6	1516	4.1	2103	1.0
31 W	0320	4.3	0933	0.7	1551	4.0	2136	1.1

Chart Datum: 2·25 metres below Ordnance Datum (Newlyn). HAT is 4·8 metres above Chart Datum.

》》 FREE monthly updates. Register at 《
www.reedsnauticalalmanac.co.uk

STANDARD TIME (UT)
For Summer Time add ONE hour in **non-shaded areas**

ABERDEEN LAT 57°09′N LONG 2°04′W
TIMES AND HEIGHTS OF HIGH AND LOW WATERS

Dates in red are **SPRINGS**
Dates in blue are NEAPS

YEAR 2022

SEPTEMBER

Day	Time m	Day	Time m
1	0356 4.2 / 1008 0.8 / TH 1628 3.9 / 2212 1.2	**16**	0444 3.9 / 1046 1.3 / F 1714 3.7 / 2302 1.5
2	0437 4.1 / 1047 1.0 / F 1712 3.8 / 2256 1.3	**17**	0534 3.6 / 1127 1.7 / SA 1804 3.5 / ◑2358 1.8
3	0527 3.9 / 1137 1.3 / SA 1807 3.6 / ◑2355 1.5	**18**	0637 3.4 / 1225 2.0 / SU 1909 3.3
4	0633 3.7 / 1244 1.6 / SU 1916 3.5	**19**	0118 1.9 / 0756 3.2 / M 1352 2.2 / 2028 3.3
5	0119 1.7 / 0758 3.6 / M 1411 3.7 / 2036 3.5	**20**	0313 1.9 / 0930 3.2 / TU 1549 2.1 / 2153 3.4
6	0259 1.6 / 0930 3.6 / TU 1546 1.7 / 2158 3.6	**21**	0428 1.7 / 1045 3.4 / W 1647 1.9 / 2254 3.6
7	0428 1.3 / 1053 3.8 / W 1658 1.5 / 2306 3.9	**22**	0514 1.4 / 1133 3.6 / TH 1727 1.7 / 2338 3.8
8	0530 1.0 / 1153 4.1 / TH 1750 1.2 / 2358 4.2	**23**	0550 1.2 / 1210 3.8 / F 1801 1.5
9	0620 0.6 / 1242 4.3 / F 1835 1.0	**24**	0013 4.0 / 0623 1.0 / SA 1242 4.0 / 1832 1.2
10	0043 4.4 / 0705 0.4 / SA 1324 4.4 / ○1916 0.8	**25**	0045 4.2 / 0654 0.8 / SU 1312 4.1 / ●1902 1.1
11	0123 4.6 / 0746 0.3 / SU 1403 4.4 / 1955 0.8	**26**	0115 4.3 / 0726 0.6 / M 1342 4.2 / 1933 0.9
12	0203 4.6 / 0825 0.3 / M 1441 4.4 / 2031 0.8	**27**	0146 4.4 / 0758 0.6 / TU 1413 4.3 / 2004 0.9
13	0242 4.6 / 0901 0.4 / TU 1518 4.2 / 2107 0.9	**28**	0219 4.4 / 0830 0.6 / W 1446 4.3 / 2037 0.9
14	0321 4.4 / 0936 0.7 / W 1555 4.1 / 2142 1.0	**29**	0255 4.4 / 0904 0.7 / TH 1521 4.2 / 2111 1.0
15	0401 4.2 / 1010 1.0 / TH 1633 3.9 / 2220 1.2	**30**	0334 4.3 / 0939 0.9 / F 1559 4.1 / 2150 1.1

OCTOBER

Day	Time m	Day	Time m
1	0418 4.1 / 1021 1.2 / SA 1644 3.9 / 2238 1.3	**16**	0501 3.6 / 1042 1.8 / SU 1714 3.6 / 2321 1.7
2	0514 3.9 / 1114 1.5 / SU 1740 3.7 / 2345 1.5	**17**	0602 3.4 / 1134 2.1 / M 1817 3.4 / ◑
3	0629 3.7 / 1230 1.8 / M 1857 3.5	**18**	0034 1.9 / 0717 3.2 / TU 1259 2.3 / 1935 3.3
4	0117 1.6 / 0759 3.5 / TU 1408 1.9 / 2023 3.5	**19**	0212 1.9 / 0841 3.1 / W 1452 2.2 / 2058 3.4
5	0303 1.5 / 0935 3.6 / W 1543 1.8 / 2148 3.7	**20**	0344 1.7 / 1002 3.4 / TH 1608 2.0 / 2209 3.5
6	0422 1.2 / 1049 3.9 / TH 1646 1.5 / 2253 4.0	**21**	0434 1.5 / 1054 3.6 / F 1651 1.8 / 2258 3.7
7	0517 0.9 / 1142 4.1 / F 1734 1.3 / 2342 4.2	**22**	0512 1.2 / 1133 3.8 / SA 1726 1.5 / 2336 4.0
8	0603 0.6 / 1224 4.3 / SA 1815 1.1	**23**	0546 1.0 / 1206 4.0 / SU 1758 1.3
9	0023 4.4 / 0644 0.5 / SU 1301 4.3 / ○1854 0.9	**24**	0010 4.2 / 0619 0.8 / M 1238 4.2 / 1831 1.1
10	0101 4.5 / 0721 0.5 / M 1336 4.4 / 1929 0.8	**25**	0043 4.3 / 0652 0.7 / TU 1310 4.3 / ●1904 0.9
11	0138 4.6 / 0756 0.5 / TU 1410 4.3 / 2004 0.8	**26**	0118 4.5 / 0727 0.6 / W 1343 4.4 / 1939 0.8
12	0216 4.5 / 0828 0.7 / W 1443 4.2 / 2039 0.9	**27**	0155 4.5 / 0802 0.6 / TH 1418 4.4 / 2015 0.8
13	0253 4.3 / 0900 0.9 / TH 1517 4.1 / 2113 1.1	**28**	0235 4.5 / 0839 0.8 / F 1456 4.3 / 2055 0.9
14	0332 4.1 / 0931 1.2 / F 1551 3.9 / 2149 1.3	**29**	0319 4.3 / 0920 1.0 / SA 1538 4.2 / 2141 1.0
15	0413 3.9 / 1004 1.5 / SA 1629 3.8 / 2229 1.5	**30**	0410 4.1 / 1007 1.3 / SU 1626 4.0 / 2237 1.2
		31	0514 3.9 / 1107 1.6 / M 1727 3.8 / 2350 1.4

NOVEMBER

Day	Time m	Day	Time m
1	0632 3.7 / 1226 1.9 / TU 1845 3.7 / ◑	**16**	0636 3.3 / 1207 2.2 / W 1843 3.4 / ◐
2	0119 1.5 / 0757 3.6 / W 1358 2.0 / 2007 3.7	**17**	0111 1.8 / 0744 3.3 / TH 1335 2.2 / 1955 3.4
3	0250 1.3 / 0924 3.7 / TH 1521 1.8 / 2127 3.8	**18**	0229 1.7 / 0856 3.4 / F 1456 2.1 / 2104 3.5
4	0402 1.1 / 1030 3.9 / F 1622 1.6 / 2230 4.0	**19**	0333 1.5 / 0958 3.5 / SA 1556 1.9 / 2203 3.7
5	0455 0.9 / 1120 4.0 / SA 1710 1.4 / 2319 4.2	**20**	0422 1.3 / 1046 3.8 / SU 1641 1.6 / 2251 3.9
6	0539 0.8 / 1200 4.2 / SU 1751 1.2	**21**	0503 1.1 / 1126 4.0 / M 1720 1.4 / 2332 4.1
7	0000 4.3 / 0619 0.8 / M 1236 4.2 / 1830 1.0	**22**	0541 0.9 / 1203 4.2 / TU 1759 1.2
8	0039 4.4 / 0654 0.8 / TU 1309 4.3 / ○1906 1.0	**23**	0012 4.3 / 0621 0.8 / W 1240 4.3 / ●1838 1.0
9	0117 4.4 / 0727 0.8 / W 1342 4.3 / 1942 0.9	**24**	0054 4.4 / 0700 0.7 / TH 1318 4.4 / 1919 0.9
10	0154 4.3 / 0759 1.0 / TH 1414 4.2 / 2017 1.0	**25**	0137 4.5 / 0742 0.8 / F 1357 4.4 / 2003 0.8
11	0232 4.2 / 0830 1.2 / F 1447 4.1 / 2052 1.1	**26**	0223 4.5 / 0825 0.9 / SA 1439 4.4 / 2050 0.8
12	0311 4.0 / 0901 1.4 / SA 1520 4.0 / 2128 1.3	**27**	0313 4.4 / 0911 1.1 / SU 1524 4.3 / 2141 0.9
13	0351 3.8 / 0935 1.6 / SU 1556 3.9 / 2208 1.4	**28**	0410 4.2 / 1003 1.4 / M 1616 4.1 / 2240 1.0
14	0437 3.6 / 1013 1.8 / M 1639 3.7 / 2255 1.6	**29**	0515 4.0 / 1102 1.6 / TU 1718 4.0 / 2349 1.1
15	0533 3.5 / 1100 2.0 / TU 1734 3.5 / 2356 1.7	**30**	0624 3.8 / 1212 1.8 / W 1828 3.9 / ◑

DECEMBER

Day	Time m	Day	Time m
1	0103 1.2 / 0737 3.7 / TH 1327 1.9 / 1940 3.8	**16**	0017 1.6 / 0651 3.4 / F 1224 2.0 / ◑1855 3.6
2	0217 1.2 / 0852 3.7 / F 1441 1.8 / 2053 3.8	**17**	0120 1.6 / 0750 3.4 / SA 1336 2.0 / 1957 3.6
3	0327 1.2 / 0958 3.8 / SA 1547 1.7 / 2159 3.9	**18**	0222 1.5 / 0852 3.5 / SU 1445 1.9 / 2059 3.6
4	0425 1.1 / 1050 3.9 / SU 1641 1.5 / 2253 4.0	**19**	0321 1.4 / 0951 3.6 / M 1546 1.8 / 2200 3.8
5	0512 1.1 / 1134 4.0 / M 1728 1.4 / 2340 4.1	**20**	0416 1.3 / 1044 3.8 / TU 1641 1.6 / 2256 3.9
6	0553 1.1 / 1212 4.1 / TU 1809 1.2	**21**	0507 1.1 / 1131 4.0 / W 1731 1.3 / 2348 4.1
7	0022 4.1 / 0630 1.1 / W 1247 4.1 / 1849 1.1	**22**	0555 1.0 / 1215 4.2 / TH 1820 1.1
8	0102 4.1 / 0704 1.2 / TH 1321 4.2 / ○1927 1.1	**23**	0038 4.3 / 0643 0.9 / F 1258 4.3 / ●1908 0.9
9	0141 4.1 / 0738 1.2 / F 1354 4.2 / 2003 1.1	**24**	0127 4.4 / 0730 0.9 / SA 1342 4.4 / 1957 0.7
10	0219 4.0 / 0810 1.3 / SA 1427 4.1 / 2038 1.1	**25**	0218 4.4 / 0818 1.0 / SU 1428 4.5 / 2048 0.6
11	0257 3.9 / 0843 1.4 / SU 1500 4.1 / 2114 1.2	**26**	0311 4.4 / 0906 1.1 / M 1516 4.4 / 2140 0.6
12	0336 3.8 / 0917 1.6 / M 1536 4.0 / 2152 1.3	**27**	0406 4.3 / 0955 1.2 / TU 1607 4.4 / 2235 0.7
13	0417 3.7 / 0953 1.7 / TU 1615 3.9 / 2234 1.4	**28**	0503 4.1 / 1047 1.4 / W 1702 4.2 / 2332 0.9
14	0503 3.6 / 1034 1.8 / W 1700 3.7 / 2322 1.5	**29**	0601 3.9 / 1144 1.6 / TH 1801 4.1
15	0554 3.5 / 1123 1.9 / TH 1754 3.6	**30**	0031 1.0 / 0702 3.7 / F 1244 1.7 / ◑1904 3.9
		31	0133 1.2 / 0806 3.6 / SA 1350 1.8 / 2011 3.8

SE Scotland

Chart Datum: 2·25 metres below Ordnance Datum (Newlyn). HAT is 4·8 metres above Chart Datum.

》FREE monthly updates. Register at 《
www.reedsnauticalalmanac.co.uk

203

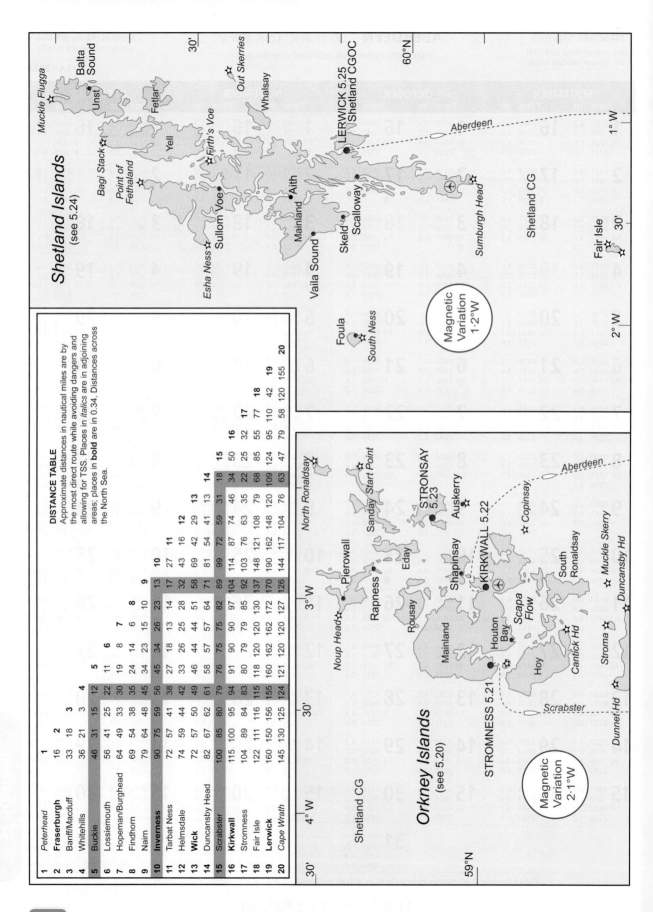

Shetland Islands
(see 5.24)

Magnetic Variation 1·2°W

Muckle Flugga · Balta Sound · Unst · *Out Skerries* · Whalsay · *Fetlar* · Yell · *Bagi Stack* · *Firth's Voe* · *Point of Fethaland* · Aith · Mainland · Scalloway · LERWICK 5.25 · Shetland CGOC · Aberdeen · Sullom Voe · Skeld · Vaila Sound · *Esha Ness* · *Sumburgh Head* · Shetland CG · *Foula* · *South Ness* · Fair Isle

Orkney Islands
(see 5.20)

Magnetic Variation 2·1°W

North Ronaldsay · *Start Point* · Sanday · STRONSAY 5.23 · Auskerry · Pierowall · Rapness · Eday · Shapinsay · KIRKWALL 5.22 · *Copinsay* · Rousay · Mainland · Houton Bay · Scapa Flow · South Ronaldsay · *Muckle Skerry* · Hoy · *Cantick Hd* · *Stroma* · *Duncansby Hd* · *Noup Head* · STROMNESS 5.21 · *Scrabster* · *Dunnet Hd* · *Aberdeen* · Shetland CG

DISTANCE TABLE
Approximate distances in nautical miles are by the most direct route while avoiding dangers and allowing for TSS. Places in *italics* are in adjoining areas; places in **bold** are in 0.34. Distances across the North Sea.

	1	2	3	4	5	6	7	8	9	10	11	12	13	14	15	16	17	18	19	20
1 *Peterhead*	1																			
2 **Fraserburgh**	16	2																		
3 Banff/Macduff	33	18	3																	
4 Whitehills	36	21	3	4																
5 Buckie	46	31	15	12	5															
6 Lossiemouth	56	41	25	22	11	6														
7 Hopeman/Burghead	64	49	33	30	19	8	7													
8 Findhorn	69	54	38	35	24	14	6	8												
9 Nairn	79	64	48	45	34	23	15	10	9											
10 Inverness	90	75	59	56	45	34	26	23	13	10										
11 Tarbat Ness	72	57	41	38	27	18	13	14	17	27	11									
12 Helmsdale	74	59	44	42	33	26	25	28	32	43	16	12								
13 **Wick**	72	57	50	46	44	44	51	58	69	42	29	13	13							
14 Duncansby Head	82	67	62	61	58	57	57	64	71	54	41	13	14	14						
15 **Scrabster**	100	85	80	79	76	75	75	82	89	72	59	31	18	15	15					
16 **Kirkwall**	115	100	95	94	91	90	90	97	104	114	87	74	46	34	50	16				
17 Stromness	104	89	84	83	80	79	79	85	92	103	76	63	35	22	25	32	17			
18 Fair Isle	122	111	116	115	118	120	120	130	137	148	121	108	79	68	85	55	77	18		
19 **Lerwick**	160	150	156	155	160	162	162	172	190	162	148	120	109	124	95	110	42	19		
20 *Cape Wrath*	145	130	125	124	121	120	120	127	126	144	117	104	76	63	47	79	58	120	155	20

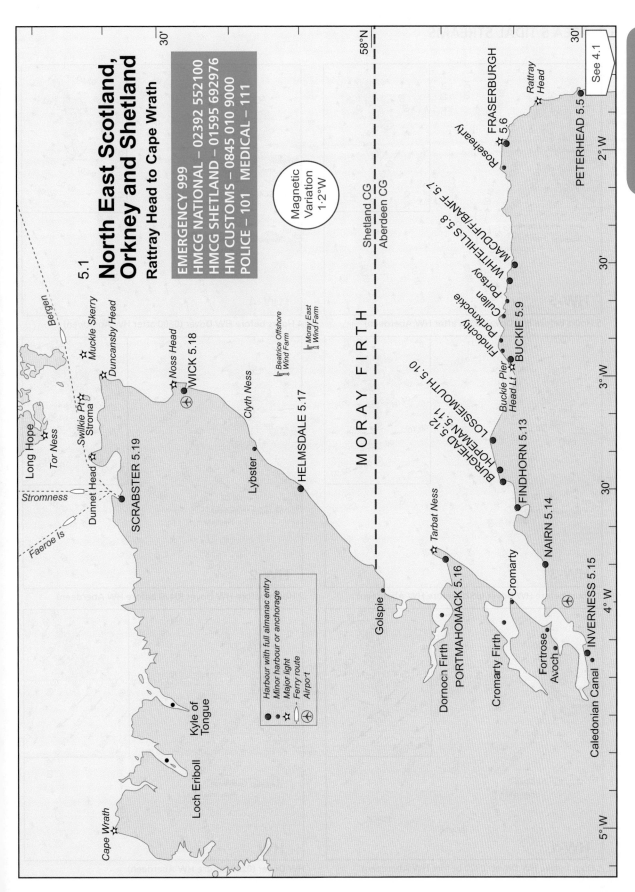

5.2 AREA 5 TIDAL STREAMS

5 Hours before HW Dover (0500 after HW Aberdeen)

4 Hours before HW Dover (0600 after HW Aberdeen)

3 Hours before HW Dover (0520 before HW Aberdeen)

2 Hours before HW Dover (0420 before HW Aberdeen)

1 Hour before HW Dover (0320 before HW Aberdeen)

HW Dover (0220 before HW Aberdeen)

Southward 4.2

HW+1
1 Hour after HW Dover (0120 before HW Aberdeen)

HW+2
2 Hours after HW Dover (0020 before HW Aberdeen)

HW+3
3 Hours after HW Dover (0040 after HW Aberdeen)

HW+4
4 Hours after HW Dover (0140 after HW Aberdeen)

HW+5
5 Hours after HW Dover (0240 after HW Aberdeen)

HW+6
6 Hours after HW Dover (0340 after HW Aberdeen)

5.3 LIGHTS, BUOYS AND WAYPOINTS

Bold print = light with a nominal range of 15M or more. CAPITALS = place or feature. *CAPITAL ITALICS* = light-vessel, light float or Lanby. *Italics* = Fog signal. ***Bold italics*** = Racon. Some marks/buoys are fitted with AIS (<u>MMSI No</u>); see relevant charts.

BUCHAN NESS TO INVERNESS

PETERHEAD and RATTRAY HEAD
Buchan Ness ☆ Fl 5s 40m **18M**; W twr, R bands; ***Racon (O) 14-16M***; 57°28'·23N 01°46'·51W.
Kirktown Ldg lts 314°. Front, Oc R 6s 14m 10M; Or △ on lattice mast; 57°30'·22N 01°47'·21W. Rear, Oc R 6s 21m 10M (sync with front); Or ▽ on lattice mast.
S Bkwtr Hd ⚓ Fl (2) R 12s 24m 7M; 57°29'·79N 01°46'·54W.
N Bkwtr Hd ⚓ Iso RG 6s 19m 11M; W tripod; vis: 171°-R-236°-G-171°; *Horn 30s;* 57°29'·84N 01°46'·32W.
Rattray Hd ☆ 57°36'·61N 01°49'·03W Fl (3) 30s 28m **18M**; W twr; ***Racon (M) 15M***; *Horn (2) 45s.*
Smith Bank Met Mast ⬦ Mo(U) 15s 17m 10M Mast (101); *Horn Mo(U) 30s;* 58°10'·93N 02°49'·22W.

FRASERBURGH
Balaclava Bkwtr Head ⚓ Fl (2) G 8s 26m 6M; dome on W twr; vis: 178°-326°; 57°41'·51N 01°59'·70W.
N Pier ⚓ WRG 2s 7m 8M; metal post; 285°-G-287°-WG-289°-W-293°-WR-295°-R-297°; 57°41'·54N 01°59'·99W.
Kinnaird Hd ☆ 57°41'·87N 02°00'·26W Fl 5s 25m **22M**; vis: 092°-297°.

MACDUFF, BANFF and WHITEHILLS
Macduff Pier Hd ⚓ Fl (2) WRG 6s 12m W9M, R7M; W twr; vis: shore-G-115°-W-174°-R-210°; 57°40'·26N 02°30'·01W.
Macduff Ldg Lts 130°, Front FR 28m 3M; 57°40'·18N 02°29'·85W. Rear, 220m from front, FR 55m 3M; both Or △ on mast.
Banff Ldg Lts 295°, Front Fl R 4s; 57°40·30N 02°31·36W. Rear, QR; both vis: 210°-345°.
Whitehills Pier Hd ⚓ 57°40'·80N 02°34'·88W Fl WR 3s 7m W9M, R6M; W twr; vis: 132°-R-212°-W-245°.

PORTSOY and FINDOCHTY
Portsoy Pier Ldg Lts 173°, Front Fl G 4s 20m 3M; post; 57°41'·09W 02°41'·40W; Rear Q G 22m 3M; R △ on BW post.
Findochty Middle Pier Ldg Lts 166°, Front FR 6m 3M; 57°41'·90N 02°54'·20W. Rear FR 10m 3M.

BUCKIE
West Muck ⚓ QR 5m 7M; tripod; 57°41'·06N 02°58'·01W.
N Pier Ldg Lts 096°, Front, FR 6m 9M; 57°40'·83N 02°57'·71W.
Rear ☆, 60m from front, Oc R 10s 15m 15M; W twr.

LOSSIEMOUTH, HOPEMAN and BURGHEAD
Lossiemouth S Pier Hd ⚓ Fl R 6s 11m 5M; 57°43'·42N 03°16'·69W.
Halliman Skerries ⚓ Q; ***Racon M***, 57°44'·33N 03°18'·57W.
Hopeman Ldg Lts 081°, Front, FR 3m; 57°42'·71N 03°26'·18W. Rear, 10m from front, FR, 4m.
Burghead N Bkwtr Hd ⚓ Oc 8s 7m 5M; 57°42'·09N 03°30'·03W.

FINDHORN, NAIRN and INVERNESS FIRTH
Findhorn Landfall ⚓ LF 10s 57°40'·34N 03°38'·77W.
Nairn E Pier Hd ⚓ Oc WRG 4s 6m 5M; 8-sided twr; vis: shore-G-100°-W-207°-R-shore; 57°35'·62N 03°51'·65W.
Riff Bank E ⚓ Fl Y 10s 3m 5M 57°38'·38N 03°58'·18W; <u>AIS</u>.

SOUTH CHANNEL
Riff Bank S ⚓ Q (6) + L Fl 15s; 57°36'·73N 04°00'·97W.
Chanonry ⚓ 57°34'·45N 04°05'·56W Oc 6s 12m 12M; W twr; vis: 148°-073°.
Munlochy ⚓ L Fl 10s; 57°32'·91N 04°07'·65W.
Petty Bank ⚓ Fl R 5s 57°31'·58N 04°08'·98W.
Meikle Mee ⚓ Fl G 3s 57°30'·26N 04°12'·02W.

Longman Pt ⚓ Fl WR 2s 7m W5M, R4M; vis: 078°-W-258°-R-078°; 57°29'·99N 04°13'·31W.
Craigton Point ⚓ Fl WRG 4s 6m W11M, R7M, G7M; vis: 312°-W-048°-R-064°-W-085°-G-shore; 57°30'·05N 04°14'·09W.
Bridge Centre , Or △; ***Racon (K) 6M***; 57°29'·97N 04°13'·79W.

INVERNESS and CALEDONIAN CANAL
R. Ness Outer ⚓ QR 3m 4M; 57°29'·83N 04°13'·93W.
Carnarc Pt ⚓ Fl G 2s 8m 4M; G lattice twr; 57°29'·72N 04°14'·25W.
Clachnaharry, S Tr'ng Wall Hd ⚓ Iso G 4s 5m 2M; tfc sigs; 57°29'·43N 04°15'·86W.

INVERNESS TO DUNCANSBY HEAD

CROMARTY FIRTH and INVERGORDON
Fairway ⚓ L Fl 10s; ***Racon (M) 5M***; 57°39'·96N 03°54'·19W.
Cromarty Bank ⚓ Fl (2) G 10s; 57°40'·66N 03°56'·78W.
Buss Bank ⚓ Fl R 3s 57°40'·97N 03°59'·54W.
Cromarty – The Ness (Lt ho disused W tr 13m); 57°40'·98N 04°02'·20W
Nigg Oil Terminal Pier Hd ⚓ Oc G 5s 31m 5M; Gy twr, floodlit; 57°41'·54N 04°02'·60W.

DORNOCH FIRTH to LYBSTER
Tarbat Ness ☆ 57°51'·88N 03°46'·76W Fl (4) 30s 53m **18M**; W twr, R bands; ***Racon (T) 14-16M***.
Met Mast ⚓ Mo(U) 15s 17m 10M; FR (101m), *Horn Mo(U) 30s;* 58°10'·93N 00°49'·22W.
Helmsdale ⚓ Dir lt 313° WRG 2s 7m 6M (1M day); post; vis: 308°-Iso G-311°-Al WG-312°-Iso W-313°-Al WR-314°-Iso R-318°; 58°06'·91N 03°39'·04W.
Lybster, S Pier Hd ⚓ Oc R 6s 10m 3M; 58°17'·79N 03°17'·41W.
Clyth Ness Lt Ho (unlit); W twr, R band; 58°18'·64N 03°12'·74W.

WICK
S Pier Hd ⚓ Fl WRG 3s 12m W12M, R9M, G9M; W 8-sided twr; vis: 253°-G-270°-W-286°-R-329°; 58°26'·34N 03°04'·73W.
Dir lt 288·5° F WRG 9m W10M, R7M, G7M; col, N end of bridge; vis: 283·5°-G-287·2°-W-289·7°-R-293·5°; 58°26'·54N 03°05'·34W
Noss Hd ☆ 58°28'·76N 03°03'·09W Fl 20s 53m **W18M**; W twr; vis: 073°-045° (332°).

DUNCANSBY HEAD TO CAPE WRATH

Duncansby Hd ☆ 58°38'·65N 03°01'·58W Fl 12s 67m **21M**; W twr; ***Racon (T)***.
Muckle Skerry ☆ 58°41'·41N 02°55'·49W Fl (3) 30s 52m **23M**; W twr; <u>992351086</u>.
Lother Rock ⚓ Fl 2s 13m 6M; ***Racon (M) 10M***; 58°43'·79N 02°58'·69W.
Swona ⚓ Fl 8s 17m 9M; vis: 261°-210°; 58°44'·25N 03°04'·24W.
Swona N Hd ⚓ Fl (3) 10s 16m 10M; 58°45'·11N 03°03'·10W.
Stroma ☆, Swilkie Point 58°41'·75N 03°07'·01W Fl (2) 20s 32m **20M**; W twr; <u>992351092</u>.
Dunnet Hd ☆ 58°40'·28N 03°22'·60W Fl (4) 30s 105m **23M**.

THURSO, SCRABSTER and CAPE WRATH
Thurso ⚓ FG 5m 4M; Gy post; 58°35'·91N 03°30'·80W.
Scrabster Q. E. Pier Hd ⚓ Fl (2) 4s 8m 8M 58°36'·66N 03°32'·31W.
Strathy Pt Lt Ho (disused) W twr on W dwelling; 58°36'·04N 04°01'·12W.
Sule Skerry ☆ 59°05'·09N 04°24'·38W Fl (2) 15s 34m **21M**; W twr; ***Racon (T)***.
Sule Stack ⊙; V-AIS; *ℐ*; 59°01'·45N 04°30'·40W; <u>992356017</u>.
Nun Rock ⊙; V-AIS; *ℐ*; 58°52'·65N 04°58'·30W; <u>992356016</u>.
North Rona ☆ 59°07'·27N 05°48'·91W Fl (3) 20s 114m **22M**.
Sula Sgeir ⚓ Fl 15s 74m 11M; □ structure; 59°05'·61N 06°09'·57W.
Loch Eriboll, White Hd ⚓ Fl WR10s 18m W13M, R12M; W twr and bldg; vis: 030°-W-172°-R-191°-W-212°; 58°31'·01N 04°38'·90W.
Cape Wrath ☆ 58°37'·54N 04°59'·99W Fl (4) 30s 122m **22M**; W twr <u>992351087</u>.

ORKNEY ISLANDS

Tor Ness ☆ 58°46'·78N 03°17'·86W Fl 5s 21m **17M**; W twr.
Cantick Hd (S Walls, SE end) ⚡ 58°47'·23N 03°07'·88W Fl 20s 35m 13M; W twr.

SCAPA FLOW and APPROACHES

Long Hope, S Ness Pier Hd ⚡ Fl WRG 3s 6m W7M, R5M, G5M; vis: 082°-G-242°-W-252°-R-082°; 58°48'·05N 03°12'·35W.
Hoxa Head ⚡ Fl WR 3s 15m W9M, R6M; W twr; vis: 026°-W-163°-R-201°-W-215°; 58°49'·31N 03°02'·09W.
Nevi Skerry ⚓ Fl (2) 6s 7m 6M; 58°50'·67N 03°02'·70W.
Flotta Grinds ⚓ Fl (2) R; 58°50'·97N 03°00'·77W; 992351083.
Rose Ness ⚡ 58°52'·33N 02°49'·97W Fl 6s 24m 8M; W twr.
Copinsay ⚡ Fl (5) 30s 79m 14M; W twr; 58°53'·79N 02°40'·33W.
Barrel of Butter ⚡ Fl (2) 10s 6m 7M; 58 53'·40N 03°07'·62W.
Cava ⚡ Fl WR 3s 11m W10M, R8M; W ○ twr; vis: 351°-W-143°-196°-W-251°-R-271°-R-298°; 58°53'·21N 03°10'·70W .
Holm of Houton ⚡ 58°54'·62N 03°10'·97W; Fl R 3s 7m 5M.
Houton Bay Ldg Lts 316°. Front ⚓ Fl G 3s 8m. Rear ⚓, 200m from front, FG 16m; vis: 312°- 320°; 58°54'·97N 03°11'·56W.

CLESTRAN SOUND and HOY SOUND

Graemsay Is Hoy Sound ☆ Ldg Lts 104°. Front Low, Iso 3s 17m 12M; W twr; vis: 070°-255°, 58°56'·42N 03°18'·60W. **High Rear**, 1·2M from front, Oc WR 8s 35m **W19M**, R14M; W twr; vis: 097°-R-112°-W-163°-R-178°-W-332°; obsc on Ldg line within 0·5M.
Skerry of Ness ⚡ Fl WG 4s 7m W7M, G4M; vis: shore -W-090°-G-shore; 58°56'·95N 03°17'·83W.

STROMNESS

Ldg Lts 317°. Front FR 29m 11M; W twr; 58°57'·61N 03°18'·15W.
Rear, 55m from front, FR 39m 11M; vis: 307°-327°; H24.

AUSKERRY

Auskerry ☆ 59°01'·51N 02°34'·34W Fl 20s 34m **20M**; W twr.
Helliar Holm, S end ⚡ Fl WRG 10s 18m W14M, R11M, G11M; W twr; vis: 256°-G-276°-W-292°-R-098°-W-116°-G-154°; 59°01'·13N 02°54'·09W.
Balfour Pier Shapinsay ⚡ Fl (2) WRG 5s 5m W3M, R2M, G2M; vis: 270°-G-010°-W-020°-R-090°; 59°01'·86N 02°54'·49W.

KIRKWALL

Thieves Holm, ⚡ Q R 8M; 59°01'·09N 02°56'·21W.
Pier N end ☆ 58°59'·29N 02°57'·72W Iso WRG 5s 8m **W15M**, R13M, G13M; W twr; vis: 153°-G-183°-W-192°-R-210°.

WIDE FIRTH

Linga Skerry ⚓ Q (3) 10s; 59°02'·39N 02°57'·56W.
Boray Skerries ⚓ Q (6) + L Fl 15s; 59°03'·65N 02°57'·66W.
Skertours ⚓ Q; 59°04'·11N 02°56'·72W.
Galt Skerry ⚓ Q; 59°05'·21N 02°54'·20W.
Seal Skerry ⚡ Fl R 3s 5m 3M; platform; 59°05'·21N 02°54'·20W.
Brough of Birsay ☆ 59°08'·19N 03°20'·41W Fl (3) 25s 52m **18M**.
Papa Stronsay NE end, The Ness ⚡ Fl(4)20s 8m 9M; W twr; 59°09'·34N 02°34'·93W.

SANDAY ISLAND and NORTH RONALDSAY

Quiabow ⚓ Fl (2) G 12s; 59°09'·82N 02°36'·30W.
Start Pt ☆ 59°16'·69N 02°22'·71W Fl (2) 20s 24m **18M**.
Kettletoft Pier Hd ⚡ Fl WRG 3s 7m W7M, R5M, G5M; vis: 351°-W- 011°-R-180°-G-351°; 59°13'·80N 02°35'·86W.
N Ronaldsay ☆ NE end, 59°23'·34N 02°22'·91W Fl 10s 43m **24M**; R twr, W bands; *Racon (T) 14-17M*.

EDAY and EGILSAY

Calf Sound ⚡ Fl (3) WRG 10s 6m W8M, R6M, G6M; W twr; vis: shore-R-215°-W-222°-G-301°-W-305°; 59°14'·21N 02°45'·82W.
Backaland Pier ⚡ 59°09'·43N 02°44'·88W Fl R 3s 5m 4M; vis: 192°-250°.
Egilsay Graand ⚓ Q (6) + L Fl 15s; 59°06'·86N 02°54'·42W.

WESTRAY and PIEROWALL

Noup Head ☆ 59°19'·86N 03°04'·23W Fl 30s 79m **20M**; W twr; vis: about 335°-282° but partially obsc 240°-275°.

Pierowall E Pier Head ⚡ Fl WRG 3s 7m W11M, R7M, G7M; vis: 254°-G-276°-W-291°-R-308°-G-215°; 59°19'·35N 02°58'·53W.
Papa Westray, Moclett Bay Pier Head ⚡ Fl WRG 5s 7m W5M, R3M, G3M; vis: 306°-G-341°-W-040°-R-074°; 59°19'·60N 02°53'·52W.

SHETLAND ISLES

FAIR ISLE

Skadan South ☆, 59°30'·84N 01°39'·16W Fl (4) 30s 32m **22M**; W twr; vis: 260°-146°, obsc inshore 260°-282°.
Skroo ☆ N end 59°33'·13N 01°36'·58W Fl (2) 30s 80m **22M**; W twr; vis: 086·7°-358°.

MAINLAND, SOUTH

Sumburgh Head ☆ 59°51'·21N 01°16'·58W Fl (3) 30s 91m **23M**.
Lt Ho disused 59°51'·48N 01°16'·28W; W twr.
Mousa, Perie Bard ⚡ Fl 3s 20m 10M; 59°59'·84N 01°09'·51W.

BRESSAY and LERWICK

Bressay, Kirkabister Ness ⚡ 60°07'·20N 01°07'·31W; Fl (2) 10s 18m 10M. Adjacent Lt Ho disused.
Maryfield Ferry Terminal ⚡ Oc WRG 6s 5m 5M; vis: W008°-R013°-G-111°-008°; 60°09'·43N 01°07'·45W.
North Ness ⚡ Iso WG 4s 4m 5M; vis: shore-W-158°-G-216°-W-301°; 60°09'·57N 01°08'·77W
Loofa Baa ⚓ Q (6) + L Fl 15s 4m 5M; 60°09'·72N 01°08'·79W.
Soldian Rock ⚓ Q (6) + L Fl 15s 60°12'·51N 01°04'·73W.
N ent Dir lt 215°, Oc WRG 6s 27m 8M; Y △, Or stripe; vis: 211°-R-214°-W-216°-G-221°; 60°10'·47N 01°09'·53W.
Rova Hd ⚡ 60°11'·46N 01°08'·60W; Fl WRG 4s (sync) 12m W12M, R/G9M; W twr; vis: 090°-R-182°-W-191°-G-213°-R-241°-W-261·5°-G-009°-R-040°; same structure: **Dir** ☆ 186·5° Fl WRG 4s (sync) 14m **W16M**, R/G13M; (sync) vis: 176·5°-R-182°-W-191°-G-196·5°.
Dales Voe ⚡ Fl (2) WRG 8s 5m W4M, R3M, G3M; vis: 220°-G-227°-W-233°-R-240°; 60°11'·79N 01°11'·23W.
Hoo Stack ⚡ Fl (4) WRG 12s 40m W7M, R5M, G5M; W pylon; vis: 169°-R-180°-W-184°-G-193°-W-169°. Same structure, Dir lt 182°. Fl (4) WRG 12s 33m W9M, R6M, G6M; vis: 177°- R-180°-W-184°-W-187°; synch with upper lt; 60°14'·96N 01°05'·38W.
Mull (Moul) of Eswick ⚡ Fl WRG 3s 50m W9M, R6M, G6M; W twr; vis: 028°-R-200°-W-207°-G-018°-W-028°; 60°15'·74N 01°05'·90W.
Inner Voder ⚓ Q (9) 15s; 60°16'·44N 01°05'·18W; AIS.

WHALSAY and SKERRIES

Symbister Ness ⚡ Fl (2) WG 12s 11m W8M, G6M; W twr; vis: shore-W-203°-G-shore; 60°20'·43N 01°02'·29W.
Suther Ness ⚡ Fl WRG 3s 10m W10M, R8M, G7M; vis: shore -W-038°-R-173°-W-206°-G-shore; 60°22'·12N 01°00'·20W.
Bound Skerry ☆ 60°25'·47N 00°43'·72W Fl 20s 44m **20M**; W twr.
South Mouth. Ldg Lts 014°. Front, FY3m 2M; 60°25'·33N 00°45'·01W. Rear, FY 12m 2M.
Muckle Skerry ⚡ Fl (2) WRG 10s 15m W7M, R5M, G5M; W twr; vis: 046°-W-192°-R-272°-G-348°-W-353°-R-046°; 60°26'·41N 00°51'·84W.

YELL SOUND

S ent, Lunna Holm ⚡ Fl (3) WRG 15s 19m W10M,R7M,G7M; W ○ twr; vis: shore-R-090°-W-094°-G-209°-W-275°-R-shore; 60°27'·34N 01°02'·52W.
Firths Voe ☆, N shore 60°27'·21N 01°10'·63W Oc WRG 8s 9m **W15M**, R10M, G10M; W twr; vis: 189°-W-194°-G-257°-W-261°-R-339°-W-066°.
Linga Is. Dir lt 150° ⚡ Q (4) WRG 8s 10m W9M, R9M, G9M; vis: 145°-R-148°-W-152°-G-155°. Q (4) WRG 8s 10m W7M, R4M, G4M; same structure: vis: 052°-R-146°, 154°-G-196°-W-312°; synch; 60°26'·80N 01°09'·13W.
The Rumble Bn ⚡ R Bn; Fl 10s 8m 4M; *Racon (O)*; 60°28'·16N 01°07'·26W.

Yell, Ulsta Ferry Term. Bkwtr Hd ☆ Oc RG 4s 7m R5M, G5M; vis: shore-G-354°, 044°-R-shore. Same structure; Oc WRG 4s 5m W8M, R5M, G5M; vis: shore-G-008°-W-036°-R-shore; 60°29'·74N 01°09'·52W.

Toft Ferry Terminal ☆,Dir lt 241° (H24); Dir Oc WRG 10s 8m **W16M**, R10M, G10M; vis: 236° -G-240°-W-242°-R-246°; by day W2M, R1M, G1M. 60°27'·96N 01°12'·34W.

Ness of Sound, W side ☆ Fl (3) WRG 12s 18m W9M, R6M, G6M; vis: shore-G-345°-W-350°-R-160°-W-165°-G-shore; 60°31'·34N 01°11'·28W.

Brother Is. Dir lt 329°, Fl (4) WRG 8s 16m W10M, R7M, G7M; vis: 323·5°-G-328°-W-330°-R-333·5°; 60°30'·95N 01°14'·11W.

Mio Ness ☆ Q (2) WR 10s 12m W7M, R4M; W ○ twr; vis: 282°-W-238°-R-282°; 60°29'·66N 01°13'·68W.

Tinga Skerry ☆ Q(2)G 10s 9m 5M. W ○ twr; 60°30'·48N 01°14'·86W.

YELL SOUND, NORTH ENTRANCE

Bagi Stack ☆ Fl (4) 20s 45m 10M; 60°43'·53N 01°07'·54W.

Gruney Is ☆ Fl WR 5s 53m W8M, R6M; W twr; vis: 064°-R-180°-W-012°; *Racon (T) 14M*; 60°39'·15N 01°18'·17W.

Pt of Fethaland ☆ 60°38'·05N 01°18'·70W Fl (3) WR 15s 65m **W19M, R15M**; vis 080°-R-103°-W-160°-R-206°-W-340°.

Muckle Holm ☆ Fl (4) 10s 32m 10M 60°34'·83N 01°16'·01W.

Little Holm ☆ Iso 4s 12m 6M; W twr; 60°33'·42N 01°15'·88W.

Outer Skerry ☆ Fl 6s 12m 8M; 60°33'·04N 01°18'·32W.

Quey Firth ☆ Oc WRG 6s 22m W12M, R8M, G8M; W twr; vis: shore (through S & W)-W-290°-G-327°-W-334°-W-shore; 60°31'·43N 01°19'·58W.

Lamba, S side ☆Fl WRG 3s 30m W8M, R5M, G5M; W twr; vis: shore-G-288°-W-293°-R-327°-W-044°-R-140°-W-shore. Dir lt 290·5° Fl WRG 3s 24m W10M, R7M, G7M; vis: 285·5°-G-288°-W-293°-W-295·5°; 60°30'·73N 01°17'·84W.

SULLOM VOE

Gluss Is ☆ Ldg Lts 194·7° (H24). **Front**, 60°29'·77N 01°19'·44W F 39m **19M**; □ on Gy twr; **Rear**, 0·75M from front, F 69m **19M**; □ on Gy twr; both Lts 9M by day.

Little Roe ☆ Fl (3) WR 10s 16m W5M, R4M; W structure, Or band; vis: 036°-R-095·5°-W-036°; 60°29'·99N 01°16'·46W.

Skaw Taing ☆ Ldg Lts 150·5°. Front, Oc WRG 5s 21m W8M, R5M, G5M; Or and W structure; vis: 049°-W-078°-G-147°-W-154°-R-169°-W-288°; 60°29'·10N 01°16'·86W. Rear, 195m from front, Oc 5s 35m 8M; vis: W145°-156°.

Ness of Bardister ☆ Oc WRG 8s 20m W9M, R6M, G6M; Or &W structure; vis: 180·5°- W-240°-R-310·5°-W-314·5°-G-030·5°; 60°28'·19N 01°19'·63W.

Fugla Ness. Lts in line 212·3°. Rear, 60°27'·25N 01°19'·74W Iso 4s 45m 14M. Common front 60°27'·45N 01°19'·57W Iso 4s 27m 14M; synch with rear Lts. Lts in line 203°. Rear, 60°27'·26N 01°19'·81W Iso 4s 45m 14M.

Sella Ness ☆ Dir lt 133·5°; 60°26'·76N 01°16'·66W Oc WRG 10s 19m **W16M**, R3M, G3M; vis: 123·5°-G-130·5°-Al WG (white phase increasing with brg)-132·5°-W-134·5°-Al WR(R phase inc

with brg)-136·5°-R-143·5°; H24. By day Oc WRG 10s 19m W2M, R1M,G1M as above.

EAST YELL, UNST and BALTA SOUND

Whitehill ☆ Fl WR 3s 24m W9M, R6M; W clad metal frame twr; vis: 147°-W-163°-R-211°-W-352°-R-003°; 60°34'·80N 01°00'·22W.

Fetlar. Hamars Ness ☆ Iso G 6s 5m 3M; 60°37'·78N 00°55'·73W.

Balta Sound ☆Fl WR 10s 17m 10M, R7M; vis: 249°-W-008°-R-058°-W-154°; 60°44'·43N 00°47'·68W.

Holme of Skaw ☆ Fl 5s 8m 8M; white metal framework twr; 60°49'·87N 00°46'·30W.

Muckle Flugga ☆ 60°51'·32N 00°53'·13W Fl (2) 20s 66m **22M**.

Yell. Cullivoe Bkwtr Hd ☆ Fl (2) WRG 10s 3m 4M; vis: 080°-G-294°-W-355°-R-080°; 60°41'·86N 00°59'·70W.

Unst. Head of Mula ☆ Fl WRG 5s 48m W10M, G7M, R7M; metal framework twr; vis: 292°-G-357°-W-002°-R-157°-W-161·5; 60°40'·76N 00°57'·58W.

MAINLAND, WEST

Esha Ness ☆ 60°29'·34N 01°37'·65W Fl 12s 61m **25M**.

Ness of Hillswick ☆ Fl (4) WR 15s 34m W9M, R6M; vis: 217°-093°-R-114°; 60°27'·21N 01°29'·80W.

Muckle Roe, Swarbacks Minn ☆ Fl WR 3s 30m W9M, R6M; vis: 314°-W-041°-R-075°-W-137°; 60°20'·98N 01°27'·07W.

W Burra Firth Outer ☆ Oc WRG 8s 27m W9M, R7M, G7M; vis: 136°-G-142°-W-150°-R-156°. H24; 60°17'·79N 01°33'·56W.

W Burra Firth Inner ☆ 60°17'·78N 01°32'·17W F WRG 9m **W15M**, R9M, G9M; vis: 095°-G-098°-W-102°-105°; H24.

Ve Skerries ☆ Fl (2) 20s 17m 11M; W twr; *Racon (T) 15M*; 60°22'·36N 01°48'·78W.

Papa Stour Housa Voe Dir lt 228° ☆ F WRG 2m W9M, R7M, G7M; vis: 219°- G-226°- W-230°-R-239°; 60°19'·58N 01°40'·47W.

Rams Head ☆ Fl WRG 8s 16m W9M, R6M; G6M; W house; vis: 265°-G-355°-W-012°-R-090°-W-136°, obsc by Vaila I when brg more than 030°; 60°11'·96N 01°33'·47W.

North Havra ☆ Fl(3) WRG 12s 24m W11M, R8M, G8M; W twr; vis: 001°-G-053·5°-W-060·5°-R-144°, 274°-G-334°-W-337·5°-R-001°; 60°09'·85N 01°20'·29W.

SCALLOWAY

Bullia Skerry ☆ Fl 5s 5m 5M; stainless steel pillar & platform 60°06'·55N 01°21'·57W.

Point of the Pund ☆ Fl WRG 5s 20m W7M, R5M, G5M; W GRP twr; vis: 267°-W-350°-R-090°-G-111°-R-135°-W-140°-G-177°; 60°07'·99N 01°18'·31W.

Whaleback Skerry ↓ Q; 60°07'·95N 01°18'·90W.

Blacks Ness Pier SW corner ☆ Oc WRG 10s 10m W11M, G8M, R8M; vis: 052°-G-063·5°-W-065·5°-R-077°; 60°08'·02N 01°16'·59W.

Fugla Ness ☆ Fl (2) WRG 10s 20m W10M, R7M, G7M; W twr; vis: 014°-G-032°-W-082°-R-134°-W-shore; 60°06'·38N 01°20'·85W.

FOULA

South Ness ☆ 60°06'·75N 02°03'·86W Fl WR (3) 15s 36m **W18M** R14M; W twr; vis: 221°-W-255°-R-277°-W-123°-obscured-221°.

5.4 PASSAGE INFORMATION

Admiralty Leisure Folio: 5617 Fraserburgh to Inverness and the Caledonian Canal. **Bibliography:** Orkney and Shetland Islands including N&NE Scotland (Imray/Clyde Cruising Club Sailing Directions & Anchorages). *Shetland Islands Pilot* (Imray Buchanan). The *N Coast of Scotland Pilot* (Admiralty NP52).

A £75 '*Rover ticket*' (Aberdeenshire and Moray Councils) allows berthing for one week at all the ports in the scheme. Orkney Marinas 'Weekly Rover' costs £11/m, to berth in their 3 marinas or on Port Authority Harbours, piers and moorings except St Margaret's Hope (5.20) which is independent.

BUCHAN NESS TO RATTRAY HEAD

Buchan Ness (light, Racon) is a rocky peninsula. 2ca N is Meikle Mackie islet, close W of which is the small harbour of Boddam (dries). 3ca NE of Meikle Mackie is The Skerry, a rock 6m high on S side of Sandford Bay; the sea breaks on shoals extending 2ca NNE. The channel between The Skerry and mainland is foul with rocks and not recommended. Peterhead is easy to enter in almost all conditions and is an excellent passage port with a marina at SW corner of the Bay. Numerous submarine pipelines lead ashore to St Fergus Terminal in Rattray Bay. **Notes on offshore installations, see 3.4.**

Rattray Hd (light on The Ron, a rock 2ca E of the Hd) has rocky foreshore, drying to 2ca off. Rattray Briggs is a detached reef, depth 0·2m, 2ca E of lt ho. Rattray Hard is a rocky patch, depth 10·7m, 1·5M ENE of the lt ho, which raises a dangerous sea during onshore gales. Conspic radio masts with red aero lights lie 2·5M WNW and 2·2M W of lighthouse.

▶ *Off Rattray Hd the S-going stream begins at HW Aberdeen −0420, and the N-going at HW Aberdeen +0110, Sp rates 3kn. In normal conditions keep about 1M E of Rattray Hd, but pass 5M off in bad weather, preferably at slack water.* ◀

MORAY FIRTH (SOUTH COAST)

(AC 115, 222, 223) Crossing the Moray Firth from Rattray Hd (lt, fog sig) to Duncansby Hd (lt, Racon) heavy seas may be met in strong W winds. Most harbours are exposed to NE-E winds.

▶ *Tidal streams attain 3kn at Sp close off Rattray Hd. 5M NE of the Hd the NE-going stream begins at Aberdeen HW +0140; the SE-going stream at HW −0440, Sp rates 2kn. Except in the inner part of the Moray Firth streams are weak.* ◀

In late spring/early summer fog (haar) is likely in onshore winds. In strong winds the sea breaks over Steratan Rk and Colonel Rk, respectively 3M E and 1M ENE of Fraserburgh. Banff Bay is shallow and the harbour, which dries, should not be approached in fresh NE-E winds, when seas break well offshore. Macduff is an alternative avoiding Collie Rocks.

From Meavie Pt to Scar Nose dangers extend up to 3ca from shore in places. Beware Caple Rk (0·2m) 7½ca W of Logie Hd. Findochty & Portknockie are between Scar Nose and Craig Hd. Spey Bay is clear of dangers more than 7½ca from shore; ⚓ here only in offshore winds. Beware Craigenroan, an above-water rky patch 5ca SW of Craig Hd. Further West, East, and Middle and West Muck lie in approach to Buckie; Halliman Skerries (dry; bn) lie 1·5M WNW of Lossiemouth; Covesea Skerries (dry) lie 5ca NW of their lt ho (disused).

A Conservation Area SW of a line between Helmsdale and Lossiemouth protects a population of bottlenose dolphins. Mariners should proceed at a safe, constant speed through the area. Inverness Firth is approached between Nairn and S Sutor. In heavy weather there is a confused sea with overfalls on Guillam Bank, 9M S of Tarbat Ness. The sea also breaks on Riff Bank (S of S Sutor) which dries and divides the channel.

▶ *Off Fort George, on E side of the mouth of Inverness Firth (AC1078), the SW-going stream begins HW Aberdeen +0605, Sp rate 2·5kn; the NE-going stream begins at HW Aberdeen −0105, Sp rate 3·5kn. There are eddies and turbulence between Fort George and Chanonry Pt when stream is running hard. Tidal streams in the Inverness Firth and approaches are not strong, except in the Cromarty Firth Narrows, the Fort George Narrows and the Kessock Road off the entrance to the Caledonian Canal.* ◀

Fort George firing range flies red flags when in use. Much of Inverness Firth is shallow, but a rhumb line from Chanonry Pt to Kessock Bridge, via Munlochy SWM and Meikle Mee SHM carries a least depth of 2·1m. Meikle Mee bank dries 0·2m.

MORAY FIRTH (NORTH WEST COAST)

Enter Cromarty Firth (AC 1889, 1890) between North and South Sutor Hds, which are fringed by rks, some drying. Buss Bank buoy, Fl R 3s, marks the entrance, and there are good sheltered ⚓s within the firth. A buoyed deep-water channel runs to Invergordon; outside the channel there are shallows and drying banks. Beware large ships and tugs using Invergordon, Nigg Oil Terminal and Energy Park jetties. Contact Cromarty Firth Port Radio passing Buss Bank Buoy, inbound/outbound and keep listening watch (VHF Ch11).

Firths of Inverness & Cromarty

	FLOOD	EBB
(a)	Aberdeen +0430 to Aberdeen −0030	Aberdeen −0030 to Aberdeen +0430
(b)	Aberdeen +0600 to Aberdeen −0130	Aberdeen −0130 to Aberdeen +0330
(c)	Aberdeen +0605 to Aberdeen −0220	Aberdeen −0105 to Aberdeen +0440

▶ *At the entrance the in-going stream starts at HW Aberdeen +0600; the out-going at HW Aberdeen −0130, Sp rates 2·5 kn in the narrows between Nigg and Cromarty.* ◀

The coast NE to Tarbat Ness (lit) is fringed with rocks. Beware Three Kings (dries) about 3M NE of N Sutor.

▶ *Culloden Rk, a shoal with depth of 1·8m, extends 2½ca NE of Tarbat Ness, where the stream is weak.* ◀

Beware salmon nets between Tarbat Ness and Portmahomack. Dornoch Firth is shallow, with shifting banks, and in strong E'lies the sea breaks heavily on the bar E of Dornoch Pt.

At Lothbeg Pt, 5M SW of Helmsdale, a rocky ledge extends 5ca offshore. Nr Berriedale, 7M NE of Helmsdale, The Pinnacle, 61m high, stands close offshore. Beatrice oil field/wind farm (BOWL) with 84 turbines lies on Smith Bank, 28M NE of Tarbat Ness 7M off the Caithness coast. 6M further off to the E and SE of BOWL is the Moray East Wind Farm (under construction). Between Dunbeath and Lybster no dangers lie more than 2ca offshore. Clyth Ness is fringed by detached drying rks. From here to Wick dangers are close inshore. ⚓ in Sinclair's Bay in good weather, but Freswick Bay further N is better to await the tide in Pentland Firth (wreck in centre of bay). Stacks of Duncansby and Baxter Rk (depth 2·7m) lie 1M and 4ca S of Duncansby Hd.

PENTLAND FIRTH

(AC 2162, 2581) **This potentially dangerous chan should only be attempted with moderate winds (less than F4), good vis, no swell and a fair np tide.** In such conditions it presents few problems. A safe passage depends on a clear understanding of tidal streams and correct timing.

▶ *The Admiralty Tidal Stream Atlas for Orkney and Shetland (NP 209) gives large scale vectors and is essential. Even in ideal conditions the races off Duncansby Hd, Swilkie Pt (N end of Stroma), and Rks of Mey (Merry Men of Mey) must be avoided as they are always dangerous to small craft. Also avoid the Pentland Skerries, Muckle Skerry, Old Head, Lother Rock (S Ronaldsay), and Dunnet Hd on E-going flood. For passages across the Firth see CCC SDs for Orkney.* ◀

At E end the Firth is entered between Duncansby Hd and Old Hd (S Ronaldsay), between which lie Muckle Skerry and the Pentland Skerries. Near the centre of Firth are the Islands of Swona (N side) and Stroma (S side). Outer Sound (main chan, 2·5M wide) runs between Swona and Stroma; Inner Sound (1·5M wide) between Stroma and the mainland. Rks of Mey extend about 2ca N of St John's Pt. The W end of the Firth is between Dunnet Hd and Tor Ness (Hoy).

Tide flows strongly around and through the Orkney Islands. **The Pentland Firth is a dangerous area for all craft; streams reach 12kn between Duncansby Head and S Ronaldsay.** W of Dunnet Hd and Hoy flows are less with little tide within Scapa Flow. **Tidal streams reach 8-9kn at Sp in the Outer Sound, and 9-12kn between Pentland Skerries and Duncansby Hd. The resultant dangerous seas, very strong eddies and violent races should be avoided by yachts at all costs.** ◀

▶ *The E-going stream begins at HW Aberdeen +0500, and the W-going at HW Aberdeen −0105.* **Duncansby Race** *extends ENE towards Muckle Skerry on the SE-going stream, but by HW Aberdeen −0440 it extends NW from Duncansby Hd. Note: HW at Muckle Skerry is the same time as HW Dover. A persistent race off* **Swilkie Pt,** *at N end of Stroma, is very dangerous with a strong W'ly wind over a W-going stream. The most dangerous and extensive race in the Firth is* **Merry Men of Mey.** *It forms off St John's Pt on W-going stream at HW Aberdeen −0150 and for a while extends right across to Tor Ness with heavy breaking seas even in fine weather.* ◀

FLOOD	EBB
Pentland Firth & Orkneys	**Pentland Firth & Orkneys**
(a) Aberdeen +0500 to Aberdeen −0105	(a) Aberdeen −0105 to Aberdeen +0500
(b) Aberdeen +0310 to Aberdeen −0330	(b) Aberdeen −0330 to Aberdeen +0310
(c) Aberdeen +0400 to Aberdeen −0150	(c) Aberdeen −0150 to Aberdeen +0400

Passage Westward: This is the more difficult direction due to prevailing W winds. Freswick B, 3·5M S of Duncansby Hd, is a good waiting ⚓.

▶ *Here an eddy runs N for 9hrs. Round Duncansby Hd close in at HW Aberdeen −0220, as the ebb starts to run W.* ◀

Take a mid-course through the Inner Sound to appr the Rks of Mey from close inshore. Gills Bay is a temp anch if early; do not pass Rks of Mey until ebb has run for at least 2hrs. Pass 100m N of the Rks (awash).

Passage Eastward: With a fair wind and tide, no race forms and the passage is easier.

▶ *Leave Scrabster at local LW+1 so as to be close off Dunnet Hd not before HW Aberdeen +0340 when the E-going flood starts to make. If late, give the Hd a wide berth.* ◀

Having rounded the Rocks of Mey, steer S initially to avoid being set onto the rocky S tip of Stroma, marked by unlit SCM. Keep mid-chan through the Inner Sound and maintain this offing to give Duncansby Hd a wide berth. Tide turbines sit in the centre of the Sound S of Stroma with 9.9m over them.

PENTLAND FIRTH TO CAPE WRATH

(AC 1954) Dunnet B, S of Dunnet Hd (lt) gives temp ⚓ in E or S winds, but dangerous seas enter in NW'lies. On W side of Thurso B is Scrabster sheltered from S and W.

▶ *Between Holborn Hd and Strathy Pt the E-going stream begins at HW Ullapool −0150, and the W-going at HW Ullapool +0420, sp rates 1·8kn. Close to Brims Ness off Ushat Hd the sp rate is 3kn, and there is often turbulence.* ◀

SW of Ushat Hd the Dounreay power station is conspic, near shore. Dangers extend 2½ca seaward off this coast.

▶ *Along E side of Strathy Pt (lt) an eddy gives almost continuous N-going stream, but there is usually turbulence off the Pt where this eddy meets the main E or W stream.* ◀

Several small bays along this coast give temp ⚓ in offshore winds, but should not be used or approached with wind in a N quarter.

Kyle of Tongue is entered from E through Caol Raineach, S of Eilean nan Ron, or from N between Eilean Iosal and Cnoc Glass. There is no chan into the kyle W of Rabbit Is, to which a drying spit extends 0·5M NNE from the mainland shore. Further S there is a bar across entrance to inner part of kyle. There are ⚓s on SE side of Eilean nan Ron, SE side of Rabbit Is, off Skullomie, or S of Eilean Creagach off Talmine. Approach to the latter runs close W of Rabbit Islands, but beware rocks to N and NW of them.

Loch Eriboll (AC 2076) provides secure ⚓s, but in strong winds violent squalls blow down from mountains. Eilean Cluimhrig lies on W side of entrance; the E shore is fringed with rks up to 2ca offshore. At White Hd (lt) the loch narrows to 6ca. There are chans W and E of Eilean Choraidh. Best ⚓s in Camas an Duin (S of Ard Neackie) or in Rispond B close to entrance (but not in E winds, and beware Rispond Rk which dries).

The coast to C Wrath is indented, with dangers extending 3ca off the shore and offlying rks and Is. Once a yacht has left Loch Eriboll she is committed to a long and exposed passage until reaching Loch Inchard. The Kyle of Durness is dangerous if the wind or sea is onshore.

▶ *Give Cape Wrath a wide berth when wind-against-tide which raises a severe sea.* ◀

A firing exercise area extends 8M E of C. Wrath, and 4M offshore. When in use, R flags or pairs of R lts (vert) are shown from E and W limits, and yachts should keep clear.

ORKNEY ISLANDS

The Orkney Islands number about 70, of which some 24 are inhabited. They extend 5 to 50M NNE from Duncansby Hd, are mostly low-lying, but Hoy in the SW of the group reaches 475m (1560ft). Coasts are rocky and much indented, but there are many sandy beaches. A passage with least width of about 3M runs NW/SE through the group. The islands are separated from Scotland by the Pentland Firth, a very dangerous stretch of water. The principal island is Mainland (or Pomona) on which stands Kirkwall, the capital. For inter-island ferries see www.orkneyferries.co.uk.

Severe gales blow in winter and early spring. The climate is mild but windy, and very few trees grow. There are LBs at Longhope, Stromness and Kirkwall.

(AC 2249, 2250) The Islands are mostly indented and rocky, but with sandy beaches especially on NE sides.

▶*Pilotage is easy in good vis, but in other conditions great care is needed since tides run strongly. For details refer to* Clyde Cruising Club's Orkney Sailing Directions *and the* Admiralty Tidal Atlas NP 209. *When cruising in Orkney it is essential to understand and use the tidal streams to the best advantage, avoiding the various tide races and overfalls, particularly near sp.*◀

A good engine is needed since there are many places where it is dangerous to get becalmed. Swell from the Atlantic or North Sea can contribute to dangerous sea conditions, or penetrate to some of the ⚓s. During summer months winds are not normally unduly strong, and can be expected to be Force 7 or more on about two days a month. In winter the wind reaches this strength for 10-15 days per month, and gales can be very severe in late winter and early spring. Cruising conditions are best near midsummer, when of course the hours of daylight are much extended.

Stronsay Firth and Westray Firth run SE/NW through the group. The many good ⚓s include: Deer Sound (W of Deer Ness); Bays of Firth, Isbister, and off Balfour in Elwick B (all leading fm Wide Firth); Rysa Snd, B of Houton, Hunda Snd (Scapa Flow); Rousay Sound; and Pierowall Road (Westray). Plans for some of these are on AC 2622. The European Marine Energy test site with underwater turbines and large static vessels lies between Eday and Muckle Green Holm, and an offshore wave test site marked by cardinal buoys NNW of Hoy Mouth (emec.org.uk). A major oil terminal and associated prohibited area is at Flotta, on the S side of Scapa Flow.

▶ *Tide races or dangerous seas occur at the entrances to most of the firths or sounds when the stream is against strong winds. This applies particularly to Hoy Sound, Eynhallow Sound, Papa Sound (Westray), Lashy Sound, and North Ronaldsay Firth. Also off Mull Head, over Dowie Sand, between Muckle Green Holm and War Ness (where violent turbulence may extend right across the firth), between Faraclett Head and Wart Holm, and off Sacquoy Hd. Off War Ness the SE-going stream begins at HW Aberdeen +0435, and the NW-going at HW Aberdeen −0200, sp rates 7kn.* ◀

SHETLAND ISLANDS

(AC 3281, 3282, 3283) ▶ *These Islands mostly have bold cliffs and are relatively high, separated by narrow sounds through which the tide runs strongly, so that in poor vis great care is needed. Avoid sp tides, swell and wind against tide conditions. The tidal flow around the Shetland Islands rotates as the cycle progresses. When the flood begins, at −0400 HW Dover, the tidal flow is to the E, at HW Dover it is S, at Dover +0300 it is W, and at −0600 Dover it is N.*◀

Between Mainland and Whalsay passage can be made E or W of W Linga with spring rates of about 2kn with weaker streams to be found to the W in Lunning Sound.

▶ *Slack water at Lunning Sound occurs simultaneously at Lerwick, either 4hrs before or 2hrs after HW Lerwick.*◀

Passage further Northward can be made through Yell Sound or Colgrave/Bluemell Sounds with shelter at Cullivoe.

▶ *Tides in Yell Sound are slack at the same time as high and low water in Lerwick. The stream normally runs at about 4kn between the islands at the narrowest part between Yell and the Mainland but may reach 8kn at springs. Colgrave Sound to the W of Yell experiences somewhat less tidal stream.*◀

Bluemull Sound between Yell and Unst is a longer narrower passage. Well marked, passage is best attempted in daylight keeping to the middle of the channel clear of the fishing vessels en-route to Cullivoe.

▶ *The stream runs at up to 6kn at springs for longer duration and may be carried throughout a transit.*◀

Although there are many secluded and attractive ⚓s, remember that the weather can change very quickly, with sudden shifts of wind. Also beware salmon fisheries and mussel rafts (unlit) in many Voes, Sounds and hbrs. Lerwick is the busy main port and capital; other hbrs are Scalloway, Walls (Vaila Sound), Uyesound (S Unst), Mid Yell (E Yell), Cullivoe (N Yell), Burravoe (S Yell), Symbister (Whalsay), Out Skerries (Skerries Isle) and Balta Sound. Refer to the CCC's *Shetland Sailing Directions.*

▶ *Coming from the S, beware a most violent and dangerous race (roost) off Sumburgh Hd (at S end of Mainland) on both streams. Other dangerous areas include between Ve Skerries and Papa Stour; the mouth of Yell Sound with strong wind against N-going stream; and off Holm of Skaw (N end of Unst). Tidal streams run mainly NW/SE and are not strong except off headlands and in the major sounds; the Admiralty Tidal Atlas NP 209 gives detail. The sp range is about 2m.*◀

The 50M passage from Orkney can conveniently be broken by a stop at Fair Isle (North Haven).

▶ *Note that races form off both ends of the Is, especially S (Roost of Keels).*◀

Recommended Traffic Routes: NW-bound ships pass to the NE (no closer than 10M to Sumburgh Hd) or SW of Fair Isle; SE-bound ships pass no closer than 5M off N Ronaldsay (Orkney). Lerwick to Bergen, Norway, is about 210M.

FLOOD
Shetland Islands

(a) Dover −0410 to Dover +0020
(b) Dover −0400 to Dover +0030
(c) Dover −0530 to Dover +0100
(d) Dover −0400 to Dover −0200

(b) 1.5k

(c) 6.0k

(d)

(a) Violent Race

EBB
Shetland Islands

(a) Dover +0050 to Dover −0410
(b) Dover +0130 to Dover −0500
(c) Dover +0100 to Dover −0630
(d) Dover +0200 to Dover +0500

(b) 1.5k

(c) 6.0k

(d)

(a) Violent Race

5.5 PETERHEAD Aberdeenshire 57°29'·81N 01°46'·42W ✿✿✿✿🌧🌧🌸🌸

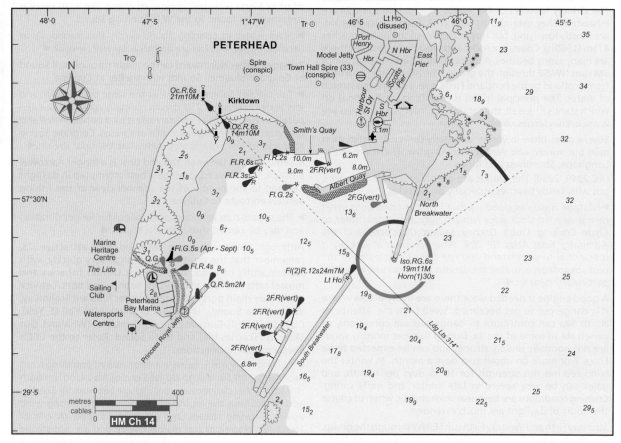

CHARTS AC 213, 1438, 5617; Imray C23

TIDES +0140 Dover; ML 2·3; Duration 0620

Standard Port ABERDEEN (⟵)

Times				Height (metres)			
High Water		Low Water		MHWS	MHWN	MLWN	MLWS
0000	0600	0100	0700	4·3	3·4	1·6	0·6
1200	1800	1300	1900				
Differences *PETERHEAD*							
−0035	−0045	−0035	−0040	−0·3	−0·2	0·0	+0·1

SHELTER Good in marina (2·8m at deepest berths) although there is 2.3m in the entrance, which should not be attempted at LW Sp, check depth with Port Control. A useful passage harbour, it is also a major fishing and oil/gas industry port. Access any weather.

NAVIGATION WPT 57°29'·44N 01°45'·75W, 314°/0·5M to ent. No dangers. 5kn speed limit in Bay; 4kn in marina. Channel between marina bkwtr and SHM lt buoy is <30m wide.

LIGHTS AND MARKS Power stn chy (183m) is conspic 1·25M S of entrance. Ldg marks 314°, front Or △, rear Or ▽, on lattice masts; lights as chartlet. Marina E bkwtr ☆ Fl R 4s 6m 2M; W bkwtr hd,

QG 5m 2M, vis 185°-300°. Buchan Ness ☆ Fl 5s 40m 28M is 1·6M S of entrance.

COMMUNICATIONS (Code 01779) Dr 474841; ⊞ 472316. Port Authority: www.peterheadport.co.uk; Hr Control (H24) 483600.

All vessels, including yachts, **must** call *Peterhead Harbour Radio* VHF Ch **14** for clearance to enter/depart the Bay up to 1·5M off the pierheads.

FACILITIES Peterhead Bay Marina marina@peterheadport.co.uk ☎483600, Mob 07803 264617. Max LOA 20m. Pontoons are 'E' to 'A' from entrance.150⊜, £13 up to 6m LOA+£1/m (7 days for 5); 🚽 🛢 🚿; ⛽ from bowser at end of Princess Royal jetty (☆ Q R); 🛒 ✕ at caravan site.

Peterhead SC ☎(01358) 751340 (Sec); Services ⚓ 🛢 ✕ 🔧 🔩 🏦 Ⓔ ▨.
Town 🏤 ⊠ 🍺 ✕ bus to Aberdeen for ⇌ ✈.

ADJACENT HARBOUR

BODDAM, Aberdeenshire, **57°28'·47N 01°46'·56W**. AC 213. HW +0145 on Dover; Tides as 5.5. Good shelter in the lee of Meikle Mackie, the island just N of Buchan Ness, Fl 5s 40m 28M Horn (3) 60s. Inner hbr dries/unlit. Beware rks around Meikle Mackie and to the SW of it. Appr from 1½ca NW of The Skerry. Yachts on S side of outer hbr. All facilities at Peterhead, 2M N.

5.6 FRASERBURGH

Aberdeenshire **57°41'·50N 01°59'·79W** 🌊🌊💧💧🌸🌸

CHARTS AC 115, 222, 1462, 5617; Imray C23

TIDES +0120 Dover; ML 2·3; Duration 0615

Standard Port ABERDEEN (←—)

Times				Height (metres)			
High Water		Low Water		MHWS	MHWN	MLWN	MLWS
0000	0600	0100	0700	4·3	3·4	1·6	0·6
1200	1800	1300	1900				
Differences FRASERBURGH							
–0122	–0118	–0115	–0115	–0·5	–0·4	–0·1	+0·2

SHELTER A safe refuge, but ent is dangerous in NE/SE gales. A very busy fishing hbr; yachts are not encouraged but may find a berth in S Hbr (3.2m). FVs come and go H24.

NAVIGATION WPT 57°41'·30N 01°58'·80W, 291°/0·57M to ent. The Outer Ent Chan is maintained to 8·9m and Inner Ent Chan 5·9m. Good lookout on entering/leaving. Yachts can enter under radar control in poor vis.

LIGHTS AND MARKS Kinnairds Hd lt ho, Fl 5s 25m 22M, is 0·45M NNW of ent. Cairnbulg Briggs bn, Fl (2) 10s 9m 6M, is 1·8M ESE of ent.

COMMUNICATIONS (Code 01346) Dr 518088. Port Office 515858; Watch Tr 515926.
Call on approach VHF Ch **12** 16 (H24) for directions/berth.

FACILITIES Port ☎515858, ⚓ ⚓£10 (in S Hbr) any LOA alongside; pontoons for 26 ⚓ inc 2 Ⓥ; 🛢 🅿 🗑 ✗ 🔧 🔲 🛞 ⛽(30t/70t mob) 🅿 🛒 ✗ 🛗.

Town ✉ Ⓑ ⚡ ✈ (bus to Aberdeen).

ADJACENT HARBOURS

ROSEHEARTY, Aberdeen, **57°42'·08N 02°06'·87W**. 🌊🌊💧🌸🌸. AC 222, 213. HW Aberdeen –1. E pier and inner hbr dry, but end of W pier is accessible at all tides. Ent exposed in N/E winds; in E/SE winds hbr can be uncomfortable. Ldg lts, 219°, on BW metal poles; rks E of ldg line. When 30m from pier, steer midway between ldg line and W pier (W round tower), Fl 4s. Port Rae, close to E, has unmarked rks; local knowledge req'd. ⚓£10 any LOA. *For details of Rover berthing ticket see 5.4.* **Town** ✉ 🛒 ✗ 🛗. Firing range: for info ☎(01346) 571634; see also 5.4. **Pennan Bay**, 5M W: ⚓ on sand between Howdman (2·9m) and Tamhead (2·1m) rks, 300m N of hbr (small craft only). **Gardenstown** (Gamrie Bay). Appr from E of Craig Dagerty rk (4m, conspic). Harbour dries, or ⚓ off.

5.7 MACDUFF/BANFF

Aberdeenshire Macduff **57°40'·25N 02°30'·03W** 🌊🌊💧💧🌸🌸
Banff **57°40'·22N 02°31'·27W** 🌊🌊💧💧🌸🌸

CHARTS AC 115, 222, 1462, 5617; Imray C23

TIDES + 0055 Dover; ML 2·0; Duration 0615

Standard Port ABERDEEN (←—)

Times				Height (metres)			
High Water		Low Water		MHWS	MHWN	MLWN	MLWS
0200	0900	0400	0900	4·3	3·4	1·6	0·6
1400	2100	1600	2100				
Differences BANFF							
–0100	–0150	–0150	–0050	–0·4	–0·2	–0·1	+0·2

SHELTER Macduff: Reasonably good, but ent not advised in strong NW winds. Slight/moderate surge in outer hbr with N/NE gales. Hbr ent is 20m wide with 3 basins, inner basin for beam <12m; depth approx 2·6m in outer hbr and 2m inner hbr. A busy fishing port with limited space for yachts and good maintenance facilities. **Banff:** Popular hbr which dries. When Macduff ent is very rough in strong NW/N winds, Banff can be a safe refuge for leisure craft; pontoon berths in both basins. Best to contact HM beforehand. In strong E/ENE winds Banff is unusable.

NAVIGATION WPT 57°40'·48N 02°30'·59W, 127°/0·4M to **Macduff** ent. WPT 57°40'·11N 02°30'·85W, 115°/0·25M to **Banff** ent. Beware Feachie Craig, Collie Rks and rky coast N and S of hbr ent.

LIGHTS AND MARKS Macduff: Ldg lts/marks 127° both FR 28/55m 3M, orange △s. Pier hd lt, Fl (2) WRG 6s 12m 9/7M, W tr; shore-G-115°-W-174°-R-210°. **Banff:** Fl 4s end of New Quay and ldg lts 295° rear Fl R 2s, front Fl R 4s.

COMMUNICATIONS (Code 01261) HM **Macduff** 832236, **Banff** hbr office 815544 (daily, 08:00-12:00). Joint HM mob 07747020496, Night mobile number 07500099570. Doctor 0345 3379933 Macduff, Banff Ch 12 (H24).

FACILITIES Macduff: Hbr £20 any LOA; ⚓ (350T) 🛢 ✗ 🔧 🔲 🛗. **Town** 🛒 🗑 ✉ 🛒 ✗ 🛗 ⚡ (bus to Keith).

Banff: Hbr www.banffmarina.com Ⓥ in Inner Hbr marina, £20 any LOA, *Rover berthing ticket see 5.4;* ⚓ 🛢 🅿 🔲 🆆🅲; **Banff SC:** 🏴. **Town** 🛒 🗑 🍴 ✗ 🛗 ⚡ Ⓑ ✈ (Aberdeen).

ADJACENT HARBOURS

PORTSOY, Aberdeenshire, **57°41'·34N 02°41'·59W**. 🌊🌊💧🌸🌸. AC 222. HW +0047 on Dover; –0132 and Ht –0·3m on Aberdeen. Small drying hbr; ent exposed to NW/NE'lies. New Hbr to port of ent partially dries; Inner Hbr dries to clean sand. Ldg lts 173°, front Fl G 4s 20m 3M, metal post; rear Q G 22m 3M, R △ on BW post. *No staff contact Macduff or Banff harbours.* Facilities: few but hosts Scottish Traditional Boat Festival late June/early July. ⚓ £10, *for details of a 'Rover Ticket' see 5.4,* 🛢 ⚓ ✉ 🛒 ✗ 🛗.

Sandend Bay, 1·7M W (57°41'N 02°44'·5W). ⚓ on sand E of hbr.

5.8 WHITEHILLS

Aberdeenshire 57°40'·80N 02°34'·87W ※❀♨♨✿✿✿

CHARTS AC 115, 222, 5617; Imray C23

TIDES +0050 Dover; ML 2·4; Duration 0610

Standard Port ABERDEEN (←—)

Times				Height (metres)			
High Water		Low Water		MHWS	MHWN	MLWN	MLWS
0200	0900	0400	0900	4·3	3·4	1·6	0·6
1400	2100	1600	2100				
Differences WHITEHILLS							
–0122	–0137	–0117	–0127	–0·4	–0·3	+0·1	+0·1

SHELTER Safe. In strong NW/N winds beware surge in the narrow ent and outer hbr, when ent is best not attempted. See HM for vacant pontoon berth.

NAVIGATION WPT 57°41'·98N 02°34'·89W, 180°/1·2M to bkwtr lt. Reefs on S side of chan marked by 2 rusty/white SHM bns. Beware fishing floats. Narrow entrance 1·7m below CD, Outer Hbr pontoon berths 2m and Inner Hbr 1·5m–1·8m.

LIGHTS AND MARKS Fl WR 3s on pier hd, vis 132°-R-212°-W-245°; approach in R sector.

COMMUNICATIONS (Code 01261) www.whitehillsharbour.co.uk, Dr 812027. HM 861291, mobile 07906 135786.

Whitehills Hbr Radio VHF Ch **14** 16.

FACILITIES Marina (47+12♥), £18 (+£2🚿) Quayside £12 ⚓ 🅿 🗑 ⛽ ▲ ✕ ⚒ 🛠 🔧 🅿 🛢 @; **Town** 🏨 ✉ 🍽 ✕ 🏦 ⇌ (bus to Keith), ✈ (Aberdeen).

ADJACENT HARBOURS

CULLEN, Moray, **57°41'·63N 02°49'·29W**. ※♨♨✿✿. AC 222. HW +0045 on Dover, HW –0135 and –0·3m on Aberdeen; Duration 0555; ML 2·4m. Shelter good, but ent hazardous in strong W/N winds. Appr on 180° toward conspic viaduct and W bn on N pier. Caple Rk, 0·2m, is 5ca NE of hbr. Small drying hbr, best for shoal draught. Bn Fl G 2s vis 114°-119° close S of the root of N pier. Beware moorings across inner basin ent. Moor S of Inner jetty if < 1m draught with Pontoons in inner hbr (1·8m at HW Np). *For details of a 'Rover Ticket' see 5.4.* HM ☎(01542) 831700. **Town** ▮ (hardware store), ✉ 🍽 ✕ 🏦.

PORTKNOCKIE, Moray, **57°42'·28N 02°51'·79W**. ※❀♨✿✿✿. AC 222. HW +0045 on Dover; –0135 and ht –0·3m Aberdeen; ML 2·3m; Duration 0555; access H24. Good shelter in one of the safest hbrs on S side of Moray Firth, but scend is often experienced; care needed in strong NW/N winds. Fl G 2s ldg lts, on white-topped poles, lead approx 151°, to ent. Orange street lts surround the hbr. Limited ABs on N Quay; most of inner hbr dries. HM ☎(01542) 831700 (home, p/time); Facilities: ⚓ 🛥; *for details of a 'Rover Ticket' see 5.4,* ⚓ ✕; Dr ☎ 840272. **Town** ⓑ ✉ 🍽 🏦.

5.9 BUCKIE

Moray 57°40'·84N 02°57'·63W ※❀❀♨♨♨✿✿

CHARTS AC 223, 1462, 5617; Imray C23

TIDES +0040 Dover; ML 2·4; Duration 0550

Standard Port ABERDEEN (←—)

Times				Height (metres)			
High Water		Low Water		MHWS	MHWN	MLWN	MLWS
0200	0900	0400	0900	4·3	3·4	1·6	0·6
1400	2100	1600	2100				
Differences BUCKIE							
–0130	–0145	–0125	–0140	–0·2	–0·2	0·0	+0·1

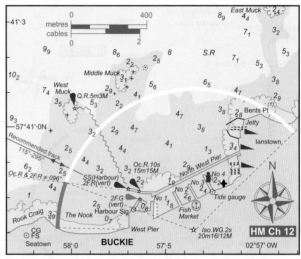

SHELTER Good in all weathers.

In strong NNW to NE winds there is a dangerous swell over the bar at hbr ent, which is 24m wide.

Access H24. Berth in No 4 basin as directed by HM.

NAVIGATION Beware W, Middle and E Muck Rks, 3ca off shore. WPT 57°41'·0N 02°58'·6W, 110°/5ca to ent. The recommended track is 3.5 cables west of West Muck and approach Harbour at 115°. Approx 2 cables from entrance alter to 100° just as the 2FR (vert) and the Oc R 10s on the N breakwater come into line (096°). Traffic is controlled by VHF.

LIGHTS AND MARKS W Muck QR 5m 2M (tripod); N bkwtr, Oc R 10s 15m 15M (W twr), N bwtr hd 2FR(vert), S bwtr hd 2FG(vert). Harbour Lt Iso WG 2s 20m 16/12M, (W tr, R top inshore of hbr).

COMMUNICATIONS (Code 01542) Dr 831555. HM 831700(H24). VHF Ch 12 16 (H24).

FACILITIES buckieharbour@moray.gov.uk ⚓ £20 ⚓ ⚓ 🛢 ▮ ▮(delivery) ⛽ ✕ 🔧 🅿 🍴 📮(50t) 🏗(15t) 🅿.

Town 🍽 🏦 ⓑ ✉, 🛢 at Strathlene caravan site 1½M E, ⇌ (bus to Elgin), ✈ (Aberdeen or Inverness).

ADJACENT HARBOURS

Findochty, Cullen and Portknockie are managed from Buckie.

FINDOCHTY (2M ENE Buckie), Moray, **57°41'·94N 02°54'·29W**. AC 222. HW +0045 on Dover, HW –0135 & ht –0·2m on Aberdeen; ML 2·3m; Duration 0550. Ent is about 2ca W of conspic church belfry. 1ca N of ent, leave Beacon Rock (3m high) to stbd. Ldg lts, FR, lead 166° into Outer Basin which dries 0·2m and has many rky outcrops. Ent faces N and is 20m wide; unlit white bn at hd of W pier. Good shelter in inner basin for 100 small craft/yachts on 3 pontoons (the 2 W'ly pontoons dry); possible ⚓ on Sterlochy Pier in 2m £21 ⚓ (£10) *for details of a 'Rover Ticket' see 5.4.* HM Buckie ☎(01542) 831700. **Town** ✉ ⓑ 🍽 ✕ 🏦.

5.10 LOSSIEMOUTH

Moray **57°43'·41N 03°16'·63W** 🌊🌊🌊🌊🌊🌊🌊🌊

CHARTS AC 223, 1462, 5617; Imray C23

TIDES +0040 Dover; ML 2·3; Duration 0605

Standard Port ABERDEEN (←—)

Times				Height (metres)			
High Water		Low Water		MHWS	MHWN	MLWN	MLWS
0200	0900	0400	0900	4·3	3·4	1·6	0·6
1400	2100	1600	2100				
Differences LOSSIEMOUTH							
–0125	–0200	–0130	–0130	–0·2	–0·2	0·0	0·0

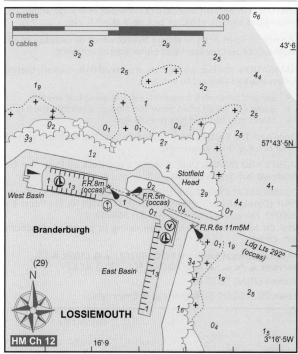

SHELTER Very good in winds from SSE to NW. Pontoon berths in both basins; marina channels dredged 1·8m below LWS (2016), berths may be less in soft mud, esp at extreme springs. HM will advise. West Basin also used by FVs.

- In N to SE winds >F6 appr can be dangerous, with swell tending to break across hbr mouth and in outer hbr. Residual swell from E to SE can be particularly hazardous.
- Near ent, beware current from R Lossie setting in N'ly direction, causing confused water in N to SE winds at sp.
- Vessels drawing >2m would have little clearance at LWS ±2.

NAVIGATION WPT 57°43'·38N 03°16'·09W, 277°/0·3M to ent. Rks to N and S of hbr ent; appr from E. Approx 1·5m in entrance at LWS.

LIGHTS AND MARKS Halliman Skerries (drying) 1M W of harbour entrance are marked by NCM, Q; *Racon M*. SPM marks outfall ½M NE of hbr. Unlit bn and disused Lt Ho on adjacent mainland shore. Ldg lts 292°, both FR 5/8m; S pier hd Fl R 6s 11m 5M.

COMMUNICATIONS (Code 01343) Dr 0345 337 1190. VHF Ch 12 16 HO.

FACILITIES Lossiemouth Marina ☎813066 (125 inc 10**Ⓥ**) ⚓£20/craft 🔧🛢️💡🗑️ wi-fi.
Hbr ⚓ (£50 pa) 🔧🛢️🏪🔨⚓🛢️🛒(25t) ⚓(1t).
Hbr Service Stn ☎813001 🛢️🛢️⚓ Mon-Fri 0800-2030, Sat 0800-1930, Sun 0930-1900.
Town ✉🅑Ⓒ🍴✕🖥️🚆(bus to Elgin) ✈(Inverness).

5.11 HOPEMAN

Moray **57°42'·70N 03°26'·31W** 🌊🌊🌊🌊🌊🌊

CHARTS AC 223, 1462, 5617; Imray C23

TIDES +0050 Dover; ML 2·4; Duration 0610

Standard Port ABERDEEN (←—)

Times				Height (metres)			
High Water		Low Water		MHWS	MHWN	MLWN	MLWS
0200	0900	0400	0900	4·3	3·4	1·6	0·6
1400	2100	1600	2100				
Differences HOPEMAN							
–0120	–0150	–0135	–0120	–0·2	–0·2	0·0	0·0

SHELTER Once in Inner Basin, shelter good from all winds; but hbr dries. Ent is difficult in winds from NE to SE. A popular yachting hbr with ⚓. HM part-time.

NAVIGATION WPT 57°42'·66N, 03°26'·59W, 083° to ent, 0·17M.

Dangerous rks lie off hbr ent. Do not attempt entry in heavy weather. Beware lobster pot floats E and W of hbr (Mar-Aug).

LIGHTS AND MARKS See 5.3 and chartlet.

COMMUNICATIONS (Code 01343) Dr 543141, HM (01542) 831700. *Burghead Radio* Ch 14 (HX).

FACILITIES Hbr ⚓£9, managed by Buckie HM; *for details of a 'Rover Ticket' see 5.4,* ⚓🔧🔨🛢️💡.
Town ✉🅑🍴✕🖥️🚆(bus to Elgin), ✈ (Inverness).

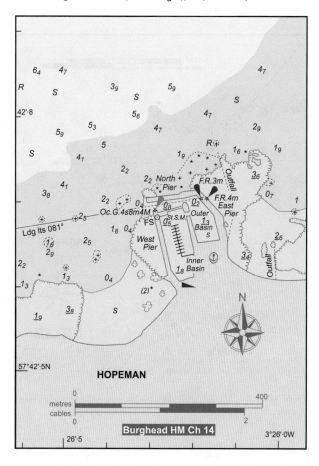

5.12 BURGHEAD

Moray 57°42'·06N 03°30'·02W ✿✿✿✿✿

CHARTS AC 223, 1462, 5617; Imray C23

TIDES +0035 Dover; ML 2·4; Duration 0610

Standard Port ABERDEEN (←—)

Times				Height (metres)			
High Water		Low Water		MHWS	MHWN	MLWN	MLWS
0200	0900	0400	0900	4·3	3·4	1·6	0·6
1400	2100	1600	2100				
Differences BURGHEAD							
–0120	–0150	–0135	–0120	–0·2	–0·2	0·0	0·0

SHELTER One of the few Moray Firth hbrs accessible in strong E winds. Go alongside where available and contact HM. Can be very busy with FVs.

NAVIGATION WPT 57°42'·28N 03°30'·39W, 137°/0·28M to N pier lt QR. 0·6m in ent chan and 1·4m in hbr, but depths variable due to sand movement. Advisable to contact HM if entering near LW. 3kn speed limit.

LIGHTS AND MARKS No ldg lts but night ent is safe after identifying the N pier lts: QR 3m 5M and Oc 8s 7m 5M.

COMMUNICATIONS (Code 01343) Dr 812277, HM (01542) 831700. *Burghead Radio* VHF Ch **14** 12 (HO and when vessel due).

FACILITIES Hbr ⊆£9, managed by Buckie HM; *for details of a 'Rover Ticket' see 5.4*, ⚓⚓✚✕⌂⌂(50t) mobile.
Town ⊠Ⓑ🛒🛏🚆(bus to Elgin), ✈(Inverness).

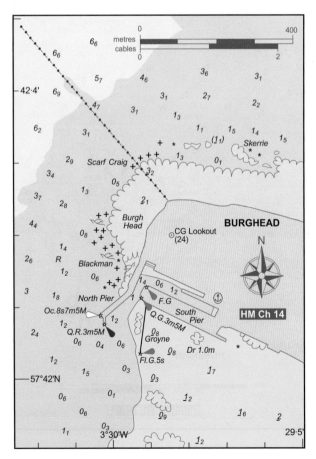

5.13 FINDHORN

Moray 57°39'·64N 03°37'·47W ✿✿✿✿✿✿

CHARTS AC 223, 5617; Imray C23

TIDES +0110 Dover; ML 2·5; Duration 0615

Standard Port ABERDEEN (←—)

Times				Height (metres)			
High Water		Low Water		MHWS	MHWN	MLWN	MLWS
0200	0900	0400	0900	4·3	3·4	1·6	0·6
1400	2100	1600	2100				
Differences FINDHORN							
–0120	–0150	–0135	–0130	0·0	–0·1	0·0	+0·1

SHELTER ⚓ in pool off boatyard or off N pier or dry out alongside, inside piers and ask at YC; or pick up Y ⚓ off N pier.

> Do not attempt entry in strong NW/NE winds or with big swell running; expect breakers/surf either side of entrance.

NAVIGATION The bar, which dries, is marked (Fl R marker); thence follow marked channel to entrance.

- Bar and sands shift frequently esp following bad weather.
- Buoys (inc SWM) often move to follow channel into the bay.
- Marks may be lifted Nov to early Apr.

Once past The Ee, turn port inside G buoys. The southern part of Findhorn Bay dries extensively.

LIGHTS AND MARKS Unlit. There is a windsock on FS by The Ee. Boatyard building is conspic.

COMMUNICATIONS (Code 01309) Dr 678866/678888; Findhorn Pilot (Derek Munro) 690802, mob 07747 840916; Findhorn BY 690099. Fairways Committee (via BY) 690099.
VHF Ch M *Chadwick Base* (when racing in progress). Findhorn BY: Ch 80.

FACILITIES Royal Findhorn YC ☎690247, ⚓⚓£10/nt✚⌂.
Services ⚓⚓⚓✚▭⌂⌂(16t)✕✎▱⌂ ACA.
Kinloss (2½M) 🅿🅿🛢.
Town 🛒✕🛏⊠Ⓑ🚆 (Forres), ✈ (Inverness).

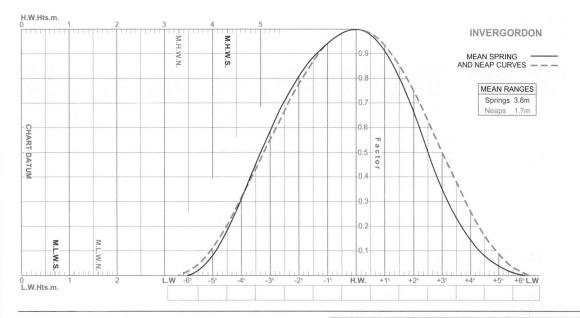

INVERGORDON

MEAN SPRING —————
AND NEAP CURVES - - - - -

MEAN RANGES	
Springs	3.6m
Neaps	1.7m

5.14 NAIRN

Highland **57°35'·61N 03°51'·65W** ✹✿♦♦✿✿

CHARTS AC 223, 1462, 5617; Imray C23

TIDES +0110 Dover; ML 2·2; Duration 0615

Standard Port INVERGORDON (→)

Times				Height (metres)			
High Water		Low Water		MHWS	MHWN	MLWN	MLWS
0100	0700	0000	0700	4·3	3·3	1·6	0·7
1300	1900	1200	1900				
Differences NAIRN							
+0005	–0015	0000	–0015	0·0	0·0	0·0	0·0
McDERMOTT BASE							
+0015	–0005	+0015	0000	–0·1	0·0	+0·1	+0·2

SHELTER Good, but entry difficult in fresh NNE'ly. Pontoons in hbr with ❶ berths. Best entry HW ± 1½. No commercial shipping.

NAVIGATION The beach dries to 100m off the pierheads. A mark is laid in the deepest water off the entrance to indicate line of approach. A gravel bar shows 200m NNW of ent at LAT. Inside, the best water is to the E side of the river chan which dries approx 1·9m.

- Buoy and sands shift frequently esp following bad weather.
- Mark may be lifted Nov to early Apr.

LIGHTS AND MARKS Lt ho on E pier hd, Oc WRG 4s 6m 5M, vis shore-G-100°-W-207°-R-shore. Keep in W sector.

COMMUNICATIONS (Code 01667) Clinic 452096; Dr 453421. Hbr Office 456008, HM mob 07821 302944.

VHF Ch M (weekends only).

FACILITIES **Nairn Basin** ⌷ £15.28/48hrs ⬎ (launch £6) ⫶⟩ (110 V) ⌕ ⌕; **Nairn SC** ☎453897, ⌂.

Town ✉ Ⓑ ⍅ ✕ ⌂ ⇌ ✈ (Inverness).

CAUTION
Depths in channel may be reduced after strong onshore winds

STANDARD TIME (UT)
For Summer Time add ONE hour in **non-shaded areas**

INVERGORDON LAT 57°41'N LONG 4°10'W
TIMES AND HEIGHTS OF HIGH AND LOW WATERS

Dates in red are SPRINGS
Dates in blue are NEAPS

YEAR **2022**

JANUARY

Time	m	Time	m
1 0436	1.0	**16** 0417	1.5
1033	4.2	1106	4.0
SA 1707	1.0	SU 1731	1.3
2301	4.3	2324	3.8
2 0530	0.9	**17** 0503	1.4
1129	4.4	1147	4.1
SU 1800	0.8	M 1806	1.1
● 2359	4.4	○	
3 0618	0.9	**18** 0003	3.9
1219	4.5	0549	1.3
M 1849	0.6	TU 1224	4.1
		1843	1.0
4 0052	4.5	**19** 0040	3.9
0704	0.9	0630	1.2
TU 1306	4.6	W 1259	4.2
1938	0.5	1921	0.9
5 0143	4.4	**20** 0116	3.9
0748	1.0	0707	1.2
W 1354	4.6	TH 1334	4.1
2026	0.6	1958	0.9
6 0233	4.3	**21** 0153	3.9
0829	1.2	0737	1.2
TH 1441	4.5	F 1408	4.1
2114	0.7	2034	0.9
7 0321	4.1	**22** 0232	3.9
0906	1.3	0753	1.3
F 1527	4.3	SA 1444	4.0
2202	0.9	2109	1.0
8 0408	3.9	**23** 0312	3.8
0936	1.5	0807	1.5
SA 1613	4.1	SU 1521	4.0
2249	1.1	2144	1.1
9 0453	3.7	**24** 0354	3.7
1008	1.7	0843	1.4
SU 1659	3.9	M 1603	3.9
◐ 2341	1.4	2224	1.2
10 0540	3.5	**25** 0439	3.6
1053	1.8	0932	1.5
M 1751	3.7	TU 1651	3.8
		◑ 2323	1.3
11 0103	1.6	**26** 0531	3.5
0632	3.4	1058	1.7
TU 1158	2.0	W 1750	3.7
1849	3.6		
12 0217	1.7	**27** 0042	1.4
0731	3.4	0634	3.5
W 1436	1.9	TH 1236	1.7
1952	3.5	1904	3.6
13 0312	1.7	**28** 0204	1.4
0832	3.5	0745	3.6
TH 1535	1.8	F 1433	1.6
2053	3.5	2026	3.7
14 0354	1.7	**29** 0317	1.3
0930	3.6	0858	3.7
F 1621	1.6	SA 1557	1.3
2150	3.6	2147	3.9
15 0344	1.6	**30** 0423	1.2
1021	3.8	1010	4.0
SA 1658	1.4	SU 1702	1.0
2240	3.7	2258	4.1
		31 0520	1.1
		1114	4.2
		M 1755	0.7
		2356	4.3

FEBRUARY

Time	m	Time	m
1 0608	0.9	**16** 0541	1.2
1207	4.5	1204	4.1
TU 1842	0.4	W 1826	0.8
●		○	
2 0046	4.4	**17** 0026	4.0
0651	0.9	0622	1.1
W 1255	4.6	TH 1240	4.2
1926	0.3	1903	0.7
3 0132	4.4	**18** 0102	4.1
0729	0.9	0700	1.0
TH 1339	4.6	F 1316	4.3
2007	0.4	1939	0.6
4 0215	4.3	**19** 0138	4.1
0804	0.9	0734	1.0
F 1422	4.6	SA 1352	4.3
2046	0.5	2015	0.6
5 0256	4.2	**20** 0215	4.1
0836	1.1	0802	1.0
SA 1503	4.4	SU 1428	4.3
2122	0.8	2050	0.7
6 0335	4.0	**21** 0253	4.0
0903	1.2	0805	1.0
SU 1543	4.2	M 1505	4.2
2153	1.1	2122	0.9
7 0413	3.7	**22** 0331	3.9
0927	1.4	0821	1.1
M 1623	3.9	TU 1545	4.0
2215	1.4	2152	1.1
8 0453	3.5	**23** 0413	3.7
0957	1.6	0900	1.3
TU 1709	3.6	W 1631	3.8
◐ 2239	1.7	◑ 2245	1.4
9 0539	3.3	**24** 0502	3.6
1051	1.9	1007	1.5
W 1805	3.4	TH 1730	3.6
2358	1.9		
10 0636	3.3	**25** 0013	1.6
1301	2.0	0604	3.4
TH 1912	3.3	F 1230	1.7
		1848	3.4
11 0150	1.9	**26** 0150	1.6
0740	3.3	0630	3.4
F 1452	1.8	SA 1432	1.5
2018	3.3	2021	3.5
12 0259	1.9	**27** 0312	1.5
0842	3.4	0833	3.6
SA 1553	1.6	SU 1554	1.2
2119	3.4	2153	3.7
13 0330	1.7	**28** 0419	1.3
0941	3.6	0953	3.8
SU 1639	1.4	M 1657	0.8
2217	3.6	2301	4.0
14 0409	1.6		
1036	3.8		
M 1715	1.2		
2307	3.7		
15 0457	1.4		
1123	4.0		
TU 1750	1.0		
2348	3.9		

MARCH

Time	m	Time	m
1 0512	1.1	**16** 0446	1.4
1103	4.2	1050	3.9
TU 1745	0.5	W 1723	0.9
2352	4.3	2326	3.9
2 0554	0.9	**17** 0525	1.1
1155	4.4	1135	4.1
W 1827	0.3	TH 1800	0.6
●			
3 0035	4.4	**18** 0004	4.1
0631	0.8	0604	0.9
TH 1239	4.6	F 1215	4.3
1905	0.2	○ 1837	0.4
4 0114	4.4	**19** 0040	4.2
0704	0.7	0641	0.8
F 1319	4.6	SA 1253	4.4
1939	0.3	1914	0.4
5 0151	4.3	**20** 0117	4.3
0735	0.8	0716	0.7
SA 1357	4.6	SU 1331	4.5
2011	0.5	1951	0.4
6 0226	4.2	**21** 0154	4.3
0806	0.8	0749	0.7
SU 1434	4.4	M 1410	4.4
2040	0.8	2027	0.6
7 0259	4.0	**22** 0232	4.2
0834	1.0	0817	0.8
M 1510	4.1	TU 1450	4.3
2101	1.1	2101	0.8
8 0332	3.8	**23** 0311	4.0
0851	1.2	0819	1.0
TU 1546	3.8	W 1532	4.1
2059	1.4	2134	1.2
9 0406	3.5	**24** 0353	3.8
0901	1.5	0854	1.2
W 1624	3.5	TH 1622	3.8
2122	1.7	2228	1.5
10 0447	3.3	**25** 0444	3.6
0938	1.7	1052	1.5
TH 1714	3.3	F 1724	3.5
◐ 2215	1.9	◑ 2358	1.7
11 0544	3.2	**26** 0546	3.4
1230	1.9	1246	1.5
F 1831	3.1	SA 1846	3.3
12 0104	2.1	**27** 0153	1.7
0656	3.1	0659	3.4
SA 1411	1.8	SU 1436	1.3
1944	3.1	2031	3.4
13 0233	2.0	**28** 0312	1.6
0803	3.3	0816	3.5
SU 1515	1.6	M 1549	1.0
2050	3.2	2158	3.7
14 0324	1.8	**29** 0412	1.3
0903	3.4	0941	3.8
M 1604	1.4	TU 1644	0.7
2151	3.5	2253	4.0
15 0406	1.6	**30** 0458	1.1
0959	3.7	1049	4.1
TU 1645	1.1	W 1729	0.5
2243	3.7	2337	4.2
		31 0536	0.9
		1138	4.3
		TH 1806	0.3

APRIL

Time	m	Time	m
1 0016	4.3	**16** 0539	0.9
0607	0.8	1146	4.3
F 1218	4.5	SA 1810	0.4
● 1838	0.3	○	
2 0051	4.3	**17** 0015	4.3
0637	0.7	0618	0.7
SA 1255	4.5	SU 1228	4.5
1907	0.4	1849	0.3
3 0123	4.3	**18** 0054	4.4
0707	0.7	0656	0.6
SU 1330	4.4	M 1310	4.5
1935	0.6	1928	0.4
4 0153	4.1	**19** 0133	4.4
0738	0.8	0733	0.6
M 1404	4.2	TU 1353	4.5
1959	0.9	2006	0.4
5 0223	4.0	**20** 0213	4.3
0806	0.9	0810	0.7
TU 1438	4.0	W 1437	4.3
2010	1.1	2043	0.9
6 0253	3.8	**21** 0254	4.1
0816	1.2	0850	0.9
W 1510	3.7	TH 1525	4.1
2014	1.4	2123	1.3
7 0323	3.6	**22** 0340	3.9
0824	1.4	0946	1.1
TH 1542	3.5	F 1619	3.8
2040	1.6	2220	1.6
8 0358	3.4	**23** 0433	3.7
0902	1.6	1107	1.3
F 1623	3.2	SA 1725	3.5
2126	1.9	◑ 2352	1.8
9 0449	3.2	**24** 0535	3.5
1027	1.8	1303	1.3
SA 1738	3.0	SU 1847	3.4
◐ 2310	2.1		
10 0607	3.1	**25** 0149	1.8
1335	1.7	0645	3.5
SU 1905	3.0	M 1426	1.1
		2027	3.5
11 0206	2.0	**26** 0258	1.6
0722	3.2	0759	3.6
M 1433	1.5	TU 1530	0.9
2014	3.2	2140	3.7
12 0259	1.8	**27** 0352	1.4
0823	3.4	0919	3.8
TU 1521	1.3	W 1623	0.7
2115	3.4	2231	4.0
13 0341	1.6	**28** 0438	1.2
0918	3.6	1025	4.0
W 1605	1.0	TH 1707	0.6
2208	3.7	2314	4.1
14 0419	1.3	**29** 0514	1.0
1011	3.9	1114	4.2
TH 1648	0.8	F 1742	0.6
2255	4.0	2351	4.2
15 0459	1.1	**30** 0543	0.9
1100	4.1	1154	4.3
F 1730	0.5	SA 1810	0.6
2336	4.2	●	

Chart Datum: 2·10 metres below Ordnance Datum (Local). HAT is 5·0 metres above Chart Datum.

STANDARD TIME (UT)
For Summer Time add ONE hour in **non-shaded areas**

INVERGORDON   LAT 57°41'N   LONG 4°10'W
TIMES AND HEIGHTS OF HIGH AND LOW WATERS

Dates in red are **SPRINGS**
Dates in blue are **NEAPS**

YEAR 2022

MAY

Day	Time m	Time m		Time m	Time m
1 SU	0024 4.2 / 0611 0.8 / 1230 4.3 / 1835 0.7		16 M	0556 0.7 / 1205 4.5 / 1827 0.5 ○	
2 M	0054 4.2 / 0641 0.8 / 1303 4.2 / 1858 0.9		17 TU	0031 4.4 / 0640 0.6 / 1252 4.5 / 1909 0.6	
3 TU	0122 4.1 / 0712 0.8 / 1336 4.0 / 1919 1.0		18 W	0114 4.4 / 0723 0.6 / 1339 4.5 / 1950 0.8	
4 W	0151 4.0 / 0741 1.0 / 1409 3.9 / 1931 1.2		19 TH	0157 4.3 / 0808 0.7 / 1429 4.3 / 2032 1.0	
5 TH	0220 3.8 / 0754 1.1 / 1441 3.7 / 1948 1.4		20 F	0243 4.2 / 0859 0.8 / 1522 4.1 / 2118 1.3	
6 F	0250 3.7 / 0808 1.3 / 1514 3.5 / 2017 1.6		21 SA	0332 4.0 / 1002 1.0 / 1619 3.8 / 2214 1.6	
7 SA	0326 3.5 / 0848 1.5 / 1556 3.5 / 2101 1.8		22 SU	0426 3.8 / 1122 1.1 / 1722 3.6 / 2335 1.7 ◐	
8 SU	0414 3.3 / 1003 1.6 / 1654 3.1 / 2219 2.0		23 M	0524 3.7 / 1249 1.1 / 1833 3.5	
9 M	0518 3.2 / 1250 1.6 / 1815 3.1 ◑		24 TU	0121 1.7 / 0627 3.7 / 1401 1.0 / 1953 3.5	
10 TU	0115 2.0 / 0632 3.2 / 1348 1.4 / 1929 3.2		25 W	0228 1.6 / 0733 3.7 / 1503 1.0 / 2103 3.7	
11 W	0216 1.8 / 0738 3.4 / 1437 1.2 / 2030 3.4		26 TH	0324 1.5 / 0842 3.8 / 1556 0.9 / 2158 3.8	
12 TH	0259 1.6 / 0835 3.6 / 1523 1.0 / 2126 3.7		27 F	0411 1.3 / 0949 3.9 / 1641 0.9 / 2243 3.9	
13 F	0341 1.4 / 0929 3.8 / 1611 0.8 / 2217 3.9		28 SA	0451 1.2 / 1044 4.0 / 1717 1.0 / 2322 4.0	
14 SA	0427 1.1 / 1024 4.1 / 1659 0.6 / 2305 4.2		29 SU	0522 1.1 / 1127 4.0 / 1742 1.0 / 2356 4.1	
15 SU	0512 0.9 / 1116 4.3 / 1744 0.5 / 2349 4.3		30 M	0549 1.0 / 1205 4.0 / 1800 1.1 ●	
			31 TU	0026 4.1 / 0620 0.9 / 1239 4.0 / 1822 1.1	

JUNE

Day	Time m		Day	Time m
1 W	0056 4.1 / 0654 0.9 / 1313 3.9 / 1846 1.2		16 TH	0058 4.4 / 0720 0.5 / 1331 4.4 / 1941 0.9
2 TH	0127 4.0 / 0727 1.0 / 1347 3.8 / 1908 1.3		17 F	0145 4.4 / 0811 0.5 / 1424 4.3 / 2026 1.0
3 F	0158 3.9 / 0753 1.1 / 1420 3.6 / 1932 1.4		18 SA	0234 4.2 / 0905 0.6 / 1518 4.2 / 2112 1.2
4 SA	0231 3.7 / 0810 1.2 / 1455 3.5 / 2003 1.5		19 SU	0324 4.2 / 1002 0.7 / 1612 4.0 / 2158 1.4
5 SU	0307 3.6 / 0845 1.3 / 1536 3.4 / 2043 1.7		20 M	0415 4.1 / 1104 0.9 / 1705 3.8 / 2244 1.6
6 M	0350 3.5 / 0946 1.4 / 1625 3.3 / 2141 1.8		21 TU	0507 3.9 / 1212 1.0 / 1801 3.6 / 2339 1.7 ◐
7 TU	0440 3.4 / 1118 1.4 / 1724 3.3 / 2259 1.9 ◐		22 W	0601 3.8 / 1324 1.1 / 1903 3.5
8 W	0539 3.4 / 1249 1.4 / 1830 3.3		23 TH	0143 1.7 / 0700 3.7 / 1428 1.2 / 2009 3.5
9 TH	0015 1.8 / 0643 3.4 / 1348 1.2 / 1938 3.4		24 F	0248 1.7 / 0803 3.6 / 1525 1.3 / 2111 3.6
10 F	0129 1.7 / 0747 3.6 / 1441 1.1 / 2039 3.6		25 SA	0342 1.5 / 0907 3.7 / 1614 1.3 / 2203 3.7
11 SA	0241 1.5 / 0849 3.8 / 1535 0.9 / 2137 3.8		26 SU	0429 1.4 / 1008 3.7 / 1652 1.3 / 2248 3.8
12 SU	0350 1.2 / 0950 4.0 / 1630 0.8 / 2232 4.1		27 M	0506 1.3 / 1059 3.8 / 1714 1.4 / 2326 3.9
13 M	0449 1.0 / 1051 4.2 / 1721 0.7 / 2323 4.2		28 TU	0536 1.2 / 1142 3.8 / 1722 1.3
14 TU	0541 0.8 / 1147 4.4 / 1809 0.7 ○		29 W	0000 4.0 / 0607 1.1 / 1219 3.8 / 1752 1.3 ●
15 W	0011 4.4 / 0631 0.6 / 1239 4.4 / 1856 0.7		30 TH	0035 4.0 / 0643 1.0 / 1255 3.8 / 1826 1.3

JULY

Day	Time m		Day	Time m
1 F	0109 4.0 / 0720 1.0 / 1331 3.8 / 1858 1.3		16 SA	0133 4.6 / 0804 0.3 / 1415 4.4 / 2012 0.9
2 SA	0143 4.0 / 0757 1.0 / 1405 3.7 / 1926 1.3		17 SU	0221 4.6 / 0852 0.4 / 1504 4.3 / 2052 1.1
3 SU	0216 3.9 / 0831 1.1 / 1440 3.6 / 1954 1.4		18 M	0308 4.5 / 0939 0.5 / 1551 4.1 / 2128 1.2
4 M	0250 3.8 / 0901 1.1 / 1517 3.6 / 2024 1.5		19 TU	0354 4.3 / 1025 0.8 / 1636 3.9 / 2201 1.4
5 TU	0327 3.7 / 0935 1.2 / 1558 3.5 / 2103 1.6		20 W	0440 4.1 / 1112 1.1 / 1721 3.7 / 2240 1.6 ◐
6 W	0408 3.6 / 1022 1.2 / 1644 3.5 / 2157 1.6		21 TH	0528 3.8 / 1215 1.4 / 1811 3.5 / 2335 1.8
7 TH	0455 3.6 / 1126 1.3 / 1737 3.4 / 2313 1.7 ◐		22 F	0624 3.6 / 1344 1.6 / 1908 3.4
8 F	0552 3.6 / 1247 1.3 / 1839 3.4		23 SA	0201 1.8 / 0726 3.5 / 1449 1.7 / 2011 3.4
9 SA	0030 1.7 / 0659 3.6 / 1400 1.3 / 1949 3.5		24 SU	0311 1.7 / 0831 3.5 / 1543 1.7 / 2113 3.5
10 SU	0150 1.5 / 0811 3.7 / 1503 1.2 / 2056 3.7		25 M	0407 1.6 / 0935 3.5 / 1626 1.6 / 2208 3.7
11 M	0322 1.3 / 0923 3.9 / 1605 1.1 / 2201 3.9		26 TU	0451 1.4 / 1034 3.6 / 1646 1.6 / 2256 3.9
12 TU	0433 1.1 / 1034 4.1 / 1704 1.0 / 2300 4.2		27 W	0525 1.2 / 1122 3.7 / 1653 1.5 / 2337 4.0
13 W	0533 0.8 / 1137 4.3 / 1757 0.9 / 2355 4.4 ○		28 TH	0555 1.1 / 1203 3.8 / 1734 1.3 ●
14 TH	0626 0.5 / 1233 4.4 / 1844 0.8		29 F	0014 4.1 / 0629 1.0 / 1239 3.9 / 1816 1.3
15 F	0045 4.5 / 0716 0.4 / 1325 4.5 / 1930 0.8		30 SA	0050 4.1 / 0706 0.9 / 1314 3.9 / 1854 1.2
			31 SU	0124 4.1 / 0742 0.8 / 1347 3.9 / 1927 1.2

AUGUST

Day	Time m		Day	Time m
1 M	0157 4.1 / 0818 0.8 / 1420 3.9 / 1954 1.2		16 TU	0244 4.6 / 0903 0.5 / 1520 4.2 / 2054 1.1
2 TU	0230 4.0 / 0850 0.9 / 1454 3.8 / 2009 1.3		17 W	0325 4.4 / 0939 0.9 / 1559 3.9 / 2125 1.3
3 W	0304 3.9 / 0919 1.0 / 1531 3.7 / 2029 1.3		18 TH	0407 4.1 / 1009 1.2 / 1638 3.7 / 2159 1.5
4 TH	0341 3.9 / 0940 1.1 / 1611 3.7 / 2107 1.4		19 F	0452 3.8 / 1036 1.6 / 1723 3.5 / 2251 1.8 ◐
5 F	0423 3.8 / 0953 1.3 / 1657 3.6 / 2205 1.6		20 SA	0546 3.5 / 1141 1.9 / 1818 3.3
6 SA	0516 3.7 / 1156 1.4 / 1755 3.5 / 2359 1.7		21 SU	0038 1.9 / 0652 3.3 / 1406 2.0 / 1924 3.3
7 SU	0624 3.6 / 1330 1.5 / 1907 3.5		22 M	0241 1.8 / 0801 3.3 / 1511 1.9 / 2028 3.4
8 M	0143 1.6 / 0748 3.6 / 1444 1.4 / 2023 3.6		23 TU	0342 1.6 / 0908 3.4 / 1558 1.8 / 2129 3.6
9 TU	0313 1.4 / 0912 3.7 / 1551 1.3 / 2135 3.9		24 W	0430 1.4 / 1012 3.5 / 1625 1.7 / 2223 3.8
10 W	0426 1.0 / 1029 4.0 / 1653 1.1 / 2242 4.2		25 TH	0504 1.2 / 1102 3.7 / 1644 1.5 / 2309 4.0
11 TH	0526 0.7 / 1133 4.3 / 1745 1.0 / 2340 4.4		26 F	0533 1.0 / 1142 3.9 / 1722 1.3 / 2349 4.2
12 F	0616 0.4 / 1226 4.5 / 1830 0.8 ○		27 SA	0605 0.8 / 1218 4.0 / 1802 1.2 ●
13 SA	0030 4.6 / 0702 0.2 / 1313 4.5 / 1910 0.8		28 SU	0024 4.2 / 0641 0.7 / 1251 4.1 / 1840 1.1
14 SU	0117 4.7 / 0744 0.2 / 1357 4.5 / 1948 0.8		29 M	0058 4.3 / 0717 0.6 / 1323 4.1 / 1914 1.0
15 M	0201 4.7 / 0825 0.3 / 1440 4.4 / 2022 0.9		30 TU	0132 4.3 / 0753 0.6 / 1356 4.1 / 1945 1.0
			31 W	0206 4.3 / 0827 0.7 / 1430 4.1 / 2004 1.1

Chart Datum: 2·10 metres below Ordnance Datum (Local). HAT is 5·0 metres above Chart Datum.

》》 **FREE** monthly updates. Register at 《
www.reedsnauticalalmanac.co.uk

221

STANDARD TIME (UT)
For Summer Time add ONE hour in **non-shaded areas**

INVERGORDON LAT 57°41'N LONG 4°10'W
TIMES AND HEIGHTS OF HIGH AND LOW WATERS

Dates in red are **SPRINGS**
Dates in blue are **NEAPS**

YEAR 2022

SEPTEMBER

Day	Time	m	Day	Time	m
1 TH	0242 / 0857 / 1505 / 2005	4.2 / 0.9 / 4.0 / 1.2	16 F	0331 / 0859 / 1553 / 2115	4.0 / 1.4 / 3.7 / 1.5
2 F	0320 / 0833 / 1544 / 2038	4.1 / 1.1 / 3.8 / 1.3	17 SA	0412 / 0906 / 1633 / 2154 ◑	3.7 / 1.7 / 3.5 / 1.8
3 SA	0403 / 0903 / 1629 / 2131 ◑	3.9 / 1.4 / 3.7 / 1.6	18 SU	0504 / 0950 / 1729	3.4 / 2.0 / 3.3
4 SU	0457 / 1130 / 1728 / 2357	3.7 / 1.6 / 3.5 / 1.7	19 M	0015 / 0615 / 1309 / 1842	2.0 / 3.2 / 2.2 / 3.3
5 M	0609 / 1316 / 1842	3.5 / 1.7 / 3.5	20 TU	0209 / 0729 / 1439 / 1951	1.9 / 3.2 / 2.1 / 3.4
6 TU	0150 / 0743 / 1438 / 2002	1.6 / 3.5 / 1.6 / 3.6	21 W	0309 / 0839 / 1529 / 2052	1.6 / 3.3 / 1.9 / 3.6
7 W	0313 / 0916 / 1546 / 2118	1.3 / 3.7 / 1.4 / 3.9	22 TH	0353 / 0944 / 1603 / 2146	1.4 / 3.5 / 1.7 / 3.8
8 TH	0421 / 1031 / 1643 / 2229	0.9 / 4.0 / 1.2 / 4.2	23 F	0426 / 1034 / 1630 / 2233	1.2 / 3.8 / 1.5 / 4.0
9 F	0515 / 1126 / 1730 / 2326	0.6 / 4.3 / 1.0 / 4.5	24 SA	0459 / 1114 / 1704 / 2315	1.0 / 4.0 / 1.3 / 4.2
10 SA	0600 / 1212 / 1809 ○	0.3 / 4.5 / 0.8	25 SU	0534 / 1149 / 1741 / 2353 ●	0.8 / 4.2 / 1.1 / 4.4
11 SU	0012 / 0640 / 1254 / 1845	4.7 / 0.2 / 4.6 / 0.7	26 M	0612 / 1223 / 1817	0.6 / 4.3 / 1.0
12 M	0055 / 0717 / 1332 / 1919	4.8 / 0.2 / 4.6 / 0.7	27 TU	0029 / 0649 / 1256 / 1853	4.5 / 0.5 / 4.3 / 0.9
13 TU	0135 / 0751 / 1409 / 1951	4.7 / 0.4 / 4.4 / 0.8	28 W	0106 / 0726 / 1330 / 1926	4.5 / 0.5 / 4.3 / 0.9
14 W	0214 / 0824 / 1444 / 2022	4.6 / 0.7 / 4.2 / 1.0	29 TH	0143 / 0759 / 1406 / 1955	4.5 / 0.7 / 4.3 / 1.0
15 TH	0252 / 0851 / 1518 / 2051	4.3 / 1.0 / 4.0 / 1.3	30 F	0222 / 0834 / 1443 / 2002	4.3 / 0.9 / 4.1 / 1.1

OCTOBER

Day	Time	m	Day	Time	m
1 SA	0304 / 0816 / 1523 / 2030	4.2 / 1.2 / 3.9 / 1.3	16 SU	0332 / 0824 / 1542 / 2107	3.6 / 1.8 / 3.6 / 1.8
2 SU	0351 / 0846 / 1611 / 2223 ◑	3.9 / 1.6 / 3.7 / 1.6	17 M	0418 / 0908 / 1634 / 2343 ◑	3.4 / 2.0 / 3.4 / 1.9
3 M	0450 / 1117 / 1712 ◑	3.6 / 1.8 / 3.6	18 TU	0531 / 1030 / 1754	3.2 / 2.3 / 3.3
4 TU	0005 / 0608 / 1313 / 1827	1.7 / 3.4 / 1.9 / 3.5	19 W	0126 / 0650 / 1401 / 1911	1.8 / 3.2 / 2.2 / 3.3
5 W	0156 / 0749 / 1437 / 1947	1.5 / 3.5 / 1.7 / 3.7	20 TH	0223 / 0800 / 1453 / 2012	1.6 / 3.3 / 2.0 / 3.5
6 TH	0310 / 0922 / 1539 / 2106	1.1 / 3.8 / 1.5 / 3.9	21 F	0305 / 0901 / 1531 / 2104	1.4 / 3.5 / 1.8 / 3.7
7 F	0410 / 1023 / 1630 / 2214	0.8 / 4.1 / 1.2 / 4.2	22 SA	0342 / 0952 / 1604 / 2152	1.2 / 3.8 / 1.5 / 4.0
8 SA	0458 / 1111 / 1711 / 2307	0.6 / 4.4 / 1.0 / 4.5	23 SU	0420 / 1036 / 1639 / 2237	1.0 / 4.0 / 1.3 / 4.2
9 SU	0539 / 1152 / 1747 / 2352 ○	0.4 / 4.5 / 0.9 / 4.6	24 M	0501 / 1115 / 1716 / 2320	0.8 / 4.3 / 1.1 / 4.4
10 M	0614 / 1230 / 1819	0.4 / 4.6 / 0.8	25 TU	0542 / 1153 / 1754 ●	0.6 / 4.4 / 0.9
11 TU	0030 / 0647 / 1304 / 1851	4.7 / 0.5 / 4.5 / 0.8	26 W	0001 / 0623 / 1229 / 1832	4.5 / 0.6 / 4.5 / 0.9
12 W	0107 / 0717 / 1336 / 1922	4.6 / 0.7 / 4.4 / 0.9	27 TH	0042 / 0701 / 1306 / 1909	4.6 / 0.6 / 4.5 / 0.9
13 TH	0143 / 0743 / 1407 / 1952	4.4 / 0.9 / 4.2 / 1.1	28 F	0123 / 0739 / 1344 / 1945	4.5 / 0.8 / 4.4 / 0.9
14 F	0218 / 0759 / 1436 / 2016	4.3 / 1.2 / 4.0 / 1.3	29 SA	0207 / 0815 / 1424 / 2024	4.4 / 1.1 / 4.2 / 1.1
15 SA	0254 / 0759 / 1507 / 2029	3.9 / 1.5 / 3.8 / 1.5	30 SU	0254 / 0851 / 1508 / 2118	4.2 / 1.4 / 4.0 / 1.3
			31 M	0347 / 0943 / 1601 / 2233	3.9 / 1.7 / 3.8 / 1.5

NOVEMBER

Day	Time	m	Day	Time	m
1 TU	0450 / 1105 / 1702 ◑	3.7 / 1.9 / 3.7	16 W	0440 / 0948 / 1656 ◑	3.3 / 2.1 / 3.4
2 W	0016 / 0607 / 1305 / 1814	1.5 / 3.5 / 1.9 / 3.6	17 TH	0027 / 0556 / 1124 / 1814	1.8 / 3.2 / 2.2 / 3.4
3 TH	0148 / 0744 / 1423 / 1930	1.3 / 3.6 / 1.8 / 3.8	18 F	0128 / 0707 / 1401 / 1923	1.6 / 3.3 / 2.1 / 3.5
4 F	0255 / 0904 / 1521 / 2047	1.1 / 3.8 / 1.5 / 4.0	19 SA	0215 / 0809 / 1448 / 2019	1.5 / 3.5 / 1.9 / 3.7
5 SA	0350 / 1000 / 1610 / 2152	0.9 / 4.1 / 1.3 / 4.2	20 SU	0257 / 0903 / 1528 / 2110	1.3 / 3.7 / 1.6 / 3.9
6 SU	0437 / 1047 / 1651 / 2244	0.8 / 4.3 / 1.2 / 4.4	21 M	0341 / 0953 / 1608 / 2159	1.1 / 4.0 / 1.4 / 4.1
7 M	0516 / 1127 / 1726 / 2328	0.7 / 4.4 / 1.0 / 4.4	22 TU	0428 / 1039 / 1651 / 2248	0.9 / 4.2 / 1.2 / 4.3
8 TU	0549 / 1204 / 1757 ○	0.8 / 4.4 / 1.0	23 W	0515 / 1123 / 1734 / 2336 ●	0.8 / 4.4 / 1.0 / 4.5
9 W	0006 / 0617 / 1236 / 1828	4.4 / 0.9 / 4.4 / 0.9	24 TH	0559 / 1205 / 1816	0.8 / 4.5 / 0.9
10 TH	0041 / 0641 / 1305 / 1859	4.4 / 1.0 / 4.3 / 1.0	25 F	0022 / 0642 / 1246 / 1859	4.5 / 0.8 / 4.5 / 0.8
11 F	0114 / 0702 / 1333 / 1929	4.2 / 1.2 / 4.2 / 1.1	26 SA	0109 / 0723 / 1328 / 1944	4.5 / 1.0 / 4.4 / 0.9
12 SA	0148 / 0713 / 1401 / 1951	4.0 / 1.4 / 4.0 / 1.3	27 SU	0157 / 0805 / 1412 / 2033	4.4 / 1.2 / 4.3 / 1.0
13 SU	0223 / 0730 / 1430 / 2006	3.8 / 1.5 / 3.9 / 1.5	28 M	0250 / 0849 / 1501 / 2131	4.2 / 1.4 / 4.2 / 1.1
14 M	0259 / 0800 / 1505 / 2046	3.6 / 1.7 / 3.7 / 1.6	29 TU	0346 / 0941 / 1554 / 2240	4.0 / 1.6 / 4.0 / 1.2
15 TU	0343 / 0844 / 1552 / 2159	3.4 / 1.9 / 3.5 / 1.8	30 W	0447 / 1042 / 1652 ◑	3.8 / 1.8 / 3.9

DECEMBER

Day	Time	m	Day	Time	m
1 TH	0001 / 0553 / 1215 / 1755 ◑	1.2 / 3.7 / 1.9 / 3.8	16 F	0457 / 1016 / 1707 ◑	3.4 / 2.0 / 3.5
2 F	0121 / 0709 / 1349 / 1902	1.2 / 3.6 / 1.8 / 3.8	17 SA	0007 / 0558 / 1131 / 1811	1.6 / 3.4 / 2.0 / 3.5
3 SA	0228 / 0824 / 1452 / 2013	1.2 / 3.7 / 1.7 / 3.9	18 SU	0115 / 0704 / 1248 / 1920	1.5 / 3.4 / 1.9 / 3.6
4 SU	0325 / 0925 / 1545 / 2120	1.1 / 3.9 / 1.5 / 4.0	19 M	0211 / 0808 / 1428 / 2023	1.4 / 3.6 / 1.8 / 3.7
5 M	0414 / 1016 / 1631 / 2218	1.1 / 4.0 / 1.4 / 4.1	20 TU	0303 / 0906 / 1531 / 2122	1.2 / 3.8 / 1.5 / 3.9
6 TU	0455 / 1059 / 1710 / 2305	1.1 / 4.1 / 1.2 / 4.1	21 W	0356 / 1001 / 1627 / 2220	1.1 / 4.0 / 1.3 / 4.2
7 W	0526 / 1136 / 1743 / 2344	1.2 / 4.2 / 1.1 / 4.1	22 TH	0451 / 1054 / 1720 / 2317	1.0 / 4.2 / 1.1 / 4.3
8 TH	0546 / 1209 / 1813 ○	1.2 / 4.2 / 1.1	23 F	0541 / 1143 / 1809 ●	0.9 / 4.4 / 0.9
9 F	0019 / 0604 / 1239 / 1845	4.1 / 1.3 / 4.2 / 1.1	24 SA	0010 / 0629 / 1230 / 1858	4.4 / 0.9 / 4.5 / 0.7
10 SA	0053 / 0626 / 1309 / 1918	4.0 / 1.3 / 4.2 / 1.1	25 SU	0101 / 0715 / 1317 / 1947	4.5 / 1.0 / 4.5 / 0.7
11 SU	0127 / 0649 / 1340 / 1949	3.9 / 1.4 / 4.1 / 1.2	26 M	0153 / 0800 / 1405 / 2038	4.4 / 1.1 / 4.4 / 0.7
12 M	0201 / 0714 / 1412 / 2013	3.8 / 1.5 / 3.9 / 1.3	27 TU	0246 / 0845 / 1454 / 2130	4.3 / 1.2 / 4.4 / 0.7
13 TU	0237 / 0745 / 1446 / 2042	3.6 / 1.6 / 3.8 / 1.4	28 W	0339 / 0928 / 1544 / 2224	4.1 / 1.4 / 4.3 / 0.9
14 W	0318 / 0823 / 1525 / 2133	3.5 / 1.7 / 3.7 / 1.5	29 TH	0430 / 1009 / 1635 / 2321	4.0 / 1.5 / 4.1 / 1.1
15 TH	0404 / 0910 / 1612 / 2242	3.4 / 1.9 / 3.5 / 1.6	30 F	0523 / 1054 / 1728 ◑	3.8 / 1.7 / 4.0
			31 SA	0033 / 0619 / 1149 / 1827	1.3 / 3.6 / 1.8 / 3.8

Chart Datum: 2·10 metres below Ordnance Datum (Local). HAT is 5·0 metres above Chart Datum.

>> FREE monthly updates. Register at <<
www.reedsnauticalalmanac.co.uk

metres
cables

0 · · · 800 · · · 1600
0 · · · 4 · · · 8

Kessock Bridge Lts: Aero FR mark tops
of 4 Trs. Oc G 6s and QG on N Trs.
Oc R 6s and QR on S Trs. FY
mark bridge centre

MEIKLE MEE

1_2
0_2
0_6

FS

North Kessock

2_1
1_2 2_1 0_6 1_5
0_3 0_6 0_6
57°30'N
4_6 15_1
24
2_4 6_1
16_5 Strong Tidal
Streams 25 Kessock Road
0_3 7_3 23 23 15_2
11_9 16_8
1_2 5_2 7_9 0_9

Beauly Firth

7_9 3_4
Q.R.5m2M
Entrance to
Caledonian
Canal
0_6 Iso.G.4s5m2M
0_3 0_6
Sea Lock
0_6 Monument
Clachnaharry
1_2

Lt Bn (conspic) Craigton Pt
Q.G
Oc.G Racon (K) Oc.R
Strong Tidal Streams 7_1
Longman Pt. Bn (conspic)
Fl.WR.2s7m5/4M
2_5
FI.WRG. 4s 13$_4$
Q.R.
Bn Outfall
Q 1_7 2_9
Carnarc Pt Q.R Longman Pt
FI.G.2s Kessock Bridge (29m)
FI.R.4s
3 Inverness Marina
FI.R.3s

SOUTH KESSOCK
Q.G
Dredged to 3.0m (2001)
Q.R INVERNESS
Clock Tower
Citadel Quay
Q.G Shore Street Quay

N
Locks Ch 74

Muirtown Basin
Swing Bridge
Clachnaharry Lock

Seaport Marina

Swing Bridge

Muirtown Locks

River Ness

Station

Town Hall Spire

Caley Marina
Caledonian Canal: see chart AC 1791

29'
16' 15' 04°14'W 13'

CALEDONIAN CANAL

Clachnaharry Sea Lock 57°29'·44N 04°15'·84W. These notes are for the convenience of those entering the Canal at Inverness.

CHARTS AC 1791, 1078, 5617. *Scottish Canals Skipper's Guide* dowload from www. scottishcanals.co.uk

TIDES Differences: Clachnaharry +0116 on Dover.

SHELTER Clachnaharry sea lock operates when depth >1·4m in canal hours; the gates cannot be opened LW±2 during Spring tides. Openings of the swing bridges are restricted – allow for delays. Seaport and Caley marinas: see Facilities.

NAVIGATION The 60M Caledonian Canal consists of 38M through three lochs (Lochs Ness, Oich and Lochy), connected by 22M of canals. It can take vessels up to 45m LOA, 10m beam, mast ht 27·4m and freshwater draught approx 4m (vessels >3·4m draught must contact the sea lock or canal office before arrival). Minimum passage time is 3½ days but allow longer.

Speed limit is 5kn in canal sections. There are 10 swing bridges; road tfc has priority at peak hrs. Do not pass bridges without the keeper's instructions. From Clachnaharry sea lock to Loch Ness (Bona Ferry lt ho) is approx 7M, via Muirtown and Dochgarroch locks.

LOCKS Operating hours subject to change – see www.scottishcanals. co.uk for latest information.

BOAT SAFETY SCHEME Visiting vessels will be checked for apparent dangerous defects eg leaking gas or fuel, damaged electrical cables, taking in water, risk of capsize. £1 million 3rd party insurance is required

LIGHTS AND MARKS Chans are marked by posts, cairns and unlit buoys, PHM on the NW side of the chan and SHM on the SE side.

COMMUNICATIONS (01463) Canal Office ☎01463 725500 Clachnaharry sea lock mob 07920 237331.
Sea locks and main lock flights operate VHF Ch **74** (HO).

FACILITIES Seaport Marina www.scottishcanals.co.uk ☎(01463) 725500, 80⌂+20♥, ⬛ ♨ ⚓ ⬛ ⬛ ⟐⬛ ◨ ✕ ✎ ⬛.
Caley Marina www.caleymarina.com ☎(01463) 236539, 25⌂+25♥ £1.50, ⬛ ✕ ✎ ⬛ ⬛(20t) ⬛ ACA.

North Kessock Pier Ideal if awaiting sea lock at Caledonian Canal. Approach on N shore to avoid shallows at Inverness. Unlit tidal slipway, suitable for leisure craft up to 20m. 2m at MLWS. Mud and rounded stones bottom, sheltered from SW by Bkwtr. Facilities: ➤ ⌂ donations in honesty box, ⚓ Jim Prentice ☎07802 915741.
Village LB(inshore), Ⓑ ⬛ ✕ ⬛ ⬛ ⬛ (coin–op), Bus.

5.15 INVERNESS

Highland 57°29'·73N 04°14'·17W ✿❋◊◊◊✿✿

CHARTS AC 223, 1077, 1078, 5617; Imray C23

TIDES +0100 Dover; ML 2·7; Duration 0620

Standard Port INVERGORDON (←—)

Times				Height (metres)			
High Water		Low Water		MHWS	MHWN	MLWN	MLWS
0100	0700	0000	0700	4·3	3·3	1·6	0·7
1300	1900	1200	1900				
Differences INVERNESS							
+0010	+0015	+0015	+0010	+0·3	+0·2	+0·1	+0·1
FORTROSE							
0000	+0010	+0010	−0010	0·0	+0·1	ND	ND
CROMARTY							
−0005	0000	0000	−0005	0·0	0·0	0·0	0·0
DINGWALL							
+0020	+0015	ND	ND	0·0	+0·1	ND	ND

SHELTER Good in all weathers. Berth at Inverness Marina (3·0m at LAT (2019)) or at one of the 2 marinas in the Caledonian Canal, entr to which can be difficult in strong tidal streams. The sea lock is normally available when depth > 1·4m in canal hours; the gates cannot be opened LW±2 during Spring tides.

NAVIGATION WPT Meikle Mee SHM By Fl G 3s, 57°30'·25N 04°12'·03W, 250°/0·74M to Longman Pt bn. Inverness Firth is deep from Chanonry Pt to Munlochy SWM buoy, but shoal (2·1m) to Meikle Mee buoy. Meikle Mee partly dries. Beware bird rafts S of Avoch (off chartlet). Tidal streams are strong S of Craigton Pt (E-going stream at sp exceeds 5kn). Ent to R Ness is narrow, dredged to 3m CD. Take care to avoid Carnarc Pt W of R mouth and its associated shoal which is marked by a lit N Cardinal buoy. For the entrance to the Caledonian Canal, keep to N Kessock bank until clear of unmarked shoals on S bank.

LIGHTS AND MARKS Longman Pt bn Fl WR 2s 7m 5/4M, vis 078°-W-258°-R-078°. Craigton Pt lt, Fl WRG 4s 6m 11/7M vis 312°-W-048°-R-064°-W-085°-G-shore. Caledonian Canal ent marked by QR and Iso G 4s on ends of training walls.

COMMUNICATIONS (Code 01463) Dr 234151, HM 715715; Clachnaharry Sea Lock mob 07920 237331; Canal Office 725500. *Inverness Hbr Office* VHF Ch 12 (Mon-Fri: 0800 –1700 LT). *Inverness Marina* Ch 12. Caledonian Canal: Ch 74 is used by all stations. Call: *Clachnaharry Sea Lock*; or for office: *Caledonian Canal.*

FACILITIES **Inverness Marina** www.invernessmarina.com ☎220501, Dredged to 3m 150⊃ inc 20♥ £2·70 + ⫶⫶⟩, £17/m wkly, short stay (4hr) £17; min chargeable length 7m. ⬚⊡♣⚓⟂(75t) ⚒⌖⌖⛽✕⌂.
City All domestic facilities, ⇌ ✈.

MINOR HARBOURS IN INVERNESS FIRTH

FORTROSE, Highland, 57°34'·71N 04°08'·04W. AC 1078. Tides 5.15. HW +0055 on Dover; ML 2·5m; Duration 0620. Small drying unlit hbr, soft silt bottom, well protected by Chanonry Ness to E; Chanonry Pt lt, Oc 6s 12m 15M, obscd 073°-shore. Follow ldg line 296°, Broomhill Ho (conspic on hill to NW) in line with school spire. Beware Craig an Roan rocks (1·8m) ESE of harbour. Stand 15m off S harbour wall until abeam centre of ent to avoid shoal marked by small Y buoy. HM mob 078 08933775; Dr ☎622000. Facilities: ⊃ £10, 2♥ (6T) £15; ⟍ ⟍ ⚓ scrubbing grid. Village ♣ © ⍾ ✕. **Chanonry SC** (near pier) ⍰ ⌖.

AVOCH, Highland, 57°34'·03N 04°09'·94W. AC 1078. It share tides with Fortrose which is larger. Hbr dries, mostly on the N side. Small craft <8m LOA can stay afloat on No 3 pontoon off South pier, where two outside berths have approx 2m water at LWS; one ♥ (max 35ft LOA) lies off harbour entrance. Appr from the East via safe channel between two pairs of lateral buoys. A rock armour groyne extends approx 30m SSE on the South side of the harbour entrance and approx 3M high. It covers at HW Springs and is marked by a small, unlit south cardinal buoy. HM ☎(01381) 622383 mob 07825667281.
Facilities: ⊃£12 (day/night) ⚓ ⫶⫶⟩. **Village** ⌖ ⌖ ⟍ ⌖ ⍾ ✕ ⌂.

CROMARTY FIRTH, Highland, 57°41'·18N 04°02'·09W. AC 1889, 1890. HW +0100 on Dover −0135 on Aberdeen; HW height 0·0m on Aberdeen; ML 2·5m; Duration 0625. See 5.15. Excellent hbr extending 7·5M W, past Invergordon, then 9M SW. Good shelter always available, depending on wind direction. Beware rks and reefs round N and S Sutor at the ent, ebb often runs longer than predicted; many unlit rig mooring buoys and lit rigs. Mussel farm 2M W of harbour marked by 4 xY SPM. *Cromarty Firth Port Radio* VHF Ch **11** 16 13 (H24) ☎(01349) 852308.

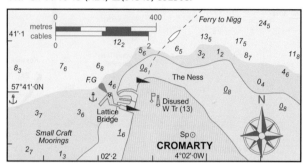

CROMARTY HARBOUR, Highland. 57°41'·00N 04°02'·35W. From WPT 57°41'·10N 04°02'·50W, 142°/1.3ca to entrance. When inside harbour beware of set towards lattice bridge, tide runs at up to 4kn. Sheltered from N through E to S. ♥⊃ at end of central pontoon, £20 o/n s/stay £10, depth approx 1·2m, max LOA 8m, no rafting. 3 ♥ 2ca W of S pier hd, in 0·5m–1·5m (free - **Cromarty Boat Club** www.cromartyboatclub.org) or ⚓ in approx 6m with good holding but exposed to the West. HM mob 07751244065 ⚓ ⫶⫶⟩ available. ⍰/⌖ ⊙ (owned by Boat Club); coin operated, key held by HM). ⌖ ⍾. Local seasonal ferry to N shore where Nigg energy park dominates the shore.

INVERGORDON WEST HARBOUR, Highland. 57°41'·12N 04°10'·05W. Mainly commercial - ⊃ on pontoons, call Cromarty Firth Port Radio Ch11; ⟍ ⚓ ⌖ ⌖ ♣ ⊙ ⟂(3t) ⌖ ⍾ ✕ ⌂. Landing at Invergordon Boat Club (1·5M W) ☎(01862) 893772 mob 07762904041.

DORNOCH FIRTH, Highland, 57°51'·28N 03°59'·39W. AC 115, 223. HW +0115 on Dover; ML 2·5m; Duration 0605; see 5.16. Excellent shelter but difficult entry. There are many shifting sandbanks, especially near the ent, from N edge of Whiteness Sands to S edge of Gizzen Briggs. ⚓s in 7m ¾M ESE of Dornoch Pt (sheltered from NE swell by Gizzen Briggs); in 7m 2ca SSE of Ard na Cailc; in 3·3m 1M below Bonar Bridge. Firth extends 15M inland, but AC coverage ceases ¼M E of Ferry Pt. The A9 road bridge, 3·3M W of Dornoch Pt, with 11m clearance, has 3 spans lit on both sides; span centres show Iso 4s, N bank pier Iso G 4s, S bank pier Iso R 4s and 2 midstream piers QY. Tarbat Ness lt ho Fl (4) 30s 53m 24M. Fl R 5s lt shown when Tain firing range active. Very limited facilities at Ferrytown and Bonar Bridge. **Dornoch**: Dr ⌖ ⌖ ⌖ ⍾ ✕ ⌂.

GOLSPIE, Highland, 57°58'·71N 03°56'·79W. AC 223. HW +0045 on Dover; ML 2·3m; Duration 068. See 5.16. Golspie pier projects 60m SE across foreshore with arm projecting SW at the head, giving shelter during NE winds. Beware The Bridge, a bank (0·3m to 1·8m) running parallel to the shore ¼M to seaward of pier hd. Seas break heavily over The Bridge in NE winds. There are no lts. To enter, keep Duke of Sutherland's Memorial in line 316° with boathouse SW of pier, until church spire in village is in line 006° with hd of pier, then keep on those marks. Harbour gets very congested; good ⚓ off pier. HM ☎01431 821692, ⊃ £25 <10m (single visit - 2nd nt free) short stay £7 ♠ ⟍.
Town ⊞ Dr ⌖ ⌖ ♣ ⌖ ⑧ ⍾ ✕ ⌂ ⇌.

LYBSTER, Highland, 58°17'·72N 03°17'·39W. AC 115. HW +0020 on Dover; HW -0150 sp, -0215 np; HW ht -0·6m on Aberdeen; ML 2·1m; Duration 0620. Excellent shelter in SW corner of inner hbr; ⊃ on W side of pier in about 1·2m, £7.00/wk. Most of hbr dries to sand/mud and is much used by FVs; no bollards on N wall. Appr on about 350°. Beware rks close on E side of ent; narrow (10m) ent is difficult in strong E to S winds. Min depth 2·5m in ent. S pier hd, Oc R 6s 10m 3M, occas in fishing season. ⚓ on W quay. ⌖ at Waterlines Visitor Centre, 01593 721520. **Town** ⍾ ✕ ⌂.

5.16 PORTMAHOMACK

Highland **57°50'·25N 03°50'·00W** ✿✿✿✿✿✿

CHARTS AC 115, 223; Imray C23

TIDES +0035 Dover; ML 2·5; Duration 0600

Standard Port ABERDEEN (←)

Times				Height (metres)			
High Water		Low Water		MHWS	MHWN	MLWN	MLWS
0300	0800	0200	0800	4·3	3·4	1·6	0·6
1500	2000	1400	2000				
Differences PORTMAHOMACK							
–0120	–0210	–0140	–0110	–0·2	–0·1	+0·1	+0·1
MEIKLE FERRY (Dornoch Firth)							
–0100	–0140	–0120	–0055	+0·1	0·0	–0·1	0·0
GOLSPIE							
–0130	–0215	–0155	–0130	–0·3	–0·3	–0·1	0·0

SHELTER Good, but uncomfortable in SW/NW winds. Hbr dries, access only at HW, but good ⚓ close SW of pier.

NAVIGATION WPT 57°53'·00N 03°50'·00W, 180°/2.7M to 1ca W of hbr ent. Beware Curach Rks which lie from 2ca SW of pier to the shore. Rks extend N and W of the pier. Beware lobster pot floats and salmon nets N of hbr. Tain firing & bombing range is about 3M to the W, S of mouth of Dornoch Firth; R flags, R lts, shown when active.

LIGHTS AND MARKS Tarbert Ness lt ho Fl (4) 30s 53m 24M, W twr R bands, is 2·6M to NE of hbr. Pier hd 2 Fl R 5s 7m 3M.

COMMUNICATIONS (Code 01862) Dr 892759. No HM; enquiries: harbours@highland.gov.uk (01349) 781612.

FACILITIES **Harbour**, ⚓ £25 <10m (single visit – 2nd nt free) short stay £6; pontoon in harbour but dries out for half its length and heavily used by local boats, ⚓ ⚓ ⚓ 🚻.
Town ✉ 🛒 🏪 ✗ ⚑ (bus to Tain), ✈ (Inverness).

5.17 HELMSDALE

Highland **58°06'·83N 03°38'·89W** ✿✿✿✿✿✿

CHARTS AC 115, 1462; Imray C23

TIDES +0035 Dover; ML 2·2; Duration 0615

Standard Port WICK (→)

Times				Height (metres)			
High Water		Low Water		MHWS	MHWN	MLWN	MLWS
0000	0700	0200	0700	3·5	2·8	1·4	0·7
1200	1900	1400	1900				
Differences HELMSDALE							
+0025	+0015	+0035	+0030	+0·5	+0·3	+0·1	–0·1

SHELTER Good, except in strong E/SE'lies. ⚓ on NW pier, approx 1m. 80m of pontoon berths through HM.

NAVIGATION WPT 58°06'·59N 03°38'·39W, 313°/0.35M to ent.

- Surface and seabed fishing gear, hazardous to navigation, extends up to 0.5M offshore and 1.0M SW of hbr.
- Keep well to seaward of ruined b'water on approach from SW.
- Beware spate coming downriver after heavy rain. Shoals both sides of chan and bar build up when river in spate.

LIGHTS AND MARKS See 5.3 and chartlet. Dir lt is wooden post, day lt vis 1M

COMMUNICATIONS (Code 01431) Dr 821225, HM 821692 (Office), mob 07767 311213.
VHF Ch 13 16.

FACILITIES ⚓ £25 <10m (single visit – 2nd nt free) short stay £7 ⚓ ⚓ (see HM); ⚓ ⚓ 🚻 🚿 (access code from HM).
Town 🔧(hardware store), ✉ 🛒 ✗ 🏪 ⑧(Brora) ⚑.

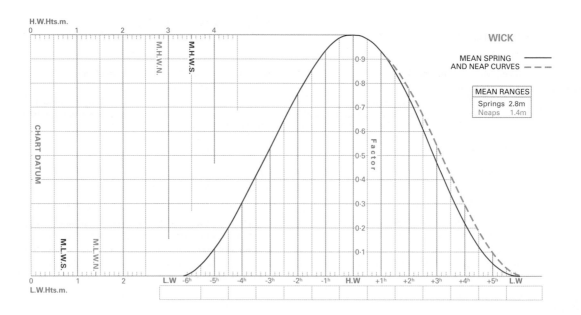

WICK

MEAN SPRING
AND NEAP CURVES

MEAN RANGES
Springs 2.8m
Neaps 1.4m

5.18 WICK

Highland 58°26′·38N 03°04′·72W ❀❀❀◊✿

CHARTS AC 115, 1462; Imray C23, C68

TIDES +0010 Dover; ML 2·0; Duration 0625. Wick is a Standard Port. Daily tidal predictions are given below.

Standard Port WICK (→)

Times				Height (metres)			
High Water		Low Water		MHWS	MHWN	MLWN	MLWS
0000	0700	0200	0700	3·5	2·8	1·4	0·7
1200	1900	1400	1900				
Differences DUNCANSBY HEAD							
–0115	–0115	–0110	–0110	–0·4	–0·4	ND	ND

SHELTER Good, except in strong NNE to SSE winds, to await right conditions for W-bound passage through the Pentland Firth (see 5.4). Berth where directed in the Outer Harbour, approx 2m, or in marina in Inner Harbour, 2·0m. Inner and Outer hbr fairways dredged 2·3m below CD (2019). NB: The River Hbr (commercial) is leased and must not be entered without prior approval.

NAVIGATION WPT 58°26′·18N 03°03′·39W, 284°/0·72M to S pier. From the N, open up hbr ent before rounding North Head so as to clear drying Proudfoot Rks. For small craft ≠ established Or △ / ▽, On N pier by tank fm and on S side of S Pier leading 287°.

> Hbr ent is dangerous in strong E'lies as craft have to turn 90° to port at the end of S pier.

On S side of bay, PHM Fl(2)R 6s lies to seaward of ruined bkwtr.

LIGHTS AND MARKS S pier lt, Fl WRG 3s 12m 12/9M, 253°-G-270°-W-286°-R-329°, Bell (2) 10s. Red sector guards shoal water marked by PHM Fl(2) R 6s. Ldg lts, both FR 5/8m, lead 234° into outer hbr. Traffic signals:

3 Oc ● (vert) on Commercial Pier = harbour closed.

COMMUNICATIONS (Code 01955) HM 602030; Ⓗ 602434, 602261.
VHF Ch 14 16 (Mon-Fri 0800-1700).

FACILITIES Poss temporary ⌣ on pontoons in Outer Harbour.
Wick Marina (Inner Harbour) dredged to 2·0m 70⌣ inc 15 ♥; £22 <10m< +£2/m + ⅏; max 25m LOA. 🅿 50m from marina 🛢.
Fish Jetty ⚓ 🛢 🅿. **Services** 🔧 🛠 🔩 ⒼⒽ(15/100t).
Town 🏬 🛢(at Heat Centre) ✉ Ⓑ 🛒 ✕ 🏧 ⇌ ✈.

STANDARD TIME (UT)
For Summer Time add ONE hour in **non-shaded areas**

WICK LAT 58°26'N LONG 3°05'W
TIMES AND HEIGHTS OF HIGH AND LOW WATERS

Dates in red are **SPRINGS**
Dates in blue are **NEAPS**

YEAR 2022

JANUARY

Time	m		Time	m
1 0326	0.9	**16**	0404	1.3
0947	3.4		1030	3.2
SA 1550	0.9	SU	1634	1.1
2215	3.5		2252	3.1
2 0416	0.9	**17**	0439	1.2
1038	3.6		1106	3.3
SU 1642	0.8	M	1710	1.0
● 2310	3.6	○	2329	3.2
3 0504	0.9	**18**	0512	1.1
1126	3.7		1140	3.4
M 1733	0.6	TU	1744	0.9
4 0002	3.6	**19**	0004	3.2
0551	0.9		0544	1.1
TU 1213	3.7	W	1213	3.4
1824	0.5		1818	0.8
5 0053	3.6	**20**	0039	3.2
0637	1.0		0617	1.1
W 1259	3.7	TH	1247	3.5
1914	0.6		1853	0.8
6 0143	3.5	**21**	0115	3.2
0721	1.1		0650	1.1
TH 1346	3.7	F	1322	3.4
2004	0.6		1929	0.8
7 0232	3.3	**22**	0151	3.2
0805	1.2		0725	1.1
F 1433	3.5	SA	1358	3.4
2054	0.8		2006	0.8
8 0322	3.1	**23**	0230	3.1
0850	1.4		0802	1.2
SA 1522	3.4	SU	1436	3.3
2146	1.0		2047	0.9
9 0413	2.9	**24**	0313	3.0
0940	1.5		0843	1.3
SU 1615	3.2	M	1520	3.3
◑ 2242	1.2		2136	1.0
10 0508	2.8	**25**	0403	2.9
1040	1.6		0932	1.4
M 1713	3.0	TU	1612	3.2
2344	1.3	◑	2237	1.1
11 0607	2.8	**26**	0501	2.9
1153	1.7		1041	1.5
TU 1815	2.9	W	1717	3.1
			2349	1.2
12 0052	1.4	**27**	0609	2.9
0711	2.8		1209	1.5
W 1315	1.6	TH	1833	3.0
1923	2.9			
13 0155	1.4	**28**	0104	1.2
0815	2.9		0721	2.9
TH 1422	1.5	F	1335	1.4
2030	2.9		1953	3.1
14 0245	1.4	**29**	0218	1.2
0908	3.0		0831	3.1
F 1513	1.4	SA	1450	1.2
2126	3.0		2110	3.2
15 0327	1.3	**30**	0319	1.1
0952	3.1		0934	3.3
SA 1556	1.2	SU	1550	0.9
2212	3.0		2213	3.4
		31	0411	1.0
			1028	3.5
		M	1642	0.7
			2307	3.5

FEBRUARY

Time	m		Time	m
1 0457	0.9	**16**	0456	1.1
1117	3.6		1121	3.4
TU 1729	0.5	W	1726	0.7
● 2356	3.5	○	2346	3.2
2 0540	0.9	**17**	0527	1.0
1202	3.7		1155	3.5
W 1814	0.4	TH	1758	0.6
3 0041	3.5	**18**	0020	3.3
0620	0.8		0559	0.9
TH 1245	3.8	F	1228	3.5
1857	0.4		1831	0.5
4 0124	3.4	**19**	0054	3.3
0659	0.9		0632	0.8
F 1327	3.7	SA	1302	3.5
1937	0.5		1905	0.5
5 0204	3.3	**20**	0129	3.4
0736	1.0		0705	0.8
SA 1407	3.6	SU	1337	3.5
2016	0.7		1941	0.5
6 0244	3.1	**21**	0205	3.2
0812	1.1		0740	0.9
SU 1448	3.4	M	1414	3.4
2055	0.9		2018	0.7
7 0325	2.9	**22**	0244	3.1
0850	1.2		0818	1.0
M 1531	3.2	TU	1456	3.3
2136	1.1		2100	0.9
8 0410	2.8	**23**	0329	3.0
0935	1.4		0902	1.2
TU 1620	3.0	W	1547	3.1
◑ 2226	1.4	◑	2155	1.1
9 0504	2.7	**24**	0424	2.9
1042	1.6		1004	1.3
W 1720	2.8	TH	1653	3.0
2333	1.5		2315	1.3
10 0608	2.6	**25**	0534	2.8
1215	1.6		1147	1.4
TH 1834	2.7	F	1819	2.8
11 0102	1.6	**26**	0049	1.4
0723	2.7		0656	2.8
F 1355	1.6	SA	1335	1.3
1959	2.7		1954	2.9
12 0221	1.6	**27**	0216	1.3
0835	2.8		0818	2.9
SA 1457	1.4	SU	1453	1.1
2108	2.8		2114	3.1
13 0312	1.5	**28**	0317	1.2
0928	3.0		0925	3.1
SU 1542	1.2	M	1549	0.8
2156	2.9		2212	3.2
14 0351	1.3			
1010	3.1			
M 1619	1.0			
2236	3.0			
15 0425	1.2			
1046	3.2			
TU 1653	0.9			
2312	3.1			

MARCH

Time	m		Time	m
1 0404	1.0	**16**	0401	1.1
1018	3.4		1018	3.1
TU 1635	0.5	W	1626	0.7
2259	3.4		2247	3.1
2 0444	0.9	**17**	0432	1.0
1104	3.6		1054	3.3
W 1716	0.4	TH	1658	0.6
● 2342	3.5		2321	3.2
3 0522	0.8	**18**	0502	0.8
1146	3.7		1129	3.4
TH 1754	0.3	F	1730	0.4
		○	2355	3.3
4 0021	3.5	**19**	0535	0.7
0558	0.7		1204	3.5
F 1225	3.7	SA	1804	0.3
1830	0.3			
5 0057	3.4	**20**	0029	3.4
0632	0.7		0609	0.6
SA 1302	3.6	SU	1239	3.6
1905	0.5		1839	0.4
6 0132	3.3	**21**	0104	3.4
0706	0.8		0644	0.6
SU 1338	3.5	M	1316	3.5
1937	0.7		1915	0.5
7 0205	3.1	**22**	0140	3.3
0738	0.9		0720	0.7
M 1414	3.3	TU	1356	3.4
2008	0.9		1953	0.7
8 0239	3.0	**23**	0219	3.2
0811	1.1		0800	0.8
TU 1451	3.1	W	1440	3.3
2039	1.1		2035	0.9
9 0316	2.8	**24**	0304	3.0
0849	1.2		0846	1.0
W 1533	2.9	TH	1534	3.0
2117	1.4		2130	1.2
10 0400	2.7	**25**	0359	2.9
0942	1.4		0957	1.2
TH 1628	2.6	F	1647	2.8
◑ 2216	1.6	◑	2301	1.4
11 0502	2.6	**26**	0513	2.7
1121	1.6		1154	1.3
F 1748	2.5	SA	1823	2.6
2358	1.7			
12 0625	2.5	**27**	0047	1.5
1320	1.5		0642	2.7
SA 1923	2.5	SU	1340	1.1
			2001	2.8
13 0151	1.7	**28**	0211	1.4
0751	2.6		0806	2.9
SU 1431	1.3	M	1447	0.9
2044	2.6		2110	3.0
14 0250	1.5	**29**	0306	1.2
0855	2.8		0911	3.1
M 1516	1.1	TU	1537	0.6
2133	2.8		2159	3.2
15 0329	1.3	**30**	0348	1.0
0940	3.0		1001	3.3
TU 1553	0.9	W	1617	0.5
2212	3.0		2242	3.3
		31	0424	0.8
			1044	3.5
		TH	1653	0.4
			2319	3.3

APRIL

Time	m		Time	m
1 0458	0.7	**16**	0433	0.7
1124	3.5		1058	3.4
F 1726	0.4	SA	1659	0.3
● 2355	3.4	○	2325	3.4
2 0532	0.6	**17**	0508	0.6
1201	3.6		1137	3.5
SA 1759	0.4	SU	1735	0.3
3 0027	3.3	**18**	0002	3.4
0606	0.6		0546	0.5
SU 1235	3.5	M	1216	3.6
1830	0.5		1813	0.3
4 0059	3.2	**19**	0039	3.4
0638	0.7		0624	0.5
M 1309	3.4	TU	1258	3.5
1900	0.7		1852	0.5
5 0129	3.1	**20**	0118	3.4
0710	0.8		0705	0.6
TU 1343	3.2	W	1343	3.4
1928	0.9		1934	0.7
6 0200	3.0	**21**	0200	3.2
0743	0.9		0751	0.7
W 1419	3.0	TH	1433	3.2
1958	1.1		2021	1.0
7 0234	2.9	**22**	0247	3.1
0819	1.1		0848	0.9
TH 1500	2.8	F	1534	2.9
2032	1.3		2124	1.3
8 0314	2.7	**23**	0346	2.9
0908	1.3		1016	1.0
F 1551	2.6	SA	1653	2.8
2119	1.6	◑	2258	1.5
9 0408	2.6	**24**	0502	2.8
1039	1.4		1159	1.0
SA 1705	2.4	SU	1823	2.7
◑ 2301	1.7			
10 0527	2.5	**25**	0035	1.5
1225	1.4		0626	2.8
SU 1837	2.4	M	1326	0.9
			1949	2.8
11 0056	1.7	**26**	0151	1.4
0654	2.5		0744	2.9
M 1346	1.3	TU	1428	0.8
2000	2.5		2050	2.9
12 0209	1.5	**27**	0243	1.2
0805	2.7		0847	3.1
TU 1437	1.1	W	1514	0.6
2055	2.7		2136	3.1
13 0252	1.3	**28**	0323	1.0
0857	2.9		0937	3.2
W 1516	0.9	TH	1552	0.6
2136	2.9		2216	3.2
14 0327	1.1	**29**	0359	0.9
0940	3.1		1020	3.3
TH 1550	0.6	F	1625	0.5
2213	3.1		2252	3.2
15 0400	0.9	**30**	0433	0.7
1019	3.3		1059	3.4
F 1624	0.5	SA	1656	0.5
2249	3.3	●	2326	3.3

Chart Datum: 1·71 metres below Ordnance Datum (Newlyn). HAT is 4·0 metres above Chart Datum.

》》 FREE monthly updates. Register at 《
www.reedsnauticalalmanac.co.uk

227

WICK LAT 58°26′N LONG 3°05′W
TIMES AND HEIGHTS OF HIGH AND LOW WATERS

Dates in **red** are **SPRINGS**
Dates in **blue** are **NEAPS**

YEAR **2022**

MAY

	Time	m		Time	m
1 SU	0507 1135 1728 2358	0.7 3.3 0.6 3.3	**16** M ○	0444 1112 1710 2337	0.6 3.5 0.4 3.5
2 M	0541 1210 1758	0.7 3.3 0.7	**17** TU	0526 1159 1752	0.5 3.5 0.5
3 TU	0028 0616 1244 1829	3.2 0.7 3.2 0.8	**18** W	0018 0612 1246 1836	3.5 0.5 3.5 0.6
4 W	0058 0649 1318 1858	3.2 0.8 3.1 1.0	**19** TH	0102 0700 1337 1923	3.4 0.5 3.3 0.9
5 TH	0130 0723 1355 1929	3.1 0.9 2.9 1.2	**20** F	0148 0754 1432 2016	3.3 0.6 3.2 1.1
6 F	0204 0802 1436 2004	3.0 1.0 2.8 1.3	**21** SA	0239 0900 1536 2122	3.2 0.7 3.0 1.3
7 SA	0244 0851 1526 2050	2.8 1.2 2.5 1.5	**22** SU ◗	0338 1020 1648 2240	3.0 0.8 2.8 1.4
8 SU	0333 1006 1629 2209	2.7 1.3 2.5 1.6	**23** M	0449 1140 1802	2.9 0.9 2.7
9 M ◗	0438 1131 1747 2349	2.6 1.3 2.5 1.6	**24** TU	0000 0601 1256 1914	1.4 2.9 0.8 2.8
10 TU	0556 1245 1859	2.6 1.2 2.5	**25** W	0113 0710 1356 2015	1.4 2.9 0.8 2.9
11 W	0105 0706 1343 2000	1.5 2.7 1.0 2.7	**26** TH	0209 0814 1443 2104	1.2 3.0 0.8 2.9
12 TH	0201 0804 1430 2050	1.3 2.8 0.8 2.9	**27** F	0254 0907 1522 2146	1.1 3.1 0.8 3.0
13 F	0244 0854 1511 2133	1.1 3.0 0.6 3.1	**28** SA	0333 0953 1556 2224	1.0 3.1 0.8 3.1
14 SA	0324 0941 1550 2215	0.9 3.2 0.5 3.3	**29** SU	0411 1035 1629 2259	0.9 3.1 0.8 3.2
15 SU	0403 1027 1629 2256	0.7 3.4 0.4 3.4	**30** M ●	0447 1113 1701 2332	0.8 3.1 0.8 3.2
			31 TU	0524 1150 1733	0.8 3.1 0.9

JUNE

	Time	m		Time	m
1 W	0004 0600 1225 1805	3.2 0.8 3.1 1.0	**16** TH	0003 0607 1239 1828	3.5 0.4 3.5 0.8
2 TH	0036 0636 1301 1837	3.2 0.8 3.0 1.1	**17** F	0050 0700 1333 1917	3.5 0.4 3.4 0.9
3 F	0109 0712 1338 1911	3.1 0.9 2.9 1.2	**18** SA	0139 0756 1427 2009	3.4 0.5 3.2 1.1
4 SA	0144 0752 1418 1948	3.0 1.0 2.8 1.3	**19** SU	0230 0857 1525 2104	3.3 0.6 3.0 1.2
5 SU	0223 0837 1504 2031	2.9 1.0 2.7 1.4	**20** M	0325 0959 1625 2205	3.2 0.7 2.9 1.3
6 M	0308 0934 1556 2128	2.8 1.1 2.6 1.5	**21** TU ◗	0424 1104 1725 2311	3.1 0.8 2.8 1.4
7 TU ◗	0401 1040 1658 2245	2.8 1.1 2.6 1.5	**22** W	0527 1211 1827	3.0 0.9 2.7
8 W	0503 1146 1803 2359	2.7 1.1 2.6 1.5	**23** TH	0020 0630 1314 1929	1.4 2.9 1.0 2.7
9 TH	0609 1246 1904	2.8 1.0 2.7	**24** F	0128 0735 1407 2026	1.3 2.9 0.9 2.8
10 F	0103 0712 1341 2001	1.4 2.9 0.9 2.9	**25** SA	0225 0836 1452 2115	1.2 2.9 1.0 2.9
11 SA	0159 0810 1431 2053	1.2 3.0 0.7 3.0	**26** SU	0313 0929 1531 2158	1.1 2.9 1.1 3.0
12 SU	0250 0907 1519 2143	1.0 3.2 0.6 3.2	**27** M	0355 1015 1607 2236	1.0 3.0 1.0 3.1
13 M	0338 1002 1605 2230	0.8 3.3 0.6 3.4	**28** TU	0435 1057 1642 2312	0.9 3.0 1.0 3.2
14 TU ○	0427 1055 1652 2317	0.7 3.4 0.5 3.5	**29** W ●	0513 1142 1716 2346	0.9 3.1 1.1 3.2
15 W	0516 1148 1739	0.5 3.5 0.6	**30** TH	0549 1211 1749	0.8 3.0 1.1

JULY

	Time	m		Time	m
1 F	0020 0625 1247 1823	3.2 0.8 3.0 1.1	**16** SA	0039 0654 1323 1904	3.6 0.3 3.4 0.8
2 SA	0053 0701 1323 1857	3.2 0.8 3.0 1.1	**17** SU	0126 0744 1412 1948	3.6 0.3 3.3 0.9
3 SU	0128 0738 1400 1932	3.2 0.8 2.9 1.2	**18** M	0213 0833 1500 2033	3.5 0.5 3.1 1.1
4 M	0205 0817 1440 2011	3.1 0.9 2.8 1.2	**19** TU	0301 0923 1549 2120	3.4 0.7 3.0 1.2
5 TU	0244 0900 1524 2054	3.0 0.9 2.8 1.3	**20** W ◗	0352 1015 1640 2215	3.2 0.9 2.8 1.3
6 W	0328 0951 1614 2146	3.0 1.0 2.7 1.4	**21** TH	0446 1112 1736 2322	3.0 1.1 2.7 1.4
7 TH	0419 1050 1711 2256	2.9 1.0 2.7 1.4	**22** F	0547 1216 1837	2.9 1.2 2.7
8 F	0519 1154 1814	2.9 1.1 2.8	**23** SA	0042 0654 1326 1943	1.5 2.8 1.3 2.7
9 SA	0010 0627 1257 1917	1.4 2.9 1.0 2.9	**24** SU	0200 0807 1425 2045	1.4 2.7 1.3 2.8
10 SU	0120 0735 1359 2018	1.3 3.0 0.9 3.0	**25** M	0258 0911 1513 2134	1.3 2.8 1.3 3.0
11 M	0226 0844 1458 2117	1.1 3.1 0.9 3.2	**26** TU	0345 1001 1553 2217	1.1 2.9 1.2 3.1
12 TU	0326 0949 1552 2212	0.9 3.2 0.8 3.3	**27** W	0424 1043 1629 2254	1.0 3.0 1.2 3.2
13 W ○	0420 1048 1642 2303	0.7 3.4 0.8 3.5	**28** TH ●	0501 1121 1702 2329	0.9 3.0 1.1 3.3
14 TH	0513 1142 1731 2352	0.5 3.5 0.8 3.6	**29** F	0535 1156 1734	0.8 3.1 1.1
15 F	0604 1234 1818	0.3 3.5 0.8	**30** SA	0003 0609 1230 1807	3.3 0.7 3.1 1.0
			31 SU	0036 0642 1303 1839	3.3 0.7 3.1 1.0

AUGUST

	Time	m		Time	m
1 M	0109 0715 1338 1912	3.3 0.7 3.1 1.0	**16** TU	0149 0758 1426 1957	3.6 0.5 3.2 0.9
2 TU	0143 0750 1413 1946	3.3 0.7 3.0 1.0	**17** W	0230 0837 1507 2035	3.5 0.7 3.0 1.1
3 W	0218 0826 1452 2023	3.2 0.8 3.0 1.1	**18** TH	0314 0918 1550 2120	3.4 1.0 2.9 1.3
4 TH	0258 0907 1536 2105	3.2 0.9 2.9 1.2	**19** F ◗	0402 1005 1641 2223	3.0 1.3 2.7 1.5
5 F ◗	0344 0958 1627 2202	3.1 1.0 2.8 1.3	**20** SA	0501 1108 1743 2356	2.8 1.5 2.7 1.6
6 SA	0441 1106 1730 2327	3.0 1.1 2.8 1.4	**21** SU	0615 1236 1856	2.6 1.6 2.6
7 SU	0554 1223 1841	2.9 1.2 2.8	**22** M	0140 0742 1403 2013	1.5 2.6 1.6 2.8
8 M	0057 0716 1341 1954	1.4 2.9 1.2 2.9	**23** TU	0244 0856 1457 2111	1.3 2.7 1.5 2.9
9 TU	0220 0837 1451 2102	1.2 3.0 1.1 3.1	**24** W	0329 0946 1538 2155	1.2 2.9 1.4 3.1
10 W	0325 0947 1547 2200	0.9 3.2 1.0 3.3	**25** TH	0407 1026 1612 2232	1.0 3.0 1.2 3.2
11 TH	0418 1044 1635 2252	0.6 3.4 0.9 3.5	**26** F	0440 1101 1643 2307	0.8 3.1 1.1 3.3
12 F ○	0507 1134 1719 2339	0.4 3.5 0.8 3.7	**27** SA ●	0512 1134 1713 2340	0.7 3.2 1.0 3.4
13 SA	0552 1220 1800	0.3 3.5 0.7	**28** SU	0543 1206 1743	0.6 3.2 0.9
14 SU	0023 0636 1304 1841	3.8 0.2 3.5 0.7	**29** M	0012 0615 1238 1815	3.5 0.5 3.3 0.8
15 M	0107 0718 1346 1919	3.8 0.3 3.4 0.8	**30** TU	0045 0647 1311 1847	3.5 0.5 3.3 0.8
			31 W	0118 0719 1345 1920	3.5 0.6 3.2 0.9

Chart Datum: 1·71 metres below Ordnance Datum (Newlyn). HAT is 4·0 metres above Chart Datum.

STANDARD TIME (UT)
For Summer Time add ONE hour in **non-shaded areas**

WICK   LAT 58°26'N   LONG 3°05'W
TIMES AND HEIGHTS OF HIGH AND LOW WATERS

Dates in red are **SPRINGS**
Dates in blue are NEAPS

YEAR 2022

NE Scotland

SEPTEMBER

	Time	m		Time	m
1 TH	0153 0754 1421 1956	3.4 0.7 3.1 1.0	**16** F	0236 0824 1501 2037	3.2 1.1 3.0 1.3
2 F	0232 0832 1503 2037	3.3 0.9 3.0 1.1	**17** SA	0320 0900 1545 2132	2.9 1.4 2.8 1.5
3 SA	0318 0919 1552 2130	3.1 1.1 2.9 1.3	**18** SU	0416 0955 1646 2313	2.7 1.7 2.7 1.6
4 SU	0418 1029 1656 2306	3.0 1.3 2.8 1.4	**19** M	0537 1138 1808	2.6 1.8 2.7
5 M	0540 1207 1817	2.8 1.5 2.8	**20** TU	0110 0713 1335 1932	1.6 2.6 1.8 2.7
6 TU	0058 0716 1341 1940	1.4 2.8 1.4 2.9	**21** W	0218 0833 1434 2038	1.4 2.7 1.6 2.9
7 W	0224 0843 1449 2052	1.1 3.0 1.3 3.1	**22** TH	0303 0921 1514 2124	1.2 2.9 1.4 3.1
8 TH	0323 0945 1539 2149	0.8 3.2 1.1 3.4	**23** F	0339 0959 1546 2202	1.0 3.0 1.3 3.2
9 F	0410 1034 1621 2237	0.6 3.4 0.9 3.6	**24** SA	0411 1032 1616 2237	0.8 3.2 1.1 3.4
10 SA	0452 1118 1659 2321	0.4 3.5 0.8 3.8	**25** SU	0441 1105 1645 2310	0.7 3.3 0.9 3.5
11 SU	0531 1159 1736	0.3 3.6 0.7	**26** M	0512 1137 1716 2344	0.6 3.4 0.8 3.6
12 M	0002 0609 1237 1813	3.8 0.3 3.5 0.7	**27** TU	0543 1209 1748	0.5 3.4 0.8
13 TU	0041 0645 1313 1848	3.8 0.4 3.4 0.8	**28** W	0018 0616 1242 1822	3.6 0.5 3.4 0.8
14 W	0120 0719 1348 1923	3.6 0.6 3.3 0.9	**29** TH	0053 0650 1317 1857	3.6 0.6 3.4 0.8
15 TH	0157 0752 1423 1958	3.4 0.9 3.1 1.1	**30** F	0131 0726 1354 1935	3.5 0.8 3.3 1.0

OCTOBER

	Time	m		Time	m
1 SA	0213 0806 1436 2019	3.3 1.0 3.2 1.1	**16** SU	0247 0815 1500 2059	2.9 1.5 2.9 1.5
2 SU	0305 0855 1528 2121	3.1 1.3 3.0 1.3	**17** M	0340 0901 1555 2232	2.7 1.7 2.8 1.6
3 M	0412 1015 1636 2317	2.9 1.5 2.9 1.4	**18** TU	0456 1040 1714	2.6 1.9 2.7
4 TU	0545 1206 1803	2.8 1.6 2.9	**19** W	0015 0628 1237 1839	1.6 2.6 1.9 2.7
5 W	0104 0723 1337 1928	1.2 2.9 1.5 3.0	**20** TH	0134 0749 1353 1948	1.4 2.7 1.7 2.9
6 TH	0218 0839 1437 2037	1.0 3.1 1.3 3.2	**21** F	0223 0842 1436 2040	1.2 2.9 1.5 3.0
7 F	0310 0932 1522 2131	0.7 3.3 1.1 3.4	**22** SA	0301 0921 1511 2122	1.0 3.0 1.3 3.2
8 SA	0352 1016 1600 2217	0.6 3.4 1.0 3.6	**23** SU	0335 0956 1542 2200	0.8 3.2 1.1 3.4
9 SU	0429 1056 1635 2258	0.4 3.5 0.8 3.7	**24** M	0407 1030 1614 2237	0.7 3.4 1.0 3.6
10 M	0504 1132 1710 2338	0.4 3.5 0.7 3.7	**25** TU	0439 1105 1647 2314	0.6 3.5 0.8 3.6
11 TU	0538 1207 1745	0.5 3.5 0.6	**26** W	0513 1140 1723 2353	0.5 3.6 0.8 3.7
12 W	0015 0611 1240 1821	3.7 0.6 3.4 0.8	**27** TH	0548 1216 1800	0.6 3.6 0.7
13 TH	0051 0642 1312 1855	3.5 0.8 3.3 0.9	**28** F	0033 0626 1253 1841	3.6 0.7 3.5 0.8
14 F	0127 0712 1344 1929	3.4 1.0 3.2 1.1	**29** SA	0116 0706 1334 1925	3.5 0.9 3.4 0.9
15 SA	0204 0742 1419 2008	3.1 1.3 3.1 1.3	**30** SU	0205 0750 1420 2018	3.3 1.2 3.3 1.1
			31 M	0302 0846 1514 2137	3.1 1.4 3.1 1.2

NOVEMBER

	Time	m		Time	m
1 TU	0416 1014 1625 2320	2.9 1.7 3.0 1.2	**16** W	0414 0941 1621 2313	2.7 1.8 2.8 1.5
2 W	0545 1153 1749	2.9 1.7 3.0	**17** TH	0531 1121 1738	2.6 1.9 2.8
3 TH	0050 0711 1314 1906	1.1 3.0 1.6 3.1	**18** F	0027 0642 1241 1846	1.4 2.7 1.8 2.9
4 F	0157 0818 1413 2013	0.9 3.1 1.4 3.3	**19** SA	0127 0743 1341 1944	1.3 2.8 1.6 3.0
5 SA	0247 0909 1457 2107	0.7 3.2 1.2 3.4	**20** SU	0213 0832 1426 2034	1.1 3.0 1.4 3.2
6 SU	0328 0951 1535 2153	0.7 3.3 1.1 3.5	**21** M	0253 0914 1505 2120	0.9 3.2 1.2 3.3
7 M	0403 1029 1612 2235	0.7 3.4 0.9 3.6	**22** TU	0330 0954 1543 2204	0.8 3.4 1.1 3.5
8 TU	0436 1105 1647 2314	0.7 3.5 0.9 3.6	**23** W	0408 1033 1622 2248	0.7 3.5 0.9 3.6
9 W	0509 1139 1723 2351	0.8 3.5 0.9 3.5	**24** TH	0446 1113 1703 2334	0.7 3.6 0.8 3.7
10 TH	0540 1211 1759	0.9 3.5 0.9	**25** F	0527 1154 1747	0.7 3.7 0.7
11 F	0027 0612 1242 1835	3.4 1.0 3.4 1.0	**26** SA	0020 0610 1236 1834	3.6 0.8 3.6 0.7
12 SA	0103 0643 1315 1911	3.3 1.2 3.3 1.1	**27** SU	0110 0656 1321 1926	3.5 1.0 3.6 0.8
13 SU	0141 0713 1349 1951	3.1 1.4 3.2 1.2	**28** M	0203 0745 1411 2027	3.4 1.2 3.4 0.9
14 M	0223 0748 1429 2040	2.9 1.5 3.1 1.4	**29** TU	0303 0844 1507 2142	3.2 1.4 3.3 1.0
15 TU	0312 0832 1518 2151	2.8 1.7 2.9 1.5	**30** W	0412 0958 1613 2301	3.0 1.6 3.2 1.1

DECEMBER

	Time	m		Time	m
1 TH	0525 1116 1724	3.0 1.6 3.2	**16** F	0432 1003 1636 2318	2.7 1.7 2.9 1.3
2 F	0018 0636 1232 1834	1.1 3.0 1.6 3.2	**17** SA	0535 1123 1740	2.7 1.7 2.9
3 SA	0125 0742 1337 1939	1.0 3.0 1.5 3.2	**18** SU	0020 0638 1233 1844	1.3 2.8 1.7 3.0
4 SU	0218 0837 1429 2038	1.0 3.1 1.3 3.3	**19** M	0117 0736 1334 1944	1.2 2.9 1.5 3.0
5 M	0301 0923 1513 2129	1.0 3.2 1.2 3.3	**20** TU	0209 0829 1428 2042	1.1 3.1 1.4 3.2
6 TU	0338 1003 1553 2214	1.0 3.3 1.1 3.4	**21** W	0257 0919 1517 2138	1.0 3.3 1.1 3.4
7 W	0412 1041 1632 2256	1.0 3.4 1.0 3.4	**22** TH	0343 1007 1605 2231	0.9 3.4 1.0 3.5
8 TH	0445 1116 1710 2335	1.1 3.5 1.0 3.3	**23** F	0429 1053 1654 2323	0.9 3.6 0.8 3.6
9 F	0518 1150 1747	1.1 3.5 1.0	**24** SA	0515 1139 1743	0.9 3.7 0.7
10 SA	0011 0552 1222 1824	3.3 1.2 3.4 1.0	**25** SU	0014 0602 1225 1834	3.6 0.9 3.7 0.6
11 SU	0048 0624 1255 1901	3.2 1.3 3.4 1.1	**26** M	0106 0650 1313 1927	3.6 1.0 3.7 0.6
12 M	0125 0657 1330 1939	3.1 1.4 3.3 1.1	**27** TU	0158 0738 1402 2023	3.5 1.1 3.6 0.7
13 TU	0204 0732 1408 2022	2.9 1.5 3.2 1.2	**28** W	0253 0829 1454 2123	3.3 1.3 3.5 0.8
14 W	0246 0811 1450 2112	2.9 1.6 3.1 1.3	**29** TH	0350 0924 1550 2225	3.1 1.4 3.4 0.9
15 TH	0335 0859 1539 2213	2.8 1.7 3.0 1.3	**30** F	0449 1027 1651 2331	3.0 1.5 3.3 1.1
			31 SA	0550 1136 1754	2.9 1.6 3.1

Chart Datum: 1·71 metres below Ordnance Datum (Newlyn). HAT is 4·0 metres above Chart Datum.

FREE monthly updates. Register at www.reedsnauticalalmanac.co.uk

229

5.19 SCRABSTER

Highland 58°36'·61N 03°32'·61W ✵✵✵◊◊✿✿✿

CHARTS AC 1954, 2162, 1462; Imray C68

TIDES -0240 Dover; ML 3·2; Duration 0615

Standard Port WICK (←—)

Times				Height (metres)			
High Water		Low Water		MHWS	MHWN	MLWN	MLWS
0200	0700	0100	0700	3·5	2·8	1·4	0·7
1400	1900	1300	1900				
Differences *SCRABSTER*							
–0255	–0225	–0240	–0230	+1·5	+1·2	+0·8	+0·3
GILLS BAY							
–0150	–0150	–0202	–0202	+0·7	+0·7	+0·6	+0·3
STROMA							
–0115	–0115	–0110	–0110	–0·4	–0·5	–0·1	–0·2
LOCH ERIBOLL (Portnancon)							
–0340	–0255	–0315	–0255	+1·6	+1·3	+0·8	+0·4
KYLE OF DURNESS							
–0350	–0350	–0315	–0315	+1·1	+0·7	+0·4	–0·1
SULE SKERRY (59°05'N 04°24'W)							
–0320	–0255	–0315	–0250	+0·4	+0·3	+0·2	+0·1
RONA (59°08'N 05°49'W)							
–0350	–0350	–0350	–0340	–0·3	–0·4	–0·2	–0·4

SHELTER Very good except for swell in NW and N winds. Yachts usually lie in the Inner (0·9–1·2m) or Centre Basins (0·9–2·7m). Pontoons in inner hbr. ⚓ is not advised.

- A good hbr to await the right conditions for E-bound passage through Pentland Firth (see 5.4).
- Beware floating creel lines in E of hbr.

NAVIGATION WPT 58°36'·58N 03°32'·09W, 278°/0·25M to E pier lt. Can be entered H24 in all weathers. Beware FVs and the Orkney ferries.

LIGHTS AND MARKS No ldg marks/lts but entry is simple once the conspic ice plant tr and/or pier lts have been located. Do not confuse hbr lts with the shore lts of Thurso.

COMMUNICATIONS (Code 01847) Dr 893154. HM 892779 mobile 07803 290366.

Call HM VHF Ch 12 16 (H24) for berthing directions, before entering hbr. From the W reception is very poor due to masking by Holborn Head.

FACILITIES www.scrabster.co.uk ⛴£13·00/night on quay, pontoon by request ⬇ ⚓ ⚓ ⬆ ⚓ ⚓ ⚓ ⚓ ⚓(15/30/99t). **Pentland Firth YC** ⚓ ⚓ ✕ ⬜ (keys held by Duty HM). **Thurso** ⬛ ⬛ ✕ ⬜ ⊠ Ⓑ ⚓ ✈ (Wick). **Ferries** Stromness 3/day 1½hrs; Northlink (www.northlinkferries.co.uk). Faroe Islands (Torshavn) weekly (seasonal) 12hrs; Bergen weekly (seasonal) 16hrs; Smyril (www.smyril.co.uk).

ANCHORAGES BETWEEN SCRABSTER AND CAPE WRATH

KYLE OF TONGUE, Highland, **58°31'·97N 04°22'·67W** (ent). AC 2720, 1954. HW +0050 on Ullapool; HW ht –0·4m; see 5.19. The Kyle runs about 7M inland.

Entry (see 5.4) should not be attempted in strong N winds.

⚓ at Talmine (W of Rabbit Is) protected from all but NE winds; at Skullomie Hr, protected from E'lies; off Mol na Coinnle, a small bay on SE side of Eilean nan Ron, protected from W and N winds; off S of Rabbit Is, protected from W to N winds. No ldg lts/marks. Facilities: Limited 🛒 at Talmine (½M from slip) or at Coldbachie (1½M from Skullomie).

LOCH ERIBOLL, Highland, **58°32'·58N 04°37'·48W**. AC 2076. HW –0345 on Dover; ML 2·7m. See 5.19. Enter between Whiten Hd and Klourig Is in W sector of White Hd lt. See 5.3.

In SW winds fierce squalls funnel down the loch.

Yachts can enter drying Rispond Hbr and dry out alongside; no lts/marks and very limited facilities. Good ⚓s at: Rispond Bay on W side of loch, ent good in all but E winds, in approx 5m; off Portnancon in 5·5m; at the head of the loch; Camus an Duin and in bays to N and S of peninsula at Heilam on E side of loch. Beware numerous marine farms in the S half of the loch.

5.20 ORKNEY ISLANDS

CHARTS AC 2162, 2250 and 2249, at medium scale. For larger scale charts, see under individual hbrs; Imray C68.

TIDES Wick (5.18) is the Standard Port. Tidal streams are strong, particularly in Pentland Firth and in the islands' firths and sounds.

SHELTER/MARINA CHARGES There are piers (fender board advised) at all main islands www.sailnorthscotland.com. For details of charges at marinas or piers throughout the Orkney Islands, except St Margaret's Hope, www.orkneymarinas.co.uk. Some of the many ⚓s are listed:

MAINLAND Scapa Bay: good except in S winds. No yacht berths alongside pier due to heavy hbr traffic. Only ents to Scapa Flow are via Hoy Snd, Hoxa Snd or W of Flotta.

St Marys (Holm/Ham): 58°53'·80N 02°54'·50W; N side of Kirk Sound; ⚓ in B of Ayre or berth E side of Pier, HW±4. 🏪 🏪 ⌧ ✕ 🍴 Bus to Kirkwall/Burwick Ferry.

Kirk Sound (E ent): ⚓ N of Lamb Holm; beware fish cages.

Deer Sound: ⚓ in Pool of Mirkady or off pier on NW side of sound; very good shelter, no facilities.

Hunda Sound: good ⚓ in all winds.

SOUTH RONALDSAY/BURRAY St Margaret's Hope/Water Sound: 🏪🏪⚓🍴🛢️🌸🌸. Ldg Lts, F.G, 174°. ⚓ in centre of bay; or 🛟 £7/day at pier (but limited space and keep clear of ferry berth on S side of pier); beware salmon farm. HM ☎01856 831440, mob 07879 688040; Dr 831206. 🔧 🏪 🏪 ⌧ 🛢️ ✕ 🍴 Bus to Kirkwall, vehicle ferry to Gill's Bay/Caithness.

Widewall Bay: ⚓ sheltered except SW'lies.

FLOTTA 58°50'·20N 03°07'·90W; berth on Sutherland Pier, SW of oil terminal. HM ☎01856 701411, 🏪 🏪 🛢️ ⌧.

HOY Long Hope: 58°48'·07N 03°12'·25W; ⚓ E of Pier, used by ferry, or berth on pier (safest at slack water). 2 🅰's < 18 tonnes close to Pier. ☎01856 701263; Dr 701209. Facilities: 🔧 🏪 🏪 ⌧ 🛢️ 🍴.

Lyness: 58°50'·20N 03°11'·40W; berth on Pier; not piles (disused); ⚓ in Ore Bay. HM ☎01856 791387, 🔧 🏪 🏪 ⌧ 🍴. Avoid fish cages.

Pegal Bay: good ⚓ except in strong W winds.

ROUSAY Wyre Sound: 59°09'·40N 02°44'·70W; ⚓ E of Rousay Pier or berth on it ⌧ 🛢️ ✕. Piermaster ☎01856 821261.

EDAY Fersness Bay: good holding, sheltered from S winds. Dr ☎ 01857 622243.

Backaland Bay: 59°09'·40N 02°44'·70W: berth on Pier clear of ferry; Piermaster ☎01856 622282; or ⚓ to NW. Beware cross-tides. 🔧 🏪 🏪 ⌧ 🛢️.

Calf Sound: ⚓ in Carrick B; good shelter from SW–NW'lies.

PAPA WESTRAY Bay of Moclett 58°21'·40N 02°26'·30W: Good ⚓ but open to S. Pier. Piermaster ☎01857 644259.

South Wick: ⚓ off the old pier or ESE of pier off Holm of Papa. Backaskaill: 🏪 🏪 ⌧ 🛢️.

SANDAY Loth Bay: 59°11'·50N 02°41'·80W; berth on Pier clear of ferry. Piermaster ☎01857 600227; beware strong tides.

Kettletoft Bay: 59°13'·90N 02°35'·80W; ⚓ in bay or berth on Pier, very exposed to SE'lies. HM ☎01857 600227, Dr 600221; 🔧 🏪 🏪 ⚓ ⌧ Ⓑ 🛢️ hotel.

North Bay: on NW side of island, exposed to NW.

Otterswick: good ⚓ except in N or E winds.

NORTH RONALDSAY South Bay: 58°21'·40N 02°26'·30W; ⚓ in middle of bay or berth on Pier. Piermaster ☎01857 633239; open to S and W and swell. ⌧ 🛢️.

Linklet Bay: ⚓ off jetty at N of bay, open to E.

MEDICAL SERVICES Doctors are available at Kirkwall, Stromness, Rousay, Hoy, Shapinsay, Eday, S and N Ronaldsay, Stronsay, Sanday and Westray (Pierowall); Papa Westray is looked after by Westray. The only hospital (and dentist) are at Kirkwall. Serious cases are flown to Aberdeen (1 hour).

NAVIGATION From the mainland, appr from Scrabster to Stromness and Scapa Flow via Hoy Mouth and Hoy Sd. From the Moray Firth keep well E of the Pentland Skerries if going N to Kirkwall. If bound for Scapa Flow via Hoxa Sd, keep close to Duncansby Hd, passing W of the Pentland Skerries and between Swona and S Ronaldsay. Keep clear of Lother Rk (dries 1·8m) off SW tip of S Ronaldsay. Time this entry for slack water in the Pentland Firth (about HW Aberdeen –1¾ and +4). Avoid tankers off Flotta oil terminal and in S part of Scapa Flow; Historic Wrecks (see 0.32) of the German WW1 Battle Fleet, classified as protected. Elsewhere in Orkney navigation is easy in clear weather, apart from the strong tidal streams in all the firths and sounds. Beware races and overfalls off Brough of Birsay (Mainland), Noup Head (Westray) and Dennis Head (N Ronaldsay). Keep a lookout for the many lobster pots (creels).

LIGHTS AND MARKS The main hbrs and sounds are well lit; for details see 5.3. Powerful lts are shown offshore from Cantick Hd, Graemsay Island, Copinsay, Auskerry, Kirkwall, Brough of Birsay, Sanday Island, N Ronaldsay and Noup Hd.

COMMUNICATIONS Area Code for islands SW of Stronsay and Westray Firths is 01856; islands to the NE are 01857. Orkney Navigation Service (*Orkney Hbr Radio*, Ch 09 11 20 16 (H24)) covers Scapa Flow, Wide Firth, Shapinsay Sound and Kirkwall Bay.

MARINE FARMS Fish cages/farms approx 30m x 50m may be found anywhere in sheltered waters within anchoring depths. Some are well buoyed, others are marked only by poles. Too many to list but the following will show the scale of the operations:

Beware **salmon cages** (may be marked by Y buoys/lts) at:

Kirkwall Bay	Toy Ness (Scapa Flow)
Rysa Sound	St Margaret's Hope
Bring Deeps	Backaland Bay (Eday)
Pegal Bay (Hoy)	Hunda Sound
Lyrawa Bay	Kirk Sound
Ore Bay (Hoy)	Carness Bay
Widewall Bay (S Ronaldsay)	Bay of London (Eday)

Beware **oysters and longlines** at:

Widewall Bay	Bay of Firth
Swanbister Bay	Damsay Sound
Water Sound	Millburn Bay (Gairsay)
Hunda Sound	Pierowall
Deer Sound	Bay of Skaill (Westray)
Inganess Bay	Longhope

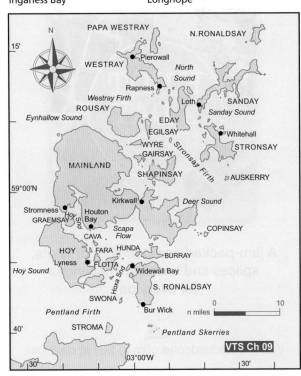

MINOR HARBOURS IN THE ORKNEY ISLANDS

HOUTON BAY, Mainland, **58°54'·85N 03°11'·33W**. AC 35, 2568. HW –0140 on Dover, –0400 on Aberdeen; HW ht +0·3m on Kirkwall; ML 1·8m; Duration 0615. ⚓ in the bay in approx 5·5m at centre, sheltered from all winds. Ent is to the E of Holm of Houton marked by bn Fl R 3s 7m 5M; chan dredged 3·5m for 15m each side of ldg line. Keep clear of shipping/ferries plying to Flotta. Ldg lts 316°: front Fl G 3s 8m, rear FG 16m; both R △ on W pole, B bands. Ro Ro terminal in NE corner marked by Iso R 4s with SHM Fl G on edge of ldg line. Bus to Kirkwall; ⚓ close E of piers. Yachtsmen may contact M.Grainger ☎01856 811397 for help.

SHAPINSAY, Orkney Islands, **59°01'·97N 02°54'·10W**. AC 2249, 2584. HW –0015 on Dover, –0330 on Aberdeen; HW ht –1·0m on Aberdeen. Good shelter in Elwick Bay off Balfour on SW end of island in 2·5-3m. Enter bay passing W of Helliar Holm which has lt Fl WRG 10s on S end. Keep mid-chan. Balfour Pier lt Q WRG 5m 3/2M; vis 270°-G-010°-W-020°-R-090°. Piermaster ☎01856 711358; tides in The String reach 5kn at sp. Facilities: ⚓ 🅿 🍴 🅼 ⊠ shop, 🛒.

AUSKERRY, Orkney Islands, **59°02'·02N 02°34'·65W**. AC 2250. HW –0010 on Dover, -0315 on Aberdeen, HW ht -1m on Aberdeen. Small island at ent to Stronsay Firth with small hbr on W side. Safe ent and good shelter except in SW winds. Ent has 3·5m; 1·2m alongside pier. Yachts can lie secured between ringbolts at ent and the pier. Auskerry Sound and Stronsay Firth are dangerous with wind over tide. Auskerry lt at S end, Fl 20s 34m 18M, W twr.

PIEROWALL, Westray, **59°19'·32N 02°58'·51W**. AC 2250, 2622. HW –0135 on Dover; ML 2·2m; Duration 0620. See 5.23. The bay is a good ⚓ in 2-7m and well protected. Marina pontoons in deep water alongside pier at Gill Pt. From S, beware Skelwick Skerry rks, and from the N the rks extending approx 1ca off Vest Ness. The N ent via Papa Sound should be approached with caution; tide race on the ebb. A dangerous tide race, The Bore Röst, runs off Mull Hd at the N of Papa Westray. Lights: E Pier Hd Fl WRG 3s 7m 11/7M. W Pier Hd 2 FR (vert) 4/6m 3M. VHF Ch 16. HM ☎01857 677216. **Marina** ☎07787364934 www.orkneymarinas.co.uk, £2.00m (see 5.4) ⚓ ⚡. Services: 🛢 🍴 🅼 ⊠ Ⓑ 🛒 🛒 ✕. Dr 01857 677209.

RAPNESS: **58°14'·90N 02°51'·50W**, berth on Pier clear of RoRo. Piermaster ☎01857 677212; Open to SSW.

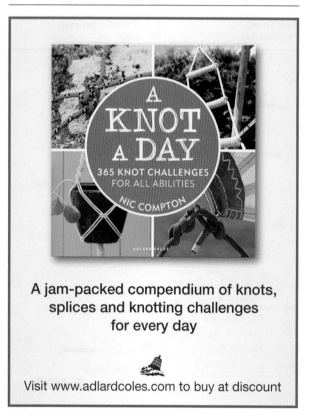
5.21 STROMNESS

Orkney Islands, Mainland **58°57'·78N 03°17'·72W**
❀❀⚓⚓⚓❀❀❀

CHARTS AC 2249, 2568; Imray C68

TIDES –0145 Dover; ML 2·0; Duration 0620

Standard Port WICK (⟵)

Times				Height (metres)			
High Water		Low Water		MHWS	MHWN	MLWN	MLWS
0000	0700	0200	0700	3·5	2·8	1·4	0·7
1200	1900	1400	1900				
Differences STROMNESS							
–0225	–0135	–0205	–0205	+0·1	–0·1	0·0	0·0
ST MARY'S (Scapa Flow)							
–0140	–0140	–0140	–0140	–0·2	–0·2	0·0	–0·1
BURRAY NESS (Burray)							
+0005	+0005	+0015	+0015	–0·2	–0·3	–0·1	–0·1
WIDEWALL BAY (S Ronaldsay)							
–0155	–0155	–0150	–0150	+0·1	–0·1	–0·1	–0·3
BUR WICK (S Ronaldsay)							
–0100	–0100	–0150	–0150	–0·1	–0·1	+0·2	+0·1
MUCKLE SKERRY (Pentland Firth)							
–0025	–0025	–0020	–0020	–0·9	–0·8	–0·4	–0·3

SHELTER Very good. Northern Lights Board have sole use of pier near to ldg lts. Marina in N of hbr; or ⚓ where shown.

NAVIGATION WPT 58°56'·93N 03°17'·00W, 317°/0·9M to front ldg lt. Turn N to pass between N Pier and Coplands Pier to marina.

- Entry from the W should not be attempted with strong wind against tide due to heavy overfalls.
- If entering against the ebb, stand on to avoid being swept onto Skerry of Ness.
- Tides in Hoy Sound are >7kn at springs. No tidal stream in hbr.

LIGHTS AND MARKS For Hoy Sound, ldg lts 104° on Graemsay Is: front Iso 3s 17m 15M, W tr; rear Oc WR 8s 35m 20/16M, ldg sector is 097°-R-112°. Skerry of Ness, Fl WG 4s 7m 7/4M; shore-W-090°-G-shore. Hbr ldg lts 317°, both FR 29/39m 11M (H24), W trs, vis 307°-327°. Coplands Pier 2 F G. Stromness Marina ent. Fl(2)R 5s.

COMMUNICATIONS (Code 01856) Police 850222; Dr 850205; Dentist 850658. HM 07810 465825; Fuel 851286. For advice Yachtsmen may contact: **Orkney Marinas** ☎871313.

VHF Ch 14 16 (0900-1700 LT). (See also 5.22.)

FACILITIES Stromness Marina: ☎07810 465825, 10 ⚓ £2.00m (see 5.4), ⚓ ⚡ ⚓ 🛢/🅼 ▲(0800-2100 ☎8851286) ✕ 🔧 🄴 Ⓔ 🛒(mob 30t). **Town** ⚓ 🛢 🍴 🅼 🛒 ⊠ Ⓑ 🛒 ✕ 🛒 ⇌ (Ferries to Scrabster, bus to Thurso), ✈ (Kirkwall).

5.22 KIRKWALL

Orkney Islands, Mainland **58°59'·30N 02°57'·70W**
❀❀❀⬧⬧❀❀❀

CHARTS AC 2250, 2249, 2584, 1553; Imray C68

TIDES –0045 Dover; ML 1·8; Duration 0620

Standard Port WICK (⟵)

Times				Height (metres)			
High Water		Low Water		MHWS	MHWN	MLWN	MLWS
0000	0700	0200	0700	3·5	2·8	1·4	0·7
1200	1900	1400	1900				
Differences KIRKWALL							
–0042	–0042	–0041	–0041	–0·5	–0·4	–0·1	–0·1
DEER SOUND							
–0040	–0040	–0035	–0035	–0·3	–0·3	–0·1	–0·1
TINGWALL							
–0200	–0125	–0145	–0125	–0·4	–0·4	–0·1	–0·1

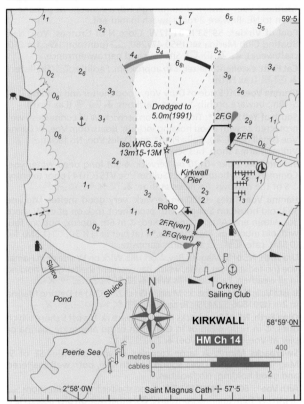

SHELTER Good except in N winds or W gales when there is a surge at the ent. Berth in marina on E of main pier, or SW end of main pier in inner hbr (very full in Jun/Jul). Safe ⚓ between pier and Crow Ness Pt. Hatston RoRo terminal in NW of bay (2 FG (vert)).

NAVIGATION WPT 59°01'·37N 02°57'·10W, 188°/2·2M to pier hd lt. Appr in W sector of pier hd lt, leaving newly extended Hatston Pier (2FG)/commercial terminal to W. Bay is shoal to SW beyond hbr.

LIGHTS AND MARKS See 5.3 and chartlet. Appr with St Magnus Cathedral (conspic) brg about 185°.

COMMUNICATIONS (Code 01856) 🛒 873802; Police 872241; Dr 888000 (Ⓗ). HM 872292; Port Office 873636; Fuel 873105.

Kirkwall Hbr Radio VHF Ch 14 16 (0800-1700 LT). Orkney Hbrs Navigation Service, call: *VTS Orkney* Ch 09 11 20 16 (0915–1715).

FACILITIES Kirkwall Marina ☎871313 (berths 07810 465835), 71 inc ♥ £2.00m (see 5.4). **Pier** ⛴🏳(HO ☎873105) ⚓ ⬟(mob 25t) ⬟; **N and E Quays** M; **Orkney SC** ☎872331, ⬟⬟⬟⬟(£15/4days). **Town** ⬟⬟⬟⬟⬟⬟⬟⬟⬟⬟⬟Ⓑ⬟⬟✕⬟@ Library(HO) Ferries to Scrabster, Aberdeen and Shetland, ✈.

5.23 STRONSAY

Orkney Islands, Stronsay **59°08'·57N 02°36'·01W** ❀❀⬧⬧❀❀

CHARTS AC 2250, 2622; Imray C68

TIDES As Dover; ML 1·7; Duration 0620

Standard Port WICK (⟵)

Times				Height (metres)			
High Water		Low Water		MHWS	MHWN	MLWN	MLWS
0000	0700	0200	0700	3·5	2·8	1·4	0·7
1200	1900	1400	1900				
Differences WHITEHALL (Stronsay)							
–0030	–0030	–0025	–0030	–0·1	0·0	+0·2	+0·2
LOTH (Sanday)							
–0045	–0045	–0055	–0105	–0·4	–0·3	+0·1	+0·2
EGILSAY (Rousay Sound)							
–0125	–0125	–0125	–0125	–0·1	0·0	+0·2	+0·1
KETTLETOFT PIER (Sanday)							
–0030	–0025	–0020	–0025	0·0	0·0	+0·2	+0·2
RAPNESS (Westray)							
–0205	–0205	–0205	–0200	+0·1	+0·1	+0·2	0·0
PIEROWALL (Westray)							
–0150	–0150	–0145	–0145	+0·2	0·0	0·0	–0·1

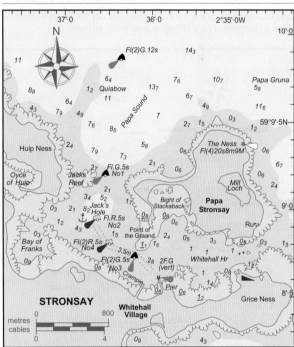

SHELTER Good from all winds. Good ⚓ between seaward end of piers, or berth on outer end of W pier and contact HM. The extended E pier head is berth for RoRo ferry. There are many other sheltered ⚓s around the bay.

NAVIGATION WPT 59°09'·82N 02°36'·31W, Quiabow SHM lt buoy, 189°/6·5ca to No 1 lt buoy. 800m NE of Huip Ness is Quiabow, a submerged rk. Jack's Reef extends 400m E from Huip Ness, and is marked by No 1 SHM lt buoy. A bank extends 350m SW from Papa Stronsay. Crampie Shoal is in mid-chan, marked by No 3 buoy. The buoyed chan to Whitehall pier is dredged 3·5m. Spit to E of Whitehall pier extends 400m N. The E ent is narrow and shallow and should not be attempted.

LIGHTS AND MARKS See chartlet.

COMMUNICATIONS (Code 01857) Piermaster 07901 984328. Police (01856) 872241; Dr 616321. See Kirkwall for VHF comms.

FACILITIES W Pier ⬟⬟⬟; **Main (E) Pier** ⬟⬟⚓⬟clear of ferry. **Village (Whitehall)** ⬟⬟⬟⬟Ⓑ⬟⬟⬟⇌ (Ferry to Scrabster, bus to Thurso) ✈.

5.24 SHETLAND ISLANDS

The Shetland Islands number about 100 islands, holms and rks with fewer than 20 inhabited. Lying 90 to 150M NNE of the Scottish mainland, the biggest island is Mainland with Lerwick (5.25), the capital, on the E side. Scalloway, the only other town and old capital, is on the W side. At the very S is Sumburgh airport, with other airstrips at Baltasound, Scalsta and Tingwall. Two offlying islands of the Shetland group are Fair Isle, 20M SSW of Sumburgh Hd and owned by the NT for Scotland, and Foula, 12M WSW of Mainland. Mariners in the vicinity of inter-island ferry ports should check carefully for ferries entering or leaving the following ports and allow them free passage. (Fair Isle North Haven, Grutness, Dury Voe, Vidlin Voe, Symbister Out Skerries, Mossbank, Ulsta, Gutcher, Belmont , NW Fetlar and West Burrafirth.)

There are LBs at Lerwick and Aith. The CGOC Lerwick ☎(01595) 692976, with an Auxilliary Stn at Fair Is.

CHARTS AC: medium scale 3281, 3282, 3283; larger scale 3271, 3272, 3292, 3293, 3294, 3295, 3297, 3298.

TIDES Standard Port Lerwick. Tidal streams run mostly N–S or NW–SE; in open waters to the E and W they are mostly weak. Rates >6kn can cause dangerous disturbances at the N and S extremities of the islands and in the two main sounds (Yell Sound and BlueMull/Colgrave Sounds). Keep 3M off Sumburgh Head to clear a dangerous race (Röst) or pass close inshore.

SHELTER Weather conditions are bad in winter; yachts should only visit Apr-Sept. Around mid-summer it is daylight H24. Some small marinas are asterisked* in the column on the right (see www.visitshetland.com); they may have room for visitors. Of the many ⚓s, the following are safe to enter in most conditions.

NAVIGATION A careful lookout must be kept for marine farms, mostly marked by Y buoys and combinations of Y lts. Clyde CC's *Shetland Sailing Directions and Anchorages* are essential for visitors. Local magnetic anomalies may be experienced.

LIGHTS AND MARKS See 5.3. Powerful lighthouses at Fair I, Sumburgh Hd, Kirkabister Ness, Bound Skerry, Muckle Flugga, Pt of Fethaland, Esha Ness and Foula. All inter-island ferry ports have leading sectored lights.

COMMUNICATIONS (Code 01595; 01806 for Sullom Voe) CGOC 692976; Sullom Voe Port Control (01806) 242551, ⌨ 242237; ⚓ 692239; Forecaster (01806) 242069; Sumburgh Airport (01950) 460654. Port Radio services see 5.25. No Coast Radio Station.

FACILITIES All stores obtainable in Lerwick and Scalloway. Elsewhere yachts should be prepared for extended offshore cruising and obtain water and diesel as and when they can:

MAINLAND (anti-clockwise from Sumburgh Head)

Grutness Voe: 1·5M N of Sumburgh Hd, a convenient passage ⚓, open to NE. Beware 2 rocks awash in mid-ent.

Pool of Virkie*: 59°53'N 01°17W; Close N of Grutness Voe. Ness Boating Club Marina ☎01950 477260, ⌑ (pontoon 1❶< 1m £10/craft/week), ⌦ ♣ ⬦ 🚾. Shallow and narrow/entrance.

Cat Firth: excellent shelter, ⚓ in approx 6m. Facilities: ⌧ (Skellister), ♣ ⌧ ⬠ (Lax Firth).

Grunna Voe: Off S side of Dury Voe, good shelter and holding, ⚓ in 5-10m; beware prohib ⚓ areas. Facilities: ♣ ⌧ ⬠ (Lax Firth).

South of Yell Sound*: Tides –0025 on Lerwick. W of Lunna Ness, well protected ⚓s with good holding include: Boatsroom Voe, W Lunna Voe (small hotel, ♣), Colla Firth* and Dales Voe. No facilities.

Vidlin: marina shop, bus service.

Sullom Voe: Tides –0130 on Lerwick. 6·5M long deep water voe, Commercial harbour. Contact Sullom Voe VTS (Ch14) prior to entry. ⚓ S of the narrows. Facilities at Brae: ♣ 🛢 ✗ ✎ ⊞ ⌧ ⬠ ⌂.

Hamna Voe: Tides –0200 on Lerwick; very good shelter. Ldg line 153° old house on S shore with prominent rock on pt of W shore 3ca within ent. Almost land-locked; ⚓ in 6m approx, bottom foul with old moorings. Facilities: ❶s, ⌦ (at pier lit Fl R 3s), 🛢 (1·5M), ⌧ (0·5M), cafe, 🚾/⬦ ⓞ at nearby campsite.

Ura Firth: NE of St Magnus Bay, ⚓ off Hills Wick on W side or in Hamar Voe (no facilities) on E side, which has excellent shelter/good holding in all weathers. Facilities: **Hills Wick** ♣ 🛢 ✗ ✎ ⊞ ⌧ ⬠ ✗ ⌂.

Busta Voe: N of Swarbacks Minn. 4 ❶ (<12m LOA) at Delting Marina in 2m (☎01806 522479); Brae (½M): 🛢 ✗ ✎ ⊞ ⌧ ✗.

Olna Firth: NE of Swarbacks Minn, beware rk 1ca off S shore which dries. ⚓ in firth, 4-8m or in Gon Firth or go alongside marina or pier at Voe. Facilities: (Voe) ♣ 🛢 ⌧ ⬠ ⌂.

Swarbacks Minn*: A large complex of voes and isles SE of St Magnus Bay. Best ⚓ Uyea Sound or Aith Voe, both well sheltered and good holding. No facilities.

Aith Voe*: 60°17·3'N 01°22·3W; Good shelter from all directions ⌑ depth LW 1.2m (marina pontoon 2 ❶s) otherwise on pier access H24, ⌦ ♣ ⬦ ✗ ✎ 🚾/⬦ (leisure centre) ⌧ ⬠ ✗ ⌂.

Vaila Sound (Walls), 60°13'·65N 01°33'·87W. AC 3295. Tides approx as Scalloway (above); see 5.25. Very good shelter. Appr to E of Vaila island (do not attempt Wester Sound) in the W sector (355°-012°) of Rams Head lt, Fl WRG 8s 16m 9/6M. Gruting Voe lies to the NE. Enter Easter Sound and go N for 1·5M, passing E of Linga islet, to Walls at the head of Vaila Voe. Navigate by echo sounder. Beware fish farms. ⚓ N of Salt Ness in 4-5m in mud. Temporary ⌑ on Bayhaa pier (covers). Close E, ⌑ £1 Peter Georgeson's pontoon. **Marina**: Sec ☎(01595) 809273, ♣. **Walls Regatta Club** welcomes visitors; ⌦ ⬦ ⌂. **Village** 🛢 🛢 🛢.

Gruting Voe*: HW –0150 on Lerwick, ⚓ in main voe or in Seli, Scutta or Browland* voes. Facilities: ⌧ ⬠ at Bridge of Walls (head of Browland Voe).

Skeld, 60°09'·65N 01°27'W. AC 3283, 3294. Tides approx as Scalloway. Appr from Skelda Voe which is subject to heavy seas and swell in strong S'lies. Beware Braga Rk (dries 2m) and drying rk 1ca S of it. At E of ent also Snap Rk (dries 3.5m) with isolated rks inshore. **Marina** offers good shelter as virtually landlocked, welcomes visitors; 8❶ £10/craft/week; James Scott ☎(01595) 860287 ♣ ⬦ 🚾/⬦ 🛢 🛢 bus to Lerwick 2/daily.

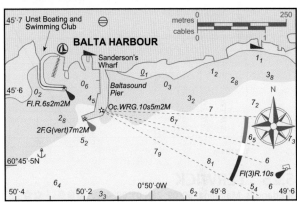

UNST Balta Sound: 60°44'·32N 00°48'·12W. AC 3293. HW –0105 on Dover; ML 1·3; Duration 0640. See 5.24. Balta Sound is a large almost landlocked inlet with good shelter from all winds. Beware fish farms and bad holding on kelp. Safest and main entry is via S Chan between Huney Is and Balta Is; inner chan marked by two PHM lt buoys. N Chan is deep but narrow; keep to Unst shore. ⚓ off Sandisons Wharf (2FG vert) in approx 6m pontoon on W side of pier is derelict and reported unsafe (Oc WRG 10s 5m 2M, 272°-G-282°-W-287°-R-297°). Small boat marina has single shallow ♥ berth. VHF Ch 16; 20 (HO or as required). Facilities: 🛥️ 🛒 ⚓ 🔧 🏪 🏨 hotel. **Baltasound village**, ⊠ 🛒 ✕ 🛏️ 🍴.

Scalloway, 60°08'·02N 01°16'·59W. AC 3294. HW –0200 on Dover; ML 0·9m; Duration 0620. See 5.25. A busy fishing port; good shelter and ⚓ in all weathers. Care is needed negotiating the islands in strong SW'lies. The N Chan is easier and safer than the S Chan, both are well lit and marked. Castle and warehouse (both conspic) lead 054° through S Chan. Dir Oc WRG 10s on hbr quay leads 064·5° into hbr (dredged 8.5m). Lts as chartlet. ♥ pontoon in 3m off SBC is best option; marina close N or new marina in E Voe (though mostly full of local boats). ⚓s in hbr 6–10m or in Hamna Voe (W Burra). Info at www.shetland.gov.uk/ports/scalloway or e-mail scalloway.harbour@shetland.gov.uk (cc to sullomvoevts@shetland.gov.uk). Call *Scalloway Hbr Radio* VHF Ch **14** 16 (Mon-Fri 0700-1830; Sat 0900-1230; Sun 1000-1200LT). Piermaster ☎(01595) 744221. Facilities: **Scalloway Boat Club** (SBC) ☎880409, 🍴 🛏️. **Town** 🔧 🛒 🏪 🏬 🍴 ⚓ 🏧 🏦 🏪 🛒 ⊠ 🛒 ✕ 🛏️ bus to Lerwick.

Hamna Voe*: 60°06'·3N 01°20·3W (West Burra) Entered between Fugla Ness and Alta Ness. Open to the NW; good shelter in small marina. Small village, bus to Lerwick and all other routes.

WHALSAY* 60°20'·60N 01°01'·60W; Fishing hbr with small marina at Symbister welcomes visitors. 🛥️ 🛒 🍴 (pontoon or pier 20♥s) £7.17/craft/4 days; ⚡ 🔧 🛥️ 🛒 🚾 🏪 🛒 🛏️ 🍴.

FOULA 60°08'·02N 02°02'·92W. AC 3283. HW -0150 on Dover; ML 1·3m. See 5.25. Highest ground is 416m. S Ness sectored Lt ho, Fl WR(3) 15s, is at the S tip. Beware both Foula Shoal (7·6m) 4·3M E of the island and Hœvdi Grund (1·4m), 2M to the SE of Ham Voe. **Ham Voe:** is a narrow inlet on the E coast with a quay; rks on both sides. Two R ▲ ldg marks, approx 270°, are hard to see. ☆ 2 FG (vert) on pierhead. Berthing or landing is only possible in settled weather with no swell. Take advice from mail boat skipper out of Walls and call Foula, ☎(01595) 753222. Small ✈. No other facilities.

OUT SKERRIES 60°25'·3N 00°45'·1W AC 3282. Good shelter at pier. The NE entrance is buoyed and is the easier and has a leading light (Local ferry port). There are two Historic Wrecks (*Kennemerland* and *Wrangels Palais*) on Out Skerries at 60°25'·2N 00°45'·0W and 60°25'·5N 00°43'·3W (see`0.3). Shops, 🚾 🏪 at pier. Beware strong tidal conditions off the NE entrance ferries approaching or leaving. Pier (£2/craft/night); 🛥️ ⚡ (by arrangement), toilet/🏪 wi-fi; **Village** ⊠ shop. Good ⚓ at Bruray.

YELL Mid Yell Voe*: 60°36'N 01°03·4W; tides –0040 on Lerwick, enter via S Sd or Hascosay Sd, good ⚓ in wide part of voe 2·5-10m. Berth at marina £5/week or Pier £7.17/4 days/craft. Facilities: ⊠ 🛥️ at pier on S side, 🛒 🔧 ⚓ 🏪 🛒. **Basta Voe**: good ⚓ above shingle bank in 5-15m; good holding in places. Facilities: 🛥️ 🍴 Hotel, ⊠. **Blue Mull Sound/Cullivoe*: 60°42'N 00°59'·7W**; Hbr with small craft marina depth 1.2m 🍴£5/craft/day, 🔧 🛥️ 🛒. Pier 🍴 20♥s £7.17/craft/4 days; 🛥️ ⚡ 🛒 🚾 🏪 🔧. **Town** ⊠ 🛒 ✕ 🛏️. ⚓ off pier. **Burra Voe*: 60°29'·8N 01°02'·4W**; Entrance to voe 2.5m bar. Good ⚓ at head of voe, but buoy ⚓ as precaution against fouling old moorings. 🍴 at small marina £5/visit or on Pier £12/visit, 🛥️ ⚡ 🚾 🏪 ⊠ 🛒 🛏️.

FETLAR Hamars Ness 60°37'·78N 00°55'·76W; small hbr with new b'water (Iso G 6s 5m 3M) at W end of rocky bay. Appr W of WCM.

FAIR ISLE 59°32'·37N 01°36'·21W. AC 3299. HW -0030 on Dover; ML 1·4m; Duration 0620. See 5.25. Good shelter in North Haven, except in NE winds. 🍴 on pier or ⚓ in approx 2m. Beware strong cross-tides in the apprs; rocks all round Fair Isle, esp in S Haven and S Harbour which are hazardous. Ldg marks 199° into N Haven: front, Stack of N Haven (a dark 'tooth' sticking up from the jumble of blocks which form the bkwtr) in transit with conspic summit of Sheep Craig (rear). Dir lt into N Haven, Oc WRG 8s 10m 6M; vis 204°-G-208°-W-211°-R-221°. Lights: N tip, Skroo Fl(2) 30s 80m **22M**, S tip, Skadan Fl(4) 30s 31m **22M**. Facilities: ⊠ 🛒 at N Shriva, ✈, bi-weekly mail boat to Grutness. No fuel or water. Bird observatory offers 🚾 🏪/meals. Use large fenders supplied against pier to protect from scend/swell.

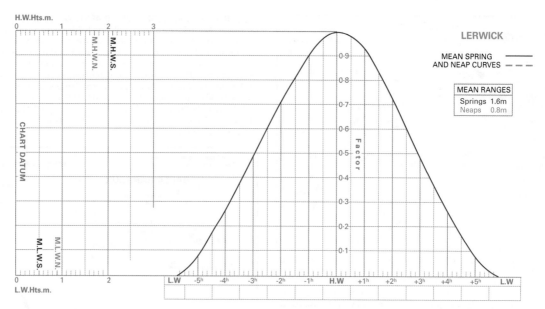

LERWICK

MEAN SPRING ——————
AND NEAP CURVES – – – –

MEAN RANGES	
Springs	1.6m
Neaps	0.8m

5.25 LERWICK

Shetland Is, Mainland 60°09'·26N 01°08'·42W ✿✿✿✿◊◊✿✿

CHARTS AC 3283, 3272, 3271

TIDES –0001 Dover; ML 1·4; Duration 0620

Standard Port LERWICK (←)

Times				Height (metres)			
High Water		Low Water		MHWS	MHWN	MLWN	MLWS
0000	0600	0100	0800	2·1	1·7	0·9	0·5
1200	1800	1300	2000				
Differences FAIR ISLE							
–0006	–0015	–0031	–0037	+0·1	0·0	+0·1	+0·1
SUMBURGH (Grutness Voe)							
+0006	+0008	+0004	–0002	–0·3	–0·3	–0·2	–0·1
DURY VOE							
–0015	–0015	–0010	–0010	0·0	–0·1	0·0	–0·2
BURRA VOE (YELL SOUND)							
–0025	–0025	–0025	–0025	+0·2	+0·1	0·0	–0·1
BALTA SOUND							
–0040	–0045	–0040	–0045	+0·3	+0·2	+0·1	0·0
BLUEMULL SOUND							
–0135	–0135	–0155	–0155	+0·5	+0·2	+0·1	0·0
SULLOM VOE							
–0135	–0125	–0135	–0120	0·0	0·0	–0·2	–0·2
HILLSWICK (URA FIRTH)							
–0220	–0220	–0200	–0200	–0·1	–0·1	–0·1	–0·1
SCALLOWAY							
–0150	–0150	–0150	–0150	–0·5	–0·4	–0·3	0·0
FOULA (23M West of Scalloway)							
–0140	–0140	–0130	–0130	–0·1	–0·1	0·0	0·0

SHELTER Good. FVs occupy most alongside space. HM allocates berths in Small Dock or Albert Dock, both prone to vessel wash. ⚓ within 2ca of the waterfront. Gremista marina in N hbr, is mainly for local boats, and is about 1M from the town.

NAVIGATION WPT 60°05'·97N 01°08'·62W, 010°/3·5M to Maryfield lt, in W sector. From S, Bressay Sound is clear of dangers. From N, WPT 60°11'·60N 01°07'·88W, 215°/1·34M to N ent Dir lt (Oc WRG 6s, 214°-W-216°). Beware Soldian Rk (dries), Nive Baa (0·6m), Green Holm (10m) and The Brethren (two rocks 2m and 1·5m).

LIGHTS AND MARKS Kirkabister Ness, Fl (2) 20s 18m 10M; Cro of Ham, Fl 3s 3M; Maryfield, Oc WRG 6s, 008°-W-013°; all on Bressay. Twageos Pt, L Fl 6s 8m 6M. Loofa Baa SCM lt bn, as on chartlet. 2 SHM lt buoys mark Middle Ground in N Hbr.

COMMUNICATIONS (Code 01595) CGOC 692976; ⚓692239; Police 692110; Dr 693201; HM 692991.

Lerwick Harbour VHF Ch **12** 16 (H24) for Vessel Information Service. Other stns: *Sullom Voe Hbr Radio* broadcasts traffic info and local forecasts on request Ch **14** 12 20 16 (H24).

FACILITIES Hbr ⚓ ⚓ ⚓ ⚓ ⚓ ⚓ ⚓ ⚓.
Lerwick Port Authority ☎692991, ⓥpontoons £1.50, ⚓⚓ ⓓ(£7.50) ⚓⚓⚓ ramps/ᴡᴄ.
Lerwick Boating Club ☎692407, ⚓ ⚓ ⚓ ⚓.
Services ⚓ ⓔ Ⓔ ⚓ ⚓ ⚓ ⚓ ⚓ ACA.
Town ✉ Ⓑ ⚓ ✕ ⚓ @ **Ferries** Aberdeen via Kirkwall; daily; overnight; North Link (www.northlinkferries.co.uk), ✈. See www.shetlandtimes.co.uk and www.lerwickboating.co.uk.

STANDARD TIME (UT)
For Summer Time add ONE hour in **non-shaded areas**

LERWICK   LAT 60°09′N   LONG 1°08′W
TIMES AND HEIGHTS OF HIGH AND LOW WATERS

Dates in red are **SPRINGS**
Dates in blue are **NEAPS**

YEAR 2022

NE Scotland

JANUARY

Time	m		Time	m
1 0308	0.7	**16**	0349	0.9
0922	2.2		1003	2.1
SA 1536	0.7	SU	1619	0.8
2153	2.2		2230	2.0
2 0359	0.6	**17**	0424	0.9
1012	2.3		1040	2.1
SU 1627	0.5	M	1654	0.7
● 2249	2.3	○	2308	2.0
3 0447	0.7	**18**	0457	0.9
1101	2.3		1115	2.2
M 1717	0.4	TU	1728	0.6
2345	2.3		2344	2.0
4 0534	0.7	**19**	0530	0.8
1150	2.4		1149	2.2
TU 1806	0.4	W	1802	0.6
5 0037	2.2	**20**	0019	2.0
0621	0.7		0604	0.8
W 1238	2.4	TH	1222	2.2
1856	0.4		1838	0.6
6 0126	2.2	**21**	0055	2.0
0706	0.8		0638	0.8
TH 1325	2.3	F	1256	2.2
1945	0.4		1915	0.6
7 0214	2.0	**22**	0131	2.0
0752	0.9		0714	0.8
F 1412	2.2	SA	1333	2.1
2035	0.6		1954	0.6
8 0300	1.9	**23**	0210	1.9
0839	0.9		0753	0.8
SA 1459	2.1	SU	1412	2.1
2127	0.7		2036	0.6
9 0349	1.8	**24**	0254	1.9
0930	1.0		0836	0.9
SU 1549	2.0	M	1458	2.0
◑ 2225	0.8		2124	0.7
10 0442	1.7	**25**	0344	1.8
1032	1.1		0927	1.0
M 1646	1.9	TU	1552	1.9
2332	0.9	◑	2220	0.8
11 0544	1.7	**26**	0442	1.8
1151	1.1		1032	1.0
TU 1756	1.8	W	1658	1.9
			2331	0.8
12 0041	1.0	**27**	0550	1.8
0651	1.7		1200	1.0
W 1309	1.1	TH	1816	1.9
1909	1.8			
13 0141	1.0	**28**	0049	0.9
0750	1.8		0704	1.8
TH 1412	1.0	F	1326	0.9
2011	1.8		1939	1.9
14 0231	1.0	**29**	0159	0.8
0840	1.9		0812	1.9
F 1501	0.9	SA	1435	0.8
2103	1.8		2050	1.9
15 0313	1.0	**30**	0300	0.8
0924	2.0		0910	2.1
SA 1543	0.9	SU	1532	0.6
2149	1.9		2153	2.1
		31	0352	0.7
			1004	2.2
		M	1623	0.5
			2249	2.2

FEBRUARY

Time	m		Time	m
1 0439	0.7	**16**	0442	0.8
1054	2.3		1057	2.1
TU 1710	0.3	W	1708	0.5
● 2338	2.2	○	2325	2.0
2 0523	0.6	**17**	0514	0.7
1141	2.4		1131	2.2
W 1754	0.3	TH	1741	0.4
			2359	2.0
3 0023	2.2	**18**	0545	0.6
0605	0.6		1205	2.2
TH 1224	2.4	F	1815	0.4
1838	0.3			
4 0105	2.1	**19**	0033	2.0
0645	0.6		0619	0.6
F 1306	2.3	SA	1237	2.2
1919	0.4		1850	0.4
5 0145	2.1	**20**	0107	2.0
0724	0.7		0654	0.6
SA 1346	2.2	SU	1312	2.2
2000	0.5		1927	0.5
6 0223	1.9	**21**	0142	2.0
0803	0.8		0731	0.6
SU 1426	2.1	M	1349	2.1
2041	0.6		2007	0.5
7 0302	1.8	**22**	0222	1.9
0844	0.9		0812	0.7
M 1507	2.0	TU	1432	2.0
2124	0.8		2052	0.6
8 0344	1.7	**23**	0307	1.8
0931	1.0		0901	0.8
TU 1553	1.8	W	1525	1.9
◑ 2214	1.0	◑	2145	0.8
9 0433	1.7	**24**	0403	1.7
1040	1.1		1004	0.9
W 1649	1.7	TH	1634	1.8
2326	1.1		2255	0.9
10 0542	1.6	**25**	0512	1.7
1220	1.1		1139	0.9
TH 1818	1.6	F	1803	1.7
11 0053	1.1	**26**	0035	1.0
0708	1.7		0640	1.7
F 1346	1.0	SA	1323	0.8
1946	1.6		1942	1.8
12 0206	1.1	**27**	0156	0.9
0813	1.7		0802	1.8
SA 1445	0.9	SU	1434	0.7
2047	1.7		2055	1.9
13 0257	1.0	**28**	0257	0.8
0902	1.8		0904	2.0
SU 1528	0.8	M	1529	0.5
2134	1.8		2152	2.0
14 0336	0.9			
0944	1.9			
M 1603	0.7			
2214	1.9			
15 0410	0.9			
1022	2.0			
TU 1636	0.6			
2250	1.9			

MARCH

Time	m		Time	m
1 0345	0.7	**16**	0345	0.8
0957	2.1		0955	1.9
TU 1615	0.3	W	1607	0.5
2240	2.1		2223	1.9
2 0426	0.6	**17**	0417	0.6
1043	2.2		1030	2.0
W 1656	0.2	TH	1640	0.4
● 2322	2.1		2257	2.0
3 0505	0.5	**18**	0449	0.5
1125	2.3		1105	2.1
TH 1734	0.2	F	1713	0.3
		○	2331	2.0
4 0001	2.1	**19**	0521	0.5
0543	0.5		1139	2.2
F 1204	2.3	SA	1748	0.2
1812	0.2			
5 0037	2.1	**20**	0005	2.1
0619	0.5		0556	0.5
SA 1241	2.3	SU	1214	2.2
1848	0.3		1824	0.2
6 0111	2.0	**21**	0039	2.0
0655	0.5		0632	0.4
SU 1316	2.2	M	1250	2.2
1923	0.5		1901	0.3
7 0143	1.9	**22**	0115	2.0
0730	0.6		0712	0.5
M 1351	2.0	TU	1330	2.1
1957	0.6		1942	0.4
8 0216	1.8	**23**	0153	1.9
0805	0.7		0755	0.6
TU 1428	1.9	W	1416	2.0
2030	0.8		2026	0.6
9 0251	1.7	**24**	0237	1.8
0846	0.8		0846	0.7
W 1509	1.7	TH	1514	1.8
2108	0.9		2120	0.8
10 0333	1.7	**25**	0333	1.7
0942	1.0		0954	0.8
TH 1600	1.6	F	1629	1.7
◑ 2204	1.1	◑	2238	1.0
11 0426	1.6	**26**	0446	1.6
1125	1.0		1146	0.8
F 1712	1.5	SA	1810	1.6
2359	1.1			
12 0553	1.5	**27**	0033	1.0
1306	1.0		0626	1.6
SA 1922	1.5	SU	1321	0.7
			1947	1.7
13 0135	1.1	**28**	0150	0.9
0741	1.6		0751	1.8
SU 1414	0.9	M	1426	0.5
2027	1.6		2050	1.8
14 0233	1.0	**29**	0245	0.8
0835	1.7		0851	1.9
M 1458	0.8	TU	1516	0.4
2111	1.7		2138	1.9
15 0312	1.0	**30**	0328	0.7
0917	1.8		0940	2.0
TU 1534	0.6	W	1557	0.3
2148	1.8		2220	2.0
		31	0406	0.5
			1024	2.1
		TH	1634	0.2
			2258	2.0

APRIL

Time	m		Time	m
1 0442	0.4	**16**	0419	0.5
1103	2.2		1033	2.1
F 1709	0.2	SA	1642	0.3
● 2333	2.0	○	2259	2.0
2 0518	0.4	**17**	0455	0.4
1139	2.2		1112	2.2
SA 1742	0.3	SU	1719	0.2
			2336	2.1
3 0004	2.0	**18**	0533	0.3
0553	0.4		1151	2.2
SU 1212	2.1	M	1758	0.2
1815	0.4			
4 0034	2.0	**19**	0012	2.1
0626	0.4		0613	0.3
M 1246	2.1	TU	1233	2.1
1847	0.5		1838	0.3
5 0104	1.9	**20**	0050	2.0
0700	0.5		0657	0.4
TU 1319	1.9	W	1319	2.0
1917	0.6		1922	0.5
6 0134	1.9	**21**	0131	2.0
0735	0.6		0745	0.4
W 1356	1.8	TH	1413	1.9
1947	0.8		2010	0.7
7 0207	1.8	**22**	0219	1.9
0815	0.7		0842	0.5
TH 1437	1.7	F	1517	1.7
2020	0.9		2109	0.9
8 0246	1.7	**23**	0319	1.7
0907	0.9		0959	0.6
F 1527	1.5	SA	1634	1.6
2107	1.1	◑	2237	1.0
9 0337	1.6	**24**	0435	1.7
1035	0.9		1145	0.6
SA 1631	1.4	SU	1811	1.6
◑ 2302	1.1			
10 0443	1.5	**25**	0018	1.0
1211	0.9		0610	1.6
SU 1836	1.4	M	1304	0.6
			1931	1.6
11 0046	1.1	**26**	0127	0.9
0642	1.5		0729	1.7
M 1321	0.8	TU	1405	0.5
1951	1.5		2026	1.7
12 0150	1.0	**27**	0221	0.8
0754	1.6		0827	1.8
TU 1413	0.7	W	1452	0.4
2034	1.6		2112	1.8
13 0234	0.9	**28**	0304	0.6
0839	1.7		0915	1.9
W 1453	0.5	TH	1532	0.3
2112	1.7		2152	1.9
14 0310	0.7	**29**	0342	0.5
0918	1.8		0958	2.0
TH 1530	0.4	F	1607	0.3
2147	1.9		2228	1.9
15 0345	0.6	**30**	0418	0.4
0956	2.0		1037	2.0
F 1606	0.3	SA	1640	0.3
2223	2.0	●	2301	2.0

Chart Datum: 1·22 metres below Ordnance Datum (Local). HAT is 2·5 metres above Chart Datum.

》 **FREE** monthly updates. Register at 《
www.reedsnauticalalmanac.co.uk

237

Lerwick tides

STANDARD TIME (UT)
For Summer Time add ONE hour in **non-shaded areas**

LERWICK LAT 60°09′N LONG 1°08′W
TIMES AND HEIGHTS OF HIGH AND LOW WATERS

Dates in **red** are **SPRINGS**
Dates in **blue** are **NEAPS**

YEAR 2022

MAY

Time m	Time m
1 0453 0.4 / 1112 2.0 / SU 1712 0.4 / 2332 2.0	**16** 0431 0.4 / 1047 2.1 / M 1654 0.2 / ○ 2309 2.1
2 0528 0.4 / 1147 2.0 / M 1743 0.5	**17** 0513 0.3 / 1134 2.1 / TU 1736 0.3 / 2350 2.1
3 0001 2.0 / 0602 0.4 / TU 1220 1.9 / 1814 0.6	**18** 0559 0.3 / 1223 2.1 / W 1821 0.4
4 0031 1.9 / 0637 0.6 / W 1255 1.8 / 1844 0.7	**19** 0033 2.1 / 0648 0.3 / TH 1317 2.0 / 1909 0.6
5 0102 1.9 / 0713 0.6 / TH 1332 1.7 / 1915 0.8	**20** 0120 2.0 / 0741 0.4 / F 1416 1.9 / 2001 0.7
6 0135 1.8 / 0755 0.7 / F 1414 1.6 / 1951 0.9	**21** 0213 1.9 / 0843 0.4 / SA 1518 1.7 / 2103 0.9
7 0214 1.7 / 0845 0.7 / SA 1504 1.5 / 2038 1.0	**22** 0314 1.8 / 0958 0.5 / SU 1626 1.6 / ☽ 2219 0.9
8 0304 1.6 / 0954 0.8 / SU 1602 1.5 / 2157 1.1	**23** 0423 1.7 / 1122 0.5 / M 1743 1.6 / 2342 0.9
9 0405 1.5 / 1118 0.8 / M 1715 1.4 / ☽ 2347 1.0	**24** 0541 1.7 / 1234 0.5 / TU 1853 1.6
10 0519 1.5 / 1225 0.7 / TU 1846 1.5	**25** 0051 0.9 / 0655 1.7 / W 1334 0.5 / 1950 1.7
11 0054 1.0 / 0648 1.6 / W 1320 0.6 / 1943 1.6	**26** 0148 0.8 / 0753 1.8 / TH 1422 0.5 / 2037 1.7
12 0145 0.8 / 0749 1.7 / TH 1408 0.5 / 2027 1.7	**27** 0236 0.7 / 0845 1.8 / F 1503 0.5 / 2118 1.8
13 0229 0.7 / 0835 1.8 / F 1451 0.4 / 2108 1.8	**28** 0318 0.6 / 0930 1.9 / SA 1539 0.5 / 2156 1.9
14 0310 0.6 / 0919 1.9 / SA 1532 0.3 / 2148 2.0	**29** 0357 0.5 / 1011 1.9 / SU 1613 0.5 / 2231 1.9
15 0350 0.5 / 1003 2.0 / SU 1612 0.2 / 2228 2.0	**30** 0433 0.5 / 1049 1.9 / M 1645 0.6 / ● 2304 2.0
	31 0509 0.5 / 1126 1.9 / TU 1717 0.6 / 2336 2.0

JUNE

Time m	Time m
1 0544 0.5 / 1203 1.8 / W 1749 0.7	**16** 0551 0.2 / 1220 2.1 / TH 1810 0.5
2 0008 1.9 / 0621 0.5 / TH 1239 1.8 / 1822 0.8	**17** 0024 2.1 / 0643 0.2 / F 1315 2.0 / 1900 0.6
3 0041 1.9 / 0659 0.6 / F 1317 1.7 / 1857 0.8	**18** 0115 2.1 / 0736 0.3 / SA 1410 1.9 / 1951 0.7
4 0115 1.8 / 0738 0.6 / SA 1358 1.7 / 1935 0.9	**19** 0208 2.0 / 0833 0.3 / SU 1504 1.8 / 2045 0.8
5 0155 1.8 / 0826 0.7 / SU 1443 1.6 / 2020 0.9	**20** 0302 2.0 / 0935 0.4 / M 1600 1.7 / 2144 0.9
6 0241 1.7 / 0919 0.7 / M 1534 1.5 / 2117 1.0	**21** 0400 1.9 / 1042 0.5 / TU 1701 1.6 / ☽ 2252 0.9
7 0336 1.6 / 1021 0.7 / TU 1631 1.5 / ☽ 2229 1.0	**22** 0503 1.8 / 1151 0.6 / W 1804 1.6
8 0436 1.6 / 1128 0.7 / W 1736 1.5 / 2349 0.9	**23** 0005 0.9 / 0612 1.7 / TH 1254 0.7 / 1904 1.6
9 0543 1.6 / 1228 0.6 / TH 1843 1.6	**24** 0112 0.8 / 0717 1.7 / F 1348 0.7 / 1958 1.7
10 0053 0.9 / 0653 1.7 / F 1322 0.6 / 1940 1.7	**25** 0209 0.8 / 0815 1.7 / SA 1435 0.7 / 2045 1.8
11 0147 0.8 / 0753 1.8 / SA 1413 0.5 / 2030 1.8	**26** 0258 0.7 / 0906 1.8 / SU 1515 0.7 / 2128 1.8
12 0236 0.6 / 0847 1.9 / SU 1501 0.4 / 2116 1.9	**27** 0341 0.7 / 0951 1.8 / M 1552 0.7 / 2207 1.9
13 0324 0.5 / 0938 2.0 / M 1548 0.4 / 2202 2.0	**28** 0420 0.6 / 1033 1.8 / TU 1627 0.7 / 2244 2.0
14 0412 0.4 / 1030 2.1 / TU 1635 0.4 / ○ 2248 2.1	**29** 0456 0.6 / 1112 1.8 / W 1701 0.7 / ● 2319 2.0
15 0501 0.3 / 1124 2.1 / W 1722 0.5 / 2335 2.1	**30** 0532 0.5 / 1150 1.8 / TH 1735 0.8 / 2353 2.0

JULY

Time m	Time m
1 0608 0.5 / 1227 1.8 / F 1808 0.8	**16** 0016 2.2 / 0633 0.2 / SA 1305 2.1 / 1846 0.6
2 0027 2.0 / 0645 0.5 / SA 1302 1.8 / 1843 0.8	**17** 0104 2.2 / 0721 0.2 / SU 1352 2.0 / 1931 0.6
3 0101 1.9 / 0722 0.5 / SU 1339 1.7 / 1920 0.8	**18** 0152 2.2 / 0810 0.3 / M 1438 1.9 / 2017 0.7
4 0138 1.9 / 0802 0.6 / M 1419 1.7 / 1959 0.8	**19** 0239 2.1 / 0900 0.4 / TU 1525 1.8 / 2105 0.8
5 0219 1.8 / 0846 0.6 / TU 1503 1.7 / 2044 0.9	**20** 0327 2.0 / 0953 0.6 / W 1613 1.7 / ☽ 2200 0.9
6 0306 1.8 / 0934 0.6 / W 1553 1.6 / 2136 0.9	**21** 0420 1.8 / 1054 0.7 / TH 1709 1.6 / 2312 0.9
7 0358 1.7 / 1030 0.7 / TH 1648 1.6 / ☽ 2239 0.9	**22** 0523 1.7 / 1204 0.8 / F 1813 1.6
8 0458 1.7 / 1134 0.7 / F 1751 1.6 / 2357 0.9	**23** 0035 0.9 / 0638 1.6 / SA 1311 0.9 / 1919 1.7
9 0606 1.7 / 1241 0.7 / SA 1856 1.7	**24** 0147 0.9 / 0749 1.6 / SU 1409 0.9 / 2016 1.7
10 0109 0.8 / 0719 1.8 / SU 1341 0.6 / 1957 1.8	**25** 0244 0.8 / 0848 1.7 / M 1458 0.9 / 2105 1.8
11 0211 0.7 / 0824 1.9 / M 1438 0.6 / 2052 1.9	**26** 0330 0.7 / 0937 1.7 / TU 1539 0.9 / 2148 1.9
12 0308 0.6 / 0925 2.0 / TU 1532 0.6 / 2144 2.0	**27** 0409 0.7 / 1020 1.8 / W 1615 0.8 / 2227 2.0
13 0402 0.4 / 1024 2.1 / W 1623 0.6 / ○ 2235 2.1	**28** 0444 0.6 / 1059 1.9 / TH 1648 0.8 / ● 2304 2.0
14 0454 0.3 / 1121 2.1 / TH 1712 0.5 / 2326 2.2	**29** 0517 0.5 / 1135 1.9 / F 1721 0.7 / 2338 2.1
15 0544 0.2 / 1215 2.1 / F 1759 0.6	**30** 0551 0.5 / 1209 1.9 / SA 1753 0.7
	31 0011 2.1 / 0624 0.5 / SU 1242 1.9 / 1825 0.7

AUGUST

Time m	Time m
1 0044 2.1 / 0659 0.5 / M 1315 1.9 / 1858 0.7	**16** 0127 2.3 / 0738 0.3 / TU 1404 2.0 / 1944 0.6
2 0117 2.0 / 0734 0.5 / TU 1350 1.8 / 1934 0.7	**17** 0208 2.1 / 0820 0.5 / W 1443 1.8 / 2026 0.7
3 0153 2.0 / 0813 0.5 / W 1429 1.8 / 2014 0.8	**18** 0250 2.0 / 0902 0.7 / TH 1524 1.8 / 2114 0.9
4 0234 1.9 / 0856 0.6 / TH 1514 1.8 / 2100 0.8	**19** 0337 1.8 / 0951 0.9 / F 1611 1.7 / ☽ 2219 1.0
5 0323 1.9 / 0946 0.7 / F 1607 1.7 / 2157 0.9	**20** 0432 1.7 / 1059 1.0 / SA 1712 1.6
6 0422 1.8 / 1047 0.8 / SA 1708 1.7 / 2314 0.9	**21** 0000 1.0 / 0555 1.6 / SU 1231 1.1 / 1839 1.6
7 0534 1.8 / 1206 0.8 / SU 1819 1.7	**22** 0127 1.0 / 0730 1.6 / M 1348 1.1 / 1951 1.7
8 0047 0.9 / 0700 1.8 / M 1323 0.8 / 1934 1.8	**23** 0229 0.8 / 0835 1.7 / TU 1443 1.0 / 2045 1.8
9 0202 0.8 / 0818 1.9 / TU 1429 0.8 / 2038 1.9	**24** 0314 0.8 / 0923 1.8 / W 1524 1.0 / 2129 1.9
10 0304 0.6 / 0924 2.0 / W 1526 0.7 / 2135 2.1	**25** 0351 0.7 / 1002 1.8 / TH 1558 0.9 / 2207 2.0
11 0358 0.4 / 1022 2.1 / TH 1615 0.6 / 2227 2.2	**26** 0423 0.6 / 1037 1.9 / F 1629 0.8 / 2242 2.1
12 0446 0.3 / 1113 2.1 / F 1700 0.6 / ○ 2316 2.3	**27** 0454 0.5 / 1111 2.0 / SA 1659 0.7 / ● 2316 2.1
13 0531 0.2 / 1200 2.2 / SA 1742 0.5	**28** 0525 0.4 / 1144 2.0 / SU 1729 0.6 / 2348 2.2
14 0001 2.3 / 0615 0.1 / SU 1244 2.1 / 1824 0.5	**29** 0557 0.4 / 1215 2.0 / M 1800 0.6
15 0045 2.3 / 0657 0.2 / M 1325 2.1 / 1904 0.6	**30** 0019 2.2 / 0630 0.4 / TU 1246 2.0 / 1834 0.6
	31 0051 2.2 / 0705 0.4 / W 1319 2.0 / 1909 0.6

Chart Datum: 1·22 metres below Ordnance Datum (Local). HAT is 2·5 metres above Chart Datum.

》》 FREE monthly updates. Register at 《
www.reedsnauticalalmanac.co.uk

STANDARD TIME (UT)
For Summer Time add ONE hour in **non-shaded areas**

LERWICK LAT 60°09′N LONG 1°08′W
TIMES AND HEIGHTS OF HIGH AND LOW WATERS

Dates in red are **SPRINGS**
Dates in blue are NEAPS

YEAR 2022

NE Scotland

SEPTEMBER

Time	m		Time	m
1 0127	2.1	**16**	0213	2.0
0742	0.5		0814	0.8
TH 1356	1.9	F	1436	1.8
1948	0.7		2034	0.9
2 0207	2.0	**17**	0257	1.8
0823	0.6		0853	1.0
F 1438	1.9	SA	1518	1.8
2034	0.8		◗ 2133	1.0
3 0255	1.9	**18**	0350	1.7
0912	0.8		0948	1.2
SA 1529	1.8	SU	1611	1.7
◖ 2131	0.9		2320	1.1
4 0359	1.8	**19**	0506	1.6
1014	0.9		1148	1.2
SU 1633	1.7	M	1738	1.6
2255	1.0			
5 0521	1.7	**20**	0056	1.0
1150	1.0		0712	1.6
M 1754	1.7	TU	1321	1.2
			1923	1.7
6 0046	0.9	**21**	0201	0.9
0703	1.7		0816	1.7
TU 1321	1.0	W	1419	1.1
1924	1.8		2019	1.8
7 0203	0.7	**22**	0246	0.8
0824	1.9		0858	1.8
W 1427	0.9	TH	1458	1.0
2032	2.0		2101	1.9
8 0301	0.6	**23**	0320	0.7
0923	2.0		0934	1.9
TH 1518	0.8	F	1530	0.9
2126	2.1		2138	2.0
9 0348	0.4	**24**	0352	0.6
1012	2.1		1007	2.0
F 1601	0.7	SA	1600	0.8
2214	2.3		2213	2.1
10 0431	0.3	**25**	0423	0.5
1057	2.2		1040	2.0
SA 1641	0.6	SU	1631	0.7
○ 2259	2.3		● 2246	2.2
11 0511	0.2	**26**	0454	0.4
1138	2.2		1112	2.1
SU 1719	0.5	M	1702	0.6
2340	2.4		2319	2.2
12 0549	0.2	**27**	0527	0.4
1216	2.2		1144	2.1
M 1757	0.5	TU	1735	0.6
			2352	2.3
13 0019	2.4	**28**	0600	0.4
0627	0.3		1216	2.1
TU 1251	2.1	W	1809	0.6
1835	0.5			
14 0056	2.3	**29**	0026	2.3
0704	0.5		0637	0.5
W 1325	2.0	TH	1249	2.1
1912	0.6		1847	0.6
15 0134	2.1	**30**	0104	2.2
0739	0.6		0715	0.6
TH 1359	1.9	F	1326	2.1
1951	0.7		1929	0.7

OCTOBER

Time	m		Time	m
1 0148	2.1	**16**	0225	1.8
0757	0.7		0805	1.1
SA 1408	2.0	SU	1434	1.9
2018	0.8		2100	1.0
2 0242	1.9	**17**	0317	1.7
0848	0.9		0852	1.2
SU 1500	1.9	M	1525	1.8
2122	0.9		◗ 2233	1.1
3 0354	1.8	**18**	0424	1.6
0957	1.1		1055	1.3
M 1610	1.8	TU	1633	1.7
◖ 2302	0.9			
4 0526	1.7	**19**	0004	1.0
1153	1.1		0630	1.6
TU 1742	1.8	W	1233	1.3
			1833	1.7
5 0047	0.8	**20**	0112	1.0
0712	1.8		0738	1.7
W 1316	1.1	TH	1336	1.2
1916	1.9		1940	1.8
6 0155	0.7	**21**	0201	0.8
0819	1.9		0821	1.8
TH 1415	0.9	F	1418	1.0
2019	2.0		2024	1.9
7 0248	0.5	**22**	0239	0.7
0909	2.0		0856	1.9
F 1501	0.8	SA	1453	0.9
2110	2.2		2102	2.0
8 0331	0.4	**23**	0314	0.6
0953	2.1		0930	2.0
SA 1541	0.7	SU	1526	0.8
2155	2.3		2137	2.1
9 0409	0.3	**24**	0347	0.5
1032	2.2		1004	2.1
SU 1618	0.6	M	1600	0.7
○ 2236	2.3		2213	2.2
10 0446	0.3	**25**	0422	0.4
1109	2.2		1038	2.2
M 1655	0.5	TU	1634	0.6
2315	2.3		● 2250	2.3
11 0521	0.4	**26**	0457	0.4
1143	2.2		1112	2.2
TU 1731	0.5	W	1710	0.6
2352	2.3		2327	2.3
12 0555	0.5	**27**	0534	0.4
1215	2.2		1148	2.3
W 1808	0.6	TH	1749	0.5
13 0027	2.2	**28**	0007	2.3
0629	0.6		0613	0.5
TH 1246	2.1	F	1224	2.2
1844	0.6		1831	0.6
14 0103	2.1	**29**	0051	2.2
0701	0.8		0654	0.7
F 1318	2.0	SA	1304	2.2
1922	0.8		1918	0.6
15 0142	2.0	**30**	0142	2.1
0732	0.9		0741	0.9
SA 1353	1.9	SU	1350	2.1
2004	0.9		2013	0.7
		31	0245	1.9
			0836	1.0
		M	1447	2.0
			2124	0.8

NOVEMBER

Time	m		Time	m
1 0359	1.8	**16**	0349	1.7
0952	1.1		0938	1.3
TU 1601	1.9	W	1551	1.8
◗ 2306	0.8		◗ 2303	1.0
2 0528	1.8	**17**	0459	1.6
1139	1.2		1126	1.3
W 1729	1.9	TH	1702	1.7
3 0031	0.8	**18**	0010	1.0
0656	1.8		0633	1.7
TH 1254	1.1	F	1235	1.2
1854	1.9		1832	1.8
4 0135	0.7	**19**	0105	0.9
0756	1.9		0729	1.8
F 1351	1.0	SA	1327	1.1
1956	2.0		1932	1.9
5 0226	0.6	**20**	0151	0.8
0844	2.0		0811	1.9
SA 1437	0.8	SU	1411	1.0
2047	2.1		2018	2.0
6 0308	0.5	**21**	0233	0.7
0926	2.1		0850	2.0
SU 1518	0.7	M	1451	0.9
2132	2.2		2100	2.1
7 0345	0.5	**22**	0312	0.6
1004	2.1		0928	2.1
M 1556	0.6	TU	1530	0.7
2213	2.2		2142	2.2
8 0420	0.5	**23**	0351	0.5
1040	2.2		1006	2.2
TU 1633	0.6	W	1610	0.6
◖ 2251	2.2		● 2225	2.3
9 0454	0.6	**24**	0431	0.5
1112	2.2		1046	2.3
W 1710	0.6	TH	1651	0.6
2328	2.2		2309	2.3
10 0527	0.7	**25**	0512	0.6
1144	2.2		1126	2.3
TH 1746	0.6	F	1735	0.5
			2357	2.3
11 0004	2.1	**26**	0556	0.7
0559	0.8		1208	2.3
F 1216	2.2	SA	1823	0.5
1824	0.7			
12 0041	2.0	**27**	0049	2.2
0630	0.9		0642	0.8
SA 1248	2.1	SU	1253	2.3
1902	0.8		1915	0.6
13 0120	1.9	**28**	0146	2.1
0702	1.0		0733	0.9
SU 1323	2.0	M	1345	2.2
1944	0.9		2013	0.6
14 0203	1.8	**29**	0247	2.0
0736	1.1		0829	1.0
M 1402	1.9	TU	1444	2.1
2035	1.0		2120	0.7
15 0252	1.7	**30**	0352	1.9
0822	1.2		0937	1.1
TU 1451	1.8	W	1550	2.0
2144	1.0		◗ 2242	0.7

DECEMBER

Time	m		Time	m
1 0504	1.8	**16**	0407	1.7
1058	1.1		0954	1.2
TH 1703	2.0	F	1612	1.8
			◗ 2303	0.9
2 0000	0.7	**17**	0508	1.7
0618	1.8		1115	1.2
F 1215	1.1	SA	1715	1.8
1818	2.0			
3 0104	0.7	**18**	0005	0.9
0720	1.9		0616	1.7
SA 1318	1.0	SU	1228	1.1
1924	2.0		1825	1.8
4 0158	0.7	**19**	0101	0.8
0811	1.9		0717	1.8
SU 1411	0.9	M	1326	1.0
2019	2.0		1929	1.9
5 0242	0.7	**20**	0152	0.8
0856	2.0		0809	1.9
M 1457	0.8	TU	1417	0.9
2108	2.1		2025	2.0
6 0321	0.7	**21**	0240	0.7
0937	2.1		0855	2.1
TU 1539	0.7	W	1504	0.8
2153	2.1		2117	2.1
7 0357	0.7	**22**	0326	0.7
1014	2.1		0941	2.2
W 1618	0.7	TH	1552	0.7
2234	2.1		2208	2.2
8 0432	0.7	**23**	0412	0.7
1049	2.2		1026	2.3
TH 1656	0.7	F	1640	0.6
○ 2313	2.1		● 2300	2.3
9 0505	0.8	**24**	0459	0.7
1123	2.2		1112	2.3
F 1733	0.7	SA	1728	0.5
2351	2.1		2355	2.3
10 0538	0.9	**25**	0546	0.7
1157	2.2		1200	2.4
SA 1811	0.7	SU	1819	0.4
11 0028	2.0	**26**	0049	2.2
0612	1.0		0635	0.8
SU 1230	2.1	M	1249	2.3
1849	0.8		1910	0.4
12 0106	1.9	**27**	0142	2.2
0645	1.0		0723	0.8
M 1305	2.1	TU	1341	2.3
1929	0.8		2004	0.5
13 0145	1.9	**28**	0235	2.0
0721	1.1		0813	0.9
TU 1342	2.0	W	1433	2.2
2012	0.8		2100	0.5
14 0227	1.8	**29**	0329	1.9
0801	1.1		0907	1.0
W 1425	1.9	TH	1528	2.1
2101	0.9		2202	0.7
15 0314	1.7	**30**	0425	1.8
0851	1.2		1008	1.0
TH 1515	1.9	F	1627	2.0
2158	0.9		◗ 2313	0.8
		31	0528	1.8
			1122	1.1
		SA	1734	1.9

Chart Datum: 1·22 metres below Ordnance Datum (Local). HAT is 2·5 metres above Chart Datum.

FREE monthly updates. Register at
www.reedsnauticalalmanac.co.uk

239

Aberdeenshire Harbours

Aberdeenshire Council operates six pleasure harbours along the east coast of Scotland. From Stonehaven, at the gateway to Royal Deeside, Johnshaven and Gourdon, to the Marina at Banff Harbour, Portsoy and Rosehearty.

These well serviced and picturesque harbours with local facilities, visitor attractions and museums, are ideally placed to explore from Royal Deeside to the Moray Firth, including the Whisky and Castle Trails.

Experience a warm welcome at the many restaurants and hotels in the area providing excellent Scottish cruising.

Macduff is Aberdeenshire's main commercial harbour involved in fishing, general cargo, vessel repair and build.

Gourdon

Johnshaven

Portsoy

Rosehearty

Stonehaven

Macduff

Aberdeenshire
COUNCIL

Harbour Authority ■ Aberdeenshire Counci
Infrastructure Services ■ St Leonards ■ Sandyhill Road ■ Banff AB45 1S
www.aberdeenshireharbours.co.u
harboursadmin@aberdeenshire.gov.u